The Russian Patriotic War of 1812 is the only publicly available translation into English of Bogdanovich's official history of the Russian forces' involvement in the fight against Napoleon and his allies in Russia in 1812. This translation also includes extracts from Ivan Liprandi's critique of Bogdanovich's work.

Volume 2 of *The Russian Patriotic War of 1812* covers Kutuzov's appointment as Field Marshal, details of the opolchenie (militia) and donations made in 1812, the meeting in Abo between Tsar Alexander I and the Crown Prince of Sweden (Jean-Baptiste Jules Bernadotte), and the situation in enemy occupied territory. Highly detailed descriptions of operations are included, from before the Battle of Borodino to the camp at Tarutino, as well as operations on the flanks by Wittgenstein and Admiral Chichagov. Outstanding feats were performed not only by prominent personalities but also by others who participated in this war. The composition of the forces are shown as clearly as possible, as are force numbers, casualties on each side, and so on. The maps attached to this work were drafted in such a way that they might serve to explain entire phases of the war. The battle plans show the locations of dominant terrain according to detailed state surveys, while villages, forests and roads have been copied from previously published plans.

Born in Sumy, Ukraine, in 1805, Bogdanovich was initially educated in the Noble Regiment, being commissioned into the artillery in 1823. Bogdanovich saw combat in the Polish campaign of 1831 and upon his return in 1833, he entered the Imperial Military Academy, becoming its Director of Operations until 1839. Thereafter, he served on committees of the General Staff. He died in August, 1882 in Oranienbaum. General Bogdanovich is famed for a number of major works, making an invaluable contribution to Russian military historiography. His *History of the Patriotic War of 1812* won the Demidov Prize for History in 1861.

Peter G.A. Phillips is a veteran of 27 years in the British Army Intelligence Corps, including working as a Russian, German, and Serbo-Croat linguist, thereafter spending five years as part of a Civil Service team training British Armed Forces personnel to serve in UK diplomatic missions. He is now retired and spends his time translating Russian military histories of the Coalition Wars. His published translations include: Mikhailovsky-Danilevsky's histories of the wars of 1805 and 1806-1807; a collaboration with renowned Napoleonic historian Dr Alexander Mikaberidze of Ilya Radozhitskii's trilogy of memoirs covering 1812-1814; and numerous articles for The Waterloo Association's website www.napoleon-series.org. Peter now lives in the Philippines with his Filipina wife of 34 years. They have two adult daughters.

The Russian Patriotic War Of 1812 Volume 2

The Russian Official History

Modest Ivanovich Bogdanovich

Translated by Peter G.A. Phillips

Helion & Company

Helion & Company Limited
Unit 8 Amherst Business Centre
Budbrooke Road
Warwick
CV34 5WE
England
Tel. 01926 499619
Email: info@helion.co.uk
Website: www.helion.co.uk
Twitter: @helionbooks
Visit our https://helionbooks.wordpress.com/

Published by Helion & Company 2024
Designed and typeset by Mach 3 Solutions (www.mach3solutions.co.uk)
Cover designed by Paul Hewitt, Battlefield Design (www.battlefield-design.co.uk)

Original text published as *History Of The Patriotic War Of 1812 According To Reliable Sources. Compiled in accordance with Supreme orders*, St Petersburg, 1861
Translation © Peter Philips 2024
Maps and diagrams by George Anderson, Anderson Subtil © Helion & Company 2024

Cover: The Battle of Krasny on 5 (17) November 1812, by Peter von Hess (Public Domain)

Every reasonable effort has been made to trace copyright holders and to obtain their permission for the use of copyright material. The author and publisher apologise for any errors or omissions in this work, and would be grateful if notified of any corrections that should be incorporated in future reprints or editions of this book.

ISBN 978-1-804514-33-7

British Library Cataloguing-in-Publication Data.
A catalogue record for this book is available from the British Library.

All rights reserved. No part of this publication may be reproduced, stored in a retrieval system, or transmitted, in any form, or by any means, electronic, mechanical, photocopying, recording or otherwise, without the express written consent of Helion & Company Limited.

For details of other military history titles published by Helion & Company Limited, contact the above address, or visit our website: http://www.helion.co.uk

We always welcome receiving book proposals from prospective authors.

Contents

List of Maps		v
15	The arrival of Kutuzov as Commander-in-Chief	7
16	The Conference at Åbo	20
17	The *Opolchenie*	29
18	Mobilisation and donations in the Governorates that were not included in the *Opolchenie*.	54
19	The situation in the enemy occupied *Oblasts* of the Empire	70
20	Prince Kutuzov joins the Army	83
21	The position at Borodino	104
22	The Battle of Borodino	128
23	The Battle of Borodino (continued)	149
24	The retreat from Borodino to Moscow	165
25	The evacuation of Moscow	187
26	The burning of Moscow	218
27	The retreat of the Russian Army from Moscow to Tarutino	236
28	The camp at Tarutino	259
29	The Guerrilla War	278
30	The arrival of reinforcements with Count Wittgenstein's Force	291
31	The union of Third Army with the Army of the Danube	307
32	The Battle of Tarutino (on the River Chernishnya)	324
Appendices		
I	Prince Bagration's correspondence with Count Arakcheev	342
II	Biography of Kutuzov	346
III	Standing Orders for the Tver *Opolchenie*	349
IV	Composition of the Don Cossack Host	351
V	Troop strengths of the *Grande Armée*	354
VI	Dispositions for First and Second Western Armies, at the village of Borodino, issued on 24 August [5 September] 1812	355
VII	Reports on the Battle of Borodino	357
VIII	Michaud's letter to former *Flügel–Adjutant* Mikhailovsky-Danilevsky	383
IX	The Tsar's general plan of operations	385
X	Prince Kutuzov's letter to the Head of Kaluga City	391
XI	Supreme Orders to the Chancellor of State Count Rumyantsev, dated 12 [24] October (archive of the M.T.D. No. 46,692, Annex 5)	392

XII	The composition of the Force from the Army of the Danube that set off from Wallachia for Volhynia on 19 [31] July	394
XIII	Order of Battle of the Third Army	396
XIV	Liprandi's assessment of Bogdanovich's four sources for the Fall of the Central Battery	398
XV	The conclusion of Liprandi's detailed assessment of available evidence on the Fall of the Great Redoubt	403
XVI	Liprandi's rebuttal of Bogdanovich's claim that there was no reliable evidence for French produced counterfeit Russian Banknotes being brought into circulation	405

Index 408

List of Maps

17	Movements from the Solovieva Crossing to Tarutino and on the Vyazma.	81
18	Plan of the position at Tsarevo-Zaimishche.	89
19	Plan of the Battle of Borodino, 7 September 1812.	103
20	Plan of the action at Shevardino, 5 September 1812.	109
21a	Operations from the occupation of Moscow by Napoleon to his retreat to Mozhaisk.	176
21b	Operations by Partisan Detachments under Wintzingerode.	177
21c	Position forwards of Moscow, 13 September 1812.	178
22	Operational Theatre for Chichagov and Tormasov, September to late October 1812.	306
23	Plan of the Battle at Tarutino, 18 October 1812.	331

15

The arrival of Kutuzov as Commander-in-Chief

> The situation during the retreat of the Western Armies from Smolensk to Dorogobuzh. – The need to select a Commander-in-Chief over all Russian armies. – The findings of the Extraordinary Committee. – The selection of Kutuzov. – His service career in outline. – His activities in accordance with the duties of the Commander of the St Petersburg *Opolchenie*. – The elevation of Kutuzov to Princely dignity. – Appointment as Commander-in-Chief. – Supreme rescript to Kutuzov as Commander-in-Chief of the armies. – Kutuzov's character. – The assessments of him by foreign historians.

Following the retreat of our Western armies from Smolensk to Dorogobuzh, the state of affairs, militarily, was infinitely more advantageous for us than at the beginning of the campaign. The Western armies, separated from each other by the enemy invasion of our borders, had managed to unite and gave battle at Smolensk and at Valutina Gora, in which we achieved the most important objective of a defensive war – weakening the enemy. The losses suffered by the Russian forces were significant, but one and a half times fewer than enemy losses, who had moved away from the well–spring of their resources and were not able to bring up reinforcements at the rate that they arrived in our army. As Napoleon's armies were crossing the borders of Russia, the strength of their forces exceeded the strength of the army put up against them more than two-fold, while after the battle of Valutina, by only one and a half times. Operations on the flanks of the main theatre of war brought us undeniable advantages and promised even more beneficial consequences: on the Dvina [Daugava], Count Wittgenstein's [Pëtr Khristianovich Wittgenstein] I Corps, outnumbered by the enemy, held them through constant successes, while the arrival of our reinforcements would soon give us the means to resume offensive operations. In Volhynia, Tormasov [Alexander Petrovich Tormasov] had been forced to retreat behind the Styr, but the Army of the Danube was already moving to his aid, with the arrival of which the superiority in numbers would pass to our side. The situation of the Russian forces, with regard to their food supply, presented some difficulties, caused by the need to retreat further than expected at the beginning of the war; the consequences of this were: the loss of some magazines, established by us in the border governorates, and the lack of a sufficient number of warehouses on the line of retreat from Smolensk towards Moscow. But all the difficulties we encountered in providing the troops with food supplies were as nothing in comparison with those experienced by the enemy army from its first steps across our borders. From intercepted French official documents, it can be seen that at the time when Napoleon's headquarters was in Vilna [Vilnius], his *Garde impériale* (who received particular attention from the quartermaster's department for their subsistence) had received insufficient rations and had indulged in marauding and looting. In an order issued on 18 (30) June, it was pointed out to the troops 'that they must save their bread, because, in all likelihood, they will not receive any the next day.' In an order dated 25 June (7 July) 'the burial of all the fallen horses lying around in the vicinity of the quartering locations of the army' was decreed. The following daily ration was allocated for the march from Vilna to Glubokoe in an order dated 27 June (9 July): less than a pound (12 *onces*) of bread; around 15 *Zolotniki* [1 *Zolotnik* = 4.26g or 0.15oz] (2 *onces*) of rice; 1⅕ pounds (*une livre*) of meat; while on the last two days of the march it was intended to issue ⅔ pound (9 *onces*) of hard tack each instead of bread. Since this ration was obviously insufficient, the unit commanders of the force were ordered to confirm the available stocks of bread, hard tack and rice issued to the soldiers every four days once they set out from Vilna.[1] The deeper the enemy army plunged into Russia, the more the hardships increased, and with them pillaging and all kinds of indiscipline.[2] This was the situation with all the troops that were part of the *Grande Armée* including those under Saint-Cyr's [Laurent de Gouvion-Saint-Cyr] command. In contrast, the Austrian and Saxon troops, located in an abundant country and remaining in the same locations for extended periods, suffered incomparably fewer losses and were in perfect order.

The troops of both Western armies, having made forced marches from the borders of the Empire to the Dnieper, were unable to maintain that excellent order, which, according to the opinions of our enemies themselves, constitutes the distinctive quality of the Russian military. Emperor Alexander, having learned about some incidents of violence and robberies by our soldiers who had absented themselves from the force without leave, ordered Barclay de Tolly [Mikhail Bogdanovich Barclay de Tolly] to conduct a thorough investigation of this and punish those responsible.[3] Barclay, during the armies' stay around Smolensk, ordered the execution of several men convicted of robbery, and these examples of severity were enough to restore order and discipline.[4] As for the morale of our troops, or, rather, of the entire

---

1 Extracted from Orders for the *2e régiment de grenadiers-à-pied* (*Vieille Garde*), intercepted by Cossacks during the French retreat from Moscow. The original copies of these Orders, issued between 1 (13) June 1811 and 24 September (6 October) 1812, are held in the Imperial Public Library; while a list of the returns are in the Archive of the Military Topographic Depot (No 47,352, folio 2).
2 Intercepted orders for the *2e régiment de grenadiers* dated 15 (27) July and 21 July (2 August).
3 '... I passed many marauders, who had straggled behind the force for the entire stage, in a most disgusting state; I ask you, General, to stop this frightful indiscipline and I expect this from your diligence for the common cause.' Extracted from a handwritten letter from Emperor Alexander I to Barclay de Tolly, dated 6 [18] July, from Lyachov.
4 '... I am striving by all means to maintain discipline and stop the disorder. I ordered the execution of seven marauders in Smolensk, who had absented themselves from the army

Russian people, neither the occupation of several of our governorates by the enemy, nor the prolonged retreat from a vast area, could shake the constant desire of each and every one to avenge the desolation of the fatherland. Letters by many of the men in the army to their closest relatives serve as evidence of the truth of our words: in these heartfelt effusions, which were not at all intended for general publication, we encounter touching expressions of devotion to the Tsar, love for the motherland, hatred for the enemy who dared to cross the cherished border of Russia. No one at that time spared either life or property, and, for the most part, not out of lust for glory, but out of a sacred sense of duty. Wilson [Robert Thomas Wilson], a British general who was in the headquarters of our army as a representative of his government, stated; 'There was no one, neither man, nor woman, nor old man, nor youth, who would not consider it contemptuous to grumble or complain about the loss of their possessions.' Everyone understood the greatness of the danger that the enemy invasion threatened; everyone was convinced of the superiority of the Genius, who, having subjugated almost all of Europe to his whims, hung heavily over Russia, but no one wanted the cost of obedience to Napoleon as the price of peace.' Wilson continued; 'When, upon my arrival from St Petersburg in the headquarters, I remarked that the Tsar had given his word not to make peace as long as at least one armed enemy remained in Russia, every warrior and non–combatant wept with joy, or rushed to kiss me, as if I had brought news of the perfect ending to the calamities of war.'

It follows from this that the benefits acquired by the enemy consisted solely in the occupation of several Russian governorates, which did not bring them any significant advantage. Napoleon, wishing to extract resources from Lithuania to feed and replenish his army, set up temporary administrations in the major locations in this country, but all these attempts were unsuccessful: postponing for the moment the presentation of the measures taken by Napoleon in relation to the administrative organisation of the regions crossed by his army, we will only say here that they presented a totally deplorable spectacle of robbery, devastation and every kind of indiscipline. In contrast, in the rear areas of the Russian army, upon the call of the Russian Monarch, hundreds of thousands of his subjects rallied together; their general eagerness, compensating for the lack of resources, found the opportunity to supply the defenders of Russia with food even where magazines arranged in advance had been lacking: huge convoys stretched from all directions onto the line of retreat of our forces, moving from Smolensk towards Moscow.

Thus, the situation of the Russian army, at that time, was in all respects more advantageous than the position of the enemy, who had gone deep into our country, was significantly weakened and enticed further onwards by the elusive phantom of a decisive victory. But these circumstances were not obvious to every Russian at that time, and neither could they be: both the people and the troops saw only the immediate consequences of retreat: the devastation of the countryside, the

---

without leave. This measure made an impression, but until the officers, and even some of the regimental commanders, are convinced of the need for strict discipline, until then the maintenance of the troops in proper order cannot be achieved…' Extracted from Barclay de Tolly's letter to Emperor Alexander I, dated 9 [21] August 1812, from Korovino.

razing of flourishing towns, the triumph of the enemy. Our troops, thirsting for an opportunity to block the onward route of the enemy with their chests, considered themselves strong enough for that; retreat seemed a betrayal of the motherland to them: such were the emotions that animated not only the soldiers, but also their commanders. Only a few, like the cautious Barclay, dared to resist the general impulse; everyone was passionate about it, and even some of our most outstanding generals did not hide their opinions: further retreat was considered pointless; as the only means to save the fatherland, the transition to decisive action was awaited with lingering impatience. These opinions, flying through Russia with the speed of lightning, reached both capitals. A general irrational hatred of foreigners became more and more evident in Moscow every day; in St Petersburg Barclay was openly condemned.[5]

On 22 July [3 August], Emperor Alexander returned to St Petersburg from Moscow. There he heard vague stories coming from the armies under Barclay de Tolly and Bagration [Pëtr Ivanovich Bagration]. As soon as they had managed to unite and report to the Tsar regarding the ending of the misunderstandings that had arisen between them, reports and letters arrived from the army with complaints about Barclay and the failure of the offensive towards Rudnya. Emperor Alexander, as the supreme commander in Russia's struggle against Napoleon, was fully aware of all the circumstances of this operation. He did full justice to the merits of Barclay de Tolly, was sure of his devotion and knew that the method of our operations had been inspired by necessity itself. Nevertheless, however, there is no doubt that success in war is possible only when a commander enjoys the absolute confidence of the troops; only with this conscious connection between the leader and the troops entrusted to him, he, owning the souls of each of his subordinates, directs the common efforts to achieve the operational objectives and can justify the hopes placed in him.

Convinced of the need to select a new Commander-in-Chief and entrust him with command over all Russian armies, Emperor Alexander entrusted the discussion of this subject to a Committee composed of His former Mentor, Chairman of the State Council, General Field Marshal Count Saltykov [Nikolai Ivanovich Saltykov]; Commander-in-Chief of St Petersburg, General of Infantry Vyazmitinov [Sergey Kuzmich Vyazmitinov]; generals: Count Arakcheev [Alexei Andreevich Arakcheev] and Balashov [Alexander Dmitrievich Balashov], and Active Privy Councillors: Prince Lopukhin [Pëtr Vasilevich Lopukhin] and Count Kochubey [Viktor Pavlovich Kochubey]. This committee, having assembled in Count Saltykov's residence on 5 (17) August (the second day of the battle of Smolensk), engaged in a discussion of the question proposed to them from seven o'clock in the evening until half-past-ten. At the beginning of the meeting, by Supreme Command, Count Arakcheev read the reports received in the Name of His Imperial Majesty from the Commanders-in-Chief of the Armies, Minister of War Barclay de Tolly, since the departure of the Tsar from the army, and from Prince Bagration, from the day of the battle of Saltanovka; after that, personal letters were presented to the Committee from Prince

---

5   Bernhardi, *Denkwürdigkeiten des Grafen v. Toll*, II, 1-2.

Bagration, Count Saint-Priest [Guillaume Emmanuel Guignard de Saint-Priest] and other generals.

From the reports by Barclay de Tolly, one could sense his lack of faith in the success of operations against the huge forces under Napoleon and his displeasure with Prince Bagration, who, in the opinion of the Minister of War, by acting decisively, should have distracted some of the enemy troops sent (as Barclay believed) in aggregate against First Army. All the plans by Barclay de Tolly were reliant on a diversion by the troops under Count Wittgenstein and Tormasov. Being swayed by public opinion prevailing in Russia which disagreed with his opinions, he had hesitated in indecision, which, without any doubt, did not promise a favourable outcome. Prince Bagration, for his part, insisted on the need for both Western armies to switch to offensive operations against the enemy, disordered by forced marches, and complained about the Minister of War, who – as Prince Bagration expressed it – 'having demanded my opinion, has rejected it.'

The disagreements between the Commanders-in-Chief were even more evident from the personal letters. Prince Bagration, informing Count Arakcheev of the current state of affairs, exposed, in the bluntest terms, the detrimental consequences that, in his opinion, a further retreat would have. Following the union of the two Western Armies, Prince Bagration wrote:

> The whole army is publicly asking me to be overall commander; but I have not given any reply; as it is in the gift of my Tsar… I confess to you frankly that however pleasing it was for me to link up with First Army, it is equally distressing; as the provisions for me are very poor. When it was just me on the march, I had everything.

Several days later he wrote:

> For God's sake, send me somewhere else, even just to command a regiment, in Moldavia, or in the Caucasus, but I can't stay here; the entire headquarters is filled with Germans, such that it is impossible for a Russian to live, if only there were some. It's up to you, or put me on leave at least so I can rest for a month.[6]

After reading all the official documents and personal letters explaining the state of affairs, the Committee unanimously recognised:

> that the lack of effect in military operations was due to the fact that there was no positive singular authority over all the active armies, and how disadvantageous such a fragmentation of power is at the present time, so in order to counter that, a common unification is necessary.

---

6 Extracted from Prince Bagration's letter to Count Arakcheev, held in the Archive of 2nd Directorate of the Department of the General Staff. For further correspondence, see Appendix 1.

In the opinion of the Committee:

> the proof of this is based both on the state of the situation in general, and on the fact that, in accordance with the operations of various armies over a considerable area, they are always obliged to coordinate their movements and operations with one another. Therefore, the Committee finds it necessary: to appoint a single overall Commander-in-Chief over all the active armies.
>
> The Commander-in-Chief of First Western Army, being, along with that, the Minister of War, has an administrative authority over the actions of other Commanders-in-Chief, senior to him in rank, which, perhaps, unduly influenced his orders, and therefore the Committee affirmatively believes that the post of Minister of War, combined with the command of an army, has produced obstacles in achieving the desired outcome.

Moving on to the matter of an overall Commander-in-Chief, the Committee decided that this should be based on a certain experience in the art of war, excellent talents, general trust and on seniority in the service. In discussing who to propose as the Commander-in-Chief, they shortlisted Bennigsen [Leonty Leontevich Bennigsen], Bagration, Tormasov and Pahlen [Pëtr Alexeevich Pahlen], who had long been retired; but it was found that none of them corresponded to all the conditions specified for selection. Eventually, when the name of Kutuzov [Mikhail Illarionovich Golenishchev-Kutuzov] was mentioned, all members of the Committee unanimously decided to entrust him with command over all the armies, to give him sole authority determined in the regulations for a large army in the field, and to order the commanders of the *opolchenie* [militia] in the governorates to report to him regarding the success of the mobilisation and about the locations where territorial forces had already been assembled.

At the same time, it was necessary:

> to give full control of the War Ministry to the head of that department, Lieutenant General Prince Gorchakov [Alexei Ivanovich Gorchakov].' He was also instructed to command the St Petersburg militia in Kutuzov's stead, 'especially since regular troops are also part of this *opolchenie*.[7]

Indeed, Kutuzov combined all the conditions determined by the Committee for choosing a Commander-in-Chief. His service began with fortunate portents: noticed by Catherine the Great in his youngest years, she would later refer to him as 'My Kutuzov,' he received a practical military education under the guidance of the most qualified of the Russian generals of the time, Bauer [Friedrich Wilhelm Bauer], Rumyantsev [Pëtr Alexandrovich Rumyantsev-Zadunaisky] regarded him as outstanding and he became a favourite of Suvorov's [Alexander Vasilevich

---

7   A copy from the original Minutes of the Extraordinary Committee for the selection of a Commander-in-Chief, is kept in the Archives of 2nd Directorate of the Department of the General Staff.

Suvorov-Rimniksky]. His name was inseparable from the memory of the most glorious deeds of Catherine's era; his two-time recovery after grievous wounds he received drew the attention of all of Russia to him.[8]

Subsequently, Kutuzov, on being appointed Ambassador Extraordinary to Constantinople [Istanbul], showed extraordinary diplomatic abilities, carried out many important missions with distinction and ended the long war with the Turks with a decisive blow inflicted on the army of the Grand Vizier and a treaty that expanded the borders of Russia to the Danube and the Prut.[9]

To all these merits, Kutuzov added the advantage of seniority in service over all the Commanders-in-Chief of our armies; finally, the name of Kutuzov, a native Russian, was Russian, which was of great importance during the Patriotic War of 1812.

By selecting Kutuzov, the Committee completely fulfilled the expectations of the Tsar, who foresaw in advance upon whom the choice would fall and, a few days before, had honoured the venerable commander with an expression of His personal favour, elevating him to princely dignity.[10] Such an award was all the more unexpected to everyone because Kutuzov, being separated at that time from command over the troops, did not enjoy the favour of Emperor Alexander. Not long before, while negotiating with the Ottoman Porte, Kutuzov had constantly received letters from the Tsar expressing the need for an immediate conclusion of peace.[11]

---

8 In 1774 and 1788, Kutuzov suffered gunshot wounds: one, hitting his left temple, exiting from his right eye; the other, hitting his cheek, exiting to the rear.
9 For a fuller biography of Kutuzov, see Appendix 2.
10 Decree to the Governing Senate: 'In expressing Our special favour for the diligent service and zealous labour of Our General of Infantry, Count Golenishchev-Kutuzov, who has contributed to the ending of the war with the Ottoman Porte and to the conclusion of a beneficial peace, which has extended the borders of Our Empire, We raise him with his descendants to the Princely dignity of the All-Russian Empire, assigning to him the title of His Grace. The Senate is commanded to prepare a diploma of Princely dignity and to present it for Our signing. Signed in original by the hand of His Imperial Majesty as: ALEXANDER. St Petersburg, 29 July [10 August] 1812.'
11 Handwritten rescript from Emperor Alexander I to General of Infantry Kutuzov, dated 22 March [3 April] 1812: 'Mikhail Ilarionovich. You will receive from this courier authority from the Chancellor regarding questions arising from the peace negotiations. The situation is becoming more critical for both Empires by the hour. You will do Russia the greatest service by concluding a swift peace with the Porte. With love for your Fatherland, I challenge you most urgently to turn all your attention and efforts towards the achievement of this objective. Eternal glory will be yours. Any loss of time under the present circumstances would be utterly harmful. Set aside all secondary distractions, and with the insight with which you are endowed, take this so very important task up yourself. For your eyes only, I inform you that if it were not possible to persuade the Turkish plenipotentiaries to sign a treaty as We desire, then, having assured yourself in advance that it would be reliant on your part to bring about the conclusion of peace, you may make the necessary concessions in the article regarding the frontier with Asia; as a last resort, I allow you to make peace by laying the border along the Prut at its confluence with the Danube. But I entrust this to your personal responsibility, and I demand that no person, without exception, be made aware of this authority from Me until the actual signing; to that end, however, I command you to agree to such an important concession under no other circumstances than by enacting a treaty of alliance with the Porte. I hope that you have grasped the full importance of this subject and do not lose sight of any means necessary in order to achieve the desired aim.' Archive of the Military Topographic Depot, No. 32,416.

Kutuzov diligently tried to fulfil the will of the Tsar, but could not overcome the intransigence of the Turkish diplomats, who, being encouraged by the intrigues of French and Austrian agents, would not agree to the conditions proposed by the Russian government. Days passed, but the matter was not advanced at all; eventually, Emperor Alexander, losing patience with the slowness of the negotiations, instructed Admiral Chichagov [Pavel Vasilievich Chichagov], both to command the Army of the Danube and to conclude peace in Kutuzov's place. Kutuzov, having discovered this, accelerated the course of negotiations by every means and the result of the active measures he took was the conclusion of the Treaty of Bucharest, on 16 (28) May, four days before the arrival of Chichagov.[12]

Emperor Alexander, in spite of the successful conclusion of peace with the Ottoman Porte, was dissatisfied with the fact that, having made many concessions in our demands, Kutuzov had not managed to conclude a defensive and offensive alliance with the Turks. In the opinion of Emperor Alexander, such an alliance alone could reward us for the loss of direct communications with the Serbs and provide us with the means to exploit their assistance against the French and their allies.[13] Although the Tsar, in doing justice to the merits of Kutuzov, had also previously elevated him to the dignity of a count, nevertheless, Kutuzov asked for a leave of absence, retired to one of the villages granted to him, and arrived in St Petersburg after the departure of the Tsar to visit the army. The successful campaign on the Danube and the peace concluded at the fateful hour of the breach with Napoleon increased Kutuzov's renown: his assessments of current military operations resonated with those in the highest circles of society, and the nation looked with rever-

---

12 Some foreign historians claim that at the very time that Emperor Alexander I was encouraging Kutuzov to conclude peace as soon as possible, Chancellor Rumyantsev, convinced of the advantages of maintaining an alliance with Napoleon at any price, considered it best, having made all kinds of concessions to him, to expand the borders of Russia at Turkey's expense. According to these historians, Rumyantsev, in correspondence with Kutuzov, advised him not to be hasty in concluding peace with the Porte, and Kutuzov, in doubt regarding the hints from the Chancellor, had postponed the execution of the will of Emperor Alexander until the Tsar directed Admiral Chichagov to replace him. But this is contradicted by the official correspondence between Rumyantsev and Kutuzov, from which it is clear that Napoleon had actually proposed dividing up European Turkey between Russia and France to Emperor Alexander, in order to put a stop all their disagreements. The Tsar, without giving any response to this proposal, ordered Kutuzov to inform the Turkish representative of Napoleon's intentions, and at the same time to make it appear that the most moderate terms of peace had been offered from our side, but that, if the desired aim was not achieved, we would be forced agree to the proposal by the Emperor of the French and contribute to the collapse of Turkey. *Mémoires tirés des papiers d'un homme d'état*, XI, 366. – Bernardi, II, 3-4. – Chancellor Count Rumyantsev's letter to Kutuzov, dated 5 [17] March 1812 (Archive of the Ministry of Foreign Affairs).
13 '... *Le général Koutousoff a négligé un point très important, c'est de n'offrir les concessions que nous avons faites dans nos prétentions, qu'à condition d'une alliance deffensive et offensive. Ce n'est que cette alliance qui pouvait nous dedommager de la gène que va mettre cette paix dans nos rapports avec les Serbes et les nations Slaves, si importants pour nous, surtout dans l'époque présente. Si un moyen pouvait encore se présenter pour obtenir l'alliance avec la Porte et sa coopération, surtout par les Serbes et les nations Slaves, contre la France et ses alliés, il ne faudrait rien negliger à cet effet...*' From the handwritten rescript by Emperor Alexander I to Admiral Chichagov, from Vilna, dated 14 [26] May 1812. In the Archive of the M.F.A.

ence upon the veteran, wounded warrior, earnestly praying in the houses of God for the salvation of the Fatherland. When the Supreme Decree on the establishment of the *opolchenie* was issued, Kutuzov was unanimously chosen as Commander of the St Petersburg Territorial Forces, on 17 (29) June, five days before the return of the Tsar to St Petersburg. Such an appointment did not correspond at all either to his achievements or to his seniority in service; but it would serve the far-sighted Kutuzov as a stepping stone to new exploits and distinctions, and therefore he accepted this position on condition: 'to leave it should he be called to other duties, or if his employment in the *opolchenie* is not pleasing to the Tsar.'[14]

Kutuzov, having become the Commander of the St Petersburg Territorial Forces, performed his duties with extreme eagerness: he spent whole days engaged in the reception of warriors, went into all the details of their equipment, training them in person and giving them instructions. All eyes were turned on Kutuzov with surprise and heartfelt concern, the brilliant former ambassador of the Russian Monarchs Catherine and Paul, the former commander of the army, enthusiastic for the common cause in the time of the Fatherland's distress. Such self-sacrifice did not go unrewarded: on 29 July [10 August], Emperor Alexander elevated Kutuzov to princely dignity, with the title of His Grace, and, following that, on 8 (20) August, summoning him to Himself, announced his appointment as the Commander-in-Chief of all armies and *opolchenie*. Kutuzov, as he himself said, on the evening of the same day, in the circle of his relatives, 'I heard the command of the Tsar with Christian humility, but without timidity, as a calling from above.' So it was that all Russians regarded this high appointment of the honoured warrior; this was how the now grateful Russia looked at this event.

On the same day, 8 [20] August, Emperor Alexander honoured Kutuzov with the following rescript:

> Prince Mikhail Ilarionovich! The present state of the military situation with Our active armies, although preceded by initial successes, nevertheless the consequences of these have not yet revealed the rapid activity with which it would be necessary to operate in order to defeat the enemy. In considering these consequences and extracting the true reasons for this, I find it necessary to appoint a single common Commander-in-Chief over all the active armies, whose selection, in addition to military talents, would be based on seniority itself. Your well-known virtues, love for the Fatherland and repeated evidence from your outstanding exploits, have gained for you the

---

14 On this occasion, Count M.I. Kutuzov wrote to Emperor Alexander: 'Most Merciful Tsar. On the 17 of this month [29 July], the St Petersburg Society of Nobility called me to their assembly, where they announced a majority desire that I accept command of the general *opolchenie* of the St Petersburg Governorate, established by the nobility. In order not to delay the eager actions of the Nobility with a refusal, I have accepted this proposal and gone into action on their part; but upon the condition that, being in Your Imperial Majesty's active military service, if I am called to another commission, or if Your Imperial Majesty does not approve of this action of mine in any way, then I must leave this position to someone else on the choice of the Nobility. Most Merciful Tsar, from Your Imperial Majesty's most humble subject, Count Mikhail G.-Kutuzov. 18 [30] July 1812, St Petersburg.'

true right to this authority from Me. In choosing you for this important work, I have asked Almighty God to bless your exploits for the glory of the Russian armed forces, and may they justify the hope for good fortune that the Fatherland places in you.

At the same time, the following rescript was sent to each of the Commanders-in-Chief of the armies: Barclay de Tolly, Prince Bagration, Tormasov and Chichagov:

> Various important dysfunctions that have occurred following the union of the two armies impose on Me the necessary duty of appointing a single overall commander for all of them. I have chosen General of Infantry Prince Kutuzov for this, to whom I subordinate all four armies. As a result, I order you, with the army entrusted to you, to follow his orders precisely. I am sure that your love for the Fatherland and eagerness for service will also open the route to new achievements for you, which I shall be very pleased to distinguish with the appropriate awards.

The news of Kutuzov's appointment as Commander-in-Chief of all the armed forces operating against Napoleon was greeted throughout Russia with inexpressible delight. Such a disposition from the whole nation in favour of a single person was sufficiently convincing of the need to appoint Kutuzov as the commander of the armed forces of the state. Foreign historians, without having delved into the state of affairs, have tried to question whether Kutuzov really deserved the place of honour which had been placed upon him by the will of the Tsar and the voice of the nation, the voice of God. For us Russians, such an inquiry is completely pointless: in Kutuzov, we honour the commander who liberated Russia from foreign invasion, we revere his memory and do not labour the issue at all: was it possible to do better than what Kutuzov had done so well? Foreigners pointlessly try to diminish the merits of our commander: the best judges of these may be those to whom they have been of benefit. They vainly suggest that the sixty-seven-year-old Kutuzov was incapable of commanding the army: yet he retained his mental faculties until his demise and, even lying on his deathbed in Bunzlau [Bolesławiec], he gave out wise advice. They vainly try to expose his shortcomings compared to our other generals: we readily admit that Kutuzov was inferior to Barclay de Tolly in administrative capability and to Prince Bagration in activity; we will not deny that Barclay's retreat paved the way for Kutuzov's subsequent successes, but at the same time, while paying tribute to all, we say that only Kutuzov could have made the decision on the unequal battle at Borodino and the abandoning of the capital, sacred to the minds of the Russian people. Foreigners have accused him of slowness, of being (in their opinion) excessively cautious in combat. Saying that he could have achieved more significant victories. It is impossible not to admit the validity of this opinion, but it is very difficult to resolve questions of what could and could not have been done in reality, and besides, there is no doubt that it was a disadvantage to have to deal with cautious military commanders for Napoleon, who bested all his opponents in tactical skill, and for the French, who were more capable of great achievements on the day of battle than of constantly enduring prolonged labour and hardship. During the entire period of the Napoleonic Wars, the generals who operated with the greatest success against French troops, Wellington [Arthur Wellesley, 1st Duke of Wellington] and Kutuzov, both were distinguished by their ability to weaken the enemy, while avoiding a decisive denouement of the issue. Some historians, in trying to diminish the reputation of our leader, accused him of cunning, duplicity, court intrigues. Indeed, Kutuzov was gifted with a very sophisticated mind, which provided him with the means to successfully extract himself from the most difficult situations. Suvorov, to whom Kutuzov was a protégé, used to say about him, without being negative: 'cunning, very cunning; even Ribas [Don Jose de Ribas y Boyons] cannot outsmart him.' Kutuzov himself, in 1812, upon leaving St Petersburg for the army, was pleased with an impolite question from one of his closest relatives: 'Uncle, do you really hope to defeat Napoleon?'

'Defeat? No! But I hope to outwit him.' He replied.

Kutuzov, throughout his life, and even more so in his advanced years, was distinguished by evasiveness, which often came to the point where he often sacrificed his own beliefs. One of the officers in his headquarters, Mayevsky [Sergei Ivanovich Mayevsky], said that when our troops had linked up on the Berezina river, he dared to report to the Field Marshal about the benefits of appointing someone as Chief of Artillery for all the Russian armies. Kutuzov responded 'Who is better than Rezvoy [Dmitry Petrovich Rezvoy]; he is a smart, experienced man, and knows this business better than anyone.' No sooner had he managed to utter these words than Count Arakcheev approached him. 'The Sovereign Emperor is pleased to combine the command of all artillery in the person of a single artillery general,' he said; 'his selection is left to Your Grace. His Majesty believes that the best thing is to entrust this post to A.P. Yermolov [Alexey Petrovich Yermolov].' Kutuzov, pointing to Mayevsky, replied 'Ask him, we just talked about this, and I myself wanted to ask the Sovereign Emperor to appoint Yermolov. And is there a better choice?'[15]

The usual secrecy of Prince Kutuzov, turning into a habit, made him sly even when there was no need for it, and the bitter experience of a long life, although it convinced him of the ingratitude of many people whom he had rewarded, nevertheless, did not protect him from the influence of persons who enjoyed his confidence and sometimes exploited his favour for evil.

Some foreign historians, including Thiers [Adolphe Thiers], by introducing the trivia of Kutuzov's private life into the epic of the war of 1812, presented him as 'extremely depraved, deceitful,' etc. Others have tried to depict him as lazy and idle, which might have been explained by his advancing years, which prevented him from personally leading regiments into action, and from engaging in correspondence, which was indeed neglected in his army. The most important documents brought

---

15 Lieutenant General Mayevsky's notes, compiled in 1812 in Prince Kutuzov's headquarters. [Liprandi is extremely sceptical of this anecdote: '…under no circumstances could an officer such as Mayevsky remain in the same room once Arakcheev, having been sent by the Tsar to Kutuzov, began to inform the Commander-in-Chief of the will of the Emperor. Everything that Mayevsky wrote about Kutuzov, Rezvoy and Yermolov, had to have been over-heard from the adjoining room, the Adjutant's Room, after he had left; indeed, for Mayevsky to remain personally present in the same room as they were talking about this, I repeat a hundred times, could not have happened, and has been included in the Notes simply as an embellishment].

for the Field Marshal's signature were left 'until tomorrow,' and this 'tomorrow' was sometimes repeated for several weeks. It took him more effort to write a few consecutive words, or to sign ten documents one after another, than for some to write several successive pages. But then in his better moods, he used to say to anyone who came with business: 'do not be angry, my dear fellow; truly, I shall sign your notes tomorrow...'[16] whereupon one could hope with almost certainty that he would keep his word. With such a strong distaste for all correspondence, Kutuzov retained the gift of the spoken word, with which he charmed everyone right up to his death. As a gifted raconteur, he captivated and enraptured even shedding tears himself, caused by the emotion. No one knew how to reward insults inflicted out of impatience or temper better than Prince Kutuzov; no one possessed the art of flattering under the guise of rudeness better than him. Once, when Konovnitsyn [Pëtr Petrovich Konovnitsyn], having introduced one of his subordinates to Kutuzov in person and praising his courage, the Field Marshal said angrily: 'I beg you not to take him with you; you have already deprived me of many worthy men.' Despite the scepticism and secrecy of his character, Kutuzov was loved by those around him; his shortcomings and weaknesses did not prevent him from gaining and keeping the general confidence of the troops. Later, on the eve of the Battle of Lützen one of the Field Marshal's aides de camp brought the news of his death, it was ordered to suppress this news in the deepest secrecy: thus, Kutuzov was no more, but the Russian army went into battle as if guided by his spirit.[17]

We shall not elevate Kutuzov at the expense of other contemporaries of Emperor Alexander I; we shall not attribute the achievements made by other personalities in the great cause of saving the Fatherland to him, but we will preserve in history the memory of the feelings that the Russians had for him in 1812, and ignore the frivolous appraisal of him by Thiers. We remain in the hope that the compatriots of this renowned historian will be more impartial than him towards our commander; many wars had been waged by them against the Russians, but, even in hostilities with each other, both nations had respected one another, and having returned to harmony, mutual sympathy was attempted and the despicable weapon of slander was never resorted to.

---

16 Kutuzov had a habit of using words in the diminutive in conversation. [Liprandi is dubious of the veracity of this story: 'I never served with him in person, but in 1812, in the appointment I held at the time, I had occasion to visit headquarters several times a day, and more than once received immediate and clear approval of verbal reports delivered to him. I might also have expected to hear of this quirk of the Field Marshal's from my comrades, but never did'].

17 [Liprandi has the following to say with regard to the spirit of Kutuzov: '...this might be taken for irony; since towards what fate was the spirit of Kutuzov leading: we lost the battle of Lützen and abandoned the Leipzig area for the Elbe; lost the battles at Bautzen and Görlitz and retreated to the Oder, while here an armistice was signed... I also doubt that they wanted to keep Kutuzov's death a secret so as not to shake the morale of the soldiers. Our soldiers do not become discouraged by such news, rather, on the contrary, they become hardened and strive for vengeance... Moreover, the troops at Lützen were commanded by Count Wittgenstein, for whom the soldier's love in 1812 far exceeded that which they had for Kutuzov for the simplest of reasons: Kutuzov had given Moscow up to the enemy, while Wittgenstein, not only then, but even now is revered among the people as the saviour of Peter the Great's city].

Kutuzov, endowed with extraordinary quick wit, fully understood that Barclay de Tolly, in avoiding a general battle, had acted in accordance with the circumstances in which he found himself. The intuition of an experienced military commander also could not hide the fact that it was necessary to continue to operate in the same way as Barclay had. But at the same time, Kutuzov knew very well what Russia expected from the commander of her armies, and therefore, from the first day of his appointment, in any event, he showed his intention to fight Napoleon.

On 11 (23) August, at the very moment that our Western armies were retreating towards Dorogobuzh, Kutuzov set off from St Petersburg on his greatest mission; saving the Fatherland.

16

The Conference at Åbo

The correspondence between Emperor Alexander and the Crown Prince of Sweden in 1812. – The arrival of the Tsar in Åbo. – The conference at Åbo. – Its consequences.

On 9 (21) August, the day after Kutuzov was appointed Commander-in-Chief of the Russian armies, Emperor Alexander went to Åbo [Turku] to meet with the Crown Prince of Sweden [Jean-Baptiste Bernadotte].

The circumstances that gave rise to the rapprochement between Russia and Sweden were as follows. Even during the time when negotiations were underway in Fredrikshamn [Hamina] in order to conclude peace between these Powers, the Swedish king Charles XIII, finding the concession of the Åland Islands very painful, turned to Napoleon, petitioning for these islands to be left in the possession of Sweden and asking for his intercession. Napoleon, instead of doing anything in favour of the king of Sweden, replied: 'Appeal to the magnanimity of Emperor Alexander.' The consequences demonstrated that the Emperor of the French, quite unintentionally, had given the king some very good advice.[1] Two years later, when Napoleon's troops invaded Swedish Pomerania, the Crown Prince, notifying our Tsar of this violation of the nation's rights, believed that the occupation of Pomerania portended a danger threatening Russia. The prince wrote: 'And therefore, it is necessary that relations between us be distinguished by perfect frankness... Only the Northern Powers can put up a barrier to the invasions that threaten to spread to the oceans themselves.'[2]

In response to this letter, Emperor Alexander expressed the hope that the alliance between Sweden and Russia and the elevated abilities of the prince would neutralise the destructive plans that threatened the general peace. The Tsar wrote: 'For my part, nothing shall be omitted in order to justify your opinions of me. The respect and friendship of Your Highness is very dear to me and I flatter myself with the hope that a personal acquaintance between us would further strengthen the ties that unite us forever.'[3]

---

1   Garden, *Histoire générale des traités de paix*, XIII, 214.Garden, *Histoire générale des traités de paix*, XIII, 214.
2   The Crown Prince's letter to Emperor Alexander, dated 6 February 1812, new style (Archive of the M.F.A.).
3   Emperor Alexander's letter dated 13 (25) February 1812 (Archive of the M.F.A.).

Following this, Count Sukhtelen [Pëtr Kornilovich Sukhtelen or Jan Pieter van Suchtelen] was sent from St Petersburg to Stockholm with instructions to present the views of our Tsar to the King and the Crown Prince. On this occasion, Emperor Alexander, expressing his desire to establish a lasting alliance between the Northern Powers, wrote to the prince:

> This alone may serve as a counterweight to the ever-increasing power of France, supported by the States which are its tributaries. Sweden and Russia shall lead by example. It is to be hoped that this will be followed by other Powers. The eminent talents of Your Royal Highness will be an essential support to this great work. It is reserved for you to play a very large role and to follow in the footsteps of Gustavus Adolphus, to complete what he could only begin. But to this political work is added another much more essential still according to my point of view. It is that of reviving liberal ideas in Europe, of preserving it from this barbarism towards which it is advancing with such giant strides, that of finally turning the design to the happiness of this unfortunate humanity oppressed so pitilessly for so many years.[4]

In response to this letter, the Crown Prince, assuring Emperor Alexander of his devotion and his animated desire to contribute to the generous efforts of our Tsar, wrote: 'All will become easy for me, as soon as my fatherland is sure of the acquisition necessary for Sweden,[5] and then I shall be able to prove in full how dearly I value Your Majesty's trust in me.' At the same time, the Crown Prince gave notice of a proposal made by the Austrian resident at the Court of Stockholm, Count Neipperg [Adam Albert von Neipperg], as a result of a letter to him from Prince Schwarzenberg [Karl Philipp Fürst zu Schwarzenberg], who, notifying him of the treaty of alliance concluded between Austria and France, instructed him to invite the Swedish government to participate in this alliance, of which, according to Schwarzenberg, the natural consequence would be the return of Finland to the Swedes. At the same time, the Prince brought to the attention of Emperor Alexander that Napoleon was trying to make him the instigator of war, and therefore, in all probability, would postpone the opening of hostilities for some time. In the opinion of the Crown Prince, this was to Russia's advantage, which, having gained time,

---

4 'Je me suis empressé d'expedier le général Souchetelen à Stockholm pour achever l'oeuvre si bien commencée d'une union etroite des puissances du Nord; s'est elle seule qui peut opposer un contrepoids à la puissance toujours croissante de la France appuyée par les États qui lui sont tributaires. La Suède et la Russie vont donner l'exemple. Il y a à ésperer qu'il sera suivi par d'autres Puissances. Les talents éminents de V.A.R. seconderont essentiellement cette grande oeuvre. Il lui est réservé de jouer un bien grand rôle et marchant sur les traces de Gustave Adolphe, d'achever ce qu'il n'a pu que commencer. Mais à cette oeuvre politique se joint une autre beaucoup plus essentielle encore d'après ma manière de voir. C'est celle d faire renaitre les idées libérales en Europe, de la préserver de cette barbarie à la quelle elle marche à si grands pas, celle enfin de tourner la conception au bonheur de cette malheureuse humanité oppressée si impitoyablement depuis tant d'années.' Extracted from Emperor Alexander's letter to the Crown Prince, dated 26 February (9 March) 1812 (Archive of the M.F.A.).
5 Norway.

could acquire new allies, meanwhile, the justness of the cause defended by them would imperceptibly attract public opinion to their side, which up to this point had been the main spring of Napoleon's successes. The Crown Prince wrote:

> The possibility of a postponement of hostilities between the Northern Powers and France should make it easier for Your Majesty to conclude peace with the Porte, to which end, in my opinion, every kind of concession should be decided upon. The Sultan, having become convinced of the danger that threatens him, might perhaps conclude an alliance with Russia, Britain and Sweden, and in order to induce him to do so, it should be enough to give him hope for the renewal of the Turkish protectorates over Ragusa [Dubrovnik] and the Septinsular [Ionian] Islands and for the acquisition of Dalmatia.[6]

Meanwhile, Count Löwenhielm [Carl Axel Löwenhielm], sent to St Petersburg by the King of Sweden, conducted negotiations that ended on 24 March (5 April) with the conclusion of a treaty of alliance between Russia and Sweden. On the basis of this agreement, Emperor Alexander undertook to assist the Swedish government in the acquisition of Norway, a consequence of which was to be the landing of a Russo-Swedish corps on the coast of northern Germany in order to mount raids against Napoleon and his allies.[7]

With regard to the conclusion of this treaty of alliance, Emperor Alexander expressed His complete delight to the Crown Prince, and, at the same time, informed him of the weakness of Austria's position towards Russia and wrote about the need to prepare for the forthcoming struggle. In the opinion of Emperor Alexander:

> The Slavic nations, warlike by nature, upon being encouraged, will form an imposing whole, and united with the malcontents of Hungary, should produce a powerful distraction for Austria and the French territories on the Adriatic. With good luck it might be possible even to penetrate far enough through Bosnia and Croatia to establish communications with the Tyroleans and through there with Switzerland. I am sending Admiral Chichagov, a leading man [*homme de tête*], to organise everything accordingly, but it is vital for Britain to want to support us powerfully both in the Baltic through its naval assets, and by taking up German battalions into its pay, which may be formed if desertion is encouraged among the troops of the Confederation, and that by supplying money and munitions to the Slavs they will act for the general cause of independence...[8]

---

6   The Crown Prince's letter dated 1 April 1812, new style (Archive of the M.F.A.).
7   The terms of this treaty are set out in [Volume 1] Chapter IV.
8   '... *Un grand plan me semble devoir être embrassé; les nations Slaves, belliqueses par leur nature, étant stimulées, formeront un ensemble imposant et réunies aux mécontents de la Hongrie, produiront une diversion puissante contre l'Autriche et les possessions françaises de l'Adriatique. Dans des chances heureuses il ne sera pas impossible même de pénétrer par la Bosnie et la Croatie assez avant pour se mettre en contact avec les Tyroliens et par-là avec la Suisse. J'envoie l'amiral Tchitchagoff, homme de tête, tout organiser en consequence, mais il serait urgent que*

At the same time, the Crown Prince, wishing to induce the Ottoman Porte to end the war with Russia, sent General Baron Tawast [Johan Henrik Tawast] to negotiate with the Turks, ordering him to go to St Petersburg to our Tsar in order to receive proper instruction.[9] Emperor Alexander, informing the prince of the news of the conclusion of the Treaty of Bucharest, which pushed the borders of the empire to the Prut and the lower Danube, expressed his gratitude for the orders given to General Tawast and of the instructions given to him.[10]

The consensus and sincerity that prevailed in relations between our Tsar and the Prince of Sweden, arousing the disbelief of the agents of other European powers and forced them to resort to intrigues. The Crown Prince was informed from Paris about a note received by the French Minister of Foreign Affairs from the Danish resident in St Petersburg, Blom, in which this diplomat wrote that the chancellor Count Rumyantsev, speaking with him about the current state of affairs, criticised the Danish government for concentrating troops on the southern borders of the kingdom and intending to form garrisons from them in Hamburg and Lübeck, and that, the chancellor is alleged on this occasion to have revealed openly Emperor Alexander's proposal to assist Sweden in the acquisition of Norway. The Crown Prince, notifying our Tsar of these rumours, which could have upset the plans of the allied northern powers, wrote at the same time about sending Narbonne [Louis-Marie-Jacques-Amalric de Narbonne-Lara] to the headquarters of our army. Warning Emperor Alexander about Napoleon's intentions, the Swedish prince wrote:

> In any event, the King and I hope that Your Imperial Majesty, once peace has been restored with France, ensure the accession of Norway to Sweden, which can bring real benefit to Russia only once this country has been added to its territories. In remaining within its current borders, Sweden would involuntarily lean in the direction of France, which would constantly tempt them with the hope of acquiring Norway or returning Finland. But the tranquillity of the north of Europe might only be ensured in such a case once Sweden has been obliged with the annexation of Norway through the influence of Your Majesty. Only then will the last traces of the former strife between the Russians and the Swedes be erased, who, in relying on the constant devotion of Russia, will be convinced that an alliance with them is more profitable than any other.[11]

---

l'Angleterre voulût nous seconder puissament tant sur la Baltique, par ses armements maritimes, et en prenant à sa solde les bataillons allemands, qu'on pourra former si la désertion s'introduit dans les trouppes de la confédération, qu'en fournissant de l'argent et des munitions aux Slaves qui agiront pour la cause de l'indépendance générale...' Extracted from Emperor Alexander's letter to the Crown Prince of Sweden, dated 9 (21) April 1812 (Archive of the M.F.A.).

9   The Crown Prince's letter to Emperor Alexander, dated 19 April (1 May) 1812 (Archive of the M.F.A.).
10 Emperor Alexander's letter to the Crown Prince, dated 24 May (5 June) 1812 (Archive of the M.F.A.).
11 The Crown Prince's note to the Tsar, dated 26 May (7 June) 1812 (Archive of the M.F.A.).

Emperor Alexander answered the prince with irrefutable evidence proving that the dispatch sent from Paris was inspired only by a desire to cause a quarrel between Sweden and Russia. The Tsar wrote, at Narbonne's expense: 'Every sentence transmitted by him is nothing but a completely distorted summary of events... It appears, we should expect the opening of hostilities soon.' At the same time, Emperor Alexander, fulfilling the wishes of the prince, authorised the Russian resident in Stockholm, General Sukhtelen, to conclude a peace treaty with Britain, but on condition that, simultaneously with the signing of this treaty, the British pledged to pay subsidies to Sweden.[12]

On 13 (25) June, notifying the prince of the passage of Napoleon's forces across our borders, Emperor Alexander wrote: 'I trust firmly in the Providence of God, in the righteousness of my cause and in the courage of my armies. I also have complete faith in the friendship of the King and of Your Royal Highness...' Two days later, on 15 (27) June, the Crown Prince, as if in anticipation of the onset of a fatal denouement, expressed his thoughts on Napoleon's method of waging war in the following terms: 'The Emperor Napoleon's habit of handling large armies must necessarily give him confidence. But if Your Majesty can manage His resources well, if He does not find Himself forced to accept a general battle and if He can reduce the war to marching and minor actions, the Emperor Napoleon will undoubtedly commit some fault from which His Majesty would be able to take advantage.'[13]

Emperor Alexander, in response to this letter, informed the prince that, following the principles set forth in his responses, the Russians were waging a war of patience (*une guerre de lenteur*) and that First Army, yielding to the superior strength of the enemy, was retreating to a fortified position on the Dvina, while Second Army was preparing to switch to the offensive, to march on the flank of the enemy army. The Tsar wrote: 'I shall continue to inform Your Highness of the events of this important war. In the meantime, you may rest assured that since this has already begun, my firm resolve is to make it last for years, even if I have to fight on the banks of Volga...'[14]

---

12 Emperor Alexander's letter to the Crown Prince, dated 3 (15) June 1812 (Archive of the M.F.A.).
13 '... *L'habitude qu'a l'empereur Napoléon de manier des grandes armées doit nécessairement lui donner de la confiance. Mais si V.M. peut bien ménager Ses moyens, si Elle ne se trouve pas forcée d'accepter une bataille générale et qu'Elle puisse reduire la guerre à des marches et des combats partiels, l'empereur Napoléon commettra indubitablement quelque faute dont V.M. pourra profiter...*' Extracted from the Crown Prince's letter to Emperor Alexander, dated 15 (27) June 1812 (Archive of the M.F.A.).
14 '*Par les notions que le comte de Löwenhielm donne à V.A.R. et par les bulletins ci-joints Elle verra, que fidèle aux principes énoncés dans les lettres de V.A. et qu'Elle me retrace encore dans sa dernière, avec tant de justesse, je fais une guerre de lenteur, et puisqu'une force superieure marche sur moi, je me retire en concentrant mes forces vers une position fortifiée que j'ai fait préparer à ce but sur la Dvina. en attendant j'ai fait prendre l'offensive à la seconde armée en la dirigeant sur la droite de celle de l'enemi qui marche sur moi, de même qu'un corps considerable de cosaques pour le harceler. Je continuerai d'instruire V.A. succesivement des évènements de cette guerre importante. En attendant, qu'Elle se persuade que puisqu'une fois elle est commencée, ma ferme résolution est de la faire durer des années, dusse-je combattre sur les rives de Wolga...*' Extracted from the Tsar's letter to the Crown Prince, dated 22 June (4 July) 1812, from Vilna (Archive of the M.F.A.).

Emperor Alexander rated the talents of the Crown Prince very highly, writing to him:

> May I be allowed to say that I very much wished that Your Highness could have been at the head of my armies, so that Your abilities and experience could guide them in their operations, directing all forces towards the achievement of the common goal. Your letters were received by me when there was no longer sufficient time to change previously issued orders. Openly acknowledging that your ideas are incomparably superior to anything we have done, I will say that, at least, we have managed to avoid general battles until now, and have maintained success in all the minor actions. I am dissatisfied with the movements of Second Army, which, operating with insufficient pace, has allowed itself to be forestalled at an important location – Minsk; but in spite of this, I hope that we can correct this error.
>
> In deciding to continue this war to the bitter end (*à outrance*), I have had to attend to the formation of new reserves…[15]

As for the plans of action for our army drawn up by the Crown Prince, as far as can be judged from his correspondence, he proposed to Emperor Alexander, that general battle be offered by concentrating forces near Smolensk. The prince wrote:

> Their loss does not threaten us with disastrous consequences, because the arrival of reserves would compensate for the casualties among the Russian troops, while Napoleon's army, weakened daily by disease and combat casualties, would soon lose their advantage in numerical terms. The enemy might perhaps win two or three battles, the fourth would be indecisive, and if Your Majesty persists in continuing the matter, then, without any doubt, the fifth will be won.

At the same time, the Crown Prince recommended sending the Army of the Danube across Napoleon's lines of communication, towards Vilna, while using the troops of the Riga garrison to launch amphibious raids behind enemy lines at Mitau [Jelgava] and beyond, and to attack the blockading corps around Riga with the aim of forcing MacDonald [Étienne (Jacques-Joseph-Alexandre) MacDonald] to split his forces.[16]

---

15 Emperor Alexander's letter to the Crown Prince, dated 17 (29) July 1812 (Archive of the M.F.A.).
16 'Je felicite V.M.I. des succés que quelqu'uns de ses corps ont obtenu. Celui du prince de Witgenstein est d'un bon augure et j'espère que les autres imiterons l'exemple qu'il vient de leur donner. Maintenant, Sire, il faut une bonne bataille et tout me fait présumer qu'elle est déjà livrée à Senno, Orza et Mohilow. Mais si elle n'a pas eu lieu, sans doute que les troupes de V.M. occupent Smolensk et qu'elles y attendent l'ennemi avec l'intention de se bien battre; quels que puissent en être les résultats, V.M. n'en doit pas être allarmée. Ses corps de réserve répareront Ses pertes, tandisque l'empereur Napoléon, s'affaiblissant tous les jours par les maladies et les combats, doit avant longtemps se trouver reduit à un nombre bien inferieur à celui de V. Majesté. Il est possible qu'il gagne la première, la seconde, la troisième bataille, la quatrième sera indecise, et si V.M. persévère, il est indubitable qu'Elle gagnera la cinquième.

Emperor Alexander, wishing to seal the alliance between Russia and Sweden, expressed to the Crown Prince, through Count Löwenhielm, his desire to meet in person. The King of Sweden, having been informed of this by the prince himself, immediately agreed to the proposal by our Tsar. The consequence of this was the meeting between Emperor Alexander and the Prince of Sweden, in Åbo. The Tsar, upon arriving in this city on 12 (24) August, at six o'clock in the afternoon, stopped in the main square, at the residence of Chief Director von Brümmer, where he was met by the Governor General, members of the Governing Council (later renamed the Finland Senate), the Supreme Court, the University, as well as the clergy, magistrates and honourable residents of the city. Every street along which the Emperor passed was filled with a dense crowd of people, expressing their joy with loud cheers, repeated every time the Tsar appeared at the windows of the chambers he was occupying. Both on this day and on the next, the city was illuminated, but there were no festivities, because the Emperor had told the deputation of Åbo citizens who were presented to His Majesty that, 'due to uncertain situation at that time, he did not consider it appropriate to accept their invitation to the ball prepared by the city.'

Three days after the arrival of Emperor Alexander I in Åbo, on 15 (27) August, the Crown Prince of Sweden arrived there on the frigate *Jarramas*.[17] The reception given to him by our Tsar was remarkable for its cordiality and attentiveness. In continuation of their conference 'on the means to counter Napoleon and to liberate Europe from the yoke imposed upon it,' the Crown Prince, fulfilling the desire of the Swedes accompanying him, petitioned for the return of the Åland Islands to Sweden. Emperor Alexander replied:

> I would gladly fulfil this request by Your Highness if I were not quite sure that such a concession would harm me in the opinion of my people. It would be better for me to give you Riga with the islands of Ezel [Saaremaa] and Dago [Hiiumaa], but only as collateral until the terms concluded between us are fully fulfilled.

> J'ai appris avec un grand contentement l'offre patriotique qu'ont fait à V.M.J. les gouvernements de Moscow, Nignie-Nowgorod, Smolensk et Twer; le veritable patriotisme s'explique par l'énergie et les sacrifices chez un peuple dont les individus ne séparent point leurs intérêts de ceux de l'Etat; l'attachement qu'on porte aux loix et au prince sont la sauvegarde de l'honneur et de l'indépendance de la nation.
> A toutes les levées que V.M.J. vient d'obtenir, je pense qu'Elle aura ajouté cette armée valeureuse et aguerrie qui a fait trembler le Croissant. Je crois que Votre Majesté devrait la faire venir en poste et la diriger sur la capitale de la Lithuanie. Cette marche intimiderait d'autant plus l'empereur Napoléon, que quand méme il serait victorieux à Smolensk, aucun de ses renforts ne pourrait plus lui parvenir et si au contraire la bataille est restée incertaine, ce mouvement audacieux le forcera ou à répasser le Niemen, ou à detacher un grand corps pour aller à la rencontre de ces braves, et des-lors V.M. peut reprendre l'offensive.
> La garnison de Riga ne devrait pas rester renfermée dans la place; elle devra faire des débarquements dans les environs de Mitau et même plus loin à fin d'arreter la marche du maréchal Macdonald et l'obliger à se disseminer, et alors saisir l'àpropos pour attaquer les troupes qui formeraient le blocus de la place.' Extracted from the Crown Prince's letter dated 11 August 1812, new style (Archive of the M.F.A.).

17 Extracted from the Åbo Gazette 1812, Nos 101 and 105 (M.T.D. No. 47,352, folio 10).

Whereupon the Crown Prince said in response that the word of our Tsar was more important for him than any material collateral, following which Emperor Alexander, shaking his hand, answered that he would never forget such a noble act.[18]

On 18 (30) August, the representatives of both Powers, Chancellor Count Rumyantsev and Count Löwenhielm, signed a convention for the following: Emperor Alexander undertook to reinforce an auxiliary corps pledging some 35,000 men to Sweden, of whom 25,000 would arrive in Scania [Skåne] by the end of September and the remaining 10,000 by the end of November, weather permitting. As soon as the 25,000 Russian troops were landed on the Swedish coast, the King of Sweden would open hostilities against the Danish islands. In the event that Denmark refused to cede Norway in favour of Sweden and to ally the Danish troops to the coalition army, for joint operations against the common enemy, the Swedish Crown Prince would land on the island of Zeeland, but after conquering it, on the matter of ownership, would agree this with His Majesty, the King of Great Britain. The Emperor of All Russia, while ceding any claims to this island in favour of the King of Sweden, nevertheless grants himself the right to approve all the conditions that are to be met on this subject between Sweden and Great Britain. The King of Sweden, for his part, undertook, in the event of expanding the boundaries of the Russian Empire to the Vistula [Wisła] at the conclusion of peace, to recognise such an increase in Russian territories as fair reparations for the sacrifices and efforts made in the war against the common enemy. His Majesty, the King of Great Britain, was invited to a similar undertaking with regards to Russia. As for the diversions to be carried out by the coalition in Germany or in any other country, it was necessary to fulfil all the orders related to these in accordance with the terms of the treaty of 24 March (5 April). His Majesty the Emperor undertook to lend Sweden 1,500,000 Roubles, within eight months from the date of the mutual ratification of this convention.

According to a separate secret clause, the contracting Powers, desiring, by mutual consent, to give the present alliance the character of a family agreement, pledged, in the event of a hostile attack by any power against Russia or Sweden, to assist one another with a corps of troops, totalling no more than 12,000 to 15,000 men.[19]

The day following the signing of this treaty, Emperor Alexander, in the presence of the Crown Prince, reviewed the troops of 6th Division, 21st Division and 25th Division assigned to assist the Swedes. The Prince of Sweden said to the Tsar: 'Your troops are excellent; they come from the elite regiments of your army. These troops would be of great use to Wittgenstein, who is weakened daily, defending like a lion against Oudinot [Nicolas Charles Marie Oudinot] and MacDonald. Send these 35,000 men to help him.'

The Tsar replied: 'Your act is chivalrous but I cannot accept your offer; if I do that, how will you acquire Norway?'

The prince continued: 'If success is on your side, I shall get it. You will keep your word. If you are defeated, Europe will be subjugated; every sovereign would be

---

18 Garden, *Histoire générale des traités de paix*, XIII, 410-411.
19 Extracted from a copy of the treaty, concluded at Åbo, 18 (30) August 1812, held in the Archive of the Ministry of Foreign Affairs.

subject to the whims of Napoleon; it would be better to be a simple ploughman than to rule under such humiliating conditions.'[20]

Emperor Alexander accepted the Crown Prince's proposal. Part of the Russian force assembled in Finland was immediately sent by sea to Reval [Tallinn], from where it moved to Riga and subsequently up the Dvina to assist Count Wittgenstein.

It must be admitted that the Crown Prince, in this case, acted as a faithful, devoted ally. His daring to place the Russian corps entrusted to him at the disposal of Emperor Alexander was all the more generous because the conference in Åbo did not create a very favourable impression in Sweden, where many, not knowing about the prince's views on Norway, believed that his only objective had been to return Finland to the Swedes and that the consequences of the negotiations in Åbo did not bring any benefits to Sweden.

The meeting between our Tsar and the Crown Prince of Sweden strengthened the mutual respect and friendship between them. Emperor Alexander continued to inform King Charles XIII and the prince about all the most important events of the war, with complete honesty.[21] Subsequently, the Crown Prince did not live up to the expectations of the coalition Monarchs who had taken up arms against France: to them, his actions were indecisive and even duplicitous; they accused him of an insatiable lust for power, striving for dominion over France. All this notwithstanding, however, Russia could not forget his friendly relations with Emperor Alexander I at a time when almost every European ruler, willingly or otherwise, had taken the side of Napoleon. Gifted with a sophisticated, prudent mind, the Crown Prince foresaw the triumph of the Russian Monarch when all of Europe was still confident in the invincibility of the arrogant conqueror.

---

20 Garden, *Histoire générale des traités de paix*, XIII, 412-413.
21 The Crown Prince's letter to Emperor Alexander, dated 4 September 1812, new style, and the Tsar's response dated 2 (14) September 1812 (Archive of the M.F.A.).

17

The *Opolchenie*

> General orders for the *Opolchenie*. – *Opolchenie* of the 1st District, the Governorates of: Moscow, Tver, Yaroslavl, Vladimir, Ryazan, Tula, Kaluga, Smolensk. General conclusions regarding the *Opolchenie* of 1st District. – *Opolchenie* of the 2nd District, the Governorates of: St Petersburg and Novgorod. – *Opolchenie* of the 3rd District. General orders. Governorates of: Kostroma, Nizhegorod, Kazan, Vyatka, Simbirsk and Penza. – Calculation of the strengths of the *Opolchenie* and donations made by the 16 governorates of all three Districts. – Understanding the spirit of the Russian people of that era.

Emperor Alexander, during His visit to Moscow, finding a complete readiness for sacrifice for the common good in every class of the population of Russia, ordered the mobilisation of territorial forces to be limited to 16 governorates, dividing them into three districts.[1] Following this, by Supreme Decree to the Governing Senate, dated 31 July [12 August], 1812, it was decided:

> In order for the centralisation and collective consideration of all matters related to the newly formed internal *Opolchenie*, recognising that it is necessary to establish an Extraordinary Committee under Our person, Orders the following to be present on this committee: General of Artillery Count Arakcheev, Minister of Police Lieutenant General Balashov, Secretary of State Vice Admiral Shishkov [Alexander Semënovich Shishkov]. Reports from this Committee shall be submitted to Us by the Minister of Police, and the executive director shall be the Minister of State, Assistant Secretary of State, State Councillor Bakkarevich [Mikhail Nikitich Bakkarevich].[2]

In order to provide the most convenient overview of the activities of each and every one of the militias in Russia, we shall first state the general, and then the specific orders.

As soon as the Supreme Manifesto was issued, by order of the Governing Senate, on 6 [18] July regarding the general *opolchenie*, the Holy Synod decided to

---

1 The Manifesto of 18 [30] July 1812 (Complete Collection of Laws, 25,188, XXXII, 397).
2 Directed Decree to the Senate, dated 31 July [12 August] (Complete Collection of Laws, 25,193, XXXII, 401).

promulgate it by reading it out in every church and offering up a prayer for victory over the adversary on their knees after each liturgy. Together with the distribution of the Supreme Manifesto, the Synod's appeal calling upon all classes in the Name of the Lord to defend the Church, the Tsar and the Fatherland was published.[3] At the same time it decided:

1. To donate 1,500,000 Roubles to the St Petersburg and Moscow *opolchenie* from the income received from the sale of candles in church.
2. To invite all the clergy and laity to make offerings within their means.
3. To release, at their own request, clerics and seminarians, no higher than the rhetorical class, into the *opolchenie*, providing them with uniforms and rations from the church and providing for the remaining families of some of them.

Regarding the general orders for the *opolchenie*, the Committee, which was constituted to the Sovereign's Person, announced the following Supreme orders:

1. To establish a special reserve of capital from all the sums donated to the *opolchenie*, which should not be spent on any items, without Supreme authority.[4] Rations were to be distributed everywhere for three months, both in the provinces that have fielded *opolchenie*, and rations for the warriors that had not been assigned at the same time; while everything taken in excess of that amount shall be off-set against the calculation of the poll tax.[5] The heads of governorates that are not part of the *opolchenie*, are to propose to their nobles about joining the *opolchenie* of other governorates.[6]
2. To allow any official accused of petty crime to join the *opolchenie*, even if the investigation into their acts has not been concluded, the only condition being that the presence of the defendant is not necessary in order to complete the investigation.[7]

Civil servants who had not previously been in military service, upon admission to the *opolchenie*, were permitted the right to wear general's uniform without holding military rank for privy and active state councillors, while state, collegiate and court councillors were equivalent to *Rottmeisters* [cavalry captains] or captains, etc.

The *opolchenie* of the first two districts, assigned for urgent action against the enemy, were assembled during August.

---

3 Directed Decree dated 25 July [6 August] (Complete Collection of Laws, 25,191, XXXII, 398).
4 Supreme Orders to the Ministry of Finance, No. 38. Senate Decree dated 23 September [5 October] (Complete Collection of Laws, 25,235, XXXII, 431).
5 Supreme Orders dated 2 [14] September, No. 54.
6 Supreme Orders dated 2 [14] September, No. 65.
7 Supreme approval of the report by the Internal *Opolchenie* Committee, dated 3 [15] September (Complete Collection of Laws, 25,216, XXXII, 419).

The *opolchenie* of the 1st District, were under the command of the Commander-in-Chief of Moscow, Count Rostopchin [Fëdor Vasilevich Rostopchin], with the exception of the Tver and Yaroslavl Territorial Forces, which remained at the disposal of Prince Georg von Oldenburg [Peter Friedrich Georg (Georgy Petrovich) von Oldenburg].

I. Moscow Governorate

Upon the promulgation of the Supreme Manifesto of 6 [18] July, on the general *opolchenie*, two committees were established in Moscow: the first for receiving and arming the men and for managing their rations, and the second for collecting donations, money, weapons, provisions and wine, as well as for their storage and release for their intended consumption.

The first committee was composed of the civil governor, the provincial marshal of the nobility, the city leadership and several officials appointed by Supreme Orders; while the second included the vice governor and two deputies, a member of the nobility and others from the merchant class. By Supreme Order, on 18 [30] July, the following were appointed to sit on these committees: in the first: generals-of-infantry Arkharov [Nikolai Petrovich Arkharov] and Obolyaninov [Pëtr Khrisanfovich Obolyaninov] and General-of-Cavalry Apraksin [Stepan Stepanovich Apraksin]; while on the second was active privy councillor Prince Yusupov [Nikolai Borisovich Yusupov] (Decree of the Governing Senate, dated 25 July [6 August] 1812).

During the Tsar's visit to Moscow, by unanimous decision of the nobility, it was intended to produce one warrior per ten souls, and within a little over a month after the publication of the Manifesto of 18 [30] July, the Moscow Governorate had 27,500 (other sources 25,800) soldiers in the territorial *opolchenie*. It consisted of regiments of mounted Cossacks, foot jägers and dismounted Cossacks.

Each of the mounted Cossack regiments was divided into ten *Sotnia* [squadrons], in each of which there was one *Sotnia* comander, two subalterns, twelve *Uryadniki* [Cossack non-commissioned officers], one hundred and twenty Cossacks and one clerk; in total, a regiment consisted of: the regimental commander, ten *Sotnia* commanders, 24 subalterns (which included two regimental adjutants, a quartermaster and a paymaster), 120 *Uryadniki*, 1,200 Cossacks and 14 clerks.

In each of the jäger and dismounted Cossack regiments there were four battalions, while each battalion had four *Sotnia*. Each *Sotnia* consisted of one *Sotnia* commander, two subalterns, 11 *Uryadniki*, 150 jägers and a clerk; in total in each regiment there were: a regimental commander, four battalion commanders, 41 subalterns (including a regimental adjutant, four battalion adjutants and four battalion paymasters) 176 *Uryadniki*, 2,400 jägers and 26 clerks.

Regiments, battalions and *Sotnia* were identified by number. Regimental commanders selected from the major generals, and colonels and lieutenant colonels, were approved by the Tsar, battalion commanders – by the commanding general of the territorial force, while *Sotnia* commanders and each of the subalterns were selected by their regimental commander. In the course of August, twelve regiments were formed and marched out: one of mounted Cossacks, three of jägers and eight of dismounted Cossacks. In addition to the weapons donated by people of various classes, 500 muskets were issued to each regiment from the arsenals and 60 cartridges to each warrior. The commander of the Moscow *opolchenie* was Lieutenant General Count Morkov [Irakli Ivanovich Morkov], and the regimental commanders were: major generals: Talyzin 1st [Fëdor Ivanovich Talyzin] and 2nd [Alexander Ivanovich Talyzin], Prince Odoevsky [Ivan Sergeevich Odoevsky], Svechin [Ivan Petrovich Svechin?], Obreskov [Nikolai Vasilevich Obreskov], Count Santi [Alexander Frantsevich Santi], Lopukhin [Pëtr Andreevich Lopukhin], Arseniev [Vasily Dmitrievich Arseniev], Laptev [Vasily Danilovich Laptev], and colonels: Prince Chetvertinsky [Boris Antonovich Chetvertinsky] and Argamakov [Alexander Vasilevich Argamakov], and Lieutenant Colonel Svechin.[8]

In addition to the twelve regiments of the provincial *opolchenie*, four Moscow landowners volunteered to form four regiments at their own expense: Counts Dmitriev-Mamonov [Matvey Alexandrovich Dmitriev-Mamonov] and Saltykov [Pëtr Ivanovich Saltykov] would form cavalry, while Demidov [Nikolai Nikitich Demidov] and Prince Gagarin [Nikolai Sergeevich Gagarin] would form infantry. The Chief Procurator of the 6th Department of the Governing Senate, Count Dmitriev-Mamonov, volunteering to form a cavalry regiment, at his own expense, formed it into five squadrons of Ulans, for which he was granted the rank of major general and appointed Colonel in Chief of the regiment, which marched out from the Yaroslavl Governorate via Moscow and, having served as part of the reserve army, participated in the foreign campaigns, and was then disbanded in 1815. Colonel Count Saltykov also proposed to recruit a cavalry regiment, from men of various classes, consisting of ten squadrons, under the title the Moscow Hussar Regiment. This regiment was first formed in Moscow and drew its weapons from the arsenal there, and then in Kazan; on the death of Count Saltykov, they were amalgamated with the Irkutsk Hussar Regiment.[9] The formation of the remaining two regiments was never carried out.

Field officers and subalterns of the Moscow *opolchenie* were issued with standard army uniforms; while those who had uniforms when they retired were granted the right to wear them. The uniform for the lower ranks consisted of a Russian caftan with a sash and trousers made of a grey peasant cloth, a Russian shirt with a slanted collar, a scarf around the neck, a cap and boots. The caftans were supposed to be loose enough that it was possible to wear a sheepskin jacket under it, which in warm weather was carried rolled up over the knapsack, as were greatcoats. Each of the warriors wore a copper cross on his cap and under it the crowned monogram of the Tsar and the inscription: '*За Веру и Царя*' [for the Faith and the Tsar]. Warriors on foot had knapsacks, while horsemen had valises and bags for oats. The contents of the knapsacks and valises consisted of one shirt, a pair of linen trousers, mittens, two foot-cloths, cloth gaiters, a spare pair of boots and hard-tack for three days.

Regimental commanders did not receive a salary, as stated in the regulations on the constitution of the Moscow military force, 'they are accorded personal authority by the Sovereign Emperor, out of zeal towards the Fatherland, according to the importance of the rank in which they serve.' From among the battalion commanders, those in need received an allowance; the rest of the subalterns were given 30 Roubles

---

8   Extracted from information supplied by local authorities, stored in the M.T.D.
9   Extracted from information held in the M.T.D. No 46,692, folios 43 and 171.

per month for *Sotnia* commanders, while the remainder got 20 Roubles a month. Cavalry officers received a one-off grant of 150 Roubles towards the purchase of a horse and forage. *Uryadniki* received one Rouble 25 Kopecks, Cossacks and jägers one Rouble each per month, while all lower ranks, in general, received a ration of hard-tack. Officers could be rewarded on a par with the officers of the regular army for distinction in combat; those invalided through wounds were granted the right to a pension from the Muscovite classes. The lower ranks could receive a special medal for bravery; each of those who received it, as well as each of those who were invalided through wounds, had the right to a pension equal to the salary laid down for irregular service.[10]

The donations by the Moscow nobility and merchants, of cash and goods, were very large and would have been much greater if the occupation of Moscow by the enemy had not halted the efforts of each and every one of its inhabitants to contribute to the sacred cause of defending the Fatherland. The committee established to accept donations, had received, by the day of its closure, 30 August [11 September], 3,293,790 Roubles (including; 19 *Pud* [one *Pud* = 16.4 kg or 36 lb], 31 pounds, 16 *Zolotniki* of silver bullion and objects, and two *Pud*, 11 *Zolotniki* of gold); four Gospels, five crosses and five monstrances; 4,843 *Arshin* [one *Arshin* = 71 centimetres or 28 inches] of cloth, 4,928 *Arshin* and seven lengths of linen, 80 lengths of *Ravenstuch* [canvas], 112 bandages, two *Pud* 25 pounds of lint; 12 brass cannon and two of cast iron, 175 muskets, 235 sabres, 326 pikes, 100,000 flints; six *Vedro* [1 *Vedro* = 12.3 litres or 2.7 gallons] of wine, two cases of rum, and so on. In addition, a few days before the opening of hostilities, when horses, oxen and provisions were required for the army, and the Moscow Governorate, due to its remoteness from the location of the troops, could not participate in the supply of these items, the noble and merchant classes contributed a million Roubles in a single day.[11]

The Moscow *opolchenie* took part in the battle of Borodino and other actions.

II. Tver Governorate

The nobility of this province, soon after the promulgation of the Supreme Manifesto on 6 [18] July, in a meeting on 18 [30] July, unanimously expressed 'full readiness, in case of need, to take part in the defence of the beloved Monarchy and Fatherland, and to sacrifice all their wealth to that end.'[12] A committee of the Tver military force was established to manage all the affairs of the *opolchenie*, and its terms of reference were granted Supreme approval on 8 [20] August; the Novgorod and Yaroslavl Governorates were guided by the same terms. The Tver nobility decided to assemble 20 warriors from every 500 souls, including one mounted, which amounted to 12,366 foot and 665 mounted warriors from all the landowners' estates. From these, six regiments were formed: five foot and one mounted. Lieutenant General Tyrtov [Yakov Ivanovich Tyrtov][13] was selected as commander of the Tver *opolchenie*,

---

10 Extracted from information supplied by local authorities, held in the M.T.D.
11 Extracted from information supplied by local authorities, held in the M.T.D.
12 The original words of the designated nobility.
13 Former commander of the Tula Infantry Regiment during Suvorov's Italian and Swiss campaigns.

while the regimental commanders were: major generals Baklanovsky [Mikhail Alexeevich Baklanovsky] and Zagryazhsky; active state councillor Poltoratsky [Alexei Markovich Poltoratsky?] and Prince Shakhovskoy, colonels Dolgopolov and Boltin, commander of the mounted regiment. In addition to the six regiments of the provincial *opolchenie*, a battalion was formed in Tver from the peasants of the Grand Duchess Yekaterina Pavlovna.[14]

As for the armament of the Tver territorial force, the nobility could only supply the warriors with pikes. Clothing and equipment were modelled on that of the Moscow *opolchenie*. The warriors were supplied with provisions for four months. The mounted men received horses with full harness and 25 Roubles a month for fodder. In mid [late] July, the Minister of War referred to the Tver governor Kologrivov regarding the procurement in Tver and Rzhev of 58,476 *Chetvert* [one *Chetvert* = 210 litres or 5¾ bushels] of flour, 5,480 *Chetvert* of cereals and 75,588 *Chetvert* of oats, in total 116,952 *Chetvert* of flour, 10,960 *Chetvert* of cereals and 151,176 *Chetvert* of oats. The Tver nobility, not having cash for such an amount of supplies, offered to bring in two *Pud* of flour from each soul on the census from rural magazines and two *Chetvert* of oats from the coming harvest, which would amount to 75,000 *Chetvert* of flour and 75,000 *Chetvert* of oats; at the same time, the nobility took on the delivery of these supplies to Tver and Rzhev. In addition to general donations, some of the nobles made significant individual donations in money and provisions. The former Governor-General of Tver, Prince Georg von Oldenburg, reporting on this to the Tsar, wrote:

> The nobility of the Tver Governorate in this case show the direct and loyal reverence for the August Will and love for the Fatherland that is a characteristic of the Russian nobility alone. They are ready, if Your Majesty pleases, and if it is necessary for the security of the state, each to shed their blood and not to spare any of their property.[15]

Over the course of several days, the merchants and citizens of Tver and other cities of the Governorate donated 308,100 Roubles for the *opolchenie*.[16] Overall, the donations from the Tver Governorate in cash and goods, according to incomplete information, amounted to 2,000,000 Roubles.[17]

The Tver *opolchenie*, being formed in locations not subjected to enemy invasion, benefited from a fairly good administration, as evidenced by some of the instructions and orders issued by its commander, General Tyrtov.[18]

The Tver mounted *opolchenie* took part in the war of 1812 and in the foreign campaigns.

---

14 Supreme approval of Grand Duchess Yekaterina Pavlovna's proposal (Complete Collection of Laws, 25,174, XXXII, 386).
15 Report to the Tsar by the Governor General of Tver, the Prince of Oldenburg, dated 22 July [3 August] 1812.
16 The most humble report by the civil governor of Tver, dated 23 July [4 August].
17 Extracted from information supplied by the local authorities, held in the M.T.D.
18 For details of their standing orders, see Appendix 3.

III. Yaroslavl Governorate

The Yaroslavl nobility, unanimously expressing its readiness 'to bring both life and all property, for the benefit of the Fatherland and the Throne, if circumstances so require,'[19] decided to select one man from every 25 souls, which amounted to 11,112 warriors. Of these, after six weeks, five Cossack regiments were formed, including: one mounted, of 670 men, and four foot, each of 2,600 men. The commander of the Yaroslavl *opolchenie* was Major General Dedulin [Yakov Ivanovich Dedulin], while the regimental commanders were: colonels Selifontov [M.P. Selifontov] and Mikhailov [N.L. Mikhailov], lieutenant colonels Sokolov [P.A. Sokolov], Kulomzin [F.S. Kulomzin] and Prince Ukhtomsky [P.D. Ukhtomsky], who was replaced by Lieutenant Colonel Omelyanov. The nobility expressed a desire to maintain the *opolchenie* with rations for a whole year. In addition, various classes from the governorate made the following donations: more than 400,000 Roubles in cash, two pounds, 41½ *Zolotniki* of gold; three *Pud*, 37 pounds, 55½ *Zolotniki* of silver; 1,430 sacks of flour, 450 *Chetvert* of oats, 100 *Chetvert* of cereals, 1,000 *Pud* of peas, and so on. With a total value of 500,000 Roubles.[20]

The Yaroslavl *opolchenie* took part in the siege of Danzig [Gdańsk].

IV. Vladimir Governorate

The nobility, from 320,000 registered souls who were on the landowners' estates, in the course of five weeks, established six foot regiments with a total of 15,086 men, who were dressed in Cossack caftans, armed with lances and sabres and supplied with provisions for three months. The commander of the Vladimir *opolchenie* was Lieutenant General Prince Golitsyn [Boris Andreevich Golitsyn], while the regimental commanders were Major General Merkulov [Pëtr Kirillovich Merkulov?], active state councillors Strakhov and Zubov [Nikolai Vasilevich Zubov], colonels Polivanov [Nikolai Petrovich Polivanov], Cherepanov and Nefediev, upon whose death was replaced by Lieutenant Colonel Kosyanskoy.

Donations of money from the Vladimir nobility consisted of: 320,000 Roubles collected for the *opolchenie* for maintenance from the landowners' estates, one Rouble per soul, and 6,705 Roubles in favour of the needs of officers entering one of the regiments formed in Vladimir, under the command of Prince Lobanov-Rostovsky [Dmitry Ivanovich Lobanov-Rostovsky]; 38,000 Roubles from donations for the allowances of needy field officers and subalterns and 3,384 Roubles for the uniforms of retired non-commissioned officers and soldiers who wished to serve in the *opolchenie*. The peasants, having heard from the local authorities about the need for rations for two regiments formed in Vladimir, donated 15,314 Roubles and 3,250 *Chetvert* of bread, and in addition took part in assembling a mobile magazine for the army of 408 wagons, 413 drivers and 900 horses, and sending it to the troops with 600 *Chetvert* of hard-tack, 56 *Chetvert* of cereal and 600 *Chetvert* of oats. In total, the donations by the Vladimir Governorate in money and supplies amounted to 800,000 Roubles.[21]

---

19 Report to the Tsar from the Yaroslavl Governor General the Prince of Oldenburg, dated 30 July [11 August] 1812.
20 Extracted from information supplied by the local authorities, held in the M.T.D.
21 Extracted from information supplied by the local authorities of the Vladimir Governorate, held in the M.T.D.

V. Ryazan Governorate

The nobility of this governorate expressed their readiness: 'to fulfil the Supreme will, sparing no sacrifice nor life itself, in order to form the *opolchenie*.'[22] It was intended to call up one warrior from every 22 souls, which in total amounted to 15,918 warriors, from which, in the course of five weeks, seven regiments were raised (one of mounted Cossacks, two of jägers and four of foot Cossacks). All of them were armed with pikes and received provisions for three months from their landlords, while in order to supply the mounted regiment with horses, one horse was requisitioned for every 250 landowner souls; totalling 1,320 horses. The commander of the Ryazan *opolchenie* was Major General Izmailov [Lev Dmitrievich Izmailov], while the regimental commanders were: Major General Shishkin [Nikolai Andreevich Shishkin], colonels: Maslov, Dubovtsky, Prince Drutskoy, Rynkevich [Yefim Yefimovich Rynkevich], Rakhmanov [Pavel Alexandrovich Rakhmanov] and Lieutenant Colonel Maslov.

In addition to the uniforms and weapons of the territorial force, the nobility of the Ryazan Governorate donated: firstly, for the purchase of saddles and *artel* cauldrons at 25 Kopecks per registered soul, for a total of 89,340 Roubles; secondly, for the construction of knapsacks, or valises and caps, five Roubles for each warrior, for a total of 89,090 Roubles; thirdly, cash for the *opolchenie* 227,848 Roubles; in addition, the nobles, merchants, tradesmen and peasants donated 107,980 Roubles. 252,936 Roubles were collected from the nobility and 27,606 Roubles from the merchants and bourgeoisie for munitions and transport for two reserve regiments forming in Ryazan; the free supply of provisions for these regiments, valued at the prices existing at the time, cost some 83,124 Roubles; in addition, military units passing through the governorate in 1812, requisitioned various goods against receipts valued at 53,519 Roubles, of which 35,429 Roubles were donated to the treasury. In September, for the formation of a mobile magazine, the nobility delivered: 292 drivers, 318 pairs of horses, 477 *Chetvert* of hard-tack, 44 *Chetvert* of cereals and 477 *Chetvert* of oats; at the same time, 20,000 pairs of boots were donated to the army. Overall, donations by the Ryazan Governorate in cash and supplies amounted to over 800,000 Roubles.

In early [mid] September, when the enemy, having occupied Moscow, headed along the Ryazan road, and the Russian army crossed onto the Kaluga road, the Ryazan governor, having made the necessary preparations for sending all business and the cash treasury by water, published an appeal to the townsfolk, in which, among other things, he wrote:

> Unity and self-sacrifice may still hold back the evil enemy, who would destroy everything with fire and sword. If it happens that the enemy attempts to move further across Russia through our governorate, then let our dead bodies cover their path first. God will punish them, and our neighbours shall take revenge on them.[23]

The Ryazan *opolchenie* took part in the blockade of Glogau [Głogów] fortress.

---

22 Report to the Minister of Police by the Ryazan civil governor, Bukharin, dated 25 July [6 August], No. 4300.
23 Extracted from information supplied by the local authorities of the Ryazan Governorate, stored in the M.T.D.

VI. Tula Governorate

Donations from the Tula nobility were very significant. It was intended to call up 15,000 warriors,[24] and to form seven regiments from these (two of mounted Cossacks, one of jägers and four of foot Cossacks) and one horse artillery company, for which guns were sent from Moscow.[25] The *opolchenie* was established in 36 days. The Tula civil governor, Privy Councillor Bogdanov [Nikolai Ivanovich Bogdanov] (who had previously served as a general in the artillery) was selected as its commander; the regimental commanders were: 1st Mounted Regiment, Major General Prince Shcherbatov, 2nd Mounted Regiment, Lieutenant Colonel Beklemishev, Jäger Regiment, Major General Miller [Ivan Ivanovich Miller]; foot regiments: Major General Rakhmanov (whose place was subsequently taken by Lieutenant Colonel Kolyubakin), colonels; Vladykin, Svechin, Bobrishchev-Pushkin [Sergei Pavlovich Bobrishchev-Pushkin]; the horse artillery company was commanded by Major Kuchin, and then, due to his illness, by Lieutenant Zybin, after whose death Lieutenant Novokshchanov took command; finally, the battalion, made up of the remaining warriors, was commanded by Major Dobroklonsky.[26]

Upon the departure of the *opolchenie* from their districts, the nobles armed their peasants with whatever they could with muskets, pikes, sabres, axes and scythes, and chose commanders from among themselves. Thus, over and above the provincial *opolchenie*, mounted and foot units were formed from the entire male population, constituting a guard force and sent on patrols. The district centres, following this example, armed some of their citizens under the command of the governors; some of the Tula townspeople, armed with pikes, was attached to the internal security battalion. The entire governorate gave the impression, as it were, of a camp composed of civilians who had taken up arms to defend the Fatherland.[27]

Even before the opening of hostilities, a Supreme Rescript had been sent, addressed to the civil governor of Tula, regarding a contribution of 700,000 Roubles from the governorate, for the purchase of oxen for the army.[28] This sum was immediately contributed by the nobility. In early [mid] July, by way of another rescript, a Supreme Order arrived for the delivery of provisions and fodder for the army from Tula to Kaluga, with payment in cash for these supplies from the treasury.[29] The nobility immediately decided to deliver 69,872 *Chetvert* of hard-tack, cereals and oats, from the village stores, without any compensation. In a report on this, the civil governor wrote:

> Bearing the current situation in mind and the needs of the dear Fatherland, with the feelings of eager sons, the nobility makes such a donation and undertakes to use their own surplus to restock the grain just taken from the stores without any payment.[30]

---

24 Decision by the Tula nobility, 20 July [1 August], 1812.
25 Report to the Minister of Police by the Tula civil governor, dated 21 July [2 August].
26 A note compiled by Colonel Bobrischev-Pushkin, who served in the *opolchenie*.
27 Extracted from information supplied by local authorities, held in the M.T.D.
28 Supreme Orders dated 3 [15] June 1812.
29 Supreme Orders dated 6 [18] July.
30 Report to the Minister of Police by the Tula civil governor, Bogdanov, dated 3 [15] August.

When, on the occasion of increased troop movements, there was a shortage of horses in the artillery of the operational army, then Field Marshal Kutuzov, on 7 [19] September, ordered the Tula governor to urge the mounted regiments to send 2,000 horses to the army, but then, cancelling this instruction with an order dated 10 [22] September, he limited himself to a requirement for 500 horses. Meanwhile, the nobility, wishing to maintain the mounted regiments in the form in which they had been established, decided to collect 150,000 Roubles for the purchase of 1,000 horses, which was sent to the headquarters.[31]

With the onset of autumn, on 13 [25] September, the Field Marshal ordered the Tula governor to prepare 20,000 sheepskin jackets and 20,000 pairs of boots for the troops, at the treasury's expense. Within one month, 18,500 sheepskin jackets had been sent to Smolensk and Vilna, at the expense of the nobles, while the remainder were given to military junior ranks discharged to the army from hospital. Subsequently, when the amount spent on sheepskin jackets was assigned as compensation from the treasury, the nobility, wishing to express their reverence for the memory of M.I. Kutuzov, donated this money to the Alexander School in Tula, so that orphans of the poor nobles of the Tula province would be brought up there, in the name of the pensioners of the late Field Marshal.[32] Overall, the amount donated by the nobility for this item was more than 90,000 Roubles.

On 11 [23] September, on the occasion of the approach of the army to the borders of the governorate, the nobility decided to collect 20 pounds of hard-tack for each of the troops from the registered souls, a total of 200,552½ *Pud*. This entire quantity, by order of the commissariat of the army, was first brought to the storage locations in the Tula and Kaluga governorates, and then, at the expense of their inhabitants, was delivered to the army in Smolensk. When the Commander-in-Chief demanded cereals for the army, then the nobility, refusing any remuneration for it, decided to collect half a *Garnets*[one *Garnets* = 3.23 litres or 5¾ pints] of grain each from the registered souls, a total of 3,691 *Chetvert*, and sent all this stock on peasant carts to Yelnya behind the troops. When the Commander-in-Chief informed the governor that the army, which was pursuing the enemy, was experiencing a shortage of food in the devastated regions, the nobility again donated 14,215 *Chetvert* of bread, which was immediately dispatched, some directly to the army in Minsk, some to the storage locations in Mosalsk and Yukhnov.

For ration demands sent from the army to the Tula Governorate, 4,494 oxen and 34,000 *Pud* of hay were donated by various estates. In addition, by order of the Commander-in-Chief dated 30 September [12 October], 100,000 *Pud* of hay were collected by the nobility for the army; but only a part of this forage managed to reach its destination; the delivery of the rest of the quantity was cancelled on the occasion of the accelerated pursuit of the French by our troops, in order to deliver a supply of hard-tack to the army donated by the nobility on the carts prepared for the transport of the fodder. In total, at various times some 40,000 carts were sent with rations to the army; while for the movement

---

31 Decision by the Tula nobility, 11 [23] September, 1812.
32 Decree by the assembly of the deputies of the Tula nobility, 6 [18] October, 1813.

across the governorate of the sick, wounded, prisoners, and for passing units by governorate-owned transport, some 105,000 carts were placed at the disposal of the governorate authorities.

When temporary hospitals were established in the cities of Tula, Odoev and Belev, each for 6,000 patients, ten kopecks per soul were collected from every landlord and state peasant, for the initial supply of firewood and straw. Merchants and tradesmen donated 25,000 Roubles for the same cause, while the nobility took on the feeding of all the sick and wounded who remained in the governorate. In addition, for the establishment and maintenance of a special hospital at the recruiting depot, the merchants donated 20 kopecks, and the townspeople and peasants four kopecks per soul.

For seven months, the Tula nobility maintained their *opolchenie* at their own expense, comprising 15,000 men and 2,746 horses, supplying them with pay, provisions and fodder, and donated, when they marched to the borders of the Empire, 59,375 Roubles for needy officers.

The total amount of cash donations made by the merchants and tradesmen of Tula reached 367,658 Roubles 80 Kopecks, and, in addition, as already mentioned, these classes contributed to many free deliveries. Donations by the nobility in cash, not counting the equipment and provision of pay and rations to the governorate *opolchenie* and other supplies, exceeded a million Roubles; and together with various deliveries in kind some 4,446,840 Roubles.[33]

The Tula *opolchenie* took part in the siege of Danzig, while 1st Mounted Regiment rode to Paris.

VII. Kaluga Governorate

As soon as the Supreme Manifesto on the mobilisation of the *opolchenie* was received in Kaluga, the nobility decided to call up 15,000 warriors, from whom six regiments (one of mounted Cossacks and five on foot) and a jäger battalion were formed. Lieutenant General Shepelev [Vasily Fëdorovich Shepelev] was selected as overall commander of the *opolchenie*, while the regimental commanders were: Major General Lvov, Brigadier Prince Lvov, colonels: Raevskiy, Yakovlev, Shepelev and Lieutenant Colonel Lvov (there is no information about the commander of the jäger battalion). At the beginning of the formation of the *opolchenie*, the Kaluga governor Kaverin [Pavel Nikitin Kaverin] issued an appeal to the inhabitants, in which, among other things, he wrote:

> The nobility will risk their lives and the lives of their children, they will lead the peasants with all their possessions, they will justify their outstanding rights and privileges through outstanding deeds. Should they spread their insolence further, the ribs and bones of the stricken enemy shall be indelible monuments to their laudable deeds. I now refer the Monarch's proclamation to you, respected citizens, knowing perfectly that you, too, will not refuse to donate your capital to equipping the *opolchenie*, which marches

---

33 Extracted from reports submitted by local authorities to General of Infantry Vyazmitinov in 1814.

to protect your children, your homes, and yourselves. The remains of your fathers will be raised up to you if you harvest your surplus to donate to the Fatherland in these troubled circumstances. The tears of your descendants will be poured out before the judgment of God to accuse you, if you refuse to take part in the challenge that is set before you.

Within a month, the *opolchenie* had been formed and supplied with everything needed. The Kaluga governor ordered that the pikes, sabres, hangers and pistols kept from the old police force be repaired, that gunsmiths be summoned from Tula and sent men to the Tula and Shostka factories to buy muskets and gunpowder.

Large stocks of provisions were assigned to be procured in Kaluga, at the expense of the treasury, and 1,125,000 Roubles were set aside for this project. But the nobility took on this resupply, without any compensation, and in addition to the required amount of 70,000 *Chetvert* of bread, donated a further 10,000 *Chetvert*. Among the many donations made by the Kaluga nobles were 710 horses for the artillery, which, together with their maintenance, cost more than 158,000 Roubles until they reached the Smolensk Governorate. The Kaluga merchants, upon receiving the Supreme Manifesto on the *opolchenie*, collected 150,000 Roubles within two days. Overall, the donations by the Kaluga Governorate, exclusive of the costs of equipping and feeding the *opolchenie* and for the provision of carts, amounted to 1,600,000 Roubles.[34]

The Kaluga *opolchenie* took part in the siege of Danzig.

VIII. Smolensk Governorate

Even before the Tsar's appeal regarding the *opolchenie*, the four Leslie brothers [Alexander, Grigory, Yegor and Pëtr Dmitrievich Leslie], retired Smolensk nobles, having learned about the approach of enemy troops to the borders of the governorate, came to Smolensk to the marshal of the nobility for the governorate, expressing their desire to offer themselves and all their property to form a militia in defence of the Fatherland. The leadership of the governorate, approving the proposal by the Leslie brothers, called together all the nobles who were in Smolensk at the time to propose to them the formation of a common *opolchenie*, and, having dispersed in perfect readiness to call up to 20,000 or more warriors, they sent Lieutenant Colonel Engelhardt [Pavel Ivanovich Engelhardt] to Drissa, with a report for the Supreme Name, regarding the desire of the Smolensk nobles to arm themselves against the enemy. Emperor Alexander, accepting this proposal as a sign of loyalty and love for the Monarch and the Fatherland, whose eagerness to serve has always been a distinction of the Smolensk nobility, His Most Graciousness deigned to express His special favour to them, in the confidence that all this would soon be carried out, and that every effort and activity would be used in supplying the warriors with weapons.[35] After that, the Tsar, during His visit to Smolensk, deigned to hand over a note on the placement of

---

34 Extracted from information supplied by local authorities, held in the M.T.D.
35 Supreme Rescript addressed to the Smolensk Civil Governor, Baron Asch, dated 9 [21] July 1812.

warriors in the various troop types, to the governor, via the leadership of the governorate.[36]

However, despite the eagerness of the citizens of Smolensk, the immediate subsequent invasion of their governorate by the enemy army, along with the delivery of various necessities to our troops and other duties, made the formation of the Smolensk *opolchenie* extremely difficult. The enemy occupation of the Porechye and Krasny districts interrupted the territorial mobilisations there; the militia of other districts assembled in Dorogobuzh. The number of warriors deployed by the Smolensk Governorate is shown as 12,143 men in the information provided by the local authorities,[37] but because many armed citizens of Smolensk joined the Russian army on the retreat of our forces from Dorogobuzh to Borodino, it may be assumed with considerable certainty that the strength of the *opolchenie* in its entirety extended to 20,000 warriors. It goes without saying that, due to a lack of time, they could not become fully operational. Their command was entrusted to Lieutenant General Lebedev [Nikolai Petrovich Lebedev], and later to Major General Vistitsky [Semën Stepanovich Vistitsky]. A small element of the *opolchenie*, assembled by the Leslie brothers,[38] was with the force under Major General Olenin [Yevgeny Ivanovich Olenin], who constituted the vanguard of Adjutant General Wintzingerode's [Ferdinand Fëdorovich von Wintzingerode] detachment, from the time it was located in Smolensk, until the Western armies were united there.[39] During the continuous occupation of the Smolensk Governorate by the enemy and their onward penetration, a people's war was waged in every district by the inhabitants and citizens.

Donations by the citizens of Smolensk in cash and various kinds of supplies were extraordinary. Without any exaggeration, we can say that they laid all their wealth upon the altar of the Fatherland. In addition to equipping the territorial forces, they donated: 52,600 Roubles in cash; 105,740 *Chetvert* of flour, 8,856 *Chetvert* of groats, 211,796 Chetvert of oats and various grains, 9,260 *Pud* of baked bread, 41,600 *Pud* of hard-tack; 2,516,000 *Pud* of hay; 31,680 head of cattle and 38,900 head of small livestock; more than 1,000 *Pud* of beef; 1,112 horses for the artillery – riding and draught, 854 carts; 1,910 sheepskin jackets; 1,000 *Arshin* of linen; 2,000 shirts. Adding to all this the amount spent on arming the men who protected the borders of the districts from enemy raids and for the maintenance of drivers and horses, with

---

36 Copy of the note issued by the Tsar to the civil governor of Smolensk:
'The forestry workers, who know how to shoot and to ride, shall form the mounted jägers. They may be joined by the gentry's game-keepers, who know how to ride.
Grooms from the kennels and stables, are to form the Cossacks, armed with pikes.
Form the jägers from those who know how to shoot, but on foot, armed with hunting firearms.
Make up a foot force from the rest, distributed to the reserve battalions assembling in Smolensk for training.
faithfully: Governor Baron Asch.' Military Topographic Depot, No. 47,352, folio 10, 318.
37 A note on the number of warriors from the Militia of 1812, signed by Anichkov, a former member of the Smolensk Governorate leadership.
38 A total of 60 mounted men. Smolensk Governorate statement, 1857, No. 9.
39 Extracted from information supplied by the local authorities of the Smolensk Governorate, held in the M.T.D.

carts requisitioned to a total of 127,000, it emerges that donations from the Smolensk Governorate, overall, amounted to over 9,800,000 Roubles.[40] No matter how significant the figures shown by us, they are still lower than reality, because this sum does not include either supplies taken for the troops from rural stores, or many supplies given by residents directly to the army, without the knowledge of the local authorities.

The number of warriors in 1st District *Opolchenie* reached over 120,000 men overall. Within a month and a half all this territorial force had been formed up and was ready to march to the locations allocated for each *opolchenie*: the Moscow to Voskresensk [Istra], Zvenigorod, Mozhaisk and Podolsk; the Tver to Klin, the Yaroslavl to Dmitrov, the Vladimir to Bogorodsk [Noginsk], the Ryazan to Kashira, the Tula to Serpukhov, the Kaluga to Vereya, the Smolensk to Mozhaisk, together with the army. The haste with which the *opolchenie* of 1st District was set up did not allow them either to be properly equipped, or to give them sufficient military training. The warriors, for the most part, were armed only with pikes and spears, and shod in bast sandals, which forced them to be used, almost exclusively, to tend to the wounded, or be placed in the third rank of the regular infantry. Later, once the people's war flared up on the enemy lines of communication, the Tver and Smolensk *opolchenie*, operating in the role of partisan detachments and inciting the peasants to arm themselves, brought great advantages to our army.

The *opolchenie* of 2nd District, was under the command of General of Infantry Kutuzov, and later under Lieutenant General Meller-Zakomelsky [Pëtr Ivanovich Meller-Zakomelsky].

I. St Petersburg Governorate

In St Petersburg, the custodian of all measures taken to compose the territorial force was unanimously selected by the nobility to command the *opolchenie*, Count Kutuzov. We have already had occasion to say how much energy he engaged in the performance of this duty.

On 17 (29) July, following the selection of Kutuzov, the St Petersburg nobility decided to call up one warrior from every 25 registered souls, but later the nobles, competing with the example of Moscow, decided to arm one man in ten, which amounted to a total of 13,405 soldiers supplied with clothes, shoes, provisions for three months and a bounty of six Roubles each; at the same time, it was decreed that their fields must be worked, the economy preserved, and taxes paid by the landowners. Nobles who had houses in the capital worth at least 5,000 Roubles were required to pay a lump sum of two percent; the owners of *dachas* in the vicinity of the capital were subject to a similar payment. The leadership of the governorate were instructed to invite nobles who had capital to participate with donations.

The organisation of the *opolchenie* at the expense of the nobility, provided everything related to this subject to the renowned commander chosen by them, who at the same time announced to the assembly that, in accordance with the Supreme will of the Tsar, while remaining in their ordinary clothes, they would have a musket,

---

40 Statement of donations by the Smolensk Governorate, for military necessities, in 1812, signed by Anichkov of the former Governorate leadership.

a cartridge pouch and a knapsack, and, moreover, in the event of constructing field fortifications, the count recognised it as necessary that each of the soldiers be equipped with an axe and a shovel. To ensure proper organisation for the militia and orders for its logistics department, at the suggestion of Count Kutuzov, two committees were established: the organisational and the logistic, which were chaired, the former by the former auditor general, Lieutenant General Prince Salagov [Semën Ivanovich Salagov], while the latter was led by former state treasurer, active privy councillor Golubtsov [Fëdor Alexandrovich Golubtsov]. The responsibilities of the organizing committee were:

1. The preliminary rulings on all general necessities for the *opolchenie*.
2. The selection of serving commanders, with Supreme approval, equally for field officers and subalterns, and in the reception of warriors.
3. Expediting everything related to their military training.

The second committee was occupied with:

1. The collection of voluntary donations, as well as pay and provisions provided by the landlords when supplying soldiers.
2. Supplying warriors with clothing and weapons.
3. Delivery of carts and horses to the *opolchenie*.
4. Summoning a sufficient number of priests and medical officers to the *opolchenie*, supplying the latter with the necessary medicines and instruments.

From 23 July (4 August) the reception of men began in the first committee, while in the second – donations of money, horses, bread, and so on. The desire to join the militia was so common that in a few days all officer vacancies were already filled. Merchants, tradesmen, craftsmen voluntarily joined the warriors.

The St Petersburg militia was not divided into regiments, but, in accordance with Kutuzov's concept, into Groups, each numbering 820 men; these Groups were in turn divided into *Sotnia*. Each Group consisted of men from the same district, or living in the neighbourhood; warriors from the same village served together. The commanders of the 15 Groups of the St Petersburg *opolchenie* were: major generals: Adadurov [Vasily Vasilevich Adadurov], Koshelev [Pavel Ivanovich Koshelev], Karpov [Yakov Ivanovich Karpov], Prince Myshetsky [Ivan Semënovich Myshetsky?], Velikopolsky [Anton Petrovich Velikopolsky], active chamberlain Mordvinov [Alexander Nikolaievich Mordvinov (1792)], Brigadier Skvortsov [Vasily Filipovich Skvortsov?], councillors of state: Bestuzhev and Nikolev and colonels: Dubyanskoy [Alexander Yakovlevich Dubyanskoy], Shemiot [Pavel Leontevich Shemiot], Alalykin, Yelagin, Chernov and Maybaum, whose Group consisted of St Petersburg and Narva tradesmen, called up to the special position through the eagerness of the merchant societies of these cities (subsequently, a 16th Group was formed from unassigned men). The entire *opolchenie* consisted of five brigades, in two formations, under the command of Senator Bibikov [Alexander Alexandrovich Bibikov] and Major General Begichev [Ivan Matveevich Begichev].

With regard to uniform, all generals, field officers and subalterns were required to wear the standard army uniform, with the provision that officers coming out of retirement could wear the uniform with which they retired. As for the clothing for warriors, it was decided, in accordance with the decision of the noble assembly, that they retain their usual clothes, and moreover, it was entrusted that each soldier should have a cross made of brass alloy on his hat, with the monogram of the Tsar and with the inscription: '*За Веру и Царя.*' All Group commanders and field officers were required to serve without pay; subalterns were intended to be paid 30 Roubles a month, *Uryadniki* and drummers 1½ Roubles each, and warriors 1 Rouble, 20 Kopecks each (Subsequently, a payment for the purchase of horses was announced by the committee, of 1,000 Roubles for Group commanders and 500 Roubles for field officers. Subalterns received, in addition to their pay, a 180 Rouble uniform allowance).

In order to hasten the training of warriors, the entire militia was entrusted to the St Petersburg commandant, Major General Bashutsky [Pavel Yakovlevich Bashutsky], who used two regiments from his division for this: the Voronezh Infantry and 2nd Marine Regiment. In order to arm the warriors, 700 muskets and 42,000 live cartridges were issued (the number of muskets deficient was made up by donations). Finally, in order to introduce the warriors to good military order, by Supreme Command, each Group was given five non-commissioned officers from the Training Battalion and twenty-five veteran soldiers from the forces of the interior; and for the initial establishment of two Cossack regiments forming up from the *opolchenie*, Count Steinheil [Fabian Gotthard von Steinheil] was ordered to send several officers and 110 men from Kiselev's Don Cossack Regiment stationed in Finland. The resources delivered from the Government to the St Petersburg *opolchenie* made it the best organised part of the territorial forces of the interior. The principles of front-line training for the warriors were very simple. The following were prescribed:

1. To inspire each of them with a solid understanding of their place in the ranks and files, and demand that the men standing together do not separate themselves from one another, while in extended line – do not lose sight of each other.
2. Training with muskets was to be limited to demonstrating how to carry it in the shoulder, loading correctly, application of fire and bayonet drills.
3. Teaching turns, marching in step, forming into line, columns and squads.

Upon the departure of His Grace Prince Kutuzov to take command of all the Russian armies, Artillery Lieutenant General Baron Meller-Zakomelsky received the Supreme appointment in his place as the commander of the *opolchenie* of 2nd District.[41]

---

41 Extracted from information supplied by the local authorities, held in the M.T.D.

On 27 August (8 September), the training of warriors began on the Preobrazhensky, Semenovsky and Izmailovsky training grounds, which was executed all the more successfully because there were no more than five new servicemen for each of the veteran soldiers. In the course of five days, or rather, 120 hours, because the warriors hardly left the training grounds, more than 13,000 men who had no idea about front-line service learned to march in step, to perform fairly even musket drills, to shoot on command and by files, form columns and squares; in particular, the 5th Group under active councillor of state Mordvinov was distinguished in its front-line training. On 1 [13] September, The Tsar, having conducted an inspection of the newly composed force, was pleased to declare Supreme favour for the good order in which he had the pleasure of seeing the *opolchenie* that day.[42] Lord Cathcart [William Schaw Cathcart], who had accompanied the Emperor to the review, pointed to the warriors and exclaimed: 'Tsar! This force has sprung from the soil.'

Two more mounted Cossack regiments were formed from huntsmen in St Petersburg: one – known as 'The Deadly' – under Count d'Oliveira, and then Colonel Yakhontov [Alexander Andreevich Yakhontov]; the other – 'Alexander's' – under Staff Captain Baron Bode [Klimenti Karlovich von Bode]. Both of these regiments, numbering 1,200 horsemen, were armed and supplied with all their needs by the committee, at the expense of donated sums, but they later became completely separate from the *opolchenie*.[43]

Simultaneously with the formation of the *opolchenie*, every estate in the St Petersburg Governorate, generously competing with each other in the sacred feelings of devotion to the Crown and love for the Fatherland, made significant donations of their property. At the first conference of the nobility, Chief Chamberlain Alexander Lvovich and Chief *Jägermeister* [Master of the Hunt] Dmitry Lvovich Naryshkin expressed a desire to donate 20,000 Roubles each, annually for the entire duration of the *opolchenie*, over and above their dues; Chief Chamberlain Count Litta 50,000, Senator Shepelev 5,000, Senator Borozdin 2,250; Admiral von Desin 2,000; overall, on this first occasion, in addition to the general contributions, 105,675 Roubles annually and a 7,200 Rouble lump sum were proposed. Her Majesty, the Dowager Empress Maria Fëdorovna [née Sophia Dorothea Auguste Luise von Württemberg], participating in the general enthusiasm for the defence of the Fatherland, deigned to send 50,000 Roubles from her income, in favour of the *opolchenie*, via a rescript

---

42 Supreme Orders dated 1 [13] September 1812.
43 Extracted from information supplied by the local authorities, held in the M.T.D. A retired lieutenant, Count d'Oliveira, having entered Russian service in 1802, took part in the campaign of 1807, was captured in the battle of Guttstadt but liberated by the famous partisan Schill, with whom he spent the rest of the campaign and was wounded several times. After that, he participated in the Finnish War, while in his spare time he was engaged in the military sciences and wrote an essay: 'regarding partisan operations.' (M.T.D. No 46,692, annex 151).
In June 1812, Baron Bode, who had previously served as a staff captain in the horse artillery, offered to form two artillery companies for the Petersburg *Opolchenie*, if only the men, horses and equipment needed for this, with harness and accessories, could be made available to him. Subsequently, the formation of these companies was cancelled, and, instead, Staff Captain Bode was instructed to form a Cossack regiment (M.T.D. No. 46,692, annex 151).

addressed to Kutuzov,[44] and ordered a similar amount to be paid annually, for the duration of the war. By the end of 1812, cash donations from the governorate had reached 4,000,000 Roubles. Among these, in addition to those mentioned by us earlier, were: 2,000,000 from St Petersburg's merchants; 750,000 from the commission for theological schools; more than 80,000 Roubles and around 7½ *Pud* of silver from the monasteries and the clergy; from Lieutenant Colonel (Retired) Sergey Yakovlev, who contributed 80,000 Roubles in April for the uniforms of one infantry regiment and 20,000 for improvements to a police unit, donated 30,000 Roubles for the needs of the state in August; 30,000 from *Rottmeister* Vladimirov; 25,000 from Prince Meshchersky and Commercial Councillor Pertsov, 10,000 from Minister of Police Balashov and so on.

But these generous donations are not the only ones worthy of attracting the grateful memory of posterity; needy people, competing in love for the Fatherland, brought their last mite as an offering. There were so many examples of this that we, of necessity, must confine ourselves to the most remarkable. Active Councillor of State Voeikov, joining the *opolchenie* with his only son, donated the pension he received, 1,800 Roubles a year, for military necessities for the entire duration of the war. Lieutenant Commander Antropov, having joined the *opolchenie* himself, presented his only servant to the warriors. Staff Captain Aller, who also joined the *opolchenie*, donated 50,000 Roubles worth of hospital supplies for their benefit, and took upon himself the delivery of them, following the army along the road to Danzig. The German colonists in the St Petersburg Governorate collected 66,900 Roubles for the *opolchenie* and expressed their readiness to arm themselves at the request of the Government. The Sofia [part of Tsarskoe Selo] merchant Persianinov, unable to make any donation due to the state of his business, presented his son to the *opolchenie*. Among the St Petersburg artisans who volunteered for service were the three Shishkin brothers, one of whom had a wife and children.[45] All these examples of generosity and outright valour were a worthy foreshadowing of the subsequent exploits of the St Petersburg *opolchenie* at Polotsk, Chashniki, Berezina and at Danzig.

II. Novgorod Governorate

The Governor General of Novgorod, Tver and Yaroslavl, Prince Georg von Oldenburg, having received the Supreme Command – to take measures to protect the Fatherland in the governorates entrusted to His Highness, arrived in Novgorod from the army on 12 [24] July. The prince reported to the Tsar:

> The Novgorod nobility, always in awe of the August will of Your Majesty, and subsequently being moved to righteous indignation against the enemy and a noble readiness to spare neither life nor property, against this invasion, with a single wave of the hand, so to speak, have suggested the formation of a corps 10,000 strong in the governorate, without the slightest delay. The governorate has taken upon itself, all the clothing for this force,

---

44 Rescript dated 28 July [9 August], addressed to Count Golenishchev-Kutuzov.
45 Extracted from information supplied by the local authorities, held in the M.T.D.

its rationing with provisions and the supply of pay, in a word, full maintenance, for a year. The merchant class, burning with desire to assist the nobility, have pledged some 200,000 Roubles for military necessities.[46]

The annual maintenance of the force cost the nobility of the governorate more than a million Roubles.[47] The Novgorod *opolchenie*, totalling 10,522 men (or 10,140 according to other sources), was divided into four brigades, each of which contained three foot units. The overall commander of the *opolchenie* was General of Infantry Svechin [Nikolai Sergeevich Svechin], with joint commander active chamberlain Zherebtsov [Alexander Alexandrovich Zherebtsov], while brigade commanders were: colonels Dirin, Count Golovin, Pogrebov and Desyatov.

Donations from various estates of the governorate, according to the very incomplete information available, amounted to 1,255,000 Roubles, of which 55,000 Roubles were received in September from the Staraya Russa and Tikhvin merchants.

The Novgorod *opolchenie* participated gloriously in the operations by the Russian army on the Berezina and during the siege of Danzig.

The *opolchenie* of the 3rd District, was under the command of Lieutenant General Count Tolstoy [Pëtr Alexandrovich Tolstoy].

Due to their remoteness from the theatre of war of the governorates that were part of this district, The Supreme command was not to drag away the villagers from their rural work in a premature assembly, limiting themselves to the preliminary identification of men and their assignment to various units of the temporary territorial force.[48]

Count Tolstoy, who was entrusted with assembling the *opolchenie* of 3rd District, requested that he be allowed to form regiments gradually rather than all at once, and that all military units located in the district entrusted to him be used to train soldiers for front-line service.[49] The Tsar deigned to express his consent to these measures, except that 3rd Training Battalion, stationed in Kazan, was not placed at the disposal of the commander of 3rd District of the territorial forces of the interior.[50]

Count Tolstoy, having assigned the selection of warriors for the entire district at four per hundred souls, proposed to form one cavalry regiment, of 600 men from, and from the rest of them, to establish foot Cossack and jäger regiments in each governorate. The reception of soldiers began in the Kostroma and Nizhny Novgorod governorates on 1 [13] September, and in the other four, on the first days [middle] of the same month.[51]

Emperor Alexander, in order to equalise the commitment of 3rd District with those governorates that had called up every tenth man, ordered Count Tolstoy to

---

46 The Prince of Oldenburg's report to the Tsar, dated 15 [27] July.
47 Report by the commander of the *opolchenie* of 2nd District, dated 15 [27] August. Order of the Commander of the Novgorod *Opolchenie* to the commander of the 6th Unit, Captain 2nd Class [naval Commander] Brovtsyn.
48 Supreme Manifesto of 18 [30] July.
49 Count Tolstoy's report to the Supreme Named, dated 24 July [5 August].
50 Supreme Instructions of 31 July [12 August].
51 The Most Humble Report by Count Tolstoy, dated 1 [13] September.

recruit ten men per hundred souls in the district entrusted to him,[52] but he was later ordered to confine himself, in addition to the previously recruited men, to collecting two additional men per hundred, with the exception of small landowner estates, not exceeding nine souls, which were exempted from additional recruitment.[53]

The additional levy of warriors, along with the men left over from the initial *opolchenie*, was referred to as the reserve *opolchenie* of 3rd District. Its formation, in the absence of Count Tolstoy, who had gone on campaign with the initial *opolchenie*, was entrusted to Major General Bulygin [Dmitry Alexandrovich Bulygin], and was subsequently cancelled and the reserve *opolchenie* was disbanded and sent to their homes.

I. Kostroma Governorate

The nobility of this governorate, by the decree of 29 July [10 August], 1812, decided to assemble 11,000 warriors; in addition to which, a later decision by the nobility, dated 15 [27] November, was intended to call up another 5,500 soldiers for the reserve *opolchenie*. In order to supply them with three months' pay and provisions, it was decided to collect 13 Roubles from the landowners' estates for each warrior. The armament of the warriors consisted of pikes. For the mounted regiment, it was intended to requisition 600 horses complete with harness, and for the transport for foot regiments, to prepare 110 carts with 110 pairs of horses with harness. From the initial call up of warriors, four foot and one mounted regiments were established, with one additional battalion. The commander of the *opolchenie* was Lieutenant General Bardakov [Pëtr Grigorevich Bardakov]; foot regiment commanders were: colonels Prince Vyazemsky [Alexander Nikolaevich Vyazemsky] and Cherevin, Lieutenant Colonel Shchulepnikov and Naval Captain 2nd Class Makaveev; the commander of the mounted regiment was Colonel Nebolsin. Donations of cash and goods, in addition to the maintenance of the *opolchenie*, before it set out on campaign, along with the compilation of a mobile magazine for the army, reached over a million Roubles, and including the *opolchenie* some 1,300,000 Roubles. The Kostroma *opolchenie*, having set out on campaign in December 1812, proceeded via Tula, Orël, Chernigov [Chernihiv], Kiev [Kyiv], Novgorod-Volynsky [Novohrad-Volynskyi] and the Duchy of Warsaw, onto Prussian territory and was part of the detachment blockading the Glogau fortress.[54]

II. Nizhny Novgorod Governorate

In pursuance of the Supreme will, the Nizhny Novgorod nobility decided to call up four men per hundred souls into the militia, from all the landowners' estates, a total of 12,924 warriors, providing them with food and pay for three months. In addition, they were to requisition transport, 25 wagons in each of the five infantry regiments, with 50 horses and harness for them, while seven wagons with 14 horses were to go to the mounted regiment, giving a total of 132 wagons and 264 horses, supplying them with fodder for two months. The commander of the *opolchenie* was active chamberlain, Prince Gruzinsky [Georgy Alexandrovich Gruzinsky]; the commanders of

---

52 Supreme Instructions of 3 [15] September.
53 Supreme Decrees dated 21 October [2 November] 1812 and 26 March [7 April] 1813.
54 Extracted from information supplied by the local authorities, held in the M.T.D.

the foot regiments were: colonels Karataev, Agalin, Prince Svenigorodsky, von Rall and Shebuev; the commander of the mounted regiment, the former *Rottmeister* of the Lifeguard Horse, active councillor of state Kozlov [Pavel Fëdorovich Kozlov]. Subsequently, a reserve *opolchenie* of 6,238 men was recruited, provided with pay and provisions for three months, and 462 riding and draught horses were requisitioned. Three more infantry regiments and three artillery companies were formed from the warriors of the second tranche. Donations of cash and goods, together with the compilation of a mobile magazine for the army, amounted to 1,075,000 Roubles.[55]

The first tranche of the Nizhny Novgorod *opolchenie*, having set out on campaign in December 1812, took part in the foreign campaigns.

III. Kazan Governorate

The number of men assigned by the nobility to comprise the *opolchenie*, according to a calculation of one warrior per 25 souls, did not exceed 3,300 men, from whom it was intended to establish a foot regiment, of six battalions, in total, some 3,000 soldiers, adding three mounted *Sotnia* to it. Upon joining the *opolchenie*, the warriors received clothes, munitions, three-months' worth of provisions and five Roubles each from their landowners. The commander of the *opolchenie* was Major General Bulygin, while the regimental commander was Lieutenant Colonel Chichagov. During the formation of the Kazan territorial force, the Sviyazhsk Archimandrite Israel [Iakinf Zvyagintsev] sent 60 pupils from the theological academy to the commander of the *opolchenie* to join the ranks of the defenders of the Fatherland. These young men, who were all assigned as *Uryadniki*, later distinguished themselves by their good behaviour and courage. The reserve *opolchenie* of the Kazan Governorate, a total of 1,000 men, made up two independent battalions. Overall, 346,000 Roubles were donated, together with a sum sent from the Vyatka Governorate (on the occasion of the Vyatka warriors joining the Kazan *opolchenie*), of which 140,000 were collected by the nobility, in addition to private donations; merchants 80,000, tradesmen 10,000, guilds 2,000; churches, monasteries, clergy and private individuals delivered some two *Pud* of silver; 72,000 Roubles were sent from Vyatka, and so on.[56]

The Kazan *opolchenie* took part in the foreign campaigns and distinguished themselves at the blockade of Dresden.

IV. Vyatka Governorate

The initial tranche of warriors, according to a calculation of four men per hundred souls, yielded 552 warriors, of whom 505 turned up. The battalion, formed from these men, was attached to the Kazan *opolchenie*, and, at the same time, money donated by various estates in the Vyatka Governorate was sent to the Kazan committee. The reserve *opolchenie* consisted of 275 men, of whom 195 were present.

Cash donations reached a total of 72,278 Roubles.[57]

---

55 Extracted from information supplied by the local authorities, held in the M.T.D.
56 Extracted from information supplied by the local authorities, held in the M.T.D.
57 Extracted from information supplied by the local authorities, held in the M.T.D.

V. Simbirsk Governorate

According to the decision by the nobility, dated 10 [22] August, 1812, it was intended to call up 9,334 men, of whom 8,679 were assembled; while by a decision of 19 November [1 December], the reserve *opolchenie* was called up, some 5,097 men, together with those remaining from the initial call up: a total of 13,776 warriors. Three foot regiments (four, according to some sources) and one mounted regiment were formed from the men of the initial *opolchenie*. The commander of the *opolchenie* was active councillor of state Prince Tenishev [Dmitry Vasilevich Tenishev]; the commanders of the foot regiments were: Naval Captain 2nd Class Filatov [Steofan Fëdorovich Filatov], Lieutenant Colonel Suvchinsky and Major Gorodetsky; Lieutenant Colonel Tretyakov [Dmitry Andreevich Tretyakov] commanded the mounted regiment.[58] The warriors were issued three-months' worth of rations. Cash, goods and weapon donations were made to a value of 63,882 Roubles; while the maintenance of the *opolchenie* cost the nobility 1,276,000 Roubles overall.[59]

The Simbirsk *opolchenie* were involved in the foreign campaigns and took part in the blockade of the fortresses of Zamość and Glogau.

VI. Penza Governorate

In order to assemble the initial *opolchenie*, 9,282 men were called up from the landowners' estates, from whom four foot regiments and one mounted regiment of 660 men were formed. The commander of the opolchenie was Major General Kishensky [Nikolai Fëdorovich Kishensky]; commanders of the foot regiments were: colonels Selunsky, Dmitriev, lieutenant colonels Koshnerov and Voinikov; commander of the mounted regiment was Colonel Bezobrazov [Lavrenty Afanasevich Bezobrazov]. In order to assemble a reserve *opolchenie*, 4,641 men were called up, of whom 330 were mounted.

The governorate's donations were as follows:

Cash: 556,891 Roubles, 80 Kopecks.
Value of horses for the mounted warriors: 121,610 Roubles.
Value of provisions: 42,900 Roubles.
In addition, value of uniforms, weapons and cost to the nobility for the maintenance of both *opolchenie*: 1,044,125 Roubles
For the uniforms of the infantry regiment formed in Tambov, donated by the nobility: 221,865 Roubles, 83 Kopecks.
For carts for this same regiment from city societies: 50,913 Roubles, 6 Kopecks.
Additional donations from various individuals: 41,323 Roubles, 32 Kopecks.

---

58 Extracted from information supplied by the Simbirsk assembly of deputies and witnessed by the former governor Khomutov. The list, signed by Count Tolstoy, shows the following regimental commanders: Major General Prince Obolensky, Colonel Samoilov, Guards Captain Topornin, Naval Captain 2nd Class Filatov; Guards Staff-*Rottmeister* Tretyakov commanding the mounted regiment (held in the M.T.D.).
59 Extracted from information supplied by the Simbirsk assembly of deputies.

Oxen, wagons and a mobile magazine for the army: 388,709 Roubles, 52 Kopecks.
General cash donations, goods and supplies: 2,468,338 Roubles.
In addition: six brass cannon and two cast-iron cannon, 25 muskets, and so on.[60]

The Penza *opolchenie* were involved in the foreign campaigns and particularly excelled themselves at Magdeburg.

The number of *opolchenie* soldiers fielded by each of the governorates from all three districts was as follows:

1st District:
Moscow Governorate: 25,800.
Tver Governorate: 13,300.
Yaroslavl Governorate: 11,112.
Vladimir Governorate: 15,086.
Ryazan Governorate: 15,918.
Tula Governorate: 15,000.
Kaluga Governorate: 15,000.
Smolensk Governorate: 12,143.
Total for 1st District: 123,359.
While including the Smolensk warriors who joined the army in parts, approximately: 130,000.

2nd District:
St Petersburg Governorate: 13,405.
Novgorod Governorate: 10,522.
Total for 2nd District: 24,927
3rd District:

	Initial *Opolchenie*	Reserve *Opolchenie*
Kostroma Governorate	11,000	5,500
Nizhny Novgorod Governorate	12,924	6,238
Kazan Governorate	3,300	1,000
Vyatka Governorate	505	195
Simbirsk Governorate	8,679	5,097
Penza Governorate	9,282	4,641
Total for 3rd District	45,690	22,671

Overall, the total *opolchenie* provided some 220,000 men.

The donations by the governorates, which were part of the three districts of the *opolchenie*, were varied. In addition to equipping the warriors and supplying them

---

60 Notes on the Simbirsk *Opolchenie*, compiled by the local authorities (held in the M.T.D.).

with provisions and pay for three months (and in some provinces even more), even before the opening of hostilities, they had donated significant sums to buy oxen for the army, made huge deliveries of bread and fodder to storage points, they delivered horses, sheepskin jackets, boots to the troops, set up mobile magazines, maintained hospitals for many thousands of wounded and sick at their own expense, provided uniforms and supplies for the regiments formed in the interior governorates of the Empire, under the command of Prince Lobanov-Rostovsky. Many gave all this property as a gift to the Fatherland, silver and gold inherited from their ancestors, weapons of all kinds, and even cannon. The amount of linen and various goods sent by private individuals was very significant. Unfortunately, there is no way to calculate all these offerings, nor to determine their value. All the information available on this subject is very incomplete. And it could not have been otherwise: in a difficult time with danger threatening our Fatherland, each and everyone was so busy participating in its defence that it never occurred to anyone to keep an accurate account of the donations; and later – time destroyed the materials that might have served to achieve this aim. In addition, some of the donations were delivered to the governorate committees; while others went to the main committee established in St Petersburg. Based on the incomplete information available regarding donations made by the 16 governorates that participated in the *opolchenie* of 1812, the total amount of donations was over 36,000,000 Roubles; but it may be assumed without doubt that each of the governorates that were part of the first two districts donated at least 4,000,000 Roubles, while St Petersburg, Moscow, Smolensk and Tula governorates gave much more; among the governorates of the third district, Penza donated some 2,500,000 Roubles, and the others, with the exception of Kazan and Vyatka, some 1,500,000 Roubles. According to this rough estimate, the governorates, which fielded 220,000 warriors, donated cash, goods and supplies, worth about 60,000,000 Roubles.

The *Oblasts* of the Empire closest to the theatre of war presented the image of a vast encampment, during the period of the enemy army's advance from Smolensk to Moscow. The distinction between warriors and peaceful peasants had disappeared; every Russian was ready to abandon their usual occupation and take a personal part in the mortal struggle for the defence of the Fatherland. Gone was the concern for the preservation of any inheritance acquired through the labour of fathers and grandfathers. The peasants asked the soldiers: 'Servicemen, please say when it's time to set fire to our houses,' as they prepared to set their dwellings on fire once the enemy appeared. No one gave a thought to the generosity of such a sacrifice, did not think about its consequences; it seemed natural to everyone – to destroy the most miserable property, if only to prevent the enemy from taking advantage of it. To accept the enemy into one's home meant, in Russian terms, to betray the Tsar, to betray God. Foreigners, not comprehending the greatness of these concepts, gave us the honorific barbarians! In that sense, may we remain barbarians for a long, long time and may the borders of Russia be terrifying for any armed foreigner! As Napoleon, stretching out his hands towards Moscow, hoped to achieve his objective to subject Russia to his will; at that very moment, all the estates, all the clans of our vast Fatherland, united among themselves with one common thought – to put an end to the successes of the common enemy. No effort was needed on the part of the Government to arouse the passions of the people. The Russians found an echo in the hearts of the people in all things domestic in 1812; everything foreign was regarded with coldness, with disgust. Let us not condemn this irrational emotion; it steeled the Russians in the consciousness of their power and gave us the possibility of defending Russia.

Contemporary theatrical performances and literary works were an expression of the feelings and concepts of our people. The only performances that attracted an audience were reminiscences of the great events of Patriotic History, as were contemporary happenings. No words are able to express the delight excited at that time by Ozerov's [Vladislav Alexandrovich Ozerov] tragedy, 'Dimitry Donskoy.' No less impressive were '*Opolchenie*' and 'Love for the Fatherland.' When the 80-year-old senior Dmitrevsky [Ivan Afanasevich Dmitrevsky] appeared in the role of a grey-haired invalid, donating the last of his property to the Fatherland, three medals, the audience, enthusiastic about this scene, at the end of the performance, curtain called the venerable invalid and greeted him with loud cheers. Dmitrevsky, touched by the favour of the public, expressed his feelings by saying that: 'being unable to show my love for the Fatherland in any other way, I have decided, having gathered the remainder of my weak strength, to appear where my compatriots have previously greeted me, to present a noble example of love for the motherland.' Many pamphlets appeared filled with hatred and contempt for Napoleon and the French. These pamphlets had no merit, but were read avidly. Russia had not been subjected to enemy invasion for a hundred years, and therefore it was quite natural that the Russians could not look with indifference at the capture of their native cities. In addition, the multi-national Napoleonic force, indulging unilaterally in robbery and disrespect for the sacred, were monsters, alien to all humanity in the eyes of our peaceful villagers. Such notions were bound to incite mutual animosity and turn the war of 1812 to some extent into a people's war.

18

Mobilisation and donations in the Governorates that were not included in the *Opolchenie*.

> The Manifesto of 18 July. – Donations by the governorates of: Pskov, Lifland, Estland; mobilisation in the Ostsee Governorates. – Finland. – The governorates of: Olonets, Arkhangel, Vologda, Perm, Orenburg, Saratov and Astrakhan. – Mobilisation and donations in the Lands of the Don Host. – The governorates of: Caucasus, Tauride, Kherson, Yekaterinoslav, Tambov, Orël, Kursk, Kharkov. – Poltava and Chernigov; *Opolchenie* of these provinces; formation of the Malorussia Cossack Force. – The governorates of Kiev and Podolia; formation of the Ukraine Cossack Force. – Siberia Governorate. – A complete summary of the mobilisation and donations made by governorates not included in the three *Opolchenie* Districts.

The Manifesto of 18 (30) July declared that, with the exception of the 16 provinces that were part of the *opolchenie*, all others would not take any part in it: 'until there is a need to use them for uniform donations and services for the Fatherland.' Nevertheless, however, upon the first appeal by the Tsar for a general mobilisation, all of Russia unanimously united in defence of their Tsar. In addition to the western *Oblasts*, which had been invaded by the enemy at the very beginning of the war, all the others took an active part in the great work of Emperor Alexander I. The image of Russia, called to arms by its Tsar, would present a spectacle of striking grandeur to the world, but, unfortunately, it is not possible to calculate all the donations, all the virtuous deeds committed by the Russians in this time of sorrow for the Fatherland, and therefore, instead of a complete representation of them, we shall confine ourselves to a summary of the efforts made for this lofty goal – to defend the honour, glory and independence of Russia.

Pskov Governorate

Although this governorate did not participate in the *opolchenie*, nevertheless, they made huge donations.

In a Supreme Rescript dated 6 [18] July, addressed in the name of the Pskov civil governor, Prince Shakhovskoy [Pëtr Ivanovich Shakhovskoy], supply depots for the troops were ordered to be established in the Pskov Governorate and residents invited to make whatever donations they could, and in return, the province would be exempted from participation in the *opolchenie*. In pursuance of the Supreme will, the following donations were made: 127,000 *Chetvert* of flour; more than 36,000 *Chetvert* of oats; 200,000 *Pud* of hay; more than 6,000 head of cattle; 983 cavalry, artillery and draught horses; 400 casks of wine; 15,434 sheepskin coats and jackets. In addition, the inhabitants of the cities of the Pskov Governorate donated 69,125 Roubles; the clergy of the Pskov diocese gave 12,313 Roubles and 62 Roubles, 50 Kopecks of silver. The Pskov Bishop's Household gave 1¼ *Pud* of silver objects and 81½ *Zolotniki* of gold. Provisions and fodder were delivered to the troops on peasant carts, some 100,000 of which were constantly on the move. Supplies were sent from every location, and very often without being entered on any official list; in particular, hay was delivered without being billed. It can be stated positively that rations for the troops under Count Wittgenstein came exclusively from the Pskov Governorate, which, moreover, provided the other corps of First Army with supplies during their movement from Dünaburg [Daugavpils], via Vitebsk, to Smolensk. All Wittgenstein's requirements were carried out by the people of Pskov with absolute diligence. Overall, all donations from the Pskov Governorate, in cash and goods (not counting rations and fodder taken from rural magazines and whose value is not recorded anywhere), amounted to 1,766,784 Roubles; or 14 million Roubles taken together with the contents of the carts and horses called up for the army.[1]

Lifland Governorate

Although the assembly of the *opolchenie* in this governorate was cancelled, on the basis of the Manifesto of 18 (30) July, nonetheless, 2,260 warriors were called up from the Lifland Governorate, and moreover, by order of the Riga military governor at that time, Lieutenant General Essen 1st [Ivan Nikolaevich Essen], the Livonian Mounted Cossack Regiment was formed at the expense of the Lifland nobility, by the Courland civil governor, Privy Councillor von Sievers [Fëdor Fëdorovich Sievers or Friedrich Wilhelm von Sievers], comprising 2,000 men,[2] which, having come under von Sievers' command, was initially stationed along the Dvina, to protect the governorate from penetration by enemy patrols, and then joined Lieutenant General Löwis' [Fëdor Fëdorovich Leviz or Friedrich von Löwis of Menar] detachment.[3] In addition, 200 marksmen were assembled in the Dorpat [Tartu] and Pernov [Pärnu] districts[4] and, with Supreme authority, independent detachments under lieutenants Schmitt [K.K. Schmitt] and Nieroth [K. von Nieroth] were formed by recruitment, the first of 330 men, and the second of 70. Finally, 200 coastal residents were recruited

---

1   Calculation of donations in the Pskov Governorate for military necessities (this statement was signed by the former civil governor in Pskov in 1812, Prince Shakhovskoy). A note on the donations of the Pskov Governorate during the Patriotic War, submitted by the former Pskov civil governor Peshchurov.
2   Memo from the Minister of Police to the military governor of Riga, dated 10 [22] August 1812.
3   Information for the History of 1812, signed by the former civil governor of Livonia von Fölkersahm.
4   Supreme Orders for Lieutenant General Essen 1st, dated 3 [15] September.

from Ezel Island [Saaremaa] to serve in the port of Riga.[5] Elsner [Fëdor Bogdanovich Elsner or Friedrich Gottlieb von Elsner], Professor of military sciences at Dorpat University (formerly a major), and all the students studying military sciences, a total of 27, were determined to serve in the military. Thirty students from the medical faculty joined various regiments of the army as surgeons.[6]

Donations from Livonia in cash and goods were significant. The equipping and maintenance of the mounted regiment cost the nobility 392,942 Roubles. Overall, voluntary offerings and deliveries, together with equipment for recruits, in 1812 amounted to 2,618,902 Roubles. The nobility of Ezel Island donated, in addition, some 150,000 Roubles.[7]

Estland Governorate

The nobility of this province, believing that the Latvians might take the assembly of the *opolchenie* as a unilateral act on the part of the landowners, petitioned for the replacement of the territorial force with conscription tranches and, in the course of 1812, provided 17 recruits per 500 souls.

They donated: 13,010 Roubles in money and silver objects, 146,687 Roubles worth of bread; 200 head of cattle worth 16,080 Roubles; 189 draught horses for the artillery valued at 39,690 Roubles; supplies for the conscripted workers for Riga, Reval and Narva, 57,577 Roubles. In addition, the nobility donated: 14,500 Roubles to equip the nobles who were joining the services; 14,500 Roubles annually to assist them, throughout their service; supplies worth 290,758 Roubles. In total, the Estland Governorate donated 593,902 Roubles for military necessities.[8]

Finland

Despite the fact that this country had been annexed by Russia only three years before the war of 1812, the Finns, driven by a sense of gratitude to Emperor Alexander, volunteered to participate in the defence of Russia, petitioning, through the Governor General of Finland, Count Steinheil, to form a Finnish army.[9] Emperor Alexander, deigning to form three Finnish jäger regiments, paid for by voluntary donations, permitted the completion of the necessary sum from the revenue of the country.[10] In the course of 1812, only one regiment, the Vyborg Jägers, managed to form, consisting of two battalions, which, under the command of the then *landsgevding* (civil governor) of the Vyborg Governorate, Stjernvall [Carl Johan Stjernvall], marched to St Petersburg on 1 [13] March, 1813, for internal security duties.[11]

---

5 Information for the History of 1812, etc.
6 *Notizen aus den Acten der kaiserlichen Universität von Dorpat in Beziegung auf den Krieg des Jahres 1812* (held in the archives of the M.T.D.).
7 Returns submitted by the former civil governor von Fölkersahm.
8 Returns submitted to the secretary of the noble assembly, Helfreich, and other information delivered by the local authorities, stored in the archive of the M.T.D.
9 Most Humble report to Emperor Alexander I by Count Steinheil, dated 15 [27] July.
10 Supreme orders to Count Steinheil, dated 1 and 18 [13 and 30] August, and appointing General of Infantry Armfelt as civil Governor General of Finland, dated 6 [18] September.
11 Information on the Grand Duchy of Finland relating to the History of 1812 (this note was signed by the commander of the first expedition by the office of Governor General Fersmann).

Donations of cash and goods from the people of Finland consisted of:

1. A concession by the merchants of Helsingfors [Helsinki] and other cities, hired to transport the independent Finland Corps to Reval on their ships, and a significant part of the agreed payment for the formation and arming of a Finnish army.
2. Voluntary donations, in the amount of some 200,000 Roubles, in addition to cash donated by the landowners of the Vyborg Governorate for the recruitment of 1,200 men, from whom the Vyborg Jäger Regiment was formed.

In addition, every estate supplied a certain amount of bread, hospital supplies, and so on.[12]

Olonets Governorate

By a decree dated 27 July [8 August], the Olonets nobility decided to call up one warrior per 500 souls from all the landowners' estates, in total 120 soldiers, providing them with pay for a year and provisions for six months. Subsequently, according to Supreme Orders, 570 marksmen were recruited from the province, who were sent to St Petersburg. Donations from each of the classes of the governorate, in addition to the equipment of the marksmen, at the nobility's expense, amounted to about 11,000 Roubles.[13]

Arkhangelsk Governorate

Upon the promulgation of the manifesto of 6 (18) July, on the widespread assembly of the *opolchenie*, the urban communities of Arkhangelsk, Kholmogory, Pinega and Mezen, the communities of the settlements of Nënoksya, Una and Luda and state peasants from the counties of: Kholmogory, Mezen and Kem, called up 389 warriors from among themselves who voluntarily came to defend the Fatherland. Upon the disbandment of the *opolchenie* in the governorate, the inhabitants donated 76,583 Roubles in cash, 7,500 Roubles worth of cloth and 2,316 Roubles worth of other goods, for a total of 86,399 Roubles. The most important donations were made by Arkhangelsk merchants of 1st Commercial Guild, councillors Popov and Brant, and the merchants Bekker and Amburger from Reval. The clergy donated 3,188 Roubles; five sailors of the 33rd Naval Crew 50 Roubles. Moreover, 5,000 Roubles and two *Pud* of silver were delivered from the Solovetsky Monastery.[14]

Vologda Governorate

Upon the promulgation of the Manifesto of 6 (18) July, on the widespread assembly of the internal *opolchenie*, the nobility of the Vologda Governorate decided to call up six men per hundred souls, from all landowner estates (which would have raised

---

12 Information on the Grand Duchy of Finland etc.
13 Information submitted by the local authorities of the governorate, signed by the former head of Chancellery of the Olonets Governorate, Filemonov.
14 Information submitted by the Arkhangelsk Governorate, held in the M.T.D.

more than 5,000 warriors), taking on the supply of their provisions for six months and deciding, in the event of the movement of the *opolchenie*, to levy 50 Kopecks per registered soul; At the same time, the nobles, wishing to give their landless comrades the opportunity to join the ranks of the defenders of the Fatherland, opened a voluntary subscription in favour of them and collected some 9,000 Roubles, half a *Pud* of silver and a hundred sacks of flour.[15] Later, when the call up of the *opolchenie* was restricted to the 16 governorates, Supreme Orders followed for the enlistment of 500 marksmen, from those due for call up from the Vologda Governorate, who were sent to St Petersburg.[16]

Perm Governorate

Upon receipt of the Supreme Manifesto of 6 (18) July in Perm, the local governor, taking into account both the lack of nobles owning large estates resident in the governorate, and the loss of time that might occur in anticipation of their assembly, invited all the chief officials of the governorate to a General Assembly, to take steps to assemble the *opolchenie*. By a resolution from this Assembly, dated 23 July [4 August], it was decided:

> In order for an initial decision on the defensive forces, from all landowner estates in general, to call up five men per 500 souls, leaving the landlords to call up these men and more at will, and, at the same time, to offer an invitation to state owned peasants, tradesmen and wagon drivers to volunteer for this *opolchenie*.

In pursuance of the Supreme will, announced in the Manifesto of 18 (30) July, this *opolchenie*, which was intended to consist of some 4,000 men, was disbanded. Donations by the inhabitants of the Perm Governorate in 1812, for the uniforms for one of the regiments forming up in Kostroma, for the transportation of this regiment and for the *opolchenie*, reached 150,000 Roubles.[17]

In the course of 1812, the Cossack lands called up 23 regiments each of 500 men and one of 1,000 men (two Orenburg, one Ural, 18 Bashkir, two Meshcheryak and one Teptyar) to reinforce the army. The number of nobles, Tatar princes and *murza* [emir] who joined Cossack regiments reached 400: among them was the remarkable Murza Absalyam Utyashev, who joined the service with all his family, 21 including himself; 17 nobles and princes entered line regiments, including four sons of the Tatar prince Yusney Kudashev. The desire of civil servants to enter military service was so general that the criminal justice and chambers of state found it difficult to release officials who wanted to go to the defence of the Fatherland.

Cash donations comprised:

---

15 Information submitted by the former leader of the Vologda Governorate, Bryanchaninov.
16 Complete Collection of Laws, 25,200, XXXII, 406.
17 Information submitted by the local leadership of the Perm Governorate, held in the M.T.D. The statement of donations was compiled from the reports by the Perm Treasury.

1. 65,000 Roubles donated by the nobility for uniforms for the second Kostroma Infantry Regiment.
2. 1,375 Roubles collected by merchants and townspeople of the city of Ufa, to supply the regiment with transport.[18]

Saratov Governorate
Upon the promulgation of the Manifesto of 6 (18) July, the nobility decided to levy, from all landowner estates, two warriors per hundred souls, and in order to supply them with everything they needed, one Rouble per soul. Of the foreign colonists settled in the Saratov province, 271 men expressed a desire to enter the services, who, by Supreme Command, were invited to be assigned to the Russo-German Legion. Due to the restriction of the *opolchenie* to the 16 governorates, some of the Saratov nobility joined the Simbirsk or Penza *opolchenie*. According to a report to the Minister of Police of the civil governor of Saratov at that time: 'the small and, for the most part, insufficient nobility of the province was ready to mark their enthusiasm for the Tsar and the Fatherland through all kinds of sacrifice.'

At the start of the war, the Saratov nobility collected 124,800 Roubles for uniforms for 2nd Jäger Regiment forming up in Voronezh, while the city societies donated 28,200 Roubles for the preparation of a wagon train for this same regiment. Moreover, all the estates of the province contributed to the sending of thousands of pairs of oxen with wagons to the army, for heavy transport, and thousands of oxen for food for the troops.[19]

Astrakhan Governorate
As early as April 1811, by Supreme Decree addressed to the Caucasus military governor, Lieutenant General Rtishchev [Nikolai Fëdorovich Rtishchev], two Kalmyk regiments were ordered to be formed, each of 500 men. The will of the Tsar was carried out with such energy that 20 days after the decree was received, in July, both regiments set off for Voronezh. One of these was assembled by the owner of Khomut, Captain (later Colonel) Prince Tyumen [Serebjab Tyumen], who spent 96,900 Roubles of his own money on this unit and supplied 150 horses to the army, worth 15,000 Roubles.

Donations throughout 1812:

Nobility:	291,462
Astrakhan tradesmen:	78,972
Orthodox clergy:	15,000
Astrakhan Armenians:	100,340
Tatar societies:	23,000
Indians and Persians:	37,800
Total:	546,574 Roubles.

---

18 Notes provided by the Orenburg Governorate in 1812, submitted to General Mikhailovsky-Danilevsky in 1836 by the former Military Governor of Orenburg, Perovsky.
19 Extracted from information submitted by the local leadership of the Saratov Governorate, held in the M.T.D.

In addition, donations were made of cloth, weapons, and so on.

The Kalmyk regiments participated in the operations of the Russian army from the beginning of the war until the return of the troops from the foreign campaigns in 1814.[20]

Lands of the Don Host

At the time when the Supreme Manifesto of 6 (18) July was issued regarding the compilation of a general internal *opolchenie*, 60 regiments with two Cossack artillery companies had already been sent from the Don to serve.[21] Having heard the Manifesto, the Military Chancellery decided to draft lists according to each settlement of all field officers and subalterns, *Uryadniki*, clerks, Cossacks and teenagers, up to and including 17 years of age, with the exclusion only of the very decrepit, totally disabled and seriously ill, completely incapable of campaign service. All healthy men were ordered to arm themselves, with the poor borrowing weapons from those who had more than they needed, to supply each of the Cossacks with a lance at least, and to organise them into *Sotnia*, so that, at the first request, they could set out on campaign wherever they were directed. The weapons that the Cossacks had in Novocherkassk, Starocherkassk and Aksai settlements were listed and evaluated, with a prohibition on exceeding the set price when selling them. The local police chiefs over the Kalmyks and the Tatar elders were ordered to report on all men capable of going on campaign, including those 17 years of age, and try by all means possible to arm them. The Cossack artillery half-company that remained with the army was ordered to equip itself for campaign, staffing it with men and horses. The estate owners had to call up the special *opolchenie*.[22] *Ataman* Platov [Matvey Ivanovich Platov] approved all the orders by the Military Chancellery, with the exception of the sending out of 17 and 18 year olds on campaign, who, in his opinion, should be left at home, both to carry out various rear-area duties and to look after property. At the same time, the entire force was ordered to assemble in Moscow, marching by the shortest route, without rest, covering stages of at least 60 Versts [1 verst = 1,067m or ⅔ mile] per day.[23] The formation of 26 new regiments, numbering 15,000 men, with six guns, was so swift that they all set out on the march throughout September and early [mid] October. The nobility supplied 3,074 warriors from 76,768 souls who were on the landowners' estates, supplying them with clothing, weapons and provisions for six months (this *opolchenie*, following the Manifesto of 18 (30) July, was disbanded). In addition, the nobles of the Don region donated 1,500 riding horses for impoverished Cossacks. The merchant Cossacks of the Ust-Aksai and Starocherkassk settlements, a total of 234 men, collected 93,600 Roubles in favour of their needy colleagues.[24]

---

20 Information submitted by the local leadership of the Astrakhan Governorate, held in the M.T.D. Notes by Prince Tyumen on 2nd Kalmyk Regiment.
21 For details of the composition of the Don Host, see Appendix 4.
22 Memo from the military chancellery to the military *ataman* Platov dated 23 July [4 August], No 14,171.
23 Proposal by the military *ataman* Platov to the Military Chancellery, dated 22 August [3 September], No 1,080.
24 From information submitted by the local authorities, held in the M.T.D.

Caucasus Governorate

Despite the meagre resources of the nobility of this governorate, they made large donations to the common cause. It was intended to call up every tenth man from all the landowners' estates, which amounted to 487 warriors. Three Roubles were levied from each registered soul for armaments, supply of horses and their rations, making a total of 14,604 Roubles; Nobles and landowners who had independent commercial establishments donated ten percent of their income and created a subscription of voluntary offerings in cash, weapons and provisions.[25]

Tauride [Crimea] Governorate

Upon receipt of the Manifesto regarding the general *opolchenie*, it was decided in the General Assembly of deputies of the governorate that all the nobles, with their peasants following them, were considered warriors, ready to go to the defence of the Fatherland at the first call of the Government, supporting themselves at their own expense, and through voluntary donations for impoverished warriors. In order to speed up the assembly of at least some of this total mobilisation, it was necessary, in the first instance, to assemble in the Dnieper and Melitopol districts – closer to the theatre of war, three warriors per hundred souls from all landowner estates, half mounted and half on foot; nobles with fewer than 33 souls and owners of gardens, vineyards, forests and uninhabited lands, had to make donations in cash of not less than a tenth of their annual income; while the nobles, who had called up warriors, undertook to arm and supply them with provisions and pay, and in general to donate goods and cash also not less than a tenth of their income. The state peasants undertook to call up three warriors per hundred souls, supplying them with provisions for ten months, and to hand over horses for half the total of warriors. The Tatars agreed to maintain the four Tatar cavalry regiments that were already with the active army. Finally, every ethnic group inhabiting Taurida offered to open voluntary subscriptions for donations in cash.

Upon the promulgation of the Manifesto of 18 (30) July, the inhabitants of the Taurida Governorate, having been released from the *opolchenie*, made the following donations:

Nobility:	50,956
Orthodox clergy:	1,228
Town dwellers:	47,300
Russian settlers:	50,322
Tatar settlers & Muslim clergy:	299,633
Kyrgyz:	40,000
Nogai:	74,945
Colonists:	399
From the military treasury of the Black Sea Forces:	100,000
From voluntary donations of the Black Sea peoples:	14,378
Total:	679,161
Including from other sources:	756,000

---

25 Status of the nobility of the Caucasus Governorate, 9 [21] August.

In addition, donations of various goods were made.[26]

Kherson Governorate

In pursuance of the Supreme Command, for the general formation of the internal territorial forces, it was intended to call up one warrior per 50 registered souls in this governorate. Following the cancellation of the *opolchenie*, a collection of voluntary donations was made, among which the inhabitants of Odessa collected 300,000 Roubles in a short period. The Bug Cossack Host, notwithstanding the three regiments already with the army, called up a unit of five *Sotnia*, and the landowner Skarzhinsky formed a squadron at his own expense that joined the army and participated on campaign.[27]

Yekaterinoslav Governorate

Upon receipt of the Supreme Manifesto of 6 (18) July, by a decree from the nobility, it was determined to assemble one warrior per 25 souls, armed to whatever extent was possible; among these warriors, 500 mounted men were to be called up, for whom the supply of horses and harness was taken on by those who had at least 100 souls in their possession. Together with the supply of men for the *opolchenie*, the nobles volunteered to supply them with a ten-day ration of hard-tack and flour for three months, holding a similar amount of provisions in readiness. Those landlords, who owned fewer than 25 souls, pledged to contribute five Roubles per soul. Having taken these measures in the first instance, the nobility announced that: 'being always filled with eagerness and zeal for the fulfilment of the Monarch's will and for the defence of the Fatherland, and preferring the common good and tranquillity of the Empire to personal gain, have set ourselves an indispensable duty to offer up all men capable of service, all property and ourselves, to defeat the enemy of the Fatherland.'[28] Simultaneously with this decision, 25,284 Roubles were collected from the nobles, in one day. Upon the disbandment of the *opolchenie* in the Yekaterinoslav Governorate, the nobility decided, in addition to the donations already made, which amounted to 50,000 Roubles, to place 250,000 Roubles at the disposal of the government.

Overall donations:[29]

Nobility:	325,284
Mariupol Greeks:	50,000
German colonists:	1,796
Retired soldiers settled in Novopavlosky, numbering 75 families, all the money they had:	1,120
Total:	378,200

---

26 Information for the History of 1812, signed by the governor of Tauride, Kaznacheev. Report by the leader of the nobility of the Tauride Governorate, Taranov-Belozerov to the Duc de Richelieu, dated 29 August [10 September].
27 Extracted from information submitted by the local authorities, held in the M.T.D.
28 Decision of the Yekaterinoslav nobility, 23 July [4 August].
29 Extracted from information submitted by the local authorities, held in the M.T.D.

Tambov Governorate

By a decision from the nobility, of 25 July [6 August], it was determined to assemble warriors, one per 50 souls, arm them and supply them with provisions for four months. Upon the disbandment of the *opolchenie*, the Tambov nobility showed their readiness to donate towards the common cause in practice. When the announcement by Count Rostopchin was received in Tambov during the enemy advance on Moscow, calling on the people, to go to Trigory to defend the capital, then the nobles, having gathered, at the invitation of Governor Nelidov [Arkady Ivanovich Nelidov?], decided to form an *opolchenie* of 12,000 men, of whom half were on foot and half mounted, and to keep a similar number of men in readiness. These measures were put into effect, despite the conscription that was being carried out in the governorate at the time. The enemy evacuation of Moscow forced Prince Kutuzov to suspend this *opolchenie*, in which every class, following the example of the nobles, had taken part.[30]

Orël Governorate

Following the disbandment of the general *opolchenie*, the nobility of the Bryansk and Trubchevsk districts, being closest to the theatre of operations, voluntarily formed an *opolchenie*, at their own expense, in order to protect the borders of the governorate from the enemy.[31]

Kursk Governorate

In order to form an internal territorial force, the nobility decided to assemble 14,000 foot and 900 mounted warriors, while 780 nobles expressed a desire to serve in the *opolchenie*. Cash donations by the nobility for armaments and maintenance of the *opolchenie* amounted to 576,313 Roubles; in addition, 29,755 *Chetvert* of flour, 2,445 *Chetvert* of grain, 2,308 *Chetvert* of oats, 2,210 *Pud* of hay were collected; 193 muskets, 1,341 sabres, 48 pistols and 8,053 pikes. The nobles of the Rylsk and Shchigry districts expressed a desire to double the donations from themselves. Even before the opening of hostilities, and again in September 1812, the Kursk nobility donated 106 war horses and 425 draught horses for the artillery, to the value of 84,650 Roubles, and 419 horses for the assembly of a mobile magazine, with harness, drivers and food, worth 77,558 Roubles. In November, at the behest of Prince Kutuzov, 7,200 carts were requisitioned in order to transport provisions prepared in Trubchevsk, for the maintenance of which 155,176 Roubles were collected. The following were also donated: 310,352 *Pud* of hard-tack, a commensurate amount of cereals, 4,850 *Chetvert* of oats, and 75,000 casks of wine.

The merchants of the Kursk Governorate, according to the general distribution, undertook to collect 100,000 Roubles, and in addition, many merchants made personal offerings, in the total amount of 20,545 Roubles (including the city leader, 2nd guild of merchants, Vasily Gladkov who donated 5,000 Roubles); the townspeople made a subscription of 6,579 Roubles. Upon the promulgation of the

---

30 Extracted from information submitted by the local authorities, held in the M.T.D.
31 Reports by the former leadership of the Orël Governorate nobility, dated 1 [13] August and 4 [16] September.

Manifesto on general mobilisation, eight of them expressed a desire to join the ranks of the defenders of the Fatherland.

Overall, in 1812, the following were donated by the various classes of the Kursk Governorate:

Nobility (excluding weapons, rations & forage):	893,727
Tradesmen:	120,545
Merchants:	9,579
Total: over	1,000,000 Roubles.[32]

Kharkov Governorate

Upon receipt of the Manifesto on the general *opolchenie*, the nobles, in a General Assembly, decided to call up one warrior per 50 souls in the landowners' estates, expressing their readiness to double this number, if necessary; thereafter, the state-owned peasants and merchants volunteered to take part in the mobilisation along with the landlords' peasants: in total, 13,211 men were assigned to be called up, of whom 1,350 were mounted Cossacks. It was intended to levy one Rouble per registered soul towards the costs of the *opolchenie*; for the initial provisioning of men and horses, two *Chetvert* of flour and one and a half *Garnets* of cereals for each warrior, and a *Chetvert* of oats and fifteen *Pud* of hay for each horse. The Kharkov merchants donated 23,315 Roubles towards the *opolchenie* and expressed their readiness to make similar donations in the future.[33] Once the Manifesto of 18 (30) July abolished the *opolchenie* in the Kharkov Governorate, and instead a conscription tranche was made for one warrior per 50 souls, meanwhile, the enemy had occupied Moscow, whereupon, according to a decision by the nobility, it was necessary to form a similar *opolchenie* to protect the borders of the governorate and open a new subscription to give each and everyone the opportunity to participate in Russia's common cause.[34]

Poltava Governorate

In pursuance of the Supreme Manifesto of 6 (18) July, from all the landowner, state and specified peasants, merchants and gentry, one warrior per 25 souls were assembled into the *opolchenie*, a total of 16,116 men armed with pikes, sabres and some with firearms. The following were formed from these warriors: six foot and six mounted regiments, a 600 strong service support unit, a battalion of hospital orderlies and an artillery unit with 24 guns of various calibres.

Uniforms, armaments and supplies for the *opolchenie* with horses with harness, provisions and transport cost the nobility and other classes 1,026,800 Roubles. 537,911 Roubles were collected for the officers' and warriors' pay, the purchase of fodder, and so on. Many of the nobles donated guns and a variety of weapons. Moreover, by order of Kutuzov, of December 1812, the residents of the Poltava

---

32 Extracted from information submitted by the local authorities, held in the M.T.D.
33 Information submitted by the former governor of Kharkov, Prince Trubetskoy.
34 Decision by the assembly of noble leaders, of 25 September [7 October].

Governorate, were to deliver flour, cereals and oats worth 883,904 Roubles, at the beginning of the following year, to the army in Minsk and Slonim.

The regiments of the territorial *opolchenie*, setting out from their assembly area on 1 [13] November, took part in the blockade of the fortresses of Zamość and Glogau.[35]

Chernigov Governorate

The nobility of this governorate, at the invitation of the marshal (leader), decided to call up one warrior per 15 registered souls and to supply the soldiers with clothing, weapons, as well as provisions and pay, for six months. The *opolchenie* was divided by *Povet* (district) and the *Povet* units into *Sotnia*. Upon the departure of the Chernigov *opolchenie* on campaign, it was divided into ten foot and five mounted regiments, totalling 26,000 men with forty guns.[36] There is no reliable information regarding cash donations by the inhabitants of the governorate.

The Cossack class of the Poltava and Chernigov governorates, being called up, by the Supreme will, by the Malorussian Governor General, Prince Ya.I. Lobanov-Rostovsky [Yakov Ivanovich Lobanov-Rostovsky], to mobilise in defence of the Fatherland, called up 15 regiments totalling 18,000 horsemen from 454,983 souls. Uniforms, weapons, supply of horses and food for the Malorussian mounted regiments, before they went on campaign, were made at the expense of the Cossack societies, which later made significant donations for these items. Prince Lobanov-Rostovsky, reporting to the Tsar regarding the eagerness of the Cossacks, who had volunteered to make up, if necessary, double the number of regiments, and even to enlist without exception,[37] petitioned for their release from conscription and from certain taxes, imputing to them constantly the obligation to appear on demand for active service.[38] Emperor Alexander, by Rescript of 30 July [11 August], leaving Prince Lobanov to put into effect the proposals regarding the Malorussian Cossacks, wrote: 'whatever they are happy to do.'[39]

Of the 15 Cossack regiments formed by Prince Lobanov, five were left to guard the Chernigov Governorate; the other ten regiments were sent to Mozyr.[40]

---

35 Information submitted by the former governor of Poltava, Mogilevsky.
36 In a work titled: 'Review of Malorussia in the summer of 1812,' by Prince Ya.I. Lobanov-Rostovsky, the number of *opolchenie* in both Malorussian governorates, Poltava and Chernigov, is shown as 42,182 men; while, according to other sources, 16,116 warriors were called up from the Poltava Governorate, it may be concluded that the Chernigov *opolchenie* reached 26,000 men.
37 'Нехай тогда и батько иде' (Let our fathers also go then), said the Cossacks.
38 Proposal by Governor-General Prince Lobanov-Rostovsky to the leadership of the Poltava and Chernigov governorates, dated 16 [28] July.
39 Proposal by Governor-General Prince Lobanov to the leadership of the Chernigov Governorate, dated 23 August [4 September] (held in the archive of the M.T.D. No 46,692.
40 Supreme Rescript addressed to Prince Lovanov-Rostovsky, dated 1 [13] September 1812.

Kiev Governorate

In accordance with the Supreme Order, issued in June 1812, three Ukrainian Cossack regiments, of eight squadrons each, for a total of 3,600 men, were formed in this governorate, by Colonel Count de Witt [Ivan Osipovich de Witt]. These Cossacks were recruited from landowners' and state-owned peasants, dependent (taxable) gentry and merchants, one warrior per 152 registered souls. Each of the Cossacks called up by the landowners was equivalent to two conscripts. The donors of men were obliged to supply them with linen, shoes and a horse with full harness; clothing and munitions were issued from the treasury, for which the donor was intended to be charged 75 Roubles for each man. Weapons (pikes, pistols and a number of sabres and muskets) were issued from the Kiev arsenal.

Upon receipt of the manifesto of 6 (18) July, the nobles of the Kiev Governorate decided to assemble, in order to call up three warriors per 500 registered souls for the internal territorial force, supplying them with clothing and provisions for 20 days and arming them with pikes. Following this, the nobility of the Chigirin and Cherkasy districts and several of the landowners from the Kiev, Zvenigorodka and Boguslav districts volunteered to call up five soldiers per 500 souls; the Kiev and Boguslav magistrates appointed 100 warriors: overall, it was intended to assemble 4,490 men from the governorate. Following the disbandment of the *opolchenie*, a conscription was made of ten men per 500 registered souls. In addition, 3,458 drivers joined a mobile magazine for Second Army and the Army of the Danube and 390 men in Third Army, to form escort units. Finally, for the work on the fortification of Kiev, several thousand men were gathered from the governorate, who received food from the donors.

Cash donations consisted of:

1. 50,000 paper Roubles, offered by the nobility on the formation of the Ukrainian Cossack force.
2. 36,000 paper Roubles, 2,606 silver Roubles and four *Chervonets* [3.47g gold coin] contributed by various classes.
3. Nine *Pud*, 33 pounds of silver and 3½ pounds of gold, were received by the treasury from the monasteries and the clergy.

Moreover, one artillery horse per five hundred souls, for a total of 1,069 horses were delivered and sent from the Radomysl district, and 52,000 *Pud* of hay for 2nd Reserve Corps.[41]

Podolsk Governorate

Even before the opening of hostilities, by Supreme Rescript dated 4 [16] March, addressed to the civil governor of Podolsk, Count Saint-Priest [Karl Frantsevich

---

41 Information on the war of 1812, collected from acts of the Kiev Governorate, signed by the former civil governor Pereverzev. This work shows the value of the deliveries made by the inhabitants of the Kiev Governorate, during the years 1812 and 1813, at about four million Roubles.

Saint-Priest or Armand-Charles-Emmanuel de Guignard, comte de Saint-Priest], it was imperative to collect one artillery horse from each five-hundred man conscription site in the Podolsk Governorate. In pursuance of this Supreme Command, 1,042 horses were sent out from the governorate.

Thereafter, 1,142 carts with 2,520 horses and 1,152 drivers were collected to form a mobile magazine for the army,[42] and in addition, 7,000 oxen with 1,000 carts and 594 drivers were sent to the army, for carrying military baggage and as food for the troops.[43]

By Supreme Command, issued in June 1812, one of the Ukrainian Cossack regiments was to be formed from 1,200 men from the inhabitants of four districts of the Podolsk Governorate: Vinnitsa, Bratslav, Gaisin [Gysin] and Balta.[44]

In addition, 3,500 horses were delivered to the army[45] and 1,719 two-horse carts were collected for the continuous supply of food and fodder to the troops.[46]

Siberian Governorates

Despite the remoteness of these governorates from the theatre of military operations, they played a useful part in the delivery of resources for the protection of the Empire. The Supreme Manifesto dated 1 (13) July ordered that cash was to be collected, instead of conscripts, from the Siberian governorates, of 2,000 Roubles from each.[47] But, soon after, the collection of this cash was cancelled so as not to over-burden the inhabitants of Siberia,[48] and a conscription tranche ordered. Since the Siberian governorates could not take an active part in the defence of the state, their inhabitants were invited to voluntarily donate cash. These offerings could not have been significant, due to the sparsely populated region, and especially due to the poor grain harvest in Siberia and the extremely high prices of the most essential supplies. But eagerness for the common cause made many give up their last possessions. Even with the strong ties that connected them with the Fatherland, broken by their crimes, they responded to the voice of the motherland, crying out for help to her sons: the workers of the Telma state-owned factory donated a fairly significant amount of money. Of the many moving examples of the general eagerness of the Siberian inhabitants, let us cite the act of one of the workers of the Barnaul plant, Belkin, who presented five silver Roubles to the factory office. The official who accepted the money was completely aware of Belkin's situation, who was very poor and burdened with a large family, and therefore expressed surprise that he was making such a donation, being in need of help himself. 'The Tsar feeds me, and my family will not die of hunger,' answered the worker. 'This money was left to me

---

42 Prince Bagration's orders to the former civil governor of Podolsk, Count Saint-Priest, dated 3 [15] May, No 180.
43 Supreme Command addressed to the former Podolsk civil governor, Count Saint-Priest, dated 25 May [6 June].
44 Complete Collection of Laws, 25,129, XXXII, 339.
45 Complete Collection of Laws, 25,211, XXXII, 414.
46 Admiral Chichagov's orders dated 31 August [12 September], No 1,409.
47 Complete Collection of Laws, 25,172, XXXII, 385.
48 Letter from the former Siberian governor general Pestel, to the former Tambov civil governor Marchenko, dated 15 [27] July 1812, No 1318, from St Petersburg.

by my father, on his deathbed, bequeathing it to me to save it for a rainy day. On hearing of the state of our holy Russia, I reasoned that for all of us there could be no blacker days than at present, and therefore, fulfilling the last wish of my father, I ask you to accept my money.[49]

The native Buryats and their Lamas, comprehending the beneficent patronage of the Russian Government, were keen and offered money, furs, bread, and so on. To say that even the nomadic Tungus [Evenki], having not heard about the occupation of Moscow by the French until two years later, were preparing to ride on reindeer against Napoleon.[50]

Donations from the Siberian governorates, according to the available, albeit very incomplete records, reached over 300,000 Roubles in cash, gold and silver ingots, fur goods, and so on.[51]

From our brief review of mobilisation, and donations made by the governorates that were not part of the three districts of the *opolchenie*, it emerges that these governorates voluntarily fielded the following forces:

Lifland *opolchenie*:	2,260
Lifland Cossack Regiment:	2,000
Marksmen:	200
Schmitt's & Nieroth's detachments:	400
From the island of Ezel:	200
Total:	5,060 men.

Estland, special conscription tranche of 17 men per 500 souls.

Finland, Vyborg Jäger Regiment:	1,200
Olonets, marksmen:	570
Vologda, marksmen:	500
Orenburg, 24 Cossack regiments:	12,500
Astrakhan, two Kalmyk regiments:	1,000
Lands of the Don Host:	
26 Cossack regiments, half-company of horse artillery and 3,000 warriors:	18,000
Kherson, Skarzhinsky's unit of 5 Sotnia & 1 squadron:	650
Malorussia governorates:	
(Poltava & Chernigov) 15 Cossack regiments & opochenie:	60,000
Kiev & Podolsk: 4 Ukrainian Cossack regiments:	4,800
Total: 104,280 men.	

---

49 Information submitted by the local authorities, held in the M.T.D.
50 Description of the Yenisei Governorate. St Petersburg, 1835, II, 73.
51 Register of donations held in the archive of the M.T.D.

It is much more difficult to calculate the donations from these governorates in cash, provisions and weapons. From the information that has come down to us about this glorious era, we can conclude that the offerings of the governorates, which were not part of the three *opolchenie* districts, amounted to at least 25 million Roubles. But as many of the donations in kind were not evaluated, and not even placed on the available records, there is no doubt that these deliveries, together with cash offerings, exceeded the indicated total by at least half as much again.

Consequently – despite several levies made during 1811 and the first half of 1812,[52] and despite the devastation of many regions of the Empire by the enemy, at the call of the Tsar, Russia voluntarily called up some 320,000 soldiers (of which 50,000 were mounted), and benefited from a total of at least 100 million Roubles.

Take heart, Russia! Have faith in your sons! Never have you shown your strength more than at the time when your enemies considered you dead. As in the days of Pozharsky [Dmitry Mikhailovich Pozharsky] and Minin [Kuzma Minich Minin], so in the days of the glorious struggle between Alexander I and Napoleon, every Russian was ready to sacrifice everything even themselves: this readiness was a sure guarantee of success.

---

52 From June 1811 to August 1812, three general levies were made in the Empire: the first for four conscripts per 500 souls, the second for two and the third for ten conscripts.

19

The situation in the enemy occupied *Oblasts* of the Empire

Establishment by the French of the Provisional Government of Lithuania, Administrative Commissions, sub–prefectures and municipal administrations. – Formation of the General Confederation in Warsaw; accession of the Lithuanian *oblasts*. – Composition of the Provisional Government, Administrative Commissions and municipal administrations. – Auxiliary Commissions. – Government of the parts of Belorussia and Volhynia, occupied by enemy troops.

Mobilisation of Lithuania: the various types of newly organised forces. – Causes of delay in the formation of these forces. – The establishment of magazines and hospitals. – Unrest in the rear areas of the French *Grande Armée*. – Disaster in Lithuania and Belorussia. – The subsequent fate of the Lithuanian forces.

Napoleon's army, having passed through Lithuania, left only small detachments there, barely sufficient to guard the most important locations along its lines of operations. For this very reason, only part of the country that was to the rear of the French *Grande Armée* was dependent on Napoleon, and although his troops occupied the governorates of Vilna, Grodno, Courland, Białystok, most of the Minsk Governorate and parts of Mogilev, Vitebsk and Volhynia, however, only in Lithuania and in the Mogilev Governorate did he succeed in introducing an administration and forming a small number of troops.

After the occupation of Vilna by the French, Napoleon, having established a provisional government for Lithuania in this city (*gouvernement provisoire de la Lithuanie*), or, as it was usually referred to, the Government Commission, subordinated it to one of his adjutants general, Comte Hogendorp [Diderik (Dirk) van Hogendorp], appointed as the Governor General of Lithuania. This commission, chaired by the former Lithuanian Marshal Sołtan [Stanisław Sołtan], with seven members, a general secretary and a French commissioner (Baron Bignon [Louis Pierre Édouard Bignon]) was entrusted with the administration of the country and the disposal of its financial resources; but the main subjects of their business were the provisioning of Napoleon's army and the training of Lithuanian forces.[1]

In every governorate capital occupied by the enemy, administrative commissions for the governorate were established and renamed *departments*; all these commissions were subordinated to the supreme government of Lithuania and consisted of three members, under the chairmanship of an intendant (a French national); later, they became reliant upon the Governors General: in Vilna, General of Brigade Baron Jomini [Antoine-Henri, baron de Jomini]; in Grodno, Baron Brun [Jean-Antoine Brun]; in Minsk, initially General Barbanègre [Joseph Barbanègre], later Bronikowski [Nicholas Bronikowski]; in Białystok, General Ferrier [Gratien Ferrier]. The districts [Uezd] were governed by sub-prefectures, consisting of a sub-prefect and two members, and a municipal government was established in each town. For the collection and analysis of documents related to the former administration of the region, special archival commissions were established in governorate capitols.[2]

Meanwhile, in Warsaw, with the consent of the King of Saxony and Duke of Warsaw, a general confederation was formed, under the control of Prince Adam Czartoryski [Adam Kazimierz Czartoryski], the purpose of which was to generate an uprising and reunite all the *Oblasts* that had once belonged to Poland. A deputation from the Warsaw Sejm [legislature], having arrived in Vilna, formally invited the provisional government to proceed with the confederation. The consequence of this was the signing of the Act of Confederation in Vilna on 2 (14) July. Other cities joined the confederation as they were occupied by Napoleon's troops: such as the Act signed in Slutsk *Uezd* in mid [late] July; in Minsk on 7 (19) July; Disna [Dzisna] joined the confederation during Napoleon's stay in Glubokoe; Bobruisk on 27 July (new style) after the occupation of Rozhnetsky Glusk; the *Uezds* of Vileyka, Igumen and Borisov were slow to join, but were eventually forced to follow the example of others, by early [mid] October.[3] Sołtyk [Roman Sołtyk] himself, an historian very biased in relation to his fellow countrymen, admits that the existence of the Warsaw Confederation was marked only by proclamations and exclamations.[4]

An immediate consequence of the Act of Confederation was the destruction of the customs border line between Lithuania and the Duchy of Warsaw on 16 (28) July, 1812. Soon after, by order of the provisional Lithuanian government, it was intended to elect deputies to the Sejm in Warsaw from the cities and districts, but this measure was not carried out.[5]

The provisional Lithuanian government was divided into committees (ministries) consisting of a chairman and several councillors. The government had seven committees:

---

[1] Comte Sołtyk, *Napoleon en 1812*, 52-53. *Notice historique sur les armemens qui eurent lieu en Lithuanie pendant l'occupation française en 1812, par Lensky*.
[2] A note containing information about the war of 1812, signed by the former Grodno governor Doppelmeier (held in the archive of the M.T.D.).
[3] Notes on the war of 1812, submitted by the local authorities of the Minsk Governorate (held in the archive of the M.T.D.).
[4] Sołtyk, *Napoléon en 1812*, 51.
[5] Notes on the war of 1812, submitted by the local authorities of the Minsk Governorate (held in the archive of the M.T.D.).

1. Justice.
2. Internal affairs.
3. Policing.
4. Finance.
5. Military affairs.
6. Spiritual affairs and public education.
7. Provisions.[6]

The military committee or ministry was run by Prince Alexander Sapieha [Aleksander Antoni Sapieha], and after his death, Brigadier General Grabowski [Stefan Grabowski], who held this position until the retreat of the *Grande Armée* from Russia.[7] In general, all matters were first considered in committee, and then submitted to a general assembly of chairmen (ministers). The administrative commissions were divided into three departments:

1. Justice, internal affairs and policing.
2. Military and provisioning department.
3. Finance, spiritual and public education.

Each department was run by one of the members of the commission, who was provided with assistants. Municipal (city) administrations in governorate capitals consisted of four branches:

1. Policing.
2. Finance and food.
3. Quartering.
4. Charitable affairs.

Municipal administrations in *Uezd* towns were entrusted to sub-prefects.[8]

Both the supreme administration and the administrative commissions acted through other subsidiary commissions. The most important of which were the following:

1. Military hospitals.
2. Public hospitals and charitable institutions.
3. Quartermaster's, which was in charge of the estates abandoned by their Russian landowners.
4. Food.
5. Tax collection.
6. Verification, for the investigation of damages suffered by the residents.

---

6   A note containing information about the war of 1812, signed by the former Grodno governor Doppelmeier (held in the archive of the M.T.D.).
7   *Notice historique sur les armemens qui eurent lieu en Lithuanie* etc.
8   A note containing information about the war of 1812, signed by the former Grodno governor Doppelmeier (held in the archive of the M.T.D.).

7. Forestry.
8. Customs etc.⁹

After the enemy occupied parts of Belorussia and the western districts of the Volhynia Governorate, various government places were introduced: in Mogilev an administrative commission was established; in Vladimir-in-Volhynia a commandant was appointed; the Vladimir *Uezd* was governed by a commission composed of local landowners, and that part of the Lutsk *Uezd* occupied by the enemy was administered by commissioners, also from the inhabitants of the region.[10]

One of the primary concerns of the new government was the formation of armed forces in Lithuania. Prince Alexander Sapieha, who had been entrusted with the military department in this country, assured Napoleon that all its inhabitants would rise up against Russia, but the consequences showed the groundlessness of Sapieha's assumptions, based more on obsequiousness towards the Emperor of the French than on profound knowledge of the matter. Napoleon, during his stay in Vilna, decided to form five infantry and four cavalry regiments at Lithuania's expense.[11] The provisional government immediately proceeded to assign and conscript *Kantonists* (recruits), numbering 14,000 (10,000 as infantry and 4,000 as cavalry). Each of the governorates was obliged to raise a number of these conscripts in proportion to its population; in order to constitute the infantry regiments, the following were recruited: 3,000 in the Vilna and Minsk governorates; 2,500 in the Grodno and 1,500 in the Białystok governorates, provided with linen, clothes and provisions for 15 days.[12] In order to constitute the Lithuanian cavalry, one man with a horse per 75 households was ordered to be conscripted, which should have produced 4,000 horsemen, for whose equipment it was intended to collect 486½ Złoty (73 silver Roubles) per 50 households. Both infantry and cavalrymen were required to serve for six years.[13]

As the Lithuanian regiments were to become part of the Polish forces, they were organised and uniformed according to the model of Polish regiments and were designated by the following numbers in sequence, the infantry were: 18th, 19th, 20th, 21st and 22nd, while the cavalry were: 17th, 18th, 19th and 20th. Each of the infantry regiments comprised three battalions, while a battalion had six companies. The cavalry (lancer) regiments had an establishment of four squadrons. Lithuanian landowners were appointed as regimental commanders, some of whom had no idea of military service.[14] In contrast, just as with every senior commander, so it was

---

9 A note containing information about the war of 1812, signed by the former Grodno governor Doppelmeier (held in the archive of the M.T.D.).
10 Information supplied by the local authorities of the Mogilev and Volhynia governorates, held in the M.T.D.
11 *Notice historique sur les armemens qui eurent lieu en Lithuanie* etc.
12 Orders from the provisional government of Lithuania to the administrative commissions, dated 25 June [7 July] 1812.
13 Orders from the provisional government of Lithuania to the administrative commissions dated 1 [13] July.
14 *Notice historique sur les armemens qui eurent lieu en Lithuanie* etc. We enclose a list of Lithuanian regiments with their designated commanders: 18th Infantry, Count Chodkiewicz;

with all subaltern officers and non-commissioned officers, who were appointed from veteran servicemen from the Polish army. In August, Napoleon appointed *général de division* Prince Giedroyć [Romuald Tadeusz Giedroyć] as Inspector General of all Lithuanian regiments; while *généraux* de brigade, Count Niesiołowski [Franciszek Ksawery Niesiołowski] and Wawrzecki [Tomasz Antoni Wawrzecki?], were appointed as inspectors of the Lithuanian infantry and cavalry. At the same time, the Governor General of Lithuania, Comte Hogendorp, was charged with supervising the formation of Lithuanian forces.[15]

Napoleon, wishing to attract the numerous Lithuanian gentry to his Eagles, instructed *général de brigade* Comte Wincenty Krasiński [Wincenty Jan Krasiński][16] to recruit a new regiment from the nobility, designated *3e chevau-légers lanciers de la Garde* (*1er chevau-légers lanciers polonais* having been formed back in 1806, in Warsaw, from Polish nationals by Comte Krasiński; *2e chevau-légers lanciers de la Garde*, the Dutch Red Lancers, in Comte Colbert's brigade [Pierre David de Colbert-Chabanais], were formed a little later). Each of the nobles joining the service was required to have a horse and uniform at his own expense. General Konopka [Jan Konopka] was appointed regimental commander of this regiment.[17]

Simultaneously with the formation of these regiments, battalions of marksmen (*bataillons des chasseurs-tirailleurs*) were recruited from the forestry gamekeepers and hunters who knew how to shoot.[18]

To keep the peace in the country, Napoleon, by decree of 1 July, new style, ordered the formation of a gendarme unit, of 30 to 60 men from the settled gentry, in each *Uezd*: all of these were under the overall command of Colonel Prince Radziwiłł [Dominik Hieronim Radziwiłł]. The gendarmes received fodder and a Zloty (15 silver Kopecks) per day.[19] In every governorate capital, a guard force was established, which was trained in marching and musket drill on holidays.[20]

It was not easy to equip and supply nine regiments with horses at the expense of the *Oblasts*, already impoverished from the movement of huge armies through them and completely devastated by marauders who wandered in the rear areas of Napoleon's forces. The delight shown by the inhabitants of Lithuania when they met the conqueror gave way to ambivalence as soon as they learned by experience to what extent the weakening of discipline in the army increased the disasters inevitably associated with war. It was impossible to expect either loyalty or self-sacrifice

---

19th Infantry, Count Tiesenhausen; 20th Infantry, Baron Bisching; 21st Infantry, Giełgud (killed during the campaign of 1831); 22nd Infantry, Czapski; 17th Ulans, Count Tyszkiewicz; 18th Ulans, Count Przezdziecki; 19th Ulans, Rajeckis; 20th Ulans, Obuchowicz.
15 *Notice historique* etc.
16 Died in 1858 as Adjutant General and General of Cavalry.
17 Proclamation by Comte Krasiński, from Beshenkovichi. Orders from the Provisional Government of Lithuania and the Vilnius Administrative Commission. *Notice historique* etc.
18 A note containing information about the war of 1812, signed by the former Grodno governor Doppelmeier (held in the archive of the M.T.D.). *Notice historique* etc. Orders from the Provisional Government of Lithuania and the Vilnius Administrative Commission.
19 Orders from the Provisional Government of Lithuania and the Vilnius Administrative Commission. *Notice historique* etc.
20 Orders from the Provisional Government of Lithuania and the Vilnius Administrative Commission. Information supplied by the local authorities, held in the M.T.D.

from those whose country was ruled as a region conquered by force of arms by the French. It is difficult to calculate the many taxes introduced in Lithuania during the ephemeral French rule in this country. We shall confine ourselves to indicating the most important:

1. Income tax, from which no one was exempt, from the capitalist, who was obliged to pay a seventh [14.28%] of the interest he received, to the poorest casual labourer (decided by the Provisional Government of Lithuania, 22 August, new style, 1812).
2. A tax on beverages (including vinegar), cattle, meat, fish, oil, tobacco, etc. (table of fees compiled by the Minsk Administrative Commission).

It goes without saying that such extortion could not win over the people of Lithuania in favour of the French. In addition, Emperor Alexander's visit to Vilna had left unforgettable memories and condemned many orders by his opponent to inaction.[21] In the Lithuanian Courier, a newspaper published in Vilna at the time, there were descriptions of enthusiastic greetings offered to the French by the frivolous inhabitants of Lithuania, and the festivities on the occasion of Napoleon's birthday, 15 (27) August; But all this news, for the most part exaggerated, did not express public opinion in the least, which was disappointed by the oppression by the illusory patrons of Poland. the conscription was relatively successful, especially in the Grodno governorate;[22] but a lack of money delayed the clothing and equipping of the troops. Finding remounts was also troublesome. As a result of this, infantry itself was formed before the cavalry. By the middle of September (new style) all five infantry regiments had been manned and almost completely equipped; in each of them an internal economy commission was established, following the example of the French army. At the same time, muskets were issued from the arsenals located in Vilna and Kovno [Kaunas] for these regiments. Following this, a sixth infantry regiment began to be formed, which received the designation 23rd, which was intended to be recruited from the southern part of the Minsk Governorate, but this order could not be executed.[23]

The formation of the cavalry proceeded infinitely more slowly. In addition to the lack of horses, the reasons for this were; the impossibility of obtaining horse harness in a short time and the difficulty of training newly recruited cavalrymen before the onset of winter and the reoccupation of Lithuania by Russian troops. One of the main reasons for this was also the lower aptitude of the Lithuanian peasants for cavalry service, compared with the inhabitants of Poland, where mounted regiments were formed more easily and more quickly than infantry. However, despite all the difficulties encountered, General Wawrzecki managed to complete the formation of *17 Pułk Ułanów, 18 Pułk Ułanów* and *19 Pułk Ułanów* by the time the French *Grande Armée* retreated from Russia. The *20 Pułk Ułanów* could not be completely

---

21 *Notice historique* etc.
22 A note containing information about the war of 1812, signed by the former Grodno governor Doppelmeier (held in the archive of the M.T.D.).
23 *Notice historique* etc.

manned. In addition to the aforementioned troops, a horse battery was also formed in Vilna, which later joined Poniatowski's *5e Corps* [Józef Antoni Poniatowski]. Konopka's *3e chevau-légers lanciers de la Garde*, quickly manned by huntsmen from the gentry and students from Vilna University, was considered the best of all the Lithuanian troops. It had been intended to form it with six squadrons, but only four squadrons could be completely manned; a Tatar squadron [*Tartares lituaniens de la Garde impériale*] was later added to it, recruited by Murza Captain Achmatowicz [Mustapha Achmatowicz] from Mohammedans who had long been settled in Lithuania. In addition to these regiments, it had been intended to form a cavalry regiment designated *21 Pułk Strzelców Konnych* in Vilna, from huntsmen. Its formation, entrusted to Colonel Moniuszko [Ignacy Moniuszko], was not completed.[24]

We have already had occasion to mention that the most successful mobilisation was effected in the Grodno Governorate, where 5,968 men of various troop types were assembled and more than 900,000 Zlotys (135,000 silver Roubles) were collected for their equipment.[25] In contrast, in the Minsk Governorate, the orders from the Lithuanian provisional government were carried out slowly and reluctantly: only a few of the gentry wished to join the *3e chevau-légers lanciers de la Garde impériale*; the corps of gendarmes in the governorate consisted of just 70 men with 19 horses; the national guard was unable to form; while in Nesvizh [Niasviž] a handful of foresters joined the marksmen. Only Count Stanisław Czapski [Stanisław Hutten-Czapski] managed to form *22 Pułk Piechoty* from conscripts, which was destroyed in its first encounter with Russian troops under Comte Lambert [Karl Osipovich de Lambert or Charles de Lambert].[26]

The provision of life-supporting supplies to Napoleon's *Grande Armée* was the subject of particular concern for the administrative commissions and was a heavy burden for the region. The huge extortion of various supplies, together with a lack of discipline in the multi-national enemy horde, was one of the main reasons for the failure to mobilise Lithuania and the cooling off of many of Napoleon's collaborators. All these requisitions and deliveries were made without any consideration for the resources of the region. The only scalar for the requirements from the administrative commission and the force commanders was the actual or perceived needs of the army. Thus, the King of Westphalia [Jérôme Bonaparte], immediately after the occupation of Grodno, demanded half a million rations of bread, beef and vodka, and ordered not only the provisions seized in Russian magazines to be taken away, but also all the bread found on six landowners' estates. Similar incidents were repeated incessantly. Some of the stock seized in the Grodno Governorate was sent to Vilna, at the request of Quartermaster General Dumas [Mathieu Dumas], and, meanwhile, in every city and large town, magazines of 10,000 rations or more were prepared in case of passage by troops. In order to replenish these reserves, under the guise of a voluntary donation, 40 Garnets of rye, 40 Garnets of oats, two

---

24 *Notice historique* etc.
25 A note containing information about the war of 1812, signed by the former Grodno governor Doppelmeier (held in the archive of the M.T.D.).
26 A note about the war of 1812, submitted by the local leadership of the Minsk Governorate (held in the archive of the M.T.D.).

Garnets of peas, two *Pud* of hay and two *Pud* of straw were collected from each household. All this notwithstanding, other significant deliveries of hay, straw, cattle and vodka were made, according to the proportions from every *Uezd*. The ruin of the inhabitants of the Grodno Governorate was completed as early as late October [early November] by the establishment of a reserve magazine of 50,000 *Chetvert* of rye, 73,000 *Chetvert* of oats, 6,500 *Berkovets* [1 *Berkovets* = 164 kg or 360lb] of hay and a similar amount of straw, by order of Napoleon. Shortly afterwards, part of the governorate was re-occupied by Russian troops, and therefore, in order to meet this demand, it was necessary to collect, from the remaining *Uezds* an additional 1⅔ *Chetvert* of rye, two *Chetvert* of oats and two *Pud* each of hay and straw, from each household. Despite the enormity of this resupply, however, half of the required goods were collected within four weeks. The French ate a large amount of meat, and therefore, during the five-month occupation of the Grodno Governorate by the enemy, it lost an entire third of its cattle. Requisitions of horses for the cavalry and wagons for the transport of various loads for the troops were also very significant, but there is no way to determine them exactly.[27]

The governorates of Vilna and Minsk and the Białystok *Oblast* were forced to make huge deliveries, to feed the passing troops, to maintain standing stores of supplies on all major routes and to establish reserve magazines, to the same level as Grodno. The Vilna and Minsk administrative commissions, in September 1812, received an order to collect immediately, for the reserve magazines, from each governorate: 200,000 cwt (more than 60,000 *Chetvert*) of rye; 200,000 *Korets* (around 100,000 *Chetvert*) of oats; 50,000 *Pud* each of hay and straw.[28] Residents of the Minsk Governorate, in addition to all the deliveries made in kind, were required to pay 9½ Zlotys (1 silver Rouble, 42 Kopecks) per soul, which amounted to about 539,000 silver Roubles, and pay all arrears that had been due to the Russian government, within seven days.[29]

Large hospitals had been set up in every provincial town, for 1,200 or more men. Patients were placed in government buildings, monasteries and private homes. The Vilna Administrative Commission, wanting the hospitals to be maintained at the expense of urban and rural inhabitants, at first would not release any sums for this matter, but later took over the supply of furnishings and linen; everything else was provided at the expense of the inhabitants of the region. Russian prisoners of war were used as hospital orderlies. The subsistence for patients in each of the provincial cities cost at least half a million Roubles. In addition to the main hospitals, smaller ones were set up in every county town and large village.

The supply of firewood for bakeries and hospitals was one of the most difficult local duties in the enemy occupied territory. In Grodno, where ovens had been built for the daily preparation of 100,000 portions of hard-tack, 27,000 wagon loads were used up throughout the summer; 19,000 cubic *Sazhen* [1 *Sazhen* = 2.13m or 7'] were

---

27 A note containing information about the war of 1812, signed by the former Grodno governor Doppelmeier (held in the archive of the M.T.D.).
28 Instructions from the provisional government of Lithuania to the administrative commissions.
29 A note about the war of 1812, submitted by the local leadership of the Minsk Governorate (held in the archive of the M.T.D.).

delivered for the heating of Grodno hospitals, and then another cart load per soul was ordered to be collected.[30]

No matter how painful the exactions imposed on Lithuania by the voracity of its supposed liberators, this country suffered incomparably more from the robbery and violence of stragglers from Napoleon's *Grande Armée*, who roamed the enemy occupied area, singly and in gangs. Complaints were constantly filed with the sub-prefects, with the administrative commissions and with the provisional Lithuanian government about harassment by the troops, but almost all the requests from the inhabitants remained unsatisfied, under the pretext of the ambiguity of the incidents described. The main reason for the unrest was the multi-national composition of Napoleon's forces, preventing the introduction of a uniform, strictly enforced discipline, which alone could have tied the soldiers to their Colours and prevented looting, which had spread in the army to such an extent that it was necessary to send large units to pursue the fugitives who plundered the countryside and killed its inhabitants. According to Sołtyk, the number of marauders from the *Grande Armée* reached 50,000.[31] It was also quite a common occurrence for significant units from the force, in their entirety, to plunder and devastate the countryside. Contemporaries of the war of 1812 swear that these violent acts were carried out mainly by the Westphalian troops, which was facilitated by the indulgence of every kind of indiscipline by their commander, General Vandamme [Dominique-Joseph-René Vandamme]. On 26 June [8 July], the sub-prefect of Lida lodged a complaint against Vandamme, that he had personally sent his soldiers out to plunder; while two days later, a Westphalian detachment, numbering 500 men, having arrived in the town of Szczuczyn and having received the full amount of bread, meat, vodka and fodder demanded from the inhabitants there, they began, with the permission of their superiors, to rob houses and shoot at the inhabitants who begged for mercy: this violence, which lasted all night, cost the lives of three people; 12 were wounded and many were mutilated and beaten.[32] In general, the enemy, almost everywhere, not content with the devastation of peasant homes, mowed or deliberately trampled crops in the fields, depriving the villagers of any means of subsistence.

Napoleon, wanting to put an end to desertion by the marauders and the devastation of the countryside he had taken under his protection, during his stay in the town of Glubokoye, ordered that any military rank, who arbitrarily abandoned the force, should be immediately handed over to the nearest court-martial commission and be executed.[33] But, despite that, the robberies and violence did not decrease at all.

---

30 A note containing information about the war of 1812, signed by the former Grodno governor Doppelmeier (held in the archive of the M.T.D.).
31 Sołtyk, *Napoleon en 1812*, 52.
32 A note containing information about the war of 1812, signed by the former Grodno governor Doppelmeier (held in the archive of the M.T.D.).
33 'Ordre du jour du 21 juillet, 1812. Article 1er. *Tout individu français, allemand ou italien, qui sera trouvé à la suite de l'armée sans autorisation suffisante, sera arrêté et traduit devant la Commisiion Prévôtale la plus voisine, qui condamnera à mort tout ceux qui seront convaincus de pillage et maraude.*

With the entry of Napoleon's *Grande Armée* into Belorussia, the enemy troops, irritated by the absence of most of the inhabitants hiding in the forests or leaving after the Russian army, indulged in even greater fury than before. Having ransacked the houses and churches, smashed the furniture, plundered the cattle and horses, the enemy very often completed the devastation with arson. Despite these acts, however, in Mogilev there were at least a few collaborators with the French who attempted to form a National Guard, but they managed to recruit, mostly by force, no more than 400 men of all kinds of scum, dressed as best they could, and armed with shoddy pikes. The Mogilev commandant, Reminsky, had been diligently training this miserable rabble, but as soon as the first Russian troops appeared during the French retreat, the entire new force fled, leaving their commander to be killed by Cossacks near the town of Knyazhitsy.[34]

The residents of Mogilev, being browbeaten by the administrative commission into swearing allegiance to Napoleon, justified themselves of this, taking on the view of the French collaborators that it was still unknown to which side the victory would go, but later they took the oath together with the clergy, not only Catholic, but also Orthodox: the latter being carried away by the criminal example of Archbishop Varlaam [Grigory Stepanovich Shishatsky], seduced by the reassurances of the enemy. The betrayal of the clergy brought discouragement to the inhabitants of Mogilev, but could not serve to shore up the shaky Napoleonic government in Belorussia.[35]

The situation in the part of the Vitebsk Governorate occupied by the enemy was no less disastrous: huge requisitions of supplies for the troops, the fury of marauders and their attempts to turn the peasants against the landowners, defined the French occupation and left indelible marks on the countryside subjected to their incursion.[36]

Article 2e. Tout habitant du pays, de quelque qualité qu'il soit, arreté avec les pillards ou maraudeurs et prevenu de les avoir excité, conduit, ou de les avoir aidé, de quelque manière que ce soit, dans leur brigandage, sera traduit devant la Commission Prévôtale la plus proche, et en cas de conviction sera condamné à mort.'

34 From information submitted by the local authorities of the Mogilev Governorate (held in the archive of the M.T.D.).

35 We attach the original order by the Mogilev commission: 'His Eminence of the Greek-Eastern Churches, Archbishop Varlaam of Mogilev. This Commission, drawn up by order of His Highness, Gentleman Marshal of the Grand Army of the French and Allied Forces, prince d'Eckmühl and many orders of Chivalry, hereby informs Your Eminence that tomorrow, at 9 o'clock, that is, on the twenty-sixth of July, according to the new calendar, in the local Greek-Eastern Cathedral Church, it will be the duty of all the Mogilev clergy, nobility and other classes of the Greek confession to take an oath of allegiance to the Emperor of the French and King of Italy, the Great Napoleon and the Divine Liturgy, to be celebrated by you personally, as the pre-eminent arch-pastor of the Governorate of Mogilev, commemorating in it, from now on, as well as in the prayers of thanksgiving to the Most High, instead of Emperor Alexander, the Emperor of the French and King of Italy, the Great Napoleon, with such diligence that it should be immediately fulfilled with decent solemnity, as well as in all the parishes of your diocese, and to send an order from yourself and notify this Commission that it has been carried out. Signed in original: Jerzy Luskina. Jan Makowieski. Marcin Nibostawski. No 6. July 25th, 1812.'

36 From information submitted by the local authorities of the Vitebsk Governorate (held in the archive of the M.T.D.).

It is impossible to determine with absolute certainty the losses inflicted on the inhabitants by enemy troops. How much may be judged from information collected on the ground – information, partly incomplete, partly exaggerated, each of the Belorussian governorates had suffered damages to the value of some 18 million Roubles. The loss in population was also very significant, the number of male souls on the landowners' estates of the Mogilev Governorate, according to the register of 1811, extended to 359,946, while according to the register of 1816, only some 287,149. In the Vitebsk Governorate, overall, according to the 1811 register there were 352,474 souls, while on the 1816 register there were 315,481 souls.[37]

The situation in the western *Oblasts* of the Russian Empire, occupied by the enemy horde, presented a deplorable vision of a country that had been anticipating Napoleon as a liberator and paid for their error with every kind of calamity. In the course of several months, all the resources for the subsistence of millions of people were exhausted, the wealth accumulated over many generations was plundered, factories and workshops were destroyed, and the heritage of the sciences, arts and crafts was wiped out. All this was sacrificed, without providing the subsistence for Napoleon's *Grande Armée*. The greatest military genius of our century, embracing all parts of the World with his political and military considerations, could neither curb the excesses of his troops, nor use to advantage the huge resources of the regions occupied by his armies. This striking example convinces us that the local and climatic properties of the country can present obstacles insurmountable for the most brilliant commander. Operations in a vast sparsely populated area are associated with the need to have extremely large baggage trains with the army, for the maintenance of which, in turn, resources will be required that go beyond the limits of the possible. The time had long passed when thirty or forty thousand soldiers were considered the maximum strength of an army, but Napoleon, despite his extraordinary talent and many years of experience in warfare, could not easily manage a half a million strong army.

All that remains is to cast a cursory glance at the fate of the Lithuanian mobilisation, made, or just started, in the continuation of Napoleon's invasion of Russia. The advance of Admiral Chichagov's Army of the Danube into the rear of the French *Grande Armée* caused extreme alarm in Lithuania. immediately every Lithuanian regiment was ordered to concentrate in Vilna. From the reports submitted at that time to the Lithuanian Governor-General, Comte Hogendorp, it emerges that in this force there were more than 19,000 men overall under arms, not counting the regiment under General Konopka; but some of the conscripted men were poorly armed, or even had no weapons at all. Konopka's regiment, attacked by surprise on 8 (20) October, in Slonim, by Russian cavalry under General Chaplits [Yefim Ignatevich Chaplits], was completely destroyed; The regimental commander himself was taken prisoner. The squadron of *Tartares lituaniens de la Garde impériale* were attached to 1er *régiment de chevau-légers lanciers polonais* until 1814, and were then disbanded. Some of the infantry which had assembled near Vilna, was

---

37 From information submitted by the former head of the nobility of the Mogilev Governorate, Golynsky. Statement of the number of souls in the Vitebsk Governorate, signed by Councillor Gorodetsky (held in the archive of the M.T.D.).

THE SITUATION IN THE ENEMY OCCUPIED *OBLASTS* OF THE EMPIRE 81

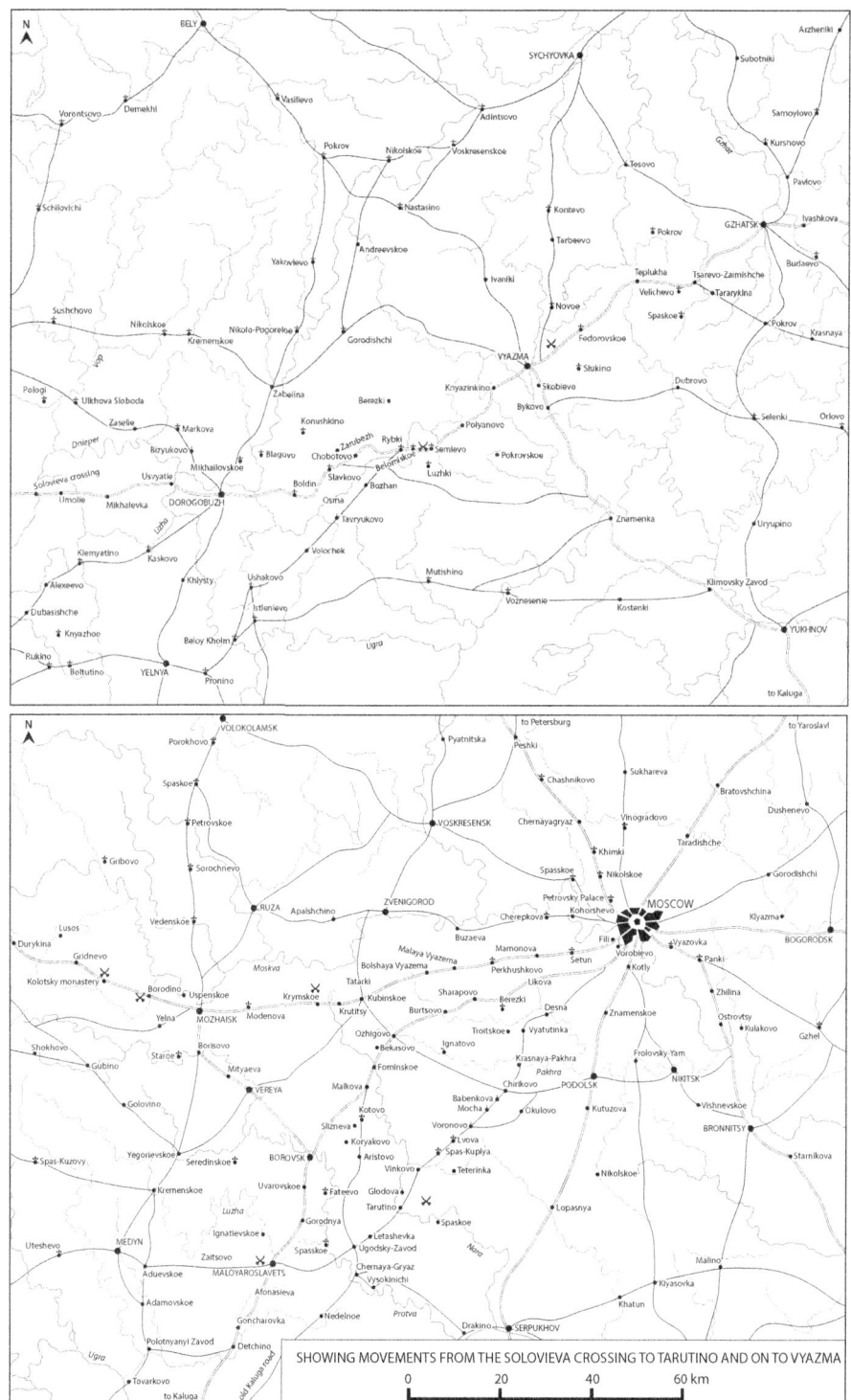

Top and Bottom: Movements from the Solovieva Crossing to Tarutino and on to Vyazma.

sent to Minsk to protect this important location with *18 Pułk Ułanów*. Of this force, *22 Pułk Piechoty, 18 Pułk Ułanów* and the marksman battalion were subsequently scattered by Comte Lambert. *18 Pułk Piechoty, 19 Pułk Piechoty, 20 Pułk Piechoty* and *21 Pułk Piechoty* joined *5e Corps* under Prince Poniatowski, and retreated with him towards Warsaw and, numbering between 5,000 to 6,000 men, made up most of the garrison of the Modlin fortress, during its siege by General Paskevich [Ivan Fëdorovich Paskevich], in 1813.

As for the cavalry, it has been stated above about the fate that befell *18 Pułk Ułanów. 20 Pułk Ułanów* in which only two squadrons had horses, and a small part of *19 Pułk Ułanów* retreated, along with MacDonald's *10e Corps*, to Danzig and became part of *9 Pułk Ułanów*, stationed in this fortress. *17 Pułk Ułanów* and *19 Pułk Ułanów* whose formation had been totally completed, covered the retreat of the remnants of the French *Grande Armée*, through Prussia, to the Elbe, and then joined the corps under Marshal Davout [Louis Nicolas Davout], which was holding Hamburg. When Denmark was forced to take part in the war and send some of its troops to Napoleon's army, then both Lithuanian regiments became part of the French detachment stationed in Holstein and Schleswig, and after the conclusion of the Paris Peace, they returned to Poland and became part of the new Polish army, which was being formed under the command of Grand Duke Konstantin Pavlovich. Finally, *21 Pułk Strzelców Konnych* under Colonel Moniuszko, whose formation was at the very start, served as replacements for *5 Pułk Strzelców Konnych* of the troops of the Duchy of Warsaw.[38]

---

38 *Notice historique sur les armemens qui eurent lieu en Lithuanie.*

20

Prince Kutuzov joins the Army

Operational objectives of the Russian Commander in Chief following the battle of Lubino. – The position at Lubino. – The position at Usvyatye. – The retreat to Dorogobuzh. – The advance of the enemy army. – The situation of the Russian forces at Dorogobuzh. – Its disadvantages. – The retreat to Vyazma. – Measures taken by Napoleon to secure the lines of communication of the *Grande Armée*. – The enemy advance on Vyazma. – The action on the river Osma. – The retreat to Tsarevo–Zaimishche. – Thoughts on the position at Tsarevo–Zaimishche.

Kutuzov's arrival at Tsarevo–Zaimishche. – The continuation of the retreat by our army. – Kutuzov's report to the Tsar on this matter. – The predicament for both sides with regard to rations for the troops. – Kutuzov's initial orders. – The retreat of the Russian army towards Borodino. – The rearguard action at Gzhatsk. – Napoleon's preparations in Gzhatsk for a general battle. – His assessment regarding a halt. – His advance on Borodino. – The withdrawal of our rearguard to the Borodino position.

Upon the retreat of the Western armies from Lubino, along the Moscow road, the objective of our Commanders-in-Chief was to find an area favourable for a defensive battle.[1] The desire to offer a decisive battle, manifested itself more strongly in the nation and the troops after the fall of Smolensk, and even those who did not expect any beneficial consequences from it, considered a general battle to be necessary. Such was the opinion of Barclay de Tolly. Yielding to the forces of circumstance, he sent several General Staff officers to survey the area along the route to Moscow and to look for positions that would be advantageous in a defensive sense; from the reports by these officers it emerged that two positions had been found in the area between Smolensk and Gzhatsk [Gagarin]: at Usvyatie, behind the river Uzha, and at Tsarevo-Zaimishche.[2] Colonel Toll [Karl Fëdorovich Tol or Karl Wilhelm von Toll], having received orders to inspect them, found the position at Usvyatie very advantageous: its right flank adjoined the Dnieper; the front was covered by the Uzha river, which, although insignificant and flowing through

---
1   See Map showing the movements from the Solovieva crossing to Tarutino.
2   *Denkwürdigkeiten des Grafen v. Toll*, I, 399.

a shallow valley, nevertheless presented an obstacle to the enemy, delaying their advance under artillery fire located in the position. The ground to the front is open with good lines of sight, while to the rear there are obstructions that help to conceal the force. But the left flank of the position was subject to envelopment; besides which, an enemy, heading from Smolensk to Dukhovshchina towards Dorogobuzh, on the far side of the Dnieper, could also envelope the position from the right flank, which would assist them in cutting the line of retreat of the Western armies towards Moscow. Since the enemy would have to detach some of their force for a considerable distance (which could expose them to defeat in detail) for such an envelopment, the colonel simply considered it sufficient, having posted the right flank against the Dnieper, to position a significant part of the force, in the form of a reserve behind the main body, in order to protect the position from the left flank. To that end, on 9 (21) August, First Army took up its chosen position, while Second Army fell back to Dorogobuzh.[3]

Upon the arrival of the headquarters of First Army in Usvyatie, both Commanders-in-Chief, wanted to survey the position and set off for a reconnaissance, together with Grand Duke Konstantin Pavlovich, accompanied by all the corps commanders and other generals. During this inspection, Prince Bagration noticed that there was dominant high ground facing the right flank of the position that the enemy could exploit. But Barclay, although he did not place much hope in the strength of this position, nevertheless decided to wait for the attack and suggested that Prince Bagration bring Second Army closer to the left flank of First Army.

On 11 (23) August, the rearguard, under the command of Platov and Rosen [Grigory Vladimirovich Rosen], being pursued by the enemy, crossed to the right bank of the Uzha and settled in position along with the main body of First Army, while Bagration, leaving Major General Neverovsky [Dmitry Petrovich Neverovsky] with a strong detachment at Dorogobuzh, attached Second Army to the left wing of First Army. The enemy, approaching to within cannon range, opened a strong bombardment. Whereupon Prince Bagration expressed concerns for his left flank, which was subject to envelopment, arguing that the position at Dorogobuzh was more advantageous than the one on which our armies currently stood. At the same time, reports were received from Generals Wintzingerode and Krasnov [Ivan Kozmich Krasnov] about an advance by the Viceroy of Italy [Eugène Rose de Beauharnais] from Dukhovshchina towards Dorogobuzh. All these factors forced Barclay to withdraw both armies towards Dorogobuzh, on the night of 11 to 12 (23 to 24) August.[4]

Indeed, although Napoleon had halted for three days in Smolensk, using this time for various governmental and military orders, and although his troops were in dire need of rest, the enemy advance continued unabated. On 10 (22) August, Murat's cavalry [Joachim Murat], followed by *1er Corps* and *3e Corps* under Davout and Ney [Michel Ney], reached Pnevo Sloboda and crossed the Dnieper: the cavalry via a

---

3 Clausewitz, *Der Feldzug von 1812 in Russland*, 127. Barclay de Tolly's report to the Tsar, No 690, dated 14 [26] August, from Semlevo.
4 Condensed War Diary of the movements of First Western Army, compiled by Toll. Description of military operations by First Army (Notes compiled by Barclay de Tolly). *Denkwürdigkeiten des Grafen v. Toll*, I, 401-403.

ford, the infantry over two pontoon bridges; Junot [Jean-Androche Junot] followed them. The weather was hot; the troops, the carts and herds of cattle that followed the army, were enveloped in thick clouds of dust. Meanwhile, most of Napoleon's army was heading along the direct route to Dorogobuzh, some of them had been preparing to set out from Smolensk in the same direction, while the troops under the Viceroy and Poniatowski were moving along country roads in envelopment: the former, with *4e Corps*, followed the Dukhovshchina road to Pomogailovo, and then, taking country lanes to the road leading from Dukhovshchina to Dorogobuzh, crossed the Vop river and arrived at Zaselie on 13 (25) August and linked up with Grouchy's [Emmanuel de Grouchy] *3e Corps de cavalerie* there, which had advanced from Dukhovshchina; Poniatowski, with *5e Corps*, proceeding to the right of the course of the Dnieper, to Belkino, keeping level with Murat's vanguard, at a distance of several *versts* from the main road; while *4e corps de cavalerie* under Latour-Maubourg [Marie Victor Nicolas de Faÿ de Latour-Maubourg], after a four-day rest in Drybin, rode to Mstislavl towards the town of Yelnya and had been intending to arrive there on 16 (28) August. Napoleon himself, having learned that the entire Russian army had halted in front of Dorogobuzh, and hoping to engage in a general battle, dispatched his *Garde impériale* on 12 (24) August and left Smolensk the very next night. The number of troops in the *Grande Armée* reached 155,000 men, excluding *1re division de la Jeune Gard*, numbering 4,500 men, under the command of General Delaborde [Henri François Delaborde] which had been left in Smolensk, in anticipation of the arrival of march battalions there.[5] The small amount of food supplies found in Smolensk was sent after the troops. Some 6,000 to 7,000 wounded remained without food for several days; but two weeks later, after the departure of the *Grande Armée*, significant magazines of flour, cereals and other supplies were established.[6]

Upon the retreat of the Russian force to Dorogobuzh, on 12 (24) August, First Army settled in a position in front of the city, except for II Corps and I Cavalry Corps, which were detached to the right bank of the Dnieper, to counter the Viceroy. Platov's rearguard withdrew to a position 7 *versts* forwards of Dorogobuzh.[7]

The position occupied by the main body of the Russian army near Dorogobuzh, according to Barclay de Tolly, presented many important disadvantages: firstly, it had been necessary to detach an entire corps onto the right bank of the Dnieper to face the Viceroy; secondly, the army was forced to be strung out over a considerable distance in order to fix its right flank on the Dnieper and occupy the high ground that dominates the surrounding country on the left wing; thirdly, the city, lying a short distance behind the army, on very rugged terrain, would make it difficult for the troops to retreat from this position; finally, Second Army was located too far from First Army.[8] Another eyewitness stated: 'This position, in my opinion, was worthless (*abscheulich*); the area to its front did not present any obstacles to the enemy and was inconvenient for observation; behind the right wing lay a city on

---

5   For a breakdown of French troop strengths, see Appendix 5.
6   Puibusque, *Lettres sur la guerre de Russie*, 57 & 74-75.
7   Condensed War Diary, compiled by Toll.
8   Description of operations by First Army.

hilly terrain; Baggovut's II Corps [Karl Fëdorovich Baggovut or Carl Gustav von Baggehufwudt] occupied an even worse position.'[9]

Fortunately, our armies did not remain near Dorogobuzh for long. The very next night, of 12 to 13 (24 to 25) August, the troops were ordered to retreat to Vyazma, in three columns: the right (turning its front in the direction of the enemy), consisting of II Corps and I Cavalry Corps, with three Cossack regiments, moved to Konushkino and Afonasyevo; the centre, of III Corps, IV Corps, V Corps and VI Corps, with the entire reserve artillery of First Army, to Chobotovo and Semlevo; the left, of the troops of Second Army, to Bozhan and Luzhki. The rearguard of the right column, consisted of the Irkutsk Dragoons and Siberia Dragoons, 30th Jägers and 48th Jägers and one Cossack regiment, under the command of Major General Kreutz [Cyprian Antonovich Kreutz]; the centre under General Platov, while the left was under Adjutant General Vasilchikov [Illarion Vasilevich Vasilchikov]. As the area from Dorogobuzh to Vyazma is rather open, II Cavalry Corps and III Cavalry Corps were left behind to support the rearguard; the detachment under Adjutant General Wintzingerode, to protect the line of communications with Tver, headed from Dukhovshchina towards Bely; while to maintain links with the main body of the army, Major General Krasnov was sent to the road leading from Dukhovshchina to Vyazma, with three Cossack regiments, supported by two battalions and eight dragoon squadrons, under the command of Major General Shevich [Ivan Yegorovich Shevich].[10]

In the meantime, Napoleon had arrived in Dorogobuzh on 13 (25) August. In preparing to take the last step towards his objective – a decisive victory, the occupation of our capital, the conquest of Russia, Napoleon redoubled the precautionary measures to secure the flanks and rear of his army. Victor [Claude-Victor Perrin], on Prussian territory with *9e Corps*, had been ordered to go to Kovno and Vilna towards Smolensk; every detachment from the *Grande Armée* that had been left in Vilna, Minsk, Mogilev, Vitebsk and Smolensk was subordinated to him.[11] All these troops were intended to be used exclusively to secure the main line of operations from Vilna to Smolensk and beyond. Orders were sent to Schwarzenberg – to push Tormasov back as far as possible. Napoleon wrote to him: 'You will have time to reach Kiev and Kaluga (*sic*), while we go on to Moscow.'[12] Marshal Saint-Cyr was ordered to pin down Wittgenstein, while MacDonald was ordered to proceed with

---

9 Clausewitz, 129.
10 Condensed War Diary, compiled by Toll. Barclay de Tolly's report to the Tsar, No 690, dated 14 [26] August. Ker-Porter *Histoire de la campagne de Russie pendant l'année 1812*, 132.
11 Composition and number of troops under Marshal Victor's command: Partouneaux's Division, 21 battalions; Daendels' Division, 13 battalions; Girard's Division, 20 battalions; Light Cavalry Division, 16 Sqns; 33,000 men at the start of the campaign. Dąbrowski's Polish Division, detached to Bobruisk, had 7,000 to 8,000 men. Garrisons in Lithuania and Belorussia. Fain, *Manuscrit de 1812*, I, 361.
12 '*Poussez plus vivement Tormassow. Après l'avantage que vous venez d'obtenir à Ghorodeczna, vous pouvez lui faire éprouver des grandes pertes dans la longue retraite qui le ramenera sur Louck. Les secours, qu'on lui envoie, dit-on, des bords du Danube, sont encore bien loin. Vous aurez le temps de pénétrer sur Kiow et sur Kalouga, tandisque nous irons à Moscou... Mais surtout faites en sorte que les Russes que vous avez devant vous ne se portent pas sur moi.*' Fain, *Manuscrit de 1812*, I, 356-357.

the siege of Riga. At the same time, the siege park, still located in Tilsit [Sovetsk, Kaliningrad *Oblast*], was to advance to the Dvina immediately. Napoleon wrote:

> After capturing Riga, MacDonald's corps is to take part in general operations, and thereafter Marshals MacDonald and Saint-Cyr may threaten St Petersburg, while we are in Moscow. If Saint-Cyr is defeated, then the duc de Bellune (Victor) is to move to support the troops operating on the Dvina. But the main mission for his army is to serve as a reserve for the Army of Moscow.[13] In the event of communications from Smolensk to my headquarters being cut, they must immediately be restored; it is also essential that the duc de Bellune, with his entire army, moves to meet us, if this proves necessary. Perhaps if I do not find peace there, I shall go after them. But then, having a strong reserve behind me stationed in the appropriate place, I shall withdraw safely, and nothing will force me to hasten the retreat.[14]

Augereau's *11e Corps* [Charles Pierre François Augereau] received orders to occupy the area between the Vistula and the Neman.[15] Some *garde nationale* cohorts were headed for the Rhine and further on to the Elbe. Finally, the conscription class of 1813 were ordered to be called up.[16] Thus, in Napoleon's gigantic struggle with Russia, his enormous resources were gradually evolving. Following the occupation of Dorogobuzh, the main body of Napoleon's army moved along the high road towards Vyazma, while the Viceroy, with his *4e Corps* and Grouchy, went around our right flank towards Blagovo and Berezki; while Poniatowski with the Polish *5e Corps*, moved around our left, to Brazhino and Luzhki. At the head of the vanguard, Murat was always the first into action. His appearance in front of the troops served as a signal for battle. In a green and gold embroidered jacket and a hat with a long feather, on a black horse, surrounded by a brilliant retinue, among whom was a black man dressed as a Mameluke, flaunted as a fearless warrior, arousing the delight of

---

13 i.e. *9e Corps* with the subsumed detachments.
14 'Quant aux Russes de Wittgenstein, le maréchal St-Cyr a pris sur eux l'avantage (?), et le siége de Riga va compléter leurs embarras. Dès que les trente mille hommes du duc de Tarente se seront rendus maîtres de la place qui les retient sur la Basse-Dwina, ils rentreront alors dans les grandes opérations de la campagne, et si nos deux maréchaux Saint-Cyr et Macdonald s'entendent, ils peuvent menacer Petersbourg quand nous serons à Moscou… Cependant je veux tout prévoir. Si Saint-Cyr éprouvait un échec, le duc de Bellune irait à son secours et le soutiendrait sur la Dwina; ce cas excepté, il ne doit pas perdre de vue la route de Smolensk à Moscou, et je reviens à l'idée principale qui devra constamment l'occuper. L'armée qu'il commande forme la réserve de l'armée de Moscou. Si la route de Smolensk au quartier impérial venait à être interceptée, il faudrait la rouvrir sur-le-champ; il faudrait même que l'armée entière du duc de Bellune s'avançât au-devant de nous, si cela était nécessaire. Je puis ne pas trouver la paix où je vais la chercher. Mais alors, appuyé sur une réserve aussi forte et aussi bien postée, ma retraite se ferait avec sécurité et rien ne saurait la précipiter.' Fain, I, 360.
15 The composition of Marshal Augereau's *11e Corps* was: Heudelet's Division in Hamburg; Morand's Division in Stettin; Durutte's Division in Berlin; Detres' Division in Danzig; Loison's Division in Königsberg; Cavaignac's Cavalry Division in Hanover & Dresden. According to returns dated 15 [27] July, numbering 56,000 men. Fain, I, 361.
16 Fain, I, 362.

his own and the astonishment of the Cossacks, who often greeted him with loud cheers.

On 15 (27) August, both columns of First Army linked up at Vyazma, while Second Army was located near the village of Bykovo; the rearguard, upon reaching the Osma River, near the village of Rybki, was attacked by Murat, holding out for seven hours near the village of Belomirskoe, near Semlevo, and by the evening of the 15th (27 August) was ordered to retreat. Only the detachment under Kreutz, still remaining 15 *versts* back from Vyazma, in order to cover the retreat of the main body through the city on the right, was swiftly attacked by the enemy, and almost lost their guns, but managed to retreat after the other troops. Our casualties overall reached 230 men.[17]

By retreating to Vyazma, Barclay intended to take advantage of the separation of enemy forces and switch from defence to the offensive. To that end, Toll and the Chief of Engineers, Truzson [Khristian Ivanovich Truzson], had been ordered to go to Vyazma on 13 (25) August, to choose a position there and fortify it so that a 20,000 or 25,000 strong corps could hold it against superior enemy forces, while both armies were to counter attack them. But as Vyazma did not have any suitable positions, the Russian armies retreated on 16 (28) August to Fedorovskoye, and the next day to Tsarevo-Zaimishche. The rearguard, retreating towards Vyazma on the 16th (28 August), was attacked by superior forces under Murat and Davout, but held out until nightfall. The following day [29 August, new style], General Konovnitsyn, having taken command of the rearguard, reinforced by 3rd Division and II Cavalry Corps, retreated half the distance from Vyazma to Tsarevo-Zaimishche.[18] According to one of the eyewitnesses, the retreat of our rearguard was carried out in such a manner that at every location that was advantageous for the operation of artillery, several horse guns were set up, under the protection of cavalry on open ground or light infantry on rugged terrain. These guns, firing at the approaching enemy, forced them to set up stronger counter batteries and to deploy troops in battle formation, the guns would then quickly move back and draw the attacker on to other guns, which operated in the same manner as the first. Meanwhile, the Cossacks vigilantly shadowed every move by the enemy and gave forewarning of their outflanking attempts. By evening, the troops were located in a most advantageous position and held on to it until nightfall.

On 17 (29) August, on the very day that both Western armies linked up in positions at Tsarevo-Zaimishche, where Barclay de Tolly intended to give battle, the enemy occupied the city of Vyazma, set on fire in several places by the inhabitants themselves, who had left after the troops. Murat's vanguard positioned themselves facing Konovnitsyn; the Viceroy was at Novoe; Poniatowski was at Pokrovskoe.[19]

There was much talk of the advantages and disadvantages of the position at Tsarevo-Zaimishche, approved by Barclay de Tolly and rejected (as we shall see

---

17 Diary of the movements of First Army, compiled by Toll. Return of killed, wounded and missing, signed by *Flügel-Adjutant* Kikin. In Platov's report our losses were shown as 400 to 500 men.
18 Diary compiled by Toll.
19 *Denkwürdigkeiten des Grafen v. Toll*, I, 408.

PRINCE KUTUZOV JOINS THE ARMY 89

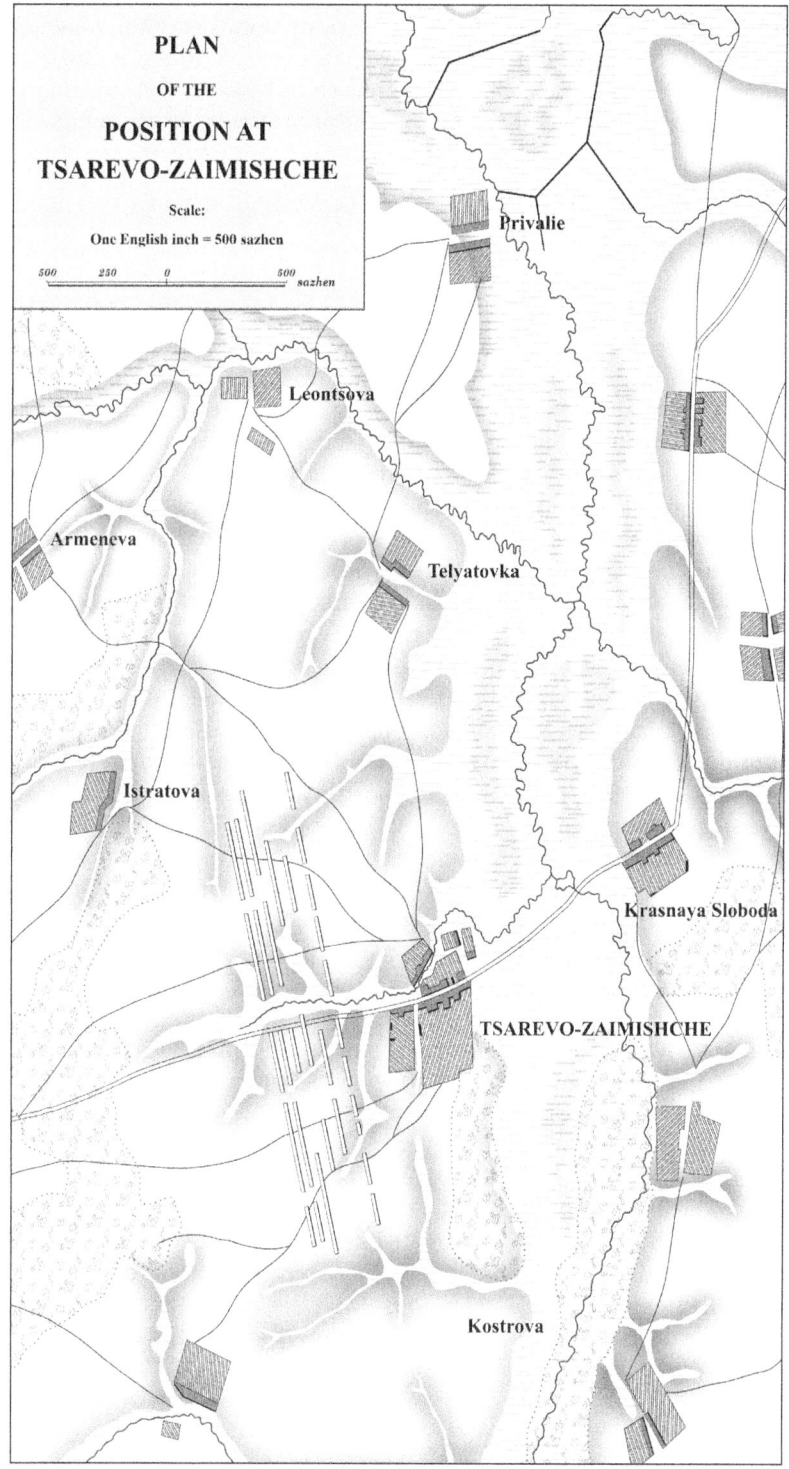

Plan of the position at Tsarevo-Zaimishche.

later) by his successor, Kutuzov. The well-known military historian, Major Blesson [Johann Ludwig Urban Blesson], who surveyed this area, considers it the best defensive position in the entire stretch from Smolensk to Moscow.[20] According to him, a causeway leads to it, several *versts* long (*mehrere Stunden*), through a swamp, stretching in all directions for an immense distance (*in unabsehbarer Ferne*). The position itself – he stated – is formed by gentle hills, enveloping the exit from the causeway, in the form of an arc.

According to Blesson, there was no way to cross this causeway by force, while an outflanking movement around the position was associated with the removal of the detachment assigned for this from the remaining troops and would lead to their defeat by the entire mass of the forces of the Russian army. Obviously, Blesson's judgment was based on his somewhat exaggerated ideas of the length of the causeway and the extent of the swamps near Tsarevo-Zaimishche. In reality, this causeway was no more than a *verst* long, and the swamps extend to the right of the position for five *versts*, and to the left about three *versts*: consequently, although they seem boundless from the highway, they would not prevent an envelopment at such a distance that the reserve located near the road could support the flanking force. These swamps, in dry weather, do not constitute an obstacle at all, which is most convincingly evidenced by the location of the Russian armies at Tsarevo-Zaimishche, in 1812, not behind the swamps, but in front of them, with their rear to the swamps themselves that Blesson, and after him Bernhardi [Theodor von Bernhardi] and Beitzke [Heinrich Ludwig Beitzke] had considered impassable. Barclay de Tolly himself, in assessing the advantages of this position, stated that: 'the armies had an open place in front of them, upon which the enemy could not conceal their movements, and that 12 *versts* behind this position, near Gzhatsk, another was found also suitable;' but does not mention the impregnability of the location at Tsarevo-Zaimishche, and even from the orders he issued to the chiefs of engineers of both armies – to build several redoubts on the front and flanks of the position – it is apparent that he did not consider it impregnable either from the front or from the flanks.

This was the position in which the Russian troops were preparing to give battle. But the hope of a decisive engagement with the enemy, already dashed more than once, seemed an unrealisable dream to everyone, as long as the command of the army remained in the hands of Barclay de Tolly. For several days, rumours had been circulating in the army about the appointment of Kutuzov as Commander-in-Chief. In the present day, no one doubts that Barclay, having preserved the army entrusted to him, is worthy of the gratitude of posterity along with Kutuzov, but in 1812 things were judged differently. Since, in the opinion of many, the operations by our troops had been conducted extremely badly by Barclay, then any change in command over the army seemed beneficial. In addition, the irrational distrust of all foreigners, and even of Russian nationals who bore foreign surnames (such as Barclay himself), had by then reached extreme levels. Even those who did not harbour any displeasure towards Barclay de Tolly attributed the unfortunate star of the omens that gravitated over Russia to him.[21] In such circumstances, the arrival of a new commander,

---

20 See the Plan of the position at Tsarevo-Zaimishche.
21 Clausewitz, 132.

Russian by heritage and name, a favourite of Catherine the Great and Suvorov's colleague, it seemed like an epoch in which victory would constantly accompany the Russian forces.

Barclay de Tolly himself, having received information about the appointment of Kutuzov as Commander-in-Chief of all Russian armies, did not allow his ardour for the common cause to cool. Expressing his readiness to risk his life, no matter what duties he was entrusted with, Barclay wrote to the Tsar:

> As Commander-in-Chief subordinate to Prince Kutuzov, I know my duties and shall carry them out conscientiously. But I am still in the dark about my relationship as Minister of War. Perhaps, Tsar, the reason for this is Your Imperial Majesty's benevolence towards me, having previously been honoured with complete authority by the Monarch. I dare to suppose that this reason alone prompted Your Majesty to postpone the assignment of the duties of Minister of War that I have been performing to someone else. I beg you, Tsar, do not pay attention to me, so that the good of the service does not suffer for a single moment. Your Majesty knows my convictions on this subject, expressed by me at the opening of the war. My way of thinking not only has not changed, it has become even more resolute. Accept my words, Tsar, as the expression of boundless devotion to Your Sacred Person by a loyal subject who seeks nothing and does not want anything other than the opportunity to be useful in the service of his Monarch.
>
> I shall not talk about the operations by the army entrusted to me at the present time, when the decisive resolution is so close. The consequences will show whether I could have done more to save the state. If my actions had been guided by frivolous vanity, then Your Imperial Majesty would have received reports from me about the battles I gave, while the enemy, in spite of this, would be under the walls of Moscow, facing forces insufficient to defend it.[22]

Emperor Alexander, having received this report and considering it with the opinion of the Committee assembled to select the Commander-in-Chief, commanded:

> General of Infantry Barclay de Tolly, on account of being with the field army, is to be released from the appointment of Minister of War, while the Ministry of Armed Land Forces is to be managed by Lieutenant General Prince Gorchakov.[23]

At the same time, the Tsar honoured Barclay de Tolly with the following rescript:

> As a result of your report of 16 [28] August, I find your military activities in the army so important and difficult that I consider it impossible for you to

---

22 Barclay de Tolly's letter to Emperor Alexander I, from Vyazma, dated 16 [28] August.
23 Decree to the Governing Senate, dated 24 August [5 September].

hold the post of Minister of War, due to a complete lack of time, but equally according to the distance you are from me.

Taking into account these factors, I find it useful that the execution of the post of Minister of War is carried out by the head of the departments of this ministry, Lieutenant General Prince Gorchakov. About which I have issued a decree on this date to the Governing Senate.[24]

The reasons that prompted Emperor Alexander I to appoint a new Commander-in-Chief are set out in a letter from the Tsar to Barclay de Tolly as follows:

> ... Fate favoured us in Smolensk, where, beyond our expectations, both armies were united. The retreat should have been stopped then. But the lack of intelligence on the enemy and their movements, through the lack of which you have experienced adverse consequences throughout the entire campaign, had forced you to make an erroneous advance towards Porechye against the left wing of the enemy army, meanwhile, they concentrated on their right flank at Lyadi and crossed the Dnieper there. You corrected this error by forestalling the enemy in Smolensk. But thereafter it was necessary to decide in Smolensk on how the two armies were united there and how you meant to give general battle, without retreating to Tsarevo-Zaimishche. Our troops were in better condition then than after the fighting on 6 and 7 [18 and 19] August and the following days before arriving at Tsarevo-Zaimishche. As for the fear of outflanking, it is difficult to avoid this disadvantage anywhere, and having settled down at Tsarevo-Zaimishche, you were also subjected to envelopment. The troops would have fought with extreme passion, because Smolensk would have been the first Russian city that they had the opportunity to defend.

The fall of Smolensk had an immense moral impact on the whole of Russia. The detractors of our plan of action believed that the disasters they had predicted had come to pass and that the Empire was in imminent danger. And as everyone interpreted and judged, each in his own way, about the mistakes I have summarised, they accused me of sacrificing the salvation of the Fatherland out of pride, defending you, just because you were chosen by me. Moscow and St Petersburg have unanimously pointed to Prince Kutuzov as the only person who could save the Empire, and so on. In such difficult circumstances, the capital of the State has been in danger for the first time, and I thought it necessary to agree with public opinion, however, I ordered that the matter be discussed firstly in a Committee composed of the chief dignitaries of the Empire. In taking the measure they suggested, I have sacrificed my own conviction...'[25]

---

24 Rescript No 86, dated 24 August [5 September].
25 'Le sort nous a favorisé à Smolensk, car contre toute probabilité la jonction des deux armées s'y est faite. C'était le moment d'arreter les mouvemens rétrogrades. Mais le manque de connaissances dans le quel vous étiez sur l'ennemi et ses mouvemens, manque, dont vous avez éprouvé malheureusement les effets pendant toute la campagne, vous a fait commettre

On 11 (23) August, Kutuzov set off for the army, accompanied by the fervent prayers of every Russian. On the eve of his departure, Kutuzov attended a prayer service in the Kazan Cathedral, on his knees, and laid the image of Our Lady of Kazan upon himself, given to him by Archpriest John. The next morning, the people, having gathered on the palace embankment, near the home of their defender, escorted him along the route from which his mortal remains were destined to return, with even greater triumph. Upon his arrival in Torzhok on the morning of the 16 (28), he met with General Bennigsen, who, having been removed from all influence by Barclay de Tolly, had asked for permission to go to St Petersburg. Kutuzov, intending to appoint him as his Chief of Staff, announced to him the Supreme Command – to return to the army. Kutuzov's onward route was directed via Staritsa and Zubtsov to Gzhatsk. Upon his arrival in the vicinity of this city, on 17 (29) August, at 11 o'clock in the morning, he was met by a crowd of local residents who, having stopped his carriage, five *versts* from Gzhatsk, unharnessed the horses and dragged the carriage by themselves to the residence prepared for him. His first task here was to send the officers of the general staff, who had been sent to inspect positions along the Moscow road, back to the armies. 'We don't need any positions behind the army; we have already retreated too far.' said Kutuzov. During the hour and a half halt in Gzhatsk, he was busy sending instructions and replies to documents with which couriers were waiting for him there, and then went to Tsarevo-Zaimishche, where the headquarters of both armies were located at the time. Upon arrival there at 3 o'clock in the afternoon, Kutuzov, having greeted the guard of honour prepared for him, said, as if to himself, but rather loudly: 'Well, how can you retreat with such good fellows!' After that, having had a quick meal, he went to the camp on horseback, in an undress coat without epaulettes and a white forage cap with a red band, with a sash over one shoulder and with a riding crop on a belt over the other. The troops greeted their commander, familiar to all veteran servicemen, with friendly cheers!

---

la faute de marcher sur Porétchié pour attaquer sa gauche tandis qu'il s'était concentré à sa droite à Liady, où il passé le Dnieper. Vous aviez reparé cette faute en prenvenant l'ennemi à Smolensk. Mais puisque les deux armées y étaient réunies et puisqu'il entrait dans vos plans de livrer à Smolensk qu'à Zaréwo-Saimistché; vos forces y auraient été plus intactes, car toutes les pertes que vous avez faites depuis dans les journées du 6,7 et les suivantes jusqu'à Zaréwo-Saimistché, n'auraient pas eu lieu. Quant à la crainte d'être tourné par les flancs, elle est à peu près la même partout, et à Zaréwo-Saimistché, vous n'en auriez pas été exempt. L'ardeur du soldat eut été extrême à Smolensk, car c'était l'entrée de la première ville vraiment russe qu'ils auraient défendue à l'ennemi. La perte de Smolensk produisit un effet moral immense dans tout l'empire. A toute la désapprobation générale qu'avait notre plan de campagne se joignaient des reproches. 'L'expérience, disait-on, démontre combien ce plan est desastreux; l'Empire est dans le plus imminent danger.' Et comme malheureusement les fautes que je viens de citer plus haut, étaient dans la bouche de tout le monde, j'étais accusé de sacrifier le salut de la patrie à l'amour-propre, de vouloir soutenir mon choix dans votre personne. Moscou et Petersbourg à l'unisson nommaient le prince Koutousoff comme le seul individu, qui pouvait, d'après leur dire, sauver l'Empire, etc. Les circonstances étaient trop critiques. Pour la première fois le capitale de l'Empire était ménacée et je n'ai pu faire autre chose que me rendre à l'opinion générale aprés avoir fait débattre cependant le pour et le contre dans un Comité composé des principaux dignitaires de l'Empire. En cedant à leur opinion, j'ai du imposer silence à mon propre sentiment.' Copy from the Handwritten Notes by Emperor Alexander I, held in the Military Topographic Depot, No 47,352, folio 3.

'Kutuzov has come to beat the French,' our soldiers said among themselves. With the speed of lightning, the news spread to every corner of vast Russia, that, at that very moment, a huge eagle had soared above Kutuzov's head, accompanying him as he went around the camp. This event, whether true or fictitious, has remained in folk legends, as symbolic of the hopes aroused by the new Commander in Chief.[26] Having inspected the position together with Barclay, Kutuzov found it very advantageous, expressed his determination to give battle there and gave orders to speed up the construction of fortifications, which had been started by his predecessor.[27] The strength of our army, not counting 7,000 Cossacks, reached some 95,734 men, while together with reinforcements that arrived at that time in Gzhatsk, under the command of Miloradovich [Mikhail Andreevich Miloradovich], were some 111,323 men.[28]

The enemy was a short march from the positions occupied by the Russian force; we readied ourselves to stop them. No one in our army doubted that the fateful hour was at hand... On 18 (30) August, the troops remained in position; the next day, unexpectedly for everyone, the order was given to withdraw.

The factors that prompted Prince Kutuzov to do this have been explained in various ways. Barclay de Tolly attributed the sudden reversal in Kutuzov's resolution, to give battle at Tsarevo-Zaimishche, to the influence of men who exploited his trust, but it can be interpreted much closer to the truth through his usual *modus operandi*. In general, Kutuzov did not like to reveal his intent to anyone until the very moment it was about to be carried out, and therefore, when examining the Tsarevo-Zaimishche position, although he found it quite strong (as it actually is), nevertheless, he did not consider it necessary to announce a further withdrawal in advance, the true reason for which was, as before, the significant numerical superiority of the enemy force. After retreating for several stages, we hoped to be bolstered by reinforcements. Kutuzov, informing the Tsar of his taking over command of the armies, wrote:

> Upon my arrival in the city of Gzhatsk, I found the troops retreating from Vyazma and the men of many regiments were absolutely exhausted from frequent fighting, as yesterday alone was the only day that has passed without combat. I took the decision of replenishing their missing numbers with those brought yesterday by General of Infantry Miloradovich who

---

26 General Mikhailovsky-Danilevsky speaks of this incident as an undoubted occurrence that happened at the moment of Kutuzov's first appearance in front of the troops, at Tsarevo-Zaimishche, while in his Notes on the War of 1812, Prince A.B. Golitsyn, who was in constant attendance on Kutuzov, the flight of an eagle over the Commander-in-Chief is attributed to another occasion. Prince Golitsyn wrote: 'As Kutuzov surveyed the position at Borodino for the first time – it was after lunch – a giant eagle soared above him. Wherever he was, there was the eagle. Anstett [Ivan Osipovich Anstett] was the first to notice this, and then there was no end to the rumours.'
27 Description of operations by First Army.
28 Combatant return on the troop composition of the Western Armies, attached to Kutuzov's report to the Tsar, dated 19 [31] August.

henceforth arrived with a force of 14,587 infantry and 1,002 cavalry, such that they were distributed among the regiments.

To improve the manning even further, I have ordered a retreat of one stage from Gzhatsk, and, depending on the circumstances, one more, in order to link the army up, on the aforementioned basis, with a sufficient number of fighting men sent from Moscow; besides, I found the location at Gzhatsk, in my opinion, to be highly unfavourable for a battle.

Strengthening ourselves in this way, both through the replacement of lost troops, and through the inclusion in the army of some of the regiments formed by Prince [D.I.] Lobanov-Rostovsky, and some of the Moscow *opolchenie*, I shall be able to submit to the vicissitudes of battle in order to save Moscow, which, however, will be undertaken with every precaution which the importance of the circumstances may require.[29]

In this same report, Kutuzov wrote about a significant number of our soldiers who had absented themselves from the army without leave. But as far as can be judged from other information about the state of the Russian forces at the time, this report by the Commander-in-Chief, written shortly after his arrival with the army, when he had not yet had time to fully familiarise himself with the state of affairs, contained some exaggerated statements. Although looting occurred among our troops, it was however, incomparably less than among the French. Prinz Eugen von Württemberg [Friedrich Eugen Karl Paul Ludwig von Württemberg], an impartial recorder of the events he witnessed, stated:

Differences of opinion in the headquarters were reflected in the army, but the spirit and discipline of the troops remained impeccable. The rearguard fought with constant courage and success; everyone watched their every move; regiments vied with each other for the honour of participating in an action; on the march and in bivouacs, the men were always upbeat and cheerful, expressing concern only for the peasants, whom the war had deprived of shelter and the last of their property. I am prepared to swear by oath that all this was so, and not otherwise.[30]

Bernhardi, not at all partial to the Russians, stated:

Upon reaching Tsarevo-Zaimishche, the Russian armies calculated that they had lost 16,000 or 17,000 men since they had linked up at Smolensk: therefore, the entire wastage of troops consisted of those men who had been lost in combat: a striking example of order, discipline and fortitude.[31]

---

29 Prince Kutuzov's report to the Tsar, dated 19 [31] August.
30 Prinz Eugen von Württemberg, E*rinnerungen aus dem Feldzuge des Jahres 1812 in Russland*, 64-65.
31 *Denkwürdigkeiten des Grafen v. Toll*, I, 409.

The reason for the outbreak of looting in our army was the lack of food on the march from Smolensk to Moscow. As no one could have foreseen that we would have to retreat so far into the interior at the opening of hostilities, so all of our large magazines had been established in the western regions of the Empire, and therefore, when retreating from Smolensk, it was necessary to resort to all kinds of *ad hoc* methods: to requisitioning, or the collection of stocks against receipts. The lack of fodder forced Prince Kutuzov to instruct in an order (dated 21 August [2 September], No. 5) that the regiments mow down the oats that were still ripening at the time. But all these methods for feeding the troops, inevitably associated with the devastation of the countryside, were still insufficient to meet the needs of a 100,000 strong army.[32] Barclay de Tolly, during his leadership of the army, reported to the Tsar more than once about the disorder that existed in the force and took measures to halt it by strict measures; but the force of circumstances sometimes overcame the iron will of the commander. Prince Kutuzov, immediately after taking command of the armies, also drew attention to the eradication of this evil: his first orders serve as evidence of this.[33]

No matter how great the difficulties encountered in the ration supply for the Russian force at every step, the position of the enemy army, in strategic and economic terms, was incomparably worse. The Russians found some supplies on the way, mowed oats in the fields for their horses and, proceeding further, devastated the countryside together with the inhabitants who set fire to their homes, leaving a wasteland for the enemy that did not present any means for subsistence. The convoys of Napoleon's army, some dragged by oxen, some consisting of heavy wagons, constantly lagged behind the troops. The enemy infantry were forced to leave the road for a considerable distance off to the sides and became extremely fatigued, while the cavalry and artillery exhausted their horses with long-range foraging and did not have chance to feed themselves. The entire menu of a French soldier consisted of a piece of beef and a handful of flour, or even wheat bread boiled in water without salt. There was not always enough time to bake bread, especially since all the mills on the route from Smolensk to Moscow had been demolished, and hand mills had not yet been sent

---

32 *Graf* Cancrin, *Über die Militaire-Öconomie*, I, 84-85.
33 Original orders for the army under Prince Kutuzov: 'From Headquarters, at Staraya Ivanova. 18 [30] August 1812, No. 2. Today, some 2,000 lower ranks have been caught straggling in the shortest period. This was accomplished not by senior commanders, but by the assistance of the military police. Such an extreme number of soldiers who have left their units, in order to evade service, proves the unusual weakening of the supervision of the gentlemen regimental commanders. The custom of looting, seeded by the weakness of the commanders, having had its effect on the morale of the soldiers, has turned it almost into a habit, which must be eradicated by the most severe measures. The main duty of First Army is to send the stragglers caught today with lists to the regiments, whom I order in the first instance to be punished in the strictest manner. To that end, I must hope that the gentlemen regimental commanders, for the benefit of the service and their own honour, will take measures and efforts to stop this harm that has already crept in to a great extent. In the future, those caught will draw lots for execution.'
'From Headquarters, at Kolotsk Monastery, 21 August [2 September] 1812, No. 5. Announce to the regiments and units that any lower rank, after 24 hours following this order, who would be apprehended half a *verst* or more from the verges of the main road, shall be punished as a deserter.'

from Paris. Occasionally, the enemy came upon Russian hard-tack, but this was not to French tastes. The lack of water, with the temperature reaching up to 26 degrees in the shade (according to Réaumur), had more effect upon Napoleon's troops than upon ours, because we usually located near rivers, halting the enemy in places where there was no water at all, or where, due to its poor quality, it could not serve in favour of the troops.[34] And therefore, it is not at all surprising that those same corps (Davout's, Ney's, the Viceroy's, Poniatowski's, Junot's, *réserve de cavalerie* and *Garde impériale*), which, when crossing the Neman, had counted 280,000 men in their ranks, after eleven weeks, losing no more than 40,000 battle casualties, had diminished to 134,000. The Westphalians under Junot suffered especially, moving at the tail of the *Grande Armée*, along the highway, and did not encounter anything but ruins along the way. A consequence of this were the extraordinary losses of the Westphalian *8e Corps*, which on the day of the battle at Lubino had counted 13,600 men in its ranks, and two weeks later, on 21 August (2 September), only 8,868.[35]

Kutuzov's initial orders for the Russian armies entrusted to him were as follows:

1. Notifying Admiral Chichagov and General Tormasov of his resolute intention to give general battle at Mozhaisk, immediately after receiving the expected reinforcements, Kutuzov wrote to both Commanders-in-Chief that, as the enemy was already in the heart of ancient Russia, the operational objectives of Third Army and the Army of the Danube should not be the protection of distant Polish provinces, but the distraction of enemy forces directed against First Army and Second Army. Therefore, Prince Kutuzov ordered Tormasov, having linked Third Army up with the troops under Ertel [Fëdor Fëdorovich Ertel] from Mozyr and Saken [Fabian Wilhelmovich Osten-Saken] from Zhitomir, to turn against the right wing of Napoleon's *Grande Armée*, while Chichagov, with the troops moving up from Moldavia, was to succeed Third Army and fulfil all the duties that until that time had been in Tormasov's care.[36]
2. General of Cavalry Bennigsen was appointed Chief of Staff of the combined Western Armies; General of Infantry Miloradovich took over command of II Corps and IV Corps; Major General Vistitsky became Quartermaster General of the Western Armies; Colonel Toll was ordered to accompany Prince Kutuzov; and appointed Colonel Kaiserov [Paisy Sergeevich Kaiserov] in the army as Duty General.[37]

---

34 Chambray, II, 37. Beitzke, *Geschichte des Russischen Krieges im Jahre 1812*, 152 and 168. *Das Buch vom Jahr 1812*, II, 234-237. Denniée, *Itinéraire de l'empereur Napoléon*, 59.
35 Chambray, II, 33. Returns on the numerical strength of the *Grande Armée*, dated 2 September (new style). It does not include the troops under Delaborde, Pino and Dąbrowski, in total some 18,000 men. Consequently – the losses of the *Grande Armée*, excluding those who were lost in battle, from crossing the Neman to arriving in Gzhatsk, reached 90,000 men. Lossberg states there were only 8,400 men in the Westphalian Corps in early September, new style.
36 Orders for General of Cavalry Tormasov, dated 20 August [1 September], No. 47, and memo to Admiral Chichagov, of the same date, No. 48.
37 Prince Kutuzov's orders, dated 18 [30] August, No. 1, and 19 [31] August, No. 3.

Meanwhile, our armies continued to retreat. On 19 (31) August, the Russian troops, having withdrawn from their position at Tsarevo-Zaimishche, passed through Gzhatsk and settled down, on the night of the 19 to 20 [31 August to 1 September], at Ivashkova, where they were joined by troops brought from Kaluga by General Miloradovich, who set off to replenish the regiments of both Western armies, while their cadres (field officers, subalterns and non-commissioned officers, veteran privates and drummers) were immediately sent to Kaluga to form new regiments.[38] The Russian rearguard, retreating to Gzhatsk, on 19 (31) August, stopped often to delay the enemy troops pursuing them, and fell far behind the main forces. Murat and Davout, taking advantage of this, attacked Konovnitsyn persistently, every time that they were passing through the vast forest near Gzhatsk, and then through the city and the bridge over the Gzhat river. General Konovnitsyn, wishing to secure his right flank from being outflanked by the enemy left hand column advancing along the road from Bely, ordered Major General Kreutz to take up positions on this road, with the Irkutsk Dragoon Regiment and one Cossack regiment, the right flank on the Gzhat river, and the left on the forest occupied by our infantry. As the road from Bely formed the most direct route to the bridge, the enemy, if they could push Kreutz back and seize the bridge, would sever the line of retreat for all the rest of the rearguard. Konovnitsyn, noticing the danger that threatened him, sent Lieutenant Colonel Gaverdovsky, who was accompanying him, to inform Kreutz that: 'in order to save the many, it is necessary to sacrifice the few, and therefore Konovnitsyn asks Kreutz if he agreed to hold out until all the other troops have crossed the bridge, and perhaps to die.' Kreutz replied: 'Agreed,' and asked only that, in the event of the destruction of the detachment, he would not vainly be blamed for this.

The enemy launched an attack on the troops holding the forest, drove them back to the city and pushed on towards the river. Kreutz, being surrounded on all sides, raced into the river with his dragoons and Cossacks, crossed it via a ford and dragged his two guns along the bed of the river. Meanwhile, the enemy, having already managed to get across the bridge after the troops under Konovnitsyn, again blocked the path of Kreutz's detachment once more. Whereupon Kreutz raced across the fields, smashing the fences separating them, outpaced the enemy cavalry and, approaching a village (Mashkov?), he left the Irkutsk Dragoons to catch their breath there, while the Cossack regiment concealed themselves in dead ground. The enemy cavalry, approaching the village, was unexpectedly attacked from the front by dragoons, and from the flank by Cossacks, and fled, with the loss of about 500 prisoners alone, including several officers.[39]

Napoleon, having arrived in Gzhatsk on 20 August (1 September), received intelligence from Murat about the arrival of the new Commander-in-Chief of the Russian army. This circumstance once more aroused the hope of engaging in a decisive battle in him, and this time he was not mistaken in his assessment.[40] In preparing for

---

38 Condensed War Diary, compiled by Toll. Prince Kutuzov's orders, dated 20 August [1 September], No. 4.
39 From Kreutz's notes (archive of the M.T.D. No. 47,352, folio 2).
40 Thiers states that Napoleon received this intelligence, about the intention of the Russians to accept a pitched battle, from spies. *Histoire du Consulat et de l'Empire, XIV, Edit. de Bruxelles*, 332.

battle with our main forces and wanting to give the disordered troops of the *Grande Armée* a rest, Napoleon postponed the advance of his vanguard, placed the corps under Ney and Davout around the city, which was held by the *Garde impériale* , brought the Viceroy and Poniatowski closer to the highway, and ordered Junot, who had remained in Dorogobuzh, to rejoin the army. On the following day, 21 August (2 September), instructions were sent to each of the corps commanders to grant the troops a rest day, to bring in the stragglers and report on the number of available men; at the same time, an inspection review of all parts of the force was ordered and to make an announcement to the soldiers that they were preparing for a decisive battle. Napoleon wrote to Berthier [Louis-Alexandre Berthier]:

> It is essential that returns be delivered to me no later than ten o'clock this evening: showing the number of men, guns, charges and cartridges; about the number of infirmary wagons, surgeons and available dressings. These returns should also show the number of men who are absent from their units and are unable to take part in a battle, a forecast for tomorrow, as well as whether they would have time to rejoin the force if we were to postpone the action for two or three days. This information must be compiled with all possible accuracy, because my orders will depend upon them… Give orders also to report on the number of untrained horses to me and about the time needed for their breaking in…'[41]

In an army order issued on the same date, Napoleon ordered: firstly, that private carriages, transport, and supply wagons are to proceed behind the artillery and infirmary wagons; secondly, that any private vehicle that impedes the movement of the artillery or infirmary wagons would be destroyed by fire; thirdly, that artillery and field hospitals only are to proceed directly behind the vanguard, while all other wagon trains are to travel no closer than eight *versts* (*deux lieues*) from the vanguard. After dark, private vehicles could join the vanguard, but not before any cannonade or firefight had ended; fourthly, that carts are not to be left on the highway during rest halts, and so on. The supervision of the precise execution of all these orders was entrusted to the Chief of Staff of the vanguard force, General Comte Belliard [Augustin-Daniel Belliard], and, in addition, it was announced that the Emperor, on 3 September [new style], would order all wagons that have violated the prescribed rules to be burned in his presence.[42]

On 2 September (new style), Napoleon, reminding his Chief of Staff of the instructions on the order of march the transport, writing to him: 'I ask you not to let the first wagons that I burn be those of the headquarters. It is impossible to imagine greater disorder than that which reigns (*Il est impossible de voir un plus mauvais ordre que celui qui règne*).'[43]

---

41 Napoleon's letter to the Chief of Staff of the *Grande Armée* (*major-général*), dated 2 September (new style).
42 *Ordre du jour, du 2 Septembre 1812*.
43 Napoleon's letter to the Chief of Staff of the *Grande Armée*, dated 3 September, new style.

The execution of Napoleon's strict instructions was impossible, because every commander in the force strove not to lose sight either of their own vehicles or the ration carts. Napoleon, for example, personally ordered the burning of two carriages belonging to officials from his main headquarters (one of which belonged to Comte Narbonne), but later nothing had changed.[44]

Napoleon gave his army another day of rest, on 22 August (3 September), having in mind to allow the stragglers to rejoin the army, to get some food and fodder and give the troops time to recover, especially the cavalry and artillery, and even, according to French historians, intended to halt the offensive completely. During the three days he spent in Gzhatsk, constant bad weather completely ruined all the roads; the damp, cold bivouacs had a detrimental effect on the men's health; horses were dying by the thousand from fatigue and hunger. Napoleon, losing patience at the disastrous state of the troops, expressed his displeasure to Ney, whose *3e Corps*, having been forced to subsist by banditry, was losing many men and was noticeably dissolving. Having received an undeserved reprimand and not finding any opportunity to help his cause, the ardent Ney wrote in response that it was impossible to go further without exposing the army to destruction. Murat reported in a similar vein. Berthier, offended by Napoleon the day before for frankly expressing his thoughts about the campaign in Russia, confirmed the opinions of his comrades with gloomy silence; while Davout refused to support Murat; 'for fear of disordering the infantry as the cavalry has already been disordered.' Napoleon, bowing to the convictions of his most reliable colleagues, answered them: 'Well, there is nothing to be done! If the weather doesn't change tomorrow, we shall go no further.' It is rather difficult to believe that every future action by Napoleon had depended on a single clear morning; but, be that as it may, the next day, 23 August (4 September), the sun rose in all its splendour, and Napoleon, hoping that the roads would dry out in a few hours, ordered Murat and Davout to set out at noon for Gridnevo, while all other troops were to follow the movements of the vanguard.[45]

Meanwhile, the Russian army, having been reinforced by 15,000 men, led by General Miloradovich,[46] retreated to Durykina on 20 August (1 September), on the 21 [2 September] to the Kolotsky Monastery, and on the 22 [3 September] to the village of Borodino, where the two *opolchenie* joined our forces: that of Moscow, numbering 7,000 men, under the command of General Morkov, and that of Smolensk, some 3,000

---

44 Chambray, II, 34.
45 Ségur, 354-355.
46 Subsequently, during the retreat to Borodino, some 2,000 men joined the Russian armies, overall, 17,000 had arrived from Kaluga (Prince Kutuzov's report to the Tsar, dated 23 August [4 September]). The troops that arrived with the army on 18 and 19 [30 and 31] August consisted of 1st, 2nd, 3rd, 4th and 5th Infantry Regiments and 1st and 2nd Jäger Regiments formed by General Miloradovich; in addition, the battalions of the Yelets Infantry Regiment, regular and 4th (recruit), and the Recruit Battalions of 28th and 32nd Jäger Regiments. On 23 and 24 August [4 and 5 September], 20 Replacement Squadrons arrived, used, for the most part, to reconstitute the regiments, and 12th, 13th and 14th Infantry Regiments, formed by Lieutenant General Kleinmichel (Statement attached to Prince Kutuzov's memo to Count Arakcheev, dated 6 [18] December 1812, No. 1,128, archive of the M.T.D. No. 46,692, folio 2).

strong, led by General Lebedev.⁴⁷ As our other reinforcements were still very far from the army, Kutuzov decided to give battle at the position near Borodino, chosen by General Vistitsky (while, according to Bernhardi, it was Lieutenant Colonel Harting [Martin Nikolaevich Harting] of the General Staff), and approved by Bennigsen.⁴⁸ We stopped at this position solely because there was none better until Moscow itself. In general, good defensive positions are very rare in Russia. Where there are still vast swamps that might serve as protection for the front and flanks of the army, the countryside is so wooded that it is difficult to find sufficient space for the deployment of significant forces; in the open, flat locations there are no obstacles that might serve to delay the enemy; the villages in which the houses are built of wood and covered with straw do not represent a means for stubborn defence.

The retreat of the Russian army, over a distance of about 300 *versts*, from Smolensk to Borodino, is one of the most remarkable examples of the preservation of order and discipline in the forces. The enemy did not succeed in capturing any of the stragglers, not a single wagon from our convoys. The main body of the army was not exhausted by tiring marches, thanks to the skilful actions of our rearguard, which retreated step by step, slowing down the advance of the enemy vanguard. According to Konovnitsyn himself, wherever plains were encountered, our cavalry greeted the enemy, formed in a chessboard pattern, while to their rear, on the high ground, batteries were located so that they could conveniently defend the space in front of them with crossfire, while in the forests infantry ambushes had been set up. By the evening of 22 August (3 September), the Russian rearguard had retreated to a position at Gridnevo, 15 *versts* ahead of Kutuzov's main body. The next day at noon, Murat, with most of the *Réserve de cavalerie* and with Compans' Infantry Division [Jean Dominique Compans], approaching Gridnevo, attacked Konovnitsyn, reinforced by I Cavalry Corps. The troops of our rearguard, which at that time included almost all the cavalry from First Army, consisted of 25 battalions and 96 squadrons.⁴⁹ After a sharp action that lasted for several hours, by evening Cossacks sent

---

47 We took this statement from Buturlin, but, in all likelihood, the number of *opolchenie* that arrived was greater. Kutuzov had hoped for the arrival of 15,000 warriors from Moscow. Barclay de Tolly writes that a total of 16,000 men arrived from both militias (Description of the operations by First Army). On 23 and 24 August [4 and 5 September], the following arrived: 1st and 4th Battalions of 1st Jäger Regiment; 2nd and 3rd Battalions of 3rd Jäger Regiment; 1st and 3rd Battalions of 3rd Foot Cossack Regiment; 3rd and 4th Battalions of 4th Foot Cossack Regiment. In addition, those remaining after reconstituting the *opolchenie* regiments arrived from Volokolamsk and Vereya with 946 warriors, and so on (Statement attached to Prince Kutuzov's memo to Count Arakcheev, dated 6 [18] December 1812, No. 1,128).
48 *Denkwürdigkeiten*, II, 18. Clausewitz (§ 137) attributes the choice of position to Toll. [Liprandi explains the process of selection of fighting positions and the responsibilities of various officers involved, concluding: 'who selected the position at Borodino? Vistitsky of course, while Bennigsen and Toll approved it. Perhaps Harting was used to review its details; but that he should select it is unfounded, even though he was an officer of great talent'].
49 In Buturlin 25 battalions and 98 squadrons are shown; in Bernhardi (*Denkwürdigkeiten des Grafen v. Toll*) 25 battalions and 48 squadrons. As the rearguard included I, II and III Cavalry Corps at that time, as well as the light cavalry of the infantry corps from First Army, the statement by General Buturlin is very close to the truth.

out laterally had passed Konovnitsyn intelligence of a flanking movement to his right by the Viceroy's *4e Corps* to Lusos, so he withdrew, on the night of 23 to 24 August [4 to 5 September], to the Kolotsky monastery. At the same time, the main body of the enemy army (the corps under Davout, Ney, *Garde impériale* and Junot) were located between Gridnevo and Gzhatsk.

On 24 August (5 September), at six o'clock in the morning, the French advanced from Gridnevo towards the Kolotsky monastery. Murat's vanguard, at three o'clock in the afternoon, attacked the force under Konovnitsyn, deployed in front of the Kolotsky monastery; our rearguard held the enemy back very successfully; in particular, the Izyum Hussar Regiment distinguished itself, which, with the assistance of the Cossacks, scattered three enemy squadrons from *3e régiment de chasseurs à cheval italiens*.[50] But when the Viceroy went around us on the right flank once more, Konovnitsyn was forced to withdraw the troops entrusted to him behind the Kolocha river, where they joined the corps in position. Among those killed was General Krasnov. Meanwhile, the vanguard under Murat, supported by the main body of the *Grande Armée*, abandoning the pursuit of our rearguard, crossed the Kolocha, at Fomkino and Valueva, and turned to their right towards Shevardino, where troops detached by Kutuzov, under the command of Lieutenant General Prince Gorchakov 2nd [Andrey Ivanovich Gorchakov] were stationed forwards of our main position on the high ground.[51] Napoleon, wanting to seize this advanced position immediately, sent part of Davout's *1er Corps* (three divisions) and Murat's *Réserve de cavalerie* against it and, at the same time, ordered Poniatowski's *5e Corps*, advancing on the village of Yelnya, along the old Smolensk road, to envelope the Shevardino position on its left flank; meanwhile, the Viceroy with his *4e Corps* was moving to the left of the main body of the enemy army to the village of Bolshiye Sady.[52]

The result of the offensive by Napoleon's troops against the position under Prince Gorchakov was the battle of Shevardino. But since this action marks the beginning of the Battle of Borodino, then, before proceeding to its presentation, we shall describe the area occupied by our armies and the location of Kutuzov's troops upon it.

---

50 Labaume mentions this skirmish, but does not admit to the defeat of *3e régiment de chasseurs à cheval italiens*. Eugène Labaume, *Relation circonstanciée de la campagne de Russie en 1812*, 4e edit. 127-128.
51 Prince Andrey Ivanovich Gorchakov, one of Suvorov's subordinates in the Italian and Swiss campaigns of 1799.
52 Buturlin, 309-310. *Denkwürdigkeiten des Grafen v. Toll*, II, 29-30.

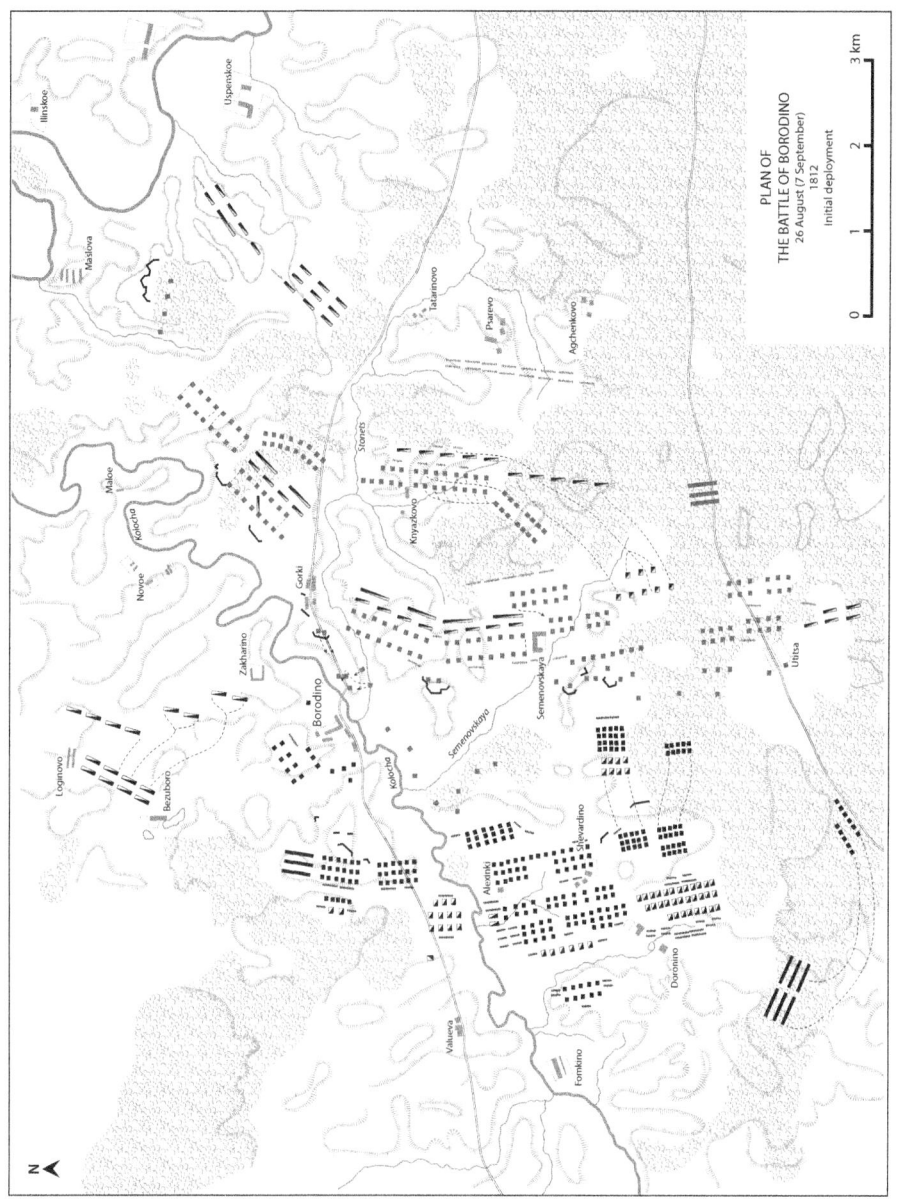

Plan of the Battle of Borodino, 7 September 1812.

21

The position at Borodino

A description of the Borodino position. – Fortifications. – Initial deployment of Russian forces in the positions at Borodino and Shevardino. – The action at Shevardino on 24 August (5 September). – The deployment of Napoleon's forces during the night of 24 to 25 August (5 to 6 September). – The rearrangement of the Russian force. – The composition and strength of Russian forces at the battle of Borodino. – The composition and strength of Napoleon's forces. – Comparison of the strengths of both sides. – Napoleon's preparations for the forthcoming battle. – The dispositions by the enemy army. – The eve of the battle of Borodino in the Russian camp. – Napoleon's orders before the battle.

The area on which the Borodino position was chosen stretches overall from the old Smolensk road, or left wing, to the Moskva river, or right wing.[1]

The Kolocha river, covering the right wing of the position, flows along a swampy valley along its upper part, parallel to the new Smolensk road, as far as the village of Borodino, where it is crossed by this road, and then, until its confluence with the Moskva river, it is in a deep valley with steep banks, of which the right, constantly dominating the left and having a height in many places of some five *Sazhen*, forms the strongest part of the position. Three streams flow into the Kolocha near Borodino: opposite the village, on the right bank is the Stonets [Stanitsa] stream, between which and the Kolocha stretches a narrow ridge with a high mound near the village of Gorki; upstream of Borodino, the Voinka stream flows into the Kolocha on the left bank, flowing sluggishly in a swampy valley; between them a hill is formed, in the form of a spur with steep slopes, on which part of Borodino lies. Further upstream, the Kolocha river receives the almost waterless Semenovka stream from the right, flowing out of the forest on the old Smolensk road; the banks of the Semenovka are flat on the upper part, and somewhat steeper on the lower part; between the courses of this stream, the Kolocha and the Stonets, there is high ground that dominates the surroundings; on top of this is the remarkable location of the so-called Kurgan battery, or Raevsky battery. On the lower reaches of the Semenovka, from the village of Semenovskaya to its confluence, the right bank dominates the left, while upstream of Semenovskaya, in contrast, the left bank dominates. All the streams mentioned

---

1   See Plan of the Battle of Borodino, 26 August (7 September).

dried up in the era of the battle of Borodino, due to the strong heat in that summer of 1812, and there was very little water in the Kolocha itself.

To the left of Semenovskaya, as far as the fields of the village of Utitsa, stretched a plain, overgrown for the most part with alder and birch scrub, no taller than one and a half *arshins*. The fields of Utitsa are surrounded on three sides by extensive forests, enveloping the left wing of the position occupied by our troops from the rear. The old Smolensk road, leading from the village of Yelnya towards Mozhaisk, runs through these forests and through the village of Utitsa. A significant mound rises in the forest behind Utitsa, by the road itself.

From the Kamenka stream, a dried-up tributary of the Semenovka, towards the direction from which the enemy was expected, the ground rises very gradually. Two *versts* from the Kamenka, three mounds rise which constituted a continuation of the front of our position, near the village of Shevardino.

The Kolocha river, flowing partly parallel and partly in a meandering direction to the new Smolensk road, served as protection only for the right wing of the position as far as the village of Gorki; to the left of this point, it was possible to hold the rest of the position such that its front moved away from the Kolocha and the Semenovka, along a straight line from Gorki to Utitsa, or along a salient, from Gorki to the high ground between the Stonets and the Semenovka and back at a shallow angle towards Utitsa. In any case, we could not disregard the significant high ground, within canister range of the forward edge of our front line, and therefore it was necessary to occupy it with a heavily armed fortification, which, when taking a position in a straight line, could serve as a support for the centre, in the form of a forward outpost, or if located at the tip of a salient, it would form part of the position itself. Bennigsen expressed his opinion in favour of taking a position in a straight line, proposing to build a strong enclosed fortification with embrasures all around on the dominant height, in case of an enemy attack, from whatever direction it may be directed. Such a fortification, he argued, should be armed with 24 or 36 heavy guns, without horses, and occupied by several battalions. On the contrary, Toll preferred to construct a lunette at this point, arm it with 18 guns and include it in the general layout of the position. Kutuzov preferred Toll's idea, and thus the disposition of our armies was directed from Gorki to the high ground, and from there to the left, at a shallow angle,[2] through Semenovskaya to Utitsa. From our brief description of the area, it is clear that the centre and left wing of the Borodino position were not protected by any natural obstacles, and that the left flank could be bypassed along the old Smolensk road. Consequently, this position did not present significant terrain advantages in a defensive sense at all, and could even lead (as actually happened) to the weakening of the left wing from a desire to take advantage of the ground on the right flank of the position. Instead of confining ourselves

---

2   According to other sources [Liprandi demands to know which other sources, when even the original source is not named], the position of Second Army was initially selected by General Vistitsky with the position of First Army in a straight line, while on 24 August [5 September], when examining the position, having found a ravine behind the left wing, Bennigsen laid out Second Army at a shallow angle, at the same time naming the mound at its tip the key to the position.

to monitoring the course of the Kolocha and deploying troops between Gorki and Utitsa, and holding strong reserves behind the left wing, we stretched the army two additional *versts* to the right of Gorki, and through this, at the very beginning of the battle, we deprived ourselves of the use of a whole third of the force.[3]

Several fortifications were built to reinforce the position. Starting from the right flank, on the right side of the road, a battery for three guns (because it was impossible to place more artillery at this point) was constructed on the mound near Gorki,[4] and another for nine guns, ahead of the first, at a distance of 200 *Sazhen* from it, on the slope descending from Gorki towards Borodino. Both of these emplacements were occupied by a Battery Company under Major Dietrichs. The wooden bridge over the Kolocha was left intact and the village of Borodino was partly adapted for defence. In the centre it was intended to construct a strong fortification, in the form of a bastion with *demi-tenaille* on its flanks;[5] but there was neither time nor materials for this, and therefore this point, contrary to the statements by foreign historians, was very weakly fortified. The guns placed there could not properly fire across the terrain ahead; the ditch was on a slope, from which the counterscarp was much lower than the scarp and the side of the ditch facing open ground was much too shallow. The construction of this fortification was begun no earlier than five o'clock in the afternoon of 25 August [6 September], i.e. it was already almost the evening of the eve of the battle of Borodino, because the soldiers of the Moscow *opolchenie*, sent as labourers, had not been equipped with shovels or picks,[6] and did not have the slightest idea about the preparation of hurdles and gabions. By dawn, embrasures for only ten guns were ready, and the lunette was far from finished. The artillery that occupied it was under the command of Colonel Schulmann [Gustav Maximovich Schulmann].

In general, earthworks were very difficult to dig due to the many stones with which all the high ground on the battlefield at Borodino was strewn, and therefore there was no way to give the profiles of the fortifications sufficient height; a lack of gabions prevented making revetments; all the slopes were very gentle, which, on the one hand, slowed down the raising of parapets, and on the other, allowed an escalade; palisades and other artificial obstacles were out of the question.

Further to the left – in front of Semenovskaya, there were three emplacements, the so-called Bagration *flèches*, whose construction was also very poor. The village

---

3 [Liprandi raises the question of whether Kutuzov's over-strengthening of his right wing was a deliberate ruse to induce Napoleon, under threat of a potential counter-attack from there, to keep back a stronger reserve and not detach a large flanking force around the Russian left, concluding 'everything that relates to the above circumstances can only be understood with an approximate balance of probability once all the data and materials have been critically assessed… Otherwise, everything remains unsubstantiated, obscure, confusing'].
4 [Liprandi points out that Gorki formed the right flank of VI Corps, not the entire army. He also notes that the total number of guns is at odds with Barclay's report].
5 [Liprandi comments that Toll favoured a lunette, Bennigsen an enclosed redoubt and bemoans the lack of a reference for the idea of a bastion flanked by *demi-tenaille*].
6 [Liprandi comments: 'This is not why it was begun so late, as the historian will state elsewhere himself; the *opolchenie* assigned to this work were immediately supplied with picks and shovels by regiments from VI Corps'].

of Semenovskaya, completely incapable of being brought into a defensive state, was partially demolished. Ahead of the Borodino position, at a distance of about 900 *Sazhen*, near the village of Shevardino, a pentagonal redoubt for 12 guns was built at the suggestion of Toll. This fortification served as a strong-point for the advanced position, which we intended to occupy not so much to delay the enemy, but to monitor their forces and reveal their initial deployment from the dominant Shevardino high ground. The construction of the redoubt there had also not been completed.

In addition to the fortifications we have described, a screen of fortifications were built near the forest, behind the right wing of the position. This construction, fronting the Moskva river, was of no benefit.

Upon the arrival of the Western Armies at the Borodino position, the light cavalry attached to the infantry corps were detached from them and became part of the cavalry corps. The Moscow and Smolensk *opolchenie*, which had joined the army with more than 10,000 men, was poorly armed and had not had time to receive proper tactical training and were assigned to evacuate the wounded from the battle-field and to escort the wagon trains.[7]

Our troops, in accordance with the disposition issued by Prince Kutuzov on 24 August (5 September), were deployed as follows:[8] in each of the infantry corps placed in the battle line, one of the divisions formed the right wing and the other the left; and in each division, the infantry regiments were drawn up in battalion columns arranged in two echelons, so that sufficient intervals were left between the columns for their deployment.[9] The jäger regiments from the divisions were initially scattered in a screen forwards of the front fighting line, and were thereafter to retreat into the position, with the exception of two regiments that were stationed in the forest on the right wing, and six regiments, in the scrub between the Bagration *flèches* and Utitsa, which operated in open order throughout. Behind each infantry corps stood one of cavalry, formed in two echelons, in extended order. Thus, in addition to the skirmisher screen, supported by reserves, there were four fighting lines: two each of infantry and cavalry. Behind them were the reserves.

Let us move on to a detailed description of the initial positions of the Russian force in the Borodino position and the subsequent changes.

The right wing and centre were formed from the troops of First Army under Barclay de Tolly, while the left were from Second Army under Prince Bagration. II Corps and IV Corps, under Miloradovich's command, constituted the right wing protected by the Kolocha; the right flank of II Corps, standing on a plateau somewhat further back than IV Corps, was 600 *Sazhen* from the Moskva river, while the left flank of IV Corps was anchored on the Stonets stream, near the village of Gorki. The village of Borodino was occupied by three battalions of Lifeguard Jägers. At a fairly significant distance behind II Corps, behind the woods, stood I Cavalry Corps and to the left of them, Platov with nine Cossack regiments; II Cavalry Corps were behind

---

7   Prince Kutuzov's orders for the armies, dated 23 August [4 September], No. 6.
8   See the Plan of the battle of Borodino, 26 August (7 September).
9   [Liprandi states emphatically that VI Corps first echelon regiments were deployed in line, and casts doubt on other front line corps being deployed differently].

IV Corps. Further to the left was VI Corps with III Cavalry Corps to their rear, both under Dokhturov's [Dmitry Sergeevich Dokhturov] command, forming the centre, deployed from Gorki to the large fortification on the Kurgan (the Raevsky redoubt). Second Army formed the left wing of the overall deployment: the troops of this army included, VII Corps with IV Cavalry Corps to their rear, holding the sector from the Raevsky redoubt to Semenovskaya; while the Combined Grenadier Division under Count Vorontsov [Mikhail Semënovich Vorontsov] (VIII Corps) held the Bagration *flèches*. The jäger regiments of those infantry corps in the fighting lines, were scattered forwards of the frontage of this force, with the exception of 20th Jägers, 21st Jägers, 11th Jägers and 41st Jägers (subsequently reinforced with 49th Jägers and 50th Jägers), who occupied the scrub along the Kamenka stream and to the left of the *flèches* towards the old Smolensk road, while two regiments, 4th Jägers and 34th Jägers, were stationed in the woods, behind the right wing, between II Corps and I Cavalry Corps. Five Cossack regiments monitored the course of the lower Kolocha as far as its confluence with the Moskva river; while six more Cossack regiments, under Major General Karpov's [Akim Akimovich Karpov] command, were monitoring the sector on the left wing around the village of Utitsa. The Bagration *flèches* were occupied by infantry and artillery; all the other fortifications were defended by artillery alone; it had been intended to protect all the infantry stationed in the front line with breastworks, but this intention remained unfulfilled.[10]

The reserves were deployed in the following manner: behind the village of Knyazkovo, the main reserve, of III Corps and V Corps (Lifeguards) and the cuirassier division under Depreradovich [Nikolay Ivanovich Depreradovich] (the cuirassier corps under Prince Golitsyn [Dmitry Vladimirovich Golitsyn] consisted of two cuirassier divisions). The main artillery reserve, of 26 companies and batteries,[11] were stationed behind Psarevo. Second Army had its own reserve, consisting of 2nd Grenadier Division under Prince Carl zu Mecklenburg [Carl August Christian zu Mecklenburg-Schwerin], located behind Semenovskaya, and, subsequently, reinforced by troops detached to defend the Shevardino position and five companies of horse artillery sent from the main reserves.[12] The headquarters was located in Tatarinovo.

The troops entrusted to Lieutenant General Prince Gorchakov 2nd, to defend the position at Shevardino, consisted of 27th Division under Neverovsky, 5th Jäger Regiment from Paskevich's 26th Division, four cavalry regiments (Kharkov

---

10 [Liprandi comments: '... an entrenchment had already been started from Gorki in front of the Pskov Musketeers, and some of the Moscow Musketeers, but then I was ordered to stop but only so as not to tire the men, proposing to use the *opolchenie* as labour; but thereafter in the evening of 25 August [6 September], the left flank of VI Corps was to move forward towards the central battery, leaving the right at Gorki, whereupon the proposal to continue the entrenchment further was completely abandoned; it even had to be filled in across the sector on which it had already been completed; as it intersected the line of regiments, particularly that of the Moscow Regiment'].
11 The Lifeguard Horse Artillery companies were referred to as Batteries consisting of eight guns each.
12 For the full Dispositions for First and Second Western Armies, at the village of Borodino, issued on 24 August [5 September] 1812, see Appendix 6.

THE POSITION AT BORODINO 109

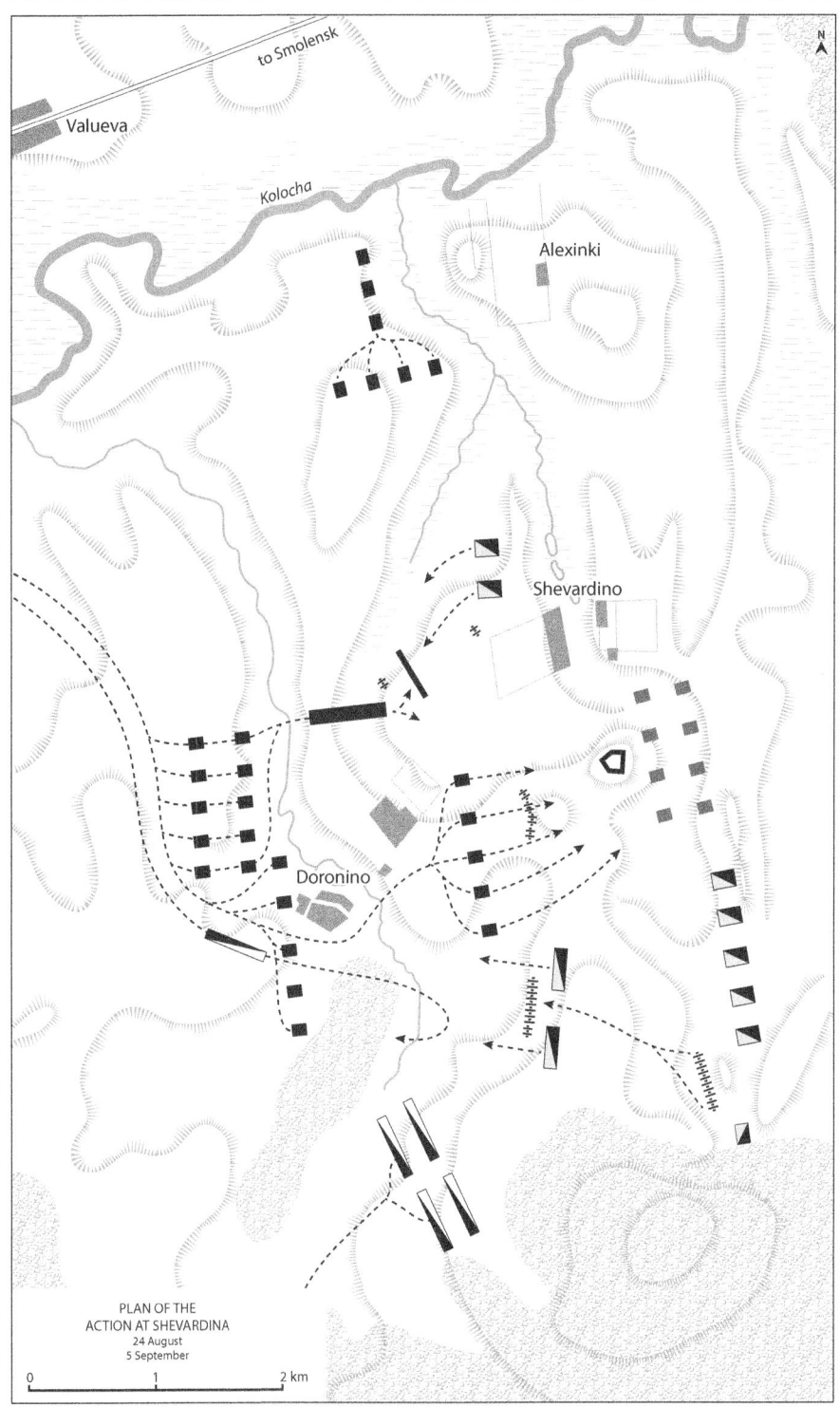

Plan of the action at Shevardino, 5 September 1812.

Dragoons, Chernigov Dragoons, Kiev Dragoons and Novorossiya Dragoons), two squadrons of Akhturka Hussars and 2nd Cuirassier Division under Duka [Ilya Mikhailovich Duka]; a total of 14 battalions and 38 squadrons. Subsequently, this force was increased by two (or according to other sources four) combined grenadier battalions from Vorontsov's Division and the troops of 2nd Grenadier Division under Prince Carl zu Mecklenburg, who arrived to relieve them.[13]

On 24 August [5 September], at the very moment that the enemy, following the action at Kolotsky monastery, were approaching Borodino, the troops assigned to defend the advanced Shevardino position were located as follows:[14] 5th Jägers, 49th Jägers and 50th Jägers were scattered in a screen from the village of Alexinki up the Kolocha to Fomkino, and further up the Doronino ravine and in the scrub towards the village of Yelnya; eight battalions of the Vilna Infantry, Simbirsk Infantry, Odessa Infantry and Tarnopol Infantry were formed up in battalion columns behind the redoubt occupied by 12 Battery guns; to the right of the infantry were the Kharkov Dragoons and Chernigov Dragoons with four horse artillery pieces; to the left of the infantry and somewhat to their rear, was the cuirassier division, in regimental columns, with eight horse artillery pieces, escorted by the Akhturka Hussars, while the Novorossiya Dragoons and Kiev Dragoons had advanced forwards to the left of the Shevardino redoubt in support of the jägers (the combined grenadier battalions arrived on the battlefield later). The number of our troops participating in the battle at Shevardino reached 11,000 men, according to Prince Gorchakov himself.[15]

As soon as the enemy, pursuing our rearguard along the highway, following the action at Kolotsky monastery, had approached Valueva, our skirmisher screen, scattered along the ravine and scrub on the right bank of the Kolocha, opened heavy fire into the flank of the advancing columns. Napoleon, seeing at first glance the inaccessibility of the right wing of our position, ordered the cavalry corps under Nansouty [Étienne Marie Antoine Champion de Nansouty] and Montbrun [Louis Pierre de Montbrun] and three divisions from Davout's *1er Corps* to be sent over the Kolocha, with the objective of ejecting the Russian marksmen from their natural cover and seizing the redoubt. Poniatowski's *5e Corps*, moving along the old Smolensk road, was intended to cooperate in this attack.[16] Consequently, over 35,000 men were directed against the Shevardino position.[17] Compans' Division, following the cavalry at the head of Davout's Corps, turned off the highway to the right, before reaching Valueva, crossed the Kolocha and captured the village of Fomkino at two o'clock in the afternoon, while the cavalry, moving back along the highway, crossed the river a little after the infantry, while Friant's [Louis Friant] and Morand's [Charles Antoine Louis Alexis Morand] divisions crossed downstream at Alexinki. After occupying Fomkino, Compans placed a strong battery in front of the village,

---

13 *Denkwürdigkeiten des Grafen v. Toll*, II, 27. Buturlin, I, 308-309. In one of the letters by Count (later Prince) Vorontsov it is stated that four combined grenadier battalions were in action at Shevardino and suffered quite significant casualties.
14 See Plan of the action at Shevardino, 24 August (5 September).
15 Prince Andrey Ivanovich Gorchakov's letter to General Mikhailovsky-Danilevsky. This total of troops shows neither 2nd Grenadier Division, nor the combined grenadier battalions.
16 Chambray, II, 43-44.
17 Chambray, II, 33.

which opened fire on our redoubt; at the same time, his infantry was lining up for battle and Murat's cavalry was approaching. After a fairly heated mutual bombardment, which lasted about two hours, the French columns attacked Doronino and the nearby woods, while Poniatowski's leading troops began to press the 5th Jägers from the direction of Yelnya. Colonel Emmanuel [Georgy (Yegor) Arsenevich Emmanuel (Manuilovich)], noticing this movement, threatening us with envelopment, charged at the enemy *voltigeurs* coming out of the bushes with the Kiev Dragoons and drove them off; while the division [pair of squadrons] of the Akhtyrka Hussars, under the command of Captain Alexandrovich, escorting the artillery on the left flank of the position, struck the infantry column which was moving to attack our guns, and forced it to pull back. After that, General Count Sievers [Karl Karlovich Sievers or Carl Gustav, Graf von Sievers], noticing the retreat of our jägers on the right wing, sent the Novorossiya Dragoon Regiment, under the command of Major Terenin, to assist them and, having passed between the village of Doronino and the woods, scattered two infantry columns advancing on this village, and drove off the enemy cavalry. But then the Poles enveloped our jägers on the left flank and pushed them back into the forest between Shevardino and Utitsa; whereupon the Novorossiya Dragoons withdrew to their original position. Taking advantage of this, Compans took possession of Doronino and the woods, while Poniatowski's cavalry, emerging from the scrub, attached themselves to the right flank of the French. Shortly thereafter, six *voltigeur* (marksmen) companies, supported by a battalion from *61e régiment de ligne*, occupied the mound in front of Doronino, at a distance of about 250 paces from the redoubt, and with their well-aimed fire caused great harm to the artillery crews who were in this fortification. The remaining battalions of *61e régiment de ligne* were also sent there with eight guns, which stationed themselves on the mound, while the infantry, formed in battalion columns, took cover behind them on the reverse slope facing Doronino. The canister fire of the French artillery caused great disorder in our redoubt; Compans, taking advantage of this, led *57e régiment de ligne* and *61e régiment de ligne* in an attack on the left wing of Neverovsky's 27th Division, while General Duppelin [Jean Duppelin], moving to his left with *25e régiment de ligne*, attacked the right wing of Neverovsky's force, while *111e régiment de ligne*, directed even further to the left, began to envelope our infantry's flank; at the same time, Friant and Morand were heading towards Shevardino. A violent close quarter battle ensued; first the French moved forward, then the Russians pressed the French; eventually, the superior enemy numbers prevailed: Compans took possession of the redoubt, while Morand took Shevardino village.

This was the situation at about eight o'clock in the evening. At this point, 2nd Grenadier Division under Prince Carl zu Mecklenburg, on Prince Bagration's orders, arrived in time to relieve Neverovsky's force. Bagration himself led his grenadiers into action; two enemy columns moved towards their flank; whereupon Colonel Tolbuzin 1st [Mikhail Ivanovich Tolbuzin], deploying the Malorussia Cuirassiers and Glukhov Cuirassiers, struck these columns, drove them off and captured the French battery stationed forwards of Doronino, but only managed to drag away three guns. At the same time, on our right wing, the Kharkov Dragoons and Chernigov Dragoons attacked *111e régiment de ligne*, which had moved away from the other troops, forced it to form up in square and captured two regimental guns that were accompanying it, this regiment also suffered significant casualties, but was rescued by the Spanish Régiment de Joseph Napoléon [Regimiento de José Napoleón] (Friant's Division). Night was falling, but the battle still raged, and that is why the sources on this action are so inconsistent with each other. Notwithstanding the statements by foreign historians, there is no doubt that the redoubt changed hands more than once and that the successful actions by our cavalry helped the grenadiers to destroy one of the battalions of the French *61e régiment de ligne* stationed in it. Meanwhile, Poniatowski's troops had enveloped the left flank of the Shevardino position; General Karpov, who was with the Cossack detachment on the old Smolensk road, reported the appearance of significant forces facing him, and that enemy numbers were noticeably increasing from the direction of the Kolocha. The unfinished redoubt had been destroyed during the fighting and did not present the means for a stubborn defence, and therefore Kutuzov ordered Prince Bagration to withdraw to the main position. Bagration, having received this order at 11 o'clock at night, withdrew at the very moment that strong enemy columns moved into the attack once more; while Compans, occupying the redoubt, took possession of the guns there. According to Barclay himself, we lost only three guns. The darkness of the night, concealing the withdrawal of our troops, prevented the enemy from pursuing them.[18]

It is difficult to state anything definitively about the casualties in the forces of both sides in the Shevardino action. Buturlin calculated the losses at more than 1,000 men on each side. Thiers states that the French lost 4,000 to 5,000 and the Russians 7,000 to 8,000. According to Barclay, our casualties were shown as 6,000 men. Bernhardi believes that some 6,000 of our men were rendered *hors de combat*, in the actions at Gridnevo, Kolotsky monastery and Shevardino, while the French, lost some 4,000. Judging from the course of these actions and from the troop losses on both sides, from 22 to 24 August [3 to 5 September], the losses were even.

During the night of 24 to 25 August (5 to 6 September), the enemy forces were located as follows: three of Davout's divisions around Shevardino, Murat, with Nansouty's, Montbrun's and Grouchy's corps, between Shevardino and the Kolocha; Poniatowski's *5e Corps* between Yelnya and Doronino. On the left bank of the Kolocha: the Viceroy's *4e Corps*, whose leading troops, during the course of the fighting at Shevardino, had attempted to capture Borodino, remained in view of this village; two of Davout's divisions (Gérard's [Étienne Maurice Gérard] and Dessaix's [Joseph Marie Dessaix]), Ney's *3e Corps* and the *Garde impériale*, together with Napoleon's main headquarters were either side of Valueva; while Junot's *8e Corps* were to their rear with Latour-Maubourg.[19]

On our side, at dawn on 25 August [6 September], in order to support the jäger regiments holding the woods on the left wing of the position and the ravines to its front, the combined grenadier battalions of 11th Division, 23rd Division,

---

18 *Denkwürdigkeiten des Grafen v. Toll*, II, 32-36. Buturlin, I, 310-314. Gourgaud. Ségur, *Histoire de Napoléon et de la Grande armée*, 4me édit, I, 370-372. Major General Sievers' report to Prince Kutuzov, dated 26 September [8 October], No. 276. Description of the operations of First Army (Barclay de Tolly).
19 *Denkwürdigkeiten des Grafen v. Toll*, II, 37. Buturlin, I, 314-315.

7th Division and 24th Division were sent forward. Count Vorontsov, with his combined grenadier division, occupied the *flèches* forwards of Semenovskaya; 27th Division stood behind the *flèches*; 2nd Grenadier Division, behind Semenovskaya; 2nd Cuirassier Division, behind 2nd Grenadier Division; the dragoon regiments and Akhtyrka Hussars, who had been in the action at Shevardino, rejoined IV Cavalry Corps.

The concentration of a significant part of the enemy force against the centre and left wing of the Borodino position forced us to pay attention to the danger threatening our left flank, which could be bypassed being unprotected by any significant obstacles. As early as 24 August (5 September), Prince Kutuzov, at Toll's suggestion, sent the engineer Captain Felkner [Völkner] to seek out an area convenient for the covert concentration of part of the army in the forests behind the left wing on the old Smolensk road, with the objective of launching a surprise counterattack on the enemy in the event of their advance enveloping our left flank. Captain Felkner soon returned with a report that just such an area existed behind the Utitsa Kurgan, on the upper part of the Semenovskaya ravine. Colonel Toll, finding this position totally suitable for the aim of this operation, transferred III Corps there, on the orders of Prince Kutuzov, from the general reserve, followed by 7,000 warriors from the Moscow *opolchenie*; the remaining battalions of the Moscow and Smolensk *opolchenie* were placed behind the battle lines to give assistance to the wounded. In order to preserve communications between III Corps and the army, Major General Prince Shakhovskoy [Ivan Leontevich Shakhovskoy] was ordered to occupy the scrub between Semenovskaya and Utitsa, with 20th Jägers, 21st Jägers, 11th Jägers and 41st Jägers.

The location of III Corps, under Tuchkov [Nikolay Alexeevich Tuchkov], in the form of a shoulder, behind the left flank of the position, gave us the opportunity to counterattack an enemy envelopment; but thereafter it was changed by Bennigsen, who, ignorant of the orders issued by Kutuzov and executed by Toll, ordered Tuchkov 1st to bring III Corps up to the village of Utitsa, level with the jäger regiments, holding the scrub to the left of the *flèches*. Thus, this part of the army was located on open ground, on a forward slope subsequently occupied by Poniatowski's troops, subjected both to envelopment and the actions of enemy artillery, which would be all the more destructive because our infantry was formed in four echelons: the first two consisted of the troops of 3rd Division, while 1st Grenadier Division were behind them. It is absolutely incredible that Bennigsen did not inform Kutuzov about his orders at the expense of III Corps, and as Tuchkov 1st was killed in the Battle of Borodino, many accused him of pointlessly and wilfully changing the position of the troops entrusted to him.[20]

---

20 Bernhardi assures us that Bennigsen, having advanced III Corps to Utitsa, did not report the orders he had made to Kutuzov and that many blamed Tuchkov 1st for this (who was killed in the battle of Borodino). But one of the young officers of the General Staff, Lieutenant Shcherbinin, who was with Tuchkov when Bennigsen ordered III Corps to go to Utitsa, believing that this order had been promptly reported to the Commander-in-Chief, a few months later, when he was in the headquarters in Kalisz, he let slip the secret he was privy to, in the presence of Toll and several of his comrades. *Denkwürdigkeiten des Grafen v. Toll*, II, 42-43. Shcherbinin's notes.

The composition and numbers of Russian troops at the Battle of Borodino were as follows:

Under the command of General of Infantry Barclay de Tolly:

Right Wing, General of Infantry Miloradovich.
II Corps, Lieutenant General Baggovut.

Formation & Commander	Units	Size
4th Division Major General Prinz Eugen von Württemberg	Tobolsk Infantry	2 battalions
	Volhynia Infantry	2 battalions
	Kremenchug Infantry	2 battalions
	Minsk Infantry	2 battalions
	4th Jägers	2 battalions
	34th Jägers	2 battalions
	4th Battery Artillery Company	1 company
17th Division Lieutenant General Olsufiev [Zakhar Dmitrievich Olsufiev]	Ryazan Infantry	2 battalions
	Belozersk Infantry	2 battalions
	Brest Infantry	2 battalions
	Wilmanstrand Infantry	2 battalions
	30th Jägers	2 battalions
	48th Jägers	2 battalions
	17th Battery Artillery Company	1 company

Total for II Corps: 24 battalions with two artillery companies, 10,300 men and 24 guns.

IV Corps, Lieutenant General Count Osterman-Tolstoy [Alexander Ivanovich Osterman-Tolstoy].

Formation & Commander	Units	Size
11th Division Major General Bakhmetev 2nd [Nikolay Nikolaevich Bakhmetev]	Kexholm Infantry	2 battalions
	Pernov Infantry	2 battalions
	Polotsk Infantry	2 battalions
	Yelets Infantry	2 battalions
	1st Jägers	2 battalions
	33rd Jägers	2 battalions
	combined grenadiers (6 companies)	2 battalions
	11th Battery Artillery Company	1 company
23rd Division Major General Bakhmetev 1st [Alexey Nikolaevich Bakhmetev]	Rylsk Infantry	2 battalions
	Yekaterinburg Infantry	2 battalions
	Selenginsk Infantry	2 battalions
	18th Jägers	2 battalions
	combined grenadiers (6 companies)	2 battalions
	44th Light Artillery Company	1 company

Total for IV Corps: 23 battalions with two artillery companies, 9,500 men and 24 guns.

I Cavalry Corps, Adjutant General Uvarov [Fëdor Petrovich Uvarov].

Formation & Commander	Units	Size
	Lifeguard Dragoons	4 squadrons
	Lifeguard Hussars	4 squadrons
	Lifeguard Ulans	4 squadrons
	Lifeguard Cossacks	4 squadrons
	Nizhin Dragoons	4 squadrons
	Yelisavetgrad Hussars	8 squadrons
	5th Horse Artillery Company	1 company

Total for I Cavalry Corps: 28 squadrons with one artillery company, 2,500 men and 12 guns.

II Cavalry Corps, Adjutant General Baron Korf [Fëdor Karlovich Korf].

Formation & Commander	Units	Size
	Pskov Dragoons	4 squadrons
	Moscow Dragoons	4 squadrons
	Kargopol Dragoons	4 squadrons
	Ingermanland Dragoons	4 squadrons
	Poland Ulans	8 squadrons
	Izyum Hussars	8 squadrons
	4th Horse Artillery Company	1 company

Total for II Cavalry Corps: 32 squadrons with one artillery company, 3,500 men and 12 guns.

Centre, General of Infantry Dokhturov.
VI Corps, General Dokhturov.

Formation & Commander	Units	Size
7th Division	Moscow Infantry	2 battalions
Lieutenant General Kaptsevich	Pskov Infantry	2 battalions
[Pëtr Mikhailovich Kaptsevich]	Sofia Infantry	2 battalions
	Libau Infantry	2 battalions
	11th Jägers	2 battalions
	36th Jägers	2 battalions
	combined grenadiers (6 companies)	2 battalions
	7th Battery Artillery Company	1 company

24th Division Major General Likhachëv [Pëtr Gavrilovich Likhachëv]	Ufa Infantry	2 battalions
	Shirvan Infantry	2 battalions
	Butyrsk Infantry	2 battalions
	Tomsk Infantry	2 battalions
	19th Jägers	2 battalions
	40th Jägers	2 battalions
	combined grenadiers (6 companies)	2 battalions
	24th Battery Artillery Company	1 company

Total for VI Corps: 28 battalions with two artillery companies, 9,900 men and 24 guns.

III Cavalry Corps, Adjutant General Baron Korf (due to the illness of Lieutenant General Count Pahlen [Pëtr Petrovich Pahlen]).

Formation & Commander	Units	Size
Major General Kreutz	Courland Dragoons	4 squadrons
	Orenburg Dragoons	4 squadrons
	Siberia Dragoons	4 squadrons
	Irkutsk Dragoons	4 squadrons
	Sumy Hussars	8 squadrons
	Mariupol Hussars	8 squadrons
	9th Horse Artillery Company	1 company

Total for III Cavalry Corps: 32 squadrons with one artillery company, 3,700 men.

Reserve of the Right Wing and Centre.
V Corps, Lieutenant General Lavrov [Nikolay Ivanovich Lavrov].

Formation & Commander	Units	Size
	Lifeguard Preobrazhensky Regiment	3 battalions
	Lifeguard Semenovsky Regiment	3 battalions
	Lifeguard Izmailovsky Regiment	3 battalions
	Lifeguard Lithuania Regiment	3 battalions
	Lifeguard Jäger Regiment	3 battalions
	Lifeguard Finland Regiment	3 battalions
	Lifeguard Marines (Equipage)	1 battalion
	combined grenadiers 4th Division	2 battalions
	combined grenadiers 17th Division	2 battalions
	combined grenadiers 1st Division	2 battalions
	combined grenadiers 3rd Division	2 battalions

Total for V Corps: 27 battalions, 13,000 men.

Formation & Commander	Units	Size
1st Cuirassier Division Major General Borozdin 2nd [Nikolay Mikhailovich Borozdin]	Chevalier Garde Regiment	4 squadrons
	Lifeguard Horse Regiment	4 squadrons
	His Majesty's Cuirassiers	4 squadrons
	Her Majesty's Cuirassiers	4 squadrons
	Astrakhan Cuirassiers	4 squadrons

Total for 1st Cuirassier Division: 20 squadrons, 2,400 men.

Formation & Commander	Units	Size
Artillery Reserve Major General Löwenstern [Karl Fëdorovich Löwenstern] & Colonel Euler [Alexander Khristoforovich Euler]	Lifeguard Artillery Brigade	6 companies
	battery artillery	6 companies
	light artillery	9 companies
	horse artillery	5 companies
	pioneers	1 company
	pontoniers	2 companies

Total for the Artillery Reserve: 26 batteries (300 guns)[21] and three companies, 8,400 men.

General of Cavalry Platov's Force: 14 Cossack regiments with two Don artillery batteries, 5,500 men and 24 guns.

Left Wing, General of Infantry Prince Bagration with Lieutenant General Prince Gorchakov 2nd and Prince Golitsyn.

VII Corps, Lieutenant General Raevsky [Nikolay Nikolaevich Raevsky].

Formation & Commander	Units	Size
26th Division Major General Paskevich	Ladoga Infantry	2 battalions
	Poltava Infantry	2 battalions
	Nizhegorod Infantry	2 battalions
	Orël Infantry	2 battalions
	5th Jägers	2 battalions
	42nd Jägers	2 battalions
	26th Battery Artillery Company	1 company
	47th Light Artillery Company	1 company

---

21 In each of the Lifeguard Horse Artillery Batteries there were 8 guns; there were two guns from the Lifeguard Marines attached to 1st Lifeguard Light Artillery Company.

12th Division	Narva Infantry	2 battalions
Major General Vasilchikov	Smolensk Infantry	2 battalions
	Novoingermanland Infantry	2 battalions
	Alexopol Infantry	2 battalions
	6th Jägers	2 battalions
	41st Jägers	2 battalions

Total for VII Corps: 24 battalions with two artillery companies, 10,800 men.

VIII Corps, Lieutenant General Borozdin 1st [Mikhail Mikhailovich Borozdin].

Formation & Commander	Units	Size
2nd Grenadier Division	Kiev Grenadiers	2 battalions
Major General Carl zu Mecklenburg	Astrakhan Grenadiers	2 battalions
	Moscow Grenadiers	2 battalions
	Fanagoria Grenadiers	2 battalions
	Siberia Grenadiers	2 battalions
	Malorussia Grenadiers	2 battalions
	2nd Battery Artillery Company	1 company
	3rd Light Artillery Company	1 company
27th Division	Vilna Infantry	2 battalions
Major General Neverovsky	Simbirsk Infantry	2 battalions
	Odessa Infantry	2 battalions
	Tarnopol Infantry	2 battalions
	49th Jägers	2 battalions
	50th Jägers	2 battalions

Total for VIII Corps: 24 battalions with two artillery companies, 11,200 men.

IV Cavalry Corps, Major General Count Sievers 1st.

Formation & Commander	Units	Size
	Kharkov Dragoons	4 squadrons
	Chernigov Dragoons	4 squadrons
	Kiev Dragoons	4 squadrons
	Novorossiya Dragoons	4 squadrons
	Akhturka Hussars	8 squadrons
	Lithuania Ulans	8 squadrons
	10th Horse Artillery Company	1 company

Total for IV Cavalry Corps: 32 squadrons with one artillery company, 3,800 men.

Reserve of the Left Wing.

Formation & Commander	Units	Size
Combined Grenadier Division Major General Count Vorontsov	combined grenadiers 26th Division	2 battalions
	combined grenadiers 12th Division	2 battalions
	combined grenadiers 2nd Division	2 battalions

Total: six battalions,[22] 2,100 men.

Formation & Commander	Units	Size
2nd Cuirassier Division Major General Duka	Yekaterinoslav Cuirassiers	4 squadrons
	Military Order Cuirassiers	4 squadrons
	Glukhov Cuirassiers	4 squadrons
	Malorussia Cuirassiers	4 squadrons
	Novgorod Cuirassiers	4 squadrons

Total: 20 squadrons, 2,300 men.

Reserve Artillery of the Left Wing: Artillery – seven companies; Pioneers – one company; Pontoniers – one company; total: 2,400 men.

III Corps, Lieutenant General Tuchkov 1st (On the Old Smolensk Road).

Formation & Commander	Units	Size
1st Grenadier Division Major General Count Stroganov [Pavel Alexandrovich Stroganov]	Leib Grenadiers	2 battalions
	Arakcheev's Grenadiers	2 battalions
	Pavlov Grenadiers	2 battalions
	St Petersburg Grenadiers	2 battalions
	Yekaterinoslav Grenadiers	2 battalions
	Tauride Grenadiers	2 battalions
	1st Battery Artillery Company	1 company
	1st Light Artillery Company	1 company
	2nd Light Artillery Company	1 company
3rd Division	Murom Infantry	2 battalions
	Reval Infantry	2 battalions
	Chernigov Infantry	2 battalions
	Kaporsk Infantry	2 battalions
	20th Jägers	2 battalions
	21st Jägers	2 battalions
	3rd Battery Artillery Company	1 company
	5th Light Artillery Company	1 company
	6th Light Artillery Company	1 company

---

22 The combined grenadier battalions of 7th Division and 24th Division had been sent to support the jägers in front of the position [see listing for VI Corps].

Total for III Corps: 24 battalions with six artillery companies, 8,000 men and 72 guns.

> **Major General Karpov's Force**: Six Cossack regiments, 1,500 men.
> **Moscow Opolchenie**, under Lieutenant General Count Morkov.
> **Smolensk Opolchenie**, under Lieutenant General Lebedev.

Overall, the Russian army consisted of: 180 battalions, 164 squadrons, 55 artillery companies and batteries, one pioneer and three pontonier companies, 103,800 men, 640 guns in total with an additonal 7,000 Cossacks and 10,000 militiamen.[23]

The composition and numbers for Napoleon's forces in the battle of Borodino were:

Davout's *1er Corps*, of five infantry divisions, totalling 84 battalions, 36,402 men and 147 guns, not including the light cavalry brigade of 16 squadrons detached to Murat's *Réserve de cavalerie*.

Ney's *3e Corps*, of three infantry divisions, totalling 33 battalions, 10,314 men and 69 guns, not including the light cavalry brigade of 16 squadrons detached to Murat's *Réserve de cavalerie*.[24]

The Viceroy's Italian *4e Corps*, of two infantry divisions, two cavalry brigades and the *Garde royale italienne,* 39 battalions and 28 squadrons, 23,528 men and 88 guns.[25]

Prince Poniatowski's *5e Corps*, of two infantry divisions and one cavalry division, 18 battalions and 12 squadrons, 10,068 men and 50 guns in total.

Junot's *8e Corps*, of two infantry divisions and one cavalry brigade, 14 battalions and 8 squadrons, 8,868 men and 30 guns in total.

Murat's *Réserve de cavalerie* of Nansouty's *1er Corps de cavalerie* of three divisions, 60 squadrons; *2e Corps de cavalerie* under Montbrun, of three divisions, 60 squadrons; Grouchy's *3e Corps de cavalerie* of two divisions, 32 squadrons; Latour-Maubourg's *4e Corps de cavalerie* of one division and one brigade, 30 squadrons;[26] the total, together with the light cavalry brigades detached from Davout's and Ney's corps, was 17,600 men and 94 guns. *Garde impériale, Vieille* and *Jeune,* of two infantry divisions, one of cavalry, and several attached units, 31 battalions and 32 squadrons, in total, 18,862 men and 109 guns.[27]

---

23 In Toll's original Notes and in Bernhardi's work the number of regular Russian troops is given as 103,800 men. *Denkwürdigkeiten des Grafen v. Toll*, II, 54. In Buturlin and Wollzogen, the total for regular troops is given as 115,000, while including the Cossacks and *opolchenie* it is 132,000. According to Prinz Eugen it is 96,000 infantry, 18,300 regular cavalry, 640 guns, 5,000 Cossacks and 15,000 *opolchenie*. Mikhailovsky-Danilevsky shows 113,000 regulars. Clausewitz states 120,000 overall; Chambray gives it as 130,000.
24 Pelet, *Bataille de la Mosowa*. According to Schreckenstein (*Die Kavallerie in der Schlacht an der Moskwa*, 163) there were 24 squadrons with *3e Corps*.
25 Pelet. Schreckenstein shows 40 squadrons.
26 Pelet. Schreckenstein (162) shows 48 squadrons.
27 Statements on the composition of Napoleon's *Grande Armée*, placed in the works by Buturlin and Chambray and in the notes by Pelet (*Spectat milit.* 1830). The number of troops with the

In general, French historians have estimated the strength of Napoleon's forces at the Battle of Borodino to be between 120,000 and 130,000 men.[28] In the returns submitted to Napoleon in Gzhatsk, on 2 September, new style, the available number of troops was 126,498; the following rejoined before the battle of Borodino: Latour-Maubourg's corps that had been left behind, some 3,000 men strong; Pajol's division [Pierre Claude Pajol] (from Montbrun's corps) which had been detached from the army in the vicinity of Smolensk, of 1,400 men and some of the units sent out with a total of 7,320 men to find food supplies, in total, at least 10,000 men rejoined. But from this number we should exclude the troops left to garrison Gzhatsk,[29] and the losses of those who were casualties in the actions at Gridnevo, Kolotsky Monastery and Shevardino, as well as the sick and stragglers, which in total would not exceed 6,000 to 8,000. Therefore, it is possible to determine accurately the number of troops on both sides as follows:

	On our side	On the enemy side
Infantry	72,000	86,000
Cavalry	17,500	28,000
Artillery, pioneers and so on, with	14,300 640 guns	16,000 587 guns[30]
Cossacks	7,000	
Opolchenie	10,000	

In total, the Russian force numbered 120,800 men, and with the exception of irregular troops, who for the most part did not participate in the battle at all, and the *opolchenie*, mostly armed with pikes and who would not be of much use in battle, we had about 104,000 men against 130,000 men of the enemy force. Taking into account that, during the advance by Napoleon to Smolensk, the number of troops in the *Grande Armée* reached 180,000 men, it is obvious that at Borodino they should have had at least 140,000 men remaining. In addition, the Russian army had some 15,000 recently-trained recruits who had never been under fire, while Napoleon's army consisted of veteran soldiers: these were the most reliable men out of the 300,000 warriors who had crossed the borders of Russia, who had endured all the difficulties and hardships of a rigorous campaign and left all the weak conscripts behind them along the way. Consequently, from Napoleon's point of view there

---

corps is taken from a list submitted to Napoleon on 2 September new style, because the losses suffered by his troops between 2 and 7 September new style, in all likelihood, were made up by the return of stragglers and foragers.

28 Information extracted from documents captured from the enemy. Chambray, II, 60. Baron Fain, II, 18.
29 Namely; *8e régiment de ligne de Westphalie* (2 Bns), 3rd Battalion, *1er régiment d'infanterie de la Légion de la Vistule* and the depots of *1er Corps* and *3e Corps*. Extracted from a return submitted by the commandant of Gzhatsk, Urguel.
30 This conclusion is drawn approximately from the available number of men in the units of the forces of both sides, but it is very close to the statements by Gourgaud. The cavalry total shown in Schreckenstein (ours of 19,550 and the enemy's of 29,400 men) is obviously exaggerated (*Die Kavallerie in der Schlacht an der Moskwa*, 21).

was an undoubted superiority in numbers. As for the enemy cavalry, although they were much more numerous than ours, however, they were not greatly superior in reality, because their horses, constantly suffering from a lack of fodder, were in poor condition. We had a decisive advantage in artillery over the enemy, not only in the number of guns (640 versus 587), but also in their calibre. Among our batteries, a quarter consisted of heavy guns, while the rest were all of light six-pounder and ¼ *Pud* calibres; in contrast, only a tenth of Napoleon's were heavy guns, while the total of the remainder included 160 regimental guns.

The whole of 25 August (6 September) was spent in preparations for the battle. The appearance of significant enemy forces on the right bank of the Kolocha during the Shevardino battle, dispelled any doubts that Napoleon planned to direct his main effort against our left wing, the weakest point of the Borodino position. It was obvious that Tuchkov's III Corps, with a total of 8,000 men, could not hold the enemy. Some of the Russian generals suggested to Prince Kutuzov that, after dark, a transfer of troops be made so that the right flank of First Army would rest on the high ground by the village of Gorki, and the left would adjoin the village of Semenovskaya; Second Army should be placed where III Corps stood; while eight or ten battalions supported by I Cavalry Corps and Platov's Cossacks should be left to monitor the sector to the right of Gorki. This arrangement offered many benefits: the occupation of shorter battle lines made it possible to retain reserves; Prince Bagration, if not being attacked, or having incomparably smaller forces facing himself, could strike at the flank of any enemy attacking First Army. Kutuzov apparently approved this proposal, but did not execute it.[31]

Even before dawn on 25 August (6 September), Napoleon went to reconnoitre our positions. He was concerned that the Russian army would again evade battle. But his concerns were groundless: Kutuzov had decided to fight and had very good reasons for that. He would not flatter himself with the hope of winning a decisive victory; but it was enough for him to hold his position and block the enemy's route to Moscow, and even an indecisive battle was beneficial for the Russians, because it forced Napoleon to seek a further battle. In contrast, it was necessary for Napoleon to deal a blow such that would induce our Government to conclude peace. As soon as he was deprived of the opportunity to quickly decide the fate of the war, the success of his operations, by moving away from the source of his means for waging war, with the onset of an unfavourable season and the incessant strengthening of the Russian army, became very doubtful. Kutuzov fully comprehended the advantages of his situation; besides which, he could not retreat without fighting in defence of our capital city.

Throughout the day of 25 August (6 September), Napoleon barely dismounted his horse, surveying the environs of Borodino. First of all, he went to the Italian *4e Corps* and examined in minute detail the course of the Kolocha and the Voinka stream that flows into it. Here, facing Borodino, he ordered the construction of several fortifications. Then, he went to Shevardino and the redoubt taken the day before, visited Poniatowski's troops in the forest, on the right wing of his army,

---

31 Description of the operations by First Army (Barclay de Tolly).

surveyed the position of our left wing from the high ground between Doronino and Utitsa and returned to the Italian corps. During lunch, Colonel Fabvier [Charles Nicolas Fabvier] arrived from Spain with the news of Marmont's [Auguste Frédéric Viesse de Marmont] defeat at Salamanca. Thereafter, Napoleon once again surveyed the surroundings of Borodino, during which several canister rounds were fired at him, and returned to his headquarters in the evening, where, on the basis of the information he had gleaned, he issued orders for the impending battle.

French historians assure us that Davout, having surveyed the area on the right wing of the location of the French army and having become convinced of the possibility of enveloping our position on its left flank, proposed to Napoleon, to carry out this flanking move along the old Smolensk road with his five divisions during the night, to strike the flank of the Russian army from this direction and drive it into the angle formed by the Moskva river and the Kolocha. Napoleon judged differently: he was concerned that, as Davout's *1er Corps* was moving through the forest, the French army would be divided into two parts, for the course of several hours, completely isolated from one another, and besides, he believed that the Russians, on seeing themselves outflanked, would retreat and abandon a general battle, the success of which was the last hope of this conqueror who had overreached himself. Taking into account that the flanking movement proposed by Marshal Davout required a night march through unfamiliar wooded terrain, one cannot help but doubt the success of such an operation, incomparably more difficult than Junot's abortive flanking march during the battle of Valutino.

Napoleon, having the intent of attacking the Bagration *flèches* using the troops under Compans, summoned him in order to announce this flattering mission to him personally. Compans offered to lead the division entrusted to him through the forest, so as not to expose the troops to effective canister fire from our *flèches*. Marshal Ney, in whose presence this opinion was expressed, contested it, believing that a move through the forest would disorder the troops; but when Compans remarked that this forest had been examined by him and found to be passable, then Napoleon approved his proposal. General Compans expressed a worry that Russian troops might move around him on his right and occupy the forest, isolating him from Poniatowski. Napoleon replied: 'You are right, take the troops of Dessaix's Division to prevent this happening.'[32]

To give an idea of Napoleon's preliminary orders for the battle of Borodino, we offer the disposition issued on his orders on 6th September (new style) by the Chief of Staff of the *Grande Armée*, the Prince of Neuchâtel (Berthier).

No. I.
At dawn, two new batteries,[33] set up during the night on the plain held by the prince d'Eckmühl,[34] are to open fire on the two opposing enemy batteries.

---

32 Gourgaud. Thiers, XIV, 343-345. Ségur, I, 380-381.
33 Each of 24 guns. Their construction was entrusted to Generals Lariboisière and Chasseloup [François Charles Louis, marquis de Chasseloup-Laubat] (Disposition No. 2, signed by Chief of Staff Berthier).
34 Davout.

At the same time, the Chief of Artillery of *1er Corps*, General Pernety [Joseph Marie de Pernety], with 30 guns from Compans' Division and all the howitzers of Dessaix's and Friant's divisions, are to move forward, open fire and bombard the enemy battery with shell, against which the following are to operate: 24 guns from *Artillerie de la Garde impériale*, 30 guns from Compans' Division, eight guns from Friant's and Dessaix's divisions, 62 guns in total.

The Chief of Artillery of *3e Corps*, General Foucher [Louis François Foucher de Careil], is to place all the howitzers of *3e Corps* and *8e Corps*, 16 in total, on the flanks of the battery, and is tasked to fire at the left fortification, which will have a total of 40 guns against it.

General Sorbier [Jean Barthélemot de Sorbier] must be at immediate readiness to move out with all the howitzers of the *Artillerie de la Garde* against either of the fortifications.

Throughout the bombardment, Prince Poniatowski is to move on the village, into the forest, and outflank the enemy position.

General Compans is to move through the forest to take possession of the first fortification.

Having gone into action in this way, orders will be issued in response to the actions of the enemy.

The bombardment of the left flank is to begin as soon as the bombardment of the right wing is heard. The marksmen from Morand's and the Viceroy's divisions are to lay down heavy fire upon seeing the right wing attack begin.

The Viceroy is to take possession of the village and cross using his three bridges,[35] proceeding level with the divisions under Morand and Gérard, who, under his direction, are to move towards the redoubt in line with the rest of the army.

All this must be carried out in methodical order [*le tout se fera avec ordre et méthode*], holding the troops in reserve as much as possible.

From the imperial camp near Mozhaisk, 6th September, 1812.

No. II.
From the imperial camp near Mozhaisk, 6th September, 1812.

Monsieur maréchal, prince d'Eckmühl.

The Emperor wishes that tomorrow, the 7th, at five o'clock in the morning, the division under Compans is to form up by brigade in the woods in front of the redoubt taken yesterday, having 16 reserve artillery guns in front of them from *1er Corps* and 14 guns belonging to this division, 30 guns in total. Dessaix's Division is to be positioned by you, *monsieur maréchal*, in the same manner, between the redoubt taken yesterday and the forest, with

---

35 Most likely meaning Borodino.

14 guns located next to it, placed on its left wing. Friant's Division is also to form up by brigade, level with the redoubt.

Maréchal duc d'Elchingen[36] is ordered to take command of *8e Corps*. He is to place three divisions from *3e Corps* behind the redoubt taken yesterday, forming them up by brigade and placing their artillery on the left wing. Behind these three divisions from *3e Corps* there are to be two divisions from *8e Corps*, each by brigade, with their own artillery also on the left wing. As for the *Garde impériale*, it is all to be formed up by brigade, to the left behind the redoubt, the *Jeune Garde* in front of the *Vieille Garde* and the *Artillerie de la Garde*. The entire *Artillerie de la Garde* is to be located on the left wing.

The cavalry under the roi de Naples [Murat], consisting of *1er Corps de cavalerie*, *2e Corps de cavalerie* and *4e Corps de cavalerie*, is to form up by regiment in squadron columns (*en bataille par escadrons*) to the right of the redoubt.

All troops are to be in their designated places by five o'clock. In communicating to you the orders regarding the artillery and engineers, I thought it also useful to make you aware of all the orders relating to the right wing of the army.

prince de Neuchâtel, *chef d'état-major*

P.S. Tomorrow Morand's and Gérard's divisions are to come under the Viceroy's command.

The disposition for the troops under Prince Kutuzov outlined the deployment of the force into fighting echelons and in reserve. In conclusion, it was stated:

> Placing all faith in the assistance of the Almighty and upon the courage and fearlessness of the Russian soldiers, upon a fortunate repulse of enemy forces, I shall issue my own orders to pursue them, to which end I shall expect incessant reports on operations, being located behind VI Corps.
>
> In any case, I consider it not superfluous to present to the gentlemen Commanders in Chief that the reserves should be preserved for as long as possible, because a general who still retains a reserve will not be defeated. In the event of a counter-offensive during the action, it should be carried out in attack column, in which case they are not to engage in a firefight at all, but to act swiftly with cold steel.
>
> In the intervals between infantry columns, there are to be some cavalry units, also in columns, which should support the infantry.

Although the Kolocha was fordable along almost its entire course, nevertheless, the French constructed several trestle bridges over this river, for more convenient communications. Two large batteries were constructed to the right of Shevardino, in order to bombard the Bagration *flèches*; a third battery, forwards of the Viceroy's

---

36 Ney.

force, was to open fire against the great redoubt. All of these batteries were built too far from the locations against which they were supposed to operate and did not bring any benefit.[37]

The enemy troops were left in place all day on 25 August (6 September), so as not to reveal prematurely the direction of the main attack proposed by Napoleon. But as soon as it got dark, every unit of the force set out for the locations allocated to them, and by three o'clock in the morning they had already completed their movements. On their right wing, in the Utitsa forest, was Poniatowski's 5e *Corps*, tasked to attack along the old Smolensk road. In the centre, the following troops were stationed: three divisions from Davout's *1er Corps*, under his personal command, some in the wood-line of the forest, forwards of the Shevardino redoubt (Compans' and Dessaix's divisions), some to the left of the redoubt behind the village of Shevardino (Friant's Division); Ney's *3e Corps* to the left of Friant; Junot's *8e Corps* behind Ney's; Morand's Division (from Davout's Corps, together with Gérard's Division remained under the Viceroy's command), moving to the right bank of the Kolocha, was stationed forwards of the village of Alexinki; Nansouty's, Montbrun's and Latour-Maubourg's cavalry corps were forwards of Doronino:[38] all the troops of the centre were tasked to attack the Bagration *flèches* and the Kurgan battery. On the left wing, behind the Kolocha were: Gérard's Division, the Viceroy's *4e Corps*, the *Garde royale italienne* and Grouchy's *3e Corps de cavalerie*. The French *Garde impériale*, having crossed to the right bank of the Kolocha, positioned themselves behind Friant's Division, to the left of Doronino; Napoleon's headquarters was moved over the Kolocha before dawn and placed to the left of the Shevardino redoubt.[39]

And for our part, the whole day of 25 August [6 September] was spent in preparations for battle. Prince Kutuzov ordered the miraculous icon of the Madonna to be carried along the line of troops, which had been saved by the efforts of our soldiers during the enemy occupation of Smolensk and since then had constantly accompanied the Russian force. Just as had happened once before the Battle of Kulikovo, an army of 100,000 in orderly ranks greeted the face of their Intercessor. The clergy walked in rich robes, stopping from time to time and offered up prayers; the censer smoked, the candles glowed, the holy icon proceeded slowly; thousands of pious warriors fell to their knees, making the sign of the cross and praying with fervour. The Commander in Chief, surrounded by his entire staff, met the icon and bowed to the ground.[40] During that day, he rode up to some regiments and spoke to the soldiers: his words were quickly passed on through the army and strengthened the general readiness to lay down their lives in defence of Moscow and Russia.[41] Foreign historians write of a double ration of food and wine, allegedly issued to our soldiers on this day on Kutuzov's orders. Indeed, thanks to the energy of the good Russian

---

37 Chambray, II, 47-48.
38 Nothing reliable is known about the location of these corps, due to the conflicts between the sources available about this. For example, Schreckenstein says that Latour-Maubourg's Corps was stationed behind the intervals between Nansouty's and Montbrun's corps.
39 Chambray, II, 46.
40 Study of the Battle of Borodino, F.N. Glinka, I, 38-39.
41 Mikhailovsky-Danilevsky, II.

people and the proximity of Moscow, our troops had everything they needed in abundance at this time; but eyewitnesses say that many of the soldiers replied to the call of the quartermasters for a drink: 'we are not readying ourselves for that; not with a day such as tomorrow will be.'[42] Such was the general sentiment of the thoughts in our army: there was no despondency among them, but there was also no rowdy delight. The imminent battle, sacred in Russian terms, caused a solemn stillness and silence. Despite the dampness in the air, which penetrated to the bones of our warriors, they kindled their bivouac fires with seeming reluctance.

In contrast, in the enemy army, at night huge bonfires blazed throughout the area held by Napoleon's troops. Despite a lack of provisions, the French were excited by the hope of an end to the exertions and privations, which had beckoned them for so long, and was finally ready to be realised. Only those troops that had made their movements at night did not have time to build fires and spent the rest of the time lying on the damp ground, waiting for the battle.[43]

Such were the preparations for the greatest battle since the invention of gunpowder. There were 250,000 men, over 60,000 horses, and over 1,200 guns in the space of a square *Meile*. On the one side, there were warriors who came from the extreme limits of the west and south of Europe, for the most part experienced, who had participated in many battles, and at their head was the greatest commander of our time; on the other, there were warriors from every region of the vast Russian Empire, who had arrived from the Arctic Sea, the Urals and the Caspian, from distant Siberia and the Caucasus, inferior in combat experience to their opponents, but tempered by exertion and hardship and led by a commander in whom all of Russia had faith.

At three o'clock in the morning, Napoleon, after a short rest, in spite of a cold that he had felt since evening, again indulged in vigorous activity, which was a distinctive feature of his character. His first words were: 'What are the Russians doing?' Having heard in response that our troops remained in place, he was very pleased and, leaving his tent with the duty adjutant general Caulaincourt [Armand de Caulaincourt], he said to the officers who had gathered around him in a group: 'It is a little cold today, but it is clear: here comes the sun of Austerlitz.'[44]

At five o'clock, Napoleon mounted his horse and galloped to the right flank of the troops tasked with the main assault. All was ready. Orderlies with orders rushed in all directions. The army stood to arms; company and squadron commanders read the following order to the units entrusted to them:

> Soldiers! This is the battle you have been longing for. The victory depends upon you. It is essential for us; it will provide us with everything we need, comfortable quarters and a speedy return to the homeland. Behave as you did at Austerlitz, Friedland, Vitebsk and Smolensk. May posterity proudly remember your future exploits on this day. Let them say of each of you; he was in the great battle near Moscow!

---

42 Study of the Battle of Borodino, F.N. Glinka, I, 40-41.
43 Chambray, II, 52.
44 Fain, II, 16.

22

The Battle of Borodino

Napoleon's plan. – Napoleon and Kutuzov. – The bombardment at the beginning of the battle. – Davout's attack on the Bagration *flèches*. – Delzons' attack on Borodino. – The advance by Ney and the enemy *Réserve de cavalerie*. The reinforcement of our left wing. – The attacks by Ney, Davout and Murat on the Bagration *flèches*. – The arrival of Konovnitsyn with 3rd Division. – The bombardment of the high ground at Semenovskaya. – Bagration is severely wounded. – The final French occupation of the *flèches* and the Russian withdrawal to Semenovskaya. – The cavalry attack by Nansouty and Latour Maubourg. – The heroic resistance of the Lifeguard Izmailovsky and Lifeguard Lithuania (now Moscow) regiments. – The French occupation of Semenovskaya. – The situation on the left wing of our army.

Tuchkov 1st's deployment at the Utitsa *kurgan*. – Poniatowski's seizure of the *kurgan*. – The Viceroy's seizure of the Raevsky battery. – Yermolov's response. – Barclay de Tolly. – The death of Kutaisov. – The death of Monakhtin. – The flanking march of II Corps. – Operations by Prinz Eugen von Württemburg. – Tuchkov 1st's capture of the Utitsa *kurgan*. – Kutuzov's orders for an attack on the enemy left wing and for the reinforcement of our centre. – Napoleon's decision to renew the attack on the centre of our position.

Descriptions of pitched battles are, for the most part, incomplete and disappointing. The reasons for this are the very essence of a subject which requires the reconciliation of factors that conflict with, and even contradict each other. On the one hand, it is necessary to preserve the sequence and interdependent links between every action on the battlefield and the great drama, often deciding the fates of realms and nations; on the other hand, it must show the individual exploits of the many people who took part in it. It is necessary to observe consistency in creating an image of the actions of the various units of the forces, during every single moment of the battle, and to enter into details, without which the story of the battle is incomplete and colourless. And all this must be recreated, reproduced, from fragmentary, incoherent information passed on by eyewitnesses, in the heat of battle, under intense stress, from whom it is unreasonable to expect unbiased observations. Taking into account the influence of prejudices, which are not alien even to great people, the historian greets the testimony of eyewitnesses with incredulity, but they cannot do without their help, and therefore, having assumed the sacred duty of a priest of Truth, they are placed in the painful position of confirming that of which they themselves are not convinced. It is not only difficult, but almost impossible, to assess the relative impact on the outcome of a battle of: the decisions of a Commander in Chief, the resourcefulness of individual commanders, the firmness of the morale of the troops and, finally, the events that play such an important role in all battles. No less difficult is the precise calculation of time and space, on which the delivery of information to the Commander in Chief and formation commanders, passing it on to the troops and the execution of orders received, are based. Everything that we have said shows why clear descriptions of great battles are so rare and can at least partly explain why the battle of Borodino is presented not entirely satisfactorily even in the best works of military history.

The course of the Battle of Borodino, accordingly, may be divided into two parts: the first, from the beginning of the battle until the enemy's eventual occupation of the Bagration *flèches* and Semenovskaya, or from six o'clock in the morning until noon, and the second, which includes the enemy capture of the Raevsky battery and subsequent events until the end of the battle, or actions from noon to six o'clock in the evening.[1]

1. From the Beginning of the Battle Until the Enemy Occupation of the *Flèches* and Semenovskaya

Having opened the battle with an intensive bombardment directed at the Bagration *flèches*, the Raevsky and Borodino batteries, Napoleon planned to direct two main assaults, one on the *flèches*, the other on the Raevsky battery, while leaving a small part of the force facing Borodino and our right wing, for observation and for diversionary attacks. Poniatowski had been directed to move along the old Smolensk road and, having drawn level with the *flèches*, assault them from the flank. It has been said that Napoleon did not know about the transfer of Tuchkov 1st to the old Smolensk road and therefore sent Poniatowski along it, enveloping our left wing, while the other formations were going to move in sequence in waves from the right flank. The corps under Davout and Ney, supported by Junot's Westphalians, were to go straight at the Bagration *flèches*. The Viceroy was instructed, after waiting for the beginning of this attack, to take possession of Borodino, cross the Kolocha with most of his force and assault the Raevsky battery. The cavalry corps under Nansouty, Latour-Maubourg and Montbrun were tasked to support Davout and Ney; Grouchy's Corps was to follow the Viceroy's troops, while the *Garde impériale* were to remain in reserve.[2]

During the battle, Napoleon was located for the most part in front of the Shevardino redoubt, on the high ground, about a *verst* and a half from the front line

---

1 Hoffmann, *Die Schlacht von Borodino*, 48.
2 Bernhardi, *Denkwürdigkeiten des Grafen v. Toll*, II, 62-64. Chambray, II, 55-58. Soltyk, *Napoléon en 1812*, 212, 215 and 217.

of our force; the Bagration *flèches* were visible to his right; the Raevsky battery was to his left. The *Garde impériale* were stationed around him in full parade dress. Here he walked alongside the redoubt, together with his Chief of Staff, Berthier, stopping from time to time and sending out orders in various directions; all the movements of his *Grande armée* were made according to his orders, but many of those who had the chance to see Napoleon on this fateful day did not recognise him as the hero of Lodi and Wagram; the former determination was not noticeable in him; he did not appear, as he used to, wherever it was necessary for him to win over an uncertain victory in his favour. It is believed that the reasons for this were a cold and his fatigue on the eve of battle.[3]

Kutuzov set off at dawn from Tatarinovo to Gorki, where he stayed, together with General Bennigsen, until the very end of the battle.[4] Since the success of the battle was decided on the left wing and in the centre, our Commander in Chief would not have a direct influence on the course of the battle, especially since the debilitations of his age forced him to remain in one place the whole time and limit himself to issuing orders that, due to his distance from the locations of the decisive enemy assault, were not always timely. This factor, depriving our army of the essential unity of command, had an unfavourable effect on the course of the battle.[5]

In the morning, on the stroke of nine [sic, six] o'clock, the right French battery under General Sorbier, emplaced opposite our endmost *flèche*, having been driven up level with the batteries under General Pernety, opened fire together; thereafter, the bombardment by the left enemy battery under General Foucher, emplaced facing the right Bagration *flèche*, was heard. The operation of these 102 guns, due to their extreme range from our fortifications, achieved nothing, and therefore all the batteries were moved forward and, approaching our *flèches* at a range of about 1,600 paces, reopened the strong barrage once more. A few minutes later, shots were fired from a battery emplaced facing Borodino, and then in the centre. On our side, the guns stationed in the fortifications and the batteries pushed up to the same level as them responded to the enemy. Under the thunder of the mutual bombardment, the enemy infantry moved into the assault. Davout, leaving Friant's troops in reserve, marched towards the *flèches* with the other two divisions: Compans, having attached 30 guns stationed by their position to his infantry, moved to the right of Sorbier's battery, through the forest, while Dessaix moved somewhat to his left, along the edge of the forest. As the enemy troops were forced to form up in columns at a range of about 800 paces from our *flèches* upon leaving the forest, their spearheads were driven back into the forest several times, struck by canister from the artillery

---

3   Chambray, II, 65-66 and 77. Ségur, I, 391-392 and 421. Fain, II, 19-20.
4   See Plan of the battle of Borodino, 26 August (7 September). [F.N. Glinka's eyewitness account states that Bennigsen did not remain with Kutuzov all day, rather that he: 'appeared on the left flank wherever the fighting was hottest' and added that, in the midst of the battle, 'Bennigsen galloped from redoubt to redoubt (Semenovskaya), encouraging the troops'].
5   Hoffmann, 54. [Liprandi points out that Kutuzov's command post was not in Gorki, rather, about a *verst* behind the second echelon of VI Corps, and that Kutuzov briefly visited Gorki at around noon before returning to his command post. Liprandi points out that he had visited Kutuzov's command post repeatedly that day, and should be given more credence than Hoffmann].

under the command of Colonel Boguslavsky [Alexander Andreevich Boguslavsky], who was holding the *flèches*, and fire from the jägers, scattered in front of our position under Prince Shakhovskoy. After a bitter firefight, the French brigade under General Teste [François Antoine Teste] (*25e régiment de ligne* and *57e régiment de ligne*) managed to debouch from the forest and charged at the endmost *flèche*,[6] but at that very moment the brave Compans was seriously wounded by canister shot. Davout, having remained by Sorbier's battery and following the unfolding of events, noticing the wavering of the advancing troops, galloped towards them and taking direct command of Teste's Brigade, directed *57e régiment de ligne* against the endmost *flèche*. The French, emboldened by his presence, burst into our fortification, but Prince Bagration immediately pushed several battalions from 27th Division forwards to assist the grenadiers under Count Vorontsov, and they drove the enemy out of the *flèche*. The commander of IV Cavalry Corps, Major General Count Sievers, noticing the disorder among the French, sent Colonel Vasilchikov [Dmitry Vasilevich Vasilchikov] to pursue them with the Akhtyrka Hussars along with Major Terenin with the Novorossiya Dragoons, who cut into the enemy infantry and captured 12 guns, but did not have time to drag them away, because they were engaged and held up by the light cavalry brigades under Mourier [Pierre Mourier] and Beurmann [Frédéric Auguste de Beurmann]. However, despite the superiority of enemy numbers, our dragoons and hussars drove off *Nr. 4* Leib-Chevauxleger-Regiment *(Württemberg)* and Nr. 2 Leib-Chevauxleger-Regiment *(Württemberg)* and did not pull back behind the *flèches* until they were ordered to retreat. During this fighting, the following generals were seriously wounded: Dessaix and Teste. Marshal Davout, having suffered a severe contusion himself, fell from his horse as it was killed under him and was rescued from death by the soldiers surrounding him.[7] The loss to the French of all their main commanders, at the decisive moment of the assault, exacerbated the wavering in their ranks and prevented them from exploiting the success won at the beginning of the battle.[8]

Simultaneously with the beginning of the bitter fighting on the Semenovskaya high ground, the Viceroy attacked Borodino. At six o'clock in the morning, along with the opening of the bombardment, the troops of Delzons' Division [Alexis Joseph Delzons] were sent towards this location; *106e régiment de ligne* were leading. Taking advantage of the thick mist that covered the surroundings of the marshy Kolocha, the French approached Borodino and took the Lifeguard Jägers stationed there by surprise. While part of Delzons' Division was advancing along the highway, another crossed the Voinka upstream of Borodino and broke into the village from that direction from which we had not expected an attack at all. Despite the efforts of the valiant Colonel Bistrom [Karl Ivanovich Bistrom] to hold out in Borodino, the Lifeguard Jägers were driven out of there and retreated in disarray across the bridge over the Kolocha; *106e régiment de ligne* were hot on their heels and crossed

---

6   The left hand one, from our point of view.
7   Chambray, II, 61-62. Thiers, XIV, *Edit. de Brux*, 355 and 357-358. Fain, II, 20-21. Hoffmann, 49. Major General Count Sievers 1st's report to Prince Kutuzov, dated 26 September [8 October], No. 728. Notes on the battle of Borodino (Military Topographic Depot, No. 29,177).
8   Fain, II, 21-22. Gourgaud, *Examen critique de l'ouvrage du comte Ségur, Livre 7*, Chap. IX.

the river, emerging near Gorki. Barclay de Tolly, who was at the Gorki battery with his retinue at the time, directed 1st Jäger Regiment under Colonel Karpenko [Moses Ivanovich Karpenko] (11th Division) at the enemy together with the Jäger Brigade under Colonel Vuich [Nikolay Vasilevich Vuich] (19th Jägers and 40th Jägers from 24th Division).[9] The French, engaged frontally by the Lifeguard Jägers who had turned against them and attacked from the flanks by Karpenko and Vuich, were driven back, losing General of Brigade Plauzonne [Louis Auguste Marchand de Plauzonne], their commander, and retreated in disorder behind the Kolocha, under the protection of *92e régiment de ligne* who had come to help them.

Despite the short duration of this action, which had lasted no more than a quarter of an hour, the losses of our Lifeguard Jägers reached 30 officers and half of the lower ranks present.[10] Among those killed was one of the most outstanding officers of the General Staff, Colonel Gaverdovsky. Here is an appraisal of him by General Konovnitsyn, in a letter to his wife, dated 27 August [8 September]:

> I share my sorrow for my good comrade, for that glorious officer, for that man devoted to me. They have just brought me the horse of my superb Gaverdovsky: he has either been killed or captured. To discover for certain, I shall try to send a *parlementaire*. This has upset me so much! He served me in the vanguard so well!

Colonel Makarov [Pëtr Stepanovich Makarov] of the Lifeguard Jägers was among those wounded.

Our troops, having recaptured the bridge over the Kolocha, demolished it on the orders of Barclay. This work was carried out by the skirmishers of the Lifeguard Marines, under the command of Midshipman Lermontov [Mikhail Nikolaevich Lermontov], who, having been sent to the bridge in advance, had prepared it for destruction even before the enemy attack on Borodino. Thereafter the Viceroy, on the basis of the general plan of action, limited himself to the capture of Borodino. Delzons' Division and the Bavarian cavalry were stationed behind the village; a strong battery was positioned to the left of Borodino in order to bombard the high ground near Gorki and the Raevsky battery; while further to the left, in front of the village of Bezubovo, on the plains, was a light cavalry division under General d'Ornano [Philippe Antoine d'Ornano]; all the Viceroy's other troops, who remained near Borodino, were moved to their right, to the bridges over the Kolocha built upstream of Borodino, and crossed there to the right bank of the river under

---

9 [Liprandi laments the lack of references here as Barclay's report and Buturlin do not mention Karpenko's involvement but Mikhailovsky-Danilevsky does and Bogdanovich, despite including Barclay's report in the appendices, offers no evidence to back up his decision to include Kapenko's 1st Jägers].

10 [Liprandi adds: 'the Lifeguard Jägers, having occupied Borodino, were delighted to find a spacious bathhouse in this prosperous village, and were waiting to take turns to use it. An entire battalion was in the baths at the very moment the French attacked. This is the real reason for the loss of 30 officers and half of the men. Many, leaping out of the baths, only managed to don their cartridge pouch and grab a musket, and went into action just so. Several were found dead in this order of dress. The whole army knew of this unfortunate incident'].

cover of the marksmen from Morand's Division, who had started a heated firefight with our jägers at the foot of the Raevsky mound.[11]

Meanwhile, Napoleon, having received a report of the wounding of Compans, sent his Adjutant General Rapp [Jean Rapp] to replace him, but even before his arrival, General Duppelin, who had taken command of Compans' force, was wounded. Soon afterwards, Rapp was also hit. Sorbier, who was with Davout at the very time moment he fell from his horse, believed he had died and rode to Napoleon with the news of the death of the marshal. Napoleon, stunned by this report, did not say a word, but a few minutes later sent an order to Murat to take command of the troops of *1er Corps*; but the King of Naples, on his arrival there, found Davout, despite the severe contusion he had received, ready to mount his horse once more and resume the assault. Napoleon, having learned of this from an officer reporting to him, was extremely pleased; but even earlier, at the first report of the difficulties encountered by Davout's force during the assault on the *flèches*, he had ordered Ney to assist *1er Corps* with *3e Corps*. At seven o'clock, Ney's force advanced through the village of Shevardino: Ledru's Division [François Roch Ledru des Essarts] was leading, with those of Marchand [Jean Gabriel Marchand] and Razout [Louis-Nicolas de Razout] following. The former was deployed in four waves, each of the first three consisted of a regiment in battalion columns, while in the third wave, a regiment advanced in a single column, formed from battalions in line, placed one behind the other. Following that, at about half-past seven, Junot's *8e Corps* edged forwards and settled to the left of Shevardino. At the same time, the cavalry set out from their overnight camp to support the assault by *1er Corps* and *3e Corps*; the corps light cavalry brigades and Nansouty's Corps followed Davout's Corps, while Latour-Maubourg's Corps followed Ney's; the corps under Montbrun followed up behind and somewhat to the left of Latour-Maubourg, in order to maintain communications between Ney and the Viceroy.[12]

Prince Bagration, watching the advance by Ney's force, which threatened an intensive assault on our left wing, took measures to counter the enemy. Neverovsky's 27th Division occupied the *flèches* together with Count Vorontsov's grenadiers; eight battalions from Raevsky's Corps were directed to their left to support the defence of the *flèches*; Prince Carl zu Mecklenburg's 2nd Grenadier Division was positioned to the left of Semenovskaya, while Duka's 2nd Cuirassier Division was to the left of the grenadiers; all the batteries held in reserve were pushed forward to the front line. Prince Bagration, correctly calculating that this force would be insufficient to repulse the superior enemy numbers, ordered Tuchkov 1st (despite the fact that III Corps was not under his command), to detach Konovnitsyn's 3rd Division to assist him and sent a request to Barclay de Tolly to reinforce the left wing with some of the

---

11 Description of the operations of First Army (Barclay de Tolly). Major General Löwenstern's notes. Chambray, II, 63. Hoffmann, 51. Thiers, XIV, 356-357. Bernhardi, II, 65-66.
12 Bernhardi, II, 67-68. *Stellung der Franzosen* (see the Legend of the Borodino battle at the end of volume two). According to Schreckenstein, between the corps under Latour-Maubourg and the Viceroy there was a significant area devoid of troops, *Die Kavallerie in der Schlacht and der Moskwa*, 50.

troops from First Army.¹³ Barclay ordered II Corps to be transferred from the right flank of the position to assist Tuchkov 1st (probably having reported the orders he had issued to Kutuzov), and after that, upon a second request from Prince Bagration, the following regiments were sent to Semenovskaya from the reserve: Lifeguard Izmailovsky, Lifeguard Lithuania, and Lifeguard Finland, His Majesty's Cuirassiers, Her Majesty's Cuirassiers and Astrakhan Cuirassiers from 1st Cuirassier Division, eight combined grenadier battalions, His Highness' Lifeguard Battery Artillery Company, Count Arakcheev's Lifeguard Battery Artillery Company and 1st Lifeguard Horse Artillery Battery under Colonel Kozen [Pëtr Andreevich Kozen].¹⁴ But it took between 1½ to 2 hours to deliver the orders from the Commander-in-Chief to these troop formations and for the arrival of these reinforcements on the left wing, while the troops under Davout and Ney were already preparing to resume the assault.

Meanwhile, from the very beginning of the battle, the bombardment of the *flèches* did not let up for a single moment, Ney's Corps, on the stroke of eight o'clock, attacked Bagration's troops. The enemy was greeted with the fiercest canister and musket fire, but continued to advance. Ney, at the head of *24e régiment léger* himself, in conjunction with *57e régiment de ligne* (from Compans' Division), captured the leftmost *flèche*; the other regiments of Ledru's Division broke into our right-hand *flèche*. Only then did they notice our third *flèche*, constructed behind the fortifications they had taken, and drove our grenadiers out of it. Hand-to-hand combat ensued; Count Vorontsov was seriously wounded by a bayonet,¹⁵ the grenadier battalions under his command were wiped out. As Vorontsov stated in describing his actions at Borodino: 'My resistance would not last long, but it did not stop until after the destruction of my division.' At nine o'clock, Prince Bagration ordered the entire 27th Division under Neverovsky to retake the *flèches* and directed four battalions from 12th Division, the grenadiers under Prince zu Mecklenburg, Duka's 2nd Cuirassier Division and the following regiments of Count Sievers IV Cavalry Corps

---

13 Prince Bagration asked for help directly from Barclay de Tolly, and not via Kutuzov, probably to save time. Anyone who is at all familiar with the practice of military operations knows how the execution of orders is sometimes delayed by the untimely re-transmission of orders.

14 With regard to the reinforcements sent from the reserve to assist the left wing, the sources vary. Toll's original notes state that Prince Kutuzov sent three regiments from 1st Cuirassier Division, eight guns from the Lifeguard Horse Artillery, Lifeguard Izmailovsky and Lifeguard Lithuania regiments, His Highness' Battery Company and Count Arakcheev's Battery Company. Buturlin gives the combined grenadier brigade in addition to these troops, who are also mentioned in Commander V Corps, Lieutenant General Lavrov's report to General Dokhturov, dated 3 [15] September, No. 1116 (M.T.D. No. 29,177). The History of the Lifeguard Finland Regiment, compiled by Marin, mentions the transfer of this regiment to the left wing, at the very beginning of the Battle of Borodino. Bernhardi calculated the following force: Lifeguard Izmailovsky, Lifeguard Lithuania and Lifeguard Finland regiments, eight battalions of combined grenadiers and both Lifeguard Battery Artillery companies, *Denkwürdigkeiten des Grafen v. Toll*, II, 69.

15 [According to Mikhail Antonovich Markus, who was serving as Divisional Surgeon in General Neverovsky's 27th Division: 'Count Vorontsov suffered a gunshot wound to the thigh; the ball penetrated deep, as far as the femoral artery, but did not damage it, because, when dressing the Count's wound in the battery, I pulled the ball out with tongs, and then with my finger in the depths of the wound I could feel the artery pulsing'].

to engage the enemy: Novorossiya Dragoons, Akhtyrka Hussars and Lithuania Ulans, with five horse artillery pieces; on the French side, the light cavalry under Beurmann and Bruyère [Jean Pierre Joseph Bruguière, *dit* Bruyère] were sent to help Davout and Ney. As soon as the Russian infantry moved forward to retake the lost *flèches*, Murat led the Württemberg chevauxleger (Beurmann's Brigade) to engage our troops, who, being attacked by Duka's cuirassiers, were driven off; our cavalry, pursuing the enemy, burst into the earthworks behind them and drove the French infantry out of there. The Novorossiya Dragoons (or, according to other sources, Duka's cuirassiers) captured a horse artillery battery that had accompanied the chevauxleger of Beurmann's Brigade, but did not have chance to drag them away. Murat, surrounded by our cuirassiers, barely escaped captivity himself, dismounting from his horse and finding refuge in our left-hand *flèche*, at that time still held by one of the Württemberg battalions. Following this, our cuirassiers captured six French horse artillery pieces from Nansouty's Corps, but, on being attacked by *6e régiment de lanciers polonais* [6 Pułk Ułanów] (Bruyère's Division), they were forced to abandon their trophies.[16] At around ten o'clock, after a new, desperate battle, in which Prince Gorchakov and Neverovsky were wounded, Ney's troops took possession of the *flèches* once more; but at that precise moment Konovnityn's 3rd Division was just approaching the high ground at Semenovskaya. His troops, with support from the Sumy Hussars, Mariupol Hussars, Courland Dragoons and Orenburg Dragoons from III Cavalry Corps, under the command of Major General Dorokhov [Ivan Semënovich Dorokhov], sent by Barclay to assist the left wing,[17] ignoring the fierce fire from the enemy batteries, charged with fixed bayonets and with loud cheers of 'Hurrah', overwhelmed the French and drove them out of the *flèches*.[18]

As early as nine o'clock, Napoleon, having received a report that our *flèches* had been taken by Ney's troops, and believing that they no longer needed the assistance of the Westphalian *8e Corps*, ordered Junot to move between Davout and Poniatowski, in order to maintain communications between the assaults directed on the *flèches* and on Utitsa. But soon after that an officer rode up with news of Ney's repulse and with a request to support him with fresh troops. Napoleon did not make up his mind to do this for some time, he consulted with Berthier and eventually instructed the officer to convey orders to Claparède [Michel Marie Claparède] – to advance with the *Légion de la Vistule* to assist Ney. But as soon as the officer was about to

---

16 Major General Count Sievers' report to Prince Kutuzov, dated 26 September [8 October], No. 278 (M.T.D. No. 29,177). Bernhardi, II, 70-71. Hoffmann, 50.
17 Buturlin, I, 330. However, General Kreutz's notes state that the Orenburg Dragoons were under his command, in the centre of our position.
18 Hoffmann, 50. Lieutenant General Konovnitsyn's report to Prince Kutuzov, dated 19 September [1 October], No. 57. '... the Chernigov Infantry, Murom Infantry, Reval Infantry and Selenginsk Infantry from 3rd Division, even before that, were demanded on the left flank of Second Army, as reinforcements for General of Infantry Prince Bagration, where, having arrived, they were immediately used to seize the vital high ground held by the enemy. This was accomplished with complete success. The above mentioned regiments, disdainful of the absolute brutality of the enemy fire, charged with fixed bayonets and upon the shout of 'Hurrah', overwhelmed the superior enemy, which led to extreme confusion in their columns, and reoccupied the high ground so stubbornly defended from the very beginning of the battle.'

head off in the direction where Claparède's troops were stationed, Napoleon called him back and, in consultation with his Chief of Staff, ordered Friant's Division to reinforce Ney. Through such indecision, more than half an hour was lost and it was already 11 o'clock before Friant's force moved from their place, which no doubt had a detrimental effect on the success of the operations by the enemy army.[19]

With the arrival of Friant's Division on the scene of the fighting, the enemy had about 26,000 infantry facing the high ground at Semenovskaya, not counting the troops fighting to their right in the scrub, against 18,000 Russians. Huge batteries were deployed on both sides; the bombardment was as continuous as the most rapid combat fire, and at times merged into a rumble, from which the whole neighbourhood shook. Here, Colonel Kozen's 1st Lifeguard Light Horse Artillery Battery distinguished itself in particular, operating with great success for more than two hours against Junot's troops, who were attempting to outflank our *flèches* on their left side. This battery, having lost 60 men (including the valiant Captain Zakharov, who was mortally wounded by shell splinters), was withdrawn to the reserve.[20] The troops of both sides, vying with each other in self-sacrifice, suffered enormous losses, but we were destined to experience the most painful loss: the main defender of the *flèches* fell, the hero, Bagration, 'a general in the image and likeness of Suvorov,' as Count Rostopchin called him.[21] Hit in the leg by canister shot, which shattered his tibia, he fell from his horse and was carried away as if dead;[22] the Chief of staff of Second Army Saint-Priest, having received a severe contusion, was forced to retire from the battlefield. Among those killed was the commander of the combined grenadier brigade attached to V Corps, Prince Kantakouzen [Nikolay Yegorovich Kantakouzen], who had recaptured several of our guns taken by the enemy. General Konovnitsyn, after the evacuation of Prince Bagration, being the senior general with the troops defending the high ground at Semenovskaya, invited Raevsky, who was in the centre of our position, to take command of Second Army and sent a request to Prince Kutuzov to support him with fresh troops. The Commander in Chief, already aware of the efforts made by the enemy against our centre, and concerned about weakening it by detaching troops to the left wing, refused reinforcements. Then, turning to Prinz Alexander von Württemberg [Alexander Friedrich Karl von Württemberg], who was in his retinue, Kutuzov offered him command of Second Army, but before the Prinz managed to reach the left wing, command of Second Army had been entrusted to General Dokhturov. At the same time, Kutuzov sent Toll there to find out about the progress of the battle.[23]

---

19 Fain, II, 24-25. Chambray, II, 65-66. Chambray states that Ney asked for reinforcements later, namely, after Baggovut's arrival on the left wing of our position.
20 Extracted from History of the Lifeguard Artillery compiled by Ratch (manuscript).
21 [Liprandi points out that Bagration looked nothing like Suvorov, concluding: 'it is also without a reference through which the Gentleman Professor could have absolved his responsibility for this awkward expression'].
22 [Prince N.B. Golitsyn, who was an orderly for Prince Bagration, described this moment as follows: 'At 11 o'clock in the morning, a fragment from a shell struck our beloved General in the leg and knocked him from his horse.' Prince Golitsyn is a most reliable witness because he took the wounded general to Sima where Prince Bagration died on 14 September, new style. Notes On The Campaigns Of 1812, 1813 And 1814, page 16].
23 Bernhardi, II, 78. Toll's original notes.

Meanwhile, the courageous Konovnitsyn had exhausted every effort by the troops to hold the enemy, who, for their part, desperately stormed the high ground at Semenovskaya. The rumble of guns, the shouts of the commanders, the cheers of victory, the groans of the wounded, merging with the firefight and the clash of cold steel, called to mind the apocalypse. A participant in the Battle of Borodino, General Pelet [Jean-Jacques Germain Pelet-Clozeau], describing the memorable battle at the *flèches*, stated:

> As reinforcements approached Bagration's troops, they marched forward with the greatest courage, over the corpses of the fallen, to recapture the lost positions. Russian columns, in our line of sight, advanced, under the orders of their commanders, like moving ramparts glinting with steel and flame. Over open ground, struck by our canister fire, attacked either by cavalry or by infantry, they suffered enormous losses, but these brave warriors, having summoned the last of their last strength, attacked us as before.[24]

At about 11 o'clock, the French, having been driven out of the *flèches* by our troops, made a desperate effort, took possession of the *flèches* once more and captured the guns emplaced in them; but not for long. Lieutenant General Borozdin 1st led a bayonet charge with the Kiev Grenadiers, Astrakhan Grenadiers, Siberia Grenadiers and Moscow Grenadiers, supported by regiments from 3rd Division, overwhelmed the enemy and pushed them back as far as the forest. In this courageous exploit, the following casualties were taken on our side: Shatilov [Ivan Yakovlevich Shatilov], Colonel of the Moscow Grenadiers [wounded] and Buxhoeveden [Ivan Filippovich Buxhoeveden], Colonel of the Astrakhan Grenadiers, who, having suffered three wounds, continued to advance and fell dead in the battery we had just recaptured. Other wounded included Prince Carl zu Mecklenburg and colonels Driesen [Fëdor Vasilevich Drizen or Friedrich Wilhelm von der Osten-Driesen] and Ushakov [Ivan Mikhailovich Ushakov]. From the French side, the Chief of Staff of *1er corps*, Romeuf [Jean-Louis Romeuf], was mortally wounded. The enemy, despite the losses they had suffered, attacked the Semenovskaya fortifications again and drove our troops out of there, at about half-past eleven. Right at that moment, Toll, having passed Semenovskaya, encountered the Colonel in Chief of the Reval Regiment, Major General Tuchkov 4th [Alexander Alexeevich Tuchkov], who, shortly thereafter, was mortally wounded by round shot.[25] The enemy, having finally conquered the *flèches*, forced us to retreat behind the Semenovskaya ravine, where Konovnitsyn rallied the remnants of the troops defending the high ground, under the covering fire of powerful batteries and the Lifeguard Izmailovsky, Lifeguard Lithuania (now Lifeguard Moscow) and Lifeguard Finland regiments posted along the ravine. 3rd Division was located to the left of the village of Semenovskaya, resting their left flank

---

24 Pelet. *Bataille de la Moscowa*.
25 [Liprandi comments that the day after the battle, officers of the Reval Infantry told him that Tuchkov 4th was killed outright by a bullet to the forehead through his hat, and that his aide de camp, Miller, who was also wounded by a bullet, was killed by round shot as he was being carried away].

on the Lifeguard; the remnants of 2nd Grenadier Division and 27th Division were placed to the right of the village.[26]

After taking the *flèches*, Ney, with the assistance of Friant's Division, attacked 2nd Grenadier Division, which was holding Semenovskaya, but was repulsed.[27] Thereafter Murat, in consultation with Ney, decided to commit a huge mass of cavalry to action: Nansouty was ordered to attack our infantry to the right of Semenovskaya, with Saint-Germain's [Antoine Louis Decrest de Saint-Germain] and Valence's [Jean-Baptiste Cyrus de Timbrune de Thiembronne de Valence] cuirassiers, while Latour-Maubourg, having crossed the Kamenka, was directed to the left of the village, with Rozniecki's [Aleksander Antoni Jan Rożniecki] and Lorge's [Jean Thomas Guillaume Lorge] divisions. Davout and Ney, having the facilitation of the success of the cavalry in mind, advanced strong batteries to the very edge of the Semenovskaya ravine, whose fire was all the more destructive because the left bank of the Semenovka upstream of the village continuously dominates the right and that the enemy position, wrapping around ours, contributed to the French artillery operations with a crossfire. Our troops, stationed forwards of Semenovskaya, were partially protected by a low ridge upon which part of the village lay, but on the other hand, having retreated to the reverse slope of this high ground, they could not fire effectively down the forward slope, which made it easier for the enemy to cross the ravine; conversely our troops, which were to the left of Semenovskaya, were completely in the open and exposed to the fire of enemy batteries located on the commanding high ground, at a distance of no more than 600 paces from our position. To give an idea of the extent to which our troops suffered losses at this point, it is enough to say that the Lifeguard Lithuania Regiment, in the course of about an hour, lost 956 out of 1,740 men, and that only a couple of horses each remained with many of our guns.[28]

This was the situation of the Russian troops in position at Semenovskaya, as the enemy directed a cavalry attack upon them. The ground trembled under several thousand horsemen, led into battle by the dashing Murat. Nansouty, having crossed the Semenovka upstream of the village, with the cuirassiers under Saint-Germain and with Breuyère's light cavalry division, at a point where the banks of the ravine are very flat, was engaged by the fiercest fire of our batteries. At the same time the Lifeguard Izmailovsky and Lifeguard Lithuania regiments, lining the ravine on the left wing, under the command of Colonel Khrapovitsky [Matvey Yevgrafovich Khrapovitsky], formed themselves into six squares, in one of which was Konovnitsyn himself.[29] These outstanding infantrymen, weakened but not disordered by the devastating enemy bombardment, delivered rapid fire on the enemy horsemen and repelled their attack. The formidable cuirassiers, whom Napoleon nicknamed the iron men (*hommes de fer*), supported by light cavalry, attacked our guardsmen twice

---

26 Toll's original notes. Buturlin, I, 330-331. Bernhardi, II, 80.
27 Bernhardi, II, 81.
28 Bernhardi, II, 88-92. Beitzke, 203-206. Colonel Udom's report to General Konovnitsyn, dated 31 August [12 September], No. 462.
29 The remnants of the combined grenadier brigade stood in clumps between the Lifeguard squares (History of the Lifeguard Izmailovsky Regiment, 173).

more, and each time they were repulsed. These attacks, during which the French artillery stopped firing, were like a break for our infantry, who proceeded to litter the field with enemy corpses and did not suffer the slightest damage from the cavalry raids. The soldiers of the Lifeguard Lithuania Regiment, carried away by success, lunged at the enemy cavalry with their bayonets, shouting 'Hurrah!' Their success was greatly facilitated by 1st Light Artillery Company and both Lifeguard battery artillery companies. So long as the enemy went on the attack and there was no danger of hitting our own, our gunners fired; as the stormy waves of the cuirassiers crashed against the granite squares, and the scattered horsemen, losing direction in the heat of battle, burst into the batteries, then the gun crews fought them off with rammers, knocking their adversaries off their horses with deft blows. Meanwhile, our 2nd Cuirassier Division, following the fighting on the high ground at Semenovskaya, having retreated to the edge of the forest, had managed to recover; as soon as the enemy cavalry turned back, they were pursued and caught by Major General Kretov [Nikolay Vasilevich Kretov], with the Military Order Cuirassiers and Yekaterinoslav Cuirassiers. After that, on the left flank of the Lifeguard Izmailovsky and Lifeguard Lithuania regiments, in the forest, a skirmish began, during which the enemy began to smash our troops with artillery once more. It was here that colonels Khrapovitsky and Kozlyaninov [Ivan Timofeevich Kozlyaninov], who was commanding the Lifeguard Izmailovsky Regiment that day, were hit by canister fire, and the commander of the Lifeguard Lithuania Regiment, Udom [Ivan Fëdorovich Udom], was wounded by a musket ball.[30]

Latour-Maubourg encountered considerably greater difficulties while advancing across the ravine, and therefore entered the battle a little later than Nansouty, but with more success. His cavalry crossed the Semenovka in two columns: with Lorge's Division on the right (with eight Saxon squadrons from the Saxon *Garde du Corps* and *Kürassier Regiment von Zastrow*, two Polish squadrons from *14 Pułk Kirasjerów* under Małachowski [Stanisław Małachowski] and eight Westphalian squadrons from *1. Westfälisches Kürassier-Regiment* and *2. Westfälisches Kürassier-Regiment*), while on the left was Rozniecki's *4e division de cavalerie légère*, of three Polish lancer regiments, consisting of 12 squadrons. The advance over the boggy bed of the Semenovka forced the riders to break ranks and move in single file via those parts where it was less marshy. But our artillery, having moved away from the edge of the ravine, could not hit the enemy effectively, and only a few round shot, by chance, hit the long columns stretching across the Semenovka. The leading elements of the cavalry, which consisted of Saxons, having climbed the reverse slope of the ravine, saw, a few hundred paces away, near the ruins of Semenovskaya, a battery under escort from the remnants of 2nd Grenadier Division, which, at that very moment, was being reformed into three squares. Whereupon General Thielmann [Johann Adolf von Thielmann], who commanded the Saxon cuirassiers, decided to immediately charge into the attack with the two and a half squadrons that had managed to

---

30 Toll's original notes. Reports by the regimental commanders: Colonel Udom of the Lifeguard Lithuania Regiment, and Colonel Kutuzov of the Lifeguard Izmailovsky Regiment (M.T.D. No. 29,177). History of the Lifeguard Artillery, compiled by Ratch (manuscript). History of the Lifeguard Izmailovsky Regiment.

cross the ravine; the rest were ordered, as they emerged over the lip of the ravine, to deploy to the left, eventually to go on the attack: thus the advance took the form of echelons from the right flank. Our grenadiers, weakened by the previous fighting, were overrun, while Sievers' dragoons, who rushed to help them, also could not hold off the *Sächsische Garde du Corps*, who, although they were engaged at 400 paces by canister fire from 2nd Lifeguard Light Artillery Company, which was under the command of Lieutenant Stolypin [Afanasy Alexeevich Stolypin], nevertheless raced past Semenovskaya and galloped off behind the Lifeguard Izmailovsky and Lifeguard Lithuania squares. But at this very moment, General Borozdin 2nd attacked the Saxon cuirassiers with His Majesty's Cuirassiers, Her Majesty's Cuirassiers and Astrakhan Cuirassiers; Thielmann himself fought against our horsemen; eventually, the issue here was decided by an attack on the enemy flank by the Akhtyrka Hussar Regiment (armed with lances, according to Shreckenstein and Bernhardi). Lorge's Division was forced to retreat behind the crest of the high ground. The wounded on the enemy side included the Westphalian General of Brigade Lepel [Eugen August Hellmuth von Lepel], whose arm was torn off by round shot just as Latour-Maubourg's troops were advancing from the Kamenka to the Semenovka ravine. During the cavalry battle, Friant resumed the assault on the ruins of Semenovskaya, with *15e régiment légère* and *48e régiment de ligne*, took possession of them and was seriously wounded. His force established themselves on the right bank of the Semenovka, forcing the remnants of our infantry, who had previously defended the *flèches*, to retreat out of effective cannon range from the ravine. Only the Lifeguard Izmailovsky, Lifeguard Lithuania and Lifeguard Finland regiments were holding out at the edge of the forest on the upper Semenovka.[31]

After occupying Semenovskaya, Ney deployed strong batteries, which opened fire frontally against our left wing and into the flank of the troops stationed in the centre of the position.

The left wing of our army was completely disordered. Barclay de Tolly wrote:

> Second Army, in the absence of the wounded Prince Bagration and many generals, was driven back in the greatest disorder; all the fortifications had fallen to the enemy with some of the batteries. Only 26th Division still held its position near the high ground forwards of the centre; they had repulsed the enemy twice; this happened at around 11 o'clock. The infantry was scattered in small groups, already rallied by the headquarters on the Mozhaisk road; the three Lifeguard regiments had retreated in good order and were nearing the other Lifeguard regiments...[32]

Fortunately, the thick dust that had risen in a pillar during the cavalry attacks, and the smoke from numerous artillery fires, of which most (as was reported, some 700 guns) were concentrated by both sides in the vicinity of Semenovskaya, prevented the enemy from seeing to what extent the left wing of our army had been weakened

---

31 Chambray, 66-67. Bernhardi, II 89-92. Schreckenstein, 51-73. History of the Lifeguard Artillery, compiled by Ratch.
32 Extracted from Operations by First Army (compiled by Barclay de Tolly).

and disordered. Davout, Ney and Murat, whose troops had also suffered huge losses, considered themselves no longer able to exploit their successes, and, halting at Semenovskaya, they again sent requests to Napoleon for reinforcements from his fresh forces. Napoleon, who comprehended, albeit too late, the difficulty of the feat he had undertaken, did not want to deplete his reserves, hesitated, and eventually sent forward *2e division de la Jeune Garde* under General Roguet [François Roguet], however, ordering them to halt at the Kamenka.[33]

Meanwhile, on the old Smolensk road and in the centre of our position, the advantage switched first to one side, then to the other.

In accordance with the overall plan of action by Napoleon, Poniatowski set out from his overnight camp at five o'clock in order to attack our left wing from the flank upon the first shots. But his advance along the rough tracks through the forest was so slow that, despite the urgings of Napoleon, who constantly sent orderlies to him, one after another, Krasiński's *16e Division* [Izydor Zenon Tomasz Krasiński], marching at the head of the Polish *5e Corps*, did not reach the highway until eight o'clock. These troops, under covering fire from several guns, captured the village of Utitsa, held by our jägers; but having encountered 1st Grenadier Division behind Utitsa, in front of whom strong batteries had been emplaced, they halted. Tuchkov, taking advantage of the enemy inaction, pulled his force back and placed them in a more advantageous position, near a high mound, upon which, due to the confines of the crest, only four heavy guns could be placed; to the right, at the foot of the mound were the Leib-Grenadier Regiment and Count Arakcheev's Grenadier Regiment; behind them, in reserve, was the Pavlov Grenadier Regiment; to the left of the mound were the Yekaterinoslav Grenadier Regiment and St Petersburg Grenadier Regiment, between whom was a battery of 12 guns. The Tauride Grenadier Regiment was very much detached to the right to hold the scrub, together with four regiments of jägers under Prince Shakhovskoy and two (49th Jägers and 50th Jägers) detached from Neverovsky's 27th Division, who helped the jägers to hold out in the scrub for about two hours against the skirmishers from Davout's *1er Corps* and the Polish *5e Corps*. Behind III Corps, on both sides of the highway, were the warriors of the Moscow *opolchenie*, armed, for the most part, with pikes. Meanwhile, Poniatowski, not knowing about the departure of Konovnitsyn's Division to the high ground at Semenovskaya, did not dare to go forward for some time, out of concern for being enveloped on his left flank and cut off from the French army. It was only at about half-past ten, before Junot's troops, having entered the forest, began a bitter fight with our jägers, Poniatowski, placing a battery of forty guns to the right of Utitsa, brought both his divisions into action, pushed Tuchkov 1st back and took possession of the mound that served as the keystone of our left flank. Tuchkov's troops withdrew a short distance in anticipation of reinforcements moving from the right flank.[34]

---

33 Hoffmann, 53. Bernhardi, II, 94.
34 Hoffmann, 52-53 and 58. Bernhardi, II, 73. In his report to Prince Kutuzov, Konovnitsyn wrote that Tuchkov 1st withdrew towards the mound even before the attack upon him, and that the mound had six guns on it, from Colonel Glukhov's company.

The Viceroy, for his part, led the attack on the Kurgan battery in the centre of our position. The defence of this fortification was entrusted to General Raevsky, who, having sent his jäger regiments forward and detached, at the request of Prince Bagration, his entire support line (eight battalions) to the high ground at Semenovskaya, placed the rest of the troops in the shallow ravine behind the fortification, as follows: on the right of the battery, four battalions from 26th Division under Paskevich's command, on the left, four more battalions from 12th Division under Vasilchikov's command, such that, once the enemy troops attacked, he could strike them on both flanks; also dispatched to assist Raevsky were 19th Jägers and 40th Jägers from VI Corps, and 18th Jägers from IV Corps, under Colonel Vuich's command, who were also placed in the ravine behind the battery.[35] Forwards of the battery, almost at the very start of the battle, a stubborn firefight ensued between our jägers, who held the scrub at the foot of the mound, on the far bank of the Semenovka, and Morand's skirmishers. Broussier's *14e Division* [Jean-Baptiste Broussier], having crossed the Kolocha, also took part in this action; the enemy set up strong batteries and, inflicting heavy casualties on our jägers, forced them to retreat across the river towards the mound. Broussier's *14e Division* followed them and formed up in the ravine between Borodino and the mound; Morand's *1re Division* advanced straight at the battery; Gérard with his *3e Division* was left in reserve across the river, while Montbrun's *2e corps de cavalerie* was ordered to cross it to the right of Morand and assist his attack. At ten o'clock, Broussier attempted to take possession of the battery, but being repulsed, he retreated into the ravine in order to reorganise his troops. After this failure, the enemy, intending to succeed with a new attack following an artillery preparation, intensified the bombardment against our battery and had already renewed the attack by 11 o'clock with Morand's troops. Bonnamy's Brigade [Charles-Auguste Bonnamy de Bellefontaine] (*30e régiment de ligne* and *badischen 2. Infanterieregiment*, for a total of seven battalions), at the head of the advancing column, rushed at the battery; its attack was facilitated by the fact that we did not have enough artillery ammunition and our guns were forced to slacken their fire at this most decisive moment. The French charged at these guns and took them, driving their escorts from the fortification and pushing them behind the Gorki ravine.[36] Thus, the enemy captured one of the most important points of the Borodino position; our line was broken, and had the troops under the Viceroy consolidated on the mound and pressed on in considerable strength, we would have been placed in a perilous position. Already Morand, witnessing the success of his leading troops, hastened to support them with artillery and several infantry columns. But before he had chance to close up to the mound, things took a new, favourable turn for us.[37]

---

35 Raevsky's report to Dokhturov, dated 11 [23] September, No. 280. Raevsky's letter to General Jomini, about the battle of Borodino. Bernhardi states, that Paskevich, to whom the immediate defence of the redoubt was entrusted, had the Poltava Infantry occupy the ditch in front of the battery; of the others, the Nizhegorod Infantry and Orël Infantry were to the right, while the Ladoga Infantry were to the left of the battery; 18th Jägers (from IV Corps), and later, 19th Jägers and 40th Jägers (from VI Corps) were in reserve. Finally, the jäger regiments from VII Corps were defending the foot of the mound.
36 [Liprandi suggests this should read 'towards the Gorki ravine'].
37 Hoffmann, 51-52. Bernhardi, II, 84-85. Fain, II, 25. Thiers, XIV, 362-363.

The main instigator for this was the Chief of Staff of First Army, General Yermolov. Shortly before then, Prince Kudashev [Nikolay Danilovich Kudashev] had ridden up to Kutuzov, on the right wing of the position, with the news of the dangerous situation of Second Army (at that point, Prince Bagration had already been wounded). The Commander-in-Chief said to Yermolov, who was with him at the time: 'My dear fellow, see if there is anything you can do to encourage the army.' Yermolov immediately set off in that direction and, meeting Colonel Nikitin [Alexey Petrovich Nikitin] on the way, invited him to assist in the defence of the left wing. Yermolov told him: 'Teska, take three horse artillery companies with you, and do not lose sight of me.' A few minutes later the guns came up (according to Nikitin himself, two horse artillery companies), and rode after Yermolov. At that very moment, Count Kutaisov [Alexander Ivanovich Kutaisov] accosted him and, having learned about the instructions given to him, expressed a desire to accompany them. It has been said that Yermolov wanted to refuse Kutaisov's suggestion, but could not dissuade him. While both generals were riding side by side across the open ground, Yermolov noticed an extraordinary commotion to his right around Raevsky's battery. Our troops, driven back by the enemy, were streaming from there in complete disorder. The perceptive Yermolov instantly realised that, having literally completed the mission given to him, that is, riding to the left flank, he could not achieve better results than could be brought by holding the enemy in the centre of the position. The horse artillery was ordered to deploy in line to the right, facing the lost battery, and open fire on the French, who had not yet had chance to look around in the fortification and could not use the guns they had captured against us, due to the lack of ammunition with them; Yermolov, grabbing the first organised unit that had come across, Third Battalion, Ufa Infantry, under Major Demidov [Flegont Pavlovich Demidov], led him directly at the battery himself. This battalion, standing to the right of Raevsky's troops, at the edge of First Army, had not been attacked by the enemy and stood in column at immediate readiness for action. But Yermolov, wishing to slow down and bring back the crowd that was fleeing towards them from the mound, deployed the battalion into line, led it forward and, rallying the fugitives, raced with them at the Frenchmen who had captured the mound. Yermolov stated in his own report:

> On this high ground, which commanded the entire area upon which both armies were located, 18 guns had been acquired by the enemy, and were too important a factor not to make a try for, to recover the losses. I took it on. I needed to be audacious and to my good fortune, I succeeded. Taking only Third Battalion, Ufa Infantry Regiment, I also stopped the fleeing crowd, forming them into a column, and charged with bayonets fixed. The enemy defended themselves desperately, their batteries made terrible execution, but nothing could stop us. Third Battalion, Ufa Infantry with 18th Jägers rushed straight at the battery, 19th Jägers and 40th Jägers, went to the left of it, and in a quarter of an hour the impertinence of the enemy had been punished. The battery was under our control, the entire high ground and its surroundings were covered with bodies, and General of Brigade Bonnamy was one of the enemy who was granted mercy.

The troops that reoccupied the mound, under the direct command of Yermolov, were joined by all the closest units, and among them was a battalion of Tomsk Infantry, brought up by Major Löwenstern [Vladimir Ivanovich Löwenstern], who, having been sent by Barclay de Tolly to reconnoitre the course of the battle, participated in the action personally. The enemy, driven off the mound, were attacked on the flanks by troops from 26th Division and 12th Division, under the command of generals Paskevich and Vasilchikov, and were pursued for a considerable distance; but Yermolov, not wanting to expose his disorganised troops to unexpected encounters with Morand's regiments, which were in full formation, supported by the fire of strong batteries posted on the far side of the Semenovka, halted the pursuit. Unable to stop his soldiers, carried away by success, Yermolov ordered Kreutz's dragoons, who were stationed to the left of the battery, to ride ahead of our infantry and round them up. Simultaneously with the defeat of Bonnamy's Brigade, General Kreutz, with the Siberia Dragoons, Orenburg Dragoons and Irkutsk Dragoons, under covering fire from a horse artillery battery, repeatedly attacked the remaining troops from Morand's Division, who were supported by carabiniers, drove off the carabiniers and delayed the advance of the enemy infantry. During these attacks, Major General Dyatkov [Stepan Vasilevich Dyatkov] was wounded by a sabre, and Kreutz, having received two musket ball wounds, remained at the front until, being wounded by canister shot, he fell from his horse. On the French side, Montbrun was killed while Generals of Division Morand, Pajol and Defrance [Jean-Marie Antoine Defrance] were wounded. Barclay, whose imperious calm in this battle amazed all his colleagues and who appeared wherever the greatest danger was developing, arrived at the battery. Almost everyone who was with him was killed or wounded. He sought death, but death spared him; it seemed that fate was saving him for the day that Russia would have chance to pay due tribute of gratitude to their commander. Noticing the total depletion of Raevsky's force defending the battery, Barclay relieved them with seven battalions from 24th Division [VI Corps] under Major General Likhachëv, upon their timely arrival at this location. The troops of VII Corps were withdrawn behind the cavalry, which was in reserve, so that, having rallied there, they could rejoin the left wing of 24th Division , but despite all the efforts of General Paskevich, they could not be returned to action until the evening.[38]

The unsuccessful French attempt on Raevsky's battery cost them some 3,000 men. Général de brigade Bonnamy, having suffered multiple bayonet wounds, was taken prisoner. But this feat cost us dearly; among the dead was Count Kutaisov, who had such promise of brilliance. At 28 years of age, having already reached the rank of general, highly decorated, gifted, educated, modest, Kutaisov, holding the appointment of Chief of Artillery of First Army, had brought great advantage with his orders during the battle of Smolensk. Without any doubt, his death was the reason that many of our batteries stood idly in reserve during the Battle of Borodino and that

---

38 Major General Yermolov's report to Barclay de Tolly, dated 20 September [2 October], No. 151. Lieutenant General Raevsky's report to Dokhturov, dated 11 [23] September, No. 280. Description of the operations by VII Corps in Raevsky's letter to General Jomini. Chambray, II, 68. Thiers, XIV, 367-369. Bernhardi, II, 86-87. Extracts from Operations by First Army (Barclay de Tolly). Barclay de Tolly's report on the battle of Borodino. Kreutz's notes.

our artillery did not show its full strength in this gigantic battle. Kutuzov himself was of that opinion and later said that the Battle of Borodino would have had an incomparably better outcome for us if Kutaisov had survived. It is not known how or where he died; the troops only learned of his death from the bloody saddle of his horse, which ran to them. Gifted with a handsome appearance, showered with gifts of fortune, respected and loved by all who knew him, Kutaisov, as if foreseeing his fate, was often deep in thought. It has been confirmed that the evening before the battle of Borodino, while talking with a number of close friends about the upcoming battle, he said: 'I wish I knew which of us will be alive tomorrow.' A few minutes after the recapture of the battery by our troops, a gifted officer, Chief of Staff of VI Corps, Colonel Monakhtin [Fëdor Fëdorovich Monakhtin], was seriously wounded. 'Boys,' he said to the soldiers from VI Corps assigned to protect the guns 'this battery represents Russia; we shall defend it with our heroic chests,' and with these last word fell hit in the stomach by canister shot.[39]

General Yermolov, having handed over the battery to Likhachëv, went to the left flank of the position and was also seriously wounded in the neck.[40]

At around noon, in the centre of the Borodino position, our troops having brilliantly wrested victory from the hands of the enemy, II Corps were completing their flank march to the left wing of the position. Upon receiving orders to go there, Baggovut had left the jäger regiments of his corps in the woods, on the right flank of the position and in the Kolocha ravine as before, and set out with the rest of the force. 17th Division had set off at about nine o'clock, under Baggovut's personal command, while Prinz Eugen von Württemberg set off a little later with 4th Division. Both divisions initially proceeded in the same direction, along a country lane leading to the right of the Knyazkovo manor; as they passed this location, the corps divided: Baggovut moved to the left through the woods himself with 17th Division, *en route* to the left wing, while Prinz Eugen von Württemberg, on Toll's orders, turned to the right with 4th Division, led the troops out of the scrub into the open, at a distance of about a *verst* from the Raevsky battery, and formed his regiments up facing it in two waves, in battalion columns. At about 11 o'clock,[41] having received orders in the meantime via an aide de camp sent to him by Barclay, to retake the fortification captured by the enemy, the prince quickly led the first wave forward, consisting of the Kremenchug Regiment and Minsk Regiment (Major

---

39 [Liprandi was a witness to Monakhtin's wounding and states that he 'was wounded inside the battery itself, in a melee, as it was being recaptured from Bonnamy's force… and having been stabbed twice in the thigh with a bayonet, he continued to give orders… He was wounded not by canister shot, but by a musket ball in the abdomen, as it later emerged, with only the omentum being shot through… He did not fall to the ground, but was immediately lifted from his horse, with the assistance of others, by his senior adjutant, Dubelt. Thereafter, he was taken to the first dressing station, where our corps Doctor, Koshcherevsky, was located, who bandaged him up and told us that the wound to the abdomen was not mortal, and therefore, not serious'].
40 [Liprandi comments that Yermolov's wound was painful but not serious, as he remained active and was rarely out of the saddle over the following days].
41 In Prinz Eugen von Württemberg's manuscript, under the heading: *Extrait de mon journal militaire des campagnes de 1812, 13 et 14* (M.T.D. No. 47,344), it suggests that the prince received Barclay's orders at ten o'clock.

General Pyshnitsky's Brigade [Dmitry Ilych Pyshnitsky]). Enemy round shot had already begun to reach these troops, tearing out entire ranks from their frontage, when Barclay de Tolly himself, riding up to the prince, told him that Yermolov had already recaptured the battery and that 4th Division should take up positions to the left of the troops located on the mound and move towards a strong enemy infantry column advancing between the Kurgan battery and Semenovskaya. Shortly thereafter, the prince was ordered to deploy his troops into line in order to reduce the casualties inflicted upon them by enemy round shot.[42]

At the same time that Prinz Eugen was advancing to occupy the place indicated to him in the position – the area between the Kurgan battery and Semenovskaya, which had previously been occupied by Second Army and had already been completely abandoned by our troops, therefore the prince, reforming the Tobolsk Infantry and Volhynia Infantry (de Rossi's Brigade [Ignaty Petrovich Rossi]) into column for the attack, pushed them forward to protect a battery emplaced to the left of the mound. It was here that Major General de Rossi suffered a severe contusion to the head; three horses were killed under Prinz Eugen. Despite heavy casualties from the enemy artillery fire, which caught them in crossfire, and attacks by Murat's cavalry, the troops of 4th Division forced the enemy infantry to retreat. At this time, Barclay, returning to the prince, ordered him to move the second brigade (Kremenchug Infantry and Minsk Infantry) to the right, where Miloradovich needed them. At the same time, Miloradovich's aide de camp, Bibikov [Dmitry Gavrilovich Bibikov], galloped up, insistently demanding that Prinz Eugen go to his commander. When asked by the prince where he might find him, Bibikov raised his arm to point, and at that very moment it was torn off by round shot; he raised the other, and pointing out where the prince was to go, replied: 'Over there! Please hurry!' Prinz Eugen, having entrusted the first brigade to Major Wolf, the only field officer remaining with them, galloped to Miloradovich, who was already with the second brigade. On his orders, in anticipation of a strong cavalry attack that threatened us, the regiments of 4th Division formed up in battalion squares, in which Barclay, Miloradovich, Raevsky and other commanders took refuge. The enemy cavalry charged at our infantry, which repelled all of their attacks, but, after that, the artillery opened up again, crushing the troops under Prinz Eugen with such force that in the course of half an hour Pyshnitsky's Brigade alone lost some 300 men killed. In the meantime, Baggovut was constantly sending orderlies, one after another, demanding 4th Division. Eventually (once the troops of IV Corps had already been transferred to the centre to support 24th Division, which was defending the Raevsky battery), Barclay decided that the prince should go to the left wing with the Kremenchug Infantry and Minsk Infantry; the remaining regiments of this division, which were under Major Wolf's command, attacked once more by French cavalry, remained in their original position, to the left of the mound, until the following morning.

At around noon, the Kremenchug Infantry and Minsk Infantry, under Prinz Eugen's command, moved via an indirect route through the scrub, to the right of Psarevo, to the old Smolensk road.[43]

---

42 Prinz Eugen von Württemberg, *Extrait de mon journal militaire* etc.
43 Prinz Eugen of Württemberg, *Erinnerungen aus dem Feldzuge des Jahres 1812 in Russland, v. dem Herzog Eugen v. Württemberg*, 80-84. *Extrait de mon journal militaire* etc.

Meanwhile, the troops under Tuchkov 1st (as we have already mentioned) had been forced to yield the position they had occupied on the mound to the enemy. But reinforcements were already approaching our left wing. Baggovut, having passed the top of the Semenovka ravine himself, with four battalions of Brest Infantry and Ryazan Infantry, turned to the right through the scrub facing the Westphalians, who were putting Prince Shakhovskoy under heavy pressure; the remaining four battalions of Wilmanstrand Infantry and Belozersk Infantry, under the command of Lieutenant General Olsufiev, continuing to move directly to the old Smolensk road, arrived to help Tuchkov at the very moment that 1st Grenadier Division was pushed back from their position near the mound. Taking advantage of the emergence of fresh troops, Tuchkov decided to attack Poniatowski in order to prevent him from consolidating himself on the locations he had seized. Tuchkov halted the enemy himself with the Pavlov Grenadiers, ordering Lieutenant General Olsufiev to relieve the regiments that had previously stood on the right wing of 1st Grenadier Division, with newly arrived troops and envelope the Poles' left wing; at the same time, Major General Count Stroganov was directed around the right wing of Poniatowski's force, with the St Petersburg Grenadiers and Yekaterinoslav Grenadiers, followed by the Leib Grenadiers and Count Arakcheev's Grenadiers. As soon as the enemy had been pushed off the mound by the united efforts of our troops, we hastily brought six heavy guns up and, placing them at reduced intervals, opened fire on Poniatowski's retreating troops and forced them to pull back to Utitsa, at long cannon range and limit themselves to a cannonade. Tuchkov, having been mortally wounded, was replaced by Baggovut; Major General Count Ivelich [Pëtr Ivanovich Ivelich] was also among the wounded.[44]

Thus, at around noon, after six hours of bitter combat, the Russian troops were holding on to all points of the position held at the beginning of the battle, except for the *flèches* and the Semenovka ravine. In the meantime, somewhat earlier, an offensive operation was launched on our part against the left wing of the enemy army, placed across the river Kolocha by the Viceroy. Platov, who was stationed on the left flank of I Cavalry Corps with most of the Cossacks, behind the woods, in the morning, during the battle, had sent patrols to look for fords on the Kolocha several times,[45] and had the opportunity to confirm that very few troops remained in Borodino, on the left wing of the enemy position. Believing it possible to bypass the French on the left flank[46] and take advantage of the surprise of this movement to do them harm, Platov sent Colonel Prinz Ernst von Hessen-Philippsthal [Ernst Konstantin von Hessen-Philippsthal], who was serving as a volunteer, to Kutuzov, proposing to advance with a significant cavalry force to attack the enemy via a ford

---

44 Toll's original notes. Prinz Eugen von Württemberg, *Extrait de mon journal militaire* etc. Bernhardi, II, 81-82. Soltyk, 227-228. Chambray, II, 63.
45 [Liprandi points out that: 'on the 22nd [3 September], five Cossack regiments had been specifically sent out to monitor the lower reaches of this river, where several jäger regiments had been deployed with them in order to guard our position from this direction; therefore, it goes without saying that those places where the enemy could cross more easily, in particular, were immediately sought out, and there is no way that Platov was only permitted to get acquainted with the river on the morning of the 26th [7 September]'].
46 [Liprandi point out that this should read: 'bypass the French left flank'].

across the Kolocha. Prinz Ernst von Hessen first turned to Toll, who, having become convinced of the usefulness of this attack, as a diversion that could draw some of the enemy forces away from the decisive points of their attack, sought permission from Prince Kutuzov to use the entire I Cavalry Corps under General Uvarov, numbering 2,500 men, for the proposed operation. This would have been at about nine o'clock. It took some time to deliver the issued orders, and their execution, i.e. the advance by I Cavalry Corps from behind the woods to the river Kolocha and its passage through a deep ravine could have only been concluded at around noon.[47] Once the enemy intention to conduct an intensive assault on the left wing and centre of our position had been identified, then Prince Kutuzov, at the suggestion of Barclay de Tolly, issued orders (at about nine o'clock) to transfer II Cavalry Corps and IV Corps closer to the centre of our position, to General Miloradovich, which was done in stages; at around noon, the troops of IV Corps were still in reserve behind VI Corps. Meanwhile, Napoleon was preparing to resume the assault on the Raevsky battery with the Viceroy's troops, supporting them with elements of the *Réserve de cavalerie* and *Garde impériale*.[48] This would be the opening of the second act of the battle of Borodino.

---

47 General Clausewitz believes that the raid launched by Uvarov was undertaken under the influence of an exaggerated perception of the successes gained by our troops, as we had recaptured the Raevsky battery, and had news of the capture of the King of Naples (Murat). But, in that case, Uvarov could not have crossed the Kolocha before two o'clock in the afternoon. Bernhardi suggests (II, 74-75) that the news of the capture of Murat came to Kutuzov from our left wing. In reality, Kutuzov did not intend to conduct a decisive offensive with Uvarov's Corp at all, and this is convincingly proved by Uvarov's report itself, where he writes: 'On the day of the battle, on that latterly unforgettable, 26 August [7 September], 1812, from the overall Commander-in-Chief of all armies, His Grace the Prince, I was personally sent with I Cavalry Corps to cross the river and attack the enemy left flank, in order to delay their forces for a while at least, which were so strong and sought to attack our Second Army, which was on the left flank of the position. Having received this mission,' etc... Lieutenant General Uvarov's report to Barclay de Tolly, dated 3 [15] September, 1812. Military Topographic Depot, No. 29,177. [Liprandi refutes Clausewitz's version, including the involvement of Prinz Ernst von Hessen, stating that the orders were Kutuzov's alone, following a survey of the French left wing conducted from the Gorki batteries, and cites Buturlin (Vol. 1, page 277-280) and Mikhailovky (Vol. 2, page 225) in support of his argument].
48 Chambray, II, 69. Fain, II, 27.

23

The Battle of Borodino (continued)

The powerful bombardment of the centre of our position. – The raid on the left flank of the enemy army by Uvarov and Platov. – Its effect on the course of the battle. – Napoleon's preparations for a second assault on the Raevsky battery. – Steps taken by Barclay de Tolly for a counter-attack. – Caulaincourt's attack and the enemy seizure of the Raevsky battery. – The attack on the infantry of our centre. – Actions by the Chevalier Garde and Lifeguard Horse regiments. – The death of Löwenwolde. – The cavalry battle. – The situation of the Russian forces during the withdrawal of the left wing from Semenovskaya, and the centre from the Raevsky battery. – Poniatowski's seizure of the *kurgan* on the Old Smolensk road. – The situation of our army at the end of the battle. – The inactivity of the *Garde impériale*. – Preparations by our side to continue the battle. – The state of the Russian forces. – The order to retreat. – The losses on both sides. – The reasons for the huge loss of life. – The strengths of the forces on both sides following the battle of Borodino. – Napoleon's thoughts on the battle of Borodino. – Comments on the operations by both sides.

2. From the Capture of the *Flèches* and the Village of Semenovskaya by the Enemy Until the End of the Battle

At one o'clock in the afternoon, the Viceroy's troops were ordered to attack the Raevsky battery once more; the *Réserve de cavalerie* and *Jeune Garde* advanced to support this attack. Meanwhile, General Comte Sorbier, noticing the strengthening of our centre with fresh troops (these were the regiments under Prinz Eugen von Württemberg and both divisions under Osterman [IV Corps], which arrived after them), believing that this movement had been made with a counter-offensive objective, therefore increased the fire from the artillery operating against this point and sent 36 guns from the reserve from the *Artillerie de la Garde impériale* and 49 horse artillery pieces from Nansouty's *1er Corps de cavalerie* and Latour-Maubourg's *4e Corps de cavalerie*. These huge batteries, lining up in front of Semenovskaya, opened fire against the troops under Osterman and Prinz Eugen von Württemberg, who were hit by a bombardment from the Viceroy at the same time. Napoleon, considering our centre sufficiently weakened, hoped to crush it with a decisive blow; huge masses of enemy troops enveloped our position like menacing clouds; behind them stood the French *Garde impériale*, not yet in action. But at this very moment, the intended enemy attack was halted by a commotion among the Viceroy's troops left at Borodino and beyond the Kolocha. From a distance, the disorder among the transport standing on the highway, in the vicinity of this point, could be seen. Many carts and service support troops were seeking salvation in flight.[1]

The reason for this alarm was the attack by General Uvarov on the left wing of the enemy army. As stated in his report, having received orders from Prince Kutuzov to go across the river with I Cavalry Corps and attack the enemy left flank in order to draw away their forces, which were so eager to attack our Second Army,[2] by 12 o'clock, Uvarov had forded the Kolocha, near the village of Maloe, with I Cavalry Corps, consisting of 28 squadrons and 12 horse artillery pieces, and headed up the Voinka, in order to go around the source of this swampy tributary of the Kolocha. Upon reaching the Voinka at around noon, at the time that the Raevsky battery had just been recaptured by Yermolov, Uvarov's force had the village of Borodino to their left, strongly held by the enemy, and to their front the French *84e régiment de ligne* and d'Ornano's light cavalry brigade, consisting of several hundred horsemen. General Uvarov immediately attacked the enemy with the Yelisavetgrad Hussars and Lifeguard Cossacks, followed by the Lifeguard Dragoons, Lifeguard Ulans, Lifeguard Hussars, Nizhin Dragoons and 2nd Horse Artillery Company. As soon as the advance by our troops was noticed, d'Ornano's cavalry moved through the village of Bezubovo crossed the watermill causeway on the Voinka, while *84e régiment de ligne* formed up in front of the causeway in square, where the Viceroy also took refuge, having just arrived on the left flank. At the same time, the *6e chasseurs à cheval*, *8e chasseurs à cheval* and *25e chasseurs à cheval* from Chastel's Division [Louis Pierre Aimé Chastel] (Grouchy's *3e Corps de cavalerie*), La Houssaye's *6e division de dragons* [Armand Lebrun de La Houssaye] (of the same Corps) and the *Garde royale italienne* were transferred to the left bank of the Kolocha. Whereupon Uvarov ordered the Lifeguard Hussars to attack. Clausewitz [Carl Philipp Gottlieb Clausewitz], serving with I Cavalry Corps at the time, suggested first disordering the French with artillery fire, but this proposal was not accepted, for fear of the enemy escaping and losing the opportunity to defeat them. Three times our hussars went on the attack and each time they were beaten off by the musketry of the French infantry; eventually, once the guns had been ordered to unlimber and open fire, the French withdrew behind the causeway, leaving a gun in our hands, captured by the hussars.[3] The Viceroy himself was in grave danger, a horse was killed under him; one of his aides de camp, Méjean, was wounded. But our entire success was limited to a retreat by the French behind the Voinka, because Uvarov could not cross the causeway with

---

1 Fain, *Manuscrit de 1812*, II, 26-27. Beitzke, 208-209.
2 Lieutenant General Uvarov's report to Prince Kutuzov, dated 27 September [9 October] 1812.
3 General Uvarov's report. None of the foreign historians mentions the capture of a gun by our hussars, and even General Buturlin does not write about it. Schreckenstein has written about the troops temporarily sent to the left bank of the Kolocha: *Die Kavallerie in der Schlacht an der Moskwa*, 37-38.

cavalry alone, within view of significant enemy forces stationed on the right bank of the Voinka; while an attack on Borodino, strongly held by enemy infantry, also did not promise success. Meanwhile, Platov, who had crossed the Kolocha with several Cossack regiments at the same time as Uvarov, finding a convenient place to cross the Voinka upstream of Bezubovo, transferred his Cossacks to the far bank of this river, who spread out in the scrub between the enemy columns and moved into their rear. The Viceroy's infantry, holding the end of the causeway, concerned about being pushed into the swamps, moved away from the river, which helped the Lifeguard Cossack Regiment to rush over the causeway into the scrub and race into the rear of the enemy infantry. Taking advantage of the consternation that this unexpected attack produced, our Cossacks withdrew back across the causeway. Meanwhile, the regiments under Uvarov, having received orders from Barclay de Tolly to return to the right bank of the Kolocha, withdrew towards Gorki, together with Platov's Cossacks, at about four o'clock in the afternoon.[4]

Napoleon, having learned of the counterattack by our troops on the left wing of his army, suspended the Viceroy's advance on the Raevsky battery, ordered Roguet's *2e division de la Jeune Garde* to make a lateral move to their left from the Kamenka river to the Kolocha, and Claparède's *Légion de la Vistule* to move towards the Kamenka, and galloped across the Kolocha onto the highway, where, having confirmed Uvarov's withdrawal, he returned to Shevardino. At the same time, the Viceroy returned to the right bank of the Kolocha, to where La Houssaye's Division proceeded behind him.[5]

In general, Uvarov's counterattack on the left wing of the enemy army, carried out without infantry support, which was vital due to the nature of the ground around Borodino, had no decisive outcome, but brought us great benefit by forcing Napoleon to lose about two hours to inaction, during which we managed to reinforce our centre with troops from the right wing and from the reserves and fill the gap that had opened between the Raevsky battery and Semenovskaya.[6] Prince Kutuzov believed that our

---

4   Clausewitz, 155-159. Uvarov's attack on the left wing of the enemy army is described in detail in the work by Clausewitz, a former chief quartermaster in I Cavalry Corps [Liprandi is dubious of Clausewitz's ability to function in such appointments as he spoke no Russian at that time]. Fain, II, 28. From the Cossack force, the following units took part in this action: Ilovaysky 5th's Regiment, Grekov 18th's Regiment, Lieutenant Colonel Kharitonov 7th's Regiment (which, according to Platov himself, 'was at the front of every charge'), Denisov 7th's Regiment, Zhirov's Regiment, Vlasov 3rd's Regiment, the Simferopol Tatars and some of the Ataman's Regiment (General of Cavalry Platov's report to Prince Kutuzov) [Liprandi notes: 'It is a shame that General Bogdanovich did not cite this in its entirety or even in extract and did not provide either a serial number or a date… Of the nine Cossack regiments with Platov, Bogdanovich names only seven and some of the Ataman's who took part in this mission, and does not say a word about what happened to an entire Cossack regiment and most of the Ataman's… they seem to have disappeared from History']. Schreckenstein, *Die Kavallerie in der Schlacht an der Moskwa*, 37-39.
5   Beitzke, 207. Pelet. Schreckenstein, 38.
6   Chambray, II, 70. Thiers, XIV, 376. [Liprandi points out that Bogdanovich's assessment is self-contradictory, since the two hour reprieve was absolutely vital for the Russians to be able to stave off an inevitable and crushing defeat and did, therefore, have a decisive outcome – in favour of the Russians].

cavalry could have achieved a more decisive result with this attack;[7] from Uvarov's report it is clear that he had been ordered to divert the enemy from attacking Second Army, but that he later received orders from Barclay and from Kutuzov himself to return to the main position. This operation by our detachment could have had more important consequences only if it had been in significant strength and consisted of all arms of the armed forces, or if Uvarov had received explicit instructions in which it was clearly expressed that his detachment was assigned to deliver a decisive blow into the enemy rear and that this counterattack was to have been executed even in the event of our detachment being subjected to total destruction.[8]

Napoleon, having confirmed that his left wing was being attacked by insignificant forces, decided to resume the attack on the Raevsky battery with the troops under the Viceroy and some of the *Réserve de cavalerie*. Broussier's *14e Division*, Morand's *1re Division* and Gérard's *3e Division*, supported on their left by the troops of Chastel's *3e division de cavalerie légère* (Grouchy's *3e Corps de cavalerie*), were assigned to attack from the front and our right flank, while Wathier's *2e division de cuirassiers* [Pierre Wathier or Wattier] from Montbrun's *2e corps de cavalerie* (under Caulaincourt's [Auguste Jean-Gabriel de Caulaincourt] command) and Lorge's *7e division de cuirassiers* from Latour-Maubourg's *4e corps de cavalerie*, which had moved to their left after the French capture of Semenovskaya, their mission being to envelope our fortification from its left flank. Barclay de Tolly, noticing the storm about to break over us, ordered IV Corps under Count Osterman, who was in reserve near the mound, to enter the front line to the locations held by the remnants of VII Corps, to the left and rear of the Raevsky battery; behind IV Corps were the Lifeguard Preobrazhensky Regiment and Lifeguard Semenovsky Regiment, and behind them the cavalry was ordered to form up in two waves: the first of II Cavalry Corps and III Cavalry Corps, under Korf's overall command, while the second had the Chevalier Garde Regiment and Lifeguard Horse Regiment. But II Cavalry Corps, delayed by the crossing of the Stonets, had not yet arrived from the right flank, and most of III Cavalry Corps, under Dorokhov's command, had been detached to support the left wing. The convergence of the reserves into the battle lines, necessary to counter the concentration of enemy masses by reinforcing the vital ground, exposed us to extremely severe damage from the fire of the huge unmasked enemy batteries, some along the lower Semenovka, which separated us from the troops under the Viceroy, and some forwards of the ruins of Semenovskaya. Our reserve horse artillery, consisting of eight companies, being constantly under fire, contributed greatly to delaying the enemy and suffered heavy losses; in particular, the company under Colonel Nikitin, in which 93 men and 113 horses were killed and seven guns were damaged.[9]

---

7 [Liprandi claims that, in the absence of a source showing that this was Kutuzov's stated belief, this is merely speculation on Bogdanovich's part].
8 [Liprandi was horrified at the concept of a detachment commander being ordered to subject his command to complete destruction: 'with a success like that, the enemy would be inspired, and despondency would proceed in our ranks, the first step towards a collapse of morale, which is the primary quality of a warrior'].
9 Toll's original notes. Count Nikitin's notes. Schreckenstein, 124.

At two o'clock in the afternoon, Caulaincourt led Wathier's *2e division de cuirassiers* into the attack, while the intensified bombardment continued, which forced our infantry to reform into square under the fiercest fire from the enemy batteries. The commander of 23rd Division, Major General Bakhmetev 2nd [Alexey Nikolayevich Bakhmatiev], lost his leg; major generals Bakhmetyev 1st [Nikolay Nikolayevich Bakhmatiev] and Aleksopol [Fëdor Panteleimonovich Aleksopol] were wounded. Osterman, having suffered a severe contusion himself, was forced to retire from the battlefield. The enemy also suffered huge losses. French historians have compared our Kurgan fortification to a mass of steel sparkling with flame. Wathier's cuirassiers, having crossed the Semenovka downstream of its confluence with the Kamenka, headed by the direct route to the left of the battery and drove back elements of VI Corps, which were to the right of the fortification, into the Gorki ravine, while the *5e régiment de cuirassiers*, proceeding in the final wave, turning to the right, crossed over the ditch and parapet into the battery. But the musketry of the infantry positioned behind the fortification immediately forced the cuirassiers to abandon it, and Caulaincourt himself was killed by a musket ball, in the gorge of the battery. Defrance's *4e division de cuirassiers*, leaving the battery to their left, had been intended to attack our position simultaneously with the cuirassiers, but they were somewhat late, while in the meantime, Latour-Maubourg's *4e corps de cavalerie* also went on the attack, enveloping the battery from its left flank: Rozniecki's *4th division de cavalerie légère* deployed in two waves, formed the right wing, while the cuirassier regiments advanced one behind the other on the left; horse artillery batteries formed the centre. The Saxon *Garde du Corps* went into the assault directly on the battery ahead of everyone, while the *Kürassier Regiment von Zastrow* and Małachowski's *14 Pułk Kirasjerów*, supported by the Westphalian brigade, struck the Pernov Infantry, Kexholm Infantry and 33rd Jägers, which were stationed on the left side of the battery, somewhat behind its gorge, in a ravine; but these courageous regiments, having allowed the enemy to close to a range of about 60 paces, greeted them with volleys and turned them back in complete disorder. Meanwhile Thielmann, with the Saxon *Garde du Corps*, having crossed the ditch and parapet, broke into the fortification. Our infantry, occupying the battery, defended themselves desperately.[10] In a corner of the fortification, on a camp chair, the commander of the defenders of the mound, General Likhachëv, sat exhausted by his wounds, but strong in spirit. Raising his weak voice, amid the thunder of gunfire and the shouts of those fighting, he aroused his subordinates to heroic deeds. Eventually, when there was no longer any hope of defending the battery, Likhachëv gathered his last strength and ran into the enemy crowds hoping to perish following the failure of his pledge to protect the Fatherland. This brave warrior, already stabbed several times by bayonets, was thrown to the ground, but the enemy, recognising him as a Russian general, held back from the lethal blow, in readiness to attack him.[11] During this fighting, the Viceroy

---

10 Hoffmann, 61. Bernhardi, II, 103-104. Buturlin, I, 342-343. Schreckenstein, 84-124 [*sic*, 81-94]. [Liprandi points out that Buturlin's account is at odds with the other three sources. See Appendix 14. for Liprandi's full assessment of these four sources].
11 Emperor Alexander I and His contemporaries in 1812, 1813, 1814 and 1815. T.I. Likhachëv's Biography. Sent to France as a prisoner of war, Likhachëv died *en route* in Königsberg.

approached the mound with the infantry divisions under Broussier, Morand and Gérard and occupied our battery with their leading battalions (from *9e régiment de ligne*).[12] Barclay de Tolly, wanting to retake the mound, withdrew the nearest battalions of 24th Division from the ravine; at that very moment, Małachowski's cuirassiers descended into the ravine in column of threes in order to outflank our infantry, and although this attempt failed, it forced Barclay to abandon the counterattack on the mound and accelerated the retreat of the Russian forces behind the Gorki ravine.[13] The enemy cavalry, encouraged by this, decided to attack the infantry of IV Corps and VI Corps, which, meanwhile, had formed up in battalion squares behind the ravine: the Saxon *Kürassier Regiment von Zastrow* went around them moving to the right; whereupon, the entire cavalry under Latour-Maubourg, with the assistance of Defrance's *4e division de cuirassiers*, who had arrived at the scene of the battle, raced to attack our infantry. The Polish lancers, having withstood the fire of one of our batteries, began to cut down the gunners with whom the Chief of Artillery of VI Corps, General Kostenetsky [Vasily Grigorevich Kostenetsky], was located at the time. Kostenetsky, endowed with extraordinary physical strength, grabbed a rammer himself, knocked several lancers off their horses and, with the help of his artillerymen, fought off the enemy.[14]

Barclay de Tolly, having noticed that the cavalry was depleted, of which a significant part was on the left wing at the time, decided to hold the enemy with infantry alone. In describing the Battle of Borodino, he states himself:

> The high ground together with some of the artillery was taken by storm;[15] 24th Division fell back in the greatest disorder, but was immediately rallied and formed up. Whereupon the enemy cavalry raced at our infantry with combined forces. It seemed as though the fateful moment of decision for the battle had just arrived; my cavalry could not hold back the weight of the forces moving towards them, and I did not dare to lead them against the enemy, believing that, on being driven off, they would retreat in disarray and drive the infantry into disorder.[16]

At this decisive moment, the Chevalier Garde Regiment and Lifeguard Horse Regiment, under their brigade commander, Major General Shevich, arrived just

---

12 [Liprandi is highly critical of Bogdanovich's entire account of the attacks on Raevsky's redoubt and researched 63 published accounts, as well as his own contemporaneous diary, to produce a more comprehensive narrative; see Appendix 15. for his conclusions].
13 [Liprandi suggests this should read 'towards the Gorki ravine'].
14 Thiers, XIV, 379-380. Bernhardi, II, 103. Kostenetsky's feat is described in the work: Emperor Alexander I and His contemporaries in 1812, 1813, 1814 and 1815. T.I. General Kostenetsky's biography. In the same place we find that the success of this hand-to-hand fighting gave Kostenetsky the idea to propose the introduction of iron rammers into the artillery to Emperor Alexander, and that the Tsar said in response: 'I may have iron rammers, but where can I get the Kostenetskys to wield them?'
15 'The enemy eventually took possession of the lunette, from where, however, we had managed to extract most of the guns.' Toll's Original Notes.
16 Extracted from Operations of First Army, compiled by Barclay de Tolly.

in time, having been summoned from the reserve on the orders of Barclay delivered by his aide de camp. Both regiments, having arrived at a trot, were stationed behind a small rise in front of Knyazkovo. Meanwhile, the enemy, having captured the Raevsky battery for a second time and wanting to exploit this success, attacked Kaptsevich's 7th Division from the front and right flank with some of the Viceroy's infantry and *3e corps de cavalerie* (namely, the troops from Defrance's and Chastel's divisions and *7e régiment de dragons* from La Houssaye's *6e division de dragons*). One of our squares from the 19th Jäger Regiment was broken by an attack from the French carabiniers of Defrance's *4e division de cuirassiers*.[17] At that moment, to the right of the Chevalier Garde Regiment, the second half of the 2nd Lifeguard Horse Artillery Battery, which had arrived from the reserves, was deployed under the command of Sub Lieutenant Baron Korf [Nikolay Ivanovich Korf]. Noticing the disordering of our square, without waiting for orders, he raced out with his guns to engage the enemy. As soon as our infantry had moved to the sides, the guns opened fire with canister at the enemy infantry from a range of about 100 *sazhen* and scattered them, carpeting the ground in front of the battery with a pile of corpses. But Chastel's light cavalry, in spite of the deadly work of the canister, continued to advance and rushed from all directions at our guns, which, being without their limbers at the time, retreated rather slowly. The French horsemen were just reaching the intervals between Korf's guns, when he, riding up the slope, shouted to the commander of the leading platoon of the right-flank squadron of the Chevalier Garde Regiment: 'Bashmakov [Dmitry Yevlampevich Bashmakov]! Save the guns!' In an instant, the entire Chevalier Garde Regiment struck the French and saved the artillery. Following this, Barclay de Tolly, approaching the commander of the Chevalier Garde Regiment, Colonel Löwenwolde [Karl Karlovich Levenvolde or Friedrich Karl Johann Freiherr von Löwenwolde], ordered him to go on the attack. Löwenwolde formed the regiment *en echelon* from the flanks, and, under canister fire, led them through the line of squares of the 19th Jägers and 40th Jägers and struck the enemy who were advancing towards him in two waves: the first consisted of the Saxon *Garde du Corps* and *Kürassier Regiment von Zastrow*, while the second was of Polish lancers. Löwenwolde had intended to attack the enemy from the front with 1st Squadron, while 4th Squadron, riding to the left of him, were to go into the Saxon flank. The command was given: 'at the gallop!' Löwenwolde shouted to the commander of 4th Squadron, Captain Davydov: 'Yevdokim Vasilevich, lead the left shoulder,' and at that very moment he fell from his horse, mortally wounded in the head by canister shot. His death, at this most decisive moment, weakened the blow of our elite horsemen, but in spite of this, the Chevalier Garde, under the command of Colonel Levashov [Vasily Vasilevich Levashov], engaging Latour-Maubourg's

---

17 [Liprandi claims: 'They were not broken. In this so-called square there were barely 180 men including the Colonel in Chief himself, Colonel Vuich. Having seen the onrushing mass of cavalry to his rear and having no time to form square properly, he gave the command to lie flat. Some of the Shirvan Musketeers who were still in extended order did the same; one of the participants in this action is still alive (now Lieutenant General Beloguzhev). Their line was passed without causing any harm; whereupon the jägers opened fire from the rear; fortunately, our cavalry arrived in the nick of time to rescue them.'

cavalry with several repeated charges, prevented the enemy from resuming their attack on our infantry.[18] The charges by the Chevalier Garde were supported by the Lifeguard Horse Regiment.[19]

Meanwhile, enemy reinforcements were continually approaching, and therefore Barclay ordered Adjutant General Baron Korf to hurry back to assist the centre, with II Cavalry Corps. No sooner had elements of this corps arrived, than Korf directed Major General Panchulidzev 2nd [Semën Davydovich Panchulidzev] to attack Wathier's cuirassiers and Defrance's carabiniers with the Izyum Hussars and Poland Ulans, but before our regiments had time to turn around, they were attacked by the enemy and thrown into disarray. Whereupon the Chief Quartermaster of II Cavalry Corps, Captain Schubert [Fëdor Fëdorovich Schubert], and the corps commander's aides de camp, Captain Yakovlev and Captain Lashkarev, having rallied the disordered regiments, helped to hold the enemy cavalry back. General Korf ordered the Pskov Dragoon Regiment, under Colonel Zass [Andrey Andreevich Zass or Gideon Heinrich von Saß], to attack to the right of the mound, while the Moscow Dragoons were to be held in reserve. Colonel Zass, noticing that the enemy infantry and cavalry (Korf's report mentions horse grenadiers) had quickly moved forward, threatening the right flank of the Izyum Hussars and Poland Ulans, which had not yet had chance to recover, attacked the enemy (probably *7e régiment de dragons*), drove them back and, having withdrawn his squadrons, rallied them under enemy fire in perfect order; some of Grouchy's cavalry, which had remained in reserve, raced to attack the Pskov Dragoons, but were also thrown into disarray and were pursued right up to their infantry; Colonel Zass, exploiting this success, struck the last battalion on the left flank and cut through them. The success of Zass' dragoons was facilitated by the firing of canister, from very close range, by the first half of 2nd Lifeguard Horse Artillery Battery, under the direct command of Colonel Kozen (who had been recalled from the left wing to the centre). The enemy cavalry were thrown into confusion, but after that, these guns, moving even further forward, on the instructions of Colonel Kudashev, stumbled upon an enemy 12-gun battery and suffered heavy losses; among those mortally wounded was the commander of 2nd Lifeguard Horse Artillery Battery, Captain Rahl.[20]

During these actions, the Sumy Hussars, Mariupol Hussars, Orenburg Dragoons, Siberia Dragoons and Irkutsk Dragoons from III Cavalry Corps arrived on the battlefield, as well as regiments from II Cavalry Corps. A bitter action began here: attacks followed quickly one after another with varying degrees of success. Riderless horses ran about in herds. Barclay himself participated in the fighting with his staff and was forced to draw his sabre in self defence. One of his aides de camp, Count Lamsdorf [Konstantin Matveevich Lamsdorf], was shot dead with a pistol. On the enemy side, *Général de Division* Chastel [sic] and *généraux de brigade* Huard [Léonard Jean Aubry Huard de Saint-Aubin] and Gérard [sic] were

---

18 History of the men of the Chevalier Garde and the Chevalier Garde Regiment, 88-90.
19 History of the Lifeguard Horse Regiment, II, 72. Buturlin, I, 344.
20 Adjutant General Korf's report to Barclay de Tolly, dated 9 [21] September 1812 (Military Topographic Depot, No. 29,177). Toll's original notes. History of the Lifeguard Artillery, compiled by Ratch.

killed; the wounded included Grouchy, the commander of 3e *corps de cavalerie* and *Général de Brigade* Dommanget.²¹ For the duration of the cavalry action, the Viceroy strongly consolidated the Kurgan battery and the areas to either side, while the Russian troops, having finally retreated behind the Gorki ravine, settled down, at four o'clock in the afternoon, at a range of about 400 *sazhen* from the fortifications taken by the enemy, resting their right flank on the village of Gorki.²² By this time, our left wing was located at cannon range from Semenovskaya resting its flank against the forest lying along the sides of the old Smolensk road.²³ The troops of both sides, exhausted and weakened by the prolonged fighting, little by little ceased their efforts. The infantry stood in small columns, containing barely a third of the men brought into action at the beginning of the battle; all the rest were killed, wounded, evacuating their wounded comrades, or rallying to the rear of the battle lines; the cavalry executed their half-hearted charges at the trot; the artillery, which had been shaking the whole area with its thunder, gradually fell silent. Only on our left wing a very heated firefight was still going on.²⁴

A bitter action had begun there, in the scrub. At about four o'clock in the afternoon, one of the Westphalian columns, under Ochs' command [Adam Ludwig von Ochs], broke through between Baggovut's force, which was in position near the mound, and the left wing of the rest of the army. Prinz Eugen, noticing that the advancing infantry were in white coats,²⁵ mentioned this to Baggovut, who, however, doubted that it was the enemy. Prince Shakhovskoy undertook to check out these troops that had appeared, with his jägers and the Minsk Infantry stationed nearby, but no sooner had the Minsk Infantry, moving towards the Westphalians, emerged from the scrub onto open ground, they were pelted with canister and having suffered significant losses, were forced to retreat.

---

21 Extracted from Operations of First Army. Barclay de Tolly's report to Prince Kutuzov, dated 26 September [8 October]. Toll's original notes. Adjutant General Korf's report to Barclay de Tolly. Chambray states: '*Cependant les Russes s'avançaient, mais lentement, accablés par le feu d'artillerie le plus violent qu'aucune troupe ait peut-être jamais essuyé. Leur cavalerie chargea les batteries à plusieurs reprises; quelques unes tombèrent même en son pouvoir, mais la cavalerie française, qui les soutenait, les reprit aussitôt...*' (Meanwhile the Russians were advancing, but slowly, overwhelmed by the fiercest artillery fire that perhaps any force had ever encountered. Their cavalry charged the batteries several times; some even fell into their hands, but the French cavalry, in close support, immediately recaptured them...). Bernhardi, II, 104.
22 [Liprandi points out that this arrangement was impossible if the troops were actually behind the Gorki ravine].
23 Barclay de Tolly's report to Kutuzov, dated 26 September [8 October]. Hoffmann, 62-63. Chambray, II, 66-67. In our official sources and in the work by General Mikhailovsky-Danilevsky it states that at the end of the battle our front line passed from Gorki to the Semenovskaya village, in which our troops allegedly held out, and onwards up the right bank of the Semenovka. But, according to the unanimous testimony of all participants in the battle on the left wing of the Russian army, the ruins of Semenovskaya were abandoned by us at around noon. Buturlin himself states: 'at nine o'clock (in the evening) the enemy launched their final attack and, emerging from Semenovskaya, occupied the forest behind this village, but were driven out from there by the Lifeguard Finland Regiment, which struck with fixed bayonets and threw the enemy back into the village.' Buturlin, I, 345-346.
24 Clausewitz, 158-159.
25 Westphalian troops wore white coats.

Whereupon Baggovut, convinced of the gravity of his situation, retreated more than a *verst* along the old Smolensk road and at about five o'clock in the afternoon brought his troops into alignment with the left wing of the army. As soon as Poniatowski noticed the Russian troops falling back, he sent both of his infantry divisions against the position at the mound, while Colonel Toliński's [Józef Toliński] *13 Pułk Huzarów*, supported by the other three cavalry regiments of *5e Corps*, were directed around our left flank. The Cossack formation under Karpov, having fallen back to Baggovut's force, had settled down somewhat ahead of their left flank. Meanwhile, Prinz Eugen remained on the mound with four guns and their escort, consisting of the Kremenchug Infantry, numbering no more than 300 men, and then, concerned about being cut off by the Westphalian column, retreated to Baggovut's new position. Poniatowski's troops occupied the mound, but Prinz Eugen, noticing that some of our generals regretted the loss of this point, expressed his intention to retake it once more. Baggovut and Konovnitsyn dissuaded him from this undertaking, but eventually allowed him to attack the enemy. Whereupon the prince, taking with him the Kremenchug Infantry and Minsk Infantry, in which there were only about 500 men left, with four guns, led them towards the enemy; they were followed at some distance by the Ryazan Infantry and Brest Infantry. As soon as the Minsk Infantry ascended the mound, they were greeted by a volley from the leading enemy infantry unit, and after that, upon being attacked by *12 Pułk Ułanów*, they retreated taking losses.[26] In spite of this, however, Poniatowski limited himself to occupying the mound, within cannon range of Baggovut's new fighting position, and withdrew the main body of his corps to Utitsa.[27]

Thus, at about six o'clock in the evening, our troops occupied the following locations: VI Corps stood with their right flank on the battery forwards of the village of Gorki, from where the front line stretched in the direction of Semenovskaya; IV Corps adjoined the left flank of VI Corps at a shallow angle; further to the left were the remains of Second Army's infantry, resting on the scrub were the Lifeguard Izmailovsky Regiment and Lifeguard Finland Regiment; finally, III Corps and the majority of II Corps, under Baggovut's command, were stationed separately on both sides of the old Smolensk road, continuing the line held by the troops of Second Army, forming an acute angle with them. The cavalry corps formed the second line, while V Corps (Lifeguard) were in reserve.[28] On our side, throughout the duration of the battle, only four regiments of jägers did not take part in it, standing on the right flank of the position from the beginning of the battle;[29] while on the enemy side, their entire *Garde impériale*, numbering around 20,000 elite troops were uncommitted. In addition, the Russian troops had been pushed back to a position

---

26 Prinz Eugen von Württemberg's diary (manuscript in the Military Topographic Depot, No. 47,344. Hoffmann, 64-65. Sołtyk, 238-239.
27 Hoffmann, 65.
28 Extracted from Operations of First Army, by Barclay de Tolly. Hoffmann, 62-63. In General Raevsky's report to General of Infantry Dokhturov, dated 11 [23] September, No. 280, it states: 'Major General Vasilchikov, having assembled the scattered remnants of 12th Division and 27th Division and together with the Lifeguard Lithuania Regiment, held the vital high ground at the left extreme of our line until evening...'
29 30th Jägers, 48th Jägers, 4th Jägers and 34th Jägers.

that did not present any advantages in defence terms; behind them, at a distance of about 2,000 paces, the line of retreat to Moscow ran parallel with it. Under such circumstances, an offensive by Napoleon's *Garde impériale*, supported by elements of the forces already in battle, could have had very decisive consequences. The sun was still high when Murat sent General Belliard to Napoleon with a request for the assistance of the *Garde impériale*. Marshal Ney had also given orders to inform him that the participation of the *cavalerie de la Garde* in the battle would complete the dispersal of the Russian army. It has been confirmed that Berthier and Bessières [Jean-Baptiste Bessières], with Napoleon at the time, dissuaded him from a further offensive. Wanting to confirm Murat's and Ney's reports personally, he galloped to the fighting troops, first to the high ground at Semenovskaya, then to the Raevsky battery: everywhere he could see the Russians, pushed back towards their line of retreat, but standing firm in anticipation of a new fight. He said: *'Je ne ferai pas démolir ma garde. A huit cents lieues de France, on ne risque pas sa dernière réserve.'* (I will not have my guard demolished. One does not risk one's last reserve eight hundred leagues from France).[30]

On our side, an offensive by Napoleon's justly illustrious *Garde impériale* was anticipated at any moment. But the enemy was limited to a bombardment, which, little by little, subsided.[31] Meanwhile, Barclay de Tolly was making efforts to rally the troops disordered by combat and sent *Flügel-Adjutant* [Equerry] Wolzogen [Justus Philipp Adolf Wilhelm Ludwig Freiherr von Wolzogen] to Kutuzov, ordering him to explain the current situation of the army to the Commander-in-Chief and to ask for orders for subsequent operations. Wolzogen, presenting himself to Kutuzov, reported that all the most important points of our position were in enemy hands and that our troops were in complete disarray. Kutuzov was not enamoured of such a somewhat exaggerated presentation of the state of affairs, in the presence of many personalities at army headquarters, who, in expressing his displeasure to Wolzogen, said to him very sharply: 'As for the battle, I know its course as well as anyone. The enemy has been repulsed at all points; Tomorrow we shall drive them from sacred Russian soil.' Whereupon, Wolzogen, fulfilling Barclay de Tolly's instructions, asked for written order from the Commander-in-Chief. Kutuzov, approving all of Barclay's orders, notified him of his intention to resume the battle and ordered him to make all preparations for that during the night. General Dokhturov, who was in temporary command of Second Army, received orders from the Commander-in-Chief in the evening: to bring the troops entrusted to him into good order, resupply the artillery with ammunition and prepare for a resumption of the battle.[32] At the same

---

30 Ségur, I, 415-416. Gourgaud, *Examen critique de l'ouvrage de M. le comte de Ségur*. Pelet, *Bataille de la Moskowa*. Berhhardi II, 106.
31 Bernhardi, II, 106.
32 Wolzogen, *Memoiren*, 145-146. Bernhardi, II, 107-109. From the resolute preparations by Barclay de Tolly for a resumption of the battle and from everything written by Barclay (Description of the operations by First Army), it emerges that Wolzogen, in explaining the state of our army to Prince Kutuzov, was carried away by the ardour of his imagination and reported completely contrary to what Barclay had entrusted to him to the Commander-in-Chief. In Raevsky's notes it states: *'N'ayant rien à faire dans ce moment j'allais le trouver (le Prince Koutousoff). Nous conservions nos positions, le feu de l'ennemi se ralentissait, mais*

time, General Yermolov's aide de camp, Staff Captain Grabbe [Pavel Khristoforovich Grabbe], was sent to warn the troops about the forthcoming battle.³³ Meanwhile at dusk, upon returning to his original headquarters at Tatarinovo manor, Prince Kutuzov instructed Toll to inspect the state and dispositions of Second Army, and the left wing in general. Having travelled along the line of these troops, Toll found them in disarray everywhere, having not quite had chance to rally, and became convinced of the impossibility of resuming the battle. To give an idea of the state of Second Army after the Battle of Borodino, it is enough to say that out of their troop totals, some 20,000 men were out of action, and those that remained present, in 54 battalions, 52 squadrons and 12 artillery companies, all in all were 14,000 strong, of whom between 8,000 to 9,000 were infantry, therefore, there were on average fewer than 200 men in each battalion. The six battalions of combined grenadiers under Vorontsov, who had taken part in the defence of the *flèches*, in total had some 300 men in their ranks. The Astrakhan Cuirassier Regiment, which had gone into action with about 400 mounted men, was reduced to 95 men with a similar number of horses. It has already been mentioned above about the huge losses among the horse artillery reserves. It has been said that Toll, having approached one of the units of the force, had asked: 'What regiment is this?' and had received the reply: 'This is 2nd Grenadier Division.'³⁴

Such was the information about the state of Second Army, collected by Toll. Upon reporting to the Commander in Chief about everything he had found, the intention

---

notre artillerie manquait de cartouches. J'allais lui presenter l'état des choses; il me reçut avec d'autant plus de bonté, qu'un moment avant moi quelqu'un lui avait presenté les affaires sous un mauvais point de vue. Il faut que je dise qu'étant encore lieutenant j'avais fait mes premières armes dans la guerre de Turquie du tems du maréchal Prince Potemkine près de la personne du Prince Koutousoff. Il me concervoit un souvenir favourable; il me dit: 'vous pensez donc que nous ne sommes pas obligés de nous retirer.' Je lui repondis que 'tout au contraire il fallait attaquer l'ennemi le lendemain; que dans les affaires indécises c'était toujours le plus opiniâtre qui restait victorieux.' Ce n'était pas une bravade de ma part; je me trompais peut-être, mais je pensais ainsi dans le moment où je parlais. Le Prince Koutousoff dicta de suite, en présence du P-ce Alexandre de Württemberg, un ordre à son aide-de-camp Kaissaroff sur l'attaque du lendemain et m'ordonna en attendant de le porter de bouche au général Doctoroff. Je courus le remplir et allais l'annoncer à toutes nos lignes, connaissant parfatiement l'effet qu'il produirait sur l'esprit du soldat.' (Having nothing to do at the time, I went to find him (Prince Kutuzov). We had held our positions, the enemy fire was slackening, but our artillery lacked ammunition. I was about to present this state of affairs to him; he received me with all the more kindness because a moment before someone had presented matters to him from a pessimistic point of view. I must say that I had made my debut as a mere lieutenant close to the person of Prince Kutuzov in the war with Turkey in the time of Marshal Prince Potemkin. He retained a favourable memory of me and said: 'So you think we don't have to retire.' I replied that; 'on the contrary, the enemy must be attacked the following day; that in indecisive actions it was always the most tenacious who emerged victorious.' It wasn't bravado on my part; I was perhaps mistaken, but it was what I was thinking when I spoke. In the presence of Prinz Alexander von Württemberg, Prince Kutuzov immediately dictated orders to his aide-de-camp Kaiserov for an attack on the following day and, in the meantime, ordered me to inform General Dokhturov verbally. I ran to carry this out and announced it across our lines, knowing full well the effect it would produce on the minds of the soldiers).

33 History of the Lifeguard Artillery, compiled by Ratch.
34 Bernhardi, II, 109-110. Hoffmann, 66.

to resume the fight once more was cancelled. Meanwhile, Barclay had taken steps to build a redoubt near the village of Gorki (for which 2,000 *opolchenie* were used), and to re-occupy the Kurgan battery, which had been abandoned by the enemy after dark. General Miloradovich received orders to place a battery with several battalions on this high ground.[35]

But at midnight, orders were received from Prince Kutuzov to retreat beyond Mozhaisk. Barclay stated that he had wanted to go to the prince with a request to cancel the issued orders, but having received information about Dokhturov's departure, he was forced to carry out the command from the Commander in Chief with a heavy heart. At first glance, it seems that Barclay de Tolly, knowing the situation of our army, had good reason to seek a new battle, but this desire is easily explained by the fact that no matter how great our losses were, we considered them fewer than those of the enemy. The stubborn resistance by the Russian forces on the unforgettable day of the battle of Borodino inspired the hope in our soldiers of blocking the enemy's route to Moscow, and that made the impossible seem possible.

In reality, although the enemy successes in the battle of Borodino were limited to capturing part of the battlefield and capturing several fortifications that were quickly filled in, nevertheless, his superiority in troop numbers and the preservation of a significant reserve did not give us the slightest probability of success. It is difficult and even almost impossible to calculate with precise accuracy the losses of both sides in the Battle of Borodino. The casualties from First Army in official sources for 24 and 26 August [5 and 7 September] are shown as: three generals, 213 field officers and subalterns, 9,036 lower ranks killed, for a total of 9,252 men; 14 generals, 1,223 field officers and subalterns, 17,989 lower ranks wounded, for a total of 19,226 men; one general (probably Likhachëv), 46 field officers and subalterns, 9,981 lower ranks missing, for a total of 10,028 men (from whom many are believed to have been killed or died of wounds, because no more than 1,000 men were taken prisoner by the French in total); while the casualties from First Army reached 38,000 men overall. There is no such information about the losses from Second Army, because all the formation and many unit commanders had been killed or wounded, and there was no one to compile the returns. The casualties from Second Army can be put without doubt at 20,000 men as follows: from the action at Shevardino and the battle of Borodino, about 58,000 men were out of action; but from this total the following should be excluded: firstly, the losses suffered by our troops at Shevardino (reaching, according to Barclay de Tolly, some 6,000 men) and secondly, some 8,000 to 10,000 men, who, scattered in the heat of battle, subsequently rejoined the force, and therefore the losses to our armies in the battle of Borodino overall may be determined without doubt as some 44,000 men.[36] Among those who laid down their lives in defence of the Fatherland were many outstanding generals: Prince Bagration, a hero

---

35 Description of Operations by First Army: 'I ordered a reconnaissance to see if the enemy still occupied the high ground in the centre; only small sub-units were found there, preparing to fall back. As a result, I instructed General Miloradovich to reoccupy this high ground with several battalions and one battery at dawn.'
36 Hoffmann, 66. Casualty returns for First Army for the battle were compiled by Duty General Kikin.

deserving of his place of honour in military history;[37] Tuchkov 1st, an educated as well as a courageous warrior; the gifted Kutaisov and Tuchkov 4th, one of the three brothers who shed their blood in the Patriotic War of 1812; the wounded included: Yermolov, having written the glorious feat he accomplished with his blood – the recapture of the Kurgan battery; Count Vorontsov, who fought with his grenadiers almost to the point of their total annihilation; Saint-Priest, Prince Gorchakov, Prince Carl zu Mecklenburg, the Bakhmetev brothers, one of whom (commander 23rd Division) had a leg torn off; Likhachëv, Neverovsky and another nine generals.[38]

On the part of the enemy, the casualties extended, according to Denniée, to over 28,000 men. 12 generals, ten colonels, 6,547 officers and lower ranks were killed; 37 generals, 27 colonels, 21,453 officers and lower ranks wounded. General Staff Surgeon Larrey [Dominique-Jean Larrey] calculated Napoleon's losses in the Battle of Borodino and in the action at Shevardino at 22,000, while Thiers gave 30,000 men. Taking into account that after the battle there were fewer than 100,000 men left in Napoleon's army, it emerges that the enemy losses were no fewer than ours.[39] Among those who were rendered out of action on 5 and 7 September (new style) were *généraux de divison*: Montbrun, Caulaincourt, Chastel, Rapp, Nansouty, Grouchy, Morand, Friant, Dessaix, Compans, Belliard, Tharreau [Jean-Victor Tharreau], Saint-Germain, Bruyere, Pajol, Defrance and Scheler [Johann Georg Freiherr von Scheler], of whom the first three were killed and the rest wounded; nine *généraux de brigade* were killed and 23 wounded.[40]

As for trophies, in comparison to the bitterness and bloodshed of the Battle of Borodino, they were few indeed. On each side some 13 to 15 guns were captured in battle, according to various sources that do not completely agree with each other; in addition, some of the guns that were in our fortifications fell into the hands of the enemy.[41] Foreign historians claim that we lost as many as 40 guns overall, but, after

---

37 Prince Bagration was evacuated to Moscow, and from there to the village of Sima, in Vladimir Governorate, Alexandrov district, where he died, in severe pain, on 12 [24] September. Shortly before his death, he had the consolation of receiving the following Rescript: 'Prince Pëtr Ivanovich. Having heard with pleasure of your exploits and diligent service, I was very saddened by the wound you have suffered, diverting you from the field of battle for a while, where your presence in the current military situation has been so necessary and useful. I hope and pray that God will grant you a speedy recovery to add to your deeds with new honours and glory. In the meantime, not as a reward for your merits, which will be delivered to you shortly, but as a certain allowance for your condition, I have granted you a lump sum of 50,000 Roubles. I remain grateful to you. St Petersburg, 31 August [12 September] 1812. Alexander.'
38 Those killed or mortally wounded were: Prince Bagration, Tuchkov 1st, Tuchkov 4th, Count Kutaisov; wounded or suffering severe contusions: Yermolov, Count Osterman, Prinz Carl zu Mecklenburg, Saint Priest, Prince Gorchakov, Bakhmetev 1st, Bakhmetev 2nd, Neverovsky, Count Vorontsov, Likhachëv, Stavitsky [Maxim Fëdorovich Stavitsky], Kern, de-Rossi, Schroeder [Pëtr Petrovich Schroeder], Matsnev [Mikhail Nikolayevich Matsnev], Count Ivelich, Tsybulsky [Ivan Denisovich Tsybulsky], Aleksopol.
39 P. Deniée, 80-81. Ségur, II, 28. Thiers, XIV, 386.
40 The following *généraux de brigade* were rendered out of action: Romeuf, Lanabere, Marion, Compere, Comte Plauzonne, Damas, Bessières [sic] and Gérard [sic] were killed; Gratien, Bonnamy, Boye, Duppelin, Teste, Gengoult, Mourier, Almeras, Beaulieu, Guilllon, Guilleminot, Krasiński, Borstell, Kennot, Russel, Souberwijk, Beurt, Chouart, Doummanger, Lacroix, Teri, Bordesoult and Leppel were wounded.
41 Toll's original notes. Chambray, II, 75-76.

clearing the enemy from the Moscow Governorate, only 17 Russian guns were found in the vicinity of Borodino (namely near the Kolotsky monastery), then it should be assumed that these were the limit of the trophies acquired by the French in the Battle of Borodino.[42]

The reasons for the huge loss of life on our part were: firstly, insufficient tactical training for the Russian troops, among whom were many recruits who did not know how to use the terrain to reduce the casualties caused by enemy musketry, and secondly, the positioning of our troops in several waves standing in close proximity one behind the other: the infantry second wave stood no more than 200 paces behind the first; the cavalry 300 or 400 paces behind the infantry, while the reserves were not more than 1,000 paces from the cavalry, which exposed not only both infantry echelons, but also the cavalry, and sometimes even the reserves, to enemy artillery fire. This arrangement, adopted to counter intensified assaults, forced us to leave the troops inactive for several hours, under a crossfire from powerful batteries. The enemy columns advancing against our position were also concentrated in a small area and suffered huge losses, especially at the beginning of the battle, until they were supported by numerous and cleverly placed batteries. To give an idea of the strength of the fire at the battle of Borodino, it is enough to say that on the part of the enemy, according to the most conservative estimates, 60,000 artillery rounds and 1,400,000 musket rounds were fired. The fire from our side was so strong that on some occasions during the battle Ney ordered his soldiers to lie down in order to protect them as much as possible from the attentions of our artillery.[43]

After the battle of Borodino, the Russian army, having lost about half of the available total of regular troops (44,000 killed and wounded and several thousand missing), counted no more than 52,000 men in its ranks, while Napoleon had more than 95,000 men, to whom the divisions under Pino [Domenico Pino] and Delaborde would soon arrive from Vitebsk and Smolensk respectively: consequently, the enemy forces were almost twice as strong as ours.[44]

---

42 Beitzke, 214. Information regarding the events of 1812, delivered by the local authorities of the Moscow Governorate.
43 'Quant à l'énorme consommation de poudre, les états remis par M. le général comte de Lariboisière, premier inspecteur-général de l'artillerie, attestent qu'il a été tiré 60,000 coups de canon et brulé 1,400,000 cartouches dans la journée du 7 septembre. Or, la bataille, ayant duré environ dix heures (?), c'est par minute 100 coups de canon et 2,300 coups de fusil, sans parler du feu des Russes...' Denniée, 80-81. (As for the enormous consumption of gunpowder, the statements submitted by General Comte de Lariboisière, Premier Inspector-General of Artillery, attest that 60,000 cannon rounds were fired and 1,400,000 cartridges burned during the day of 7 September. Now, the battle, having lasted about ten hours (?), there were 100 cannon rounds and 2,300 musket rounds fired per minute, not to mention the fire from the Russians...). 'L'artillerie française tira dans cette bataille quatre vingt onze mille et quelques cents coups de canon.' Gourgaud. (During this battle, the French artillery fired ninety-one thousand and a few hundred cannon rounds). In one of the statements submitted to Napoleon, we find that 43,578 artillery rounds and more than two million cartridges were fired in the Battle of Borodino. Artillery Journal, 1859, II.
44 Bernhardi, II, 112-114. Bernhardi states that the strength of Napoleon's army, after the battle of Borodino, reached 90,000 men. If that were the case, the enemy would have lost at least 33,000 men in this battle.

Such were the consequences of the Battle of Borodino, one of the most important in modern times. Napoleon himself said more than once: 'Of all my battles, the most terrible was the one I gave near Moscow. In it, the French showed themselves worthy of victory; while the Russians acquired the right to be invincible.' Later, once on the island of St Helena, he expressed the opinion that, 'of the 50 battles I have given, the most valour was shown in the battle near Moscow and the least advantage was won.'[45] The reason for this was the indecision from Napoleon himself, who did not dare to complete the success he had gained by committing his *Garde impériale* to battle. Although nothing in military matters is subject to exact mathematical calculations, nevertheless, judging by the course of the battle, it can be concluded that the participation in this battle of 20,000 men of an elite French force would have delivered a decisive victory for Napoleon,[46] which, being associated with the complete destruction of the Russian army, would have produced a stronger influence on the morale of our nation than the occupation of Moscow by enemy troops. Even assuming that the desperate resistance of our army might have forced Napoleon to retreat, he was not in any danger during this retreat, because he would be protected by numerous cavalry,[47] while upon reaching Smolensk, Napoleon would have strengthened himself by uniting his army with the force under Victor, who had arrived there on 15 (27) September. Any delay in the outcome of the action was as harmful to the enemy as it was beneficial to us: meanwhile, as we were strengthened by reinforcements, the unfavourable season for the conduct of an offensive war drew near and became one of the reasons for the destruction of Napoleon's army.

We have already had occasion to notice that the position at Borodino was occupied by us erroneously, out of a desire to take advantage of its strongest sector, behind the Kolocha river. By deploying almost a full third of the army between Gorki and the Moskva river, where it would have sufficed to place several thousand light troops to monitor the enemy, we exposed the centre, and especially the left wing of our position; remaining in Gorki throughout the entire duration of the battle, Kutuzov would not have a direct influence on the course of the action, but all his orders were very sound, and despite the disadvantages of the initial deployment of the Russian army, the steadfastness of our troops and the self sacrifice of their commanders helped us to hold on to each of the attacked points until reinforcements arrived.[48]

---

45 Pelet, *Bataille de la Moskowa*.
46 [Liprandi claims that Bogdanovich has overstated the *Garde* strength by at least 1,500 men, and states that it is pure speculation that the committal of the *Garde* would have secured a decisive victory, since the Russians still had significant uncommitted or partially used reserves of men and artillery].
47 [Liprandi disputes Napoleon's potential to have retreated in relative safety, stating: 'The efforts of Napoleon's cavalry at Borodino were their last: they were its swan-song. Yet General Bogdanovich suggests that Napoleon could have retreated, having… numerous cavalry to cover his retreat, along a route where everything had been desolated and supplies had not yet been collected nor magazines established'].
48 For the reports by Russian commanders from the battle of Borodino, see Appendix 7.

24

The retreat from Borodino to Moscow

> The situation following the battle of Borodino. – Kutuzov's report to the Tsar. – Awards. – Kutuzov and Rostopchin. – Napoleon's orders following the battle of Borodino. – The state of the forces of both sides on the route from Borodino to Moscow. – Steps taken by Napoleon for the pursuit of the Russian army. – The action at Mozhaisk. – The appointment of Miloradovich as commander of the rearguard. – The action at Krymskoe. – Manning of the Russian forces with Moscow militiamen. – Changes to the establishment of our forces. – The arrival of the Russian army in Moscow. – Wintzingerode's operations.
>
> The position near Moscow. – Barclay de Tolly's thoughts on it. – The meeting on Poklonnaya Gora. – The council of war at Fili. – Kutuzov's subsequent orders.

Following the battle of Borodino, the Russian army was weakened and disorganised, as troops usually are who have endured bitter combat with a powerful enemy, but they had not dismissed the possibility of giving battle once more. The enemy force, with the exception of the *Garde impériale*, being no less disordered than ours, withdrew a little under cover of the thick mist. The French, having forced the troops of our left wing and centre to pull back, considered themselves victorious; The Russians, having retained sectors of the battlefield, did not yet acknowledge themselves as having been defeated.[1] But the superiority of enemy troop numbers prompted us to abandon the fight. Kutuzov foresaw that a retreat from the Borodino position would entail the fall of Moscow, but his only choice was to sacrifice the capital, or the army entrusted to him. And, if we had indeed accepted battle at Borodino for a second time, in all probability, we could not have withdrawn in good order and maintained proper cohesion in the army. On the other hand, there was no doubt that, having undertaken a further retreat, we could neither build ourselves up with significant reinforcements on the way to Moscow, nor find a position of sufficient natural strength that would negate the enemy's double superiority in numbers. In deciding to retreat back along the Moscow highway, Kutuzov was following the guidance of prudence, but was concerned that the retreat of our army and the loss

---

1 From the renowned partisan, Major General Löwenstern's notes.

of Moscow would have a harmful effect on the morale of the nation, and therefore tried to disguise his intentions until the last minute by expressing readiness to give battle again.

The enemy army, despite the advantages it had gained at the battle of Borodino, was in an awkward situation. Napoleon's troops were in dire need of food and fodder; all accommodation from Smolensk to Gzhatsk was filled with sick and wounded; reinforcements and the parks were lagging behind the army. There were only a few stages to Moscow, but already, little by little, the hopes for peace were disappearing and a decline in morale was noticeable among the troops who could see no end to their misfortunes. The further Napoleon's army advanced, the more it became separated from its flanking corps, which, instead of providing support from the rear of the main force, were forced to pay attention exclusively to our own forces operating on the Dvina and in Volhynia, who were constantly strengthening with new reinforcements. From all this it follows that the battle of Borodino satisfied the impatient expectations of the Russian people without changing the relative positions of the opposing sides. Prinz Eugen von Württemberg, setting out the consequences of this event, stated;

> One of my closest friends later left a work which contains a lot of wonderful things about the battle of Borodino. It ends with the following words: 'To be honest, there was no reason for either Kutuzov to proclaim a victory to Emperor Alexander, or for Napoleon to notify Marie-Louise [Maria Ludovica Leopoldina Franziska Therese Josepha Lucia, Erzherzogin von Österreich] about it. If we, the warriors of both sides, putting the enmity of our masters aside for a while, were to appear before the altar of truth tomorrow, then Glory, of course, would recognise us as brothers.'[2]

The reports by our Commander in Chief about the battle of Borodino are neither accurate nor definitive, but are incomparably less exaggerated than the bulletins with which Napoleon misled France and the whole of Europe. Bernhardi pointlessly criticises General Mikhailovsky-Danilevsky [Alexander Ivanovich Mikhailovsky-Danilevsky] for deliberately correcting Prince Kutuzov's report to the Tsar. This report, held in the archives of our Military Topographic Depot, runs as follows:

> Following my report that the enemy made an attack on the 24 [5 September] on the left flank of our army with significant forces, the 25 [6 September] passed in that they were not engaged in significant activity, but yesterday, taking advantage of the mist, at four o'clock, at dawn, they directed all their forces against the left flank of our army. The battle was general and continued right up until nightfall; the losses on both sides were great; the enemy casualties, judging from their tenacious attacks on our fortified positions, must greatly exceed ours. The troops of Your Imperial Majesty fought with incredible valour: the batteries passed from hand to hand and

---

2 Herzog v. Württemberg, *Erinnerungen aus dem Feldzuge des Jahres 1812*, 96.

it ended with the enemy gaining not a single foot of land anywhere with their superior forces. *If it please Your Imperial Majesty to agree that even after 15 hours of the most bloody, continuous combat, ours and the enemy armies could not help but be dismayed about the losses suffered this day, the positions previously occupied naturally became too extended and inappropriate for the force, and therefore, as this is not merely a matter of the glory of battles won, but the entire objective being directed at the destruction of the French army, having spent the night on the field of battle, I took the decision to withdraw six versts, which would put us beyond Mozhaisk,* and having rallied the troops scattered by the fighting, replenishing my artillery and strengthening myself with the Moscow *opolchenie*, in the warm hope of the help of the Almighty and the incredible courage shown by our troops, I shall see what I might be able to do against the enemy. Unfortunately, Prince Pëtr Ivanovich Bagration was wounded by a bullet in the left leg; lieutenant generals Tuchkov and Prince Gorchakov, major generals Bakhmetev, Count Vorontsov, Kretov are wounded. Enemy prisoners and guns and one *général de brigade* were taken: it is currently nighttime and I cannot yet calculate the losses on our part.

27 August [8 September] 1812, the Borodino position.

This same report, by order of the Minister of War, Prince Gorchakov 1st, was printed for public consumption in the 70th issue of the *Severnaya Pochta*, dated 31 August [12 September], 1812, but not in the form in which it was sent by Kutuzov, and with the exception of the lines marked in italics.[3] Consequently, the report to the Tsar by our Commander in Chief was completely justified, except for the statement; 'with the enemy gaining not a single foot of land anywhere.' Emperor Alexander could not have been misled about the consequences of the battle of Borodino by such a report, but wanting to maintain national confidence in himself and confidence in Kutuzov, he accepted this report as news of a victory. Having received it on His saint's name day, 30 August [11 September], the Tsar with both Empresses, the Grand Dukes and Grand Duchess Anna Pavlovna went to the Nevsky Monastery and listened to the Divine Liturgy there, after which Prince Gorchakov, who was head of the Ministry of War, read out Kutuzov's report, and after that, they took to their knees to offer a prayer of thanksgiving. The news of the battle of Borodino was received with enthusiasm; everyone had been waiting for a decisive engagement with the enemy for a long time, and as usual, rumour attributed a decisive victory to us.

Emperor Alexander, in recognition for the achievements of Prince Kutuzov, promoted him to General Field Marshal and granted him 100,000 Roubles.[4] The

---

3   Prince Kutuzov's report to the Tsar, dated 27 August [8 September] (Military Topographic Depot, No. 46,692).
4   Rescript addressed to the Commander in Chief of the armies, General Prince Golenishchev-Kutuzov: 'Prince Mikhail Ilarionovich. Your famous feat in repulsing the main enemy force, which dared to approach our ancient capital, has drawn my and the entire Fatherland's attention to these new achievements. Complete the work you have begun so successfully, exploiting the advantages thus gained and not allowing the enemy to recover. May the hand of the Lord be over you and over our brave soldiery, from whom Russia awaits its glory and

following awards were granted to his main colleagues: Order of St George, 2nd class to Barclay de Tolly, 50,000 Roubles to Prince Bagration, the Order of St Alexander Nevsky with diamonds to Miloradovich and Dokhturov, the Order of St Alexander Nevsky to Count Osterman and Raevsky. Kaptsevich, Lavrov, Prince Golitsyn, Borozdin 1st, Borozdin 2nd, Prince Gorchakov, Prinz Eugen von Württemberg, Laptev, Kostenetsky, Olsufiev, Foch [Boris Borisovich Foch], Count Sievers, Kretov and Löwenstern all received the Order of St George 3rd class. Swords with diamonds were awarded to; Herzog Alexander von Württemberg, Prinz von Oldenburg, Konovnitsyn, Prince Shakhovskoy, Count Ozharovsky [Adam Petrovich Ozharovsky] and Panchulidzev. Yermolov, Vistitsky, Prince Guryalov [Ivan Stepanovich Guryalov], Paskevich, Count Vorontsov, Duka, Tsvilenev [Alexander Ivanovich Tsvilenev], Baron Rosen, Shevich, Ivashev [Pëtr Nikiforevich Ivashev] and Förster [Yegor Khristianovich Förster] all received the Order of St Anne, 1st class. Prinz zu Mecklenburg, Bakhmetev 2nd, Korf, Vasilchikov, Neverovsky, Dorokhov and Count Stroganov were all promoted to lieutenant general. All lower ranks who were present at the battle were granted five Roubles each. *Feldwebel* Zolotov, from the 18th Jäger Regiment, was promoted to sub-lieutenant for the capture of General Bonnamy.[5]

It is rather difficult to say anything definitive about Kutuzov's intentions following the battle of Borodino. On 19 (31) August, at the moment that Kutuzov was retreating from Tsarevo-Zaimishche towards Borodino, Rostopchin asked him to clarify whether he intended to defend Moscow, or to retreat to save the army. In the latter case, Count Rostopchin intended, having taken measures to save the inhabitants, to go to join the army with the entire armed population. But even before receiving this letter, Kutuzov, in a reply to Rostopchin, from Gzhatsk, dated 17 (29) August, asking him to send the *opolchenie* to Mozhaisk and to supply the warriors with muskets, wrote:

---

all Europe its tranquillity. As a reward for your virtues and labours, We entrust you with the rank of General Field Marshal, We grant you the sum of 100,000 Roubles, and Command that your wife, the princess, attend Us at court as a Lady of State. We grant five Roubles per man to all the lower ranks who were at the battle. We await the special report from you regarding the main commanders who worked alongside you, and after that, about all the other ranks, such that, according to your opinion, appropriate rewards may be made. We remain grateful to you. Signed in original by My Own Hand Signed: Alexander His Imperial Majesty, 31 August [12 September] 1812.'

5 Supreme Orders. Army Orders by Prince Kutuzov. On the occasion of the award of 50,000 Roubles to Prince Bagration, a Supreme Rescript in his name was issued, with the following content: 'Prince Pëtr Ivanovich. Having heard with pleasure of your exploits and diligent service, I was very saddened by the wound you have suffered, diverting you from the field of battle for a while, where your presence in the current military situation has been so necessary and useful. I hope and pray that God will grant you a speedy recovery to add to your deeds with new honours and glory. In the meantime, not as a reward for your merits, which will be delivered to you shortly, but as a certain allowance for your condition, I have granted you a lump sum of 50,000 Roubles. I remain grateful to you. Signed in original by My Own Hand His Imperial Majesty Signed: Alexander St Petersburg, August 1812.' Collection of Supreme Manifestos, Letters, Decrees, Rescripts, etc. issued during 1812, 1813, 1814, 1815 and 1816. St Petersburg, 1816.

> Having not yet seen the Minister of War, who hitherto was commanding the armies, and not being sufficiently informed about all the resources available to them, I cannot say anything conclusive about future plans regarding operations by the armies. The question has not yet been resolved: should we sacrifice the army, or lose Moscow? In my opinion, the loss of Moscow is comparable to the loss of Russia.

Thereafter, Kutuzov, being in constant communication with Count Rostopchin, on occasion wrote to him several times a day: in all these memos, our Commander in Chief turned to Rostopchin with demands for the delivery from Moscow of bread, entrenching tools, carts and, in general, everything needed for the army, and informed him of his intentions. Upon arrival at the Borodino position, Kutuzov wrote to him:

> Having found a position for a general battle that is most advantageous to our side near the village of Borodino, having established myself in it and hoping, with the help of Almighty God, to drive the enemy away, I consider it necessary to anticipate and most humbly ask Your Excellency: firstly, to return the 32 doctors sent to Moscow with a convoy of sick to the army without delay, and seek out, if possible, some more freelance practitioners, and secondly, from the Sovereign Emperor, I have a verbal Supreme Command to establish mobile magazines using civilian drivers, to that end you are to hire them with wagons up to a thousand or more in order to use them for supplies, but more importantly to resupply the pursuit of the enemy, should the Almighty bless our armed forces with success. I entrust all this to your Excellency's peerless diligence and look forward to your sending them here.[6]

In subsequent memos to Count Rostopchin, Kutuzov repeated his request for the dispatch of carts (a thousand for each stage from Moscow to Mozhaisk), informed him of the outcome of the action at the Kolotsky monastery, about the measures taken to protect Tver from the enemy and about the action at Shevardino.[7] Thereafter, on the orders of the Commander in Chief, Kaiserov wrote to Rostopchin from the field of battle at Borodino:

> I ask you in God's name, Count Fëdor Vasilevich, give orders for us to be sent immediately complete resupply loads of ammunition for 500 guns from the arsenal, mostly of heavy types. No. 69, 26 August [7 September] 1812. The village of Borodino, at two o'clock in the afternoon.[8]

---

6   Kutuzov's memo to General of Infantry Count Rostopchin, dated 22 August [3 September], No. 17.
7   Memos dated 23 August [4 September], No. 25, dated the 24 [5 September] No. 31, dated the 25 [6 September], dated the 26 [7 September], No. 68 (the latter two were signed by Kaiserov).
8   [Since the village of Borodino had been occupied by the French since dawn, Liprandi suggests this should read 'position at Borodino'].

Kutuzov himself added:

> This battle is of the bloodiest. We shall hold on. So far it is going fairly well.

On the same day, probably at a time when he was still hoping to resume the battle of Borodino, Prince Kutuzov wrote:

> Today's was a very heated and bloody battle. The Russian army, with the help of God, has not yielded a single step during it, although the enemy has been operating against them in very superior numbers. Tomorrow, placing my faith in God and in the Moscow Shrine, I hope to fight with renewed vigour. I am relying upon Your Excellency to deliver to me as many troops as possible from the forces under your command. From the field of battle at the village of Borodino. No. 70, 26 August [7 September] 1812.

On the following day, in a memo to Count Rostopchin regarding the outcome of the battle, using almost the same wording as was in his report to the Tsar, Kutuzov wrote:

> The sincerity with which I tell you this, and my intentions should calm Moscow, and after an appeal made by Your Excellency, from your well-known love for the Fatherland I shall await all the donations that the capital may be able to give to the army.[9]

Having decided to retreat after the battle of Borodino, in all his subsequent orders, Kutuzov showed the hope of again giving battle in defence of Moscow. The concession of the ancient capital to the enemy seemed so incredible to every Russian that both Kutuzov and Rostopchin, wishing to reassure each other on account of the fate of Moscow, exaggerated the resources at their disposal and involuntarily misled not only each other, but also themselves. On the very day that our army arrived at Borodino, Rostopchin wrote to Kutuzov:

> … Count Morkov should already be with Your Grace by now, and I, with the exception of an unknown number of residents from Moscow and its environs have some 10,000 men in uniform and more than half of them trained recruits. I have already sent couriers to the neighbouring governorates, such that their *opolchenie* should come to Moscow.[10]

For his part, right up until his arrival in the capital, Prince Kutuzov did not cease to reassure Rostopchin of his intention to defend it to the bitter end. On 27 August [8 September], the day after the battle of Borodino, the Commander in Chief wrote:

> After the most bloody of battles that took place yesterday, in which our troops suffered understandably significant losses, in proportion to their

---

9   Prince Kutuzov's memo, dated 27 August [8 September], No. 71, from the position at Borodino.
10 Rostopchin's memo dated 22 August [3 September].

courage, although the battle is completely won, my intention is that, in order to inflict the strongest effect on the enemy, having drawn to myself as many resources as possible from Moscow, it may be possible to chance a decisive battle with an already partially defeated enemy force. The assistance that I require is varied, and therefore I am sending Colonel Prince Kudashev to present it personally to Your Excellency and ask that everything that Moscow is able to give, in terms of troops, a resupply of artillery, ammunition and horses, and supplies, which are to be expected from faithful sons of the Fatherland, everything that might be sent to an army expecting to fight the enemy. And to whom can I turn with greater reliance for all these needs, if not to the one known for his love and zeal for the Fatherland, the worthy governor of the ancient capital.[11]

On 30 August (11 September), Kutuzov, already at Vyazema, 35 *versts* from Moscow, wrote to Count Rostopchin:

We are anticipating a general battle near Moscow, but the thought that I will not have the means to evacuate the wounded on carts appals me. I ask Your Excellency in God's name for assistance as soon as possible.[12]

Count Rostopchin had done everything he could: he had sent Count Morkov to Mozhaisk with elements of the Moscow *opolchenie*, attended to the dispatch of a thousand carts to each stage on the route between the army and Moscow, sent a complete resupply load of ammunition for 125 guns and entrenching tools to the troops and reinforced the army with two newly formed regiments, totalling 4,000 men.[13] But all this was not enough to hold an enemy almost twice our strength. We had already made many sacrifices in defence of the Fatherland; it remained to make the last, great sacrifice.

After the battle of Borodino, Napoleon initially turned his attention to the care of the wounded, but all his attentions were ineffective due to a lack of resources, and many patients only received their first field dressing 72 hours after the battle. At the same time, Napoleon instructed General Lariboisière [Jean Ambroise Baston de Lariboisière] to deliver ammunition to the army from Smolensk. To that end, he was allowed to use between 600 to 800 horses from the pontoon parks left in Smolensk. The shortage of ammunition almost forced Napoleon to stop short of Moscow. Various troop formations, who were *en route* to the *Grande Armée*, from Smolensk, Minsk, Vilna, Kovno, Königsberg [Kaliningrad], and in particular, march battalions and squadrons assigned to replenish the force, were ordered to close up to the army.[14]

---

11 Kutuzov's memo, dated 27 August [8 September], from Zhukovo.
12 Prince Kutuzov's memo dated 30 August [11 September], from Malaya Vyazema.
13 Rostopchin's letters to Kutuzov dated 25 and 27 August [6 and 8 September].
14 Thiers, XIV, *Edit. de Brux.* 390-391. In Berthier's memo to Marshal Bessières dated 15 (27) September 1812, regarding the French operation for the advance on Moscow, it states: 'Kutuzov, retreating towards Moscow, has done as he should: he has entrenched himself in good positions, as if he has the intention of giving battle for a second time. If the returns filed by the Chief of Artillery Lariboisière had shown fewer than 20,000 rounds, then the Emperor

The retreat from Borodino to Moscow was carried out by our troops with good discipline, as much as could be expected after a bitter, bloody battle. Barclay de Tolly asserts the opposite,[15] but, despite his truthful reputation, such an assessment was hardly impartial. If all the infractions described by Barclay really had happened, then the Russian army, pursued by the indefatigable Murat, could not have retreated step by step, leaving neither transport nor stragglers behind for the enemy.[16] Our troops, as before, had bread or hard-tack, cereals, meat and wine rations delivered from Moscow and Kaluga, and they could get fodder everywhere along the way. Only the cavalry who were in the rearguard were in a worse condition than the other troops, being unable to unsaddle their horses, and therefore almost all of them were rubbed raw.[17]

The enemy troops, as they penetrated deeper into our country, encountered great difficulties. The carts carrying food could not keep up with the troops, or were depleted without any hope of replenishing them with further supplies. The Russians, as they were retreating, destroyed not only the pre-stocked magazines in the towns behind them, but the towns and villages themselves. The countryside, already sparsely populated, had been abandoned and presented the image of a desert to view. The cavalry was forced to search for fodder, deviating from the roads off to the sides for a considerable distance. The shortage of drinking water, from which our troops also suffered in the hot summer of 1812, was even more painful for the enemy, who were often held up by our rear guard in places where they considered it good fortune to find a muddy puddle. They had to repair bridges destroyed by our rear guard at every stage. To all these factors which hampered the operations of Napoleon's army, ignorance of the area had to be added. Our troops, retreating along the highway, demolished sign posts and thus deprived the enemy of the basic means of navigating in an unknown country. All these things, delaying and hampering the French army, helped Kutuzov to restore good order in our force on the road from Borodino to Moscow.[18]

On 27 August (8 September), even before dawn, the Russian troops, having withdrawn from the Borodino position, retreated beyond Mozhaisk to the village of Zhukovo. The Cossacks, four jäger regiments from II Corps with the Tobolsk Infantry and Infantry Regiment from 4th Division remained in position until 11 o'clock in the

---

would have halted, no matter how advantageous the battlefield might have been, because the capture of redoubts would be impossible without more artillery and shells.'
15 Description of Operations by First Army, compiled by Barclay de Tolly.
16 The distance of about 120 *versts* between Borodino and Moscow was covered in six short stages. Chambray states: '*Depuis Mojaisk Koutouzof se retira sur Moscou, apportant tous ses soins à retablir l'ordre dans son infanterie et à lui rendre une confiance qui devait être ébranlée par les revers de Borodino. La lenteur que mit Napoléon dans sa poursuite et la bonne contenance de Miloradowitz lui permirent d'atteindre ce résultat.*' Histoire de l'éxpedition de Russie, II, 97. (From Mozhaisk Kutuzov withdrew to Moscow, taking every care to re-establish order in his infantry and to restore their confidence which must have been shaken by the reverse at Borodino. Napoleon's sluggishness in the pursuit and the good showing by Miloradovich enabled him to achieve this objective).
17 Clausewitz, *Der Feldzug von 1812 in Russland*, 169.
18 Clausewitz, 167-172.

morning.¹⁹ Our main force retreated from the battlefield in two columns: the first consisted of troops from the right wing and centre, moving along the road leading from Borodino to Mozhaisk, while the left [wing], of troops under Dokhturov,²⁰ went along the old Smolensk road. To cover this retreat, the rearguard under Platov's command, was composed of most of the Cossack regiments, four regiments of jägers from II Corps and one hussar regiment, with 12 horse artillery pieces.

Meanwhile, as our troops retreated to Mozhaisk, the French spent the night in bivouacs, among the dead, wounded and dying, without fires and without bread. After all the discomfort and hardship suffered by the troops of Napoleon's army, after all the feats of self-sacrifice and courage they had shown, there were none of the usual accompaniments to a victory; neither a discernible sense of joy nor triumph in them. On the contrary, the French remained in some state of shock, seeing no end to their misfortunes.²¹ For the pursuit of the retreating Russian army, the vanguard, under Murat's command, was composed of the four corps of the *Réserve de cavalerie* and Dufour's *2e Division* [François Marie Dufour] (formerly Friant's). They were followed by Mortier [Adolphe Édouard Casimir Joseph Mortier] with the *Jeune Garde* and Davout's *1er Corps*, and behind them, Ney's *3e Corps* and the *Vieille Garde*. Poniatowski marched along the old Smolensk road and then turned right towards Borisovo; while the Viceroy's *4e Corps*, having been rejoined by Pino's *15e Division* even crossed the Moskva river, downstream of its confluence with the Kolocha, at the village of Uspenskoe, marching to the left of the main force towards Ruza. The troops of the Westphalian *8e Corps* under Junot were left on the field of the battle of Borodino, in order to care for the wounded, and then to go to Mozhaisk until Napoleon's army returned there from Moscow.²²

Napoleon, intending to move his *État-major général* into Mozhaisk immediately after the battle of Borodino, ordered Murat to eject our troops from the city. Kutuzov, noticing the advance by the enemy in significant numbers, ordered Major General Rosen commanding the jägers in the rear guard to hold the city with Platov. The infantry and artillery occupied Mozhaisk, the Cossacks were stationed more to the left, while both of our armies were located on the high ground behind the city in order to support these troops. The enemy, approaching Mozhaisk, at five o'clock in the afternoon, opened a strong cannonade, but did not manage to capture the city.²³

On the following day, 28 August (9 September), the Russian army set off for Zemlino (18 *versts* from Zhukovo). The rearguard, reinforced by I Cavalry Corps, which had suffered the least in the battle of Borodino, being fiercely attacked by Murat, was forced to yield Mozhaisk to the enemy and retreat to Modenova, at a distance of no more than three *versts* from the location of the main body of our army. Upon leaving Mozhaisk, we did not have enough carts to evacuate our wounded, and therefore

---

19 *Erinnerungen aus dem Feldzuge des Jahres 1812*, 97. Bernhardi asserts that II Cavalry Corps also remained behind, facing the Raevsky battery until nine o'clock in the morning.
20 [Liprandi states that Dokhturov had returned to command VI Corps by this time and was, therefore, not with this column].
21 Chambray, II, 82.
22 Chambray, II, 82-83. Bernhardi, II, 125-126.
23 Condensed War Diary, maintained by Colonel Toll.

many of them were left in the city. Chambray puts the number of these unfortunates at 10,000. The enemy, having occupied Mozhaisk, threw the Russians out of their homes onto the streets in order to clear a space for their sick and wounded, with whom not only this city was littered, but the Kolotsky monastery, Gridnevo and the entire surrounding area. For three days after the battle, the maimed were discovered in barns and outbuildings, where they lay without water and without food. The situation for our wounded abandoned in the city was even worse.[24] Kutuzov, concerned that the rearguard might be thrown back onto the main body of the army, reinforced it with four infantry and two jäger regiments with one heavy artillery company.[25] At the same time, being not entirely satisfied with Platov's orders, who had not managed to keep the enemy at a suitable distance from the army that day, Prince Kutuzov entrusted the command of the rearguard to General Miloradovich.[26]

On 29 August (10 September), the Russian army, having made a march of 18 *versts*, pulled back across the Nara River, to the village of Krutitsy, while Miloradovich settled down, not quite four *versts* from this village with the rearguard in positions near the village of Krymskoe. The left wing of the position, resting on a swamp, was held by one of the battalions from 11th Jäger Regiment, scattered across a scrub covered hillside; 4th Jäger Regiment held the scrub and a small wood to the right of the road, at Krymskoe; the 30th Jägers and 48th Jägers made up the right wing, under Colonel Potëmkin's command [Yakov Alexeevich Potëmkin], formed in battalion columns, to the right of the forest. Three batteries defended the approaches to the position. 34th Jägers formed the reserve of the right wing,[27] while 36th Jägers and Second Battalion, 11th Jägers formed the reserve of the left. As the frontage of the position was very limited, then, in order not to hamper the troops, all the other regiments of the rear guard withdrew beyond the river Polga. The Cossack regiments and regular cavalry remained in contact with the enemy.

At five o'clock in the afternoon, Murat's vanguard, pushing back our leading troops, approached Miloradovich's position. Some of our cavalry and Cossacks posted themselves on the right wing; the rest of the cavalry withdrew behind the centre and formed its reserve. Whereupon the enemy attacked Miloradovich's force. Murat's attempts against the left wing and the centre of our position assured him of the inaccessibility of these points; in particular, it was difficult to attack the centre, along a narrow ravine, under enfilading fire from a battery. The enemy, deciding to turn their efforts against our right wing, directed strong infantry columns out of the scrub, under covering fire from batteries, and hurried them towards Krymskoe. In order to support 4th Jägers and Potëmkin's Brigade, 34th Jägers (33rd?),[28] were gradually fed into action from the right, followed by the Libau Infantry and Sofia Infantry stationed behind the Polga.

---

24 Lemasurier, *Medicinische Geschichte des Russischen Feldzuges von 1812*.Lemasurier, *Medicinische Geschichte des Russischen Feldzuges von 1812*. Bernhardi, II, 125. Chambray, II, 90-91.
25 The Libau Infantry, Sofia Infantry, Butyrsk Infantry, Tomsk Infantry with 11th Jägers and 36th Jägers, all from VI Corps, with Gulevich's Battery Artillery Company (Condensed War Diary, maintained by Colonel Toll).
26 Condensed War Diary, maintained by Colonel Toll.
27 According to General Buturlin, it was 33rd Jägers rather than 34th Jägers.
28 [Liprandi comments, dryly: 'Mikhailovsky-Danilevsky also referred to 33rd Jägers, while there is no mention of 34th Jägers. In any case, the brackets and question mark are unprofessional'].

The Butyrsk Infantry and Tomsk Infantry, also crossing the Polga, made up the reserve of the centre. The enemy were driven back into the scrub; and their cavalry, attacked by Uvarov's regiments, retreated in disorder. In this action, about 2,000 of our men were put out of action; among them was Prinz Ernst von Hessen-Philippsthal, who lost a leg; the French casualties were even heavier than ours.[29]

On that same day [10 September, new style], Prince Kutuzov sent a report to the Tsar about his retreat to the Nara river and about his intention to retreat even further, which was prompted both by the extraordinary losses suffered by our troops in the battle of Borodino and the failure of the expected reinforcements to arrive.[30] At the same time, 14,000 warriors from the Moscow *opolchenie* were assigned to infantry regiments to form their third ranks. At the same time, an Army Order was issued instructing them:

> to accept the soldiers of the *Opolchenie*, not as soldiers permanently assigned to this rank, but as men volunteering themselves temporarily for the defence of the Fatherland. And therefore, the soldiers of the Moscow *Opolchenie* will not change their dress, will not shave their beards and, in a word, remain in their former state, and upon fulfilment of this sacred duty they will return to their homes.[31]

Murat's persistent attacks in the action at Krymskoe forced Kutuzov to withdraw the main body of our army 25 *versts* back to Bolshaya-Vyazema (the village of Nikolskoe) on 30 August (11 September), and the next day [12 September, new style] to the village of Mamonova, while the rearguard retreated initially to Kubinskoe, and then to Malaya-Vyazema.[32] Prince Kutuzov, located in the village of Setun, no more than 10 *versts* from Moscow, was convinced of the impossibility of holding the enemy, but could not accept the idea of abandoning our ancient capital to be sacrificed to the enemy. The losses we suffered at Borodino were great, but every Russian believed that it was necessary to chance the fortunes of battle once more: to defend Moscow, or, at least, to sell it at a high price. The Commander in Chief, yielding to the instinctive emotions of the nation and the troops, sent the most experienced General Staff officers to seek out an advantageous defensive position. Meanwhile, throughout the duration of the march from Borodino to Moscow, measures were taken to put in order the most disrupted elements of the army. Those infantry regiments in which fewer than 300 fighting men remained, were reconstituted into a single battalion each. The number of squadrons in the cavalry regiments was also reduced. II Cavalry Corps and III Cavalry Corps were amalgamated into a single corps under the command of Adjutant General Baron Korf. Konovnitsyn took over command of III Corps while Prince Shakovskoy took over 3rd Division in Konovnitsyn's place, Choglokov [Pavel Nikolaevich Choglokov] took over 11th

---

29 Buturlin, I, 353-356 [Liprandi points out: 'It was not Buturlin who wrote about the wounding of Prinz Ernst, but Mikhailovsky-Danilevsky, and yet he is not referenced].
30 Kutuzov's report dated 29 August [10 September], from the village of Naro.
31 Prince Kutuzov's Army Order dated 30 August [11 September], No. 14.
32 Condensed War Diary, maintained by Colonel Toll.

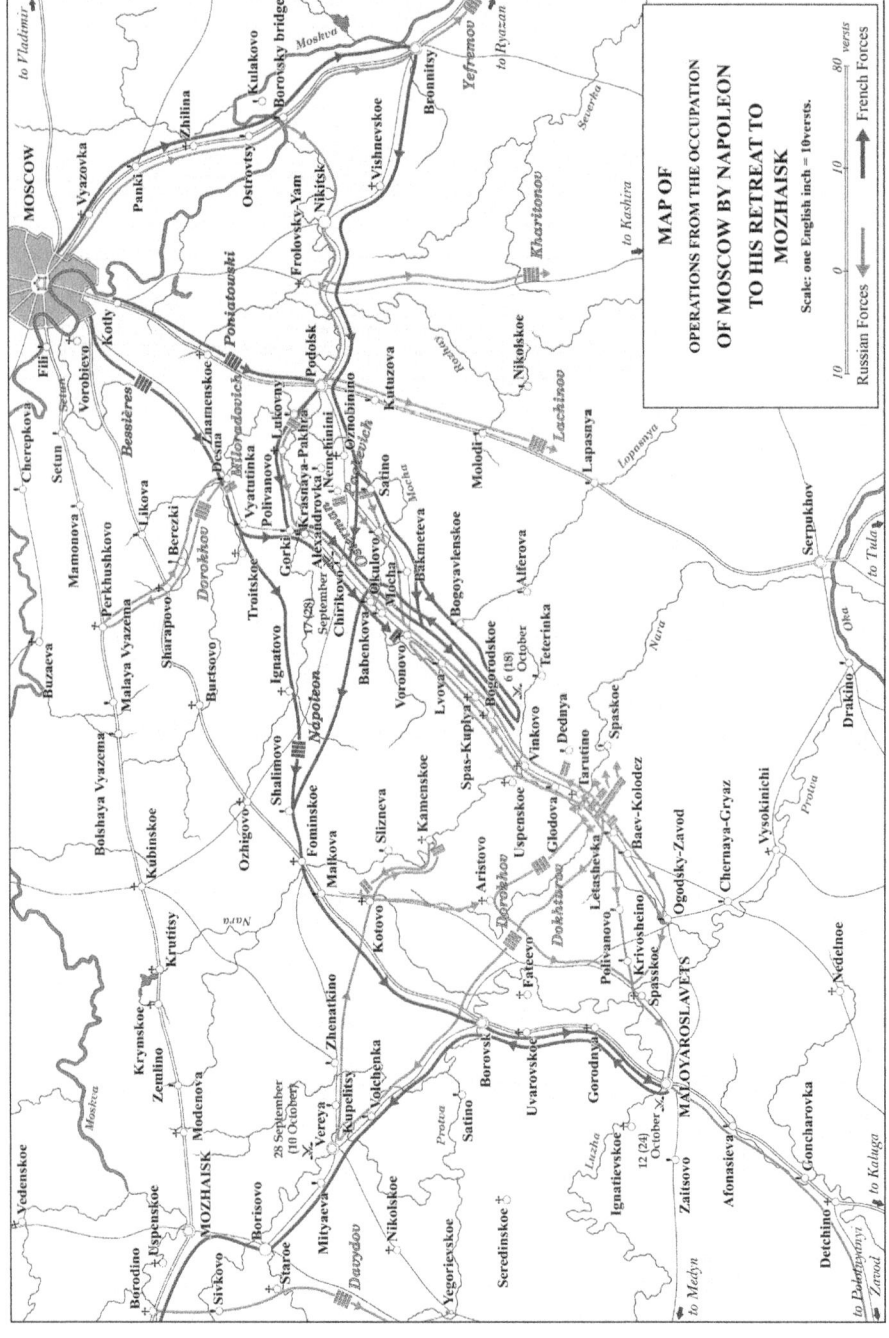

Operations from the occupation of Moscow by Napoleon to his retreat to Mozhaisk.

THE RETREAT FROM BORODINO TO MOSCOW 177

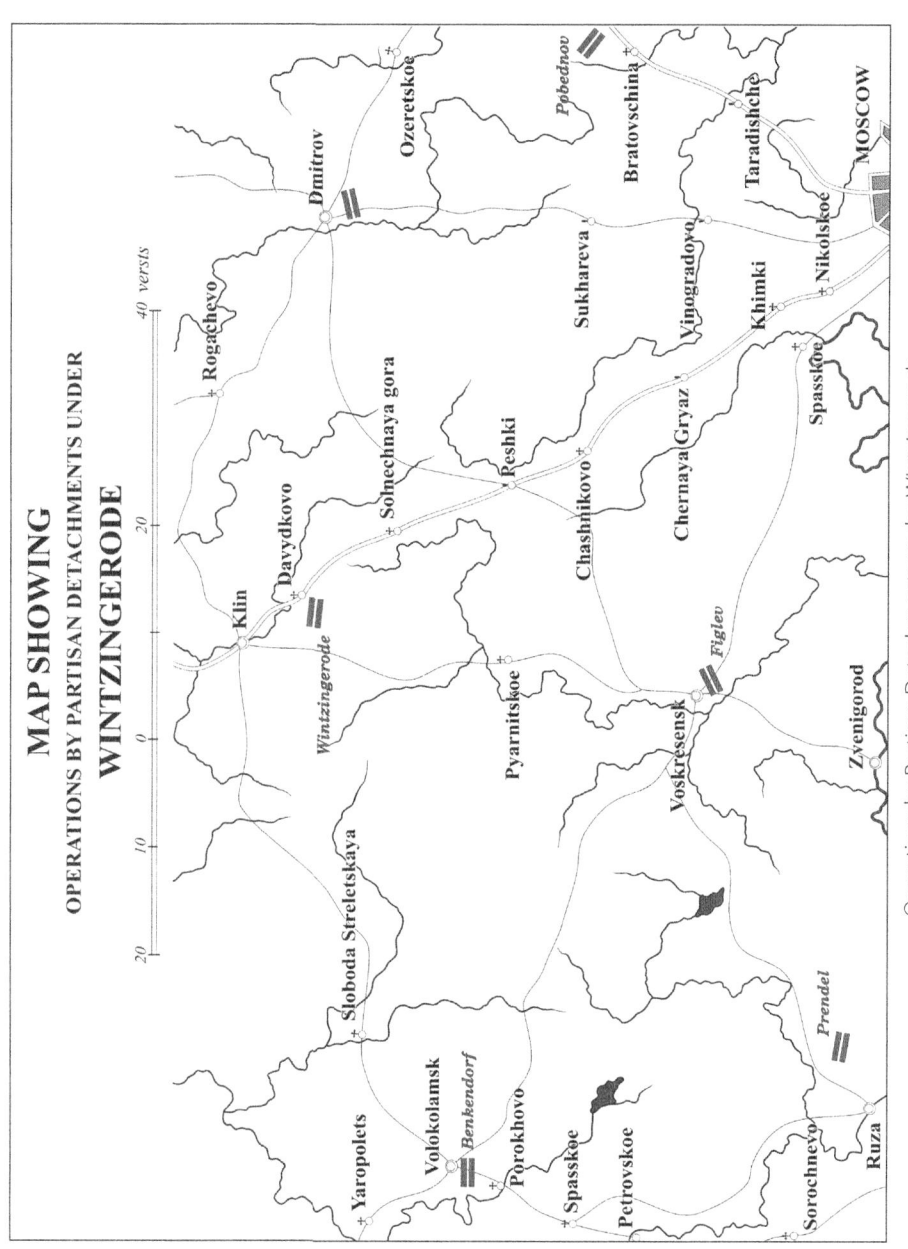

Operations by Partisan Detachments under Wintzingerode.

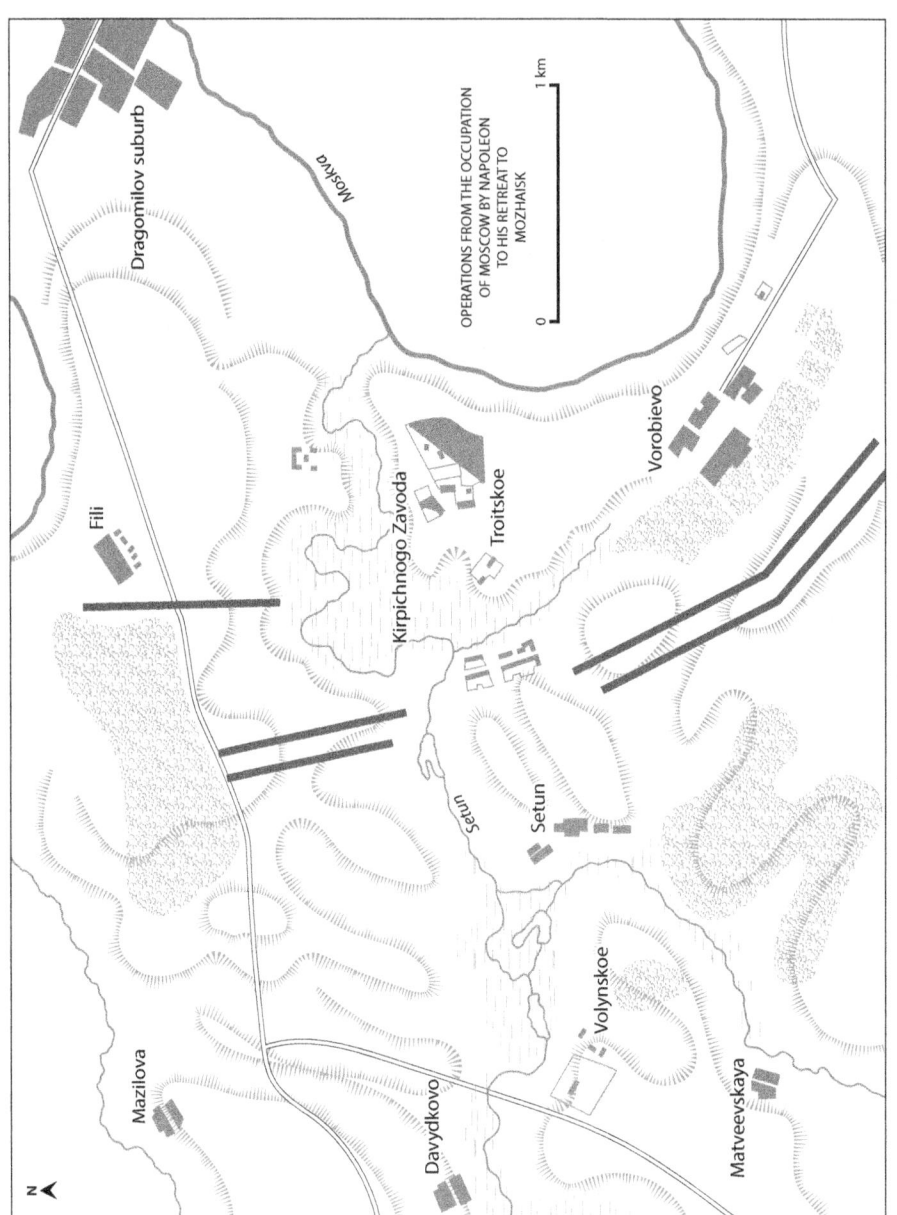
Position forwards of Moscow, 13 September 1812.

Division from Bakhmetev 2nd, Laptev replaced Bakhmetev 1st at 23rd Division and Foch took over 24th Division from Likhachëv.

On 1 (13) September, the Russian army, having set out from Mamonovo, moved towards Moscow and settled in bivouacs, just short of the capital, two *versts* from the Dorogomilov gate. In general, following the battle of Borodino, the enemy pursued us rather weakly, and after the action at Krymskoe in particular. This aroused concerns in Kutuzov's headquarters that the Viceroy might bypass us on our right flank and occupy Moscow, to the rear of our army. To counteract any such envelopment, a detachment under Adjutant General Wintzingerode was established, temporarily supported by the Izyum Hussars and two Cossack regiments.

On the very same day as the battle of Lubino, 7 (19) August, Wintzingerode, closing up to Vitebsk, captured some 800 prisoners; after that, on the orders of Barclay de Tolly, having assembled his detachment and sent Rodionov's [Mark Ivanovich Rodionov] Cossack Regiment to rejoin Wittgenstein's force, he set out for Porechye and on to Dukhovshchina, from where he moved towards Bely. Shortly thereafter, Wintzingerode again closed up to the army and upon arrival in the village of Sorochnevo (half way between Mozhaisk and Volokolamsk), on 27 August (8 September) he heard about the battle of Borodino from enemy marauders captured by Cossacks. Wintzingerode immediately paid a visit to Kutuzov, received orders from him to cover the army from the right flank and to move on Ruza, but on approaching this town, he saw the Viceroy's vast camp nearby, and therefore, waiting for nightfall, moved around the enemy via a circuitous route to the left and, on departing Velkino along the road to Zvenigorod, he forestalled the enemy on the road to Moscow. Meanwhile, the Viceroy marched towards Zvenigorod, while Wintzingerode, delaying his advance, crossed the Moskva river at Spasskoe and, upon arrival at Cherepkova, established communications with the main force and was ordered to move onto the Vladimir road.[33]

As the men of the Russian army approached Moscow, they were placed in a position chosen by General Bennigsen. The right wing rested on a bend of the Moskva river in front of the village of Fili, the centre was between the Volynskoe and Troitskoe villages, while the left wing was stationed on the Vorobievo Hills [Sparrow Hills]; the rearguard remained at Setun.[34] Meanwhile, Kutuzov arrived at Poklonnaya Gora ahead of the troops, where a stool had been set up for him,[35] and most importantly, the formation commanders hurried to familiarise themselves with the ground on which they had to give decisive battle, and gathered on the hill around their Commander in Chief.

The position selected by Bennigsen presented many disadvantages.[36] The high ground on which the troops were intended to be stationed, in the direction from which the enemy was advancing, was formed of fairly gentle slopes, rising like

---

33 Adjutant General Wintzingerode's reports to the Tsar.
34 Condensed War Diary, maintained by Colonel Toll.
35 [Liprandi describes Kutuzov's camp-stool thus: 'whenever the Field Marshal… had the intention of staying in place for some time, he often asked for a stool (it was a low, unpainted stool, almost square, about two or three hands square. There was a hole in the top to make it easier to pick up with one hand), and then one was brought for him; but as long as he did not ask for it, none would be brought and it remained with the escort].
36 See Plan of the Position Forwards of Moscow, 1 (13) September.

terraces; while on the opposite side, just behind the centre and left wing of the position, they are very steep. The position itself is intersected by several ravines that would not permit free communications between the parts of the army, in particular, the right wing was separated from the centre by the Setun river, which flows with much meandering into the Moskva river. The reserves could not be positioned in cover behind the high ground due to the steep slopes, at the foot of which the Moskva flows, while beyond it the capital extends into the distance, and therefore both battle lines and the reserves could only be located on the forward slopes facing the direction of the enemy, which, due to the very limited depth of the position, would expose every echelon to enemy artillery fire. In the event that our army was forced out of this position (which was only to be expected, judging by the great superiority of enemy numbers), our troops would be ejected down the steep cliffs into the river or driven back into the city.[37]

Barclay de Tolly himself, exhausted from a fever at the time, mounted his horse and went to reconnoitre the chosen position. Barclay stated, in his own notes:

> I was astonished. Many of the divisions were isolated by impassable ravines, in one of which a river flowed, completely severing communications. The right wing adjoined a forest that stretched several *versts* in the direction of the enemy, which gave them the opportunity, exploiting the superiority of their marksmen, to take possession of this forest and envelope us from the right flank. Behind the front line of the left wing there was a ravine, between 10 to 15 *sazhen* deep, with such steep slopes that it was barely possible to negotiate it in single file. The reserve of the right wing was so close that every enemy round shot would hit each of our four echelons; while the reserve of the left wing, isolated from the battle lines by the aforementioned ravine, would have remained an idle spectator of the defeat of the troops standing in front, without being able to support them. The infantry of this reserve could at least shoot at the enemy, but hitting their own at the same time; the cavalry, deprived of any opportunity to take part in the battle, would have had to immediately take flight, or remain inactive until it was destroyed by enemy artillery fire. The position extended for almost four *versts*; the army, weakened by the battle of Borodino, having occupied its entire length, would have been stretched out as thin as spider silk… To the rear was the river, and beyond that a vast city. Eight bridges of boats had been constructed on this river, upstream and downstream of the city; but it should be noted that the slopes down to the bridges built upstream of the city were so steep that only infantry could negotiate them. In the event of a defeat, the entire army would have been wiped out to the last man…[38]

Aware of the disadvantages of the proposed position, Barclay de Tolly hurried to the right flank to Prince Kutuzov, and meeting Bennigsen, passed his comments on

---

37 Bernhardi, II, 134-135.
38 Description of Operations by First Army, compiled by Barclay de Tolly.

to him. Bennigsen was apparently taken aback by this and announced to Barclay that he was going to the left wing immediately himself, but instead retired to his quarters in the village lying behind the centre of the position. When, after that, Barclay de Tolly explained the situation of the army to Kutuzov, the Commander in Chief expressed a desire to know Toll's opinion, who confessed that he would never have proposed such a position and that by taking it, we were in peril.[39] Whereupon, the Commander in Chief, turning to Yermolov, asked: 'what do you think of the position?' and received in reply that 'although it is difficult to assess the ground in order to position 60,000 or 70,000 men at first glance, nevertheless, one can see great shortcomings in it and I doubt our ability to hold it.' As this opinion was expressed by Yermolov with his usual passion, Kutuzov, taking his wrist and feeling his pulse, asked him: 'Are you alright, my friend?' But straight afterwards ordered him, together with Toll and with Colonel Crossard [Jean Baptiste Louis baron de Crossard], who had transferred to our service from the Spanish,[40] to inspect the position and report on its shortcomings.

Meanwhile, the construction of fortifications on Poklonnaya Gora continued, traces of which were still visible in the 1850s. But the movement of troops assigned to the occupation of the Vorobievo hills was suspended. Many of their commanders gradually gathered around Kutuzov. Rostopchin also arrived. It was not difficult for him to recognise at a glance the impossibility of defending Moscow. All units in the force were noticeably weakened; there were differences of opinion between their commanders. An eyewitness to the events we are describing, Prinz Eugen von Württemberg, stated:

> Kutuzov listened to the assessments from the generals around him without saying a word, but it was impossible not to notice his genuine agitation. And, in fact, it required a great deal of determination, taking upon oneself all the responsibility for the cession of the ancient capital of the Empire to the enemy, contrary to the opinions of the nation and the troops, to yield following a successful battle, as all of Russia was convinced at the time, and after a completely unforced retreat, to yield, finally, having an army the numerical strength of which reached 90,000, including Cossacks and the *opolchenie*, as was claimed.[41]

Yet it was even more difficult to give battle in which defeat was beyond doubt. Kutuzov, having weighed the consequences of both courses of action, had decided to sacrifice Moscow, but did not want to be the first to say a word about the necessity for this sacrifice, and even argued with Rostopchin, who, having guessed the intentions of the old commander, explained to him that the enemy, having captured Moscow, would not gain any significant benefit, because most of the state and private property had already been evacuated from the city, where there were no more than

---

39 Description of Operations by First Army.
40 [Born in France, Crossard served as a counter-revolutionary *emigré*, in the Dutch and Austrian armies before serving as an Austrian military attaché in Spain].
41 *Erinnerungen aus dem Feldzuge des Jahres 1812*, 98.

40,000 residents by this time. It is claimed that Count Rostopchin even let slip that the troops, having passed through Moscow, would see it in flames.[42]

Upon Yermolov's return from reconnaissance, he reported in detail to the Commander in Chief about the disadvantages he had noticed around the position. Kutuzov asked him: 'Would it not be possible to retreat from here to the Kaluga road?'[43] and received in response: 'the enemy, attacking us in this position, will get close to that road and prevent us from retreating along it,' he fell silent and at one o'clock in the afternoon left for the village of Fili, to the quarters prepared for him, whispering covertly to Prinz Eugen von Württemberg on the way out: *'ici, ma tête, fut-elle bonne ou mauvaise, ne doit cependant s'aider que d'elle même.'* (here, in my head, for good or ill, I must however only rely upon myself). Following this, Count Rostopchin, approaching the prince, said with feeling:

> If you asked me what to do, I would answer: destroy the capital before you cede it to the enemy. That is my opinion, as Count Rostopchin; but as the governor bound to look after the welfare of the capital, I cannot offer such advice.[44]

Upon Kutuzov's departure, all the generals who had gathered on the Poklonnaya Gora dispersed.

Following this meeting, Prince Kutuzov, having decided to abandon Moscow, but not wanting to take on sole responsibility for such a decision, convened a council of war for five o'clock in the afternoon. The question of the fate of Moscow was decided in a cottage, which to this day has been preserved in the same state as it was during the council by the defenders of Russia.[45] On receipt of the summons from the Commander in Chief, Barclay de Tolly, Dokhturov, Uvarov, Count Osterman, Konovnitsyn, Yermolov and Kaiserov arrived immediately, Toll arriving shortly thereafter. They waited for Bennigsen until six o'clock, while Raevsky arrived after everyone else. Miloradovich did not attend, as he was unable to leave the rearguard. Bennigsen opened the meeting by posing the question: 'Is it better to fight under the walls of Moscow, or to abandon it to the enemy?' Kutuzov interrupted Bennigsen's speech with a criticism of the incongruity and mindlessness of the question he had raised, which, in his opinion, was utterly pointless without a preliminary statement of all the facts of the matter. After explaining in detail all the information regarding the position on the Vorobievo hills presented to him by Barclay, Yermolov and Toll, the Commander in Chief said:

> As long as the army exists and as long as it retains the ability to resist the enemy, then there remains a hope of ending the war successfully; in contrast, following the destruction of the army, not only is Moscow lost, but also Russia.

---

42 [As Liprandi asks: claimed by whom? There is no reference].
43 [Liprandi believes that this mention of the Kaluga road indicates that Kutuzov was already considering a line of retreat along the latter; even before the council of war at Fili].
44 [Liprandi bemoans the lack of a source for this quote, considering its importance].
45 [The cottage burned down in 1868, was restored in 1887, and since 1962 has been a branch of the Borodino Panorama Museum].

He concluded by proposing for the consideration of the Council: 'should we await the assault in a disadvantageous position, or cede Moscow to the enemy?'

It seemed that the question thus proposed would not allow for differences of opinion: it turned out otherwise. Barclay de Tolly, with his customary bluntness, explained that, in giving battle in the position in front of Moscow, it was impossible to avoid a total defeat, and therefore recommended a retreat along the road towards Nizhny Novgorod in order to maintain communications, both with St Petersburg and with the southern governorates of the Empire. Colonel Toll expressed his agreement with everything that was said about the disadvantages of the position, proposing to occupy another with the right wing on the village of Vorobievo, and the left on the new Kaluga road, directed between the villages of Shatilova and Voronovo, and then, if necessary, to retreat towards the old Kaluga road. After that, Kutuzov ordered Yermolov to speak, who was aware of the thoroughness of the retreat proposed by Barclay de Tolly and disagreed with him only in the direction of Nizhny Novgorod, which exposed us to the danger of losing communications with our central governorates and with the armies under Tormasov and Chichagov, but understanding the general mood and the mindset of the people and the army, he proposed to fight in defence of Moscow. Bennigsen, taking advantage of the differences of opinion, continued to argue against the need for a retreat. Unable to say anything in favour of his chosen position, for which the disadvantages were obvious, he spread about the undesirable consequences of leaving Moscow, about the losses associated with it, about the impact of such an event on the morale of the nation. He stated:

> It is shameful to give up the capital without a shot; if we decide on this, will it not be an admittance that we lost the battle of Borodino? It is easy to foresee what effect the enemy occupation of Moscow will have in foreign courts and in Europe in general! I don't understand on what basis it is assumed that we will certainly be defeated and lose all our artillery, since we have received reinforcements following the battle of Borodino, while the enemy army has not been strengthened at all. We are still Russians and will fight as bravely as before. Our casualties were great, but the enemy's were no less than ours; if our army is disordered, then the enemy is in a no better situation. Napoleon has weakened his army by detaching the Viceroy to Ruza and another corps to the new Kaluga road. We must take advantage of these circumstances. I propose, leaving one of the corps on the Mozhaisk road, transferring all the remaining troops to our left wing and to attack the enemy on their right flank. In the event of a reverse, we can retreat to the Kaluga road.

Count Osterman, having heard this opinion, asked Bennigsen: 'Do you guarantee the success of this operation?' and received the response: 'If there was no doubt about it, the Council of War would not have been assembled and you probably would not have been summoned here.'

Dokhturov, Uvarov and Yermolov agreed with Bennigsen's proposal (according to Buturlin, Konovnitsyn also). In contrast, Barclay believed that:

> If it was intended to act offensively, this should have been ordered in advance, and the army positioned accordingly; there was still plenty of time for that this morning, after my first explanation of the disadvantages of this position to General Bennigsen; and now it's too late. It is difficult to redeploy troops concealed in deep ravines at night, and, in the meantime, the enemy might assault them. The army has lost many of its generals and field officers; many of the regiments are commanded by captains. Our troops, with the courage characteristic of Russian soldiers, can fight at the halt in positions and repel the enemy, but are unable to execute manoeuvres in contact with the enemy.

Kutuzov recognised the validity of this opinion and cited the battle of Friedland as an example of the disaster that might result from an untimely offensive.

Raevsky, who had been with the rearguard, arrived at the meeting last of all. The Commander in Chief said 'I'm tired of speaking. General Yermolov, explain what the matter is about.' Raevsky, having learned for the first time what the subject of the meeting was: whether to give battle, or abandon Moscow, asked: 'What sort of position is the army occupying?' Yermolov answered; 'that this position is unfavourable, the army is divided in two by a deep ravine and the reserve cannot support the troops stationed at the front.' Raevsky said;

> If our position does not allow us to bring our forces into action, and, meanwhile, it has already been decided to give battle, then it is more beneficial to engage the enemy than to wait for them. By operating in this manner, it should be possible to disrupt their intended offensive, but since our troops are not sufficiently capable of manoeuvring, we should limit ourselves to delaying the enemy around Moscow. A retreat through the vast city after a lost battle may disorder the army; Moscow is not the salvation of Russia, and therefore, having the preservation of the army in mind, the capital should be abandoned without a fight. However, I am arguing as a soldier, I leave it to Prince Mikhail Ilarionovich to decide what political impact the enemy occupation of Moscow might have.

According to Raevsky, Kutuzov, having listened to all the opinions presented by the members of the council and having already decided to abandon Moscow beforehand, ended the meeting with the following statement: *'Je sens que je payerai les pots cassés, mais je me sacrifie pour le bien de ma patrie. J'ordonne la retraite.'* (I sense that I shall be paying for the smashed crockery, but I shall sacrifice myself for the good of my fatherland. I order the retreat). But in the War Diary of the main operational army we are told that Kutuzov, addressing the members of the Council, said:

> Russia is not yet lost, even with the loss of Moscow; I have made it my primary duty to save the army, to move closer to our reinforcements, and to prepare the enemy for inevitable destruction through the surrender of

Moscow itself, and therefore I intend, having passed through Moscow, to retreat along the Ryazan road.⁴⁶

As for the question of whether Kutuzov already intended to switch to the Kaluga road at that point, or came up with this movement later, once already on the Ryazan road, a question that is very important in historical terms, then, in all likelihood, it will remain unanswered. Kutuzov never expressed his intentions to anyone prior to their execution, and therefore it is difficult to say exactly when the skilful flank march by our army from the Ryazan road to the Kaluga road was conceived. A retreat to a flanking position (as we have already seen) was proposed by Toll, and therefore there is no reason to doubt that he proposed this movement later, after the arrival of the army on the Ryazan road (as Bernhardi asserts), or, at the very least, had a hand in the drafting of this appreciation.⁴⁷

In deciding to leave Moscow, the Commander in Chief had to ensure the supply of food to the army along the route he had chosen and take measures to save the wounded who were in the capital and to remove the remaining state and private property from there. Kutuzov, calling on Quartermaster General Lanskoy [Vasily Sergeevich Lanskoy], ordered him to take care of the distribution of rations. 'Where are we going?' asked Lanskoy.

'To the Ryazan road.'

'It will be hard to get supplies there. They have been collected in the Kaluga Governorate, Tula Governorate, Orël Governorate and Simbirsk Governorate; while the ration convoys, for the most part, have been directed to Serpukhov.

Kutuzov replied; 'Very well. We will discuss this tomorrow, once we have got to the place.'⁴⁸ Indeed, there was no need to rush into the adoption of any new measures for the movement of supplies, which could be delivered from Serpukhov with equal convenience, both to the Ryazan road and the Kaluga road. It was much more difficult to manage the departure of the inhabitants and the deprivation of the opportunity for the enemy to use the huge stockpiles in Moscow within a few hours at the expense of the evacuation of the wounded. Many of the inhabitants had left in advance with the majority of their goods and chattels, despite the reassuring news from the army and the appeals by Rostopchin, who had assured the Muscovites that the enemy would not reach the capital; the rest remained in the city, some out of lack of concern, some due to lack of means to leave. The Commander in Chief ordered the army Provost Marshal, Shulgin [Alexander Sergeevich Shulgin]; 'herd them all into Ryazan.'⁴⁹

---

46 All information about the council of war in Fili was extracted from reports to Emperor Alexander I by Barclay de Tolly and Bennigsen, Raevsky's Notes and private letters.
47 According to Bernhardi, *Flügel-Adjutant*, Colonel Michaud, before the meeting in Fili, drew the attention of Prince Kutuzov to the fact that the Oka, overflowing in the autumn, would flood the vicinity of this river, and that, in this case, our army, moving along the Nizhny Novgorod road (as suggested by Barclay de Tolly), would be isolated from the southern regions of the Empire. Bernhardi believes that this observation prompted Kutuzov to retreat along the Ryazan road. II, 142-143.
48 General Mikhailovsky-Danilevsky. Description Of The Patriotic War Of 1812.
49 Notes On The War Of 1812, compiled by Prince A.B.Golitsyn, appointed permanent orderly attending Prince Kutuzov.

As for the salvation of the wounded, in The Story Of The Razing Of Moscow In 1812, we find that 7,000 of our wounded were left in the main military hospital.[50] Bernhardi believes their number was over 10,000.[51] Perhaps these statements are exaggerated, but there can be no doubt that there was no way to evacuate the many wounded sent there from the Borodino battlefield, from Moscow, in the course of several hours, and that several thousand of the maimed remained in the city, incapable of marching along with the troops.[52]

Regarding the weapons stored in the arsenal, it is stated in the War Diary of the main operational army that: 'of the remaining weapons some were selected, some destroyed,' but, in all likelihood, there was not enough time for this. From the records of the Artillery Department, it is clear that we abandoned as booty for the enemy: 156 guns of various calibres, more than 80,000 firearms, of which half required repair; over 60,000 broadswords, sabres and swords, 20,000 *Pud* of gunpowder 27,000 rounds of artillery ammunition and two and a half million Roubles worth of various commissariat and provisions stocks.[53] In contrast, in one of Count Rostopchin's reports to the Tsar we find: 'Everything has been evacuated: from the commissariat, from the arsenal.' Some of the firearms were looted as our troops abandoned Moscow; all the rest, for the most part unserviceable weapons, fell into the hands of the enemy, or were destroyed by fire throughout the duration of the Moscow conflagration. It is rather difficult to understand why the muskets that were in the arsenal were not used by the Moscow *opolchenie* instead of the poor quality pikes issued to the warriors. But, in all probability, the serviceable weapons were kept in case they were required by regular troops.

At the end of the Council in Fili, Prince Kutuzov ordered:

1. The wagon trains were to be sent out at once to the Ryazan road; and after midnight, the troops were to proceed after them.
2. Miloradovich's rearguard were to hold the enemy in order to buy the army time to pass through Moscow.
3. Wintzingerode's detachment was to retreat to the Vladimir road.[54]

Despite his firm conviction that it was necessary to abandon Moscow, Kutuzov could not overcome the grief that had taken possession of him, he did not sleep all night and, according to Kaiserov's statements, who was with him, he broke down in tears several times.[55] Indeed, the sacrifice made by the Russians was great; but its consequences were the liberation of Russia from a formidable invasion and the eternal glory of the Blessed leader of the struggle we endured, Emperor Alexander I.

---

50 *Histoire de la destruction de Moscou en 1812, etc. par A.F. de B…ch, ancien officier au service de Russie. Traduit de l'allemand par M. Breton*, 84.
51 *Denkwürdigkeiten des Grafen v. Toll*, II, 143.
52 Chambray, II, 124.
53 *Denkwürdigkeiten des Grafen v. Toll*, II, 143.
54 War Diary of the main operational army. Benkendorf's notes.
55 [Liprandi points out that there is no reference provided, even though this event is mentioned in Mikhailovsky-Danilevsky's work, who was also present at the headquarters at the time, and names Kaiserov as the source].

25

The evacuation of Moscow

Count Rostopchin. – His actions. – The monitoring of foreigners. – Rostopchin's notices. – The arrival of the wounded in Moscow after the battle of Borodino. – Schmidt (Leppich) and his flying machine. – The activities of Metropolitan Platon. – Rostophchin's report to the Tsar. – Moscow on the eve of the French occupation. – Rostopchin's orders. – His departure.

Moscow on the day the French arrived. – The march through Moscow of the main body of the Russian army. – Miloradovich's operations. – Akinfov's mission to Murat. – Terms concluded with the enemy. – Napoleon's arrival at the Dragomilov gate. – His deployment into the suburbs. – The enemy seizure of the Kremlin. – Miloradovich's heroic deeds. – His service on the day Moscow was evacuated.

Count Rostopchin's report of the fall of Moscow. – Colonel Michaud's arrival in St Petersburg with Prince Kutuzov's report. – His conversation with the Tsar. – Kutuzov's report on the evacuation of Moscow. – Bennigsen's letter to Count Arakcheev. – The steadfastness of Emperor Alexander I. – Measures taken for the protection of St Petersburg. – Instructions in the event of an enemy attempt on St Petersburg. – Emperor Alexander I's composure.

Upon the departure of the Tsar from Moscow for St Petersburg, on 18 (30) July, all the thoughts of the residents of the capital were turned to mobilising against the enemy. Anyone who could handle a weapon tried to acquire one. Sabres, muskets and pistols became five times more expensive than the price at which they had been sold before. Count Rostopchin, wishing to contribute to the general *opolchenie*, ordered the sale of cheap old weapons, which were mostly faulty, but in spite of this, the arsenal was full of buyers from morning to evening.[1]

---

1 Manuscript notes by Bestuzhev-Ryumin. On 18 [30] August, the Commander in Chief of Moscow, Count Rostopchin, announced: 'Many of the residents wish to arm themselves, and there are 10,000 weapons in the arsenal, which were bought cheaply at the Makaryev fair; every morning, those who wish to may buy muskets, pistols and sabres in the arsenal; prices

It is quite natural that the measures taken by Count Rostopchin, during the difficult time of the enemy invasion of Russia, departing from the usual order of affairs, and, as it were, violating them, were the subject of many different rumours. It is impossible not to admit that the tenacity and passion of Count Rostopchin's personality sometimes involved him in unwise acts. In addition, having received an excellent secular education, but having no profound understanding of anything, he could be the soul of society, but was insufficiently experienced in holding important public appointments. His devotion to the Tsar was boundless, while his love for the Fatherland reached the point of rapture and during Napoleon's invasion of Russia turned into xenophobia, which was all the more remarkable in his character because, having been surrounded in his youth by French tutors, he preferred French literature to anything else.[2]

The main subjects of his attentions, once the enemy had invaded the Empire, were strict surveillance of foreigners and pacifying the population, agitated by the impending threat.

The situation for foreigners in Moscow at that time was very difficult. The people, having the sketchiest concept of the heterogeneous nature of Napoleon's forces, believed that all of Europe had taken up arms against the Russians, and therefore imagined a foe in every foreigner, a traitor, or at best someone enjoying *Schadenfreude* at Russia's expense. To utter a few foreign words, or speak Russian badly, was enough to arouse suspicion against oneself, and if this happened to people not well known in the city, then they were subjected to every kind of insult. The government tried by all possible means to provide protection for foreigners; there were more than 3,000 French living in Moscow at that time, of whom only a few were expelled from the city. This measure was not initiated on a whim, but on the basis of the following decrees drawn up in the Ministry of Police and approved by Emperor Alexander I:

1. In the governorates, only those foreigners should be allowed to remain for whose trustworthiness the governors have taken responsibility.
2. Send undesirable foreigners abroad by sea.
3. Those who, through their disclosures, could give rise to unfavourable consequences for Russia, are to be sent to the internal governorates.[3]

Only 40 (according to other sources 65) people, noticed in particular for their poor behaviour and harmful opinions, were sent by boat to Makaryev.[4] Foreign writers

---

are listed here. For this they will thank me, while some with musketeer status will be angry; but that is their choice, may God forgive them.' Rostopchin's memoirs, 1853, 170.
2 [Liprandi comments: 'to describe the character and qualities of Fëdor Vasilievich, who played such an important role in the Patriotic War, based solely on the unreferenced authority of a person who did not know Count Rostopchin personally is insufficient to utter such an opinion'].
3 Memo from the Commander in Chief of St Petersburg, Vyazmitinov, to the Moscow military governor, Count Rostopchin, dated 5 [17] July, No. 258.
4 Count Rostopchin's memos to the minister of police, dated 18 and 23 August [30 August and 4 September].

have criticised Rostopchin for the high-handed insults and oppression suffered by their compatriots, but, according to his own statements, all those expelled from Moscow were extremely badly behaved people.[5]

As for defusing the fears that agitated the capital, at the beginning of the war this did not present any problems. Although there were exaggerated rumours among the people about the huge mobilisation by Napoleon, nevertheless, history appeared to guarantee the inviolability of the borders of Russia: for more than 100 years, no enemy had crossed the sacred frontiers of our Fatherland! But as the enemy invasion progressed, unthinking arrogance gave way to an equally irrational fear. The Napoleonic hordes, made up of people from various nations, seemed like new Vandals to the Russians, ready to flood the East, just as the barbarians had once inundated the West. In Moscow, the heart of Russia, news of the successes of the enemy invasion flooded in, and, promulgated from there to all parts of the Empire, often in an exaggerated form, they disturbed the general peace. Count Rostopchin countered this evil with equally exaggerated announcements of the successes won by our troops. In order to give an idea of the style and content of Rostopchin's announcements (or so-called flyers), I consider it not superfluous to place here the most remarkable of these news-sheets.

I.

On the 4th,[6] having concentrated his entire force with a total of 100,000 men, Emperor Napoleon was approaching Smolensk, where he was engaged, six *versts* from the city, by the corps under Lieutenant General Raevsky. The fighting began at six o'clock in the morning and by noon it had become bloody. The courage of the Russians overcame their numbers, and the enemy was driven back. The corps under General Dokhturov, who relieved Lieutenant General Raevsky's tired, but victorious corps, went into battle on the 5th [17 August] at dawn, which continued until late at night. The enemy forces were repulsed everywhere, and Russian soldiers, with the valour and courage that are characteristic of them, marched with fury to destroy the enemy and defend the Fatherland, invoking the name of the Lord for help. But by this time the city of Smolensk was in flames, and our troops took up positions from the Dnieper towards the village of Pnevo and Dorogobuzh. Both armies stand together. The enemy, disordered by such a strong reverse, halted, and, having lost more than 20,000 men, took the ancient city of Smolensk like prey, turned into ashes in their hands. The residents had exited the city in the days before the battle. On our side, the losses in killed and wounded reached 4,000 men; among the former were two brave generals: Skalon [Anton Antonovich Skalon] and Balla [Adam Ivanovich Balla]. Many troops were taken prisoner and entire enemy battalions threw down their arms in order to save their lives. Three regiments of

---

5 'Those who have chosen to be the worst of rogues,' as Rostopchin described them in a memo to the minister of police, dated 23 August [4 September].
6 4 [16] August.

our cavalry and three of Cossacks drove off 60 squadrons of enemy cavalry under the command of the King of Naples.[7]

II.
Our vanguard is near Gzhatsk; the position held by our troops is strong, and here His Grace the Prince intends to give battle; we are now equal with the enemy in the number of troops. In two days we will have 20,000 more, but our Russian troops, under one law, one Tsar, defending the Church of God, our homes, wives, children and the churchyards where our fathers lie. The enemy, fighting for bread, die as brigands; if they once chance a battle, then all of them will be dispersed, and, will remember your name!

You know that I know everything that is going on in Moscow; but what happened yesterday was not good, and it is something to be disapproved of: two Germans came to exchange money, and the people did them over; one almost died. They thought that they were spies, and to that end they should have been interrogated; that is my business. And you should know that I will not release my Russian brothers either; and what a novelty for 100 people to pin down a bony Frenchman, or a German in a smoky wig. In a hunt to dirty your hands! And whoever embarks on this will not stand up for themselves in this case. If you think that they are spies, well, come to me, and do not beat them and do not draw criticism to the Russians; the French troops should be buried, but not by putting out the eyes of riff-raff. Those injured were brought here; they are lying in the Golovinsky Palace; I watched over them, gave them a drink, fed them and put them to rest. After all, they fought for you; don't abandon them; visit and talk. You even feed convicts, yet these are the Tsar's loyal subjects and our friends; is there no help for them![8]

Despite all the efforts by the Moscow Commander in Chief to dispel the fears of the residents, many of them left the city, so the following announcement was made public:

There is a rumour here, and there are people who believe it and repeat it, that I forbade leaving the city. If this were so, then sentries would have been posted at the checkpoints and several thousand carriages, carts and wagons would not be leaving in every direction. And I am pleased that ladies and merchants' wives are departing from Moscow for their peace of mind. Less to fear, less to hear, but one cannot praise husbands, brothers, and relatives who set off with the women without returning, with the times to come. If it is indecent because they were in danger, then if there is none; it is obscene, then it becomes shameful. I must answer with my life that the Antichrist shall not reach Moscow, and here's why: in the armies there are

---
7   Notes on military operations, printed and published in Moscow, by order of Count Rostopchin.
8   Notes on military operations.

130,000 glorious troops, 1,800 guns and His Grace Prince Kutuzov, truly the Tsar's chosen *Voivod* [generalissimo] for the Russian forces and overall commander; he has Generals Tormasov and Chichagov behind the enemy, with 85,000 glorious troops; General Miloradovich has arrived in Mozhaisk from Kaluga with 36,000 infantry, 3,800 cavalry and 84 cannon from the foot and horse artillery. Count Morkov will arrive in Mozhaisk in three days with 24,000 from our military force, and the remaining 7,000 will follow him. In Moscow, in Klin, in Zavidovo, in Podolsk, there are 14,000 infantry. And if this is not enough for the destruction of the Antichrist, then I shall say again; well, fellow Muscovites! Let us go too! And we shall march out as 100,000 fine fellows, taking the Iberian Mother of God, and 150 guns and finish the job all together. The enemy has his own scum, even 150,000 men; they feed on boiled rye and horse meat. This is what I think and declare to you, so that some will rejoice, while others will be reassured, and even more so by the fact that our Sovereign Emperor will deign to return to his loyal capital one of these days. Read on; everything is understandable to you, and there is nothing to decipher.[9] 1812, 26 August [7 September].

Having received news from Prince Kutuzov of the battle of Borodino, in which it was stated that the Russian army had not yielded a single step and that it was intended to fight the enemy again, Count Rostopchin ordered that this news be made public, adding on his own behalf:

I.
The enemy losses are innumerable. They were given orders not to take prisoners (yet there were none to take), and that the French must win or die. When today, with the help of God, they are repulsed once more, then the Antichrist and his demons shall perish from hunger, fire and the sword.

I am sending 4,000 locally trained soldiers to the army, ammunition for 250 cannon and provisions.

Orthodox Christians! Stay calm. Our blood is shed for the salvation of the Fatherland; ours are ready, and if the time comes, we shall support the troops. God will boost our strength and the demons will lay their bones in Russian soil.

27 August [8 September] 1812.

II.
His Grace the Prince, in order to quickly link up with the troops that are advancing towards him, has passed through Mozhaisk and stands in a strong location where the enemy cannot immediately attack him. 48 cannon are on their way to him from here with ammunition. And His Grace has stated: that he will defend Moscow to the last drop of blood, and is ready to fight even in the streets. My brothers, you should see nothing in the fact

---

9 Rostopchin's memoirs, 171-173.

that government offices have been closed; this business is to be cleared up, while we shall deal with the Antichrist in our own courts. When it comes down to it, I need good fellows, both urban and rural; I shall make the call, for two days; and presently if it is not necessary; I will be silent! If you are good with an axe, not bad with a spear, but best of all with a pitchfork; a Frenchman is no heavier than a sheaf of rye. Tomorrow after dinner, I will raise the Iberian Mother of God at the hospital for the wounded: we will bless the water there; they will recover sooner; and I am well now; my eye was hurting, and now I can see in both.

30 August [11 September] 1812.[10]

Everyone rejoiced, all was triumph in Moscow at the rebuff given to the enemy, but soon a host of wagons began to appear in the capital with the wounded. Their suffering aroused general concern; Muscovites hurried to meet them and escorted them to the Lefortovo Palace, which was turned into a hospital, granting the sufferers whatever they could. His Grace the Vicar of Moscow Augustine [Alexei Vasilyevich Vinogradsky], wishing to bring supreme consolation to the Orthodox soldiers, sent the clergy to them, on 31 August (12 September), with the miraculous icons of the Iberian and Smolensk Madonnas (the latter, which had previously been in Smolensk Cathedral, was transferred to Moscow before the battle of Borodino by Bishop Irenaeus [Ivan Akimovich Falkovsky]). The groans, exhaled through excruciating pain, ceased. The tormented, maimed warriors, having gathered their last strength, hastened to venerate the sacred face of the Comforter of the unfortunate; some of them died as soon as they had chance to offer a final prayer.[11] Count Rostopchin, as before, tried to dispel the fears of Moscow residents, ordering the removal of state property from the city only at night, but since more than 60,000 carts were used for this, the orders of this Commander in Chief could not remain a secret. Anyone who was able was in a hurry to leave. Moscow was visibly emptying.

As early as the occasion of Napoleon's *Grande Armée* approaching Smolensk, a Dutch national, Schmidt (Franz Leppich),[12] came to the Moscow Commander in Chief, proposing to build a huge airship, which, according to the inventor, could be armed with firearms, in the form of war rockets, and could serve to destroy the enemy; his collaborator in this enterprise was the physician Dr Schäffer [Georg Anton Aloysius von Schäffer], from Würzburg. It is hard to believe, especially taking into account Rostopchin's distrust of foreigners, that he really was convinced of the utility of the machine proposed by Schmidt; it is much more likely that he meant only to divert general attention from the impending threat and stop the migration of Moscow residents. Schmidt himself, fanatically confident in the value of his invention, used a huge amount of iron, timber, taffeta, nitric acid, and so on for the construction of a flying machine and for filling the airship with gas. Many workers

---

10 Rostopchin's memoirs, 174-175.
11 A study of the life of the Moscow Archbishop Augustine, compiled by Snegirev [Ivan Mikhailovich Snegirev], 1841, 3rd edition, 27-28.
12 [Franz Xaver Leppich, born in Bavaria, led a colourful life, including a brief period of service in the British army in 1805].

and seamstresses were engaged in this business under the direction of Schmidt, in the village of Vorontsovo, six *versts* from Moscow, along the Kaluga road, where there was a sub-unit of 160 infantrymen and several dragoons, in order the divert the curious and for the protection of Schmidt from malicious attempts on his person. The Tsar himself, in a letter to the Moscow military governor, gave orders for Leppich to be provided with all necessary assistance, to form a crew of capable and sound men for his airship, and to enter into correspondence with Prince Kutuzov on the use of the flying machine.[13] But, apparently, the police were not particularly concerned about keeping this intricate undertaking a secret. All Moscow started talking about him; many took it as a joke. Rostopchin, who, on the contrary, wanted to attach as much importance to Schmidt's work as possible, ordered the following announcement to be printed in the newspapers:

From the Commander in Chief of Moscow.
I have been instructed herewith by the Tsar to construct a large balloon, in which 50 men can fly wherever they want, both downwind and against the wind, and you shall learn and rejoice at whatever becomes of it. If the weather is good, then tomorrow or the day after tomorrow I shall have a smaller balloon for testing. I declare to you that once you see it, you must not think that this is from the Antichrist, but it was made to do him harm and destruction.[14]

The small balloon actually rose, which did not surprise anyone present at the experiment; the machine itself stubbornly remained on the ground; but Schmidt, with no loss of confidence, continued to work. Eventually, once the enemy was already closing in on Moscow, the large balloon with all the chemicals and workers belonging to it were transported on 130 wagons to Nizhny Novgorod.[15]

The closer the enemy came to the capital, the more eagerly the Orthodox clergy, as guardians of the Faith, affirmed the strong and strengthened the weak in their devotion to the Tsar and love of the Fatherland. At the forefront of our spiritual pastors at that time, the Moscow Metropolitan Platon [Pëtr Georgievich Levshin] shone with lofty intelligence and greatness of spirit. Emperor Alexander I, while still in Moscow, received the image of St Sergius as a blessing from this Saint, who

---

13 From Emperor Alexander I's letter to Count Rostopchin: '*Aussitôt que Leppich sera pret, compsez lui un équipage pour sa nacelle d'hommes surs et intelligents et dépéchez un courrier au général Koutousoff pour l'en prévenir. Je l'ai instruit de la chose. Recommandez, Je vous prie, à Leppich d'être bien attentif sur l'endroit où il descendra la première fois, pour ne pas se tromper et ne pas tomber dans les mains de l'ennemi. Il est indispensable qu'il combine ses mouvemens avec le général en chef.*' A copy of this is kept in the Archive of the M.T.D. No. 47,352, folio I.
14 Rostopchin's memoirs, 170-171.
15 In October 1812, Schmidt moved from Nizhny Novgorod to St Petersburg with all his apparatus and worked in Oranienbaum, under the supervision of Count Arakcheev's aide de camp, Captain Tiesenhausen, developing his flying machine, but without success, he left the country at the beginning of 1813. *Histoire de la destruction de Moscou en 1812, par A.F. de B...ch*, 49-51. Information on Schmidt's (Franz Leppich's) machine, in the M.T.D. No. 46,692, folio 2.

had accompanied Peter I on his campaigns, and a message in which Platon, inspired from above, foretold Russia's victory over the enemy.[16] The Tsar, already in Tver on the return journey replied to him:

> Most Reverend Platon! I have received the letter from you and with it the image of St Sergius. I accepted the former with pleasure, as from a renowned pastor of the Church and much respected by me, and the second with reverence. I have given orders for the image of the holy champion of the Russian armed forces to be given to the Moscow *opolchenie*, which is being formed to defend the Fatherland: may he preserve them with his intercession at the Throne of God, and may he prolong your days, decorated with honour and glory, with his prayers. Submitting myself to your prayers, I remain grateful to you.

In response to this message, the reverend orator wrote to the Emperor on 23 July (4 August):

> August Monarch, Sovereign Most Merciful! Elder Simeon had the most blessed destiny in life to receive the Eternal Child in his arms, and from the depths of the sacred souls sang the sacred hymn to the Ruler of the world. I, the unworthy, have been honoured by the reply from your August person, in delight I kiss the High Monarch's right hand; I carry the burden of a tedious old age, but as if I were young in sweet feelings, reverent for the dearest name Alexander. Tsar! You, in the spirit of Christian piety, have blessed the newly armed heroes with the icon of the miracle worker Sergius brought to you from me. *Much may be helped by righteous prayer.* The grasping foe has extended his evil weapons to encroach beyond the Dnieper, but this Pharaoh will founder here with his hordes, as if in the Red Sea. He has come to the banks of the Dvina and the Dnieper to draw a third new river, frightful to utter, a river of human blood! Oh! Every drop of blood will cry to the heavens from earth. *I shall exact the blood of thy brother from thine hand.* France will recognise the Lord of vengeance in God, while Russia will feel, profess, sing to him: Ave, Father! King of Heaven! Ye shall bring forth, into the light, the truth of the Monarch and the fate of Russia as at noon.

---

16 'Most Merciful Sovereign Emperor! The capital city of Moscow, the new Jerusalem, accepts its Christ, like a mother, into the arms of its zealous sons, and emerging through the darkness, passing the brilliant glory of Your Power, sings in delight: Hosanna, blessed is he who comes! Let the impudent and arrogant Goliath from the borders of France be enveloped by deadly horrors on the edges of Russia; may gentle faith, this sling of the Russian David, suddenly strike down the head of his bloodthirsty pride. This image of St Sergius, an ancient zealot for the good of our Fatherland, is brought to Your Imperial Majesty. I am pained that my weakening strength prevents me from enjoying your most kind consideration. I send a warm prayer to heaven, that the Almighty may exalt the just race and fulfil Your Majesty's righteous desires.'

Thus spoke Platon to the Blessed guardian of the honour and glory of Russia. But not content with the word of eternal truth, the great Saint prepared to arouse general enthusiasm by personal example. On the same day as the battle of Borodino, when many Moscow residents, frightened by the news of the approaching enemy, were in a hurry to leave the city, the 75 year old Metropolitan Platon arrived in the ancient capital from his peaceful refuge of Bethany, exhausted by illness. A year before, he had handed over the administration of the diocese to his vicar Augustine; but the news of the danger that threatened to fall upon Moscow called out the magnanimous Saint, who quite rightly considered his presence in the capital useful in the days of disaster for the Fatherland. The news of the Metropolitan's arrival gave hope to a despondent nation. Many of the inhabitants of Moscow, animated by his example, decided to take part in the defence of the capital, resigned themselves to die and partook of the Holy Mysteries. On the appeal by Rostopchin, Muscovites wanted to go to Trekhgorka field with religious banners; many of them, mounted and on foot, hurried there armed with whatever they could find. A rumour spread that Platon himself would come to Trekhgorka, or to Poklonnaya Gora, to bless the Russian army before the decisive battle. Indeed, he was ready for any sacrifice; but the physical strength of the Saint betrayed him; nevertheless, in spite of this, upon seeing Moscow filled with the wounded, abandoned by the inhabitants, he did not want to leave the city. His vicar, Augustine, and other people devoted to him vainly tried to induce him to do this, reminding him that the enemy was already close. 'What can they do to me?' repeated the fearless old man; finally, by 31 August (12 September), he agreed to leave for Bethany.[17]

Moscow at that time was like a condemned man. Rostopchin, convinced of the impossibility of defending the capital himself, reported to the Tsar:

> Up until the 26th [7 September], I used every means to placate the inhabitants and encourage morale generally, but the hasty retreat by the army, the approach of the enemy and the many wounded arriving, with whom the streets are filled, has produced horror. Seeing for myself that the fate of Moscow had hung on this battle, I decided to facilitate the departure of the small number of remaining residents. I swear with my life that Bonaparte will find Moscow as deserted as Smolensk. Everything has been removed from the commissariat and the arsenal. Currently I am taking care of the wounded; 1,500 of them are brought daily.[18]

On 1 (13) September, on the day of the meeting in Fili, which decided the fate of Moscow, the entire capital with its environs resembled an immense military encampment: our troops, protecting it on the side facing the enemy, built fortifications; the inhabitants fled in droves to the arsenal, where on that day weapons were being distributed for free, and then, with shouts of: 'Long live our father Alexander Pavlovich!' they hurried to Trekhgorka, expecting to find the military governor

---

17 The life of Moscow Metropolitan Platon, compiled by Snegirev, 1856, II, 47-50.
18 Rostopchin's report dated 1 [13] September.

there.[19] On this day, Bishop Augustine, celebrating the Liturgy in the Uspensky Cathedral, prayed to the Lord in tears, for the overthrow of the enemy, for the salvation of Moscow and Russia. The cathedral was full of people; it seemed as though every remaining resident of Moscow had gathered to mourn the calamities that lay ahead of them. At the end of the liturgy, Augustine wanted to send the treasures, holy relics and miraculous icons that remained in the Uspensky Cathedral to Vologda, but Count Rostopchin would not allow him to carry out this plan, for fear of 'instilling despondency among the people.'[20]

Evening came. Some Moscow residents set off, with weapons in hand, for the Dragomilov gate; others saved their families and left the capital, not knowing if they would be able to find shelter anywhere. In the city a sepulchral silence settled over the few remaining residents. Hope and despair, fear of unknown disasters and grim determination, all these emotions, chased one another, stirring the mood of Moscow's residents. At night, just after the end of the Council in Fili, Count Rostopchin received the following letter from Prince Kutuzov:

> The enemy, having detached columns to Zvenigorod and Borovsk, and the unfavourable local terrain, with sorrow, are forcing me to abandon Moscow. The army is to march to the Ryazan road. Therefore, I humbly ask you to send me as many police officers as possible, with my aide de camp, Montresor [Karl Lukyanovich Montresor], who could lead the army via various routes to the Ryazan road.[21]

This was the first definitive information regarding Prince Kutuzov's intent to abandon Moscow received by Rostopchin. Until that time, it had been impossible to either destroy or remove from the city those resources that might still be useful to our army, and therefore Rostopchin had ordered only the most valuable state property and the most important files from the archives to be sent out; everything else remained in the city. With just a few hours remaining before the enemy entered the capital, Count Rostopchin ordered extraordinary actions. Orders went out to use all the carts that were to be found in the city for the evacuation of the sick and wounded. Every military unit that was in Moscow immediately set out along the Ryazan road. The fire brigades were sent to Vladimir with their fire-extinguishing pumps. Police units, under the direction of intelligent officials, were instructed to breach the barrels of wine in the wine warehouses, burn all the barges containing state and personal property on the Moscow River and destroy commissariat stocks, and then also move to Vladimir.[22] Some of the police officers were left in the capital to set it alight at several points.[23] By condemning Moscow to the flames, Count Rostopchin imposed a heavy responsibility upon himself, because he had not received such a

---

19 Manuscript notes by Bestuzhev-Ryumin.
20 Study of the life of the Moscow Archbishop Augustine, compiled by I. Snegirev, 1841, 32.
21 Prince Kutuzov's memo, dated 1 [13] September.
22 Information submitted by the former Moscow detective police chief Voronenko.
23 Diary of the French commission for the court martial on the Moscow fires. Of the 26 people brought to trial, nine were members of the Moscow police.

command from the gracious Tsar. But having been granted full authority to act by the Monarch and placed in extraordinary circumstances, he decided to carry out that which he considered useful and glorious for the Fatherland.

During the day, Bishop Augustine had requested updates on the situation several times from Count Rostopchin; eventually, just at midnight, he received the news of the evacuation of Moscow; at the same time, he was given the assignment to leave on the road to Vladimir. On a dark autumn night, the bishop, accompanied by several clergymen, took the icon of the Mother of God of Vladimir with him from the Uspensky Cathedral, as well as the Iberian icon from the chapel at the Voskresensk gate and set off from Moscow in the indicated direction. The glow of burning farms and villages spread around the capital; on the Smolensk road, bivouac fires were visible and occasional gunshots were heard. Wagon trains stretched along the Vladimir road, crowded with people on foot and horseback. The peasants who encountered the bishop, instead of the usual respect, expressed displeasure towards him, criticising him for abandoning his flock like a contemptible hireling. These reproaches were unjust, but it was not malice that inspired them, but the deep sorrow of the people, accustomed to regarding Moscow as the heart of Russia.[24]

Meanwhile, the capital seethed with extraordinary activity. Count Rostopchin, having dismissed the police from the city and ordered the withdrawal of the Moscow garrison, remained with a small team, as loyal guardians of public peace and order. Unfortunately, Count Rostopchin's final act when leaving the capital was incompatible with the dignity of his nature. A few days earlier, all the detainees held in the city gaols had been sent to Vladimir (contrary to the statements by some foreign historians who claim that Count Rostopchin released all the criminals, instructing them to set fire to the city). Only two remained in custody in Moscow: some Frenchman, who took it upon himself to condemn the actions of the Russians, and the son of the merchant Vereshchagin [Mikhail Nikolaevich Vereshchagin], who had translated Napoleon's Russo-phobic proclamations from the Hamburg newspapers into Russian, and gave them to his friends to read. At eight o'clock in the morning on 2 (14) September, at the very moment that Rostopchin was preparing to leave the city, a large crowd of people gathered at his house, announcing their intention to go to Trekhgorka to face the enemy, and asking the Commander in Chief to lead them. Rostopchin's response was: 'Wait, brothers, just let me deal with these traitors.' After that, having given orders to bring both prisoners, turning to Vereshchagin, he said: 'You are unworthy of being called Russian and have dared to betray your Fatherland and dishonour your family. Your crime has surpassed every penal ordinance under the law. I condemn you to the vengeance of the people. Beat the traitor; Moscow is dying because of him.' The unfortunate was beaten and tortured by the people around him, condemned to death by the outraged, violent mob. While the general attention of the people was drawn to this bloody spectacle, Rostopchin, ordering the guilty foreigner to be brought to him, said to him: 'As for you, a French national, I ask you to speak more carefully at the expense of a nation that has accepted you with good grace.' When the Frenchman began to try to justify himself, the Commander

---

24 Study of the life of the Moscow Archbishop Augustine, 33-34.

in Chief, ordering him to be silent, continued: 'Go, I forgive you; I pray that when the robbers, your countrymen, come here, you tell them how traitors are punished in our country.' Following that, Count Rostopchin left the capital.[25]

On the morning of 2 (14) September, Moscow presented a hazy view. The few inhabitants who remained were hurriedly leaving the city, saving their most valuable possessions, or hiding in homes and cellars; the price of hiring horses was now as much cash as it used to cost to buy them. All order was gone. Evil minded people, taking advantage of the departure of the police, scattered around the houses and, in the absence of their owners, looted other people's properties; others, with the same purpose, went into the alleys and carried away anything that came to hand; no one resisted, no one interfered with them. Merchants, encountering soldiers on the streets, invited them into their shops and invited them to take whatever they liked. They commented to our servicemen: 'Rather let our goods go to you than to the French.' A deep silence reigned in the city, interrupted at times only by violent shouts from the taverns and the sobs of the unfortunates who left homes where they had hoped to spend their entire lives in peace; the main streets, cluttered with every kind of carriage and wagon, between which pedestrians made their way with difficulty, presented a picture of complete chaos. Entire families wandered the streets, asking anybody they encountered: 'in which direction should we go, so as not to bump into the enemy.' Others doubted the possibility of the enemy entering the capital and claimed that a Swedish auxiliary corps was proceeding to our army. But most of the people hurriedly left the city and, in the first instance, sought refuge in the nearest villages. Although it is impossible to say for certain how many residents remained in Moscow at that time, nevertheless, in Count Rostopchin's memo to Field Marshal Prince Kutuzov, dated 28 October [9 November], 1812, No. 41, it appears that there were some 10,000, but no more than 3,000 when the enemy evacuated Moscow.[26]

Let us turn to operations by the troops.

At the same time as the Council of War was convening in Fili, Napoleon approached Moscow with the main body of the *Grande Armée*, to a distance of about 30 *versts*, and settled down at Perkhushkovo. The flanking columns, on the night of 1 to 2 (13 to 14) September, had almost drawn level with the main body: Poniatowski's *5e Corps* was on the new Kaluga road, at Likova, while the Viceroy's *4e Corps*, having marched along the Zvenigorod road, on the right bank of the Moskva river, was at Buzaeva.[27]

On our side, on the night of 1 to 2 (13 to 14) September, the army trains left their locations. Behind them, at three o'clock in the morning, just before dawn, the troops

---

25 Manuscript notes by Bestuzhev-Ryumin [Liprandi point out that, according to an examination in Readings From The Imperial Society Of Russian History And Antiquities, 1866, book 4: The Vereshchagin Case, page 258, this is not found in Bestuzhev's Notes]. *Histoire de l'incendie de Moscou en 1812, par M. l'abbé Surugue, copiée mot-à-mot sur les registres de la paroisse de St Louis à Moscou* [Liprandi comments: 'what Surugue narrates is integral to the History Of The Patriotic War, especially Moscow. It is a shame that the honourable author does not paint a picture of the violence, as it is depicted by the French themselves'].
26 Ker-Porter, 176. Chambray, II, 104-105. *Histoire de la destruction de Moscou en 1812*, 78.
27 General course of movements and operations by Russian forces during the war of 1812, compiled by General Khatov [Alexander Ilych Khatov], Archive of the M.T.D. No. 37,640.

entered the capital through the Dragomilov gate: the cavalry in the lead, then the *opolchenie*, and finally, the infantry, artillery and Cossacks: our entire army moved in a single column, extending across the city. It is easy to imagine how the movement of the troops, crossing the Moskva river over the only wooden bridge, was delayed at every step, and even that bridge collapsed and could not be fixed quickly, which forced some of the cavalry and the Moscow *opolchenie* to cross the river by fording.[28] Barclay de Tolly stated that our retreat was disorganised; and indeed, the yielding of Moscow without a fight shocked the army and, as it were, severed the restraints of the customary discipline of our troops. An eyewitness to the evacuation of Moscow, Prinz Eugen von Württemberg wrote:

> In the opinion of most of the top commanders, further retreat seemed inconsistent with the rules of honour itself: they believed that Moscow was meant to represent to the Russian warrior what the grave is for every mortal. Beyond it was another world.[29]

The troops at first believed that they would be led by a roundabout route against the enemy via Moscow: 'We are outflanking,' the soldiers reasoned among themselves. But the very spectacle of Moscow, abandoned by most of its former residents, did not permit them to doubt the sad truth. 'The ranks of soldiers silently and sadly stretched along the deserted streets of the capital.'[30] As 2 (14) September fell on a Monday, there were gloomy discussions among the people about leaving Moscow; others, on the contrary, foretold (and this time they were not mistaken) that Napoleon would not fare well from a Monday house-warming in Moscow.

Kutuzov, having arrived at the Dragomilov gate himself by eight o'clock in the morning, found the streets in the city completely cluttered and, wanting to get through as soon as possible, turned to the retinue surrounding him with a question: 'Who among you knows their way around Moscow?' The Field Marshal's permanent orderly, Prince A.B. Golitsyn [Alexander Borisovich Golitsyn]. presented himself. Kutuzov said: 'Guide me so that we don't have to engage with anyone,' and, together with Prince Golitsyn, rode on horseback from the Arbatsky Gate, along the boulevards, to a bridge over the Yauza. There he bumped into Count Rostopchin, who, with a riding crop in his hand, was trying to clear a passage across the bridge for the artillery, between the crowds of troops and residents. The encounter between the Field Marshal and Rostopchin was extremely cool; Kutuzov, without acknowledging him, interrupted him several times with orders to clear the bridge. The further movement of the troops mixed with refugees to the Kolomna checkpoint was likened to a tidal surge. As the army left the city, it was positioned at the halt on both sides of the road. The Field Marshal, having passed the gates himself, sat down on a bench by the road itself, near the Old Believer's cemetery. Here he remained, as if listening to Moscow's last words, waiting for news from the rearguard. Eventually, Miloradovich's aide

---

28 Wolzogen, 155.
29 *Erinnerungen aus dem Feldzuge des Jahres 1812 in Russland, v. dem Herzog Eugen v. Württemberg*, 98.
30 *Erinnerungen aus dem Feldzuge des Jahres 1812*, 100.

de camp arrived with a report that if Murat would not accept the proposals made to him, then he would have to fight in the city, and that in this case the rearguard would need reinforcements. This news alarmed the old Field Marshal, but a quarter of an hour later Colonel Potemkin arrived with another report from Miloradovich, regarding the negotiations with the enemy, which ensured the safe passage of our rearguard. Kutuzov immediately ordered the main body of the army to continue the march to the village of Panki, 17 *versts* distant from Moscow, while he proceeded there himself along with the troops who had managed to pass the Kolomna gate.[31]

Meanwhile, Barclay de Tolly remained at the Yauza bridge, letting the troops pass by and trying to maintain order among them. His activity and patience this day were extraordinary. For eighteen hours straight he remained on horseback, sending his aides de camp with Cossack patrols along all the streets where the troops were passing, to force the pace of their march and to round up the stragglers.[32] The heroic fearlessness demonstrated by Barclay in front of the entire army at the battle of Borodino, and the prudent measures he took during the retreat by our troops across Moscow, won him the loyalty of the Russian army and the respect of all Russia.

The situation was even more difficult for our rearguard.

At dawn on 2 (14) September, at the same time as the Russian army, having withdrawn from its positions in front of Moscow, was retreating through the capital, our rear guard was ten *versts* from the Dragomilov gate, near the porcelain factories. Miloradovich, as already mentioned, had been instructed to hold the enemy for as long as possible in order to give the army time to retreat with all its baggage and evacuate the Moscow residents. Kutuzov sent him a letter addressed to Berthier, signed by Kaiserov, in which the fate of 9,000 of our wounded and sick, who could not be taken out of the city, was entrusted, in accordance with custom, to the protection of the enemy. Miloradovich was authorised: 'to honour the ancient walls of Moscow with a token battle.'[33] To that end, falling back, he placed his right flank at Poklonnaya Gora and extended the left flank to the Vorobievo hills. Having thus shown his strength, Miloradovich hoped that the enemy would begin to assemble forces for an assault and in doing so would give us the opportunity to gain some time.

As our rearguard withdrew, the enemy vanguard gradually edged forwards. Napoleon, having spent the night in the village of Vyazema himself, which belonged to Prince Golitsyn, 40 *versts* distant from Moscow, set off from there on 2 (14) September, at dawn, in a carriage, together with Berthier, but not being able to cross a deep ravine in it, where the bridge had been burned, got on his horse and continued on horseback the rest of the way to Moscow. Upon arrival at a dacha on the right side of the main road, not quite 12 *versts* from Moscow, at ten o'clock in the morning Napoleon was met by Murat, talked with him in the courtyard near the church for more than an hour before ordering him to move onwards, took a quick

---

31 Notes on the war of 1812, compiled by Prince A.B. Golitsyn, appointed Field Marshal Kutuzov's permanent orderly.
32 Description of operations by First Army, compiled by Barclay de Tolly. Major General Löwenstern's manuscript notes.
33 Senator Akinfov's notes.

meal and with a small escort quickly set off behind the vanguard.[34] In the meantime, Murat had directed his force against Miloradovich in several columns, who, having received a report about an offensive by a significant enemy force outflanking his rearguard, could not remain in place without exposing himself to the danger of being cut off, and especially from the direction of the Kaluga road, because the troops stationed on his left wing were few in number and occupied very unfavourable ground; on the other hand, by retreating hastily, he would not be executing the orders given to him to hold the enemy back. Miloradovich decided to resort to negotiations and, turning to the Lifeguard Hussar Regiment stationed nearby, called for an officer who could speak French fluently. Staff Captain Akinfov [Fëdor Vladimirovich Akinfov] presented himself. Miloradovich, handing him the note sent from headquarters, ordered him to hand it over personally to the King of Naples and announce to him that:

> if the French want to occupy Moscow intact, then let them give us time to pass through the city unhindered; otherwise, we shall fight to the last man and leave only ruins for the enemy.

It is claimed that one of Miloradovich's aides de camp said: '*On ne brave pas ainsi l'armée française,*' (The French army cannot be bluffed in this manner) and was told in response: '*C'est à moi à la braver, et à vous – à mourir.*' (The bluffing is up to me, while the dying is up to you). In sending Akinfov, Miloradovich ordered him to try to stay with the enemy as long as possible in order to gain time.

Akinfov, taking a trumpeter with him, rode up to the enemy outpost screen, which consisted of *chasseurs à cheval*. At the signal blown by the trumpeter, the colonel [Pierre Antoine François Huber] of the French *1er régiment de chasseurs à cheval* rode up to the screen. When asked about the reason for his arrival, our *parlementaire* replied that he had been sent on a mission to the King of Naples by the commander of the vanguard of the Russian army, General Miloradorvich. Akinfov was led to General Sébastiani [Horace François Bastien Sébastiani], who was in command of the outposts, who asked what he wanted and ordered him to be taken to Murat. Having passed by five cavalry regiments, stationed in a chessboard formation ahead of the infantry, Akinfov caught sight of Murat in a brilliant uniform, surrounded by a large retinue. The king raised his hat, embroidered with gold and adorned with feathers, dismissed his retinue, and, placing his hand on the neck of our officer's horse, asked him: 'Captain! What have you got to say?' Akinfov, handing Murat the note sent from headquarters, which conveyed Miloradovich's statement to him, demanding a halt to the advance by the French columns to give us time to pass through Moscow; otherwise, we would fight to the last man and leave not a stone standing in the city. After reading the letter, Murat said: 'There is no need to commit the sick and wounded to the humanity of the French forces; we do not regard prisoners as enemies.' As for our other demand, he responded initially

---

34 Korbeletsky. A Short History Of The French Seizure Of Moscow And Their Occupation Of It Until 27 September [9 October], 1812, [Краткое повествование о вторжении французов в Москву и о пребывании их в оной] 21-22.

to having a lack of authority to halt the advance without first asking Napoleon's permission, but then he announced to Akinfov that, wanting to save Moscow, he would agree to Miloradovich's proposal and that we could proceed in peace, as we pleased, with the only condition being that Moscow would be occupied by French troops on that same day. Having received in response that Miloradovich would agree to this, Murat immediately sent an order to the forward screen to halt and desist from skirmishing. Then, turning to Akinfov, he asked: 'Do you know Moscow well?' and having received in reply that he was a native of Moscow, he continued: 'I ask you to persuade the residents to remain calm. Not only will we do them no harm, but we will not take the slightest contribution from them and we will take care of their security in every possible way… Is it true that Moscow has been abandoned by its residents? Where is Count Rostopchin?' Akinfov replied: 'I have been with the vanguard the whole time and therefore know nothing about what's happening in Moscow or Count Rostopchin.' When asked where Emperor Alexander and Grand Duke Konstantin Pavlovich were, our *parlementaire* responded with ignorance, being concerned (as he himself states in his notes) that the enemy, having received intelligence about the Tsar's whereabouts in St Petersburg, might send an independent corps towards our northern capital. Murat continued: 'I respect your Emperor, I am friendly with the Grand Duke, I regret that I have to fight against you. Tell me, how many casualties has your regiment suffered?' Akinfov replied: 'Being in action almost daily, it is impossible to do so without loss.' The king observed: 'War is tough!'

'We are fighting for the Fatherland and do not notice the rigours of the campaign.'

'Why not make peace?'

'Your Majesty knows this better than I do; as far as I can see, neither of the opposing sides can yet boast of a complete victory.'

'It is time for a reconciliation,' Murat said with a smile, repeating once more that the French forces would take care to preserve Moscow. 'Tell General Miloradovich that I agreed to his proposal purely out of respect for him,' he added, releasing our negotiator. Akinfov set off to return, accompanied by the same colonel who had led him to the king; wanting to buy time, he rode at a gentle canter and expressed a desire to watch the two hussar regiments stationed nearby in admiration, to which the colonel who accompanied him agreed. Having approached our screen force, Akinfov announced to their commander, Colonel Yefremov [Ivan Yefremovich Yefremov] of the Lifeguard Cossack Regiment, that the French would not press our rear guard and galloped on to Miloradovich.[35]

Meanwhile, Sébastiani, having sent Akinfov to Murat, had gone to the outpost screen, where he met Miloradovich, whom he had met in Bucharest, during the war between Russia and Turkey. Both generals rode side by side for quite some time along the highway, talking among themselves about the preservation of Moscow.[36] In the city the confusion and disorder increased more-and-more; no sooner had the army passed than every street along which it had moved was jammed with wagon trains. In order to clear the way for the rearguard, Miloradovich sent officers with cavalry

---

35 From Akinfov's notes.
36 Clausewitz. *Der Feldzug von 1812*, 173.

sub-units, but, in spite of this, the movement by the retreating troops was hampered at every step and was very slow. Miloradovich, having arrived at the Dragomilov gate himself at about three o'clock in the afternoon, hurried on to his infantry, which was already in the city. Having approached the Kremlin with his retinue, he saw the commander of the Moscow Garrison Regiment, Lieutenant General Brozin, with two battalions that had set out from the Kremlin and marched through the city with bands playing, which in the circumstances of that time was completely inappropriate. There was criticism from all sides; both soldiers and residents commenting aloud: 'What treachery is this, rejoicing at our misfortunes?' Miloradovich, turning to Brozin himself, who did not understand the mistake he was making, shouted at the top of his voice: 'Which c… [expletive?] ordered you to march with bands playing?' Brozin innocently replied: 'If a garrison, upon surrendering a fortress, receives permission to exit freely, then it is to march out with bands playing: it says so in Peter the Great's regulations.' Miloradovich shouted back: 'But is there anything in Peter the Great's regulations about surrendering Moscow? I command you to silence your band.'[37]

Just as Miloradovich was approaching the Yauza, Akinfov, catching up with him, informed him of Murat's consent to our demands. Miloradovich responded: 'It seems that the French really want to have Moscow. Go to Murat again and offer to conclude a truce with him, in addition to the previous conditions, until seven o'clock tomorrow morning in order to give time for the wagon trains and stragglers to clear the city. Otherwise, they will defend themselves inside Moscow.'

Indeed, Napoleon's entire army, from general to soldier, was eager to get into the capital, the achievement of which had been bought at the cost of so much effort and hardship. Some thought to bask in the glory of their master, who, in their opinion, having occupied Moscow, would have bent Russia to his will, just as most of the rest of Europe had already been conquered by him; others, exhausted and disillusioned, hoped to rest in our capital before returning to their homelands. In any case, the bloodless occupation of Moscow after the terrible battle of Borodino was as much a surprise for our foe as it was for ourselves. And therefore it is quite natural that the French, in an effort to capture Moscow, were ready to make all kinds of concessions in order to acquire this important prize intact, the possession of which, judging by Napoleon's previous successes, would lead him to a successful conclusion to the difficult struggle against Russia.

Just as Akinfov was setting off to return to Murat, carrying out the instructions of his commander, the enemy troops, having already ascended Poklonnaya Gora, caught sight or our ancient capital before them in all its majestic beauty. It was all a novelty for the inhabitants of the West, everything was attractive to the warriors who had achieved their objective. Murat, having left for his forward screen himself, mixed with the Cossacks, talked with their commander and at one o'clock in the afternoon was already close to the Dragomilov gate. Akinfov encountered him there. The king, having welcomed our negotiator most cordially, unquestioningly

---

37 *Denkwürdigkeiten des Grafen v. Toll*, II, 150-151.

agreed to Miloradovich's proposal, with the only condition being that all carts not belonging to the army be left in Moscow.³⁸

As Murat's troops were approaching the Dragomilov gate, at two o'clock in the afternoon, Napoleon rode up Poklonnaya Gora and, seeing the ancient capital of the Russian Kingdom spread at his feet, turned to his retinue, saying: *'La voilà donc enfin cette fameuse ville!'* (Here it is, at last, this famous city!). And then he added: *'Il était temps!'* (It's about time!). In these few words were expressed both the joy of a conqueror who has achieved the objective of his operations, and the regret at the loss of hundreds of thousands of soldiers sacrificed to the unreachable dream of a global monarchy. After that, dismounting from his horse, Napoleon examined both the capital itself and its environs for a long time through a telescope, he ordered a detailed plan of Moscow to be spread out on the ground and asked about the locations of its most important points from one of his secretaries, Lelorgne [Lelorgne d'Iderville], who served him as a Russian language interpreter and knew the capital well.³⁹ For a long time he proceeded with the dispositions of his forces, and eventually he gave a signal by cannon shot for all the columns to continue moving towards Moscow: thus, the additional condition proposed by Miloradovich and accepted by Murat was not honoured. The enemy corps enveloped Moscow from the west like dense clouds. Murat advanced on the Dragomilov gate with the vanguard and the *Jeune Garde*, Poniatowski moved towards the Kaluga gate, the Viceroy towards the Tver gate. There were cheers from many thousands of warriors: *Vive Napoléon*! and the enemy army raced into Moscow: the cavalry galloped at full speed; the artillery tried to keep up with them; the infantry set off at the double. The clatter of horses, the creaking of wheels, the blast of muskets, the conversations of the soldiers, all mixed up in a frightful rumble. The daylight was dimmed by the dust that rose in a pillar, and within a few minutes Napoleon found himself at the Dragomilov gate with the hordes closest to him. There, dismounting from his horse once more, opposite the Kamer-Kollezhsky embankment, to the left of the gate, he paced back and forth, preparing himself to receive a deputation from Moscow. As time passed waiting in vain, his pace became faster and faster; impatience was evident from all his movements.⁴⁰ Having received news of the abandonment of Moscow from the officers sent to him from the vanguard, he had not wanted to believe it. *'Moscou déserte! Quel évènement invraisemblable! Il faut y pénétrer. Allez et amenez moi les boyards!'* (Moscow deserted! What an incredible event! You must enter it. Come on and bring me the *boyars*!) he said to comte D'Arriule [Jean-Lucq D'Arriule], sending him into the city to drag out a deputation.⁴¹

But as there were no *boyars*, and Napoleon demanded that a deputation be brought to him without fail, several foreigners were rounded up who, instead of the usual greeting to a triumphant conqueror, confirmed the news of the abandonment of Moscow by all its residents, with the exception of the French and Germans engaged

---

38 From Akinfov's notes.
39 Korbeletsky, 23-24. Fain, II, 44. Ségur, II, 36.
40 Korbeletsky, 24-27.
41 Ségur, II, 38. Denniée says that Napoleon ordered General Durosnel to bring a deputation to him. *Itinéraire de l'empereur Napoléon*, 88-89.

in trade and a small number of Russians. belonging to the lower social classes. Napoleon, without honouring this pitiful deputation with so much as a single word, mounted his horse, rode into the Dragomilov suburb and settled down in several peasant houses with his entire retinue, where, except for four caretakers, there were no Muscovites.[42] His initial orders in Moscow were that Mortier was appointed governor-general, and General Durosnel [Antoine Jean Auguste Durosnel], commandant of the capital; Lesseps [Martin de Lesseps], the former French consul in St Petersburg, received orders to perform the duties of intendant of the Moscow province; an appeal to the inhabitants of Moscow was supposed to be distributed on the same day, drafted in advance and already printed, but since there was almost no-one to read it, this intention remained unfulfilled for the time being.[43] An order was sent to Murat to pursue the Russian army without losing sight of them, and to Marshal Mortier to occupy the Kremlin with the *Jeune Garde*.[44]

Upon arrival at the Dragomilov gate, Murat detached the cavalry corps under Grouchy and Nansouty to the left, around the northern part of the city; the former was located on the road to Dmitrov, while the latter was at the Petrovsky Palace, on the Tver road; Murat entered the city himself with only the cavalry corps under Sébastiani (formerly Montbrun's?) and Latour-Maubourg, followed by the *Jeune Garde* (the divisions under Claparède and Dufour). As Claparède was following Murat's movement to the Yauza bridge, Mortier was approaching the Kremlin with Dufour's Division and was engaged there by several hundred of our straggling soldiers and Muscovites, who opened fire on the enemy with their muskets. Having fired canister to disperse this handful of the brave, who did not want to leave this ancient residence of the Russian Tsars without protection, the French occupied the Kremlin. On this day, only the troops under Murat and Mortier were brought into Moscow; all other corps were forbidden to enter the city, and the gate itself was held by a detachment of light *cavalerie de la Garde impériale*. The *Vieille Garde* with the corps under Davout and Ney settled down for the night on both sides of the Smolensk road; the Viceroy's *4e Corps* was ordered to halt at Petrevosky, while Poniatowski's *5e Corps* was at the Kaluga gate.[45]

In the meantime, by five o'clock in the afternoon, having managed to withdraw most of the rearguard from the city, Miloradovich reformed his force at a distance of about a thousand paces from the Kolomna gate. At this very moment, two regiments of enemy cavalry appeared on his left flank, which, having been directed from the city by another checkpoint, had moved to block the Ryazan road: these were the Polish 10th Lancers [*10 Pułk Huzarów*?] and Prussian Lancers [1st Prussian Uhlans?], which had been marching at the head of Murat's cavalry. Miloradovich sent an officer to the enemy, demanding a meeting with the King of Naples, but the *parlementaire* did not return for a long while, time was passing, and even if our rearguard managed to retreat without hindrance, by exploiting the uncertainty of any conditions being agreed, the French could have captured many of our stragglers

---

42 Korbeletsky, 29. Chambray, II, 117-118.
43 Chambray, II, 114.
44 Fain, II, 45-46.
45 Chambray, II, 115. Bernhardi, *Denkwürdigkeiten*, II, 154-155.

and transport remaining in the city. Miloradovich, knowing that Sébastiani was in command of Murat's leading troops, galloped up to the enemy cavalry and, turning to the Polish lancers, asked: 'Where is General Sébastiani?' Surprised by the boldness of the Russian general, the enemy pointed out to him in which direction he was likely to find their commander. Miloradovich's aides de camp, who set off after him on exhausted horses, caught up with him just as he halted, having bumped into Sébastiani. To Miloradovich's insistence that the King of Naples had concluded a truce with us until seven o'clock the following morning, Sébastiani replied that the King had not given him any word about it. During their conversation, the troops of both sides mingled with each other, yet did not violate the unofficial truce with hostile acts. From all the nearby gates, carts, stragglers and refugees, poured out onto the Ryazan road and continued to move without encountering the slightest interference from the enemy, while the Cossacks restored order in the city, and all the time the leading units of Murat's vanguard stood near the Ryazan road.[46] General Sébastiani, pointing to the troops and wagons moving past his cavalry, said to Miloradovich: 'You must admit that we are generous people; this could all be ours.' Miloradovich replied: 'You are mistaken, you could not have taken this other than by stepping over my corpse, and the 100,000 men who stand behind me would have avenged my death.'[47] Having assembled all his troops, with the exception of the Lifeguard Cossacks and Izyum Hussars, who were unable to reach the Kolomna gate and marched along the Vladimir road to join up with Wintzingerode's detachment, Miloradovich moved four *versts* from the city and settled down for the night.[48]

On this day, Miloradovich rendered an unforgettable service to the Fatherland, contributing to the retreat of the army and the departure of several thousand refugees. Suvorov's final campaigns and the whole series of wars preceding this last struggle between Emperor Alexander I and Napoleon served to form many excellent generals, of whom Russia was justly proud during the Patriotic War; some of them surpassed Miloradovich in their abilities, but none could have carried out Kutuzov's orders, to protect the army's march from Moscow, as successfully as Miloradovich did. Having acquired the burden granted to a select few, ringing renown, in his youth and having reached the rank of full general in the prime of his life, he was as well known in the French army as Murat was in ours. It seemed that nature itself

---

46 Clausewitz, 174-175.
47 Mikhailovsky-Danilevsky, Description Of The Patriotic War Of 1812. Bernhardi, *Denkwürdigkeiten*, II, 153.
48 Bernhardi, 154. General Mikhailovsky-Danilevsky, describing the departure of the Russian forces from Moscow, states that once the rearguard and wagon trains had moved four *versts* from the city and Miloradovich was settled in a nearby village, suddenly: 'Major General Panchulidzev presented himself, with a report that two squadrons of his regiment (Poland Ulans?), either were delayed, or had got lost in Moscow, and had not been able to rejoin the rearguard and were detained behind enemy lines. Miloradovich sent a demand for their safe passage, but considering the matter too important, he mounted, overtook his aide de camp, galloped alone without a trumpeter through enemy outposts, shouted a greeting to Sébastiani, and without waiting for his response, ordered our two squadrons 'by the right in threes, move on!' led them out of the enemy screen and together with them released many more carriages that had arrived from Moscow.' Description Of The Patriotic War Of 1812, compiled by General Mikhailovsky-Danilevsky, II, 340-341.

had forged Miloradovich into his military status, striking him with all the hallmarks of an excellent warrior. Handsome in appearance, dressed in battle and in the bivouacs as if on parade, a dandy, in all his decorations, with a tall plume on his hat, sometimes wrapped in a rich cape, like Murat, he appeared on his swift horse wherever he could engage the threat face to face. Always cheerful, indefatigable in wartime, the first into action, the last to take a rest, he inspired the troops subordinate to him through his courage. The more difficult the situation became, the more his customary vitality was revealed, the better became his ability to communicate with the Russian soldiers who adored him. Like Murat, throughout his entire military career, he was never wounded, despite the fact that, in the words of Yermolov: 'whoever served under Miloradovich, needed to have two lives; one his own and another as a replacement.'

The first word of the enemy occupation of Moscow reached St Petersburg through a landowner who arrived there. Nobody wanted to believe the fateful news. But soon after that, Emperor Alexander I received the following report, from Count Rostopchin, from Yaroslavl:

> Prince Kutuzov's aide de camp has brought me a letter in which he demands police officers from me in order to guide the army to the Ryazan road. He has stated that he is abandoning Moscow with regret. Tsar! Kutuzov's act has decided the fate of the capital and your Empire. Russia will shudder when it learns of the surrender of this city, where the greatness of Russia is concentrated, where the remains of your ancestors lie.
>
> I shall follow the army. I have evacuated everything: all that remains is for me to weep over the fate of my Fatherland.[49]

Emperor Alexander, having received this report, sent Adjutant General Prince Volkonsky (Pëtr Mikhailovich) to the army, with the following rescript for the Field Marshal:

> Prince Mikhail Illarionovich! I have not received any reports from you since 29 August [10 September]. Meanwhile, on 1 [13] September, I received sad notice from the Moscow Commander in Chief via Yaroslavl that you have decided to leave Moscow with the army. You can imagine yourselves the effect this news has produced, while your silence deepens my astonishment. I am sending this with Adjutant General Prince Volkonsky in order to learn about the state of the army from you and about the reasons that prompted you to make such an unfortunate decision.
>
> 7 [19] September, 1812.[50]

Two days later, on 9 (21) September, Colonel Michaud [Alexandre Michaud de Beauretour] arrived in St Petersburg from the army, sent to the Tsar by Prince

---

49 Report dated 1 [13] September.
50 From documents kept in the Classified Archives of the 2nd Branch of the Department of the General Staff.

Kutuzov, with a report on the fall of Moscow. Being immediately shown in to the Emperor on Kamenny Island, Michaud left an intriguing description of the conversation with which the Tsar graced him on this occasion, in a letter to the former *Flügel-Adjutant* Mikhailovsky-Danilevsky. As Colonel Michaud brought the fall and burning of the capital to the attention of His Majesty, Emperor Alexander, touched to the core by the misfortunes of his subjects, could not hide his grief, and said: 'From everything we have experienced, I must conclude that Providence itself requires great sacrifices from us, from me in particular. I submit to his will, but tell me: what did the troops say, abandoning my ancient capital without a shot? Have you noticed a decline in their morale?'

'Will you allow me, as a soldier, to speak frankly to Your Majesty?'

'I always demand sincerity, but now I ask you: do not hide anything from me, tell me the whole truth honestly.'

'Tsar! I confess that I left the army in indescribable dread, from Kutuzov to the last soldier…'

'What are you talking about? Have my Russians been crushed by misfortune?'

'No, Tsar, they are only afraid that you, out of the kindness of your heart, might make peace, they are burning with the desire to fight and prove their loyalty to you!'

The Emperor patted Michaud on the shoulder and said: 'You have eased my heart; you calmed me down. Return to the army, tell my loyal subjects wherever you pass, that should I have not a single soldier left, I would convene my faithful nobility and good villagers, I would lead them myself and mobilise every resource of my Empire. Russia presents me with more options than the enemy supposes. But if by fate and divine providence it is destined for my family to reign no longer on the throne of my ancestors, then, having exhausted all efforts, I shall grow a beard for myself down to here (pointing to his chest with his hand) and I'd rather agree to eat potatoes in the depths of Siberia than sign the shame of my Fatherland and my good subjects, whose sacrifices I am able to appreciate. Providence is testing us; let us hope it does not abandon us.' With these words, the Emperor, shaking the hand of the messenger, continued: 'Do not forget what I am telling you now; maybe the time will come when we will recall this with pleasure: Napoleon or I, I or he, but we cannot reign together. I have found him out; he will no longer deceive me.'

'Tsar!' replied Michaud, 'Your Majesty has underwritten the glory of your people and the salvation of Europe this minute.'

'May your prophecy be fulfilled;' said Alexander; 'go rest and be prepared to return to the army.'[51]

The report to the Tsar by Prince Kutuzov, delivered by Colonel Michaud, read as follows:

> After such a bloody, albeit victorious battle, on our part, on 26 August [7 September], I had to abandon the position at Borodino, for reasons that I had the good fortune to convey to Your Imperial Majesty. After this battle,

---

51 Michaud's letter to former *Flügel-Adjutant* Mikhailovsky-Danilevsky. A copy is held in the Archives of the Military Topographic Depot, No. 47,352, folio 2. For the text of this letter, see Appendix 8.

the army found itself in extreme disorder; Second Army is already much weakened. With such an expenditure of strength, we approached Moscow, in action daily with the enemy vanguard, and at this short distance there was no position on which I could reliably engage the enemy. The forces with whom we hoped to unite had not yet come; the enemy launched two new columns, one along the Borovsk road and the other along the Zvenigorod road, trying to operate on my communications with Moscow; and therefore I could not in any way dare to fight, the negative outcome of which would have resulted not only in the destruction of the remnants of the army, but also in a most bloody destruction and leaving Moscow itself in ruins. In such an extremely precarious situation, in consultation with our leading generals, some of whom had contrary opinions, I had to decide to allow the enemy to enter Moscow, from which all the treasures, the arsenal and almost all property, both public and private, had been evacuated, and not a single nobleman remained there.

Having outlined the factors that prompted him to abandon Moscow, Prince Kutuzov wrote that the enemy entry into Moscow was not yet the conquest of Russia, and reported on his intention to make a flank march to protect Tula, Bryansk and the most fertile governorates of the Empire, and to threaten the enemy line of operations in the sector from Moscow to Smolensk. The Field Marshal's report concludes with the following words:

As long as Your Imperial Majesty's army is intact and motivated by its renowned valour and our eagerness, the earlier loss of Moscow is reversible and does not represent the fall of the Fatherland. Your Imperial Majesty has most graciously agreed that these consequences are inseparably linked with the loss of Smolensk and with the completely disordered state of the troops in which I found them. Colonel Michaud will explain the state of affairs in greater detail to Your Imperial Majesty.[52]

The report by Prince Kutuzov about the abandoning of Moscow was vague, and even contained some contradictions: the battle of Borodino is referred to as victorious, but after that, instead of describing our army thus, another was used, the remnants of the army, which does not at all suit a force that had won a victory. The statement about the evacuation of the arsenal is not accurate, because only some of the state property located there was saved, but Prince Kutuzov, in this case, was misled by Count Rostopchin, who had assured the Field Marshal that everything had been removed, and he even wrote to the Tsar on this subject.

At the same time as delivering Kutuzov's report, Colonel Michaud delivered a letter from General Bennigsen to Count Arakcheev, expressing gratitude to the count for receiving, on his recommendation, a cash award from the Tsar and reported the following news:

---

52 Prince Kutuzov's report from Zhilina, dated 4 [16] September. Archive of the M.T.D. No. 46,692.

I believe that the submission (*Abgabe*) of Moscow has made an impact in St Petersburg. On 1 [13] September, at seven o'clock in the evening, a Council of War was assembled, at which it was decided to give up Moscow, which was immediately executed. General Barclay most energetically supported this opinion, insisting that the Tsar himself would have approved it. Time will tell to what extent this assurance is true. I would very much like it brought to the attention of the Monarch that I did not agree to this proposal in any way, explaining the reasons for my opposition and bringing to light all the harmful consequences that I foresaw. Once the opinion of General Barclay had been accepted, I left the Council. It seems that Prince Kutuzov is now convinced that he has made a huge error, and is consulting with me about further operations; I hope that our situation will improve soon. Colonel Michaud has been sent with this to report on future operations to His Imperial Majesty...[53]

The news of the enemy occupation of our ancient capital made a strong impression in St Petersburg and throughout the Empire, but did not have a harmful effect on national morale. Despite the unexpectedness of such an event after *the repulse of the enemy army at Borodino*, general confidence in the old Field Marshal did not waver at all. Only in St Petersburg did the champions of peace express loss of hope in the success of further military operations; among them were Chancellor Rumyantsev and Count Arakcheev. But Emperor Alexander I remained unshakable in his intention to defend the glory and honour of Russia. Foreign historians claim that the famous Stein [Heinrich Friedrich Karl Reichsfreiherr vom und zum Stein], at the fateful time of the enemy occupation of Moscow, raised the collapsed morale of the Russians and even had influence over the determination of our government to continue the war.[54] But this is contradicted by the general distrust of foreigners that prevailed in Russia at the time. While acknowledging in full the importance of Stein's participation in the liberation of Germany, I shall say that we Russians never needed outside influence to arouse devotion to our Tsars and love for the Fatherland in us: these feelings are innate to us and live and die with us.

Emperor Alexander I himself gave his people an example of fortitude and selflessness. The Tsar wrote the following to the Crown Prince of Sweden:

> The loss of Moscow is harsh, but it has more value morally and politically than militarily. It gives me the opportunity to present the strongest evidence to Europe of my perseverance in the struggle against the oppressor of kingdoms. Following this wound, any others would be insignificant. I repeat to Your Royal Highness the solemn assurance that now, more than ever, I and the people at whose head I stand, are determined to hold fast and bury

---

53 The original of this letter, in German, is held in the Archive of the M.T.D. No. 46,692. A note was made on the Russian translation attached to it that a reply was sent with Colonel Michaud on 14 [26] September.
54 *Das Leben des Ministers Freiherrn v. Stein*, 2e Auflage, III, 158. *Denkwürdigkeiten des Grafen v. Toll*, II, 173.

ourselves under the ruins of the Empire rather than reconcile ourselves with the Attila of our time. Irritated by the fact that he found neither the treasures he sought to possess, nor the peace he hoped to achieve in Moscow, he has burned this beautiful capital, turned now into piles of ashes and rubble.[55]

A few days later, Adjutant General Count Lieven [Khristofor Andreevich Liven or Christoph Heinrich von Lieven], by the will of the Tsar, in a note to the Prussian State Chancellor, Baron Hardenberg [Karl August von Hardenberg], having calculated all the forces we had assembled for operations against the enemy, wrote that we had made a heavy sacrifice in abandoning Moscow, but that this measure had served to weaken Napoleon's army:

> The time has come for Prussia to arm themselves against the common enemy and persuade Austria to do the same. Strictly speaking, Emperor Alexander is waging war in order to defend Russia and to restore the independence of the German powers. In order to achieve such an objective, it is necessary that General Yorck [Johann David Ludwig von Yorck] be provided with proper instructions for just such an event.[56]

The news of the fall of Moscow was made public, by Supreme Command, as follows:

> It is with the most extremely contrite heart that this sadness is announced to every son of the Fatherland, that the enemy has entered Moscow on 3 [15] September.[57] But let the great people of Russia not be discouraged by this. On the contrary, let each and every one swear to rise up with the spirit of courage, firmness and undoubted faith that all the evil and harm inflicted upon us by the enemy will finally be turned upon their heads. The enemy has occupied Moscow not by overcoming our forces, nor by weakening them. The Commander in Chief, on the advice of the leading generals, found it useful and necessary to submit for a moment to necessity, such that by using the most reliable and also the surest methods we may convert this short-term enemy triumph into their inevitable demise. No matter how painful it is for every Russian to hear that the capital city of Moscow is held by the enemies of the Fatherland, but they hold an empty shell, stripped of all treasures and population. The proud conqueror, having entered it, hoped to become the ruler of the entire Russian Realm and to dictate to us such a peace as he pleases; but he will be deceived in his hopes and will find in this capital neither means to rule, nor means to survive. Our assembled and ever increasing forces around Moscow shall

---

55 Emperor Alexander I's handwritten letter, dated 19 September [1 October] 1812.
56 A copy of Count Lieven's letter, dated 21 September [3 October], is held in the Archive of the Ministry of Foreign Affairs.
57 They entered on 2 [14] September, but in the published news it was shown as the 3rd, probably because Napoleon entered the city on that date.

continuously block all their routes and destroy the detachments sent by them for food every day, until they see that their hopes of winning over our minds through the capture of Moscow were futile, and that they will be compelled to break their way out of it by force of arms. Their position is as follows: they entered our lands with three hundred thousand men, of whom the main body consists of various nations, of peoples who serve and obey him not from enthusiasm, not for the defence of their fatherlands, but out of shameful fear and timidity. Half of this multinational army has been destroyed partly by our brave troops, partly by desertion, disease and starvation. They have arrived with the remainder in Moscow. Without a doubt, his bold, or, better said, impertinent pursuit to the very heart of Russia, and right up to our most ancient capital, has satisfied their ambitions, and given them reason to be conceited and arrogant; but their deeds shall be judged by the outcome. They have entered the wrong country, if they think one bold step strikes everyone with horror and forces both the troops and the people to bow at their feet! Russia is not accustomed to subjugation, it will not tolerate subjugation, it will not betray its laws, faith, freedom, territory. They will defend themselves to the last drop of blood in their veins. The general diligence and eagerness, evident everywhere in the willing and voluntary *opolchenie* facing the enemy, is clear evidence of how strong and unshakable our Fatherland is, protected by the cheerful spirit of its faithful sons. And let no one lose heart: is it even possible to lose heart at such a time as all institutions of the state are breathing courage and resolve? As the enemy, with the remnant of their ever more diminishing forces, are removed from his land, in the midst of a numerous people, surrounded by our armies, of which one stands facing him, and the other three are poised to block their return route and prevent any new forces coming to them? When Spain has not only thrown off their yoke, but also threatened them with the invasion of their lands? When most of Europe, exhausted and plundered by them, serving their every whim, seeks and looks forward with impatience to the moment when they might escape from under their heavy and unbearable power? When their own land sees no end to the blood shed by their own and others in the pursuit of glory? With such a disastrous state for the entire human race, will that nation not be glorified, which, having endured all the ruin inevitable from war with patience and courage, finally reach the point that not only will they acquire a firm and inviolable peace for themselves, but also deliver it to other powers, and even to those who, against their will, fight against them? It is pleasant and characteristic of this good nation to repay evil with good. God Almighty! Turn Thy merciful eyes upon the Russian Church praying to Thee upon their knees. Grant good cheer, spirit and patience to Thy faithful people who fight in righteousness. Through this, may they triumph over their enemies, may they overcome them and, in saving themselves, save the freedom and independence of Kings and Realms.

8 [20] September, 1812.

This is how the feelings of the magnanimous Tsar were expressed in the time of disasters, when the greatest commander of our century, having subjugated most of Europe, brought his hordes to Moscow, and when none could see the limits to either his bold intentions or the wondrous successes of the conqueror. Just as he, contrary to all calculations based on normal expectations, had occupied Moscow, it seemed that he might race to our other capital and take that. It became necessary to take measures to guard the St Petersburg road, where at that time there were no troops, except for the weak detachment under Wintzingerode (who had switched to this route, on the orders of the Field Marshal), and to attend to contingencies in the event of failure. And all this had to be done without giving rise to needless alarm, without disturbing the people with untimely fears.

As the detachment under Adjutant General Wintzingerode, consisting of 3,200 regular and irregular cavalry,[58] could not block access to St Petersburg, the Supreme orders were:

1. Lieutenant General Tyrtov will come under General Wintzingerode's command with the Tver *opolchenie*.[59]
2. Colonel Zhemchuzhnikov [Apollon Stepanovich Zhemchuzhnikov], with eight reserve (fourth) battalions expected in Tver, will also come under Wintzingerode's command,[60] and is to appoint as many non-commissioned officers and privates from these battalions as are needed to train the Tver warriors.[61]
3. Adjutant General Kutuzov [Pavel Vasilyevich Golenishchev-Kutuzov] is to collect from the posting stages, between Vyshny-Volochëk and Moscow, young coachmen capable of Cossack service, with their own horses and pikes, 200 men from each posting house. These temporary Cossacks were assigned to reinforce General Wintzingerode's detachment. At the same time, Adjutant General Kutuzov is entrusted with the formation of the Tver *opolchenie*.[62]
4. A corps is to be established in Novgorod consisting of two Cossack regiments from the St Petersburg *opolchenie*, three battalions of the 2nd Marine Regiment, one artillery company and the entire Novgorod *opolchenie*, with the exception of the 4,000 men who had already been sent to reinforce the troops under Count Wittgenstein. It was ordered that non-commissioned officers and privates from 2nd Marines be appointed to train the warriors. The command of the corps being

---

58 The composition of General Wintzingerode's detachment was: the Lifeguard Cossacks, Kazan Dragoons, Izyum Hussars, Lifeguard Black Sea Sotnia, two guns from 5th Horse Artillery Company, Ilovaisky 4th's Cossacks, Ilovaisky 12th's Cossacks, Chernozubov 8th's Cossacks, Ilovaisky 7th's Cossacks (the latter was on the Yaroslavl road), the Stavropol Kalmyks and Perekop Tatars (Combatant Returns dated 6 [18] September, signed by General Wintzingerode).
59 Supreme Orders dated 9 [21] September, No. 122.
60 Supreme Orders dated 9 [21] September, No. 123.
61 Supreme Orders for Adjutant General Kutuzov dated 10 [22] September, No. 125.
62 Supreme Orders for Adjutant General Kutuzov dated 10 [22] September, No. 125.

assembled in Novgorod was entrusted to artillery Major General Novak [Ivan Ivanovich Novak?]. The mission of this corps was to guard both the Moscow highway and the roads leading from Gzhatsk, via Zubtsov and Rzhev, to Ostashkov.[63]

In order to arm and supply these forces with ammunition, 40,000 muskets and 50,000 *Pud* of gunpowder had been ordered from Britain.

Emperor Alexander, wishing to provide a means of subsistence for Russian refugees from the enemy occupied western governorates of the Empire, and to use these men for the common cause, ordered the Pskov civil governor, Privy Councillor Prince Shakhovskoy, to offer them enlistment into temporary service, keeping their own clothing and issuing rations and pay from the treasury on a par with the *opolchenie*.[64] In order to facilitate the extraordinary recruitment obligation necessitated by the circumstances at that time, it was ordered:

> To accept men up to the age of forty, but not younger than the legal age, and to pay no attention to either stature or physical defects, so long as they are blessed with a strong constitution. In the absence of green cloth, it will be necessary to dress all reserve troops in grey.[65]

In taking the most active measures to protect the state and to protect St Petersburg, but without being carried away by over confidence, the Government had been concerned beforehand with the removal from this capital of everything that, in the event of an enemy invasion, might become spoils of war. Orders were issued to collect 1,000 carts at each staging post along the road from St Petersburg to Yaroslavl for the removal of heavy baggage by land, but just as before from Novgorod Governorate alone some 90,000 carts were offered, then 3,000 wagons from the Olonets Governorate and Vologda Governorate were fitted out as a donation to the residents of Novgorod. For the purpose of transporting heavy baggage by internal waterways, boats were bought and hired, which were located in significant numbers not only in St Petersburg, but in Shlisselburg [Schlüsselburg] and other places.[66] In the event of the enemy taking the northern capital by winter, Kronstadt was brought into such a state that it could be defended in winter. As the fleet stationed there was vulnerable in the winter from the landward direction, Emperor Alexander, summoning the British ambassador, Lord Cathcart, suggested that he send all our warships to Britain and place them at the disposal of the British government, for operations against Napoleon and his allies, which was done. All these measures, taken in a timely manner, showed the unlimited trust from our Tsar in His allies and His firm determination to continue the war even in the event of both capitals of the Russian Empire being occupied by enemy forces.[67]

---

63 Supreme Orders to the director of the Ministry of War, dated 12 [24] September, No. 129.
64 From the minutes of the Committee of Ministers.
65 Supreme Orders, dated 12 [24] September, No. 132.
66 Description Of The Patriotic War, compiled by General Mikhailovsky-Danilevsky, II, 399-401.
67 *Das Leben des Ministers Freiherrn v. Stein*, III, 159-160.

Preparations for the removal of government property from St Petersburg could not remain secret for long; many of the residents of the capital, following the example of the Government, tended to the evacuation of their possessions; others were leaving, or were preparing to leave. Rumours of the danger allegedly threatening St Petersburg constantly spread. It was said that the French were already in Tver, in Velikie Luki, and so on. To dispel these untruths, the following announcement was published, by Supreme will:

> Here in St Petersburg, certain measures are being taken to remove items that may be needed in the future. This is not being done because some kind of danger threatens this capital. One glance at the position of our forces should comfort and reassure everyone of this; as the enemy attempting to advance from the direction of the Pskov and Riga roads, not only is barely hanging on, being struck often by our troops, and probably, with the current increase in troop numbers there, will not be able to persist. As far as the Moscow road is concerned, although it is littered with the enemy, they have not got far; as Adjutant General Wintzingerode, having been stationed between Klin and Moscow with his detachment, is sending his patrols right up to Moscow itself; our troops are also in Tver; moreover, the Commander-in-Chief Field Marshal is monitoring the movements of the enemy with his entire army. So neither can they come here themselves, nor can a major part of their force be detached, without being hunted down. As a result of all these factors, it is obvious that the city here does not face any danger. As for the removal of necessities, as has been said, for the time being, this is being done solely as an advance precaution, that would be prevented once the rivers freeze. The present time presents no danger, but we would sin against God if we began to predict the future with undoubted certainty, about which He alone knows. Every expectation of the destruction of the enemy, regardless of the success of their advance into Russia, is with our side; nevertheless, even in the most secure circumstances, the idea of precautions should not inspire either fear or despondency. These measures are being taken at a secure time and to a single purpose, such that if danger begins to threaten this city (may God preserve us!), then the Government, with advance word of this, and having already removed all the heavy baggage, could facilitate the residents travelling from here to the interior of the land in better order and without confusion. As it has been once and firmly established (with which every Russian no doubt agrees) that no matter how successful the enemy forces are, we must first drain the entire cup of disasters, rather than betray Russia to subservience through a shameful peace.
> 20 September [2 October] 1812.

Thus the constantly magnanimous Monarch expressed his intentions once and for all, to defend Russia, or fall at the head of the valiant Russian people. By sharing the general regret about the loss of Moscow, in spite of this, He did not pay attention to the rumours from Kutuzov's ill-wishers and did not deprive him of His authority.[68] The Committee of Ministers, which received all state affairs for discussion and even reports on military operations at that time, being dissatisfied with the imprecise reports by the Field Marshal, submitted the following thoughts to the Tsar:

> The Committee of Ministers, at a meeting on 10 [22] September, 1812, had discussions that the reports by General Field Marshal Prince Golenishchev-Kutuzov, both dated 29 August [10 September] and the latter reported to the Committee, in which the first anticipates the retreat of the army from the position at Borodino, while the second gives notice of the unexpected admission of the enemy into Moscow without any resistance, they do not represent a definitive and full presentation of the facts, which are necessary in matters of such great importance and that this makes it impossible for the Government to formulate its conclusions. Considering previous examples, the Commanders in Chief not only always reported in detail about all their movements and intentions, but also delivered logs of their actions, minutes of councils of war, etc. which is why, then as they are now, the necessary officials accompany them, the Committee proposes to instruct the Commander in Chief of the Armies, firstly, to bring here the minutes of the Council, in which it was decided to abandon Moscow to the enemy without any protection, and secondly, that in the future he should always send full information about every measure and action in his reports. The opinion of the Committee on this is that orders to the Commander in Chief should be made not in the form of any ugly insinuation, but solely on the basis of the necessities, made mention of above, in reports from him.
> Signed in original:
> Sergey Vyazmitinov
> P. Lopukhin
> Count V. Kochubey
> Marquis Traversé [Jean-Baptiste Prévost de Sansac de Traversé]
> D. Guriev [Dmitry Alexandrovich Guriev]
> Count Arakcheev
> Count Alexey Razumovsky [Alexey Kirillovich Razumovsky]
> Prince Alexey Gorchakov
> Count A. Saltykov [Alexander Nikolaevich Saltykov]
> A. Balashov
> Ivan Dmitriev [Ivan Ivanovich Dmitriev]
> Osip Kozodavlev [Osip Petrovich Kozodavlev]
> Prince Alexander Golitsyn [Alexander Nikolaevich Golitsyn]
> Baron Campenhausen [Balthasar von Campenhausen].

Emperor Alexander, acknowledging the opinions of the Committee of Ministers as fair, but wanting to eliminate any reason to discuss reducing His trust in the Field

---

68 Shishkov's notes, 45.

Marshal, forwarded the minutes of the Committee to him, but, at the same time, demanded that the information delivered from the army about military operations must be more detailed than previously.[69]

Having outlined the actions of Emperor Alexander, which so clearly signify His steadfastness, I consider it my duty to point out a feature of His benevolence, which was the predominant quality of the elevated soul of the Blessed Monarch. Noticing Michaud's grief, as he reported on the fall of Moscow, the Emperor, despite being burdened by heavy cares, turned his attention to the situation of an officer who had suffered while performing his duties. Once Michaud had been sent back to the army, the following Supreme Command was sent to Prince Kutuzov:

> Renowned for his diligent service, Colonel Michaud was sent with the sad news of the admission of the enemy into the capital city of Moscow. The sorrow of this worthy officer at being the presenter of this report was obvious. I find it just, as a consolation for him, to order you to send him with the very next joyful news after his arrival.[70]

Such was Emperor Alexander I! Relentless in the struggle for the honour and glory of Russia, gracious to His subjects, He was the comforting angel of every afflicted person.

---

69 The original minutes of the Committee of Ministers and a copy of Emperor Alexander's letter to Field Marshal Kutuzov, are held in the Archives of the M.T.D. No. 46,692, folio 4.
70 Supreme Orders to Prince Kutuzov, dated 14 [26] September, No. 142.

26

The burning of Moscow

Napoleon in the Kremlin. – The fires. – Napoleon's departure to the Petrovsky Palace. – Preparations for the march on St Petersburg. – Napoleon's return to the Kremlin.

Looting. – Disaster for the Moscow residents. – Investigation of the case of the Moscow fires and the verdict of the French Courts-Martial Commission. – Who were the culprits of the Moscow fires?

The consequences of the fires. – The devastation of Moscow. – The preservation of the Orphanage. – Napoleon's conversation with Tutolmin. – Orders issued to Yakovlev by Napoleon. – Napoleon's letter to Emperor Alexander I. – The enemy's orders in Moscow. – Establishment of the Municipal Administration and the Police. – Indiscipline among the enemy troops. – The influence of the Moscow fires on the course of the war.

Upon the entry of the French into Moscow, Napoleon, having spent the night of 2 to 3 (14 to 15) September in the Dragomilov suburb, at six o'clock in the morning, moved his headquarters into the Kremlin, where he occupied a room in the chambers of the palace facing the Moskva river.[1] Even on the previous day, right from the start of the enemy entry into the city, fires had broken out. Initially, the 'Mosquito Bazaar' and the residential streets in Kitai-Gorod [Chinatown] caught fire, then flames broke out in Balchug and the Karetny Row went up in flames in Zemlyanoy-Gorod, set on fire by the owners of the workshops. The French initially attributed these individual fires to negligence and disorder, inevitable when a large city is occupied by armed force, but subsequently several men were captured with combustible materials, deliberately setting fire to buildings, who claimed that they had been ordered to do so by the police before the French entered the city.[2] All efforts to stop the outbreaks were in vain. Fires, extinguished in one place, flared up in many others, and by the night of 3 to 4 (15 to 16 September) engulfed most of the capital. Suddenly a strong wind arose; like a raging torrent, the flames raced from one street to another and rose

---

1 Fain, *Manuscrit de 1812*, II, 46.
2 Korbeletsky, A short history of the French seizure of Moscow, 29-30. Study of the life of the Moscow Archbishop Augustine, compiled by I. Snegirev, 1841, 3rd edition, 35.

in a fireball, like a fiery whirlwind, over the city buildings.³ Among the buildings destroyed by fire were several hospitals filled with our wounded.

Napoleon sent out orders to extinguish the fires, but when he was informed that several Russian incendiaries had been caught, he put aside his concern for the preservation of the city. He told his associates: 'Moscow has died! I have lost the means of rewarding my army.' Indeed, in those terrible days sacred Moscow, the cradle of our Tsars, was no more. Russian hands should not have been raised against her! Moscow remained, engulfed in flames, destroyed, abandoned to the mercy of every vile passion that dishonours humanity. The Russians were not burning Moscow... They were burning a city where their foes nested.

On the 4 (16 September), at noon, the fires reached the Kremlin; a stables near the palace caught fire and the arsenal tower flared up. Several burning embers carried away by the whirlwinds fell into the yard where all the ammunition caissons of the French *artillerie de la Garde* were standing at the time. Napoleon was in great danger himself; his fate, and with it the fate of the twenty-nation army, led away to a distant unknown country by him, was vulnerable to a single spark... Several times the Viceroy, Bessières and Lefebvre [François Joseph Lefebvre] begged him to retire; he remained, as if in disbelief that danger could threaten him. Eventually, once Berthier had pointed out that it would be impossible to move out to support the corps stationed outside the city in the event of a Russian attack on them, Napoleon decided to leave the Kremlin. Wanting to move to the Tver gate, to the troops of *4e Corps*, he ordered one of his orderlies, Captain Mortemer, to reconnoitre the streets leading there. This scout reported that there was no way to get through in this direction, but a few minutes later another officer appeared, who had arrived from the Tver gate. Napoleon, having set off on foot towards the Moskva river from the Kremlin, gave orders to fetch riding horses for himself and his retinue, and rode through the city. He was followed by the *Garde impériale*, except for one battalion left to guard the Kremlin. Piles of rubble and red-hot ashes stopped him at every stage. A member of the Moscow police, who served as a guide to Napoleon, bewildered by the general destruction, recognising neither streets nor buildings, having occasionally moved in a roundabout way to bypass the fires, had strayed from the correct bearing, and eventually, by six o'clock in the evening, the Frenchmen emerged at the Petrovsky Palace, where Napoleon took refuge among the bivouacs of *4e Corps*.⁴

It is claimed that Napoleon, convinced that the distraction of his troops by the Moscow conflagration would not induce the Russian Government to conclude peace, had the intention of making a threatening advance towards St Petersburg, sending the Viceroy's *4e Corps* there, placing the rest of the army between our two capitals and holding Moscow with a rearguard. By operating in this way, he hoped to make us more compliant; in the event that he did not succeed, he proposed to move all the trains of his army to the left, from the route leading from Moscow to St Petersburg towards the Pskov and Novgorod governorates across Count Wittgenstein's lines of communication, to absorb the troops under Saint-Cyr, MacDonald and Victor

---

3   Fain, II, 74-75. Study of the life of the Moscow Archbishop Augustine, 35.
4   Fain, II, 76-78. Chambray, *Histoire de lexpédition de Russie*, II, 119-122. Gourgaud, *Examen critique de l'ouvrage du comte Ségur*. Deniée, *Itinéraire de l'empereur Napoléon*, 93-95 & 190.

into his main force, and in mid [late] October to place his entire army on the Dvina and Dnieper, resting his right flank on Smolensk, and the left on Riga (which he hoped to have captured by that time). Napoleon had no doubts about the success of this plan of action, but all his main colleagues, with the exception of the Viceroy, were of the opposite opinion, believing that the army had the absolute necessity of rest, that, despite the fire that had devastated it, Moscow contained huge resources that should be used up and that, in the event of a retreat to Smolensk, it was far more advantageous to head south from Moscow, where the French could strike the Russians decisively, destroying the arms factory at Tula and the large storehouses at Kaluga. Napoleon, although not fully convinced by the arguments of his marshals, cancelled his proposed advance, noting, however, 'that one could not expect a great inclination towards peace from those who had burned Moscow.'[5]

After 48 hours the fires still raged in the city, while looting completed the misery of the residents. Foreigners, reduced to poverty, came to the Petrovsky Palace, begging the enemy for assistance; the Russians were getting out of Moscow. Eventually, once a large part of the city had become prey to the flames, the fires began to subside, partly from the pouring rain, partly from a lack of fuel for this destructive element. Napoleon, having been informed of this and having received a report that the Kremlin remained intact, returned to Moscow at noon on 6 (18) September. On the way, between the rows of bivouacs, he saw a strange mixture of luxury and want. Cauldrons boiled in which, for lack of beef or other choice cuts of meat, horse meat was being cooked over fires fuelled with expensive furniture, broken mirrors, torn up books and pictures, icons of the saints split into kindling; left bare under the sky, without any protection, there were sugar-loaves, bags of coffee and other exotic products, while almost no one had bread. The evidence of looting by enemy marauders was on every side. Napoleon, wanting to salvage the resources remaining in the city from rapid destruction, gave orders not to let any of the soldiers into Moscow, except for the marauding teams (*à la maraude*), provided with certificates from their formation commanders. This measure somewhat reduced the wandering and violence of the marauders, but did not bring much benefit to the troops, because specific areas were not indicated for each formation for the collection of supplies; units from various formations roamed all over the city, destroying much that would later have been of benefit to the army. As a result, there was an abundance, and even an excess of some supplies, with a complete lack of others: in one regiment there was an abundance of rice and cereals, but there was nothing to season it with; in another, whose foragers were lucky enough to find a cellar with the best wines, there was neither bread nor meat, and thus, due to the negligence and dysfunction of the military logistics department, despite the many supplies found in the city, the troops suffered extreme shortages. In particular, there was a significant lack of fodder, from which the cavalry and artillery of Napoleon's army became totally emaciated during its five-week stay in the vicinity of Moscow.[6]

In the course of 72 hours, three-quarters of the total number of buildings in Moscow had burned down; most of the churches had been destroyed or plundered.

---

5 Fain, II, 79-82. Deniée, 96.
6 Chambray, II, 131-132. Ségur, II, 66-67. Thiers, XIV, *Ed de Brux.* 427-429.

Despite the many and varied kinds of clothing found in the city, almost all the Russians who had the misfortune to remain in Moscow were stripped down to their shirts and robbed of their last pair of shoes. Many of these unfortunates survived on roots from gardens, or with barnacles obtained from the hulls of barges that had settled on the river bed.[7] Napoleon, upon his return to the Kremlin, seeing the evidence of the devastation at every turn, the like of which had not been seen in modern times, ordered a thorough investigation of the causes of the Moscow fires. To that end, a court martial commission was convened of several generals and field officers, chaired by *général de brigade* Lauer [Jean-Baptiste Lauer]. On 12 (24) September, the commission opened proceedings by reading documents presented in the Moscow fires case. After that, the president ordered that the accused be brought in, totalling 26 men of various social classes. After listening to their statements and the testimony of witnesses, various projectiles and materials were presented, such as rockets, wicks, phosphor lighters, sulphur, and so on found in the possession of the accused, or planted by them in the houses as acts of arson.

The diary of the commission claimed that, from the evidence collected, there was no doubt that the Russian Government, foreseeing the impossibility of defending Moscow, had decided to resort to the extraordinary measure of destruction by incendiaries: 'abhorrent to all civilised nations' in order to resist the French army. The commission were convinced that the proposal by the Englishman (who posed as a German) Schmidt had been accepted for this purpose, who, in the vicinity of Moscow, in the village of Vorontsovo, to be precise, had built a huge airship as a fighting machine for operations against the French army. It goes on to claim: the construction of the larger airship was done only for deception, while in the village of Vorontsovo all the workers were engaged in the manufacture of pyrotechnics and incendiary devices; that Count Rostopchin, after the battle of Borodino, had finally decided to burn Moscow, and published several appeals to the residents of the capital and in one of them he stated:

> Arm yourself with whatever comes to hand, with pitchforks in particular, very appropriate for using on the French, who are no heavier than a sheaf of straw. If we do not defeat them and they enter Moscow, then we shall burn them there.[8]

Finally, that it was alleged that Rostopchin, upon leaving Moscow, had ordered about 800 convicts to be released from the gaols, extracting a promise from them to set fire to the city 24 hours after the French entered it,[9] and that for the same purpose several officers and policemen had been left in Moscow, while all firefighting equipment had been removed in order to deny the ability to extinguish any fires.

---

7   Tutolmin's report to Empress Maria Fëdorovna, dated 11 [23] November 1812.
8   The burning of the enemy in Moscow is not mentioned in any of the announcements by Count Rostopchin.
9   There was not a single convict among those accused of arson. And was it even possible to enforce these terms on criminals?

Of the 26 defendants, ten men who were convicted by the testimony of witnesses and who confirmed their participation in incendiary actions with their own confessions were sentenced to death and shot on 13 (25) September.[10] The other 16, due to insufficient evidence, were imprisoned: 'in order to prevent any harm that they might cause if they were released.'[11]

Without attaching any particular significance to the actions of the French court martial commission and its conclusions, in which falsehoods are mixed with truth to such an extent that the very matter entrusted to the deliberations of the commission are not given proper clarity, I will try to address the issue: who was responsible for the Moscow fires?[12] The French very naturally tried to pre-empt any criticism for this disaster and attributed it to orders from the Russian Government, carried out by Count Rostopchin. Our Government had no need to justify itself in something in which it had not the slightest involvement; but attached no blame for the Moscow fires, either on Napoleon or the French. Rostopchin initially expressed regret that he had not been able to burn Moscow, and then published a pamphlet in which he tried to reject any participation in this matter; eventually, public opinion, guided by a hatred of the French in 1812, blamed them for the Moscow fire, as well as for every consequence of the enemy invasion; but then, once time had bit by bit erased the memories of past evils, the conviction arose that we ourselves, guided by an elevated feeling of love for the Fatherland, had burned Moscow in order to deprive the enemy army of the huge resources that were in this capital.

The only evidence cited by foreign historians to confirm the alleged participation of our Government in the Moscow fires is based on Schmidt's fighting machine, which, according to the conclusion of the French court martial commission, was designed for the burning of Moscow. But the commission diary states that Schmidt arrived in Russia at the beginning of May; and at that time, and even two months later, no one among us believed that the enemy could reach Moscow: consequently, Schmidt's work could not have been intended to prepare incendiaries for the burning

---

10 Diary of the session of the Court Martial Commission on the Moscow fires, published in the French Monitor [*Le Moniteur universel*] on 29 October, 1812, No. 303. Those sentenced to death were: Pëtr Ignatiev, Lieutenant of 1st Moscow Regiment (*opolchenie*); Straton Barov, painter [artist]; Alexey Karlum, Moscow policeman; Ivan Tomas, shopkeeper; Pëtr Stignevich, painter; Iliya Arakomov, blacksmith; Ivan Maximov, footman for Prince Sibirsky; Semën Akhrameev (occupation not shown); Nikolay Levutiev, painter; Fëdor Sergeev, tailor.
11 Diary of the session of the Court Martial Commission on the Moscow fires. Those remanded in custody were: Ivan Kasiyanov, sexton; Nikolay Vasiliev, blacksmith; Fëdor Midtsov, soldier; Vasily Yermovaev, craftsman; Nikolay Belsherov, footman; Semën Ivanov, interior decorator; Andrey Shestonerov, Moscow policeman; Fëdor Yefimov, Moscow policeman; Lutsian Moteyts, Moscow policeman; Seakhov, Moscow policeman; Gavrila Abramov, Moscow policeman; Nikifor Samoylov, Moscow policeman; Gavrila Beglov, Moscow policeman; Stenan Logonov, footman; Fëdor Grigoriev, Moscow policeman; Shestoperov (occupation not shown).
12 [Liprandi recommends the book: Some Remarks, Gleaned Mainly From Foreign Sources, On The True Causes Of The Demise Of Napoleon's Hordes In 1812, St Petersburg, 1855 (Некоторые Замечания, Почерпнутые Преимущественно Из Иностранных Источников, О Действительных Причинах Гибели Наполеоновых Полчищ В 1812 Году), 'a separate lengthy article on the Moscow fires is also included, in which all the accounts of this event are critically analysed'].

of the capital. The archives of our Military Topographic Depot contain all the correspondence regarding Schmidt's proposals, which leaves no doubt that it consisted of the construction of a flying machine fitted with innovative equipment, in the form of rockets, for the destruction of the enemy army. At first glance, it is not clear how they could have believed Schmidt's unrealistic promises. Indeed, if he had appeared at any other time, he would have been instantly refused. But in 1812, as the Russians were preparing to fight against the vast forces of Napoleon, having just endured a six-year war against the Turks, conventional weapons seemed insufficient; this compelled us to resort to extraordinary measures without subjecting them to rigorous examination, and that is why Schmidt's strange invention was not rejected until after the trials had been carried out, which proved the absurdity of his enterprise.

As for the participation of Count Rostopchin in the Moscow fire, there is no doubt that he considered that the burning of the capital would be beneficial for Russia. This is proved by the words he said to Prinz Eugen von Württemburg, on the day of their meeting on Poklonnaya Gora, and by two reports to the Tsar, written by Rostopchin himself, after the enemy had already occupied Moscow. In the first one we find:

> The order from Prince Kutuzov to transport provisions to the Kaluga road was issued on the 29th [10 September]. This shows that he wanted to abandon Moscow even at this point. I am in despair that he hid his intentions from me, because, not being able to hold the city, I should have set fire to it and deprived Bonaparte of the glory of taking Moscow, plundering it and then setting it on fire. I would have snatched from the French both the fruits of their campaign and the ruins of the capital. I would make them see that they have lost great treasures, and thus I would prove to them what kind of people they are dealing with.[13]

In the second report from Count Rostopchin, it states:

> Up until 30 August [11 September], Prince Kutuzov was writing to me that he would fight; On 1 [13] September, when I saw him, he told me the same thing, repeating: 'And I shall fight in the streets.' I left him at one o'clock in the afternoon. At eight o'clock, he sent me the infamous letter, demanding police officers to escort the army out of the city, leaving it, as he said, with extreme regret. If he had told me this two days before, then I would have set fire to the city, having sent the inhabitants out of it.[14]

Count Rostopchin's intention to burn Moscow, in the event that it was occupied by the enemy, was not the fleeting passion of an ardent patriot, but a consideration thought out at leisure. We are convinced of this by the following letter from Rostopchin to Prince Bagration.

---

13 Count Rostopchin's report dated 13 [25] September, from Krasnaya Pakhra. From this report, we can conclude that as early as 29 August [10 September], Kutuzov had the intention of moving down the Kaluga road.
14 Count Rostopchin's report dated 13 [25] October, from Vladimir.

As early as 12 (24) August, as news reached Moscow of the fighting at Smolensk and Valyutina Gora, Count Rostopchin wrote to Bagration:

> If you retreat to Vyazma, I shall begin to dispatch all state property… The people here, out of loyalty to their Tsar and love for their homeland, have decided to die at the walls of Moscow, and if God does not aid them in their just cause, then, following the Russian principle, *do not reward the devil*, they will turn the city into ruins and instead of rich booty, Napoleon will find only the ashes of the ancient Russian capital. It is not bad to let him know of this, so that he does not expect millions and large grain magazines, because here he will find only ruins and ashes. I embrace you in friendship and in Russian from the bottom of my heart, I remain clear-headed, but grieving from events.

In a letter from Count Rostopchin to Prince Bagration, dated 21 August (2 September), among other things, it states:

> I believe that you will fight before you give up the capital; if you are beaten and approach Moscow, I shall come out to support you with 100,000 armed residents, and if even then we fail, then instead of Moscow, the fiends will get only ashes…[15]

After all that I have stated, is it possible to doubt that Rostopchin wanted to burn Moscow, considering the razing of the occupied capital to be of benefit to Russia? If he thought otherwise, then why would he express his regret about the failure to fulfil his planned intentions before the Tsar? And it was only due to a lack of time that Rostopchin did not fulfil it. It was not possible to burn Moscow before our army retreated through it because it contained large warehouses that were used to supply our troops with military equipment and food, and besides, Rostopchin, relying on Kutuzov's assurances, hoped that the enemy would not succeed in occupying the capital. Once our army had retreated to Poklonnaya Gora, then, although there was no longer any hope of blocking access to Moscow from the French, it was still not possible to set fire to it without exposing our own troops to imminent danger, retreating in contact with the enemy through the embrace of a city in flames. While Napoleon's troops entered Moscow after the retreat of the Russian army, or, to put it better, at the same time as they left the capital. Consequently, Rostopchin could not carry out his intentions until their departure from the city, but he did everything that could be done in those few hours to achieve his objective: ordered firefighting equipment to be removed and combustible materials to be pre-positioned in many houses, instructed police units left in the city to set fire to it, with the assistance of some residents, ordered the breaching of barrels of wine, which was intended to increase turmoil and disorder; finally, on 2 (14) September, at five o'clock in the morning, he sent one of the detective police chiefs with a unit to the vintners and

---

15 A copy of the correspondence is held by Councillor of State Starinkevich, who managed Prince Bagration's affairs.

laundry compounds, to the commissariat and to the state-owned and private barges that remained at Krasny Kholm [on the left bank of the Moskva river downstream from Vshivaya Gorka] and Simonov Monastery, ordering them, in the event of the enemy entering into city, to destroy everything with fire. According to the police chief, this order was carried out in various places, as far as possible, within sight of the enemy, until ten o'clock in the evening,[16] while having crossed the Moskva river on horseback, below the Danilov Monastery at 11 o'clock, he rejoined the rearguard at about two o'clock in the morning. It is obvious that the execution of such an order would give rise to many fires, and that these fires were the first after the emergence of our army from Moscow;[17] the subsequent ones occurred quite naturally from the disorder that prevailed in the city. The inhabitants who remained there were, for the most part, homeless people, vagabonds who had nothing to lose, and who, taking advantage of circumstances, looted and at the same time set fire to houses in order to more conveniently disguise their crimes. Many soldiers from the enemy army, scattered throughout Moscow to collect supplies and plunder, often drunk, went from house to house with candles, torches, and spills, and even laid out large fires in the yards for cooking. Is it plausible to believe that they observed due caution in so doing?

Finally, a cause of some fires was the deliberate destruction of their own homes by the inhabitants. Count Rostopchin wrote that merchants, craftsmen and other trades, expressing their concern to him that Moscow would fall into the hands of the enemy, often said: 'better to burn it.' He also testifies that later, during his stay at Prince Kutuzov's headquarters, he saw many people who had escaped from Moscow after the fire, who boasted that they had set fire to their homes themselves.[18]

But it does not therefore follow from this that the Moscow fires were a deliberate act by the inhabitants of the capital, who allegedly, in a selfless outburst of love for the Fatherland, decided to make a great, general sacrifice to save it. Without entering into a study of the question of whether the Moscow fires served in favour of Russia, we would justly be proud of it if in reality all the inhabitants of the capital, or at least the majority of them, had unanimously accomplished this feat, sacrificing their property in order to harm the enemy. But this was not and could not be. A very small proportion of the householders remained in the city; all the rest left, leaving their houses empty, or leaving them in the care of estate managers, butlers, janitors, and in general people who would neither decide to burn the houses that were under their supervision themselves, nor get permission from the homeowners for such a dangerous business. It is impossible to imagine that all the inhabitants of such a vast city agreed among themselves to burn their homes; if only a few decided on this (as was the case in reality),[19] then their patriotic deed had a most unfavourable signifi-

---

16 Information submitted by the former Moscow detective police chief Voronenko.
17 [Liprandi points out that this is at odds with Bogdanovich's earlier claim that fires initially broke out in 'the 'Mosquito Bazaar' and the residential streets in Kitai-Gorod'].
18 Rostopchin's memoirs, 1853, 212-213.
19 [Liprandi disagrees suggesting that homeowners may well have left verbal orders with the caretakers for their homes to be burned down in the event of a French occupation (as had been happening in towns and cities across occupied Russia) and points out that Bogdanovich

cance in the eyes of those who, having lost all their possessions in the fire, became unwitting victims of someone else's self-sacrifice. Therefore, to present the burning of Moscow as equivalent to the self-destruction of Saguntum [219 B.C. triggering the second Punic war] is as absurd as to attribute it to the cruelty of Napoleon and the aggression of his troops. Napoleon, in the first days of his stay in Moscow, not only did not order the burning of the city, but tried to extinguish the fires; later, his troops of many nations, indulging in looting and atrocity, actually indulged in arson, but did not intend to raze Moscow at all. Even without this, they did us a lot of harm during the fateful period of the Patriotic War of 1812: the enemy were rightly vilified for the murder of civilians, for desecrating their wives and daughters, for plundering the Houses of God, we then accused them of the burning of Moscow, for atrocities that exceeded the measure of Heaven and of human patience. All of Russia, having heard the news: that the French had burned Moscow, was seething with a sense of vengeance. The conflict became a national war.

In the present day, as almost half a century has already passed since the Moscow fires, once Moscow, like a phoenix, was reborn in greater beauty from the ashes of the conflagration, without losing its former grandeur, History should attribute the disaster that befell our ancient capital neither to the malice of Napoleon nor the self-sacrifice of the Muscovites. Why should we insult the truth with a boastful account of an unprecedented act? The war of 1812 is so rich in the glorious deeds of our compatriots that we would hardly ever be able to pay due tribute of praise to all the heroes of this great era. From everything that has been said about the burning of Moscow, it is obvious that the main, or at least the initial, culprit was Count Rostopchin, although he later denied any participation in this matter.[20] He was prompted to such a denial by the fact that the inhabitants of Moscow, returning to the ruins of their homes, were indignant towards Rostopchin, as the cause of their destruction; It should also not be overlooked that Rostopchin's pamphlet, in which he tried to deny any involvement by himself in the Moscow fires, was published in Paris, at a time when Count Rostopchin, permanently resident there, did not want to be regarded as a rude Scythian in the eyes of the French, prepared to sacrifice himself and others for the benefit of his Fatherland. Fortunately for Rostopchin's honour, if there were French who took his word for it, then at least we Russians, on the basis of the above facts, remain convinced that Rostopchin had the intention of burning Moscow and that the first fires after the entry of the French into the city took place on his orders.

The consequences of the Moscow fire were terrible. The vast city, flourishing a few days previously, had turned into a desert dotted with heaps of ruins, among which towered the chimneys of razed and charred homes and a few surviving churches. Of the monasteries, churches, public and private buildings, more than two-thirds

---

himself cites many Muscovite refugees rejoicing that their destroyed properties would not be of use to the foe].

20 *La verité sur l'incendie de Moscou, Paris, 1823, Par le comte Rastoptchine* (the truth of the burning of Moscow, by Count Rostopchin). This pamphlet was published, in Russian translation and in the French original, in a book printed by Smirdin: Rostopchin's memoirs, 1853, 199-298.

burned down (there were 9,257 buildings that were registered in Moscow before the enemy invasion, 6,496 burned down); almost all the others had been looted. Like rare oases, interrupting the gloomy monotony of the boundless steppe, there were buildings preserved, as if by a miracle, from the general destruction. Among them was the Orphanage, which owed its preservation to its worthy warden, the active Councillor of State Tutolmin [Ivan Akinfievich Tutolmin]. As soon as the enemy entered Moscow, Tutolmin, prompted by a desire to save this charitable institution entrusted to him, went to the Kremlin to the French governor Durosnel, explained to him about the infants and minors left in his care and asked to be taken under protection, as an humanitarian duty.[21] General Durosnel, moved by the words of the venerable old man, sent an officer with 12 gendarmes to guard the Orphanage. During the period of the Moscow fires, Tutolmin, trying to save the institution entrusted to him from a complete disaster, placed all his subordinates and senior pupils around the building to extinguish the embers scattered by the firestorm and, with the assistance of the French gendarmes, they preserved all the buildings of the Orphanage, except for the pharmacy burned by enemy arsonists.

On 6 (18) September (Tutolmin's notes state 5 September), Napoleon, on his return to Moscow from the Petrovsky Palace, riding along the embankment past the Orphanage, asked: 'What is this building?' and having learned that it had been preserved by the diligence of the warden of the institution and his subordinates, he ordered General Dumas to find Tutolmin and announce to him the gratitude of the Emperor of the French. Following this, the secretary Lelorgne came to Tutolmin, with the news that the Emperor wished to see him. Upon arrival at the Kremlin, he was immediately introduced to Napoleon and, being received very favourably, expressed gratitude to him on behalf of several hundred unfortunates who owed their salvation to his patronage. Napoleon replied: 'I had wanted to do for the whole city what has been done for your institution. I would have dealt with Moscow as I did with Vienna and Berlin, but the Russians abandoned the city almost entirely, burned it themselves and, in wanting to harm me, within a few days have destroyed the work of many centuries. Even if I abandon Moscow, the damage that you have inflicted upon yourselves will be irreparable. Bring this to the attention of your Tsar; he truly does not know what is going on here.' Thereafter Napoleon asked: how many children were being raised in the institution? How much food storage do they have? From where will the winter supplies come? etc. Having received a statement on the number of children from Tutolmin and quickly examining it, he said with a smile: 'You have sent all the adult girls to Kazan.'

As, in the meantime, the fires were still burning and flames could even be seen across the river from the windows of the palace, Napoleon suddenly broke off his speech and began to criticise Rostopchin for all the misfortunes suffered by the Muscovites. Beside himself, he cried out: 'Misery! He has dared to add arson to all the disasters of war. It is inhumane, is it not, to abandon several thousand wounded, so many women, old people, children, to a certain death!'

---

21 All children over 11 years of age had been sent to Kazan, on the Supreme Orders of Empress Maria Fëodorovna.

Then, turning to Tutolmin, he asked: 'Has he not to ask for this?' and when Tutolmin expressed a desire to bring to the attention of the August Patroness of the institution entrusted to him that it had miraculously survived amid the general destruction, Napoleon not only allowed him to send a report to the Dowager Empress, but took advantage of this opportunity to express his personal respect for Emperor Alexander and his desire to end the war. His parting words were: 'Write to your Tsar that I wish for peace and send it with a report from your official. I shall order his safe passage through the outposts.'[22]

Three days later, Napoleon made another attempt to open relations with Emperor Alexander. Among the five or six Moscow nobles who remained in the city during its occupation by the French was Yakovlev, brother of the former Russian resident in Stuttgart. On 2 (14) September, at the very moment he was about to get into a carriage to leave Moscow, several enemy soldiers caught up with him and confiscated his horses and carriage with all his belongings. Deprived of the opportunity to leave, Yakovlev was forced to wander around burned-out Moscow, together with his family, servants and hundreds of Muscovite peasants, robbed even of their footwear and exhausted from hunger. Meanwhile, the properties belonging to Yakovlev and his family had, one by one, burned down. Deprived of his last refuge, he decided to ask for advice on passing through the French outposts with the people who were with him, from Colonel Meynadier [Louis Henri René Meynadier], who he had met by chance whilst serving in France, who responded that he would have to ask Marshal Mortier, the Moscow governor general at the time, and immediately led him to the marshal. In response to Yakovlev's request, Mortier said that he had no authority to grant it without the permission from the Emperor. Napoleon, according to the records, expressed a desire to see Yakovlev. On 9 (21) September, Lelorgne, having escorted him to the Kremlin Palace, introduced him to Napoleon in the throne room.

Almost from his first words, Napoleon, embittered by the sight of the ruins of Moscow smouldering before him, began to accuse the Russians, with his usual vehemence, of the deliberate burning of the city. 'My troops have occupied almost every European capital, but I have not burned any of them. In all my life I have burned down only one city, in Italy, and even then it was by chance in the heat of a battle that was raging through the streets. While you have decided to burn Moscow yourselves, sacred Moscow, Moscow, where the remains of every ancestor of your Tsar rest.' In response to this outburst, Yakovlev said that he did not know exactly who was to blame for the general disaster, but that he was suffering its consequences. Whereupon Napoleon asked Lelorgne: 'But who was their governor in Moscow,' and having received in reply that this position had been occupied by Count Rostopchin, he turned to Yakovlev with a question: 'What is this man?'

'He is known for his intelligence,' answered Yakovlev.

'Perhaps' Napoleon interrupted, 'but he is deranged. I had some idea of your country before, but everything I saw from the borders to Moscow has convinced me that Russia is a most beautiful country (*c'est un pays magnifique*). All of it is

---

22 Tutolmin's report to Emperor Alexander I, dated 7 [19] September, and to Empress Maria Fëodeorovna, dated 11 [23] November 1812. Fain, II, 84-87.

cultivated, populated, but I found the houses empty or in flames. And you are ruining your beautiful land yourselves! For what? It didn't stop me from moving forward. You would do the same in Poland. The Poles deserve it; they greeted us with delight. It is time to put an end to this bloodshed. It is easy for us to get along. My war with Russia is purely political. I have nothing against you; I do not demand anything from you except the obligations of the Treaty of Tilsit. I am ready to return, because my main priority is to deal with Britain. If I could take London, I would not leave it soon. I want to go back. If Emperor Alexander wishes peace, then let me know. I shall send one of my aides de camp to him, Narbonne or Lauriston [Jacques Jean Alexandre Bernard Law de Lauriston], and we will immediately be reconciled. If he wants war, we shall fight. My troops are asking me to lead them to St Petersburg. Let us go there too; in that case, St Petersburg would suffer the same fate as Moscow.'

As Napoleon paused his monologue to take a pinch of snuff, Yakovlev, taking advantage of the moment, asked him: 'Where is the main body of our army?'

'Ah! Your main army is on the Ryazan road,' replied Napoleon. To Yakovlev's question about Count Wittgenstein, Napoleon said that he was positioned towards St Petersburg and had been utterly beaten by Saint-Cyr. Speaking of our troops, he extolled their strengths and capabilities. 'Your soldiers are excellent, and your officers are good,' he said, 'but they are not able to endure what mine endure, who can endure cold and heat and all kinds of hardships equally. My soldiers have started markets in the city, they found a lot of goods, the best wines in the cellars. But if they were to write about all this to their families, all of Europe would descend upon you. People everywhere love luxuries (*le peuple partout aime la cocagne*). You wish to leave Moscow. I agree, but on condition that you, after visiting your people wherever you wish, then go on to St Petersburg. Your Tsar will be pleased to learn about everything that is happening in Moscow from an eyewitness.' When Yakovlev observed that, due to his status, he had no right to hope to be presented to the Tsar, Napoleon said: 'Present yourself to the Chamberlain Count Tolstoy; I know him to be a good man (*que je connais pour un brave homme*); order his valet to report your presence to the Emperor, or try to engage the Tsar as he is taking a walk.'

'I am in your hands at the moment,' answered Yakovlev, 'but I am a subject of Emperor Alexander's and will remain so to the last drop of blood. Do not demand from me what I dare not pledge to you.'

'Very well,' said Napoleon, 'I shall write to your Tsar. I shall say that I summoned you.' After that, having explained the content of the letter, the main subject of which was an expression of readiness for peace, Napoleon instructed Yakovlev to deliver it to Emperor Alexander. The next day [22 September, new style], Lelorgne brought Napoleon's letter and a certificate of free passage from the city through the forward posts of the French army. Having received these documents, Yakovlev, accompanied by more than 500 people, set off on foot from Moscow and in the evening arrived in Chernaya-Gryaz, where he presented himself to Colonel Ilovaisky; and from there, on the following day [23 September], he was escorted by Cossacks to Davydkovo, to Adjutant General Wintzingerode, who sent him on to St Petersburg with an officer. Upon their arrival at the Moscow gate, an order was received to bring Yakovlev directly to Count Arakcheev, who, taking Napoleon's letter from him, presented it to the Tsar.

This letter had the following contents:

> Having learned that the brother of Your Imperial Majesty's ambassador to the Court of Kassel was here,[23] I summoned him and instructed him to go to Your Majesty to express my feelings to you. Beautiful, magnificent Moscow no longer exists! Rostopchin has burned it; 400 arsonists were captured at the scene of the crime. All of them testified that they acted on the orders of the governor and the chief of police. The criminals were shot. The fire appears to have finally stopped. Three-quarters of the buildings have burned down; one quarter remains. This act was terrible and unconscionable! Was the city set on fire to deprive us of our means of subsistence? But the stores were in the cellars, where the flames did not reach. Was it worth it to achieve such an insignificant aim, to destroy one of the most beautiful cities in the world, built over the course of several centuries? This is what they did in Smolensk itself; 600,000 households driven into poverty. Moscow's fire pumps were broken or taken out of the city; some of the weapons stored in the arsenal had been distributed to the criminals. We had to drive them out of the Kremlin with gunfire. Humanity, Your Majesty's interests and those of this vast city demand that I be entrusted with this capital abandoned by the Russian army. It was vital to leave governance and civil authorities in it. As has happened twice in Vienna, in Berlin, in Madrid, and that is what we did in Milan, when Suvorov arrived there. The fires have given rise to looting: the soldiers have appropriated for themselves that which did not become a victim to the flames. I would not be writing to Your Majesty had I assumed that all this was done at your command, indeed, I consider that impossible under your reign; with your heart and enlightened mind, you have not prevented such a fury, unworthy of a great Monarch and a great nation. When the fire pumps were removed from Moscow, they left 150 field guns, 70,000 new muskets, 1,600,000 cartridges, more than 10,000 *Pud* of gunpowder, some 8,000 *Pud* of saltpetre, a similar amount of sulphur, etc. I am waging war against Your Majesty without acrimony. Had you written me a note before the last battle, or shortly thereafter, I would have halted the army and willingly given up the advantage of entering Moscow. If Your Majesty retains similar feelings towards me, at least in part, then accept my letter favourably. In any event, be grateful to me that I have informed Your Majesty about what is happening in Moscow.[24]

The response to this letter was silence from Emperor Alexander, who did not even want to see Yakovlev, so as not to give rise to rumours of any kind of relations with Napoleon. Moscow, destroyed by flames, divided the belligerents like a terrifying

---

23 As it states in Napoleon's letter; Baron Fain states that Yakovlev's brother was the Russian Resident in Stuttgart.
24 Yakovlev's manuscript notes. At the end it states that this may serve to refute the false narrative about the conversation between Yakovlev and Napoleon, which is placed in the work by Baron Fain.

chasm. The Tsar, having ordered Napoleon's message to be shown to the Swedish Resident, Count Löwenhielm, also wrote to the Crown Prince that there was nothing in it but hubris.[25]

But once Napoleon had returned to the Kremlin, measures were taken, at his command, to protect the headquarters and to re-establish order in the city as much as possible.

A constant guard-force was established in the Kremlin from one of the *Garde impériale* regiments, from which 106 men were formed up for each of the two gates in use; the rest of the gates were blocked up completely and were under the supervision of pickets of eight men each, under the command of a sergeant. No Russians were allowed to enter the Kremlin, with the exception of those whom Napoleon had summoned himself. The sentries were ordered to shoot at any Russians who might dare to violate this prohibition. There was a screen of sentries all along the walls; patrols constantly moved around the Kremlin and in general a routine was ordered, day and night, as is done in close proximity to the enemy.[26] Patrols from each battalion were set up to stop the looting, each of 15 men, under the command of officers who were obliged to disperse any rioters and detain all soldiers who had absented themselves from their units.[27] In one of the Daily Orders, it stated:

> The Emperor is very dissatisfied with the fact that, despite standing orders to prevent looting, gangs of marauders are constantly entering the Kremlin with looted property. At the same time, it is the duty of generals and unit commanders to supervise the execution of this command from His Majesty.[28]

A few days later, an order was issued: 'Yesterday, last night and today, soldiers of the *Garde* again indulged in disorder and looting, worse than ever.' In order to stop these shameful deeds, thorough searches were ordered to be carried out so that all the rogues who brought dishonour on this elite corps could be expelled from the *Garde impériale*. As the subunits sent to the city by the regiments to collect provisions and other supplies were looting along with the marauders, it was forbidden to send such work-parties; while in order to supply the troops with everything they needed, magazines were set up in which stores were collected from whatever was found in the houses abandoned by the residents, and then the correct distribution of provisions were to be made to various units of the army.[29] If this order had been made immediately upon the entry into Moscow by the French, or, at least, in the first days following the cessation of the fires, then Napoleon's army would have been provided with its necessary supplies for a long time, but the city, charred and plundered for two weeks, was no longer able to provide large resources for the army.

---

25 Emperor Alexander I's hand-written letter to the Crown Prince of Sweden, dated 19 September (1 October) 1812.
26 *Ordre du jour, du 18 septembre*. The original is held in the Imperial Public Library.
27 *Ordre du jour, du 20 septembre*.
28 *Ordre du jour, du 21 septembre*.
29 *Ordre du jour, du 29 septembre*.

Particularly harmful was the shortage of fodder, which consequently led to huge losses of horses in the cavalry and artillery. To compensate for these losses, all the peasant horses (*cognats*) over four feet, three inches (1 *arshin* 13 *vershok* [1 *vershok* = 4.44 cm or 1¾']) that were with the infantry and cavalry corps were ordered to be collected, except for those that were in the artillery and transport, to issue them as remounts for the light cavalry.[30]

The disorder in which Napoleon's multi-national army indulged itself in Moscow had a morally devastating effect on the troops. Discipline, the essence of any well-ordered army, was gone. The soldiers disregarded the orders of their officers, indulged in all sorts of atrocities in their presence and spat on the lists of grievances presented to them by the unfortunate residents of Moscow. The decline in respect for authority reached the point that officers participated in the violent acts of the lower ranks themselves and showed disrespect not only to their superiors, but also to Napoleon himself. In one of the orders for the *Garde* we find:

> Every officer, of whatever rank, marching past the Emperor with the troops, must salute His Majesty with their sword. Today on parade, this was not done. The duc de Dantzig,[31] invites the gentlemen officers to better remember their duties in this respect and the gentlemen commanders to supervise their execution.[32]

Napoleon was doing everything in his power to put an end to these disorders. Wishing to establish institutions in the city, he set up a municipality (*municipalité*) and a police department (*bureau de police*). The chairman of the former of these departments was Lesseps, the intendant of Moscow, a well-intentioned man, but one who could not alleviate the distress of the residents at all. The composition of the municipal government was completely heterogeneous: it consisted of Russians, French, Germans and Italians; of officials, merchants and tradesmen. Their main duty was to care for those unfortunates deprived of shelter and means of subsistence, but Lesseps himself, despite Napoleon's favour towards him, was not able to stop the indiscipline and was even forced to watch if through his fingers.[33] The looting

---

30 *Ordre du jour, du 1 octobre.*
31 Lefebvre.
32 *Ordre du jour, du 29 septembre et du 6 octobre.* In the former of these orders it states:
 'L'Empereur voit avec peine que des soldats d'élite destinés à la garde de Sa Personne, qui devraient conséquemment donner dans toutes les circonstances l'exemple de l'ordre et de la subordination, s'oublient au point de commettre des pareilles fautes. Il en est qui ont enfoncé des caves et des magasins de farine que fesait garder l'Intendant-général pour le service de l'armée; il en est d'autres qui se sont avili au point de méconnaître les consignes et de maltraiter de propos et de fait les gardes et leur chefs placés par les autorités.'
 The order dated 6 October registers: 'Tous les officiers, quelque soit leur grade, soit en ligne, soit en colonne, soit lorsqu'ils defileront, doivent saluer de l'épée Sa Majesté. C'est une marque de respect qui n'est dûe, qu'à l'Empereur. Déjà plusieurs fois cela a été ordonné et l'on a observé aujourd'hui à la parade que cela ne se faisait plus. S. Exc-ce le maréchal duc de Dantzick invite Mrs. les officiers à mieux se rappeler de leurs devoirs dans cette circonstance et Mrs. les chefs à en surveiller l'éxécution.'
33 *Histoire de la destruction de MoscouHistoire de la destruction de Moscou en 1812, etc. par A.F. de B...ch, ancien officier au service de Russie. en 1812,* 113-114.

continued as before, not only in empty houses, but also in those where locals were in residence. Resistance to violent looters very often resulted in severe beatings, torture and murder. It is impossible to imagine the terrible vision of suffering inscribed with the tears and blood of the residents during the Moscow conflagration. The enemy, driven by brutal motives, forgot both their feelings of pity for humanity and the fear of God. There was no respect for the sanctity of the altars, nor for the dignity of the clergy. Many churches were turned into barracks, magazines and stables. Soldiers of Christian nations, proud of their enlightenment, stripped the fittings from the holy icons, chopped them up, burned them, shot at targets made from religious images, and cursed at every object of worship. It was as if the era of the invasion by the pagan Tatars had come again to Russia! Moscow, famous for the number and wealth of its Houses of God, was deprived of the ultimate consolation of Orthodox martyrs for two whole weeks, to ascend above all earthly calamities through prayer in church to the Almighty Comforter. Eventually, on 15 (27) September, the gospel rang out in the deserted capital, overwhelmed by the presence of the enemy. On this day, marked by the anniversary of the coronation of the Blessed Monarch, the chaplain of the Chevalier Garde Regiment, Gratsiansky, performed the sacred liturgy in the church of Archdeacon Euplas. Having been captured during the departure of our troops from Moscow, he was the first to ask for permission to perform the Divine service through Lesseps, but with the condition that it was forbidden to pray for the Tsar and commemorate the Imperial House at litanies. The fearless spiritual shepherd, surrounded by the enemy, in the ruins of Moscow, offered prayers to the Heavens for the subjugation of all His enemies under the feet of the Orthodox Tsar and asked for the granting of victory to Him.[34] In every region of the vastness of Russia, millions of Russians prayed for their Monarch, but could anyone ascend to God in spirit more earnestly than the unfortunate inhabitants of Moscow?

Many years have passed since the Moscow fires. Time has erased both the traces and even the memory of the disasters that bore down on Russia. The memory of our enmity towards the French has disappeared. Nothing remains of Napoleon's conquests. But the glory of the righteous deeds accomplished by Emperor Alexander I will remain forever immutable. History will say that He, having defended the honour and independence of Russia, avenged the fires of Moscow by preserving Paris.[35] Napoleon, ruling over a Europe that had taken up arms against us, could not save Moscow from the rioting of his legions; in contrast, Emperor Alexander I, in preserving Paris, not only set an example of mercy and magnanimity to the Russian troops, but also prompted his allies to forget their grievances.

There is no doubt that the burning of Moscow inflicted huge losses of both public and private property. As for its influence on the course of military operations, although this fire destroyed a lot of stores that could have been used by Napoleon's army, nevertheless, it is still impossible to draw the conclusion that the preservation of these supplies would have helped the enemy spend the winter in Moscow, or, at least, make their retreat less disastrous. There can be no doubt that the burning of

---

34 From the testimony of eyewitnesses.
35 [Liprandi comments: 'After everything that the author has already written about this, he could have written: avenged the occupation of Moscow, even its ruin, but not the fires!'].

Moscow, having given rise to looting (*maraude*) on an enormous scale, had a devastating effect on the discipline of the enemy force, but it had already been in steep decline before then; and the five-week occupation of Moscow by the French only completed the turmoil and disorder that had gradually developed in Napoleon's army from its first steps into Russia.

As for the influence of the Moscow fires on the morale of the Russian troops and, in general, on the morale of our people, eyewitnesses to this event assure us that, having dispelled the despondency and hopelessness that were the immediate consequences of the fall of Moscow, it aroused a general thirst for vengeance in Russia. The news of the enemy's entry into our capital, all the more surprising after the exaggerated rumours of the successes won by the Russians at Borodino, horrified the residents of the governorates surrounding Moscow, who, no longer considering themselves secure, began to withdraw into the countryside. Some of our most outstanding generals, after the loss of Moscow, began to doubt the successful outcome of the war, and among them was even Barclay de Tolly, who, being the former Minister of War, had the opportunity to fully appreciate the military resources of Russia. It is claimed that when Lieutenant Colonel Clausewitz came to him with several officers who were leaving the headquarters for the corps under Count Wittgenstein, Barclay said: 'Thank God that you have been called away from here; we cannot expect anything worthwhile here.'[36] Some talked of peace. In contrast, Kutuzov showed confidence in future successes and a dislike for negotiations that could lead to a cessation of hostilities, and waited for the arrival of our reinforcements on the Dvina and in Volhynia, which, together with the onset of winter, would prompt Napoleon to evacuate Moscow.[37] It is difficult to say anything definitive about the thoughts and calculations of our Field Marshal at this time, because even then, as always, he did not reveal his intentions to anyone. How far did his self-confidence extend? Did he really possess inner resolve, or was he able to hide the worries that agitated him? I do not undertake to resolve these issues, but I believe that Kutuzov foresaw the inevitable influence of the situation in which the enemy army found itself, and that this was his greatest gift in the war of 1812.

Meanwhile, Emperor Alexander I publicly expressed before the face of the world his firm intention to continue the struggle against Napoleon. When the enemy entered Moscow, many thought that in order to liberate the capital, our Government would be ready to make any compromise and even conclude an unfavourable peace. But as Moscow went up in flames, at the hands of the enemy, as it was believed at the time, then it was no longer a matter of saving Moscow; every Russian, as one man, was inspired by the desire to avenge her. The unpleasant memory of previous failures had disappeared. It was not difficult for us to grasp at what cost the enemy had gained their successes; everyone now knew how strong Napoleon's army had been when it entered Russia and what losses it had suffered; little by little, the conviction

---

36 Clausewitz, *Der Feldzug von 1812 in Russland*, 184-185 [Liprandi asks who were the other outstanding generals that doubted the successful outcome of the war? He also finds Barclay's comment to be implausible – arguing that such an indiscreet statement to a relatively junior officer would be very out of character for Barclay].
37 Clausewitz, 184.

was gaining that Napoleon could neither spend the winter in Moscow, nor go deeper into our country. All that remained was to wait for his retreat. The longer he remained in the ruins of the ancient capital, the greater would be the difficulties that awaited him on the way back: autumn arrived; following it would be a harsh winter, disastrous for the sons of Western Europe who were not accustomed to enduring this cold. Everyone among us knew that Chichagov's veteran army was already approaching Volhynia to reinforce Tormasov, and that they would have a decisive superiority in numbers over the corps under Schwarzenberg and Reynier. Everyone knew that Steinheil's corps from Finland and a significant number of recruits were already moving in support of the troops under Count Wittgenstein. The successes of the Russian troops on the flanks of the theatre of war ought to have led Napoleon to hasten his return march from Moscow.

Without any doubt, all these factors could not be so precisely assessed at the time of the events described, as with present hindsight: the proximity of danger and the influence of Napoleon's previous successes did not allow a discussion of the current state of affairs at that time with serene peace of mind and with perfect clarity. But Emperor Alexander, at the head of His people, had decided, from the first enemy footsteps on Russian soil, to repel the invasion, or fall gloriously. The burning of Moscow did not change His resolve.

27

The retreat of the Russian Army from Moscow to Tarutino

Prince Kutuzov's retreat from Moscow along the Ryazan road towards the the Borovsky crossing. – The flanking march by the Russian army towards Podolsk and Krasny Pakhar. – The operations by our rearguard and their consequences. – Steps taken by Napoleon for the pursuit of the Russian army and for the security of the Smolensk road. – The first actions by Russian partisans.

The advantages accrued through the flanking march on the Old Kaluga road. – The detachment of General Dorokhov to the Smolensk road. – His first operations.

The general plan of action for the entire Russian army. – The situation in the Moscow area. – The enemy's ignorance regarding the movements of our forces. – Murat's advance on Bronnitsy and onwards towards Podolsk. – Poniatowski's advance on Podolsk, while Bessières moved on Desna. – Steps taken for the general security of the Russian army. – Prince Kutuzov's retreat along the Old Kaluga road.

The amalgamation of First Army with Second Army. – Barclay de Tolly's departure from the army. – Emperor Alexander I's letter to him.

Retreat of the Russian army to Tarutino. – Miloradovich's retreat to the river Chernishnya with the rearguard. – The deployment of the enemy army. – Their situation. – Steps taken by Napoleon on military matters during his stay in Moscow. – Reasons for the inactivity of the enemy army.

On 2 (14) September, on the day Moscow was occupied by the French, the Russian army, having crossed the capital, made a 15 *verst* march along the Ryazan road and stopped for the night near the village of Panki.[1] Miloradovich's rearguard moved

---

1   See Map Depicting Operations from Napoleon's Occupation of Moscow to his Retreat to Mozhaisk.

six *versts* from Moscow and spent the night at Vyazovka. Our troops remained in these locations throughout the following day, 3 (15) September.[2] The reason for this rest day, close to the enemy army, was the need to protect the departure of many of the refugees from Moscow who were escaping along every route leading from the capital. The troops, on the very first night after leaving Moscow, witnessed the terrible glow of the fires.[3] On the evening of 3 (15) September, Miloradovich's rearguard was relieved by VII Corps and IV Cavalry Corps, under the overall command of General Raevsky (IV Cavalry Corps was commanded by Adjutant General Vasilchikov). The regiments of the former rearguard rejoined the main body of the army. During 3 (15) September, the leading troops of both sides stood within sight of one another, without resorting to hostile actions, but skirmishing broke out between them the following day; by the evening of the 4 (16 September), Raevsky had retreated to Ostrovtsy with his infantry, while Vasilchikov moved to Panki, in the meantime, the army, having crossed the Moskva river, settled down near the villages at the Borovsky crossing and Kulakovo.[4]

On the way from Panki to the Borovsky crossing, as mentioned above, Prince Kutuzov sent Colonel Michaud from the village of Zhilina on 4 (16) September, with a report for the Tsar about abandoning Moscow, and upon reaching the Borovsky crossing, it was decided to make a flank march from the Ryazan road to the Kaluga road. Foreign historians, trying to deprive Kutuzov of the glory he deserves, have tried to prove that the original idea for this flank march did not come from our commander and that this movement itself was a mistake.[5] It could just as easily emerge that this flank march was proposed to Kutuzov by Toll, or by any other of his colleagues. General Yermolov, who knew everything that was going on in the army better than anyone, attributes the honour of this march to Bennigsen; in any case, it is sufficiently to Kutuzov's credit that he, being able to appreciate the merit of this idea, skilfully prepared the means for its implementation and sent food supplies in advance to such locations along the Kaluga road from where they would be timely for the arrival of the army. It is pointless to claim that Kutuzov did not report to the Tsar about the flank march on 4 (16) September, undertaken the following day, and even left everyone around him in the dark about his intentions, because he himself had not yet drawn up a definitive plan.[6] All this is explained by the usual *modus operandi* of our Commander in Chief, who never revealed his intentions to anyone before they were to be carried out. Everyone knows how difficult it is to keep something a secret among the many people who make up the inevitable attachments to an army headquarters. Perhaps Kutuzov, by not making anyone a participant in his

---

2   War Diary of the Main Operational Army. Buturlin, I, 366.
3   War Diary of the Main Operational Army. Wollzogen, 157.
4   War Diary of the Main Operational Army. Buturlin, I, 372-373.
5   Bernhardi, II, 166-167. Wollzogen, 159. [Liprandi comments: 'But if it was a mistake, then, after all, it was Germans that had proposed it, and therefore I do not see that this would deprive Kutuzov of the glory he deserved'].
6   Wollzogen, 159. [Liprandi states that, in this report, Kutuzov specifically wrote: 'Regarding the intent to make a flanking march in order to shield Tula, Bryansk and the most fertile governorates of the Empire, and to threaten the enemy line of operations in the sector between Moscow and Smolensk'].

decision making process, damaged his renown; on the other hand, the common cause gained a great deal.

It is also pointless to suggest that the movement made by Kutuzov was too complex, and therefore fraught with risk to our army. Bernhardi says that Toll initially suggested retreating to a flank position at Borodino, and then at the position on the Vorobievo hills. But who could be sure that the enemy would permit us, in the first instance, to make a rather lengthy move along poor country roads, from Borodino to Vereya and Borovsk, or in the second, to move across the Setun river and several deep ravines in full view of them? In contrast, having passed through Moscow, abandoned as a sacrifice to the enemy, we could easily mislead them about our future intentions. Meanwhile, as Kutuzov was executing this skilful manoeuvre, Napoleon, initially intoxicated by the prize that he had so easily won, and then in dealing with the Moscow fires, did not show his usual energy and, distracted by the elusive phantom of peace, completely lost track of the Russian army. Without any doubt, Kutuzov could not have foreseen the favourable circumstances that contributed to our flank march, but he exploited them very skilfully.

On 5 (17) September, Prince Kutuzov, leaving the rearguard under General Raevsky at the Borovsky crossing, moved the main body of the army via a forced march, to the road from Moscow towards Kashira, and the next day [18 September, new style] reached Podolsk and granted the army a rest day on 7 (19) September.[7] Throughout this march, the troops, following the right bank of the Pakhra, were protected from the enemy direction by the course of this river. At night, the huge glow of the Moscow fires illuminated our bivouacs with its ominous reflection. Meanwhile, as the main body of the Russian army was moving towards Podolsk, VII Corps, which was in the rearguard, crossed the Moskva river at the Borovsky crossing, and on 5 (17) September, deployed between this village and Kulakovo, where the main body of the army had previously stood; Vasilchikov remained on the far side of the Moskva river with IV Cavalry Corps until the evening, beating off probing attacks by enemy cavalry that had caught up with them, and at nightfall they crossed to the right bank and destroyed the bridge. After that, Raevsky, leaving Colonel Yefremov facing the enemy with two Cossack regiments on the Ryazan road, set out with the rearguard troops in the footsteps of the army, along the right bank of the Pakhra, to Frolovsky Yam (Iom?), and then on to Podolsk.[8]

During the army's stay at Podolsk, Prince Kutuzov issued the following orders: Lieutenant General Konovnitsyn was appointed Duty General for both Western Armies;[9] Admiral Chichagov was ordered to advance through Mozyr and Rogachev towards Mogilev, to co-operate with the Western Armies, while General Tormasov, was to hold on the river Styr.[10] The main body, continuing the flank march, crossed, onto the left bank of the Pakhra river on 8 (20) September, to the village of Gorki,

---

7 War Diary of the Main Operational Army (Archive of the M.T.D. No. 29,179). In another copy of this diary, it is erroneously stated that the army proceeded non-stop onwards to Gorki.
8 War Diary of the Main Operational Army. Kutuzov's report to the Tsar, dated 6 [18] September, from Podolsk.
9 Prince Kutuzov's orders, dated 7 [19] September, No. 19.
10 Prince Kutuzov's orders.

on the old Kaluga road, and recrossed to the right bank on the 9 (21 September), where they settled down near the village of Krasnaya-Pakhra. In order to shield the army from the direction of Moscow, General Miloradovich was sent from Podolsk directly to the village of Desna, on the old Kaluga road, with VIII Corps and I Cavalry Corps (coming under the command of General Meller-Zakomelsky, on the occasion of the illness of Adjutant General Uvarov). At the same time, Raevsky's infantry were located near the village of Lukovnya, between the Tula road and the old Kaluga road; his cavalry, under Vasilchikov's command, were stationed near Podolsk, on the Tula road; the Cossack regiments, which were in the rearguard under the overall command of Colonel Balabin [Stepan Fëdorovich Balabin], were distributed as follows: one regiment at Podolsk, another on the Kashira road; the other two, under Colonel Yefremov's command, on the Ryazan road. Each of these Cossack detachments received orders from General Vasilchikov, in the event of an offensive against them by superior numbers of enemy troops, not to rejoin the rearguard, but to retreat along those roads from Moscow on which they were stationed.[11]

Meanwhile, Sébastiani, moving step by step along the Ryazan road, crossed the Moskva river and, mistaking Yefremov's detachment as the rearguard of the Russian force, continued to pursue them as far as Bronnitsy. Murat, misled by the intelligence from the vanguard and the over-confidence that engulfed the enemy after they had occupied Moscow, and had remained in the capital himself, reported to Napoleon that: 'the Russian army has scattered, and that it consists only of Cossacks.' But upon reaching Bronnitsy, Sébastiani became convinced that he had been deceived by the skilful movement by the Russian detachment. On the night of 9 to 10 (21 to 22) September, as soon as Napoleon received reports, on the one hand, that his vanguard had completely lost contact with the Russian army, and on the other, that Cossacks had appeared on the Mozhaisk road and attacked the convoys moving along it,[12] he sent Poniatowski's *5e Corps* from Moscow directly to Podolsk, to assist the troops on the Ryazan road and ordered Murat, having taken command over them, to move against the Russians and to stay on their heels in pursuit.[13] Bessières, with a hastily assembled observation corps, was sent along the Tula road, from which he subsequently turned onto the old Kaluga road.[14]

---

11 Lieutenant General Raevsky's memo to the army Chief of Staff, Major General Yermolov, dated 8 [20] September, from the village of Lukovnya, No. 356.
12 Fain, II, 94. Letter from the Chief of Staff of the *Grande Armée*, Berthier, to the King of Naples, dated 22 September, new style: '*Des cosaques ont paru sur la route de Smolensk, à six ou sept lieues d'ici. Ils étaient une trentaine, qui ont surpris un convoi d'une quinzaine de caissons, qu'ils ont brûlés…*' (Cossacks have appeared on the road to Smolensk, six or seven leagues from here. They were about thirty, who surprised a convoy of about fifteen caissons, which they burned…).
13 Berthier's letter to the King of Naples, dated 23 September, new style. Murat's force consisted of: Poniatowski's *5e Corps*, Claparède's Division, Dufour's Division, the light cavalry from *1er Corps* and *3e Corps* (less one light brigade from *1er Corps*) and the *Réserve de cavalerie* (less La Houssaye's Corps, who had replaced Grouchy). Chambray, II, 145 & 216.
14 Berthier's letter to the Duc d'Istrie (Bessières) dated 22 September, new style. Bessières' corps consisted of: Friederichs' Division (formerly Dessaix's), one light cavalry brigade from *1er Corps*, La Houssaye's *3e Corps de cavalerie* and Colbert's lancer brigade from the *cavalerie de la Garde*. Chambray, II 148.

In order to secure the Mozhaisk road, Major Letort [Louis-Michel Letort de Lorville] was sent along it, with several squadrons of dragoons, who received orders to collect every march squadron along their route, totalling from 1,500 to 2,000 men; after that, on 11 (23) September, the *Dragons de la Garde impériale* were sent from Moscow along the Mozhaisk road, for a distance of about 30 *versts*, with two *Artillerie à cheval de la Garde* batteries; while a few days later, on the 14(26 September), Broussier's Division, the light cavalry of *4e Corps* and the *vélites de la Garde italienne* were positioned halfway between them and Moscow. Napoleon himself was preparing to march along the Ryazan road or Tula road with his entire army in order to push our army beyond the Oka.[15]

The attacks on French convoys, which aroused such great alarm in the enemy army, were the first actions by Russian partisans in the war of 1812. Intending to describe the nature of our partisan operations and their results later, I shall confine myself here to explaining the circumstances that gave rise to the use of these methods, which turned out to be so valid in combination with the popular uprising and brought us undoubted benefits.

As early as the moment when our Western armies, moving from Gzhatsk to Borodino, had reached the Kolotsky monastery, Lieutenant Colonel Davydov [Denis Vasilievich Davydov] of the Akhtyrka Hussar Regiment, languishing with a thirst for action, sent a letter to Prince Bagration, who knew him personally, with the following content:

> Your Excellency! You know that, since leaving the position as your aide de camp, which was so flattering to my pride, and joining an hussar regiment, I have had partisan service as an ambition, both with the strength of my relative youth, and according to my experience, and, if I dare say, according to my courage. The situation leads me to this time in the ranks with my comrades, where I am allowed no initiative of my own, and therefore I can neither undertake nor accomplish anything brilliant. My Prince! You are my only patron; let me come before you to explain my intentions. If it please you, to use me as I propose then be assured that the man who held the appointment of Bagration's aide de camp for five consecutive years, will uphold this honour with all the diligence that the plight of our dear Fatherland requires.[16]

Thereafter, having been summoned to Bagration, on 21 August (2 September), Davydov explained to him the benefits of guerrilla warfare under the circumstances in which we found ourselves at the time. Convinced by his arguments, the very next day, Prince Bagration reported to his Grace. The proposal to send a detachment behind enemy lines, completely isolated from their own troops, was completely novel; besides, Prince Kutuzov, by his very nature, did not willingly subscribe to dubious enterprises: the matter concluded with the Commander in Chief agreeing to send, as he put it, to their almost certain deaths just 50 hussars and 150 Cossacks,

---

15 Berthier's letters to Bessières, dated 22 & 23 September, new style. Chambray, II, 150.
16 Davydov's memoirs, published by A. Smirdin, 1848, 448.

on condition that Davydov took command of them personally. When Bagration conveyed the words of His Grace to Davydov, he received from him in response: 'I would be ashamed, my Prince, having proposed a dangerous enterprise, to yield its execution to another. You know yourself that I am ready for anything, but for the cause: that is the priority, and there are few men fitted for this.'

'None could do more,' said Bagration. Davydov, realising that it is not numbers that win during a surprise raid, but daring, and concerned that his proposal might be refused, he answered: 'If so, then I shall also go with that number; maybe I'll clear the way for larger detachments.'

'That is what I have come to expect from you,' said Bagration.

'Believe me when I say, my Prince' continued Davydov, 'that this patrol will be tight; I vouch for this on my honour: that is all that is needed, daring in action, decisiveness in a tough spot and vigilance at rest halts and overnight camps. This is what I am taking on... But with only a few men; give me a thousand Cossacks, and then watch what happens!'

'I would give you 3,000,' he answered; 'I don't like to do such things blindly, but there is no point discussing it. The Field Marshal himself designated the strength of the patrol... One must obey.'[17]

Many of the Russian partisans went on to become famous; some surpassed Davydov in their exploits, but, having said that, he has the glory of introducing us to a completely new method of partisan operations. When Davydov presented himself to Adjutant General Vasilchikov with a letter from Prince Bagration regarding the assignment of his best hussars to the partisans, some of the generals who were in attendance teased him: 'Give our compliments to Pavel Tuchkov,' (who was then in captivity) they said: 'may he dissuade you from being a partisan.' Others expressed their condolences to Davydov, calculating that he was going to his certain death. But Davydov was confident of success. Having shared the dangers and glory of the Battle of Borodino with his colleagues, with 50 hussars and 80 Cossacks, he moved via a circuitous route through Sivkovo, Boris-Gorodok, Yegorievskoye and Medyn, to the village of Skugorevo (on the border between the Medyn *Uezd* and Gzhatsk *Uezd*), from where, having learned about enemy convoys following the Smolensk road, he turned via Tokarevo towards Tsarevo-Zaimishche, attacked a convoy of 30 wagons, with an escort of 215 infantry, captured about 100 men, the rest having been killed, and captured another small convoy after it had been abandoned by its escort.[18]

The flank march executed by the Russian army from the Ryazan road to the Kaluga road, gave us the opportunity to protect Kaluga, where large warehouses of ration stores had been assembled at the time, and Tula with its arms factories, as well as maintain communications with the southern regions of the Empire, which contained rich resources of manpower for the force and the supply of all necessities. But in addition to these advantages, which are very important from a defensive point of view, we acquired the means to operate against the enemy army's lines of

---

17 Davydov's memoirs, 447-451.
18 Lieutenant Colonel Davydov's report to the commander of the vanguard, Lieutenant General Konovnitsyn, dated 2 [14] September, No. 11 (in the Archive of the M.T.D. No. 29,172. Log of incoming documents).

communication, all the more so since the bend formed by the Smolensk road near Gzhatsk helped us to get closer to Napoleon's line of operations. The Field Marshal immediately took advantage of these circumstances. Having withdrawn the main body of the army to the right bank of the Pakhra, to the village of Krasnaya-Pakhra, and covering them from the direction of Moscow with the vanguard under Miloradovich, located near Desna, and from the direction of Podolsk by Raevsky's detachment, stationed at Lukovnya, on 9 (21) September, Kutuzov detached Major General Dorokhov in the direction of the Smolensk road, with the Lifeguard Dragoons, Yelisavetgrad Hussars, three Cossack regiments and with two Don Cossack guns, for a total of around 2,000 men.[19]

Dorokhov, having set out on that same day [21 September new style] from Desna, on his way towards Mozhaisk, settled on the new Kaluga road, near Sharapovo, on 10 (22) September and, moving from there onto the Smolensk road, destroyed a convoy at Perkhushkovo, blowing up 56 ammunition caissons and capturing more than 300 men.[20]

During the halt of the Russian force at Krasnaya-Pakhra, *Flügel-Adjutant*, Colonel Chernyshev [Alexander Ivanovich Chernyshev], having been despatched by the Tsar on 31 August (12 September) to Prince Kutuzov, arrived at the army headquarters with a general plan for military operations. This wide-ranging plan was intended to take advantage of Napoleon's troops being pulled deeper into the internal regions of the Empire. The essence of the intentions contained in it was that the Russian forces operating on the flanks of the main theatre of war, having been boosted with reinforcements, were to go over to the offensive, drive the enemy corps facing them from Russia and then move into the rear of Napoleon's *Grande armée*, under pressure at the same time from the front by our main body: thus the ultimate consequence of our operations would be the annihilation of the enemy main body.

The operations by our independent corps and armies, on the flanks of the main theatre of war, were to be as follows: Count Steinheil, having disembarked in Reval and moving from there to Riga, with 15,000 men drawn from the troops stationed in Finland, was intended to link up with the garrison there and open offensive operations, both against MacDonald and against the remnants of Saint-Cyr's Corps, which by then would have already been driven back behind the Dvina by Count Wittgenstein. Having driven these corps back behind the Neman, Steinheil's force was to be stationed at Vilna and serve as the reserve for an army to be assembled on the Berezina. Meanwhile, Wittgenstein, having assimilated the reinforcements sent to him, was to liberate Polotsk, drive Saint-Cyr back to the left bank of the Dvina and, entrusting his further pursuit to Steinheil, advance to Dokshitsy [Dokšycy] and establish communications with Chichagov. Simultaneously with these advances by the Russian forces gathering on the Dvina, Admiral Chichagov, who had already arrived in Volhynia with the Army of the Danube, was ordered to envelope Prince Schwarzenberg on his left flank and, having driven him out

---

19 Major General Dorokhov's report to Duty General Konovnitsyn, dated 9 [21] September, from Desna (Archive of the M.T.D. No. 29,172).
20 Major General Dorokhov's reports to Duty General Konovnitsyn, dated 10 & 11 [22 & 23] September (Archive of the M.T.D. No. 29,172).

of Lithuania, push him back beyond the Bug and leave Third Army facing him at Nesvizh; while he would advance on Minsk himself with the Army of the Danube, link up there with Ertel's corps from Mozyr and, having assimilated some 15,000 men, follow the course of the Berezina behind enemy lines and establish communications with Count Wittgenstein. The concentration of forces behind enemy lines, on the Ula and the Berezina, was intended to be completed by mid [late] October.[21] To maintain unity in the operations by these troops, the Army of the Danube and Third Army were subordinated to a single commander in Chief, Chichagov; while Tormasov was recalled to Prince Kutuzov's headquarters to take command of Second Army instead of Prince Bagration or to command the reserve in the event of both Western armies combining into one, or another force formation, at the discretion of the Field Marshal.[22]

When drawing up the general plan of action for all Russian armies, it was meant to take advantage of the impending superiority of our forces, for which, on the one hand, the strengthening of our troops, and on the other, the weakening of Napoleon's *Grande Armée* gave us hope. In order to achieve this objective, measures were taken in advance, at a time when the enemy forces were still in a formidable state, and this was the main virtue of our general plan of action.

The Supreme Orders, delivered to the Field Marshal by Colonel Chernyshev, read as follows:

> Prince Mikhail Illarionovich! From your last report I can see with what constant courage the troops entrusted to you overcame the swift attack on them on 24 and 26 August [5 and 7 September], and to what extend the enemy losses in killed and wounded reached.
>
> Based on these conclusions, I remain in hope that your military foresight, having checked the successes of the enemy, will also deter their further progress.
>
> At this very moment, I found it useful to forward to you some notes on the operational plan for offensive operations by the armies under General Tormasov and Admiral Chichagov and the corps under Count Wittgenstein

---

21 For the full text of this general plan of operations, see Appendix 9.
22 Supreme Instructions to Chichagov and Tormasov. Along with the general operational plan, the Field Marshal received, the following Supreme Orders: 'Prince Mikhail Ilarionovich! The approach of the brave Army of Moldavia to unite with Third Western, and the importance of the current situation, causes Me to pay attention to the need for a single commander to direct them. Of the two, being frank with you, I acknowledge that Admiral Chichagov is the more capable due to his resolute nature. But I don't want to disappoint General Tormasov, and therefore I find it more appropriate to summon him to the armies led by you, as if as a result of Prince Bagration's injuries. Upon the arrival of General Tormasov, his employment is up to you according to your discretion, and the drop in strength that occurred in the memorable battle at Borodino in Second Army may serve as a reason for you to no longer divide these armies in two, but to consider them as one; whereupon you may entrust General Tormasov with the reserve, or another formation at your best discretion. Keep this Rescript confidential so as not to offend General Tormasov, who is highly respected by me. St Petersburg, 1 [13] September 1812.'

and Count Steinheil, detached from Riga, where the existing corps will be reinforced by troops arriving from Finland.

If, in your opinion, you find the execution of this plan appropriate, in this case, in order to put this into action, I am enclosing drafts and instructions regarding this for you.

You will see from this plan that the main operations are intended to be carried out by the army under Admiral Chichagov, then I present to you, under My signature, the orders to be followed by him in this event, in which the timing of his operations is not determined, as this will be subject to your own assessment; while for this reason, in these orders, the dates signifying the timings have only been entered in pencil.

For the most convenient implementation of this plan, the following orders are issued:

The current forces in Riga are to be reinforced by a corps transported from Finland to Reval, numbering 14,000.

This corps, under the command of Lieutenant-General Count Steinheil, having already arrived in Reval on the 26th of this month [7 September], set out from there towards Riga via Pernau [Pärnu].

The corps under Count Wittgenstein is to be reinforced by troops leaving St Petersburg on 3 and 5 [15 and 17] September, consisting of 19,000 men, who are due to arrive in Sebezh on the 25th [7 October], having been in Velikie-Luki on 24 September [6 October].

A specific detailed note regarding the composition of these forces and about their current strength is attached.

Finally, I am enclosing copies of Admiral Chichagov's reports, similarly, the originals from Lieutenant General Ertel, and a statement on the number of troops under their command.

I am sending all this to you via My *Flügel-Adjutant*, Colonel Chernyshev, to whom I read the draft of this plan, and in accordance with his tried and tested humility known to me from previous missions, so that, at your request, he could give you all the necessary explanations. If you find this plan to be of use, then send *Flügel-Adjutant* Chernyshev on to Admiral Chichagov.

St Petersburg, 31 August [12 September] 1812. Alexander.

The Field Marshal, having received this rescript, as well as the Supreme Instructions sent for preliminary discussion to Chichagov, Tormasov, Count Wittgenstein and Count Steinheil, summoned Bennigsen, Konovnitsyn and Toll to a meeting, and ordered Chernyshev to read out the documents he had brought (which had previously been translated into French by Chernyshev for Bennigsen's benefit). Bennigsen considered all the measures contained in the general plan of action to be viable; the field marshal, for his part, having approved them, decided to proceed immediately with the execution of the plan sent to him. But just three days before receiving the Supreme Rescript, Kutuzov had sent orders to Chichagov to move towards Mogilev via Mozyr and Rogachev, in order to close up to our main army and to threaten the enemy from behind, then, in order to avoid an operation, which would be inconsistent with the general plan, the Field Marshal ordered Chernyshev to go to Chichagov and Tormasov immediately and pass the Supreme Orders on to them. On his way from St Petersburg to Kutuzov's headquarters, Chernyshev involuntarily lost several days taking a roundabout route to avoid the enemy occupied area, therefore the Commander in Chief, when committing the dates to the Supreme Orders (which was granted to him), meant each was five days later than in the Tsar's draft. In a report to the Emperor about everything that had been done on this subject, the Field Marshal wrote:

> I have left this plan, explained to me in detail by Chernyshev, in its full force. It must be said that diversions distant from the main operations of the war cannot have such an influence over it as those nearby; such that if there was any hindrance to the detailed execution of the plan issued to Admiral Chichagov, then in this case, however, he must keep in mind moving across the enemy line of operations, or considering this with the army under Count Wittgenstein, or closing up to the environs of Mogilev as soon as possible; this will make the situation of the enemy main force more precarious, and the sooner they will be forced to abandon the heart of Russia. Since Chernyshev encountered frequent delays on his way and had to make long detours, all the dates of the month assigned in the plan for the movements and operations by the troops had been set five days too soon, which I specifically instructed Colonel Chernyshev to explain.

Meanwhile, as Emperor Alexander, with hope in God and the valour of his people, took measures to crush the hostile forces, Napoleon's army, weakened, but still formidable, after occupying Moscow, remained in complete inactivity for several days. The hopes for peace raised among the enemy by their entry into our capital, and the need to reconnoitre the vast, unknown city, forced a busy Murat to suspend the pursuit, but once sight of the Russian army had been lost, it was difficult to track their movements. Our small detachments had completely disrupted communications between the various formations of Napoleon's forces, while the peasants who remained within their sphere of influence informed our detachment commanders of all their movements. Doing justice to the skill with which our detachments distracted the enemy from the direction taken by the main body under Prince Kutuzov, one cannot but admit that the negligence and inaction by the French facilitated the success of our operations. For twelve days after the occupation of Moscow, until 14 (26) September to be precise, Napoleon did not have accurate intelligence about our army.[23] Nevertheless, however, as mentioned above, this brilliant commander took measures to counter Kutuzov. But the general exhaustion, a consequence of the difficult campaign from the Neman to Moscow, struck every measure taken by Napoleon with inertia. His orders were carried out sluggishly. Two days passed between Miloradovich taking post at Desna, twenty *versts* from Moscow, before Napoleon was informed about it.[24]

---

23 Chambray, II, 149-150.
24 Bernhardi, II, 182.

As soon as Murat had taken command personally of the French troops advancing along the Ryazan road, he accelerated the pursuit, but having reached Bronnitsy, he became convinced that it was only a Cossack detachment retreating in front of him, and therefore, on 12 (24) September, having ordered Poniatowski's *5e Corps* to move towards Podolsk, he moved there the following day with all his cavalry. At the same time, Bessières was approaching Desna. The arrival of superior enemy numbers forced our forward detachments to retreat: Miloradovich to Vyatutinka, and Raevsky to Polivanovo.[25] Colonel Kharitonov, who was stationed at Frolovsky Yam with his Cossack regiment on the Kashira road, retreated along this road, as a result of orders received, diverting the enemy away from our army.[26] In a similar fashion, Major Lachinov, who was at Podolsk with a Bashkir regiment, retreated along the Serpukhov road, dragging along some 2,000 enemy cavalry.[27]

Meanwhile, at the headquarters in Pakhra, General Miloradovich delivered the intelligence he had received from Adjutant General Vasilchikov, who was stationed near the mouth of the Desna river, regarding the appearance of the enemy on the route from Podolsk towards the village of Chirikovo.[28] The Field Marshal, concerned that his right flank might get turned, sent Count Osterman to this road with IV Corps and Korf's combined (II and III) Cavalry Corps. Having emerged onto this route, Osterman stationed himself with the infantry in the forests near Nemchinino and advanced the cavalry beyond the village of Alexandrovka.[29] Raevsky, not yet knowing about this order, had sent Paskevich's 26th Division to protect the right flank of his corps, which, converging with Osterman's force in Nemchinino, received orders from him to move to the right to Satino,[30] which contributed to protecting our army from envelopment from the right flank across the entire sector along the Mocha river.

The advance by enemy forces to the Desna and Podolsk was perceived by Prince Kutuzov as the beginning of a general offensive by Napoleon's army. On 14 (26) September, the Field Marshal summoned his senior staff to a meeting on this subject; their opinions varied: some believed that Napoleon was advancing on Podolsk with the main force himself; others assessed that such an advance was unlikely, because, by operating in this direction, the enemy would leave their communications with Smolensk vulnerable. Barclay de Tolly recommended staying put, awaiting clarification of the situation. Bennigsen, in agreement with Barclay, believing that only a part of the enemy army was in Podolsk and that Napoleon could not operate in this direction, for fear of being cut off from Moscow and Smolensk, proposed assigning the defence of the course of the Pakhra and the old Kaluga road to Miloradovich,

---

25 Buturlin, I, 376.
26 Colonel Balabin's (commander of the Cossack regiments in Raevsky's rearguard) report to Adjutant General Vasilchikov, dated 13 [25] September, No. 1433 (M.T.D. No. 29,172).
27 Colonel Balabin's report to Adjutant General Vasilchikov, dated 13 [25] September, No. 1437.
28 General Miloradovich's memo to Duty General Konovnitsyn, dated 13 [25] September (M.T.D. No. 29,172).
29 Count Osterman-Tolstoy's report to Barclay de Tolly, dated 14 [26] September (M.T.D. No. 29,172).
30 Major General Paskevich's report to Duty General Konovnitsyn, dated 14 [26] September (M.T.D. No. 29,172).

while marching on Podolsk with all the rest of the forces to attack the enemy. Others considered such a movement too risky, believing that by operating in this direction, we could be cut off from Kaluga and be driven back towards Vereya and Mozhaisk. With hindsight, we would not have been at any risk by accepting Bennigsen's proposal, because we would have been attacking Murat with at least double his strength; but this factor was unknown at the time. The Field Marshal would not dare to undertake any enterprise whose success was in doubt, which forced Toll to propose a different course of action, more in line with the character of our Commander in Chief. Taking into account that the Russian army would soon be receiving significant reinforcements, it was necessary, according to Toll, to postpone offensive operations until they arrived and confine ourselves to placing the army in a position in which, without being outflanked (as in Krasnaya Pakhra), they could protect the sources of their materiel and contribute to operations against the enemy lines of communication. By adopting such a position and waiting there for a favourable turn of events, offensive operations could subsequently be launched with confidence in their success. It was necessary to attend principally to the protection of Kaluga, the location at which there were warehouses of rations and all items of equipment for the troops; the most important locations for us at this time were Tula and Bryansk. Three routes lead from Moscow to Kaluga, of which the shortest (the old Kaluga road) runs through Krasnaya Pakhra and Tarutino; to either side of this route are: the new Kaluga road, via Borovsk and Maloyaroslavets, and the Tula road through Serpukhov, from where the road to Kaluga passes through Tarusa. Having settled down on the old Kaluga road, the Russian army would be blocking the shortest route to Kaluga and be at a distance of one stage from the new Kaluga road; the distance from Tarutino to the Tula road is somewhat more, but this was not an important disadvantage, because Napoleon could not take it without immediately exposing his own line of communications. All these factors forced us to remain on the old Kaluga road, in anticipation of an attack by the enemy army, where, according to a report by Lieutenant Colonel Harting of the quartermaster's department of His Majesty's Suite, there was a good position near the village of Tarutino. Tactically, the position at Tarutino, unprotected by any significant obstacles and surrounded by forests, which would allow an enemy surprise attack, did not present great advantages, but it was hoped to negate this with fortifications and vigilance by the forward detachments.[31]

Upon receiving the initial intelligence of the enemy advance, the Field Marshal drew all his forward detachments closer in to the army. General Dorokhov, who had destroyed several enemy detachments and convoys in the course of a week (in which our troops captured some 1,500 men), was also sent orders to return to the army.[32] On 15 (27) September, Prince Kutuzov withdrew to Babenkova on the Mocha river himself, with the main body, where II, Corps III Corps, V Corps and VI Corps and

---

31 Barclay de Tolly's description of military operations of First Army. Prince A.B. Golitsyn's description of the war of 1812, who was Prince Kutuzov's permanent orderly. Bernhardi, II, 185-186.
32 Bennigsen's orders to Dorokhov, dated 13 [25] September (M.T.D. No. 29,172). Prince Kutuzov's orders, dated 19 [30] September, No. 28.

both cuirassier divisions were concentrated.[33] On that same day, the enemy offensive forced Miloradovich and Raevsky to retreat to Krasnaya Pakhra through superior numbers, while Osterman retreated to Okulovo.[34] Miloradovich was himself taken by surprise, carelessly at the outposts of two Bashkir regiments who had recently arrived in the army, and was in great danger, but was rescued by Adjutant General Vasilchikov, who charged up with the Lifeguard Hussars to engage the enemy.[35]

From the French side, on 15 (27) September, Bessières, stopped on the Pakhra, near Gorki with the main body of his corps, pushing a small part of the infantry and La Houssaye's cavalry onto the far bank of the river, while Murat, with Poniatowski's *5e Corps* at the head of his force, upon reaching Nemchinino, sent some of the infantry from there to Okulovo, and at nine o'clock in the evening, reported to Napoleon that the Russians had stopped in their positions intending to resist. As soon as this news arrived in Moscow, Napoleon issued orders to concentrate all the troops stationed in the capital and its environs on the Mocha river by the 17 (29 September). But then, Murat sent a message reporting the retreat of the Russian army. This intelligence was faulty: the Russians remained in place, and only Osterman's IV Corps withdrew behind the Mocha. But as this circumstance was unknown to Napoleon, he cancelled the proposed advance. Overall, at that time, his main objective was to provide the troops with some much needed rest after a difficult campaign.[36]

Meanwhile, on 16 (28) September, our rearguards retreated to the village of Chirikovo, near Krasnaya Pakhra, and to Satino. On the 17 (29 September), Miloradovich counter-attacked the enemy who were approaching him, at Chirikovo, and drove them out of the forest with losses, while the warriors of the Moscow *opolchenie* distinguished themselves. Among the prisoners taken by the Russian troops were the French *général de brigade* Ferrier [Gratien-Ferrier] and Prince Poniatowski's, aide de camp, Captain Count Potocki [Antoni Potocki].[37]

At this time, changes were made in the organisation of the Russian forces. Upon the assumption of command by Prince Kutuzov, the division of the forces acting collectively in the main theatre of war into two armies had become redundant, and also made it difficult to transmit and execute orders from the Commander in Chief,

---

33 War diary of the main operational army.
34 Miloradovich's memo to Konovnitsyn, dated 15 [27] September (M.T.D. No. 29,172). Buturlin, I, 379.
35 Buturlin, I, 379. Bernhardi, II, 188-189.
36 *Lettre du major-général au duc d'Istrie. Le 27 Septembre:* 'Si l'ennemi reste en position sur la Pakra, l'intention de l'empereur est de marcher pour lui livrer bataille; mais on doit supposer qu'il n'atendra pas et qu'il n'a d'autre but que de savoir si toute notre armée est devant lui... L'intention qu'a l'empereur d'épargner des fatigues à ses troupes, le porte à désirer de ne pas faire marcher son armée pour deloger l'ennemi, faites croire à tout le monde que Sa Majesté est arrivée avec toute son armée derrière elle...' (If the enemy remains in position on the Pakhra, the Emperor's intention is to march to give battle; but one must suppose that they will not wait and that their only objective is to discover if our whole army is facing them... The Emperor's intention to spare his troops fatigue, leads him to desire not to march his army to dislodge the enemy, but rather to make them believe that His Majesty has arrived with his entire army behind him...).
37 War diary of the main operational army (Archive of the M.T.D. No. 29,172). General Miloradovich's report to Prince Kutuzov, dated 17 [29] September (Archive of the M.T.D. No. 29,172). Buturlin, I, 380. Chambray, II, 153.

but they continued because the Field Marshal did not dare to change the arrangement. He knew that Emperor Alexander wanted for Barclay de Tolly, honoured by His trust, not to lose the influence over the army to which he was entitled by his earlier feats, and that the Tsar, for similar reasons, had appointed Tormasov, in Prince Bagration's place, as Commander in Chief of Second Army. But from the Supreme Rescript dated 1 [13] September it can be seen that the Emperor himself permitted the formation of a single army from the two Western armies, whereupon Prince Kutuzov, having become convinced of the need to change the chain of command and control, announced the amalgamation of Second Army with First Army in an Order dated 16 (28) September. Command of II Corps, IV Corps, VI Corps, VII Corps and VIII Corps with Meller-Zakomelsky's, Korf's and Vasilchikov's Cavalry Corps was entrusted to Barclay de Tolly, while General Miloradovich took command of the reserve, composed of III Corps and V Corps and both cuirassier divisions. Yermolov remained Chief of Staff of the main army as before; Duty General was Konovnitsyn. The provisioning of the army, by Supreme Command, was left in the care of Senator Lanskoy. The Chief of Artillery was entrusted to Major General Löwenstern; Chief of Engineers was Major General Förster. Command over all the cavalry, with the exception of the two cuirassier divisions was entrusted to Adjutant General Uvarov.[38]

Unfortunately, the new structure of the army headquarters did not bring the expected results. Barclay de Tolly was Commander in Chief in name only, meanwhile, orders for the troops entrusted to him were issued and executed without his knowledge. Bennigsen, as Chief of Staff of all Russian armies, assumed the role of assistant to the Field Marshal, but also did not have his full trust. In a letter to Emperor Alexander I from Barclay de Tolly, we find a gloomy image of the unrest that then prevailed in the headquarters of the army. According to him, the orders issued by various personalities contradicted one another; no one could give an accurate account of the distribution of troops; the delivery of rations to them was not secured; most of the army was with the rearguards, and all other troops were subjected to incessant disturbances.[39] It is possible that Barclay's strained relationship with Prince Kutuzov subconsciously forced him to exaggerate the disorder that existed in the army at the time, but from the contemporary correspondence between the headquarters and the formation commanders of the force, it turns out that they often received conflicting orders on the same day, and that our operations at that time were conducted, as it were, with hesitancy. From the orders of the Field Marshal himself, it can be seen that, despite the proximity of huge warehouses of provisions, ration convoys did not always keep pace with meeting the needs of the army, and therefore, during the deployment of our main forces at Krasnaya Pakhra, it was entrusted to corps and divisional commanders:

---

38 Prince Kutuzov's Orders, dated 16 [28] September, No. 26: 'Due to circumstances hitherto allowing the existence of Second Army, I did not proceed to unite it with First Army. Now, wishing to delegate powers, and even more so in terms of the complexity of administering the internal structure of the armies and the inevitable difficulties that destroy uniform control, henceforth, I amalgamate Second Army with First Army, retaining this name,' etc.
39 Barclay de Tolly's letter dated 24 September [6 October] from Kaluga (a copy is held in the Archive of the Department of the General Staff).

it is agreed that provisions may be purchased for the regiments in their care, for four days, at approved prices, 15 paper Roubles for a *Chetvert* of flour, and grain at 20 paper Roubles.[40]

Such embarrassments are quite natural, and may occur with the most well-organised troops; as an experienced administrator, Barclay was completely aware of all the difficulties associated with the management of the army, but being dissatisfied with the position in which he had been placed by Prince Kutuzov and those around him, in reporting to his Tsar, got carried away by his indignation beyond the limits of a level-headed and unbiased presentation of his case.

Even before the battle of Borodino, Barclay de Tolly had offered his resignation.[41] In another letter to the Tsar, repeating his request, he wrote:

> As for me personally, I resignedly submit to my fate, and as the most passionate of my wishes did not come true on 26 August [7 September] and Providence was pleased to spare my life, which has become a burden to me, then I can only beg for the fulfilment of the request, which I was privileged to submit to the discretion of Your Imperial Majesty in my last letter.[42]

After that, not finding an opportunity to leave the army, Barclay asked the Field Marshal to send him on sick leave, and having been granted this, he went via Kaluga to Vladimir, where he lived for some time, and then in late autumn he arrived at his estate, in Livonia. He wrote to the Tsar:

> I would like to express my deep sadness to Your Majesty with which I am leaving the army. I was willing to live and die with the troops under my command; but even if my illness had not prevented this, then fatigue and mental stress would not have allowed me to remain in the army under the present circumstances...[43]

Upon arrival at his estate, Barclay informed the Tsar of this and submitted a Note to the Supreme Person, which outlined his actions throughout the duration of his command of First Army. Emperor Alexander I, having received these documents, honoured Barclay de Tolly with the following Handwritten comments:

> I have received your letter dated 9 [21] November. You must hardly know Me if you could doubt that you have every right to come to St Petersburg without waiting for My permission. I will even tell you, I was anticipating

---

40 Annex to Prince Kutuzov's Orders dated 10 [22] September, No. 21.
41 Barclay de Tolly's letter to Emperor Alexander I, from Tatarinovo (near Borodino), dated 24 August [5 September].
42 Barclay de Tolly's letter to Emperor Alexander I, from Krasnaya Pakhra, dated 11 [23] September.
43 Barclay de Tolly's letter to Emperor Alexander I, from Kaluga, dated 24 September [6 October].

your arrival, because I sincerely wanted to explain myself to you face to face. But as you were not disposed to do justice to My character, I will try in a few words to explain to you the nature of My thoughts about you and about the events that have taken place. The respect and friendship that I constantly show you, give Me the right to speak frankly with you.

The plan of action we adopted, as I hitherto believed, was the only one that could guarantee success in a war against Napoleon, which was vindicated by experience itself; but it would inevitably meet with criticism among those people who do not have profound knowledge of the art of war and were boastful of the easy successes gained in previous wars over weak enemies, or over poor military commanders. It was difficult for such people to reconcile themselves to a plan of action aimed at drawing the enemy into the depths of the country. It was necessary to anticipate opposition beforehand, but I was prepared for that. But it was necessary, at the same time, to carefully avoid anything that might attract unfavourable comment, and in this respect you deserve some blame.

As soon as it was decided to operate in accordance with the concept of this plan, it was essential to prepare all resources for its implementation. We had sufficient time for that, but still much was left undone.

Shortly after My arrival in Vilna, I ordered you to send away all the unnecessary baggage of regiments that were permanently stationed in quarters in Lithuania, but in spite of this, they were sent no further than Niemenczyn [Nemenčinė], Sventsiany [Švenčionys], Wiłkomierz [Ukmergė] and Schaulen [Šiauliai], and as a result of this the troops were forced to retreat among huge convoys. I reminded you several times to construct the necessary bridges; many of the engineers from the Highways Department were with the army, yet for the most part, the bridges were in quite the worst condition. As soon as it was decided to retreat, it was necessary to withdraw the hospitals accordingly, but, on the contrary, upon my arrival in Vilna, I found several thousand patients there, about whose evacuation I reminded you constantly.

Such are the criticisms which, speaking frankly, I can make to you. All of them have come from a single mistake of yours: you are not quite convinced that issuing orders and completing the execution are two completely different things, and that there is no method of eliminating omissions by subordinates except for active supervision of them and constant confirmation by trustworthy persons.

The mistakes by Prince Bagration, which had the effect of the enemy forestalling him in Minsk, Borisov and Mogilev, forced you to fall back towards Smolensk. Fortune favoured us, beyond all expectations, to unite both armies there. It was time to end the retreat. But the lack of intelligence on the enemy, which has subjected you to unfavourable consequences throughout the entire campaign, made you mistakenly move towards Porechye against the left wing of Napoleon's army, while they concentrated on their right flank at Lyady and crossed the Dnieper. You rectified this error by forestalling the enemy to Smolensk. But since both of our armies were concentrated at this location and you had the intention of subsequently accepting a general battle, would it not have been better to decide upon this at Smolensk rather than at Tsarevo-Zaimishche? At Smolensk, your troops were in the best condition, because they had not yet suffered the losses from the actions on 6 and 7 [18 and 19] August and thereafter. As for the concerns about being outflanked, you were just as subject to this at Tsarevo-Zaimishche, as anywhere else. The enthusiasm of our troops at Smolensk was aroused in the extreme by the fact that, by fighting there, they were defending the first ancient Russian city.

The loss of Smolensk produced an extraordinary effect on morale throughout the Empire. 'Experience itself has shown the disastrous consequences of this plan,' said the detractors of your operations. 'Russia is in immediate peril,' and as, unfortunately, all the mistakes I have recounted were obvious, I was accused of sacrificing the salvation of the Fatherland out of pride, in order to support the Commander in Chief I had chosen. Moscow and St Petersburg unanimously praised Prince Kutuzov as the only commander who could preserve the Empire. In support of these assessments, it was argued that even the seniority in rank of Tormasov, Bagration and Chichagov over you, which significantly impeded the success of military operations, would be eliminated by the appointment of Kutuzov. The circumstances were very difficult. The capital was under threat and I was simply forced to agree with public opinion, following a preliminary discussion of the issue in a Committee composed of the main dignitaries of the Empire.

In yielding to their opinion, I compromised my own convictions. But I wanted you to retain the opportunity to justify My choice in the face of Russia and Europe, and prove that you are worthy to command an army. Just as at Borodino, I was sure that you would willingly remain with the troops in order to receive your share of respect even from your ill-wishers. You would inevitably have achieved this aim had you remained with the army. I have no doubts about that, and, in my unchanging friendship towards you, I was extremely saddened by the news of your departure. In spite of all the troubles you have suffered, you should have stayed, because there are times when it is necessary to put everything in the world above ourselves (*il fallait rester, car il y a des cas où on doit se mettre au dessus de toute chose au monde*).

Convinced that you would remain with the troops, I dismissed you from the post of Minister of War, because you could not have held it while in an army which was commanded by a Commander in Chief senior to you in rank. Moreover, I have learned from experience that command of an army and the position of Minister of War, combined in one and the same person, will overwhelm his powers.

I shall never forget the important services rendered by you to the Fatherland and to Me, and I remain convinced that you will demonstrate even more important ones. Although the present circumstances are very favourable for us, judging by the situation in which the enemy find themselves, the struggle is not yet over; it will present you with an opportunity to prove your military abilities, to which in general you have already done justice…⁴⁴

Having received this letter, Barclay de Tolly went to St Petersburg, but did not find the Tsar there, as he had already gone to Vilna.

Upon the departure of Barclay de Tolly from the army, Kutuzov announced that he would take over all his duties until such time as the Tsar was pleased to appoint a Commander in Chief of First Army.⁴⁵

Meanwhile, our main force was retreating in short stages to Tarutino. Bennigsen proposed waiting for the enemy at Babenkova and giving battle there. The Commander in Chief did not oppose him, but soon Bennigsen himself was forced to admit that the position he proposed did not present any advantages. On 19 September (1 October), the army retreated to Spas-Kuplya, while the troops under Miloradovich and Osterman moved to Golokhvastovo (according to other sources, behind the Mocha river).⁴⁶ On the following day, 20 September (2 October), the main body entered the camp at Tarutino, behind the Nara; Miloradovich, under threat from Murat's offensive with superior numbers, withdrew beyond the village of Voronovo,⁴⁷ which belonged to Count Rostopchin, who, as the enemy approached, ordered his expensive château there to be set on fire. On 21 September (3 October), having been outflanked on the right by some enemy troops who had moved to Bogoyavlenskoe, Miloradovich retreated to Spas-Kuplya with a rearguard composed of VIII Corps and two jäger regiments, while the troops of IV Corps and VII Corps were withdrawn to the Tarutino position; all the cavalry, under the command of Adjutant General Korf, remained with the infantry of VIII Corps. In order to hold the enemy back, who continued to advance, a battery of 14 horse artillery pieces was placed on the high ground at Spas-Kuplya, under the command of Colonel Zakharzhevsky [Yakov Vasilevich Zakharzhevsky]. The enemy, as they emerged from the forest onto open ground, being disordered by the effective fire from this artillery, set up a battery of 18 guns facing it, which opened fire at relatively short range; but our artillery, having knocked out three guns and blown up four ammunition caissons, forced the enemy battery to withdraw from its location and move away; whereupon we turned our fire on the cavalry, who were trying to outflank us, and, having disordered them with well-aimed fire, prompted the French to conceal themselves in the forest and abandon any further advance. The enemy lost ten officers and 150 lower ranks as prisoners alone.⁴⁸ On the following day [4 October new style],

---

44 Emperor Alexander I's letter, dated 24 November [6 December] 1812 (a copy is held in the Archive of the Department of the General Staff).
45 Prince Kutuzov's orders, dated 21 September [3 October], No. 30.
46 General Miloradovich's memo to Duty General Konovnitsyn, dated 19 September [1 October] (Archive of the M.T.D. No. 29,172).
47 General Miloradovich's memo to Duty General Konovnitsyn, dated 20 September [2 October].
48 General Miloradovich's memo to Duty General Konovnitsyn, dated 21 September [3 October]. War diary of the main operational army.

having been attacked once more at Spas-Kuplya, Miloradovich was forced to retreat across the Chernishnya river.[49]

On 24 September (6 October), VIII Corps and I Cavalry Corps rejoined the army. On 25 September (7 October), Miloradovich's rearguard, in which, besides the Cossacks, only II Cavalry Corps (together with III Cavalry Corps) and IV Corps remained, settled between the villages of Glodova and Dednya.[50] The strength of this force, not including the Cossacks, whose strength is not known, extended to 4,000 men.[51]

On the French side, at a distance of four *versts* from the force under Miloradovich and no further than seven *versts* from the front line of the main body under Prince Kutuzov, from the evening of 4 October (new style), Murat remained on the Chernishnya river, with four corps of the *Réserve de cavalerie*, the light cavalry from Davout's and Ney's corps, Poniatowski's force and Claparède's and Dufour's infantry divisions, numbering 26,500 men.[52] Bessières, who was in Moscow at the time, left the infantry division under Friederichs [Jean-Parfait Friederichs] and the Bavarian cavalry at Voronovo, in support of Murat's vanguard; Colbert's brigade of *lanciers de la Garde* was located between Podolsk and Moscow, while the *Dragons de la Garde* and *Chasseurs à cheval de la Garde*, who had been stationed on the Mozhaisk road, returned to Moscow. Having in mind the occupation of a large area with his troops, to facilitate foraging, Napoleon sent Ney's *3e Corps* to Bogorodsk, along the Vladimir road, while Delzons' division, from *4e Corps*, moved to Dmitrov, north of Moscow.[53]

The troops of both sides stayed in these positions for two whole weeks, from 22 September to 6 October (4 to 18 October). On our part, this time was used to great advantage in recruiting and training troops, in strengthening the army with significant reinforcements, and in partisan operations. Using the advantages of our position, protecting the sources of our own materiel and being in the vicinity of the enemy line of communications, we were able to give the main body of our army complete rest and limited ourselves to operations by light detachments, which, eluding any encounter with superior enemy forces, attacked their small units by surprise, destroyed their supplies, intercepted couriers and did not neglect the slightest opportunity to harass them. In every location they found willing accomplices in the inhabitants of the region, who, being led by them and supplied with weapons, brought great mutual benefits, serving as guides, bringing word of the appearance of the enemy and passing both intelligence from the partisans and prisoners captured by them to army headquarters. Intending to describe the *modus operandi* of our partisans and the exploits they accomplished during the Patriotic War in due course, I shall confine myself here to the comment that, in the course of ten days, from 20 to

---

49 General Miloradovich's memo to Duty General Konovnitsyn, dated 22 September [4 October].
50 War diary of the main operational army. The general track of movements and operations by the Russian forces in the war of 1812-1814, compiled by General Khatov.
51 Return, No. 13, attached to the work by General Buturlin.
52 Returns submitted to Napoleon by the Chief of Staff of the *Grande armée*, dated 28 September new style.
53 Chambray, II, 153-154.

30 September (2 to 12 October), they captured four field officers, 55 subalterns and more than 3,000 lower ranks, killing at least a similar number and losing no more than 200 men themselves.[54] Having surrounded the enemy army in Moscow with a network of their outposts, our partisans made it difficult for the French to obtain food supplies and terrorised them to such an extent that they did not dare to forage beyond five *versts* from their camps, or decided to go on distant foraging expeditions only under escort from strong detachments, which sometimes had artillery attached. Under such conditions, the already exhausted enemy cavalry fell into a disastrous state: the horses could barely keep their feet and perished, and there was no way to replace them with remounts. The infantry, during the course of the halt in Moscow, managed to rest a little and receive replacement manning who had been discharged from hospital, but deprived of support from the other branches of the military, although they could still fight with success, nevertheless, they did not have the means to exploit a victory. Napoleon's *Grande armée*, by this time, was nothing more than a formidable phantom. Napoleon saw the need to push the Russians away from his line of communications, but at the same time he recognised the impossibility of the rapid offensive operations that were the hallmark of his war-fighting. It was not hidden from his brilliant insight that a further offensive against the Russian army, not presenting the possibility of winning brilliant successes, would aggravate his difficulties; the consequences of the battle of Borodino convinced him that it was only this clash of belligerent parties, in which, having won a dubious victory, his army had been crushed by the Russians. After all this, is it possible to criticise Napoleon for stopping in Moscow and not going further, or for the fact that, after taking Moscow, he did not make a strategic withdrawal to the Dnieper? The former did not guarantee him any advantages; the latter could have been done by Napoleon if he had a gift of foresight, inaccessible to mere mortals. The advance on Moscow was undertaken by him not for the permanent conquest of our capital, but to induce Emperor Alexander I to peace. Napoleon believed that he would more surely achieve this objective by remaining in a formidable position in the ruins of Moscow than by showing his weakness through a hasty retreat and thus raising the self-confidence of the Russians. The campaign of 1812 was unsuccessful for Napoleon, not because his military assessments were unworthy of the great commander, but because of a political misjudgement: he did not fully appreciate the most important factors, the character of Emperor Alexander I and the spirit of the Russian people, and this mistake led to the demise of the *Grande armée*. Criticising Napoleon for his inaction during the halt in Moscow is pointless. The time he spent there was the period of his greatest activity, and his correspondence from that time leaves no doubt about this.

In terms of supplying the troops with rations, Napoleon was in constant communication with the duc de Bassano (Maret [Hugues-Bernard Maret]), who was in Vilna at the time, and was in charge of supervising the delivery of supplies from Danzig to Kovno and Vilna, and onwards to the army. But as the transportation of each *Zentner* (2½ *Pud*) cost 20 francs (about five silver Roubles) just from Kovno to Minsk, Napoleon ordered the duc de Bassano to buy flour in Minsk, where a

---

54 War diary of the main operational army.

Zentner cost no more than six francs (1½ silver Roubles). He was also ordered to procure hand mills in Vilna, Minsk, Warsaw and Königsberg, modelled on those sent from Paris, using which it was possible to grind some 30 pounds of grain per hour. Napoleon wanted each company to have its own hand mill. No less attention was directed by him to the arrangement of magazines, warehouses for clothing, ammunition and medical supplies. But all the measures taken by him were unsuccessful because of the incompetence and greed of the persons who had these stores in their charge.[55]

In order to provide remounts for the cavalry and artillery, Napoleon ordered the Quartermaster General to buy 14,000 horses. General Bourcier [François Antoine Louis Bourcier], who had been sent to Vilna, was issued four million francs for this same purpose.[56]

In order to find replacement manning for the artillery, Napoleon ordered the dispatch of 22 companies from France, some of whom were assigned to man the guns in the fortresses along the Elbe and Oder, while the rest were for the field artillery. General Lariboisière was ordered to reinforce the reserve artillery of Davout's *1er Corps* with eight guns and restore the reserve to the state in which it had been when it set out from Paris. Both companies of the *Marins de la Garde* were supplied with guns and ammunition caissons from the Moscow arsenal. Napoleon wanted all of the 200 ammunition caissons found in Moscow to be issued to the army, where they could be put to good use because of their lightness and could be towed by peasant horses (*L'on pourra les atteler avec des cognats*). After inspecting the laboratories established in Moscow, Napoleon was dissatisfied with the slowness of the work and expressed the desire that 6,000 artillery rounds be made in them daily.[57]

Upon first hearing news of the appearance of Russian partisans on the Smolensk road, measures were taken to secure the *Grande armée's* lines of communication. Junot, who was stationed in Mozhaisk, General Baraguey d'Hilliers [Louis Baraguey d'Hilliers] in Vyazma, and the Smolensk commandant received orders that the convoys they sent out were to move and rest tactically and with precautions against surprise attack. Convoys sent from Smolensk to the army were intended to have an escort of at least 1,500 men under the command of a field officer.[58] Marshal Victor was ordered to detain all those destined for this location in Smolensk, for the onward movement of detachments and carts to the army. The division thus assembled, numbering from 10,000 to 12,000 men, with 12 guns and ten days' supply of rations, was to be under the command of General Baraguey d'Hilliers, and, under their escort, all the carts belonging to them assembled in Smolensk were to be sent to the troops. Subsequently, similar columns would be sent to the army. All of them were to follow routes cleared parallel to the old Smolensk road, at a distance of eight to twelve *versts* (*à deux ou trois lieues*) from wherever there were still villages and other dwellings. Only couriers, officers on mission and anything that required

---

55 Fain, II, 121-123. Orders for the duc de Bassano (Maret), dated 24 September, 6 and 17 October, new style.
56 Decree regarding remounts, dated 2 October, new style.
57 Fain, II, 118-119. Orders to General Lariboisière, dated 18 September and 3 October, new style.
58 Orders to the Chief of Staff of the *Grande armée*, dated 23 September, new style.

urgent delivery, such as hand mills ordered from Paris, were allowed to be sent along the old road.[59]

In early October (new style), having summoned the Quartermaster-General, Napoleon said to him: 'Wishing to retain the option of selecting between courses of action, I want to know how many days are needed for the final evacuation of the hospitals?' Dumas replied that it would need at least 45 days. 'That is too long; your estimate is pessimistic,' Napoleon continued: 'we know from experience that three months after a battle, not even a sixth of the wounded remain in hospital. Divide all the wounded into two categories: place all those who will be able to walk within a month, and the seriously wounded who cannot be transported in the former, and all the rest in the latter. You need have no concerns about the former, and therefore turn all your attention to the evacuation of the rest. You will see that your estimate will be reduced and we will gain valuable time.'[60]

All these and many other orders by Napoleon on the military side could not exhaust his vigorous activity: from his headquarters in Moscow, decrees were sent to France and other lands subject to him daily regarding the strengthening of his army with new reinforcements, while the Emperor of the French expressed a desire that in the official news published in the newspapers, the numbers of these reinforcements should be given as twice the actual total. His other decrees dealt with various subjects; during his stay in Moscow, Napoleon even found time for a decree on the Parisian theatres, probably wanting to show the versatility of his studies, or considering this subject to be especially important for Parisians. In Moscow itself, two theatres were established on Napoleon's orders, one in the Kremlin and one in a private house, but he never attended any of them himself even once: all of his free time from official studies was spent in reviews of the troops and walks around the city. In general, the theatres were empty. Perhaps bread and games were most needed by the French, but since there was no bread, there were no chasers after games.[61]

The longer Napoleon remained in Moscow, the more obvious it became that the occupation of our capital by his troops would not induce the Russians to make peace. Little by little, the moderation, aroused in Napoleon through the weakening of his army, gave way to anger against Emperor Alexander I. Wanting to destroy the influence of the Manifestos from our Tsar, for his part, Napoleon began to issue appeals, in which he not only invited the peasants around Moscow to return to peaceful pursuits, under his patronage, but called on the Russians to unite with him! Some of the residents of Moscow captured by the enemy, were persuaded by the promise of generous rewards to go to our army to find out everything concerning it, to spread rumours that there was a lot of bread left in Moscow and that the French intended to spend the winter there, and to return with the collected intelligence.[62] It is claimed

---

59 Orders to the Chief of Staff of the *Grande armée*, dated 10 October, new style.
60 Fain, II, 125-126.
61 *Histoire de la destruction de Moscou en 1812, par de B…ch, ancien officier au service de Russie.* 141.
62 Among the Moscow residents sent by the French to the Russian army was the 3rd guild merchant Zhdanov, who later published a curious description of this proposition, under the title: 'Memorial to the French, or the Adventures of a Moscow Resident. P. Zh.' St Petersburg, 1813. The instructions given to him at the time of his departure and learned by heart, under duress by the enemy, were as follows: 'Go to Kaluga (added, but later cancelled: to Tula,

that Napoleon, wishing to undermine public confidence in our government, released a large number of counterfeit Russian banknotes into circulation, but this allegation is not based on any reliable evidence.[63]

Days, weeks passed, and there was not the slightest sign of readiness on the part of the Russians to open peace negotiations. The situation of Napoleon's army became more difficult every day. To pursue the Russian army further meant exposing their own troops to new exertions and hardships, and besides, the enemy had spent little more than a few days in Moscow when autumn came; heavy rain and cold nights were a real disaster for the French. Spending the winter in Moscow did not bear thinking about. It was easy to foresee that Napoleon's army, in this case, would be in danger of being surrounded on all sides by Russian troops. The surest way to avoid this danger was to retreat to the Neman and the Bug. But Napoleon was not so much thinking about saving his legions at that time as about ending the difficult campaign in a way that would not expose the failure of his enterprise against Russia in the face of Europe. He had already succeeded on more than one occasion, of exploiting the short-sightedness or timidity of his opponents in order to get out of the most difficult circumstances. Napoleon hoped that in the current case, Fortune would still be indulgent of the errors of this Genius.

---

and from Tula to Moscow); Estimate and ask how many are in the Russian army; Who are the army commanders; Who are the divisional commanders; Where is the army heading; Have the regiments been reconstituted since the battle of Borodino; Are there more troops on their way; What are people saying about peace; Divulge that in Moscow all the grain remains intact and was not burned; Spread the rumour that we want to spend the winter in Moscow; If the Russian army is moving towards the Smolensk road, then, return to Moscow as soon as possible without going to Kaluga; Upon returning, do not lie about anything, do not embellish, but only talk about what you saw and heard; On pain of great danger, do not to reveal these instructions to anyone, not even to tell your wife where and for what you are leaving; Upon returning, announce yourself at the first French outpost in order to be taken to the *prince d'Eckmühl*; If you return successfully, you will be rewarded with 1,000 *Chervonets*, which is worth 12,000 Roubles at the current rate; on top of that, a stone house in Moscow, whichever you want to take.' Memorial to the French, II, Zhdanov, 33-34.

63 *Histoire de la destruction de Moscou en 1812*, 135-137. [Liprandi states that he had seen these counterfeit notes himself and provides a lengthy refutation of Bogdanovich, details of which are at Appendix 16.].

28

The camp at Tarutino

The Russian mobilisation. – The Tarutino camp. – Deployment of the Russian army. – The strength of our forces on their arrival in the Tarutino camp. – Step taken to eradicate indiscipline in the army. – The composition of our forces. – Prince Kutuzov's intentions. – The course of action he adopted. – The distribution of partisan detachments around Moscow.

The characteristics of Russian partisan operations. – The actions by our partisans during Kutuzov's retreat towards Tarutino and during the occupation of the Tarutino camp by the main body of the army. – Dorokhov's destruction of two squadrons of *Dragons de la Garde*. – The defeat of an enemy detachment by Yefremov. – Davydov's operations in the Vyazma area. – Figner's operations in the Moscow area. – Several of his reports. – Features of his military career. – The defeat of a strong enemy detachment by Prince Kudashev. – Dorokhov's capture of Vereya.

The consequences of partisan operations. – The situation of the enemy army. – Napoleon's peace proposals. – Kutuzov's meeting with Lauriston. – The Tsar's displeasure. – Steps taken by Napoleon in the event of departing Moscow.

As Napoleon was exhausting the resources of Western Europe in order to bend Russia to his will, Emperor Alexander I, leading the forces of the Russian nation, directed them to launch a counter-offensive against this hitherto invincible enemy. Contemporaries and posterity have already given due justice to the resolve of our magnanimous Monarch, publicly expressed by Him at a time when the servility of the oppressed nations towards Napoleon and the 'great nation' knew no limits. But the foresight of our Tsar in preparing the resources for the successful conduct of the war is worthy of no less astonishment and gratitude. Russia was rich in forces, but the timely coordination of them in the theatre of operations, due to the vastness of the territory of our Fatherland and the lack of good roads, had always been fraught with great difficulties. Any measure that was intended to reinforce or provide the army with supplies had to be taken much earlier than its requirement could become evident. Emperor Alexander I had been preparing for war with Napoleon for a long time, and from the first enemy steps on Russian soil, he redoubled the activity of

His preparations. Measures had immediately been taken to resupply the Western Armies with recruits from the recruiting depots; the Army of Moldavia had moved into Volhynia; the formation of strong reserves has begun; the Manifesto on the *opolchenie* had been published in the 16 governorates closest to the theatre of war; specifications were drawn up for the manufacture of weapons in significant numbers at Tula and other factories, and a large number of muskets had been ordered from Britain. The nation responded to the call of their Monarch. Everyone was in a hurry to join the ranks of the army, and even infirm old men were eager to take part in the holy cause of defending Russia. Government orders were carried out with extraordinary diligence. To remain inactive during the general mobilisation by every Russian was considered shameful.

The consequences of this mentality were enormous. The formation of reserves went very quickly: infantry reserves were formed by General of Infantry Prince D.I. Lobanov-Rostovsky[1] and Lieutenant General Kleinmichel [Andrei Andreevich Kleinmichel].[2] Reserve battalions and squadrons, formed by General Miloradovich between Moscow and Kaluga, were used (as has already been mentioned) to bring the army up to strength before the battle of Borodino; after the enemy occupation of Moscow, the formation of reserve battalions was continued in Kaluga by Major General Ushakov.[3] Subsequently, once the regiments formed by Prince Lobanov-Rostovsky and General Kleinmichel had also arrived in the autumn to bring the main operational army up to strength, a Supreme Command directed Prince Lobanov to form 39 infantry and 28 jäger battalions in Arzamas, while, in Yaroslavl, General Kleinmichel was directed to form one battalion for each of the twelve grenadier regiments and twelve battalions (eight infantry and four jäger) for the regiments of 5th Division and 14th Division in Count Wittgenstein's I Corps. In St Petersburg, Major General Bashutsky formed six battalions for the Lifeguard, under the supervision of His Highness Grand Duke Konstantin Pavlovich, and eighteen for 6th Division, 21st Division and 25th Division of the Finland Corps. Cavalry reserves were formed in Murom under the supervision of the commander

---

1   The following regiments were formed: 1st and 2nd Infantry in Vladimir; 3rd and 4th Infantry in Kostroma; 5th and 6th Infantry in Ryazan; 7th and 8th Infantry in Tambov; 1st and 2nd Jäger in Yaroslavl; 3rd and 4th Jäger in Voronezh.
    A division under Major General Rusanov, consisting of six regiments: 5th, 6th, 7th and 8th Infantry and 3rd and 4th Jägers, joined the army on 18 and 27 September [30 September and 9 October]; while the division under Prince Urusov of 1st, 2nd, 3rd Infantry, 1st and 2nd Jägers arrived in December; the 4th Infantry Regiment became some of the 67 battalions formed later by Prince Lobanov.
2   The following regiments were formed: 9th Infantry in St Petersburg; 10th Infantry in Novgorod; 11th Infantry in Tver; absorbed as replacements in the army in November. 12th Infantry in Kaluga; 13th Infantry in Tula; 14th Infantry in Moscow; absorbed as replacements in the army before the battle of Borodino.
3   On 10 and 11 [22 and 23] September, the army was reinforced by infantry regiments No. 6 and No. 7 brought by General Ushakov from Kaluga, two jäger battalions and eight reserve squadrons were split up to bring infantry and cavalry regiments up to strength. The remaining regiments, formed by General Miloradovich, joined the troops formed under the command of General D.I. Lobanov-Rostovsky (returns attached to the memo by Kutuzov to Count Arakcheev, dated 6 [18] December, No. 1,128, Archive of the M.T.D. No. 46,692, Portfolio 2).

of the *opolchenie* of 3rd District, Lieutenant General Count Tolstoy; and then, once he had been ordered to march to Vladimir with the Nizhny Novgorod *opolchenie*, the formation of 94 reserve squadrons, two for each of the 47 line cavalry regiments of the operational army, and five reserves (each of two squadrons) for the Lifeguard, was entrusted to General of Cavalry Kologrivov [Andrey Semënovich Kologrivov]. The Lifeguard cavalry reserves, two squadrons for each regiment, and six horse artillery pieces were formed in St Petersburg under the supervision of His Highness Grand Duke Konstantin Pavlovich.[4] Reserve Artillery companies formed in Nizhny Novgorod by Major General Ilyin, as well as in St Petersburg, Kostroma and Tambov; the number of lower ranks in these companies reached some 10,000.[5] In general, there were sufficient men, but the formation of forces was hampered by a lack of weapons, ammunition and transport. Very serious obstacles were encountered with the formation of cavalry reserves due to the high costs and also a complete lack of war horses and saddles.[6] The *opolchenie* was very successful. The commander of the *opolchenie* of 2nd District, Lieutenant General Meller-Zakomelsky, was ordered to send fifteen St Petersburg regiments with four battalions, eight squadrons and two light artillery companies attached to them in early [mid] September to reinforce Count Wittgenstein's I Corps.[7] After that, he was ordered to send a further 4,000 to 5,000 men of the Novgorod opolchenie to Wittgenstein's Corps.[8] The *opolchenie* of 1st District, which was at the direct disposal of Prince Kutuzov, was used by him to protect the provinces near Moscow from enemy raids: to that end, the Tver *opolchenie* partly joined the force under General Wintzingerode, some located between Klin and Tver; that of Yaroslavl was on the route between Moscow and Yaroslavl, near Pereyaslavl-Zalessky; that of Vladimir was on the route between Vladimir and Pokrov; that of Ryazan was stationed at Kolomna and Yegorevsk, protecting the Ryazan and Kasimirov roads; that of Tula was stationed between Kashira and Aleksin; the Kaluga *opolchenie* was stationed some on the borders of their governorate with that of Moscow and Smolensk, some at Bryansk, with the addition of regular troops and artillery, in order to defend this location; the Smolensk and Moscow *opolchenie* were still with the army. The commander of the Chernigov *opolchenie* was ordered to support the Kaluga detachment sent to Bryansk.[9] The *opolchenie* from 3rd

---

4 Supreme Orders for General of Cavalry Kologrivov, dated 2 [14] October (Archive of the M.T.D. No. 46,692, folio 23). Orders for the Head of the Ministry of War, Prince Gorchakov, dated 20 October [1 November], No. 230.
5 Artillery journal published by the Supreme Committee, 1852. Brief review of the state of Russian artillery from 1798 to 1848, 34.
6 General of Cavalry Kologrivov's letter to the Head of the Ministry of War, Prince Gorchakov, dated 31 October [12 November], from Murom.
7 Supreme Orders dated 30 August [11 September].
8 Supreme Orders to Lieutenant General Baron Meller-Zakomelsky, dated 4 [16] September.
9 Prince Kutuzov's orders to the *opolchenie* commanders: to Lieutenant General Tyrtov, of Tver, dated 3 [15] September; to Lieutenant General Shepelev, of Kaluga, dated 30 September [12 October]; to Major General Izmailov, of Ryazan, dated 19 September [1 October]; to Lieutenant General Count Gudovich, of Chernigov, dated 25 September [7 October]; to Major General Dedyulin, of Yaroslavl, dated 9 and 25 September [21 September and 7 October]; to Major General Bogdanov, of Tula, dated 27 September [9 October]; Lieutenant General Prince Golitsyn, of Vladimir, dated 27 September [9 October].

District would be ready for action in a short time.[10] Many regiments of the Cossack forces were formed up, moving to support the main army in the field; from among them, the Don regiments had already begun to approach its locations, and therefore officers were sent to meet these regiments, for their quickest conveyance to the army. In order to direct all these forces towards the achievement of the common objective and to supply them with all the means of waging war, the extraordinary activity of the main director of our operations, Emperor Alexander I, was needed. His handwritten correspondence from the war of 1812 serves as evidence that not a single one of the orders relating to military forces and resources escaped His attention, and is a monument to the great feats He accomplished. Not limited to orders to the most important dignitaries of the Empire and the Commanders-in-Chief of the armies, He personally corresponded with the commanders of the reserves and *opolchenie*, directors of arms factories, civil governors, and so on. With a multitude of directors of armaments across the vastness Russia, there was not always the necessary unanimity between them, needed to achieve the common objective. Indulgent to the point of heavenly benevolence towards the shortcomings of some of his colleagues, Emperor Alexander used their abilities for the benefit of the Fatherland, entrusted them with duties consistent with the talent of each and rarely made mistakes in His selection of personalities.

After the retreat of the Russian army to Tarutino, the military forces and resources of our Fatherland were concentrated on this point. I have already taken the opportunity to note that the position at Tarutino offered us no tactical advantage. The Nara river, which protected our camp's frontage, in this sector had a width of 15 to 20 *sazhen*, and a depth of about half a *sazhen*. The river bed is mostly swampy; the banks are not high, but are steep. The left flank of the camp rested on a vast forest, which exposed us to a surprise envelopment, and therefore abatis were arranged on this side to protect the camp; while several *flèches* were constructed to reinforce the army frontage. Within this position, the troops were located as follows: II Corps and VI Corps stood in line, in two echelons, on the crest of the high ground of the right bank of the Nara, at a distance of about 800 paces from the river. Behind them, at a thousand paces, IV Corps, V Corps, III Corps and VII Corps were formed up in attack columns, also in two echelons. To the right and somewhat behind IV Corps, forming a salient angle with them, stood I Cavalry Corps in two echelons; VIII Corps was in reserve, behind the centre, in battalion columns. 2nd Cuirassier Division was even further back (1st Cuirassier Division, was quartered in the villages for better economy). The Artillery reserves were behind 2nd Cuirassier Division. Colonel Gogel [Fëdor Grigorievich Gogel] was stationed in the large forest on the left flank with five regiments of jägers,[11] while Colonel Potëmkin was in the forest on the right flank with two regiments of jägers.[12] The headquarters was initially in the village of Tranishcheva, opposite Tarutino, and then in Letashevka, a small village, five *versts* behind the position. II Cavalry Corps and IV Cavalry Corps, under Miloradovich's

---

10 Report by the commander of the *opolchenie* of 3rd District, Lieutenant General Count Tolstoy, dated 28 September [10 October].
11 5th Jägers, 6th Jägers, 1st Jägers, 33rd Jägers and 11th Jägers.
12 4th Jägers and 48th Jägers.

command, made up the vanguard, and was located, as already mentioned, between the villages of Glodova and Dednya, four *versts* from the camp of the main force.¹³

As the Russian army entered the Tarutino camp, it counted 2,379 field officers and subalterns and 83,260 lower ranks in its ranks, with 622 guns; among the rank and file were 15,530 *opolchenie* warriors, some armed with pikes and 7,690 recruits, thus there were some 60,000 regular troops.

Overall, the number of lower ranks was: Infantry 63,238; Cavalry 10,212; Artillery 8,680; Pioneers, Pontoniers, Lifeguard Marines 1,130.

In addition, the unassigned warriors of the Ryazan *opolchenie* had some 3,300 men.¹⁴

Prior to Kutuzov's withdrawal into the Tarutino camp, Napoleon had kept most of his army all in all close to Moscow. But as soon as he was convinced that the Russians did not intend to operate on the offensive, then, meaning to occupy a vast area and use its resources to feed his troops, he ordered Ney's *3e Corps* to move to Bogorodsk, while Delzons' Division (from the Viceroy's *4e Corps*) went to Dmitrov.¹⁵

After the occupation of the Tarutino camp, the main points of concern for Prince Kutuzov were the manning, training and supply of every necessity for the army entrusted to him. During the three-week stay at Tarutino, a general enthusiasm, making up for a lack of time, contributed to the conversion of inexperienced recruits into rather fine soldiers, trained in target shooting and in the essential evolutions. The prolonged retreat by the Russian armies from the borders into the Empire full of labour and hardship, and the heavy loss of Moscow, brought desertion and looting as a consequence. Emperor Alexander I, having learned about this from reports by Prince Kutuzov, ordered him to take the strictest measures to stop this disorder. The Tsar wrote: 'By the grace of the Almighty, the Russian army is filled with reverence for the faith and the laws of God.' Based on that, Supreme Orders and a sworn pledge were sent to the Commander in Chief, in which the lower ranks were obliged: 'not to leave their units and do not commit robbery.' At the same time, the Field Marshal was permitted to dispense with the oath by the troops if he found it unnecessary, but to issue the Supreme Order to all the armies, in which the Tsar reminded the soldiers, as defenders of the Fatherland, of their sacred duties and instructed all commanders to supervise the units entrusted to them most strictly. Kutuzov limited himself to issuing the Supreme Order. The disorder that had crept into the force was stopped by strict discipline and the regular distribution of rations.¹⁶ Carts flocked to

---

13 Buturlin, I, 386-388.
14 Returns, signed by Prince Kutuzov, attached to his report to the Supreme Person, dated 22 September [4 October].
15 Chambray, II, 154.
16 Prince Kutuzov's reports to Emperor Alexander I, dated 6 [18] September and 10 [22] October. Supreme Orders to Prince Kutuzov, dated 29 September [11 October]:
'Orders To all Our troops. 29 September [11 October] 1812. Courageous and Faithful warriors! Dear sons of the Fatherland! You are those Russian defenders of the faith, whose glory reverberates across the whole world. Recently, the field of battle was witness to your exploits, recently the Fatherland thanked you for your courage in tears, and the Church of God prayed for your salvation. But, to my great regret, I hear that there are comrades among you unworthy of you, who, absent themselves from their units without leave, roam the villages

Tarutino from various directions, satisfying the needs of our soldiers in abundance. The landowners, sending supplies for sale in the camp, ordered their clerks 'one cannot take too much.' Huge donations delivered by the residents of the Moscow and southern governorates contributed to the almost daily issue of meat and wine rations to the troops. As early as 27 August [8 September], Emperor Alexander ordered 'the forthcoming need for sheepskin coats for the army' to be put on the agenda for that same day, for discussion by the Committee of Ministers.[17] The Field Marshal, foreseeing that we would have to fight through the winter, ordered the Duty General Konovnitsyn, to write to all the heads of the neighbouring governorates about the preparation of sheepskin coats for the lower ranks, on the very first day after the army entered the Tarutino camp. Tranquillity and the abundance of every necessity raised the morale of the army and dispelled the despondency that had been the result of abandoning Moscow. In the evenings and before dawn, music played in every regiment and the sounds of distant Russian songs were heard. Many peasants came to the camp, excited by the desire to visit relatives, or association with the defenders of the motherland. The Field Marshal, wishing to bring the nature of the national struggle of the war to the attention of the French, often talked with the villagers, consoled them with the hope of an early triumph over the enemies and gave weapons to those of them who expressed their readiness to exterminate the enemy. In Tarutino, having been greeted with bread and salt by a deputation of Kaluga citizens, Kutuzov received them very kindly, and in order to dispel the fears of Kaluga, on the occasion of the approach of military operations to their city, he wrote to the Kaluga city head Torubaev [Ivan Vikulovich Torubaev], thanking him for his diligence and reassuring them that: 'the city of Kaluga is and will be perfectly secure.'[18]

The Field Marshal, as far as can be assessed from the sum of his actions at that time, had the intention of remaining in the Tarutino camp, without taking decisive action against the enemy who occupied Moscow. Subsequently, he explained his views as follows:

> *J'avais besoin de rester sur place pour organiser l'armée et pour ne pas trop inquieter Napoléon. Cette position en valait bien une autre. D'ailleurs j'étais presque sûr qu'il ne viendrait pas se casser le nez contre elle... Tous les jours*

---

and forests, under the name of marauders, a vile name, never heard among Russian troops, meaning a thief, a robber, a bandit! Should the honourable name of the defenders of the faith and the Fatherland be defiled by these contemptuous names! Russia is your mother; What could be more criminal than, having seen her plundered by her enemies, not only to fail to defend her, but also to rob her alongside them and tear apart their mother's womb with their own hands? This grave sin will never be forgiven, neither at this time nor in the future.
Every commander has been instructed to observe the eradication of this evil most strictly, and he who is noted to be negligent in this regard will be permanently dismissed from the service as an example to others and to his own shame.
Warriors! Burning Moscow will ignite the fire of vengeance in your souls; put out this fire with the blood of your enemies. May they not carry your shame and the tears of your relatives and neighbours with them. The Church desecrated by them and offended Fatherland expects this.'

17 Supreme Command, delivered by Count Arakcheev to Prince A.I. Gorchakov.
18 For the text of Prince Kutuzov's letter to the city head, Torubaev, see Appendix 10.

que nous sommes restés sur cette position étaient des jours d'or pour moi et pour l'armée et nous en avons profité.

(I needed to stay there to reorganise the army and not to aggravate Napoleon too much. This position was as good as any other. Besides, I was almost certain that he wouldn't come and break his nose against it… Every day that we stayed in this position was a golden day for me and for the army and we made the best of them).[19]

This assessment by the old commander was correct: every day the Russian army was augmented, while the enemy was diminished. Why leave the fate of the war to a gamble for success in battle under such circumstances, when the passage of time, without any effort on our part, would give us an undoubted advantage over the enemy? But the Field Marshal did not confine himself to inaction, rather, on the contrary, of all the methods of harming the enemy, he chose the most certain one. The French army, despite the losses it had suffered, being under the command of a brilliant leader, could win victories in set piece battles, but was less capable of guerilla war actions, due to insufficient knowledge of the ground in the theatre of war and due to a lack of irregular troops like our Cossacks. The Field Marshal, having grasped these factors and learning of the benefits of partisan raids from experience, from the operations by Davydov, Dorokhov and the Cossack regiments left behind by the army, during its flank movement onto the Kaluga road, sent out several brave officers in small detachments, composed of light troops and intended to operate on all the routes leading to Moscow. Lieutenant Colonel Davydov was sent to the sector between Mozhaisk and Vyazma; Colonel Prince Vadbolsky [Ivan Mikhailovich Vadbolsky], with the Mariupol Hussar Regiment and several Cossack *sotnia*, operated in the vicinity of Mozhaisk; Lieutenant von Vizin [Mikhail Alexandrovich von Vizin] was on the Borovsk road with a Cossack raiding party; Captain Seslavin [Alexander Nikitich Seslavin] was between Borovsk and Moscow; Artillery Captain Figner [Alexander Samoilovich Figner], with a small unit of Akhtyrka Hussars, Poland Ulans, Lithuania Ulans, Kharkov Dragoons and 2nd Bug Cossacks, were destroying the enemy in the Moscow area; Colonel Prince Kudashev, was operating along the Serpukhov road with Zhirov's [Ivan Ivanovich Zhirov] and Kharitonov's Cossack Regiments; Colonel Yefremov was on the Ryazan road: in this manner, the raiding detachments sent out from our main body had occupied the entire area south of Moscow, between Vyazma and Bronnitsy. Adjutant General Wintzingerode, who was stationed at Klin at the time, sent out partisans from his direction: on the right at Volokolamsk, *Flügel-Adjutant* Colonel Benkendorf [Alexander Khristoforovich Benkendorf] was stationed with the Lifeguard Cossacks; Major Prendel [Victor Antonovich Prendel] was at Ruza with two *sotnia* of Cossacks, and Lieutenant Colonel Chernozubov [Ilya Fëdorovich Chernozubov] of the Don Host, was in the Mozhaisk area with his Cossack regiment, while to the left of Klin, Cossack detachments were operating along the Dmitrov and Yaroslavl roads; the latter was guarded by the Military *Starshina* [Lieutenant Colonel] Pobednov [Grigory Petrovich Pobednov] with Denisov 7th's [Vasily Timofeevich Denisov] Cossack Regiment. On

---

19 A. B. Golitsyn's notes, who was Prince Kutuzov's permanent orderly in 1812.

22 September (4 October), Major Figlev, with five mounted *sotnia* from the Tver *opolchenie* and a *sotnia* of Cossacks, was sent to Voskresensk to maintain communications between the detachment stationed in Volokolamsk and the vanguard of Wintzingerode's Corps, which was under the command of Major General Ilovaisky 12th [Vasily Dmitrievich Ilovaisky].[20]

Thus, Napoleon's army in Moscow was surrounded on all sides by our partisan detachments, which, quite often being behind enemy lines, had no communications not only with the main body of the army, but also with the other detachments. Permitted to conduct independent operations, the Russian partisans had to resort to particular precautions: moving, for the most part, at night, along country lanes, or even along tracks, without a sound; moving swiftly from one place to another; settling down to rest in forests and ravines, without forward outposts. No one, except the commander of the detachment, knew where they were going and to what end they was operating. Having received intelligence from the peasants or from patrols about the approach of the enemy, or about their location in the vicinity of the detachment, the partisan commander would set off with several officers and Cossacks for a reconnaissance, seeking to ascertain enemy numbers in the surrounding area, and returning to base, would make plans for a raid, or, if the enemy was beyond their strength, inform the nearest of our detachments about them, and sometimes even the headquarters. The intelligence was delivered, by officers, or by peasants, who came to the partisans from the forests and other hideouts, served as their guides, passed intelligence from them to the army and armed themselves, to assist them, having received weapons captured from the enemy. A raid on the enemy was usually carried out by surprise, swiftly, from various directions. When the partisans had the opportunity to deliver prisoners they had captured to headquarters, then they sent them under escort of Cossacks and villagers; if it was impossible to escort prisoners to the army, due to the distances involved, or due to the small size of the detachment, then sometimes they were executed.[21] Justice requires the confession that some of our partisans (and Figner in particular) acted utterly mercilessly not only with any enemy who showed resistance, but also with prisoners, sacrificing them to the vengeance of embittered peasants who killed them without mercy.[22]

During the short stay of the Russian army at Tarutino, the operations by our partisans had a very important influence on the course of the war. We have already had occasion to mention the successes won by the small detachment under Lieutenant Colonel Davydov and the demolition of an artillery park on the Mozhaisk road by

---

20 War Diary of the Main Operational Army (Archive of the M.T.D. No. 46,692). Adjutant General Wintzingerode's report to the Tsar.
21 [Liprandi comments: 'True, there were cases: but then the partisans were supposed to hand them over to the adjacent *Uyezds*. Seslavin and Davydov did not execute a single one'].
22 Lieutenant Biskupsky's [Xavier Andreevich Biskupsky] letter (of the Poland Ulan Regiment, and a member of Figner's detachment) regarding partisan operations in 1812. [Figner is named. Liprandi asks: 'And who are the others?' and later 'he (Bogdanovich) is infinitely more lenient towards the enemy: in his account there is not even a tenth of the atrocities that the French indulged in, especially by their allies in Moscow, which can also be found in their own works. Why does the author not speak of the 'mercy' of the French, as a result of which they shot our prisoners? He scarcely mentions this, and even then only on one occasion, yet it was a general policy'].

the detachment under Major General Dorokhov. Following this, the movement of a significant detachment under Saint-Sulpice [Raymond Gaspard de Bonardi, comte de Saint-Sulpice] from Moscow and 4,000 infantry from Smolensk to Mozhaisk forced Dorokhov to retreat to the Borovsk road, but this did not prevent him from destroying another 20 ammunition caissons, capturing some 100 men, detaining two couriers with important dispatches and liberating several *Pud* of church silver. Two days later, he ambushed two squadrons of French *Dragons de la Garde* and, surrounding them with three squadrons of Lifeguard Dragoons and two of Yelisavetgrad Hussars, and with the assistance of Cossacks, completely scattered the enemy detachment and captured 190 men. On our side, in this action, 25 men were killed or wounded; among the mortally wounded were Colonels Sievers and Khilkov. In the course of four days, from 9 to 13 [21 to 25] September, General Dorokhov managed to capture around 1,000 prisoners, including 48 officers.[23]

Colonel Yefremov of the Don Army, who was stationed on the Ryazan road with Andryanov 2nd's Cossacks and the Simferopol Tatars, defeated the enemy on 14 (26) September, near the village of Vishnevskoe, between the Ryazan and Kashira roads, and captured 500 men.[24]

The initial successes of Davydov's partisan operations caught the attention of the Commander in Chief, who ordered his detachment to be reinforced with two Cossack regiments. Having received reinforcements in the shape of 1st Bug Regiment and 1st Teptyar Regiment on 12 (24) September, Davydov set out from Yukhnov (where he had been since 8 [20] September) for Vyazma with 360 horsemen and on the 16th (28 September), within sight of this city, attacked and defeated a strong enemy detachment escorting a convoy with fodder and artillery ammunition. In this action, the French lost 250 killed and 150 taken prisoner. Due to the impossibility of dragging the supplies away with exhausted horses, most of them were burned, while the horses and captured weapons were distributed among the peasants. On 18 (30) September, 125 prisoners were captured by the Teptyar Regiment and 100 more were killed in action, because Davydov, not being able to handle the transfer of prisoners with his detachment, had ordered: 'take as few of them as possible.' On the 19th (1 October), having received intelligence about the location of 300 Russian prisoners and an artillery park between Vyazma and Semlevo, in the village of Yurenevo, Davydov went there, meaning to free our men and take possession of the park, but the prisoners had been led away the previous night along the Dorogobuzh road, while there were three enemy battalions (two Polish and one Westphalian) in Yurenevo. Unaware of this development, Davydov attacked the incomparably stronger enemy at dawn and, after a bitter battle that lasted two hours, blew up all the decking with charges, killed some of the escort and captured some 140 men. More than 100 soldiers who had occupied the village and did not want to surrender to our partisans were burned along with the barns in which they had taken refuge.[25]

---

23 Major General Dorokhov's reports to General Konovnitsyn, dated 9, 11 and 13 [21, 23 and 25] September.
24 Colonel Yefremov's report to Colonel Balabin 2nd, dated 14 [26] September.
25 Lieutenant Colonel Davydov's report to General Konovnitsyn dated 21 September [3 October], No. 37.

Captain Figner, detesting Napoleon with all his heart, was prepared for death from the very beginning of the Patriotic War, and went to church every day praying in tears. Following the enemy occupation of Moscow, with the permission of the Commander in Chief, he went there, and during daylight hours he walked around the city, dressed in a tailcoat, and later in a peasant *sermyaga* [calf-length overcoat], found his way into the houses taken over by the French and discovered what he needed; while at night, having armed several inhabitants, he assassinated the enemy, and, as it is claimed, he looked for an opportunity to kill Napoleon himself. When partisan operations began, Kutuzov sent him into the rear of the French army with a small detachment.

In the first report by Captain Figner, about the operations by the detachment entrusted to him, it states:

> Regarding the harm caused to the enemy, I have the honour to convey the following: In the vicinity of Moscow, all provisions have been destroyed. In the villages lying between the Tula and Zvenigorod roads, some 400 men were beaten. An artillery park was blown up on the Mozhaisk road: six heavy guns were rendered completely unserviceable, while eighteen ammunition caissons belonging to these guns were blown up. A colonel, four officers and 58 privates were captured with the guns. Three officers and a large number of privates were killed.
>
> Despite the extreme difficulty of the tracks, the officers have maintained perfect order in their sub-units, as a result, even on the darkest nights, in forests barely passable during the day, the marches were fast, and the consequences of this were disastrous for the enemy. Enduring hunger and cold with indifference, fearless of the dangers in the midst of a numerous enemy, they instilled resolve and hope in the soldiers.[26]

After that, in a subsequent note about the operations of his detachment, Captain Figner reported:

> Today at noon, between the *Grande armée* and the vanguard, I struck and took several prisoners. A considerable element of the enemy cavalry, which is with the vanguard, was turned against me. I am reporting this as our army might be able to exploit this.[27]

In another note to the Duty General, Figner reported:

> Yesterday I learned that you are concerned with discovering the strength and movements of the enemy. To that end I went to the French yesterday as one of them, and today I visited them with weapons in hand, after which I

---

26 Artillery Staff Captain Figner's report to the Chief of Staff of the army, Major General Yermolov, dated 23 September [5 October] (Figner had been promoted to Captain following the action at Valutina Gora on 7 [19] August).
27 Figner's note, dated 29 September [11 October].

again had talks with them. Captain Alekseev, who I have sent to you, will tell you better about everything that happened, as I am afraid of appearing boastful.[28]

Indeed, Figner more than once changed into French uniform and, talking with the enemy, gathered such intelligence that informants could not tell him. One of the officers who was in Figner's detachment wrote that one day, disguised as a French cuirassier, in a white cloak, he led his detachment into the forest, ordered the men to dismount and maintain peace and quiet, while he rode up to a clearing along the highway himself, and stopped in the shadows at the edge of the forest. Soon there came the clatter of hooves, soldiers' voices, and French cuirassiers appeared on the road, in column of sixes. Having allowed three squadrons to pass and, probably, having already been noticed by the enemy, Figner himself called out: *qui vive?* (who goes there?); whereupon one of the officers, riding on the flank of the cuirassiers, detached himself from the squadron and rode up to our partisan, who, after exchanging a few words with him, turned his horse into the forest and returned to his own. Having crossed a fairly large area of dead-end tracks with the detachment, under the direction of peasants who served as guides, Figner again left his partisans in the forest, with orders to dismount and rest until he returned; having summoned two officers of the Poland Ulan Regiment to go with him (whose uniform resembled that of the Polish lancers serving in Napoleon's army), he ordered one of them, who spoke some French, in the event of encountering the enemy, to answer both for himself and for his comrade who did not know foreign languages at all. Then, all three, riding out of the forest, saw a rather extensive French camp about two *versts* away, in open ground, around a village. 'Let's go to them,' said Figner, and together with his comrades, rode up to the camp at a gentle trot so nonchalantly that it didn't even occur to the sentries to challenge them. Approaching the cuirassier regiment, which had passed by his detachment at night, Figner turned to the two officers standing together, wished them a good morning and entered into a lengthy conversation with them, while his officers, talking involuntarily with the cuirassiers surrounding them, despaired of getting out alive. Finally, he said goodbye to his unexpected acquaintances, turned his horse back and rode off a few paces, but suddenly returned to the French officers again, asked them a few questions before calmly heading into the forest to his detachment. On another occasion, Figner, with Sumy Hussar Lieutenant Orlov, who was in his detachment, both dressed in French uniforms, went with a peasant guide to the village of Voronovo, where the camp of the vanguard of Napoleon's army was located at the time, as was Murat's headquarters. Having made his way through the screen of vedettes undetected, Figner rode up to the bridge over the river, which protected the enemy bivouacs. The infantry sentry, standing on the bridge, greeted him with the challenge: *qui vive?* and demanded the watchword; but Figner, instead of the response (which, of course, he did not know), reprimanded the sentry for alleged incorrect protocol in relation to the calls verifying the outposts. The sentry, completely bewildered, let both

---

28 A second note from Figner, dated 29 September [11 October].

partisans into the camp, where Figner appearing to be one of their own, rode up to many fires, spoke very coolly with the officers, and having learned everything that he needed, returned to the bridge. There, he again instructed the familiar sentry that he should not dare to stop the calls, he crossed the bridge and at first made his way for a few paces, and then, approaching the screen of vedettes, raced through them together with Orlov, under fire, and returned to the detachment.[29]

Colonel Prince Kudashev, with two Cossack regiments entrusted to him, totalling 500 men, approaching the Serpukhov road on 27 September (9 October), received intelligence about the location of a large enemy force near the village of Nikolskoe and found more than 2,500 French foragers there, with an escort of six squadrons, under the command of Generals Beaumont [Marc-Antoine Bonnin de la Bonninière de Beaumont] and Bouvier [Joseph Bouvier des Éclaz]. Despite the extreme disparity in strength, Kudashev decided to attack the enemy and having previously sent one *sotnia* to their rear, attacked them frontally and put them to flight, with the loss of more than 100 men killed and 200 captured. On our side, three Cossacks were killed or wounded. Two days later, 150 Cossacks detached by Kudashev, under the command of the Commander in Chief's aide de camp Captain Kozhukhov [Alexey Stepanovich Kozhukov], crossed the Mocha River, forced the French infantry to evacuate the village of Chegodaevo, and when, having entered open ground, they formed up in square, the Cossacks charged at the enemy and broke them with the loss of 40 men killed and 60 captured.[30]

One of the most important feats accomplished by our detachments at that time was the storming of Vereya. Having received intelligence that the enemy was fortifying this city, probably with the aim of establishing themselves there and shielding the Smolensk road from our partisans, the Field Marshal ordered Dorokhov to go to Vereya via Borovsk with a detachment consisting of five battalions, four squadrons and two Cossack regiments, with eight guns,[31] to attack the enemy and, having defeated them, destroy any fortifications constructed. The detachment under Prince Vadbolsky, consisting of the Mariupol Hussar Regiment and 500 Cossacks, was ordered to link up with Dorokhov, in the vicinity of Borovsk, and become part of his task force.[32]

Upon arrival in Borovsk, on 27 September (9 October), General Dorokhov left elements of his detachment there to secure communications with the army, and sent strong fighting patrols to Kupelitsy and Mityaeva, to isolate the enemy troops who were holding Vereya from Moscow and Mozhaisk, and moved on. Having reached Volchenka, three *versts* from Vereya, the detachment cached their backpacks and, crossing the Protva in light order, closed up to Vereya, before dawn on the 28th (10 October). The city, lying on a knoll with a height of about five *sazhen*,

---

29 Extracted from Biskupsky's correspondence.
30 Colonel Prince Kudashev's reports to Duty General Konovnitsyn, dated 27 and 29 September [9 and 11 October].
31 Dorokhov's detachment consisted of: the Wilmanstrand Infantry, Polotsk Infantry, one battalion from 19th Jägers, four squadrons of Yelisavetgrad Hussars, Kommisarov's Cossack Regiment, Ilovaisky 11th's Cossack Regiment, four light guns and four horse artillery pieces.
32 Orders for Dorokhov dated 26 September [8 October] (outgoing document log, Archive of the M.T.D. No. 29,172).

was surrounded by a rampart with a palisade and occupied by a Westphalian battalion. Five residents of Vereya, a retired soldier and four tradesmen,[33] served as guides to our detachment. Having roused the morale of his soldiers with a short speech, Dorokhov led them into the assault. The troops were ordered to advance in silence and attack the enemy without firing, with fixed bayonets. The garrison, taken by surprise, stood to arms just as our soldiers broke into the city, but defended themselves rather stubbornly, firing from houses and from the church; eventually, once some of them had been killed, the rest laid down their weapons. The prisoners included: a colonel, 14 officers and more than 350 lower ranks; their Colour was taken. No sooner had our soldiers managed to capture the city, than an enemy detachment appeared from the direction of Mozhaisk, consisting of three battalions and four squadrons, with several guns; but noticing that Vereya had already been taken by Russian troops, they fell back. The number of killed in our detachment did not exceed 30 men. Several hundred armed peasants, under the command of the priest of Vereya cathedral, John Skabeev, having learned about this victory, came to Dorokhov and tore down the fortifications built by the enemy. Having distributed 500 muskets captured from the Westphalians to the unarmed residents and food supplies found in the city, Dorokhov, on the orders of the Field Marshal, moved to the village of Kamenskoe with the detachment entrusted to him.[34]

Partisan operations and the popular uprising inflicted significant casualties on the enemy. It is impossible to state with certainty how many men Napoleon's army lost during its stay in Moscow; but this can be assessed from a report to the Tsar, by Prince Kutuzov, which mentions that the troops of the main army, in the course of ten days from 9 to 19 September [21 September to 3 October], had captured more than 5,000 prisoners. From the reports by General Wintzingerode it can be seen that the partisans sent out from his detachment, in the course of twenty days, from 10 to 29 September [22 September to 11 October], captured some 1,500 men.[35] The enemy troops suffered no less harm from their inability to forage, which was a result of partisan raids; French detachments sent to obtain supplies were destroyed by our partisans and the residents of the surrounding countryside. The enemy was forced to detach significant elements of the army with artillery to protect the foragers; as a result of this, the troops located around Moscow were forced to endure almost the same amount of hard work as they had been subjected to on the march; at first, after occupying our capital, the enemy could still obtain provisions, but they constantly suffered a lack of fodder, from which they lost several hundred horses daily; later the men too were subjected to famine; not having enough bread or meat, the French in Moscow shot crows, ate cats, and were even forced to eat the meat of their dead

---

33 Grechishkin, Prokudin, Zhukov and Shushukin. All four were awarded the Military Order.
34 Dorokhov's report dated 29 September [11 October].
35 Prince Kutuzov's report to the Tsar dated 29 September [11 October]. Adjutant General Wintzingerode's reports to the Tsar dated: 10, 13, 16, 20, 24, 26 and 29 September [22, 25, 28 September, 2, 6, 11 October]. In the War Diary of the main army entry for 5 [17] October: Lieutenant General Baron Wintzingerode reported that, including prisoners taken along the Yaroslavl road, of which there were more than 250 men, in three weeks his detachment had captured 33 officers and 2,792 non-commissioned officers and soldiers.

horses.³⁶ The consequences of this were digestive diseases and colds, fevers, typhoid fever, and so on, and as the deterioration of physical strength is almost always accompanied by a breakdown in morale, many of the soldiers, and especially the recruits, were seized by depression and homesickness (*nostalgie*). Physicians seldom saw the need for anti-inflammatory (*antiflogische*) treatments, but, in contrast, almost always treated with restorative (*tonische*) agents.³⁷

After constant rain in the first half of September (new style) the weather came clear, very rarely interrupted by light showers. The temperature was moderate, but the cold nights already heralded the onset of the harsh season. The elements of the French army, located in Moscow and in the vicinity of the capital, and especially the *Garde impériale*, having had time to rest a little, stock up on warm clothes and find, from time to time, stocks of hard-tack, salted beef and vodka, was in incomparably better condition than the troops stationed in the vanguard on the river Chernishnya. There, fatigued from outpost duty and distant foraging expeditions, the soldiers had a meagre diet of cereals and horse meat. If they happened to find any rye or wheat, they cracked the grains on rocks and stewed it. As there was no salt to be found almost anywhere, it was substituted with gunpowder, and tallow candles were used for cooking instead of lard. On cold, damp nights, due to a lack of firewood, the troops sometimes did not make fires, and trembled from the cold being vulnerable to the common cold and toothache. The horses were fed with straw from the roofs, if any could be found. The weakening of the cavalry made it necessary to send infantry and artillery on foraging expeditions.³⁸

Without any exaggeration, such was the situation of the French army. Napoleon hoped that the occupation of Moscow by his troops would force Emperor Alexander I to open peace negotiations, but time was passing, and the Russian Government showed no inclination to end the war. Eventually, after twenty days had passed since the start of the French occupation of Moscow, Napoleon decided to make the first step towards peace, and considering direct communications with our Tsar to be the best way to do this, he suggested that Caulaincourt go to St Petersburg, but then abandoned this idea, having been persuaded of its futility by the objections of Caulaincourt himself. Hoping to achieve his objective through negotiations with Kutuzov, Napoleon ordered Murat to write a letter to the commander of the Russian vanguard with the following content: 'The Emperor, intending to send one of his adjutants general to Commander in Chief Kutuzov, wishes to know when and where he might be received.'³⁹ Having received an invitation to visit on the following day, Lauriston arrived at our vanguard on the morning of 23 September (5 October). There he found Prince Volkonsky, whom Kutuzov had instructed to ask Lauriston what he had been sent with, and if he had a letter from Napoleon, to take it. The reason for the

---

36 *Histoire de la destruction de Moscou en 1812*, 148 & 150. Labaume, 242.
37 Lemasurier, *Medicinische Geschichte des Russischen Feldzuges von 1812*.
38 *Ein Jahr aus meinem Leben, oder Reise von den westlichen Ufern der Donau an die Nara, und zurück an die Beresina im Jahre 1812*, 146-148.
39 Berthier's letter to the King of Naples, dated 4 October, new style: '... L'empereur étant dans l'intention d'envoyer un de ses aides-de-camp généraux en chef Koutousoff, on désire connaitre le jour, l'heure, l'endroit, où ce général veut le recevoir.'

Field Marshal's reluctance to meet with Lauriston was, in all likelihood, the fear of arousing displeasure in the army through negotiations with the enemy. Arriving at the outposts, Prince Volkonsky let the French forward screen know that he wanted to see Lauriston, who immediately came to him, but upon learning of the order given to Volkonsky by the Field Marshal, he replied that he had orders from Emperor Napoleon to speak with the Russian Commander in Chief in person. Whereupon Prince Volkonsky sent his orderly Nashchokin to inform Kutuzov of this and suggested that he and Lauriston, in anticipation of an answer, each return to their own vanguard. At that very moment, Murat rode up to them from the forward outposts from one direction, while Bennigsen and Miloradovich arrived from another, and after conversing among themselves for several minutes, parted. Kutuzov, in any event, trying to gain time, and perhaps wanting to make some preparations for receiving the enemy *parlementaire*, sent Nashchokin back with an invitation for Lauriston to visit the headquarters of the Russian army once it was completely dark. Lauriston immediately came to our vanguard and was driven to the Tarutino camp with Prince Volkonsky in a *droshky* [light carriage]. In the meantime, our troops had received orders to spread out over a wide area, for which some regiments were transferred from one location to another; big camp fires were lit; orders were issued to cook savoury porridge with meat; songs were sung and the bands played in every regiment; however, it was not necessary to raise the spirits of the soldiers, who, knowing about the arrival of the ambassador, had guessed that he had come to sue for peace. Having crossed the entire camp, Lauriston and Volkonsky arrived at Tarutino, where an *izba* [log cabin] had been prepared for the forthcoming meeting. Kutuzov himself, for the first time since his arrival in the army, put on his uniform and, as he did not have new epaulettes, he borrowed some from Konovnitsyn.[40]

Lauriston arrived at half-past ten o'clock. The Field Marshal, inviting him into the *izba*, spoke with him without witnesses, and therefore their negotiations are known to us only from Kutuzov's report to the Tsar.[41]

First of all, Lauriston began to talk about an exchange of prisoners, to which the Field Marshal did not agree. Thereafter, turning to the burning of Moscow and the devastation of the countryside, the French *parlementaire* complained of the brutality with which the war was being waged; argued that we, by ruining our own land, would not achieve our objective, and that Napoleon's troops had everything they needed in abundance; accused the inhabitants of unheard-of cruelty against the French who had fallen into their hands and suggested that our Commander in Chief take measures to stop these barbaric acts and, in general, to give the war the character of one between civilised nations. Kutuzov answered that:

---

40 [Liprandi points out that Lauriston probably passed through the vanguard's bivouacs but 'in no case could Lauriston have been driven across the entire camp, which was 800 paces from the right bank of the Nara, and Tarutino lies on the left bank of this river… Had he gone to Letashevka, he really would have crossed the entire camp. Had Kutuzov received him in Tranishcheva, on the right bank of the Nara, even then, in this case Lauriston would have seen neither the camp nor the meat, but would merely have enjoyed the singing and music being some 200 or 300 paces closer. I repeat, one has only to look at the plan to be convinced of this blunder'].
41 Prince Kutuzov's report to Emperor Alexander I, dated 23 September [5 October].

> Even if I wanted to change the opinions of the people, I could not succeed in that, because the Russians consider this war to be a second invasion by the Tatars [Mongols], and I am not able to change the perceptions of an entire nation.

Eventually turning to the true purpose of the mission given to him, Lauriston began to talk of peace. He said:

> The friendship that existed between your Tsar and Emperor Napoleon was terminated in an unfortunate manner, due to external factors, and now there is an opportunity to restore it. This war is extraordinary, unprecedented, must it last forever? My Sovereign sincerely wishes to put an end to the disagreements between the two great nations, and put it aside forever.[42]

Kutuzov replied:

> I have no instructions in that regard; when I was sent to the army, the conditions for peace were never mentioned. However, all this talk that I have heard from you, whether it comes from your own assessment, or has its origins from higher up, I, in any case, have no wish to convey to my Tsar. I would expose myself to the condemnation of posterity, if it was thought that I had been the instigator of any kind of reconciliation; such, at the present time, is the mindset of our nation.[43]

After that, Lauriston handed the Field Marshal a letter from his Sovereign, with the following content:

> I am sending to you one of my general aides-de-camp to talk to you about several matters of interest. I want Your Highness to believe what he tells you, especially when he expresses the feelings of esteem and particular consideration that I have long had for his person. This letter having no other purpose, I pray God, Monsieur le Prince, that he has you in his holy and worthy keeping. Moscow, 3 October [new style], 1812.[44]

---

42 From Prince Kutuzov's report dated 23 September [5 October]: *'Cette guerre singulière, cette guerre inouie, doit-elle durer éternellement? L'empereur mon maître a un désir sincère de terminer ce differend entre deux nations grandes et généreuses et à le terminer à jamais...'*
43 From Prince Kutuzov's report dated 23 September [5 October]: *'... Je serais maudit par la postérité si on me regardait comme le premier moteur d'un accommodement quelconque, car tel est l'esprit actuel de ma nation.'*
44 *'Monsieur le prince Koutousoff. J'envoye près de vous un de mes aides-de-camp généraux pour vous entretenir de plusieurs objets intéressants. Je désire que Votre Altesse ajoute foi à ce qu'il lui dira, surtout lorsqu'il exprimera les sentimens d'estime et de particulière considération que j'ai depuis longtems pour sa personne. Cette lettre n'étant à autre fin, je prie Dieu, Monsieur le Prince, qu'il vous ait en sa sainte et digne garde. Moscou, le 3 octobre. 1812. Signé: Napoléon. A. M-r. le prince Koutousoff, généralissime de l'armée russe.'*

At the same time, Lauriston, expressing Napoleon's unwillingness to send him to St Petersburg for negotiations, asked Prince Kutuzov to seek consent from our Tsar, and proposed a truce in anticipation of an answer. Kutuzov refused a truce, but promised to inform the Tsar about Napoleon's wishes. In calculating the time it would take for an answer to come from St Petersburg, Lauriston betrayed the urgency of receiving it as quickly as possible,[45] and even volunteered to go there himself. The Field Marshal, rejecting this proposal, said that he would convey everything to the Tsar in a report via Prince Volkonsky, who was intending to travel to St Petersburg the next day. After that, summoning Volkonsky, Kutuzov repeated in his presence what had been said before about the guerilla war. He stated: 'The Tsar has forbidden me even from uttering the words: peace or truce. Ask Prince Volkonsky: he was sent here to confirm the Monarch's will to me.' Lauriston hinted that it would be quicker for Volkonsky to travel via Moscow. Kutuzov disagreed. 'Wouldn't it be better to send a courier? He'll get there sooner!' Lauriston said. But the Field Marshal did not agree to this either.[46]

Napoleon, wishing to entice the Russian Government towards peace, issued orders indicating his intention to stay in Moscow for a long time. To that end, the rearmament of the Kremlin was started and the troops were ordered to stock up on food for six months, which was obviously impossible.[47] These ruses had no effect on the resolve of Emperor Alexander I, but they made a very unfavourable impression on Napoleon's own troops, vastly removed from the origin of their resources and surrounded by a hostile population in the countryside. The sense of hopelessness completely weakened discipline, already in decline in the French army.[48]

Emperor Alexander I, having received the report from Prince Kutuzov about his meeting with Lauriston, expressed his displeasure in the following rescript:

> Prince Mikhail Ilarionovich! From your report received via Prince Volkonsky, I was informed about your earlier meeting with the French Adjutant General Lauriston.
>
> At the time of your departure to the armies entrusted to you, from My personal briefings to you, you knew My firm and urgent desire to withdraw from any negotiations or relations with the enemy directed towards peace.
>
> Now, after this incident, I must repeat to you with the same determination: such that this principle adopted by me, must be strictly and unshakably observed by you to its full extent.
>
> On a similar note, it was with extreme displeasure that I learned that General Bennigsen had a meeting with the King of Naples, and without any grounds for this.
>
> In presenting this inconsistent act to him, I demand active and strict supervision from you, such that other generals never have any meetings,

---

45 From Prince Kutuzov's report dated 23 September [5 October].
46 Emperor Alexander and His contemporaries in 1812, 1813, 1814 and 1815, Volume IV. Biography of Prince P.M. Volkonsky.
47 *Ordre au général Lariboissière, 1 octobre 1812*. Ségur, II, 79.
48 Beitzke, 267.

and any negotiations with the enemy even more so, striving by every possible means to avoid them.

All the intelligence that comes from Me to you and all My plans in decrees addressed in your name are explained, and in a word, everything must convince you of my firm resolve that at the present time no proposals by the enemy will induce Me to break off the struggle, and thereby weaken our sacred duty: to avenge the offences to the Fatherland. I remain grateful to you.

St Petersburg. 9 [21] October 1812. Alexander.'

The meeting between Prince Kutuzov and Lauriston left no doubt that there was no inclination towards peace on the part of the Russians. Napoleon still hoped that Emperor Alexander would take advantage of his proposal to open peace negotiations, however, on the very next day after the meeting described above, he began to take precautions in the event of a retreat from Moscow, upon which he had already decided, but had postponed pending a response from St Petersburg. Having the intention to move from Moscow, via Kaluga and Yelnya, to Smolensk, Napoleon gave orders to write to Marshal Victor that, according to intelligence from Schwarzenberg, Chichagov's Army of the Danube had linked up with Tormasov's army in Volhynia; that, on the other side, Emperor Alexander was trying to strengthen Wittgenstein's army so that it could push back the corps under MacDonald, Oudinot and Saint-Cyr behind the Dvina. Under these circumstances, Victor was to position his corps between Smolensk and Orsha in order to support the troops operating in Volhynia, or those stationed on the Dvina as necessary, and, at the same time, serve as a reserve for the *Grande armée*, to provide rear area security for the main force and head to meet them during their retreat to Smolensk. Dąbrowski's [Jan Henryk Dąbrowski] Division and the brigade located in Vilna were subordinated to him. As Governor of the whole of Lithuania and Belorussia, the marshal was to speed up the preparation of provisions and fodder in these areas, so as to have a thirty-day supply of food for his corps, for however many of them were to proceed to the army.[49] In order to protect the line of operations, Napoleon ordered that, in addition to the detachments stationed between Moscow and Mozhaisk and the Westphalian *8e Corps* near Mozhaisk, significant elements of the force were to be located at Gzhatsk, Vyazma and Dorogobuzh. To that end, the Smolensk commandant, General Baraguey d'Hilliers, having collected twelve battalions *en route* to the army,[50] was ordered to place five each in Gzhatsk and Vyazma and two in Dorogobuzh.[51] Wanting to more reliably secure the progress to the army of artillery parks, Napoleon gave orders to write to Marshal Victor, such that their escorts were not to be assigned to units made up of men from various regiments (*régimens formés d'hommes isolés*), but to send

---

49 Instructions to Chief of Staff of the Grande armée, Berthier, dated 6 October, new style.
50 Two Mecklenburg battalions from Davout's Corps, which had been garrisoned in Vilna; three battalions from Claparède's *Légion de la Vistule*, also left to garrison various locations; one battalion of *33e Légère*, and two battalions each from Westphalia, Württemberg and Hessen-Darmstadt, newly arrived from Germany.
51 Napoleon's orders issued by Berthier, dated 6 October, new style.

well-established battalions or companies. Finally, instructions were sent to Marshal Junot and General Baraguey d'Hilliers, to collect all the wagons that could be found within forty *versts* (*à dix lieues à la ronde*) of Mozhaisk and Vyazma, and evacuate all the wounded from the hospitals arranged along the Smolensk road, in Mozhaisk, Ruza, Kolotsky monastery (*à l'Abbaye*) and Gzhatsk. Sending the wounded to Vyazma was assigned to Junot, while their onward journey to Smolensk, was entrusted to Baraguey d'Hilliers. Napoleon wrote: 'In any case, I want not a single wounded man in the hospitals within a week; notify the generals that I consider this a very important matter.'[52]

Such were the measures taken by Napoleon, in anticipation of a response from St Petersburg to his proposal for peace talks. And, meanwhile, he was preparing for the departure from Moscow, which, in any case, was unavoidable.

---

52 Instructions from Berthier, dated 6 October, new style.

29

The Guerrilla War

The participation by Smolensk residents in guerrilla warfare. – The exploits of the residents of the Porechye and Bely *Uezds*. – Feats of the Sychyovka residents. – Major Yemelyanov; police officer Boguslavsky; the *Bürgermeister* of Levshino. – Feats of the Yukhnov residents. – Khrapovitsky. – Feats of the Roslavl residents. – Police Chief Semichev. – Hussar Samus. – The heroic deaths of Lieutenant Colonel Engelhardt and collegiate assessor Shubin. – The *modus operandi* of soldier-peasants. – Feats of the residents of Voskresensk and Vereya. – The guerrilla war in Bogorodsk *Uezd*.

Napoleon's appeal to the residents of Moscow. – The loyalty of the Russian people. – Rostopchin's appeal. – The announcements of the Ministry of Police. – The importance of guerrilla warfare. – The general participation by each and every person in the war of 1812. – Comments on the Russians by comte Ségur.

The participation of the population in the war began with the first steps by Napoleon's hordes into the ancient region of Russia, the Smolensk Governorate. The Tsar's appeal for a general mobilisation had not yet been released, when the inhabitants of the Porechye *Uezd* rose up in defence of the Fatherland; peaceful villagers turned into brave warriors; in their hands, agricultural implements became formidable weapons. Whoever was unable to fight, escaped to places free from enemy interference, or into dense forests, as if refusing to breathe the same air as the enemy who dared to disturb the peace of their adored mother Russia. As soon as the French succeeded in invading the Smolensk Governorate, our peasants began to intercept foragers, scouts and marauders who roamed in the rear of Napoleon's *Grande armée*; from among the Porechye warrior-peasants, the tradesman Manchenkov especially distinguished himself, having captured a courier with important dispatches and was awarded the Military Order medal.[1]

Following the enemy occupation of Smolensk and the retreat of our army towards Moscow, most of the Smolensk Governorate was turned into a desert dotted with ruins. The inhabitants, hiding their families in inaccessible refuges, and everything

---

[1] From sources in the Smolensk Governorate held in the Archive of the M.T.D.

that they managed to take with them, often set fire to their houses themselves, and even put the grain in the fields to the torch so that it would not fall into the hands of the French. The towns of Bely, Sychyovka, Yukhnov and Roslavl, unoccupied by enemy troops, became the main centres of the popular uprising. In the Bely *Uezd*, notwithstanding the general governorate *opolchenie*, the peasants and townspeople armed themselves under the command of the leader of the nobility Kolenov and the mayor Adamovich. Retired Lieutenant Colonel Diebitsch, having gathered a small detachment of Smolensk residents, reinforced with deserters from the enemy army and operated successfully throughout the French occupation of the governorate. The inhabitants of Bely attacked enemy patrols that appeared in their *uezd*, killed or captured the French, and secured themselves from plunder and ruin.[2] Sychyovka *Uezd* became famous for the deaths of many of the enemy. Its inhabitants took up arms under the command of the leader of the nobility Nakhimov and police officer Boguslavsky. A warrior from the days of Suvorov, retired Major Yemelyanov, became the terror of the enemy in particular. Encouraging the first of the Sychyovka nobility and peasants into the *opolchenie*, he was elected their commander. His squad, at first armed with pikes, scythes, pitchforks and axes, later replaced them with muskets taken from the enemy and were distinguished not only by fearlessness, but also by their good discipline. The veteran Yemelyanov established signal stations, whose beacons and bell ringing gave the villagers forewarning whether to leave their houses or assemble, where to go into action, and so on. Being constantly at the front, he was mortally wounded by a bullet during a fierce firefight with the enemy, to the regret of his subordinates, who adored Yemelyanov, despite his strictness in service. In the Sychyovka *Uezd*, in the village of Tesovo, the peasants, under the command of police officer Boguslavsky, on 30 August [11 September], attacked a patrol that had appeared in their neighbourhood, laid 130 men low and captured 60. Among the Sychyovka warrior-peasants the *Bürgermeister* [steward] of the village of Levshino (15 *versts* from Sychyovka, along the Vyazma road) was known for his courage and extraordinary physical strength. On one occasion an enemy patrol of 30 men entered this village and occupied an *izba* to rest. Having learned of this, the *Bürgermeister* summoned the people, and, having asked one of the peasants to help him, moved silently up to the *izba* occupied by the French and barred the door himself. The terrified enemy began to shoot through the doors and mortally wounded the *Bürgermeister*; but the peasants meanwhile had managed to take cover, surrounded the *izba* and threatening to set it on fire, forced the enemy to surrender. Feeling his life ebbing away, the *Bürgermeister* willed his comrades not to avenge his death and to spare the captured French. Many of the inhabitants of Sychyovka were awarded the Military Order medal, while the tradespeople who participated in actions against the enemy, by Supreme command, all received five Roubles each.[3]

In the Yukhnov *Uezd*, the marshal of the nobility Khrapovitsky, a warrior from Catherine's era, having assembled an *opolchenie* of 2,000 men, assigned some of

---

2   Report from the head of the Bely nobility to Prince Kutuzov, dated 31 August [12 September]. Notes from the Fatherland, 1826, XXVI, 87-88.
3   From sources in the Smolensk Governorate held in the Archive of the M.T.D. *Severnaya Pochta*, 1812, No. 74. Notes from the Fatherland, 1826, XXV, 416-419.

them to patrolling, while he settled down on the Ugra with the rest of the warriors and halted the enemy, who were trying to get to Kaluga. When Davydov's partisan detachment arrived in Yukhnov, Khrapovitsky supplied them with food, posted warning pickets, and established a hospital at his own expense for sick and wounded soldiers.[4] The inhabitants of the city of Roslavl formed a mounted *opolchenie*, of 100 men, equipped with lances, sabres and muskets, and operating under the leadership of the city head Polozov, they not only protected themselves from enemy occupation, but also attacked enemy marauders who had devastated the Yelnya *Uezd* neighbouring them. The Roslavl police officer Semichev, blocking French access along the road to Bryansk, was killed. Prince Tenishev, being elected by the nobles to the post of cordon commander, rounded up some 400 marauders and donated all his property to establish a hospital for the wounded.[5]

In the Gzhatsk *Uezd*, right at the start of the retreat by the enemy army, one of the most remarkable Russian partisans appeared. After the battle of Smolensk, a member of the Yelisavetgrad Hussar Regiment, Hussar Samus [Fëdor Potapov], having been wounded in one of the rearguard actions, remained on the battlefield, found shelter away from the highway and, convalescing from his wounds, decided to take an active part in the war. The peasants of the surrounding villages, encouraged by him to join the *opolchenie*, formed a detachment, which subsequently increased to 2,000 men and captured a cannon from the enemy. The brave Samus, operating with extraordinary success, annihilated some 3,000 men and became known to Miloradovich, who promoted him to non-commissioned officer and recommended him for a decoration.[6]

Thus, the Smolensk Governorate, during the difficult days of the enemy occupation, presented a magnificent demonstration of the competition by all classes towards the common cause. The commanders of the squads, not limited to causing every kind of harm to the enemy, supported the improvement of services between their own and neighbouring peasants. Among the residents of Smolensk who rose up to defend the Fatherland were some of the leading landowners Engelhardt [Pavel Ivanovich Engelhardt] and Shubin [Semën Ivanovich Shubin]. During the French invasion, Lieutenant Colonel Engelhardt, remaining on his Porechye estate, helped the Cossacks to exterminate the enemy who appeared in his neighbourhood, and tried to keep his peasants in good order and obedience, while the collegiate assessor Shubin, who was also living on his estate, having learned about the arrival of a sub-unit of Kazan Dragoons in Dukhovshchina, attacked enemy marauders who had plundered the village next to him, with the dragoons and captured 21 men. Only two soldiers from this unit managed to escape to Smolensk and report on Shubin's feat. At the same time, a denunciation was made of Engelhardt for the murder of many French soldiers. Having been brought to Smolensk, imprisoned and handed over to a court martial, Engelhardt was sentenced to death and shot on 15 [27] October.

---

4   From sources in the Smolensk Governorate held in the Archive of the M.T.D. Davydov's memoirs, 464. Notes from the Fatherland, 1826, XXVI, 90-91.
5   From sources in the Smolensk Governorate held in the Archive of the M.T.D. The patriotic and heroic deeds of Prince I.G. Tenishev, 1815.
6   The exploits of General Miloradovich, by F.N. Glinka, 45-47.

When he was taken outside the Malakhov Gate, which was the appointed place of execution for the sentence by the court, the enemy tried to persuade him to enter French service, offering the rank of colonel as a reward for this betrayal. The Russian nobleman scornfully rejected the unworthy offer, 'Shoot me!' he said, pulling off the handkerchief with which they wanted to blindfold him, and fearlessly looking at the firing squad. The enemy, in order to shake his courage, first inflicted a wound to his leg, promising to spare him if he agreed to serve Napoleon: neither the pain endured by the victim, nor the tempting promises of his tormentors, could shake the firmness of spirit of the noble Engelhardt. Whereupon the French fired a salvo at him. Of the 18 rounds fired at him, two hit him in the chest and one in the stomach, but as he still continued to breathe, one of the soldiers, hastily reloading a musket, shot him in the temple and put an end to his suffering. Collegiate assessor Shubin was also asked to serve in the French forces, but he remained true to his obligations, responded sharply to the enemy, expressing his hatred for the French, and was shot on 24 October [5 November].[7]

Emperor Alexander I, having learned about all the circumstances of the heroic deaths of Engelhardt and Shubin, granted pensions to their nearest relatives.[8]

The French invasion of the Moscow Governorate was met with as much hostility by its inhabitants as it had been in Smolensk. Both the tradespeople and the peasants, upon leaving their homes, destroyed everything that might become booty for the enemy, set fire to the buildings and hid in the forests, where they set up ambushes, or went out from there to destroy the blundering enemy.[9] Often the inhabitants of an entire village, or even several villages, would take a mutual oath to exterminate the French and stand strong for each other. The slightest compliance with the enemy was considered treason. On one occasion, the peasants of a village, terrified of a French detachment that had come to them, greeted them with bread and salt. Soon after, the enemy was driven away and the peasants, who had received them respectfully, came to the nearest church for a divine service. When they, along with other parishioners, began to approach the cross, the priest met them with a severe rebuke: 'Why did you come here?' he said: 'You are not our kind, having betrayed the Faith, you accepted our enemies as welcome guests.' Sometimes the unbridled hatred of the foreigners who had surged into the Russian lands made our peasants suspicious in the extreme. In each village not yet abandoned by the inhabitants, the gates were obstructed with logs and guarded by crowds of people with pitchforks, stakes, scythes, axes, and sometimes with muskets. At that time it was not safe to

---

7 From sources in the Smolensk Governorate held in the Archive of the M.T.D.
8 Emperor Alexander I gave orders to award annual pensions: to Engelhardt's brother of 6,000 paper Roubles, and to his nephew and niece 3,000 paper Roubles each; to Shubin's widow 9,000, his mother 6,000 and his two sisters 3,000 Roubles each (Decree to the Governing Senate dated 30 August [11 September], 1813). Emperor Nikolay Pavlovich, on his way through Smolensk, in 1833, noticing the dilapidated monument erected by his relatives over Engelhardt's grave, ordered a significant sum to be allocated for the construction of a new monument, made of cast iron.
9 [Liprandi comments: 'Did the nobility not do the same? Meanwhile, only the tradespeople and the peasants are mentioned. In the Patriotic History, in my opinion, every expression, every word carries its own weight'].

appear in unfamiliar places in clothing that looked anything like a foreign uniform; often, instead of answering the questions of a passing officer, they greeted him with a swinging axe or a gunshot. Davydov wrote that the peasants of one *volost* [parish] near the village of Yegorievskoe (in the Medyn *Uezd*) exterminated 60 Cossacks of the Teptyar Regiment, mistaking them for the enemy, because they did not speak Russian clearly.[10]

On high ground dominating the surrounding area, outposts were set up by the peasants, vigilantly watching for the appearance of the enemy. If the approaching unit was few in number, then the warrior-peasants would try to surround and seize it covertly so as not to reveal their hideouts; in the event of an advance by significant forces, the sentries sent the news to the nearest village; the alarm was sounded and at a rendezvous point agreed in advance, the people gathered from all neighbouring villages, armed with whatever they could find, under the command of local leaders, retired officers, nobles, or elders elected by peasants from among themselves. Sometimes these leaders would raise the morale of their subordinates with a short speech before combat. The battle orders were very simple: the men who had guns occupied buildings, gardens, woods, and greeted the enemy with fire, or, using their perfect knowledge of the area that happened to be the field of battle, tried to envelope the enemy undetected and surround them from all sides. Having succeeded, the peasant warriors exterminated the enemy, or, having bound them, sent them under escort to the nearest town. At the same time, our peasants, who had no idea about the laws and customs generally accepted in war, sometimes acted very cruelly towards the prisoners. The captured booty was divided equally, or each used it according to their own whim; but the dominant passion that animated our guerrilla squads was a thirst for revenge on the enemy, and by no means greed. Davydov claims that the peasants once attacked a straggler in a cart with his valise, on which lay a sick hussar. The villagers, mistaking him for an enemy, beat him and left him for dead on the road, smashed the cart, and tore up his things and scattered them over the fields, without taking anything from them.[11] There were many such incidents.

Following the enemy occupation of the Zvenigorod *Uezd*, the inhabitants of Voskresensk established day and night sentries, who were placed on hills in open ground, or watched for the enemy in the forests by climbing into the treetops. The peasant-warriors repeatedly drove the French troops away, defended Voskresensk and inflicted casualties on the enemy, reaching over 2,000 men: among these heroes, the head of the Velyaminovo *volost*, Ivan Andreev, and Pavel Ivanov of the Luchinskoe village 'hundred,' who fought alongside all his sons, were especially distinguished. In the Vereya *Uezd*, the priest of the village of Dubrovo, John Skabeev, encouraged the peasants to stand firmly for the faith and their native land. In the Tver Governorate, outwith the general *opolchenie*, the inhabitants of Zubtsov, Ostashkov and Kashin armed themselves. The command over the *opolchenie* of the Zubtsov *Uezd*, which consisted of 2,500 foot and mounted warriors, was taken on

---

10 Davydov's memoirs, 445-456.
11 Davydov's memoirs, 456.

a vote by the nobles, by the landowner Tsyzyrev, who provided six light cannon, in case of an enemy incursion.[12]

In order to give an idea of the *modus operandi* of the peasant-warriors, I shall briefly describe the skirmishes of one of the squads, as recorded by its former commander.

At the end of September [early October], Ney's troops occupied the city of Bogorodsk. The peasants of the Vokhna *volost*, the village of Pavlova, having learned of this, sent all the elderly and children into the forests and to other refuges, but they themselves decided;

> to fight the enemy to the death, or take revenge on the demons for the desecration of holy churches and other shrines. One of the Vokhna villagers, Gerasim Kurin [Gerasim Matveyevich Kurin], was appointed head of the squad, because in all dealings between the peasants he showed particular promptness and courage.

Having unexpectedly assumed the position of commander of the *Zemstvo* [territorial] force, Kurin showed himself worthy of the trust of his comrades. His first priority was the armament of the squad: having assembled his soldiers, he ordered them to buy muskets or make pikes. On 25 September [7 October], a small enemy patrol appeared on the opposite side of the Klyazma, near the village of Bolshie-Dvory, at a distance of about four *versts* from the village of Pavlova. Having learned of this, Kurin ferried the peasant-warriors across the river and led them against the enemy, but noticing that, upon seeing the French 'they began to hang back, because they were unfamiliar with this business,' he gave them the following pep-talk:

> My dear friends! You are people of the Russian faith; you are Orthodox Christians! Strive or die for the faith and the Tsar. Why are we Christians, if not to suffer for the faith; why are we Orthodox, if not to serve the Tsar. Sovereign of our hearts, that he is our dear father; if he hears of us, we shall not be left without a reward.

Encouraged by these words and the example of their leader, the warriors attacked the enemy and forced them to take cover in the forest. Ten muskets and two wagons with four horses went to the victors as booty.

On the following day, 26 September [8 October], Having received intelligence about the French intention to burn the village of Gribovo, three *versts* from Pavlova, Kurin attacked the enemy, put them to flight and returned home without loss.

On 27 September [9 October], three enemy squadrons arrived in the village of Subbotino (six *versts* from the village of Pavlova). The commander of this detachment sent a note to Pavlova, proposing that the Vukhna squad remain at peace and quiet with the French; but the peasant-warriors, instead of answering this message, raced towards Subbotino at the double. The action, which began at about 11 o'clock

---

12 Notes on 1812, Sergey Glinka, 114 & 118. *Severnaya Pochta*, 1812, No. 80 & 81.

in the morning, ended at two o'clock in the afternoon with the defeat of the enemy detachment, which lost 18 killed and three prisoners; 20 horses were captured by the peasants; on our side, the casualties were limited to a few wounded.

On the 28 [10 October], at nine o'clock in the morning, having arrived at the village of Nazarova (eight *versts* from Pavlova, up the Klyazma), the enemy sent patrols into the village and towards the neighbouring villages in order to find the hussars and horses lost the day before. The commander of the Vokhna guerrillas was absent, in the city of Pokrov, where he had gone to see the commander of the Vladimir *opolchenie*, Prince Golitsyn, with a request to support his squad with a small number of soldiers or Cossacks. Having received 20 mounted men to help, Kurin rejoined his squad in Pavlova and attacked the French near Nazarova with them. The enemy, stunned by the sudden appearance of our soldiers, took flight and were pursued for several *versts*, leaving ten horses and two wagons as booty for the victors. On the following day [11 October new style], at around noon, another French patrol arrived in the village of Trubitsino, near the village of Pavlova; the French managed to round up two herds of cattle and sheep, but the peasant-warriors, having assembled in significant strength, recaptured their livestock and, having driven off the enemy, pursued them for several *versts* and captured eight two-horse wagons loaded with grain, with 16 horses. On the French side, 15 men were killed, while on our side, four were wounded.

The enemy, no longer daring to forage in small parties, sent a fairly strong detachment towards the village of Pavlova. Having learned about this on 1 [13] October, Kurin assembled the peasants from the whole neighbourhood and delivered a speech in which he convinced them; 'to stand up for the Fatherland and for the House of the Most Holy Madonna, against an enemy who threatened to burn all their villages and flay the skin from every inhabitant.' The strength of the *opolchenie* that day reached 5,800 men, of whom 500 were on horseback and the rest on foot. All of them, at eight o'clock in the morning, gathered at the church in the village of Pavlova, where, after the liturgy and prayer service, they bade each other farewell in tears and swore before the altar not to let down their comrades to the last drop of blood. After that, Kurin proposed, dividing the men who had taken up arms into three groups, to appoint, in addition to himself, two commanders, and selected the headman of Vokhna, Stulov [Yegor Semënovich Stulov] and another peasant for these positions: the former was entrusted with all the mounted men, while the latter had 1,000 foot. Kurin took on command over the rest of the men himself and the deployment of each element for the battle. Having placed detachments of his comrades in ambushes near the villages of Melenkovo and Yudinsky-ravine and ordered them to stay there and not to go into action without his orders, Kurin placed the remaining peasant-warriors covertly in the village of Pavlova. Meanwhile, at two o'clock in the afternoon, having reached the village of Gribovo, the enemy halted there and sent two squadrons towards the village of Pavlova: one halted before reaching the village, while the other entered the village and halted in the square. The commander of this squadron, through an interpreter, demanded that the elders deliver as much flour, cereals and oats as needed, promising to pay the peasants for everything at a price that they themselves set. Kurin replied that he would immediately order the preparation of the necessary supplies, and believing that the enemy did not have any other troops near the village, sent a message to Stulov to attack the squadron that was stationed outside the village; while he, having lured the enemy standing in the square into one of the peasant farmyards himself, ordered the gates to be barricaded, surrounded the French from all sides and shot down the squadron almost to the last man. Meanwhile, the peasant-warriors sent from Pavlova attacked the other squadron, enveloped by Stulov's squad from the rear, scattered them and pursued the French to Gribovo; but there, encountering a large enemy detachment, they were driven off and pursued to the village itself, where the French broke in after them and surrounded our soldiers from all sides. At this very moment, the detachment stationed in the Yudinsky ravine appeared in the enemy rear. The French, who did not expect an attack from this direction, were put to flight and pursued for eight *versts*. Only the darkness of the night saved them from complete annihilation. Kurin killed one officer and two privates himself that day, and in total eight men had fallen at his hands. The victors took 20 two-horse carts with their horses, 25 muskets, 120 pistols and 400 pouches full of cartridges.

Encouraged by this success, the guerrillas marched on Bogorodsk the next day [14 October new style], in order to clear enemy troops from this city, but they found the French were no longer there, because Napoleon, planning to abandon Moscow soon, had ordered the troops stationed at Bogorodsk and Dmitrov to return from there. Thus, not only these cities, but also their *Uezds* were liberated from the invader. The inhabitants of the village of Pavlova, rejoiced at their deliverance from the danger that had threatened them, and decided to celebrate the anniversary of their victory, on the day of the Intercession of the Mother of God, in perpetuity and donated a rich vestment with an inscription memorialising the exploits of the Vukhna warriors to decorate the image of the Holy Intercessor.[13]

Napoleon, wishing to avert the danger that a popular uprising threatened, attempted to win over the inhabitants to his cause. The Moscow intendant Lesseps published the following appeal to the inhabitants of the capital and the surrounding countryside, on behalf of the Emperor of the French.

> You, peaceful Moscow civilians, artisans and workers, removed from the city by the disasters of war, and you, misguided farmers, trapped by irrational fear in your villages, listen: calm and order have been restored in this capital; your countrymen voluntarily leave their sanctuaries without fear of insult; any violence against their persons or property is immediately punished. His Majesty the Emperor is your protector and does not consider any of you enemies, except those who disobey his orders. He wants to put an end to your calamities; he wants you to return to your homes, to your families. Be grateful for his beneficent intentions and come to us without any fear. Let each of the residents return with confidence to their homes; you will soon find the resources there to meet your needs. Workers, artisans, making a living by your trade, return to your usual occupations:

---

13 Description of the skirmishes between the peasants of the Vokhna *volost* and the enemy in 1812 (Archive of the M.T.D. No. 47,352). Kurin and Stulov were decorated with the Military Order medal.

houses, shops, protective watchmen are ready for you; you will get paid for your work. And you, peasants, come out of the forests, where you have taken refuge from horror; return to your cottages; you will find protection in them. In the city there are markets where you can sell your surplus.

To ensure their easy sale, the government has taken the following measures:

1. From now on, peasants, farmers and residents of the Moscow region can, without any fear, bring their supplies, whatever their kind, to the city, to the markets established on Mokhovaya and Okhotny Rows.
2. These supplies may be sold at such prices as the buyer and seller agree between themselves; but if the seller does not receive the actual price they demand, they are free to take them back to their village, from which no one, under any pretext, can prevent them.
3. The main markets are scheduled twice a week, on Sundays and Wednesdays, and therefore, on the eve of these days, troops will be posted in sufficient numbers on all the main roads leading into the city to guard the supplies.
4. Similar precautions will be taken such that the peasants will not encounter any difficulties on the return journey with their carts and horses.
5. Resources will be set aside immediately in order to restore normal trade.

Urban and rural inhabitants, and you, workers and artisans, whatever nationality you may be! I invite you to contribute to the paternal intentions of His Majesty the Emperor, tending towards the general welfare. Fall at his feet with respect and trust, and do not delay in joining with us (*Portez à ses pieds respect et confiance et ne tardez pas à vous reunir à nous*).

Moscow, 6th October (new style) 1812. Intendant of the city and province of Moscow: Lesseps.[14]

This seditious appeal, printed in large numbers, was distributed by the commissars of the Moscow municipality and French officers sent to the villages for forage. But all the methods used by the enemy to spread this appeal and to shake the loyalty of the Russian people towards their Tsar and the Fatherland were in vain: the enemy's enticing promises were met with distrust and contempt. To counteract his plans, the Russian clergy and local authorities sent exhortations that were read in churches and at secular meetings. Let us cite as an example the appeal by Count Rostopchin, published after the French occupation of Moscow.

Peasants, residents of Moscow Governorate!
The enemy of the human race, God's punishment for our sins, the diabolical deluder, the evil Frenchman, has ascended to Moscow, betrayed her to

---

14 Chambray, II, 172-174.

the sword, to the flames. He has plundered the houses of God, defiled the altars with indecency, the vessels with drunkenness, has made a mockery of them. They use vestments instead of blankets, tore off the casing and crowns from holy icons, led horses into the church of our Orthodox faith. Looted houses, property; dishonoured wives, daughters, young children. He has defiled the cemeteries and, before the resurrection, removed the bones of the dead, our ancestors, our parents, from the earth. He caught whomever he could, and forced them to carry stolen goods, as if they were horses. Starving our people, and now, when you yourselves have nothing to eat, then let his warriors, like predatory animals, devour around Moscow, and he thought to amicably invite you to market, craftsmen and traders, promising order, protection for everyone. Can you really rely on his words, Orthodox, faithful servants of our Tsar, the nursemaid of mother stone-built Moscow, or submit to this deception by the predatory enemy, this bloodthirsty demon? Taking away your last crumb and condemning you to die of starvation; he will lead you astray with promises, while if he gives you money, then it is counterfeit; it will bring you grief. Brothers, remain true, humble, Christian soldiers of the Mother of God, do not listen to empty words. Honour your leaders and landlords; they are your protectors, helpers; ready to clothe you, to see that you are shod, fed and watered. To exterminate the enemy's powerful force, let us bury them in holy Russia; we shall begin to strike, wherever encountered; there are very few of them left; and we are forty million people, swoop from all sides like a convocation of eagles. We shall exterminate the frogs overseas, and let us leave their bodies to the wolves and crows; while Moscow will be adorned again, golden domes, stone houses will appear; people will flood in from all directions. Will our Father Alexander Pavlovich not spare us millions of roubles for the construction of stone-built Moscow, where He anointed himself with myrrh and was crowned with the Tsar's crown? He trusts in God Almighty, in the God of Russian soil, in the people, his subjects, the heroic hearts of the valiant. He alone is God's Anointed One, and we have sworn allegiance to Him. He is our father, and we His children; while the demon Frenchman is the unchristened enemy. He is ready to sell his soul; he has already become a Turk, in Egypt he became an apostate, he has robbed Moscow, left them naked, barefoot; and now he fawns and says that there will be no robbery, but everything has been taken by him, the dog, and nothing good will come of it. Bitter tears will be shed by the fierce wolf. Another two weeks, so shout *pardon*, but we seem not to hear; they have only one ending; they will eat everything like locusts and become emaciated, unburied dead: wherever they wander, throw them down living or dead into a deep grave. The Russian soldiers will help you; whoever runs, the Cossacks will finish them off: and you, do not be reticent, brothers, daring, Moscow warriors, and wherever you can close with them, exterminate the vile, unclean scum, and then you may come to the Tsar in Moscow and boast of your deeds. He will restore you again as before and you will live in clover in the old way. But whoever of you obeys the demon and bows to the Frenchman, that unworthy son of his father, an apostate of the Law of God, a criminal to his Sovereign, must give himself up to judgment and reproach; and consign his soul to hell with the demons and burn in the fire, as our mother Moscow burned.[15]

Paying attention to the harmful actions by the enemy, who, no longer hoping to defeat the Russians by brute force, resorted to cunning and enticements, the government, published the following appeal:

> By Supreme Command. Announced by the Ministry of Police.
> It is known that the enemy has established some official posts or leadership in Moscow on the French model, trying to publicise that they are allegedly doing this to restore order and a peaceful life for residents in the city. Meanwhile, the soldiers continue to plunder and carry out acts of violence and looting. To cover up these rampages, they have managed to persuade some Russian commoners through coercion or enticements to assume these duties, to be members of these institutions established by them. We have intercepted documents containing their names. The government feels it ought to promulgate them, and pronounce a strict and righteous judgment on them; as entering into positions established by the enemy is already to recognise oneself as subject to them, and not merely a prisoner. But the Government refrains from doing so only because these documents may not be entirely reliable, and because they are concerned about insulting a person's innocence through a premature and hasty condemnation without compelling evidence in this regard. Meanwhile, paying attention and concern for the welfare of each and everyone, one cannot leave without prior admonition that everyone should be wary of believing the cunning voice of an enemy who has come here with promises of security and peace on their lips, but with arson, plunder and the destruction of our kingdom in their hands. What kind of folly or extreme corruption is required to believe in the civility of those who came here with the sword to kill us, with torches to fire our homes, with chains to put around our necks, with hampers to fill with our looted property, that they want to arrange for our security and peace? Will those who came to take these things away from us preserve our glory and honour? Will those who, not wounded by anything we have done, spare our blood, having come here to shed it? Would they leave us to observe the ancient faith of our ancestors unhindered, who, with sacrilegious hands, dare to rip off the casings from the saints and miraculous icons that we revere? What meaning do their words and promises have? Where is that son of the Fatherland, who will believe them? For these reasons, the Government deems it necessary to announce publicly:

---

15 Count Rostopchin's memoirs, 1853, 178-182.

1. That it will render all possible care for the assistance and charity for people ruined by the enemy, wandering without shelter.
2. That through this warning notice it is hoped to save those of simple gullibility from late repentance; while the insolent, and those not ashamed to violate duty and oaths, are to fear their righteous and inevitable punishment.

9 [21] October 1812.[16]

This appeal had already been published when the enemy army, having evacuated Moscow, was retreating to the Dnieper. It seemed that Almighty Providence had determined that the Russian people, following the promptings of conscience and duty, would demonstrate all their outstanding qualities in full splendour even before the appeal by the Government. It did not take much effort to motivate the inhabitants of those governorates engulfed in the flames of war to total mobilisation. The entire male population, even decrepit old men and scrawny youths, armed themselves to defend Russia.[17] Agricultural work, the transportation of military cargo, delivery of dispatches by courier, all these were performed by women. Some of them took part in the warlike feats of their husbands and brothers, and among them was the head-woman Vasilisa, famous in folk legends for capturing and delivering an entire enemy patrol to Sychyovka.

The consequences of the guerrilla war in 1812 were just as disastrous for the enemy as the exploits of our partisans. It is very difficult to fully calculate the damage inflicted by the peasant-warriors on Napoleon's army; but the importance of their actions appears from the fact that in several *Uezd* the enemy lost more than 5,000 men.[18]

The burning of Moscow was one of the main reasons for the development of the guerrilla war. The people, convinced that the French had burnt our capital, longed to take revenge on an impious enemy who had not spared the Moscow shrines, and even those who knew that the enemy had not necessarily burned Moscow were extremely embittered against the French, prompted by a sense of offended national pride, from the Treaty of Tilsit and the enemy invasion. All of Russia was like a huge military camp: no one tended to their property, no one indulged in their usual occupations; everyone was striving to take some part in the sacred cause of the liberation of the motherland; women regarded upon those who hesitated to sacrifice the comforts of life for the common cause with contempt. In every place where reserves and *opolchenie* were formed, increased activity dominated; there was no need for coercion; subordinates were not inferior in diligence to their superiors. Common dangers and common hopes made the Russians members of the same family: people completely unfamiliar with each other, upon receiving favourable news from the

---

16 Collection of the Supreme Manifestos, Charters etc. 47-48.
17 From unpublished notes by Alexander Andreevich Shcherbinin.
18 In the Mosalsk *Uezd*, 987 men were killed and 450 were captured; in that of Medyn 894 were killed and 593 were taken prisoner; in that of Borovsk 2,200 were killed and 1,300 were taken prisoner (extracted from sources held in the Archive of the M.T.D.).

army, hugged each other like brothers and congratulated each other, or wept together about the disasters of the Fatherland. Family misfortunes were brushed aside and it seemed that every emotion was swallowed up in the general grief and thirst for revenge. Many had sacrificed their entire fortunes, not at all out of vanity, and in St Petersburg there were often people who had lost hundreds of thousands in Moscow and had come from there on foot in *sermyaga* and bast shoes, who were glad that their property had perished in the fire, and had not gone to the hated enemy.

Such an enthusiastic state of a powerful, but, for the most part, uneducated, coarse people, sometimes gave rise to the cruel treatment of unarmed enemy. The people who wanted to save themselves were often ruthless to strangers who had come from distant lands in order to devastate Russia. Composed from 20 different nations in 1812, Napoleon's army was not distinguished by discipline, and therefore the Russians, seeing looting, violence and contempt for their shrines at every step, would not have any Christian feelings towards an enemy who trampled upon the objects of their reverence and avenged cruelty with cruelty. Any nation placed in the position in which our compatriots found themselves during the French invasion would have acted no better than ours: let us remember what the guerrillas did in the Iberian Peninsula and the militia under Cardinal Ruffo [Fabrizio Dionigi Ruffo dei duchi di Bagnara e Baranello] in southern Italy, and without burdening the good Russian people with an undeserved reproach for unprecedented hardness of hearts, let us pity humanity, which in the greatest epochs pays the price of its imperfections. At the very least, the Russians can feel good because they did not humiliate themselves with cowardice in a time of trial and that the enemy did not find collaborators anywhere. Only a few foreigners and a handful of native Russians belonging to the lower classes took part in the sessions of the Moscow municipality. Not a single notable personality shamed themselves through servility towards the enemy; none of the Moscow spiritual pastors prayed for Napoleon; several village elders were shot for not wanting to obey the French; the peasants, forced to serve as guides to the enemy, led them astray and perished as victims of their sacred duty. The Russian clergy, following in the footsteps of the great saint, Metropolitan Platon, affirming feelings of self-sacrifice in the Orthodox, sanctified the common cause with a blessing from above. Napoleon's hordes, instead of fighting with our armies, were forced to fight with an entire nation, encountering an abyss that was ready to swallow them up in every location in the vastness of Russia. Ségur himself, recounting the events of 1812, stated:

> Comrades! Let us do justice to the Russians. The sacrifice they made was enormous and absolute. They did not regret their losses and did not demand any reward, even after the occupation of the enemy capital, to which they owed their preservation. They have earned the fame they deserve, and once a more refined education filters down to them, then a great era will come for this great nation, and renown will become their fate.[19]

---

19 Ségur, II, 75.

30

The arrival of reinforcements with Count Wittgenstein's Force

The situation of Count Wittgenstein's force following the first battle of Polotsk. – The composition of the forces on both sides. – The movement of reinforcements to Count Wittgenstein's I Corps. – The departure of the *Opolchenie* from St Petersburg. – Partisan operations. – The arrival of the Finland Corps in Riga. – The situation on the Lower Dvina. – General Essen's operations up until the arrival of the Finland force. – Count Steinheil's operations. – Action at Mesothen. – Steinheil's retreat. – Essen's seizure of Mitau and the Russian retreat to Riga. – Steinheil's advance towards Pridruisk. – Steps taken by Count Wittgenstein to secure lines of communication with the Finland Corps. – The arrival of the St Petersburg *Opolchenie* and their distribution. – The strength of Count Wittgenstein's force in early [mid] October. – The strength of Saint-Cyr's force. – Steps taken by him in the event of an offensive by Russian troops.

After the first battle of Polotsk, the Russian force under Count Wittgenstein was located (as stated at the end of Chapter XIV), from 11 (23) August until 4 (16) October, as follows: the main body of the corps was in positions on the right bank of the river Drissa, at Sivoshina; the reserve was at the Sokolishche-Shchit manor, to where the corps headquarters had also moved; the vanguard was at Beloe. Count Wittgenstein, intending to hold the enemy on the Drissa, gave orders for the position to be strengthened with fieldworks and to bring the city of Sebezh, where the transport and significant warehouses were located, into a defensible state. Lieutenant Colonel Bedryaga remained at Kamenets with the Consolidated Hussar Regiment, on the route from Dünaburg to Rezhitsa [Rēzekne] in order to monitor MacDonald; while the area in front of the corps, in addition to the vanguard, was guarded by detachments sent up the Svolna river to the village of Filipovo, to the village of Gramoshche and along the road leading from Polotsk to Nevel.[1]

Thus, Count Wittgenstein protected our northern capital from the enemy, having secured the routes leading from the Dvina to Novgorod and Pskov. He became a

---

1 Historical Diary of I Corps. *Précis de la campagne du 1er Corps de l'armée d'Occident* (Archive of the M.T.D. No. 29,200).

household name, glorified by the constant successes of our armed forces during the difficult days of the enemy invasion. The Pskov merchants, wanting to express their gratitude to him, sent him an icon of the Holy Miracle-worker, Grand Duke Gabriel of Pskov [Vsevolod of Pskov], in an ornate frame, with the inscription: '*Защитнику Пскова, графу П.Х. Витгенштейну от купцов сего города, сентября 1-го дня, 1812 года.*' [To the Defender of Pskov, Count P. Kh. Wittgenstein from the merchants of this city, September 1 [13], 1812.]. In response to Wittgenstein's report to the Tsar, with regard to permission for him to accept this gift, as a blessing from the citizens of Pskov, a Supreme Rescript was issued with the following content:

> Count Pëtr Khristianovich! I not only permit you to accept the icon of Gabriel the Miracle-worker presented to you by the society of Pskov merchants, with the inscription: Defender of Pskov, but I also praise the merchants who expressed their gratitude to you for this act. The Saintly and Blessed Prince Gabriel has an inscription on his sword: *чести моей никому не отдам*. [I shall surrender my honour to no-one]. Through your defence of Pskov and the fatherland, with the army entrusted to you, you have proved yourself a diligent follower of this principle, and therefore I have no doubt that this saint of God, seeing his icon in your hands, would rejoice in spirit and embrace you from above.[2]

Marshal Saint-Cyr, despite his superiority in troop numbers, did not dare to attack the positions held by Count Wittgenstein. The reasons for this were exaggerated intelligence about the strength of our corps and the extreme fatigue of Saint-Cyr's troops, of whom, according to him, it was impossible to move a single battalion before 10 (22) August. A reconnaissance in force carried out by the Bavarians on this day cost them dearly and did not achieve the intended objective – to push our troops back and occupy more space from which to extract supplies.[3] This experienced marshal, wishing to avoid the over-centralisation of the provisioning department in the corps headquarters, entrusted the business of food supply to the divisional commanders; at the same time, each of the corps had been assigned specific areas for foraging. Saint-Cyr claimed that these measures ensured the correct supply of rations to his troops and contributed to the cessation of looting, but, according to the marshal, his soldiers were exhausted to such an extent that no measures could save them.[4]

In contrast, the troops under Count Wittgenstein, who from the very beginning of the war had everything they needed in abundance, continued to use requisitions from the surrounding countryside and deliveries from the Pskov Governorate. The reinforcements that arrived for our corps not only secured it from offensive operations by Saint-Cyr, but also gave us the opportunity to harass the enemy with

---

2   Count Wittgenstein's report addressed to the Sovereign, dated 7 [19] September, No. 38. Supreme Rescript dated 14 [26] September.
3   Saint-Cyr himself reported: '*l'avant-garde russe resta à Biéloé, la notre à Ghamzeleva.*' *Mémoires pour servir à l'histoire militaire sous le directoire, le consulat et l'empire*, III, 101.
4   Saint-Cyr, *Mémoires*, III, 103-104.

guerrilla operations, which served to further exhaust and weaken the Franco-Bavarian force.[5]

The most important of the reinforcements that arrived at Wittgenstein's I Corps were the *opolchenie* and reserves sent from St Petersburg and Novgorod.

On the basis of the Supreme Orders dated 30 August (11 September), addressed to Adjutant General Meller-Zakomelsky, the St Petersburg *opolchenie*, with units of regular troops attached to them, had the following composition:

1. The detachment under the command of Privy Councillor Bibikov, directed from St Petersburg to Sebezh, via Pskov: Voronezh Infantry Regiment, two battalions. First and Third *opolchenie* brigades, six groups. Attached from Tsarskoe Selo: Grodno Hussars, two squadrons. Poland Ulans, two squadrons.
2. The detachment under Major General Begichev, directed from St Petersburg towards Velikie-Luki via Porkhov: Second, Fourth and Fifth *opolchenie* brigades, nine groups. Mitau Dragoon Regiment, four squadrons. Attached from Gatchina, 1st Marine Regiment, two battalions. Departing a day later; 35th Light Artillery and 49th Light Artillery companies.

The totals for both detachments: 15 St Petersburg *opolchenie* groups, 11,567 men. Voronezh Infantry (1,283) and 1st Marines (1,000), 2,283 men. Mitau Dragoons, 575 men. Grodno Hussars and Poland Ulans, 500 men. 35th Light Artillery and 49th Light Artillery, 346 men.

For a grand total of 15,000 men with 24 guns.[6]

The first detachment departed St Petersburg on 3 (15) September, the very same day as Napoleon occupied the Moscow Kremlin, while the second detachment set off on 5 (17) September. The Tsar was present both times to send off the defenders of the Fatherland. The Metropolitan, approaching the nearest militia column, delivered a speech, blessed the army with the holy icon of the Saviour and handed it to Bibikov, and on the departure of the second detachment, he presented the icon of the Blessed Prince Alexander Nevsky to the warriors. General Begichev, having received the holy image from the hands of the bishop, raised it up and, turning to his detachment, declared: 'Swear it, my lads! as long as you live, you will not abandon him.'

---

5 See the reinforcement schedule for troops that arrived with Count Wittgenstein, indicating the date of their arrival: 7 [19] August: 4th (reserve) Battalion of the Mogilev Infantry Regiment and 23rd Horse Artillery Company. 12 [24] August: Two Lifeguard reserve battalions. 14 [26] August: Colonel Rodionov 2nd's Cossack regiment, returned from detachment to Adjutant General Wintzingerode. 1 & 2 [13 & 14] September: 1,360 convalescents from various regiments (subsequently, some 5,000 more arrived). During September: 1,400 recruits from Novgorod and Velikie-Luki. 28 September [10 October]: The first detachment of the St Petersburg *opolchenie*, with the troops accompanying them. 2 [4] October: second detachment of the St Petersburg *opolchenie*, with the troops accompanying them. 8 [20] October: two groups of Novgorod opolchenie and the Teptyar Cossack regiment (later four more groups arrived).
6 Strength returns dated 3 and 5 [15 and 17] September, from the notes by Senator Bibikov and Major General Begichev (archive of the M.T.D. No. 46,692, folio 2).

'We shall not abandon him!' the warriors answered, making the sign of the cross. 'We are glad to die for our faith and our paternal Tsar.' The people, gathered in crowds, accompanied their defenders with resounding cheers. The Tsar himself, having let all the columns pass by, caught up with the first platoon, stopped it and expressed his hopes for the diligence of the *opolchenie* in a short speech; in response to their adored Monarch, thousands of voices unanimously exclaimed: 'Happy to strive! glad to die!' Many of the inhabitants of the capital escorted the warriors to their first halt, at the 'Four Arms' [now Victory Square in St Petersburg].[7]

When departing on campaign, the warriors received: two-month's pay and ten-day's of rations; while the unit commanders and all field officers and subalterns, received a cash allowance for their commission and initial uniform. As the procurement of provisions and fodder could not be carried out by the units themselves, the commander of Second District of the *opolchenie*, Adjutant General Mellor-Zakomelsky, petitioned for the release of supplies in kind from the treasury.[8]

On 4 (16) September, a Supreme order was issued to Meller-Zakomelsky to strengthen the force under Count Wittgenstein with four to five thousand warriors from the Novgorod *opolchenie*.

The St Petersburg *opolchenie* arrived with the corps just before the second battle of Polotsk and participated in it (as will be described later); while the Novgorod *opolchenie* arrived after the battle.[9]

Guerrilla warfare was waged throughout the halt on the Drissa river by Wittgenstein's force, from 11 (23) August to 4 (16) October. On 20 August (1 September), intelligence was received by the corps headquarters about the appearance of the enemy in significant strength near Drissa, which forced Colonel Rodionov 2nd, who had arrived from the troops of First Army not long before, to search from Gramoshche to this location. The detachment entrusted to him consisted of his eponymous Cossack regiment, two squadrons of the Consolidated Lifeguard Regiment and one squadron of Riga Dragoons. The valiant Rodionov crossed over the Dvina, near Drissa on 22 August (3 September), and, catching up with a march battalion and a squadron of the *7e chasseurs à cheval*, took them by surprise, defeated them, captured more than 50 men and returned to Gramoshche. After that, turning in the direction of Nevel and adding three squadrons from the Riga, Dragoons, Ingermanland Dragoons and Yamburg Dragoons to his detachment, previously sent to him under the command of retired artillery Lieutenant Colonel Nepeitsyn [Sergey Vasilevich Nepeitsyn], Rodionov scattered several enemy patrols, and on 9 (21) September, at Kozyany, defeated quite a significant enemy detachment and pursued them for seven *versts*. More than 180 men were taken prisoner by our forces in these actions, including one field officer and four subalterns; the enemy lost some 300 men killed, while the *3e chevau-légers lanciers* suffered particularly badly. On

---

7 Notes on the establishment and campaigns of the St Petersburg *opolchenie* in 1812 and 1813, written by naval captain-lieutenant [Lieutenant Commander] B.V. Sht. I, 80-87. Stories, by R. Zotov.
8 Adjutant General Meller-Zakomelsky's report to the Tsar, dated 29 August [10 September]. Schedule for the St Petersburg *opolchenie*, from the same report (archive of the M.T.D. No. 46,692, folio 2).
9 War Diary of I Independent Corps.

our side, nine men were killed and 35 wounded. Rodionov's force captured some 5,000 *Chetvert* of flour and oats, more than 1,000 baked loaves, 40 barrels of wine and 1,000 head of cattle in Kozyany; all these stores were destroyed for lack of transport, except for the cattle and bread.[10]

Retired Lieutenant Colonel Nepeitsyn and Major (soon to be promoted one rank) Bedryaga became no less renowned for their partisan exploits. The former of these, having lost a leg during the assault on Ochakov [1788], returned to service from retirement in 1812 and, having received command of a small detachment, became a hammer of the enemy; while Bedryaga, operating independently for almost the entire campaign, distinguished himself through bold raids and earned the praise of Count Wittgenstein on more than one occasion.

On 7th (19th) September, Count Wittgenstein received the Supreme Command, in which the intentions of Emperor Alexander I were outlined regarding the participation of the troops of I Corps in the execution of the general plan of action. As has been stated previously, having been strengthened by reinforcements on the march to him, he received the mission to attack Polotsk along both banks of the Dvina, to eject the enemy corps from this city and pursue them in the direction of Sventsiany; thereafter, entrusting the further pursuit of the defeated enemy to the corps under Count Steinheil reinforced by part of the Riga garrison, he was to turn towards Dokshitsy, establish himself on the Ula river and by 10 (22) October, was to have established communications with the troops under Admiral Chichagov, and cut the line of retreat of Napoleon's *Grande Armée*.

In accordance with the general plan of action, issued on 18 (30) August by Supreme command to the force commander in Finland, Lieutenant General Count Steinheil, he was to go to Riga with a corps composed of three infantry and one jäger regiments from 6th Division, four infantry and two jäger regiments from 21st Division, the Finland Dragoons and Loshchilin's Cossack Regiment. The infantry and jäger regiments were intended to comprise one over-strength battalion, for which the first battalions of each regiment were to be brought up to strength with privates from the other field battalions remaining in Finland and reduced to a cadre of field officers, subalterns, non-commissioned officers and musicians.[11]

The composition of the corps assigned to depart to Riga was:

Infantry:
6th Division, under the command of Major General Rakhmanov [Vasily Sergeevich Rakhmanov]: Azov Infantry Regiment; Nizov Infantry Regiment; Bryansk Infantry Regiment (on the Åland islands, did not arrive); 3rd Jäger Regiment.

---

10 Colonel Rodionov 2nd's report to Count Wittgenstein, dated 9 [21] September, No. 1439. Count Wittgenstein's report to the Tsar, dated 13 [25] September, No. 45. Saint-Cyr, *Mémoires*, III, 112-118. In a report on the action at Kozyany, Colonel Rodionov 2nd wrote: 'We captured: Lieutenant Colonel and chevalier Tinel, two captains, two lieutenants, four military commissars and about 150 *chasseurs à cheval* and other lower ranks, and every single one of them are genuine Frenchmen.'
11 Supreme orders to Count Steinheil, dated 18 (30) August.

21st Division, under the command of Major General Alekseev [Ilya Ivanovich Alekseev]: Neva Infantry Regiment; Petrov Infantry Regiment; Lithuania Infantry Regiment; Podolsk Infantry Regiment; 2nd Jäger Regiment; 44th Jäger Regiment (on the Åland islands, did not arrive).

Cavalry: Finland Dragoon Regiment; Loshchilin's Cossack Regiment.

Artillery: 21st Battery Artillery Company (one half-company did not arrive); 11th Light Artillery Company.

These troops were assigned to embark in Helsingfors, Åbo and on the island of Åland, and, having landed in Reval, to continue their further advance on Riga by land, because a landing at the latter location presented great difficulties. On 24 and 25 August (5 and 6 September), part of the embarked force sailed from the harbour at Helsingfors; some of the departed ships, being caught in a powerful storm on the night of the 26 [7 September], sank with 179 dragoons, 110 Cossacks and six guns, all those who were aboard; after that, on the 26 [7 September], at seven o'clock in the morning, Count Steinheil sailed with the rest of the regiments, except for one sent from Åbo, and by 28 August (9 September) his entire corps had already landed in Reval. The number of troops in it were significantly fewer than assigned in the general operational plan, both due to the tragedy with the first transport, and due to the non-arrival of the Bryansk Infantry and 44th Jäger regiments from Åland, a deficit of 2,630 men.[12] The troops under Count Steinheil, having disembarked numbering 10,159,[13] were immediately sent to Riga in several echelons and linked up near this city on 10 (22) September.

The situation on the lower Dvina had not changed since the start of operations. MacDonald remained inactive at Dünaburg with the division under Grandjean [Charles Louis Dieudonné Grandjean], numbering 12,000 men, while the Prussian troops, who had arrived at the beginning of August (new style) under the command of General Yorck, stood near Riga, confining themselves to monitoring this fortress. General Essen 1st tried twice to push them back: on 26 July (7 August), our troops attacked the left wing of the Prussian detachment and captured the Schlock [Sloka] settlement, but then were driven out from there. On 10 (22) August, General Essen again moved against the enemy line extending for 40 *versts*, from Schlock, through Olai [Olaine], to Dahlenkirchen [near Ķekava]: our right column drove them out of Schlock, while our left column seized Dahlenkirchen in battle; the losses of the Prussian force in prisoners alone reached 650, and overall exceeded a thousand men; 600 men were killed or wounded on our side: among those killed was Lieutenant Colonel Tiedemann [Karl Ludwig Heinrich von Tiedemann], who at the beginning of the war had transferred into our service from the Prussian General Staff. Two days later, Essen evacuated both locations and withdrew his troops into the fortress.[14]

---

12 A short description of the military operations by the Finland Corps (archive of the M.T.D. No. 15,302).

13 Lieutenant General Count Steinheil's report to the Tsar, dated 27 August [8 September], from Reval.

14 General Essen 1st's report to the Tsar, dated 12 [24] August, No. 34. Chambray, I, 258.

MacDonald, having received news of the attempted sortie by the Riga garrison, sent Hünerbein's [Friedrich Heinrich Karl Georg Freiherr von Hünerbein] brigade (formerly Ricard's [Étienne Pierre Sylvestre Ricard]) to Friedrichstadt [Jaunjelgava] to support Yorck if necessary, while he remained at Dünaburg himself, with the other two brigades from Grandjean's division.[15]

Following this, General Essen undertook a demonstration towards Danzig in order to delay, albeit for a short time, the movement (as he perceived) of enemy troops sent to assist Saint-Cyr and the *Grande Armée*. To that end, British Rear Admiral Martin [Sir Thomas Byam Martin], by agreement with General Essen, set off on 9 (21) August with a squadron consisting of the warship HMS *Aboukir*, several frigates and transport ships, with 400 men from 30th Jägers and two guns under the command of *Flügel-Adjutant* Colonel Balabin [Pëtr Ivanovich Balabin]. Contrary winds, dead calm and the poor progress of some transports prevented the squadron from arriving off Danzig before 19 (31) August. Rear Admiral Martin sailed inshore under a Swedish flag to give his ships the appearance of the vanguard of a Russo-Swedish amphibious force. Their appearance caused great alarm in the city and forced the enemy to bring troops from Pillau [Baltiysk] and Memel [Klaipėda] towards Danzig. Having achieved his objective, Martin sailed back to Riga.[16]

Upon the arrival of Finland Corps in Riga, misunderstandings arose between Essen and Count Steinheil, because the former, being senior in service, considered himself offended by the appointment of Steinheil as the commander of all troops assigned to the expedition and asked to be relieved.[17] Meanwhile, on the basis of the Supreme order to Count Steinheil, they began to clear the enemy from the lower reaches of the Dvina. But it turned out that instead of the 20,000 men under General Löwis's command from the Riga garrison, who were supposed to assist Steinheil, it was impossible to detach more than 11,600 men with 12 guns from the garrison to support him. Only 5,135 men remained to guard Riga and Dünamünde [Daugavgrīva]. Consequently, instead of the 35,000 men listed in the general plan of action, our generals would have only 22,000 with whom to achieve the stated objectives.[18]

The first three days following the arrival of Finland Corps, were spent resupplying them with ammunition and rations for ten days. Thereafter, on 14 (26) September, our troops set off to face the enemy. The immediate operational objective, according to Essen, should be the occupation of Mitau; 'as the centre of the French administration in Courland.' In contrast, Count Steinheil believed that first of all it was necessary to take possession of the enemy siege artillery park, which at that time was stationed at Ruhenthal [Rundāle], near Bauska, 70 *versts* from Riga. As a consequence of this divergence of opinions, the forces assigned to the expedition were divided into three different directions: Möller's flotilla [Anton Vasilevich Moller or

---

15 Chambray, I, 258-259.
16 *Flügel-Adjutant* Colonel Balabin's report to Count Arakcheev, dated 1 [13] September.
17 Lieutenant General Essen 1st's report to the Tsar, dated 4 [16] September, No. 48.
18 Lieutenant General Essen 1st's report addressed to the Minister of War, dated 13 [25] September, No. 723, with an annex containing the troop strength returns (archive of the M.T.D. No. 46,692, att. 123).

Berend Otto von Möller], sailing from Dünamünde, along the Bolder-Aa [Buḷḷupe], on 15 (27) September, sailed to Wilderlingshof, where, at the same time, Lieutenant General Briseman von Netting [Ivan Ivanovich Briseman von Netting] had arrived by land, with 1,850 infantry, 30 dragoons, 50 Cossacks and four guns, for combined operations against the enemy troops occupying Schlock, together with the flotilla, and for the continued advance on Mitau; Colonel Baron Rosen [Fëdor Fëdorovich Rosen] was directed on Olai with 1,000 men, in order to seize the causeway on the route between Riga and Mitau; the main column, consisting of the entire Finland Corps and the rest of Löwis's troops, totalling 18,000 infantry and 1,300 cavalry, with 23 guns, on 14 (26) September, assembled on the Bauska road. On that same day, the vanguard, consisting of four battalions, three squadrons and 500 Cossacks, with six guns, totalling 3,000 men,[19] advanced to Flamenhof, drove off the Prussian outpost there and drove the detachment totalling 2,500 men under Colonel Horn [Heinrich Wilhelm von Horn] out of Dahlenkirchen, capturing three officers and 150 lower ranks and leaving more than 20 men on the field of battle; on our side, the casualties were much fewer. By evening, our main body was located at Dahlenkirchen, having sent detachments out along the road to Olai, as far as Plakanciems, and along the road to Friedrichstadt as far as Bersemünde [Bērzmente].

General Yorck, who was at Olai with the main body of his corps, withdrew most of them towards Eckau [Iecava], ordered Horn to retreat there and take up a rather advantageous position behind the river. On 15 (27) September, Count Steinheil moved against the enemy with the main body from the front, having detached Colonel Traskin [Semën Ivanovich Traskin], with two battalions and a platoon of dragoons, to Baldohn [Baldone], enveloping the right flank of the enemy position. Our troops crossed the river via a ford, which forced Yorck to retreat to Bauska with the loss of 120 prisoners.

General Yorck, realising that the force assembled by him at Bauska could not stop the advance of our corps, ordered Hünerbein's brigade, totalling 3,000 men, stationed at Friedrichstadt, and General Kleist [Friedrich Emil Ferdinand Heinrich von Kleist], with five battalions and three squadrons, totalling more than 4,000 men who held Mitau, to link up with him.

Meanwhile, as General Yorck was taking measures to concentrate his forces, on our side, on 16 (28) September, by order of General Essen, Colonel Eckeln was detached via Garoza, with two jäger battalions and 50 dragoons (Steinheil's war diary says, with 3,000 infantry, a platoon of dragoons and six guns), to assist other detachments previously sent to Mitau, to where Essen himself had set off. The force under Count Steinheil, totalling 15,000 infantry, 1,000 cavalry and 18 guns, moved towards Zohden [Code], sending the vanguard, under the command of Colonel Gerngross [Rodion Fëdorovich Gerngross or Renatus Samuel August von Gerngroß], towards Bauska. Whereupon, General Yorck, fearing that our troops, having crossed the river Aa [Lielupe], might take possession of the parks stationed at

---

19 The composition of the vanguard was: 3rd Jäger Battalion, replacement battalions of 4th Jägers, 20th Jägers and 21st Jägers, three squadrons of Finland Dragoons, 200 of Selivanov's Cossacks and 300 of Loshchilin's Cossacks, six guns from 11th Light Artillery Company (from Count Steinheil's report to General Essen 1st, dated 25 September [7 October], No. 165).

Ruhenthal, having decided, to protect them, would go to Mesothen [Mežotne] and settled down at this location, on the morning of 17 (29) September, on the right bank of the Aa, assigning Kleist's detachment that had arrived from Mitau, to the defence of the left bank, and keeping communications with him via the bridge in Mesothen and the fords on the Aa. The vanguard under Colonel Gerngross, taking advantage of the departure of the Prussian troops from Bauska, occupied this city, while a newly composed vanguard, under the command of Major General Velyaminov [Ivan Aleksandrovich Velyaminov], was located near Mesothen, within sight of Yorck's main body covering the parks at Ruhenthal. Heavy rain that continued throughout the day kept both sides inactive.

On 17 (29) September, Count Steinheil, having received intelligence about a significant strengthening of the enemy and having seen the strength of their positions behind the Aa river, decided to envelope them from the left flank, towards Zemgale [Semgallen], and ordered Gerngross to evacuate Bauska and rejoin the main body, which was done after the destruction of the Bauska magazines. Meanwhile, Yorck ordered General Massenbach [Eberhard Friedrich Fabian von Massenbach] to attack the Russians on the right bank; for his part, Steinheil, not abandoning his intention to outflank the enemy, ordered Major General Belgard [Alexander Alexandrovich Belgard], with the Azov Infantry and Nizov Infantry battalions and six guns from 11th Light Artillery Company, to cross via the ford at Zemgale and attack the Prussian position. At six o'clock in the evening, our troops attacked along the left bank of the river; Kleist's brigade was sent to hold them back. After a heated engagement, Belgard was forced to retreat to the right bank of the river with heavy losses.[20] The failure of our attack and the significant enemy superiority in cavalry and artillery forced Count Steinheil and Löwis to abandon further operations and retreat to Riga. In order to form a rearguard, the former vanguard was reinforced by the Petrov Infantry battalion, the detachment under Colonel Gerngross, who had arrived from Bauska, and part of the Riga Corps, and was entrusted to Major General Foch [Alexander Borisovich Foch]. At dawn on 18 (30) September, our main body began to retreat to Garoza. At five o'clock in the morning, the enemy attacked General Foch with their entire force, supported by the fire of 50 guns. The open country favoured operations by the numerous enemy cavalry, which we could only counter with two squadrons of Finland Dragoons, but the heroic resistance of 3rd Jäger Regiment allowed us to retreat to Annenburg [Emburga] without further losses, where the forested hills made it difficult for the enemy to advance further. Count Steinheil, having left Major General Velyaminov in the rearguard, with the Neva Infantry and Petrov Infantry battalions, the dragoons and Cossacks, retreated via Garoza to Olai, where he gathered up all the detachments sent to Mitau, who had occupied this city without meeting any resistance on 17 (29) September, capturing four brass

---

20 Liebenstein, *Der Krieg Napoleons gegen Russland in den Jahren 1812-1813*, II, 134. Liebenstein wrote that, during the attack on the position at Mesothen, the Russian force lost 500 prisoners and that the Black Hussars, pursuing our troops, destroyed the 3rd Jäger Regiment (battalion?) and the replacement battalion of the 25th Jägers. But this is contradicted by the returns for the number of troops in Finland Corps, dated 22 September [4 October] (five days after the action at Mesothen), from which it is clear that the total for 3rd Jägers was 614 men.

guns and destroying a large amount of provisions and commissariat stores collected by the enemy there, and then, when word came regarding Steinheil's and Löwis's retreat, they withdrew to rejoin them in Olai. On 19 September (1 October), our rearguard, being attacked at Garoza, repelled the enemy, where the artillery (six guns from 11th Light Artillery Company) under the command of Lieutenant Gerbel [Karl Gustavovich Gerbel (Härbel)] distinguished itself in particular. On the following day [2 October new style], all the troops participating in the expedition retreated to Riga, where the flotilla also returned. Our combat losses from 14 (26) September to 19 September (1 October), reached 1,900 killed or missing and 578 wounded. The enemy losses in prisoners alone consisted of three officers and 400 lower ranks.[21]

The expedition that we had undertaken to clear the lower Dvina of enemy did not achieve the intended objective, but forced MacDonald to move from Dünaburg to Bauska with the rest of Grandjean's division, and prevented him from assisting Saint-Cyr during the subsequent offensive by Count Wittgenstein towards Polotsk. Napoleon was very pleased with the Prussian troops, who, in doing their duty, fought very bravely for the oppressor they detested, but the valour they displayed was a foretaste of what could be expected from Prussian efforts in defence of Germany.

Upon the retreat of the Russian troops to Riga, both sides reoccupied their former positions. Count Steinheil, being unable to agree with General Essen on future plans, decided to go along the right bank of the Dvina to Pridruisk [Piedruja] and cross over to the left bank of this river in order to assist Count Wittgenstein.[22]

Emperor Alexander I, having received a report from Lieutenant General Essen about the unsuccessful offensive by our troops, expressed His displeasure to Count Steinheil, making the following comments to him:

1. 'If you foresaw that the corps entrusted to you was in too weak a condition for operations before the arrival of the rest of the regiments from Reval, then you should have waited for them.
2. In the same vein, I find it mistaken of you to leave some of the troops in Mitau when there was no need, because at that very moment the enemy troops had already left this city, which is why I consider this useless fragmentation of your corps the cause of this failure.'[23]

After receiving the report from Count Steinheil regarding the course of action taken by his force along the right bank of the Dvina, the Tsar expressed His opinion with the following rescript:

---

21 Lieutenant General Count Steinheil's report to Lieutenant General Essen 1st, dated 25 September [7 October], No. 165. Brief notes on the military operations by Finland Corps. General Essen 1st's reports to the Tsar: dated 13 [25] September, from Riga; 17 and 18 [29 and 30] September, from Mitau; 21 and 22 September [3 and 4 October], from Riga. Count Steinheil's report to the Tsar, dated 22 September [4 October]. Liebenstein, II, 132-134. According to him, the losses to the Prussian force did not exceed 1,000 men, while the Russians lost from 4,000 to 5,000.
22 Brief notes on the military operations by Finland Corps. Count Steinheil's report to the Tsar, dated 22 September [4 October].
23 Extract from the Supreme Rescript addressed to Count Steinheil, dated 24 September [6 October].

In response to your report, about the impossibility of operating independently with the corps entrusted to you and about the change in the plan of operations, undertaken by you in the direction along the right bank of the Dvina to Druya, I find it necessary to remind you that the corps, which set out from Riga on 14 [26] September, for operations against Mitau and Eckau, amounted, according to my calculations (excluding the final troops that did not arrive from Reval), to over 20,000, therefore, it could be assumed with certainty that this number of regular Russian troops could successfully fight against an equal number of enemy assembled from various nations. In military enterprises, hedging measures are very rarely successful. Their very moderation and frugality often prevents success,[24] especially with the splitting of forces, as was done in this case, leaving a detachment in Mitau, and another at Schlock. Due to the remoteness at which I find myself, however, and due to the inconvenience of changing your direction, I cannot give you any further instructions other than to express My desire that your new operations should be crowned with better results; since, without this, the implementation of the overall plan of operations will not achieve its real objectives.[25]

Having resupplied Finland Corps with ammunition and provisions, Count Steinheil marched from Riga on 23 September (5 October), with his force, totalling 8,200 infantry, 530 dragoons and Cossacks, 270 artillerymen and 40 pioneers, in total: 9,000 men with 18 guns. The advance from Riga, through Erlaa [Ērgļi] and Prely [Preiļi], to Pridruisk, over 280 *versts*, was carried out by forced marches in 11 days. On 4 (16) October (on the same day that Count Wittgenstein resumed offensive operations with his main force), the troops of Finland Corps, having crossed the bridge over the Dvina at Pridruisk, moved along the left bank of this river to continue the advance against the enemy corps occupying Polotsk. Count Wittgenstein, for his part, having it in mind to establish communications with Steinheil's force, ordered Lieutenant Colonel Bedryaga to arrive in Pridruisk by 1 (13) October with the Consolidated Hussar Regiment stationed at Kamenets, and, crossing the Dvina there, move up the left bank of the river, as the vanguard of Finland Corps approaching the Dvina; Major Bellingshausen was sent to Disna with two consolidated infantry regiments and four guns from 23rd Horse Artillery Company, where they were to cross the Dvina, over bridges laid by Colonel Count Sievers, and, having united his detachment with Bedryaga's regiment, was to join the vanguard of Finland Corps, along left bank of the Dvina, towards Polotsk.[26]

Not long before, the troops under Count Wittgenstein had been reinforced by the St Petersburg *opolchenie* and the regular troops accompanying them.

---

24 Even Napoleon said: 'half-measures are the most harmful in military affairs.' *Mémoires de Gourgaud*.
25 Supreme Rescript to Count Steinheil, dated 26 September [8 October].
26 Historical journal of the operations by I Independent Corps. Extracts selected from reports to the Tsar by Count Wittgenstein (archive of the M.T.D. No. 44,585).

The detachment under Senator Bibikov, as mentioned above, had departed from St Petersburg on 3 (15) September and arrived in Pskov on the 16th (28 September). The people of Pskov, who had made so many sacrifices for the troops of I Corps and for the transport of the wounded and sick to hospitals, welcomed these new soldiers as their defenders. The fervour of the warriors for the common cause and the desire to take revenge on the enemy reached its extreme limit the next day [29 September new style], when the fateful news of the occupation of Moscow by the French spread. On 18 (30) September, Bibikov, having received an order from Count Wittgenstein to speed up the advance of the detachment, set out from Pskov and arrived in Opochka on the 22 (4 October). The next day [5 October new style], having received new orders to proceed directly to Sokolishche, and to send only one unit to Sebezh, Bibikov went to the corps headquarters. Count Wittgenstein congratulated him on becoming the commander of the St Petersburg and Novgorod *opolchenie* and suggested that the units, during combat, be attached to infantry regiments in the role of reserves. On the 28th (10 October), at three o'clock in the afternoon, the detachment linked up with the main body of the corps. The Voronezh Infantry Regiment joined the second line; two squadrons of the Poland Ulan Regiment were assigned to the Combined Lifeguard Regiment; the 1st, 2nd, 3rd, 7th and 9th *opolchenie* groups were assigned to infantry regiments in 14th Division and to the jägers of 5th Division; the 8th *opolchenie* group, with the exception of two *sotnia* detached to Sebezh under the command of Major General Kutuzov; while Lieutenant Colonel Chernoevich was sent to Pridruisk, with two *sotnia* from 9th *opolchenie* group in order to build bridges over which Count Steinheil's corps was intended to cross.[27]

The detachment under Major General Begichev, departing from St Petersburg on 5 (17) September, took their third rest day on the 13 (25 September) at the Feofilova Hermitage. Here the news was received that Moscow had been occupied by the enemy. At first, a gloomy despondency took possession of the warriors, but then it was replaced by a thirst for revenge. They were concerned that a humiliating peace might be concluded and wished for an early engagement with the enemy. On the 16 (28 September), the detachment arrive in Porkhov; On the 20 (2 October), during a 42 *verst* stage, along a muddy road to the village of Pochaevo, the warriors met a detachment under Lieutenant Colonel Nepeitsyn, who was escorting French prisoners. 'Take a look, lads,' he said, 'I am missing one leg, but I have already managed to beat the fiends; see that you try your best.'

'No doubt, father,' answered the warriors, 'let us not fall into the hands of shame: if God would only let us get at them.'

On the 22 (4 October), General Begichev went to the corps headquarters. The next day [5 October new style], the detachment arrive in Velikie-Luki, where a two-day rest was scheduled. The inhabitants greeted their defenders with extraordinary cordiality. The merchants, even before the arrival of the *opolchenie*, agreed among themselves not to take money from the warriors for anything; the militiamen, for their part, did not maliciously exploit the selflessness of the inhabitants of the city, being content with the refreshments offered. On the 28th (10 October),

---

27 Notes on the establishment and campaign of the St Petersburg *opolchenie*, B.V. Sht. I, 90-98. Historical journal of the operations by I Independent Corps.

the detachment arrived in Nevel, where they were reunited with their commander and during the day received seven-days of rations, took an issue of wine and put their weapons in good working order. All the carts, except for ammunition caissons and infirmary carts, were left in the city, under escort of 15th *opolchenie* group. Major General Alekseev was detached against the enemy marauders who had devastated the neighbourhood of Gorodok with his Mitau Dragoons and 1st Marine Regiment, 15th Group of the St Petersburg *opolchenie* and six guns of 49th Light Artillery Company; while two squadrons of Yamburg Dragoons joined Begichev's detachment. On 1 (13) October, Begichev settled down at the Krasnopolye manor, waiting for the detachment under Major General Diebitsch 2nd [Ivan Ivanovich Diebitsch-Zabalkansky or Hans Karl Friedrich Anton von Diebitsch und Narten] to join him, consisting of four combined grenadier battalions from 5th Division and 14th Division, three battalions of the Combined Jäger Regiment, the replacement battalion of the Polotsk Infantry Regiment, four dragoon squadrons and six guns from 49th Light Artillery Company.[28]

Upon the arrival of these reinforcements to the force under Count Wittgenstein, their overall numbers reached: Infantry 20,800 men; Cavalry 5,460 men; Artillerymen 2,737 men; *Opolchenie* 10,360 men; Pioneers 144 men; Pontoniers (less pontoons) 345 men.

For a total of 39,846 men with 152 guns.[29] The number of troops that arrived with the corps after the first battle of Polotsk, not counting the returned convalescent sick and wounded, reached: Infantry 3,600 men; Cavalry 1,230 men; Artillerymen 1,026 men; *Opolchenie* 10,360 men; Total: 16,216 men.[30]

With 60 guns. In addition, 1,400 recruits arrived from Novgorod and Velikie Luki.

Taking into account that after the first battle of Polotsk the strength of Count Wittgenstein's force did not exceed 15,000 men, it appears that between 6,000 and 7,000 convalescents arrived in August and September. Consequently, the corps under Count Wittgenstein, over a period of about two months, was increased by 23,000, or 25,000 men, and together with Finland Corps moving to assist them, the number of Russian troops on the Dvina increased by 33,000, or 34,000 men and reached some 49,000 men overall, not counting the Riga garrison and the Novgorod *opolchenie* that had not yet arrived, totalling about 12,000 warriors and recruits.

---

28 Notes on the establishment and campaign of the St Petersburg *opolchenie*, B.V. Sht. I, 101-109. Historical journal of the operations by I Independent Corps. Interview with R. Zotov.
29 These numbers were extracted from strength returns for the composition of I Independent Corps (M.T.D. No. 29,200), dated 4 [16] October 1812, and is somewhat different from the returns placed in the work by Buturlin, in which the number of troops under Count Wittgenstein, on 4 [16] October, is shown as 37,944 men.
30 Following the first battle of Polotsk, by 4 (16) October, arrivals were: 4th Battalion, Mogilev Infantry Regiment, 244 men; 23rd Horse Artillery Company, 50th Battery Artillery Company, 35th, 49th and 57th Light Artillery companies, 1,026 men; Two reserve Lifeguard battalions, 847 men; Voronezh Infantry & 1st Marine regiments, 2,164 men; 1st & 2nd Pontoon companies (Without pontoons, whose carts were used to deliver a mobile magazine), 345 men; Two squadrons of Poland Ulans, 325 men; Mitau Dragoon Regiment, 575 men; Rodionov's Cossack Regiment, 330 men; Fifteen groups of St Petersburg *opolchenie*, 10,360 men.

In contrast, during the two-month occupation of Polotsk, the force under Saint-Cyr had weakened numerically. Saint-Cyr stated that in the middle of October (new style), the number of troops in *2e Corps* did not exceed 15,572 men, while *6e Corps* had 1,823 men, therefore, overall, about 17,400 men. According to the testimony of Saint-Cyr himself, after the first battle at Polotsk, there were 29,000 men in both of his corps, of whom some 6,000 soldiers were convalescents returned from hospitals,[31] therefore, accepting his testimony about the number of these troops in October as accurate, it emerges that in the course of two months, they lost more than 17,000 men to disease and in actions against our partisans. It follows from this that either the partisans under Count Wittgenstein inflicted extraordinary losses on the French, or the logistics department for the administration of Saint-Cyr's force was in an unusually poor state, or finally, that Saint-Cyr, wanting to justify the failure of his operations, deliberately presented a smaller number of troops than were present in reality. The latter assumption is confirmed by the evidence of the most unbiased of all French historians of the war of 1812, Chambray, who wrote that in the middle of October (new style) Saint-Cyr had 22,000 in *2e Corps*, and 5,000 in *6e Corps*, a total of 27,000 men, of whom 4,000 were cavalry. All these troops consisted of experienced, veteran soldiers, but the Bavarians, not inferior in valour to the French, were incapable of enduring the labours and hardships of war.[32]

The appearance of strong Russian detachments near Gorodok and Disna, on the flanks of the Franco-Bavarian forces' locations, indicated Count Wittgenstein's intentions of entering into a decisive conflict, or to cross to the left bank of the Dvina and move into the rear of the corps occupying positions around Polotsk. Saint-Cyr, having superior forces facing him, was forced to attend to fortifying his position and vigilant monitoring of the left bank of the river. The number of troops at the disposal of the French commander did not allow him to hold an extensive frontage, and therefore he limited himself to the construction of entrenchments of a rather weak profile, to protect the city on the right bank of the Polota, and the construction of a barrier of palisades, flanked by redans, on the left bank of the river. Most of this work was completed in time through the efforts of the engineer General Dode de la Brunerie [Guillaume Dode de la Brunerie], who was as skilful as he was active. In order to reconnoitre everything happening on the left bank of the Dvina and to prevent a surprise envelopment, the entire cavalry was sent there, under the command of Generals Doumerc [Jean-Pierre Doumerc] and Corbineau [Jean-Baptiste Juvénal Corbineau], with the exception of five squadrons left in positions forwards of Polotsk. At the same time, the heavy baggage and all the sick who remained in the city were sent behind the Dvina.[33]

Even before the resumption of operations around Polotsk, *9e Corps* under Marshal Victor had arrived in the theatre of war, and was assigned to form the reserve of Napoleon's *Grande Armée* and to support the corps operating on the Dvina, if necessary.

---

31 Chambray, II, 173.
32 Saint-Cyr, *Mémoires*, III, 129-130. Chambray, II, 173-174.
33 Saint-Cyr, *Mémoires*, III, 120-121 & 131-133. Chambray, II, 175.

Victor's force, consisting of 41 battalions and 15 squadrons, with 80 guns, totalling 28,000 infantry, 2,000 cavalry and 1,000 artillerymen, assembled at Tilsit on 9 August (new style), settled in the vicinity of this city and remained static for three weeks. At the end of August, the corps was ordered to set out on a further campaign, taking with it a twenty-day supply of rations and fodder, on peasant horses, which required 42 carts for each battalion. The result of such a huge task during the working hours was the complete devastation of the region, and was of no use to the troops, as a significant part of the stores fell behind the corps. Victor's force moved to Kovno, from where one battalion was sent to occupy Pillau, and continuing to proceed via Vilna and Minsk, arriving in Smolensk on 16 (28) September. In each of these cities and in the town of Dubrowna, the corps had rest days, but they gave little benefit to the soldiers, because the troops were stationed in bivouacs at a considerable distance from the magazines, and were almost as exhausted from being sent for provisions as if they had been made to march another stage.[34] During the four-week march from Tilsit to Smolensk, many men and horses died from malnutrition and cool nights interspersed with very hot days; many of the horses that fell on the road, contaminating the air with harmful gases, contributed to the spread of disease and death. A significant number of men remained in hospitals, where poor facilities robbed the sick of any hope for recovery. The artillery was forced to leave guns and ammunition wagons behind them and, in spite of this, upon arrival in Smolensk, they still did not have a sufficient number of horses.

Upon reaching Smolensk, Victor's troops were located in the vicinity of this city, where they were able to obtain provisions. But the stocks collected there were very meagre: the infantry, instead of bread or hard-tack, received stale flour in insufficient quantities; while the cavalry and artillery, foraging in large detachments over a considerable area, found fodder and provisions. Despite the scarcity of these resources, the troops under Victor, having encountered marauders from the *Grande Armée* in a most miserable condition at every step during their movement to Smolensk, took note of their situation and maintained order and discipline in their ranks. During the two-week stay at Smolensk, the soldiers managed to repair their clothing and equipment, which would be especially important as the harsh season approached.

The arrival of reinforcements with Count Wittgenstein forced Marshal Victor to send some of his troops closer to the corps under Saint-Cyr. To that end, the division under Daendels [Herman Willem Daendels], departing from the Smolensk area on 11 October (new style), arrived in Babinovichy on 3 (15) October. At the same time, the division under General Partouneaux [Louis de Partouneaux] and the cavalry of *9e Corps* were located near Mstislavl, for the most convenient foraging, while the division under Girard [Jean-Baptiste Girard] remained in Smolensk. The overall troop strength of *9e Corps* reached some 25,000 men.[35]

---

34 *Beitrag zu der Geschichte des neunten Corps der französischen Armée im Feldzug gegen Russland 1812, mit einen Anhang in besonderer Beziehung auf die Geschichte der grossherzoglich Badenschen Truppen. Oestreich. milit. Zeitschrift*, 1821, 3 Heft.
35 *Beitrag zu der Geschichte des neunten Corps der französischen Armée im Feldzug gegen Russland 1812, mit einen Anhang in besonderer Beziehung auf die Geschichte der grossherzoglich Badenschen Truppen. Oestreich. milit. Zeitschrift*, 1821, 3 Heft.

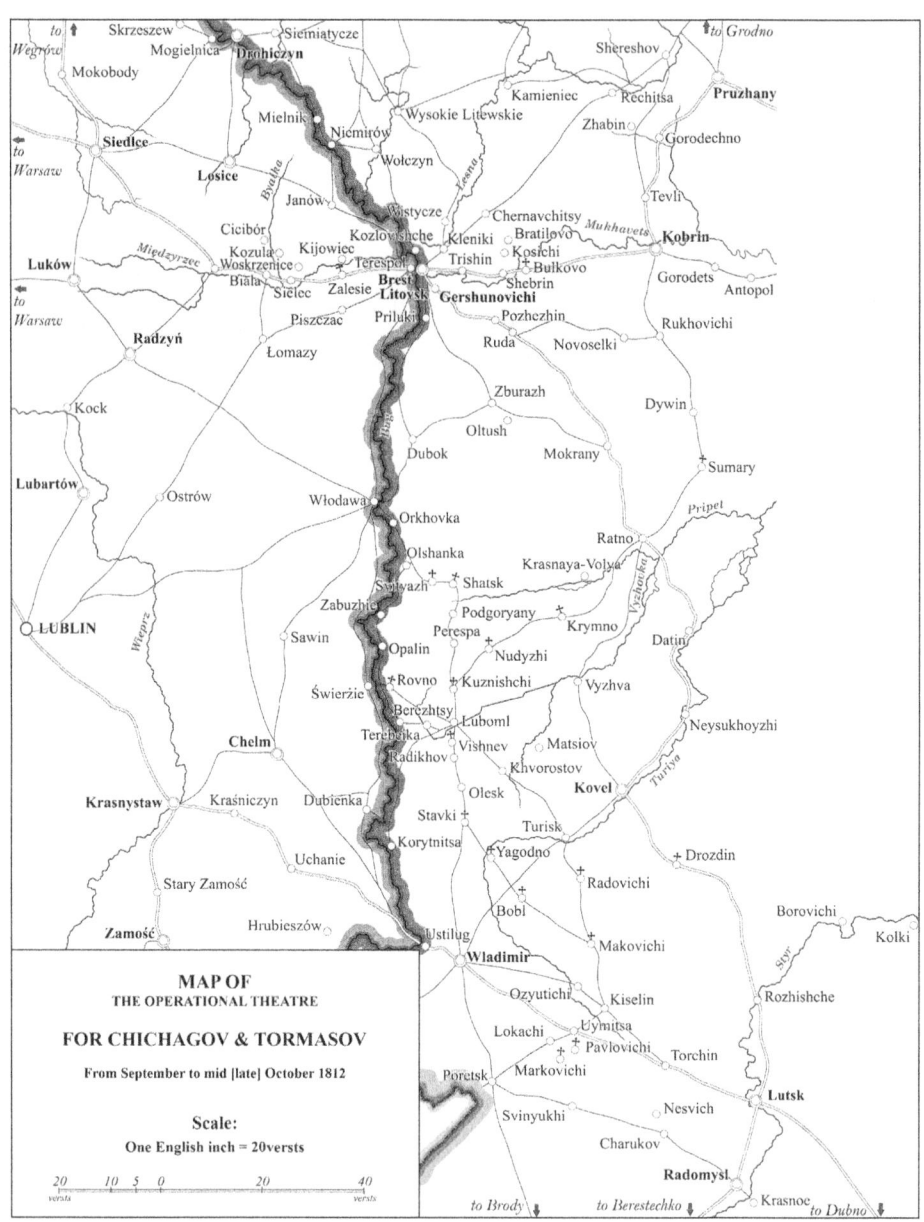

Operational Theatre for Chichagov and Tormasov, September to late October 1812.

31

The union of Third Army with the Army of the Danube

The situation of the forces of both sides in Volhynia during Tormasov's retreat to the Styr. – Guerilla warfare. – The raid on Charukov.

The arrival of the Army of the Danube. – Admiral Chichagov. – The forces of both sides. – Plan of action of the Russian forces. – Their crossing of the Styr. – The enemy retreat to the Turiya. – The action at Luboml. – The enemy retreat to the left bank of the Bug.

The arrival of Colonel Chernyshev in Chichagov's headquarters. – The departure of Tormasov. – Pursuit of the enemy detachments remaining on the right bank of the Bug by Russian troops. – Dispositions of the Austro-Saxon army in front of Brest-Litovsk. – The advance of the Russian army on Brest. – Dispositions for the assault of the enemy position. – Schwarzenberg's retreat towards Drohiczyn and onto the left bank of the Bug. – Chernyshev's expedition into the Duchy of Warsaw. – The advance of Essen 3rd's Corps towards Biała. – The action at Biała. – General Chaplits' expedition towards Slonim. – Chichagov's orders for the advance on the Berezina. – Comments of the operations by both sides.

Following the indecisive battle of Gorodechno, on 17 (29) August, on the day Prince Kutuzov arrived in Tsarevo-Zaimishche, the troops under General Tormasov retreated in perfect order behind the river Styr. The main force under Tormasov was located in the vicinity of Lutsk; forward detachments under Count Lambert and Chaplits were along the Styr: the former from the Austrian border to Lutsk, while the latter went from Lutsk to Kolki.[1] The troops under Schwarzenberg, Reynier and a Polish brigade, under the command of General Kosiński [Antoni Amilkar Kosiński],

---

1   Count Lambert's vanguard consisted of: Kozlov Infantry, Ryazhsk Infantry, Yakutsk Infantry, 10th Jägers and Alexandria Hussars with the replacement squadrons from the Tatar Ulans, Zhitomir Dragoons and Arzamas Dragoons and the Yevpatoria Tatar and 2nd Kalmuck irregular regiments, 11 horse artillery pieces and six heavy guns (diary of the vanguard of Third Army). The records for the composition of Chaplits' detachment could not be found.

who had joined the Saxon *7e Corps*, stood between the Styr and the Turiya, having advanced detachments at Torchin and Charukov.[2] The position beyond the Styr completely secured our army from attack by a powerful enemy: the Styr, throughout its entire course from the Austrian border right to the confluence with the Pripet, has no fords; all the bridges on it had been destroyed, and only the ferry near the village of Krasnoe and rubble from the dismantled bridge remained near the town of Berestechko [30 kilometres south of Radomysl]. The elevated, wooded right bank of the river helped the Russian troops to conceal their movements and approach the enemy undetected, who, occupying the swampy open side, were deprived of these advantages. Several times they made reconnaissances in force, planning to cross covertly on the left wing of our location and force us back towards the Pripet; but the keen observation of the Cossacks prevented them from achieving their intent. Schwarzenberg and Reynier, driven back by the difficulties of their operations, limited themselves to holding our army behind the Styr and covering the line of communications of Napoleon's *Grande Armée* from Volhynia.[3]

On our side, the main body under Tormasov, completely secured by the vanguards under Count Lambert and Chaplits, waged guerrilla warfare with success. On 26 August (5 September), a Cossack fighting patrol, having swum the Styr, captured an enemy officer who was scouting with the squad that was with him. On 7 (19) September, the Cossack regiments under Vlasov and Chikilev, sent to reconnoitre the enemy on the left bank of the river, towards the village of Charukov, attacked an Austrian squadron there and captured some 40 men, who unanimously gave away that General Zechmeister [Theophil Joseph Freiherr Zechmeister von Rheinau], with the O'Reilly Dragoons [*Chevauxlegersregiment Nr. 3*] and other vanguard cavalry, were to spend the night in this very village. On 8 (20) September, Count Lambert, having received this intelligence, crossed the Styr at around midnight, with a detachment consisting of several *sotnia* from Vlasov's and Chikilev's regiments, three squadrons of Alexandria Hussars, three squadrons of Tartar Ulans and the Arzamas Dragoon Regiment. In order to remove the enemy advanced outposts, 15 skirmishers from the Tatar Ulans who knew the German language, were dressed in Austrian greatcoats and helmets. On approaching Charukov, it emerged that the enemy was bivouacking at a distance of about a *verst* from there near the village of Nesvich. Our leading ulans took one Polish picket by surprise, but one of the Poles managed to fire a shot. Whereupon Count Lambert, in order not to give the enemy time to come to their senses, left the Arzamas Dragoons in reserve, and went towards the bivouacs with the remainder at the canter. Staff captain Ilyashevich, who was riding at the head of the column with his squadron of Alexandria Hussars, encountered one of the Austrian squadrons at full combat readiness on the way, rushed at them with his hussars, drove them back and put them to flight. This champion spread such terror throughout the rest of the enemy cavalry, consisting of 13 squadrons,[4] that they fled from their positions with the loss of 150 men and a number

---

2   Chambray, II, 189. Funk, *Erinnerungen aus dem Felzuge in Russland im Jahr 1812*, 98.
3   Diary of the vanguard of Third Army in 1812. Funk, 109-110.
4   The composition of the enemy force stationed at Nesvich, near Charukov was: six squadrons of Austrian O'Reilly's Dragoons, two squadrons of Saxon hussars, three squadrons of Polish

of prisoners, including nine officers. On our side, two hussars were killed and three wounded.[5] The three standards from the O'Reilly Dragoons, taken by Alexandria Hussar Lieutenant Count Buxhoeveden [Pëtr Fëdorovich Buxhoeveden], were returned to the Emperor of Austria, by order of Emperor Alexander I.[6]

On 7 (19) September, the first elements of the Army off the Danube arrived on the Styr, while the remainder assembled over the next two days [20 to 21 September new style]. The Commander in Chief of this army, Admiral Chichagov, was renowned for his abilities. Emperor Alexander I, in one of His handwritten letters to Barclay de Tolly, outlining the plan of action against Austria which had just entered into an alliance with Napoleon against Russia, wrote:

> *ce sont les nations Slaves qu'il faut seourir et lancer contre les Autrichiens en tachant de les mettre en rapport avec les mécontents d'Hongrie. Un homme de tête doit être employé pour mener cette importante opération. J'ai choisi pour cet effet l'amiral Tchitchagof, qui est enthousiasmé de ce plan. Ses capacités et son énergie me donnent l'espoir qu'il reusira dans cette commission essentielle.*
>
> *7 [19] avril 1812.*

(it is the Slavic nations that must be rescued and launched against the Austrians, trying to put them in touch with the discontented people of Hungary. A commanding figure must be employed to carry out this important operation. For this purpose I have chosen Admiral Chichagov, who is enthusiastic about this plan. His abilities and his energy give me hope that he will succeed in this vital mission).[7]

Admiral Chichagov, having received orders to go to Volhynia with the troops entrusted to him, set out from Wallachia on 19 (31) July. His army, consisting of 50 battalions, 56 squadrons, 10 Cossack regiments and 17 artillery companies (some 35,000 men with 204 guns in total),[8] was divided into five corps, commanded by

---

lancers and three squadrons of newly raised Warsaw militia (Diary of the vanguard of Third Army in 1812).

5   General of Cavalry Tormasov's report to Prince Kutuzov, dated 11 [23] September, No. 125. In the diary of the vanguard of Third Army it states: 'the enemy losses consist of three standards from the O'Reilly regiment, 15 field officers and subalterns, and 295 lower ranks; from our side, not a single man.' According to Funk: '*Der General Zechmeister liess sich bei Neswiez überfallen und verlor den grössten Theil seiner Truppen. Von dem Regimente Orelly wurden neunhundert Pferde gefangen, die Sachsen bedauerten den Verlust von hundert Husaren und Dragoner und vorzüglich im kleinen Kriege besonders ausgezeichneten Offiziere.*' 110-111. (General Zechmeister allowed himself to be attacked near Nesvich and lost most of his force. Nine hundred horses were captured from O'Reilly's Regiment, and the Saxons suffered the loss of a hundred hussars and dragoons, and, in particular, officers who had been especially skilled in guerrilla warfare).

6   For the details of the correspondence between the Russian and Austrian governments in the original French, see Appendix 11.

7   A copy of this letter is held in the archive of the General Staff Department.

8   For the composition of the leading elements of the Army of the Danube, see Appendix 12.

General of Infantry Count Langéron [Alexander Fëdorovich Langeron or Louis Alexandre Andrault, comte de Langéron] and Lieutenant Generals, Essen 3rd [Pëtr Kirillovich Essen], Voinov [Alexander Lvovich Voinov], Zass [Alexander Pavlovich Zass or Christoph Alexander Freiherr von Saß][9] and Sabaneev [Ivan Vasilevich Sabaneev]. A detachment, consisting of 11 battalions, eight squadrons, one Cossack regiment and three artillery companies, under the command of Major General Lüders [Nikolai Ivanovich Lüders], stationed in Serbia, subsequently moved to Volhynia.[10] Thirteen battalions and one Cossack regiment were left on the Danube for the time being, in order to monitor the Turkish border.[11]

Chichagov's force, having departed from their locations, moved via Focsany [Focșani], Iasi [Iași], Khotyn, Stary-Konstantinov [Starokostyantiniv] and Dubno, where they were reinforced by eight battalions from 13th Division (Saratov Infantry, 12th Jägers and 22nd Jägers), they arrived on the Styr and had concentrated by 9 (21) September.[12] The number of troops in the Army of the Danube and Third Army reached over 60,000; while the enemy army had some 43,000 men in its ranks (26,000 Austrians, 12,000 Saxons and 5,000 Poles).[13] Although Chichagov and Tormasov (as stated in chapter XX) had received orders from Prince Kutuzov, firstly to follow Third Army with the troops of the Army of the Danube, and secondly, to move against the right wing of Napoleon's *Grande Armée*; however, our Commander-in-Chief decided to operate against Schwarzenberg with a united force, moving the left wing forward, which consisted of the Army of the Danube, while Third Army, crossing the Styr a day later, was to advance more slowly: by operating in this manner, our commanders hoped to cut the enemy off from the Duchy of Warsaw, from where new reinforcements might be able to reach them.[14]

On the 10 and 11 [22 and 23] September, the troops of both armies crossed the Styr at a number of points: the vanguard of the Army of the Danube, consisting of six battalions, eight squadrons and two Cossack regiments with 12 horse artillery pieces, under the command of Major General Count O'Rourke 1st [Joseph Cornelius O'Rourke],[15] and behind them the corps under Essen 3rd, Voinov and

---

9   In his absence, Major General Bulatov [Mikhail Leontevich Bulatov] commanded this corps.
10   General Lüders detachment comprised: Nyslott Infantry, three battalions; 22nd Jägers, two battalions; 27th Jägers, three battalions; 43rd Jägers, three battalions; Volhynia Ulans, eight squadrons; Kireev's Cossacks; Turchaninov's Cossacks; 24th Light Artillery Company; 30th Light Artillery Company; 18th Horse Artillery Company. (Instructions from Admiral Chichagov to Major General Lüders, dated 30 September [12 October] and 10 [22] October).
11   The following remained to secure the border along the Danube: Okhotsk Infantry, one battalion; Mingrelia Infantry, one battalion;Vyborg Infantry, one battalion; Staroskol Infantry, one battalion; Arkhangelogorod Infantry, one battalion; Staroingermanland Infantry, one battalion; Kursk Infantry, one battalion; Crimea Infantry, one battalion; Ukraine Infantry, one battalion; Kamchatka Infantry, one battalion; one battalion each of 8th Jägers, 28th Jägers and three battalions of 39th Jägers; Astapov's Cossack Regiment. (From the Army of the Danube establishment).
12   War diary of the Army of the Danube, compiled by Lieutenant Colonel Malinovsky.
13   Buturlin, II, 105. Chambray shows a total of 26,000 Austrians and 15,000 Saxon-Polish troops, II, 190.
14   Buturlin, II, 105.
15   Count O'Rourke's vanguard consisted of: the Saratov Infantry, 8th Jägers, 39th Jägers, Belorussia Hussars, Grekov 4th's Cossacks, Panteleev 4th's Cossacks and 15 Horse

Sabaneev, crossed the river at Khrinnyky [16 kilometres south of Radomysl]; the corps under Langéron and Bulatov crossed upstream of this point at Tovpuzhin [four kilometres west of Khrinnyky] and Berestechko; the vanguard under Count Lambert, consisting of eight battalions, 18 squadrons and two Cossack regiments, with 11 horse artillery pieces,[16] and behind them, the army under Tormasov, crossed over at Lutsk and Rozhishche.

The enemy, having learned about the crossing by our forces, began to retreat behind the river Turiya. On 11 (23) September, Count O'Rourke's vanguard caught up with the Saxons at the town of Lokachi, forced them to retreat, and captured two officers and 150 lower ranks. News of the French occupation of Moscow was gained from the prisoners. This news not only failed to discourage our troops, rather, on the contrary, instilled in them such a thirst for revenge that any missed opportunity for combat was met with grumbling and an expression of a general readiness to die for the liberation of the Fatherland.[17]

The enemy force retreated in three main directions: the right column, consisting of Kosiński's brigade, towards Vladimir; Reynier moved towards Turisk, while Schwarzenberg went towards Kovel. On 12 (24) September, General Bulatov, on the march with the left column of the Army of the Danube, ejected the Poles from Vladimir, separating them from the Saxon *7e Corps*, and forcing them back towards Zamość.[18] The Saxons burned the bridges over the Turiya and tried to halt the advance by our troops, but the vanguard under Count Lambert, on the 15th (27 September), repaired the bridges, and meanwhile Lieutenant Colonel Madatov [Valerian Grigorevich Madatov] crossed via a ford near Turisk with the Cossack regiments.[19]

The forces under Schwarzenberg and Reynier, having linked up on 16 (28) September at Luboml, took up a rather advantageous position there, leaving some of the troops in the rear guard at Radikhov. Admiral Chichagov, intending to attack the enemy, instructed the vanguard under Count O'Rourke to capture the village of Radikhov, reinforced by the Dorpat Dragoons and Kireev's Cossack Regiment. On the 17 (29 September), at three o'clock in the morning, O'Rourke's force set out from their overnight camp three *versts* from Radikhov. It was necessary to pass along a narrow causeway through the marshes, making their way in single file. Taking advantage of the darkness of the night, the Cossacks and Belorussia Hussars crossed the causeway, broke into the village and, pursuing the fleeing enemy towards Luboml, killed 20 men and took 65 prisoners.[20] After that, following improvements to the causeway by the pioneers under Lieutenant Colonel Gebener, Chichagov advanced on the enemy position with the main body of the Army of the

---

Artillery Company (war diary of the Army of the Danube, compiled by Lieutenant Colonel Malinovsky).

16 Count Lambert's vanguard consisted of: the Kozlov Infantry, Ryazhsk Infantry, 10th Jägers, Alexandria Hussars, the replacement squadrons of the Zhitomir Dragoons and Arzamas Dragoons, the Yevpatoria Tatars and 2nd Kalmucks, and 12th Horse Artillery Company (war diary of Third Army).
17 War diary of the Army of the Danube, compiled by Lieutenant Colonel Malinovsky.
18 Funck, 112.
19 Diary of the vanguard of Third Army.
20 War diary of the Army of the Danube, compiled by Lieutenant Colonel Malinovsky.

Danube. The troops under Schwarzenberg and Reynier were located behind a canal, more than two *sazhen* wide, very deep and across marshy ground. These allies held the exits of the long causeways leading through the swamps, across which the canal had been dug, along the sides of the salient angle formed by the course of the canal. The bridges along the causeways had been destroyed. The right wing of the Allied force, consisting of Saxons, defended the causeway on the country road leading to the Bug from the Luboml road, on which the troops of the left wing, composed of Austrians, held the exit from another causeway with a strong battery near the town of Luboml. Chichagov, having surveyed this position, advanced 15th Horse Artillery Company onto high ground facing the enemy battery, which was firing on the causeway and Luboml, and, having ordered both the guns and the marksmen of 8th Jägers, scattered along the canal, to open fire, sent pioneers escorted by a company of marksmen to repair the bridge. At the same time, Essen 3rd's Corps was sent towards the village of Berezhtsy by the Bug, where, according to intelligence received, the enemy was crossing to the left bank of the river.

As soon as 15th Horse Artillery Company opened their cannonade on the enemy guns, our jägers raced to the causeway, but were met by strong cannon and small-arms fire and forced to retreat. Not wanting to expose the troops to unnecessary losses, Chichagov pulled them back and, believing that Schwarzenberg and Reynier would remain in their position, undertook to envelope them on both flanks. To that end, Essen, who had found no enemy by the Bug, was ordered to head from the village of Berezhtsy towards the village of Terebeika, where the corps under Count Langéron had been sent from the main body to assist Essen; this force was assigned to move around the enemy's right flank, while the other corps of the Army of the Danube army were to attack them frontally, while Tormasov was to go around the enemy left. But the enemy commanders, who had repelled the attack by the Russian force (as Funk, the Saxon historian of the war of 1812, wrote), only because they were attacked at the strongest point of their position, retreated during the night of 17 to 18 (29 to 30) September, and moving, along very difficult roads, via Rovno and Opalin, to Włodawa, where they had built a bridgehead by the Bug, they crossed to the left bank of the river on 19 September (1 October). Throughout operations from 11 to 19 September (23 September to 1 October), the enemy lost some 2,000 killed or wounded and some 500 prisoners.[21]

On 18 (30) September, our troops, having crossed over the canal at Luboml without resistance, stopped to rest, meanwhile, a vanguard under Major General Lanskoy [Sergey Nikolaevich Lanskoy], consisting of eight squadrons and two Cossack regiments with six guns,[22] was sent to pursue the enemy, while following them was the corps under General Essen 3rd, reinforced by Melnikov 5th's Cossacks and 4th Ural Cossacks and 38th Battery Artillery Company.[23] During the march

---

21 War diary of the Army of the Danube. General Tormasov's report to the Tsar and Prince Kutuzov, dated 22 September [4 October].
22 General Lanskoy's detachment consisted of: the Belorussia Hussars, Lukovkin's Cossacks, Grekov 4th's Cossacks and half of 14th Horse Artillery Company (war diary of the Army of the Danube).
23 War diary of the Army of the Danube. Diary of Essen 3rd's Corps, compiled by Lieutenant Colonel Freigang.

towards Luboml by the army, our Commanders-in-Chief received orders from Prince Kutuzov, who, instead of the previous assignment for the Danube Army, to operate in Volhynia, while Third Army was to march to link up with the main force, the Field Marshal ordered Tormasov to remain facing Schwarzenberg and Reynier as before, while Chichagov was to move via Mozyr, Rogachev and Mogilev, in order to be closer to the main army and to operate in the enemy rear areas. The immediate execution of this order was very difficult, because our Commanders-in-Chief, in anticipation of a decisive engagement with the enemy army, did not want to weaken themselves by dividing their forces. In addition, Admiral Chichagov needed to link up with the parks and mobile magazine of his force, which, being moved by ox cart from Wallachia to Volhynia, had lagged behind the army.[24] Following the receipt of these instructions from the Field Marshal, on 17 (29) September, just as Chichagov was preparing to attack the enemy at Luboml, *Flügel-Adjutant* Chernyshev arrived at the headquarters of our armies, with Supreme orders regarding the appointment of Tormasov as Commander in Chief Second Army, and about the plans for Chichagov's operations, based on the overall operational plan, which consisted of the admiral being ordered to envelope Schwarzenberg on his left flank, leaving Third Army facing him, marching to Minsk with the Army of the Danube, linking up with Ertel on the way and, having established communications with Count Wittgenstein, blocking the line of retreat of Napoleon's *Grande Armée*.

Up until our troops occupied Luboml, Chichagov and Tormasov had constantly sought to envelope the enemy on their right flank, intending to sever communications of the allied corps with the Duchy of Warsaw and push them back towards the Pripet marshes. Whereas, on the basis of the overall plan of action, it was necessary, on the contrary, to push the enemy out of the Empire and cut them off completely from Napoleon's *Grande Armée*. The enemy commanders facilitated the execution of this operation themselves by retreating behind the Bug. Upon the occupation of Luboml by our troops, the pursuit of Schwarzenberg was entrusted to Essen's Corps, reinforced by two Cossack regiments, eight heavy guns and the detachment under Major General Lanskoy, moving at the forefront of the corps, while the troops under Tormasov's command were advanced to Shatsk, in order to envelope the Allied Army on their left flank and to seize the road leading to the town of Ratno, which would serve to isolate the troops under Siegenthal [Heinrich Freiherr Bersina von Siegenthal] and Mohr [Johann Friedrich Freiherr von Mohr] from the main body under Schwarzenberg. Thereafter, Tormasov moved to Prince Kutuzov's headquarters.[25]

On 20 September (2 October), an Austrian courier was intercepted, travelling to Schwarzenberg with dispatches, from which it emerged that the detachment under General Mohr, having been ejected from Pinsk by a force under Major General Zapolsky [Andrey Vasilevich Zapolsky], was in Ratno, while Siegenthal's Division had

---

24 Prince Kutuzov's orders for Admiral Chichagov and General Tormasov, dated 6 [18] September (archive of the M.T.D. No. 47,352, Document III). Reports to Prince Kutuzov, from General Tormasov, dated 14 [26] September, No. 135, and from Admiral Chichagov, also dated 14 [26] September, No. 1486.
25 Diary of the vanguard of Third Army. War diary of the Army of the Danube.

moved from Ratno to the village of Krasnaya-Volya. It was obvious that both enemy detachments would go to the Bug to rejoin the main body under Schwarzenberg, and therefore Count Lambert, wanting to cut them off, made a forced march to the village of Dubok with the vanguard of the former Third Army and linked up with the vanguard under Major General Lanskoy there.[26] The infantry and artillery, exhausted from moving along a sandy road on a hot day, arrived at the overnight camp site at midnight. Meanwhile, Chichagov arrived in Zabuzhie, on the Bug with the main body on 20 September (2 October), having detached Voinov's Corps, reinforced by eight squadrons, one Cossack regiment and the detachment under Count O'Rourke, assigned to the vanguard of the corps,[27] to the right, towards Ratno, in order to cut off Siegenthal. On 21 September (3 October), having reached Zburazh, Count Lambert set out at midnight for Pozhezhin in order to march against the enemy from there, having also extracted intelligence from captured Hungarian hussars that Siegenthal's force, having spent the night at Mokrany, had marched towards Ruda. But the infantry, which arrived very late at their overnight halt and was exhausted from the forced march, could not complete the intended movement, and therefore the entire cavalry of the vanguard was sent to open ground near the city of Brest in order to engage the enemy force there, and the next day [4 October new style] they reached the village of Gershunovichi, while Voinov's Corps moved from Ratno to Dywin on 22 September (4 October) in order to cut off Mohr.[28]

Meanwhile, Schwarzenberg, having reached Brest-Litovsk via the left bank of the Bug, and wishing to link up with the detachments under Siegenthal and Mohr, crossed to the right bank with both allied corps on 22 September (4 October), and settled in a position forwards [east] of Brest, between the rivers Mukhavets and Lesna. On the same day, Siegenthal crossed to the right bank of the Mukhavets at Bulkovo and, having destroyed the crossing there, retreated towards Brest; Mohr's detachment continued to retreat along the road from Ratno towards Kobrin.[29]

Count Lambert remained at Gershunovichi with the vanguard until 25 September (7 October), and on this day, moving to Bulkovo, built a bridge there over the Mukhavets, crossed to the right bank of the river and on 26 September (8 October), pushing Siegenthal, who was stationed at Trishin, towards Brest, settled down within cannon range of the enemy position. At the same time, Chichagov moved up to the Mukhavets with the main body, towards Brest and Bulkovo; Essen's Corps, having arrived at Priluki on the Bug on 22 September (4 October), remained there for five days and constructed a crossing, while the leading detachment of Voinov's Corps, under the command of Major General Count O'Rourke, caught up with Mohr's detachment on 23 September (5 October), near Kobrin, ejected the Hungarian hussars from there and, having prevented the enemy from burning the magazines located there, captured 4,000 *Chetvert* of grain. General Mohr, pushed back from

---

26 Diary of the vanguard of Third Army. War diary of the Army of the Danube.
27 Voinov's Corps had been reinforced with the Dorpat Dragoons, Kinburn Dragoons and Kireev's Cossacks (war diary of the Army of the Danube).
28 Diary of the vanguard of Third Army. War diary of the Army of the Danube.
29 Diary of the vanguard of Third Army. Funck, 120. Liebenstein, *Der Krieg Napoleons gegen Russland in den Jahren 1812 und 1813*, II, 155 & 159-160.

the road to Brest, was forced to retreat to Pruzhany and further to Białowieża on 26 September (8 October). The troops of Voinov's Corps, having arrived in Pruzhany, following behind O'Rourke's detachment, were ordered to move closer to the main body stationed near Brest.[30]

Upon the departure of General Tormasov to Prince Kutuzov's headquarters, Admiral Chichagov drew up a new order of battle for all the troops entrusted to him, under the title of Third Army, divided into corps under Major General Count Lambert, Lieutenant General Markov [Yevgeny Ivanovich Markov] (later under Major General Prince Shcherbatov [Alexey Grigorevich Shcherbatov]), General of Infantry Count Langéron, Lieutenant General Essen 3rd, Lieutenant General Voinov, Major General Bulatov, Major General Engelhardt's [Grigory Grigorevich Engelhardt] detachment and the reserve under Lieutenant General Sabaneev.[31]

On 28 September (10 October), a disposition was drawn up for an attack on the enemy at Brest, the essence of which was as follows: the attack on the position was intended to be carried out by four corps: Count Lambert's, Prince Shcherbatov's,[32] Count Langéron's and Essen 3rd's; with Sabaneev's force in reserve, as well as Bulatov's Corps, upon their arrival from Kobrin, where they had been sent to bake the rations found there. Voinov's Corps was directed on Chernavchitsy against the left flank of the enemy position; Engelhardt's detachment, which had replaced Essen's corps at Priluki, was ordered to launch feints against the right flank of the position, making the force appear to be stronger than it was in reality; Chernyshev's detachment, sent onto the left bank of the Bug, in the direction of Terespol, was assigned to destroy the bridge over the Bug and, in the event of an enemy retreat, to pursue them.[33]

---

30 Diary of the vanguard of Third Army. War diary of the Army of the Danube.
31 For the full order of battle of Third Army, see Appendix 13.
32 Prince Shcherbatov was appointed to command 2nd Corps, instead of Ye.I. Markov, who was deprived of command over the force for failure to comply with orders issued by Chichagov, specifically because, having advanced his corps prematurely, he gave away the Commander-in-Chief's intention to attack the enemy. Markov, hoping for support from Prince Kutuzov, with whom he had served for a long time, went to his headquarters. Kutuzov received him as an old comrade, but did not give him any assignments until Chichagov's departure from the army in 1813.
33 Force dispositions dated 29 September [11 October]: 'Both armies in combination, in accordance with the order of battle drafted by me, are to form four corps.
    The first under the command of Adjutant General Count Lambert, is to proceed on the right, through the town of Bratilovo, along the Brest road towards Chernavitsy. While taking this route, try to discover the enemy positions, and inform me of whatever may be seen worthy of note, in particular if it is noted that the enemy has become concerned about the direction of this corps and is making changes in their dispositions; after occupying said road, inspect the ground at the location facing the enemy left flank, whether it might be suitable for launching an attack from this direction, and immediately notify me, explaining the apparent suitability of the local position. If, during the movement of your corps, the enemy brings up superior forces, then immediately notify me of this, so that I may send reinforcements. However, if you notice the opportunity to cause great disruption to the enemy through a swift attack, then immediately do this.
    The left corps, under the command of Lieutenant General Essen 3rd, constituting the left flank of the army, is to be located at the village of Vychulki.

On the following day, 29 September (11 October), the columns on the right wing, under the command of Count Lambert and Prince Shcherbatov, moved forward to attack the enemy position, but Schwarzenberg and Reynier, having guessed the intention of our Commander in Chief and concerned about being trapped against the Bug, or against the marshy river Lesna, had abandoned their positions at midnight and retreated towards the Lesna. Thus, Chichagov's intention to attack the enemy with superior forces in the disadvantageous position at Brest, had no consequences other than that he postponed the attack and gave time for Schwarzenberg and Reynier to avoid the threat that faced them. Instead of a decisive battle, the fighting was limited to a cannonade on the retreating troops from the left bank of the Lesna and the pursuit of the enemy by some of the cavalry under Count Lambert, who had crossed the river at Wistycze by swimming. But all our attempts to repair the bridges destroyed by the enemy were unsuccessful, which forced Chichagov to postpone the crossing until the following day. On our side, Major General Udom was seriously wounded by a round shot to the leg,[34] and Lieutenant Savich of the quartermaster's department was killed. The army headquarters was moved to Brest-Litovsk; the vanguard and the corps under Shcherbatov, Langéron and Essen were deployed along the Lesna, from Chernavchitsy to Kleniki; Voinov's Corps went to Kamieniec; Bulatov's Corps was stationed between the Lesna and Mukhavets, at Trishin; the reserve was in Brest.[35]

During the night of 29 to 30 September, (11 to 12 October), The enemy withdrew from the positions they had taken up behind the Lesna, and retreated to Wołczyn [Voŭčyn]. Chichagov pursued them with light troops alone,[36] while the main force

---

The two centre corps, one under Count Langéron, forwards of the village of Kosichi, while the second, Lieutenant General Markov's, is to be at the village of Bratilovo.

The main reserve corps, which is to be with me, will be located behind the village of Kosichi. Major General Engelhardt, simultaneously with the attack on the enemy position, is to demonstrate an intention to attack their right flank and the city of Brest through your movements, trying to make it appear to the enemy that you have overwhelming numbers; as soon as you notice the success of our attack, then open a bombardment, firing incendiary shells into the city, and also on their right flank, if it can be brought under fire, and meanwhile attempt to reconnoitre the crossings onto the left bank of the Bug.

Flügel-Adjutant Chernyshev's detachment (the composition of this detachment is given below) is to attempt to destroy the bridges built by the enemy, but if the enemy is making their retreat across these bridges, then try to inflict as much damage as possible on them and pursue them. Major General Bulatov, upon arrival from Kobrin, is to form the army reserve.

My starting location will be in the centre in the village of Kosichi, I shall inform you of any changes, should I decide to move.

Signed: Admiral Chichagov.'

34 Yevstafy Yevstafievich Udom, later Lieutenant General (Emperor Alexander I and His Contemporaries in 1812, 1813, 1814 and 1815, Volume III).
35 Diary of the vanguard of Third Army. War diary of the Army of the Danube.
36 The following were detached for the pursuit of the enemy: from Count Lambert's Corps: the Cossack regiment, 10th Jägers (two battalions) and four horse artillery pieces; from Count Langéron's Corps: the Cossack regiment, 29th Jägers (three battalions) and four light guns; from Essen 3rd's Corps: the Cossack regiment, two battalions of the Ukraine Infantry and four horse artillery pieces. The corps under General Voinov, advancing towards Kamieniec, was ordered to detach patrols in the direction of Wysokie-Litewskie and Kleszczele, to maintain communications with the light detachments and to reconnoitre the enemy.

remained in place, preparing provisions for the forthcoming advance on the Berezina. The retreat of the Austro-Saxon force, during which they were forced to move day and night, cost them many stragglers, captured by the Cossacks.[37] Having reached the town of Siemiatycze, the enemy crossed to the left bank of the Bug between Mielnik and Drohiczyn on bridges they had built from rafts, on 3 (15) October.[38] Thus, both allied corps had been driven back into the Duchy of Warsaw and the routes leading to the Berezina were completely open to the troops of Third Army.

Having occupied Brest, Chichagov remained inactive for two weeks with his main force, while trying to collect supplies from the Duchy of Warsaw, the Grodno Governorate and Volhynia, and waiting for supplies from the Podolsk Governorate, Kiev Governorate and Chernigov Governorate. The corps under Prince Shcherbatov, which now came under the command of Lieutenant General Saken who had arrived from Zhitomir, on 2 (14) October, received orders to move from the Lesna to Pruzhany and to prepare a ten-day supply of rations for the army there (8,000 *chetvert* of hard-tack and 800 *chetvert* of cereals) through requisitions. Throughout Chichagov's encampment at Brest, *Flügel-Adjutant* Chernyshev and General Chaplits were detached from the army: the former was instructed to carry out a raid into the Duchy of Warsaw, to destroy the magazines prepared by the enemy there, while Chaplits was directed from Pruzhany towards Slonim against the guards regiment [*3e chevau-légers lanciers de la Garde*] under General Konopka forming there from Lithuanians.[39]

Chernyshev's detachment, consisting of seven squadrons and three Cossack regiments with four horse artillery pieces,[40] set out from Terespol (opposite Brest) on the evening of 29 September (11 October) towards the town of Międzyrzec, lying at the junction of roads from Warsaw and Lublin, the occupation of which presented the opportunity to threaten these two important locations simultaneously.[41]

Upon arrival in Międzyrzec, on 1 (13) October, Chernyshev learned that an Austrian detachment, numbering 2,000 men, having passed through Łuków, was moving towards Siedlce in order to link up the troops under Schwarzenberg, who had retreated to Drohiczyn. In order to prevent the enemy from fulfilling this mission, or at least to harm this detachment, Colonel Lukovkin [Gavryl Amvrosievich Lukovkin] was sent to Siedlce with his eponymous Cossack regiment, with orders to send patrols from there to Węgrów and Drohiczyn, either to find the enemy, or to reconnoitre the movements of the Austro-Saxon army. Chernyshev himself followed Lukovkin's Cossacks with the rest of his cavalry in order to cut off the Austrian detachment, which, seeing the impossibility of linking up with the main force under Schwarzenberg, was forced to divert to Modlin. Chichagov, for his part, at the first news of the movement of reinforcements towards the enemy army, sent

---

37 Diary of the vanguard of Third Army.
38 Funck, 133-134.
39 War diary of the Army of the Danube. Chaplits' notes (archive of the M.T.D. No. 44,712).
40 Chernyshev's detachment consisted of: two squadrons of Alexandria Hussars, under Colonel Prince Madatov's command; two squadrons of Tatar Ulans; three squadrons of Chuguev Ulans; Chikilev's Cossacks, Vlasov's Cossacks and Lukovkin's Cossacks; four horse artillery pieces; for a total of 1,800 men.
41 Colonel Chernyshev's report to the Tsar from Włodawa dated 7 [19] October.

generals Melissino [Alexey Petrovich Melissino] and Dekhterev [Nikolai Vasilevich Dekhterev], with the Lubny Hussars and Olviopol Hussars, onto the left bank of the Bug via Terespol towards Drohiczyn, to assist Colonel Chernyshev and to cut off the enemy detachment.[42] Having occupied Siedlce, Chernyshev received intelligence from the patrols tasked by him that the enemy was moving in significant strength from Drohiczyn along the routes from Brest to Warsaw. Indeed, the appearance of our brave partisans to the rear of the allied army, who destroyed enemy magazines in all the cities and towns they passed through and imposed small indemnities on the inhabitants, solely for the purpose of convincing them of the impotence of the Austro-Saxons, caused Schwarzenberg concerns and forced him to send quite significant detachments towards Siedlce and Międzyrzec and to send the Saxon corps with some Austrian troops towards Biała.[43] As soon as Chernyshev learned about the enemy movements threatening to surround his small detachment and cut them off from the Bug, he immediately decided to divert towards Lublin in order to destroy the depots of the allied army, but at the same time, having in mind to spread the terror inspired by his operations to Warsaw itself, ordered Lukovkin, who had returned to Siedlce from Węgrów with his Cossacks and with 120 prisoners captured by him, to move towards Stoczek [30 kilometres west of Łuków] and Garwolin [58 kilometres west of Łuków] towards the Vistula. Chernyshev himself rode to Łuków and on to Kock, destroyed the enemy magazines in both of these towns, sending some of the supplies to the army's headquarters, recalled Lukovkin's Cossack Regiment, which returned from its sweep to the Vistula, and, moving off to Włodawa, on 7 (19) October, crossed onto the right bank of the Bug there. During the burning of the magazines in Łuków, several peasant houses burned down. Chernyshev, unable to repair the losses suffered by the inhabitants, ordered that some of the money collected in the countryside be distributed to the worst victims of the fire; the rest of the indemnities were distributed to the lower ranks who had participated in the expedition.[44]

The appearance of our partisans instilled such fear in Warsaw that the inhabitants left there in droves, carrying away whatever they could; the French commandant, General Dutaillis [Adrien Jean-Baptiste Aimable Ramon du Bosc Dutaillis], instigated protective measures, closing the checkpoints for three days and taking the horses from the townsfolk by force, trying to form a cavalry detachment and calling for mobilisation. He exclaimed: 'Poles! The great Napoleon is looking to you from Moscow's bell towers.' This unfortunate paraphrase of the well-known comment by the victor at the Pyramids[45] did not achieve the slightest success.[46]

Upon the occupation of Brest-Litovsk by our troops, an observation post of 30 Cossacks was sent to Biała and one battalion of the Schlüsselburg Infantry was sent to the village of Zalesie to provide an escort for the provisions sent by Chernyshev to the headquarters. The advance of significant enemy forces to Biała, on 5 (17) October, forced the Cossacks to retreat to Zalesie, while the Schlüsselburg Infantry

---

42 Chichagov's orders to Major Generals Melissino and Dekhterev, dated 2 [14] October.
43 Liebenstein, II, 157-158.
44 Colonel Chernyshev's report to the Tsar from Włodawa dated 7 [19] October.
45 *'Nous allons combattre. Songez que du haut de ces monuments quarante siècles vous contemplent.'*
46 Pradt, *Ambassade en Pologne,* 177 & 179. Liebenstein, II, 157.

battalion moved to Terespol. The Commander in Chief, having received a report about this, ordered Essen 3rd's Corps to pass through Brest to Biała and attack the enemy located there. Bulatov's Corps was sent to the village of Piszczac in support of Essen and to maintain communications with Chernyshev. During the night of 5 to 6 (17 to 18) October, Essen's force deployed in front of Zalesie, pushing a battalion of combined grenadiers and a squadron of Smolensk Dragoons up to the causeway and bridges on the river Krzna, on the road to Biała. Another squadron of Smolensk Dragoons was sent to the bridge over this same river on the Drohiczyn road, at the village of Kijowiec.

On 6 (18) October, the same day as the battle of Tarutino, Essen's force advanced at dawn towards Biała, having the combined grenadier battalion in the vanguard with a squadron of Smolensk Dragoons under Major Filatov's command. Approaching the village of Woskrzenice, our dragoons saw two squadrons of Saxon hussars and lancers before them, who, noticing the advance of the battalion, took off. Following this, the enemy was reinforced by two more squadrons, which, dismounting and occupying the scrub off the sides of the road, halted our dragoons. But once the grenadier battalion arrived, and another squadron of Smolensk Dragoons with two guns from 15th Horse Artillery Company, the enemy was forced to retreat across the river Byalka, where the Saxon force was deployed as follows: 2nd Division formed the right wing forwards of the town of Biała, protected by a screen of skirmishers, scattered along the Byalka marshes; 1st Division formed the left wing, guarding the crossing over the Byalka, at the mill, near the village of Kozula. The Austrian force stood upstream along the river.[47]

As he closed up to the river, General Essen ordered the three battalions of 37th Jägers, together with one combined grenadier battalion, to line the bank with skirmishers and drive off the enemy screen, clearing the crossing over the bridge on the highway; while four horse artillery pieces were placed on the road verges in support; two combined grenadier battalions with six guns from 8th Battery Artillery Company were sent to occupy the forest to the right of the village of Sielec. The Smolensk Dragoons deployed to the left of the highway, in order to protect the horse artillery, while two and a half squadrons of Zhitomir Dragoons were stationed near the forest, to the right of the road, to cover the heavy guns and to support the infantry sent into the forest. Despite the gunfire from the Saxon screen, supported by a cannonade of 18 guns, with the assistance of our horse artillery striking the enemy frontally while the heavy half-company enfiladed their right wing, our marksmen completely cleared the opposite river bank. General Funck wrote of this action: 'Here, for the first time, we became acquainted with the excellent jägers of Saken's Corps. As dexterous in their movement as they were skilled at marksmanship, they caused us great harm, engaging at double our effective range with their excellent muskets. They were particularly dangerous for our officers…'[48] General Essen was attempting to cross the Byalka on his left wing in order to establish communications with Bulatov, hoping for his arrival from Piszczac; while Schwarzenberg and Reynier believed that Essen wanted to lure them out of position, and therefore, at

---

47 Funck, 135. Diary of Essen 3rd's Corps.
48 Funck, 137-138.

the beginning, their operations were limited to defence; but then, convinced of the weakness of the Russian detachment, they decided to switch to the offensive. To that end, the Saxon force launched an attack along the causeway against the left wing of our troops with a battalion of light infantry, supported by two grenadier battalions; the enemy lost many men to the well-aimed fire of the jägers, but managed to infiltrate some of their marksmen via a ford on one side of the causeway; others crossed the river via the bridge at the mill near Kozula and took advantage of an oversight by the combined grenadier battalions who had not cleared the forest near which two of our heavy guns were stationed, capturing one of them; the other was rescued by the Zhitomir Dragoons. During these incidents, a strong Austrian column, crossing near the village of Cicibór, enveloped our right flank, which forced Essen to retreat. Our troops retreated in perfect order to Zalesie, having dismantled the bridges on the causeway over the Krzna and set fire to the buildings along the causeway in order to delay the advancing enemy. In the action at Biała, one subaltern and 125 lower ranks were killed on our side; 16 field officers and subalterns and 193 lower ranks were wounded: among the wounded was artillery Lieutenant Colonel Gebhardt [Karl Karlovich Gebhardt].[49]

The gun we lost was the sole trophy captured from us by the Saxons in 1812, and in all likelihood, was the only gun of those captured from us that reached the borders of France.[50] On the part of the allies, by their own admission, their casualties were significant.[51]

As soon as Chichagov received word from General Essen about his engagement with superior enemy numbers at Biała, Langéron's Corps was sent to Zalesie to assist him and the remaining formations of his army were ordered to concentrate at Brest in order to move against the enemy and attack them decisively.[52] But Reynier, without waiting to be attacked, marched off towards Węgrów, from where he later moved to the village of Skrzeszew, near Drohiczyn. From this location, the enemy corps could maintain communications with Warsaw and could not only monitor Chichagov's movements, but also interfere with his operations against the line of communications of Napoleon's *Grande Armée*.[53]

I have already had the opportunity to mention above that Major General Chaplits had been sent to Lithuania to disperse the militia being formed there. His detachment consisted of four battalions, 12 squadrons and 2½ Cossack regiments, with 12 guns. Modest, affable, beloved by the troops, Chaplits was one of the most outstanding generals of the glorious era of 1812.[54] His immediate operational objec-

---

49 Diary of Essen 3rd's Corps. Admiral Chichagov's report to Prince Kutuzov, dated 9 [21] October, No. 1,700.
50 Funck, 139.
51 Funck, 141. Liebenstein, II, 159.
52 Extracted from the diaries and documents of the Commander in Chief of the Army of the Danube and Third Army (archive of the M.T.D. No. 44,585, Annex 17).
53 Funck, 143. Liebenstein, II, 159.
54 Chaplits' detachment comprised: 28th Jägers, 32nd Jägers, Pavlograd Hussars, Tver Dragoons, Dyachkin's Cossacks, Kalmytsky's Cossacks and part of the Bashkir Regiment and 13th Horse Artillery Company (War Diary of the Army of the Danube). Diary kept by Martos [Alexey Ivanovich Martos], an officer serving in the Army of the Danube.

tive was to attack *3e chevau-légers lanciers de la Garde* under General Konopka in Slonim and isolate the Austrian detachment under General Mohr, who, not having the opportunity to join Schwarzenberg's army during their occupation of Brest, had retreated in a roundabout way to Pruzhany and Mosty. Departing Pruzhany on 6 (18) October, Chaplits moved by forced marches, leaving all his infantry, dragoons, two squadrons of hussars and eight guns on the route to Ruzhany, and arrived in Slonim at dawn on 8 (20) October with the rest of the hussars and Cossacks, attacked the Polish General Konopka by surprise, who was forming *3e chevau-légers lanciers de la Garde* there, killing some 100 men, capturing one general (Konopka himself), 13 field officers and subalterns and 228 lower ranks, and disbanded several thousand conscripts. Having sent the prisoners and the regimental treasury, which contained 50,000 złoty (7,500 silver roubles), to Brest-Litovsk, Chaplits remained in Slonim, at the junction of the roads leading to Grodno, Vilna, Minsk and Bobruisk.[55]

The detachment under General Mohr managed to avoid the pursuit by our troops: having crossed the Neman at Mosty on 29 September (11 October), he reached Grodno and was reunited with the main force under Schwarzenberg, which was stationed on the left bank of the Bug near Drohiczyn, via Białystok.[56]

The main force under Chichagov remained in the vicinity of Brest-Litovsk until mid [late] October.[57]

During his preparations for the march to the Berezina, Chichagov was concerned both with the provision of rations for his army on this march, and with the security of Volhynia and Podolia from enemy invasion. Admiral Chichagov has been criticised for the long delay at Brest, but one could hardly agree that this criticism was justified. In order to march an army over a distance of some 450 *versts*, through countryside devastated by the enemy, it was necessary to have a significant mobile magazine accompany the troops. The collection of supplies by means of requisition required a lot of time in itself; it was even more difficult to obtain a sufficient number of horses and wagons for the transport of provisions and parks following the army. Charles XII, during the Great Northern War, being in a most advantageous situation (because some of the inhabitants of Poland had taken his side), was forced to spend several weeks preparing food supplies and mobile magazines in Smorgon, and his subsequent operations were much slower than those by Chichagov. The time spent by the admiral in Brest-Litovsk was not wasted: significant raiding parties sent to the left bank of the Bug not only destroyed resources that could have been used by the enemy, but extracted supplies for our army by armed force, and meanwhile, with the assistance of the local authorities, grain, fodder and livestock were requisitioned in the Grodno Governorate and carts with provisions from Volhynia, Podolia and Ukraine were on their way. To secure these convoys, Chichagov ordered Major General Liders [Nikolai Ivanovich Liders], on the march to Pinsk, to leave part of

---

55 War diary of the Army of the Danube. Chaplits' notes. Admiral Chichagov's report to Prince Kutuzov, dated 20 October [1 November].
56 Liebenstein, II, 160.
57 War diary of the Army of the Danube.

his detachment in Dubno,[58] and move via Pinsk to join the army with the remaining troops. A significant part of the force was left facing the Austro-Saxon army, under the command of Lieutenant General Saken, but since the mission of this force was principally to secure the march of Chichagov's army to the Berezina, a special detachment was consequently assigned to the direct protection of Volhynia, consisting of four battalions, four squadrons and one Cossack regiment, with six guns, under the command of Major General Repninsky [Sergei Yakovlevich Repninsky],[59] who was ordered to establish a screen of Cossack outposts along the line of the Bug from the Austrian border to Orkhovka opposite Włodawa.[60] Lieutenant General Musin-Pushkin [Pëtr Klavdievich Musin-Pushkin], who had taken over command of the force in Zhitomir from General Saken, was assigned to move to Vladimir and take charge of all the troops left in Volhynia; he was also ordered to send two replacement battalions, eight replacement squadrons and six guns from 33rd Battery Company to General Ertel in Mozyr, from the force stationed in Zhitomir.[61] Orders were issued for the reserve (recruit) battalions formed up in the Novomirgorod, Yelisavetgrad [Kropyvnytskyi] and Chigirin depots, for 8th Division, 10th Division and 22nd Division, to send six battalions to Kiev, while the remaining 12 were to go to Mozyr, to reinforce the corps under the command of General Ertel.[62] In order to supply these recruits with muskets and knapsacks, weapons and ammunition were used, which had been recovered from the dead and sick, during the advance of the regiments from Khotyn, Kamenets-Podolsky and Zhitomir.[63]

Some have criticised Prince Schwarzenberg for his inaction after the battle of Gorodechno, believing that he should have taken advantage of his superior troop numbers over Tormasov's army before Chichagov's arrival in Volhynia. For a thorough discussion of operations by the Austrian commander, it is necessary, first of all, to resolve the following issue: what advantages would he have gained by

---

58 General Liders left one battalion each from the Nyslott Infantry and 43rd Jägers, one of the Ukrainian Cossack regiments formed by Colonel Count de Witt, and 13th Battery Artillery Company in Dubno. As both battalions and the artillery company were intended to arrive with the army with the first convoys, the following regiments were sent to replace them: the Feodosia Tatars from Mogilev-on-Dniester [Mogilev-Podolsky], Platov 5th's Cossacks from Tarnopol *Oblast* and 9th Black Sea Cossacks from Moldavia. In addition, the 75th Black Sea Crew and two battalions of the Velikie-Luki Infantry were intended to move from Mogilev-on-Dniester to Dubno, and proceed from there with the convoys to the army (Admiral Chichagov's instructions to Major Generals Liders and Komnin dated 4 [16] October).
59 Major General Repninsky's detachment consisted of: one battalion each from the Penza Infantry, Saratov Infantry, Okhotsk Infantry and Mingrelia Infantry, the Tiraspol Dragoons, Turchaninov's Cossacks, four heavy and two light guns. Subsequently, this force was reinforced from Liders detachment by four battalions from the Nyslott Infantry and 43rd Jägers. The Tiraspol Dragoons were sent to Repninsky's detachment from Bulatov's Corps (Admiral Chichagov's orders to Major General Repninsky, dated 30 September [12 October], and to Major General Liders, dated 10 [22] October).
60 Admiral Chichagov's orders to Major General Repninsky, dated 30 September [12 October].
61 Admiral Chichagov's orders to Lieutenant General Musin-Pushkin, dated 10 [22] October.
62 Admiral Chichagov's orders to the commander of the recruit battalions of 8th Division, 10th Division and 22nd Division, Colonel Vykhodtsevsky, dated 6 and 13 [18 and 25] October.
63 Admiral Chichagov's orders to the civil governor of Kamenets-Podolsky, Saint-Priest, and the civil governor of Volhynia, Komburley, dated 13 [25] October.

relentlessly pursuing Tormasov? The total defeat of our army, which alone could have consolidated the occupation of Volhynia and Podolia by the allied force, was hardly possible, both due to the inconclusive outcome of the battle at Gorodechna, and because Tormasov, in all likelihood, would not have accepted another battle, but would have retreated towards Chichagov. Consequently, the total benefit of a further allied offensive would have been limited to the short-term occupation of country with abundant food resources for the army. But even on the Styr, Schwarzenberg could not satisfy their requirements for food supplies, importing them from Lithuania and the Duchy of Warsaw. Was it worth moving away from one's own borders, to expose oneself to the risks of a long retreat, which was inevitable as soon as the Army of the Danube appeared in the theatre of war? In addition, the political relations between the Austrian government and Russia, despite their alliance with Napoleon, were not hostile to Emperor Alexander either. The correspondence between the St Petersburg and Viennese Cabinets was not interrupted during the entire duration of the campaign of 1812,[64] and the Austrians were generally reluctant to operate against our forces. The Saxons and Poles operated more decisively, but the weakness of their forces prevented them from having any significant influence on the outcome of the war. In considering the operations by Schwarzenberg, as a general left to protect the line of communications of the army with an independent corps, one cannot help but notice that he did not fulfil the orders issued to him; however, taking into account the political circumstances, which undoubtedly had an influence on his *modus operandi*, we may say that he achieved his primary objective completely, the preservation the army entrusted to him by the Austrian government.

---

64 The civil governor of Volhynia, Komburley's report to Barclay de Tolly, dated 7 [19] August, No. 964 (archive of the M.T.D. No. 46,692, folio 3).

32

The Battle of Tarutino (on the River Chernishnya)

Napoleon's preparations for the retreat from Moscow. – Reasons for the delay in his departure. – Orders for the march.

The deployment of Murat's force on the river Chernishnya. – Plan for a surprise attack on Murat's position. – The dispositions drafted by Toll. – Dispositions for the troops of the right wing, drafted by Bennigsen. – The battle of Tarutino (or of the river Chernishnya). – Misunderstandings between Prince Kutuzov and General Bennigsen. – Emperor Alexander I's rescript after the battle of Tarutino. – Awards made to Kutuzov and Bennigsen. – The reorganisation of the army. – Assessments by foreign historians regarding alleged Russian violations of the truce.

We have already seen (in Chapter 16) that Napoleon, having occupied Moscow and not achieving his operational objective of the subjugation of Russia to his whim, initially intended to make a feint advance towards St Petersburg, but then decided to go on a flanking movement to the Dvina. By operating in this manner, he could bring his army closer to the reserves marching towards him from Germany and mask his forced retreat with the appearance of a formidable offensive towards our northern capital. To that end, he intended to send Victor's *9e Corps*, reinforced with some of the Westphalian, Saxon and Polish troops and march battalions of some 40,000 men, and one of MacDonald's divisions to assist Saint-Cyr, which in total was intended to form an army of 70,000 men on the Dvina, meanwhile, Napoleon planned to move via Volokolamsk, Zubtsov, Bely and Velizh, to Velikiye-Luki himself, with the *Garde* and corps under the Viceroy and Davout, also totalling some 70,000, sending the corps under Marshal Ney along the Smolensk road and the force under Murat to Mozhaisk in order to cover the retreat of the main body. Thus, Napoleon hoped to concentrate some 140,000 men at Velikiye-Luki and Velizh, not including Murat's and Ney's 30,000,[1] and after wintering on the Dvina, would march on St Petersburg in the spring, with 300,000 newly assembled

---

1   Chambray, *Histoire de l'expedition de Russie*, II, 209-210. Thiers, *Histoire du consulat ed de l'empire*, XIV, Édit. de Brux. 455-457.

men.[2] But almost all of Napoleon's chief subordinates, having been summoned for a meeting on the proposed movement, expressed doubts about its outcome. In the meantime, it was necessary to decide on any plan of action as soon as possible, because the unfavourable season for military movements was already approaching. Some (including Daru [Pierre-Antoine-Noël-Mathieu Bruno Daru]) recommended wintering in Moscow; Napoleon approved of this plan himself,[3] but the foresight of this brilliant commander would not allow him to be misled regarding the dangers associated with wintering in Moscow. Even if he managed to collect provisions in the vicinity of Moscow in the quantities required to supply the army, there remained the even greater difficulty of providing fodder for the cavalry, artillery and cattle necessary for meat rations. In order to do this, it would be necessary to expand the area where the troops were quartered, but the French cavalry, already in a state of exhaustion, would not be able to protect the army from partisan raids. Was it realistic to hope for the maintenance of communications with Lithuania, which were constantly subjected to attack by our Cossacks and light detachments?

With his characteristic insight, Napoleon saw not only the obvious impossibility of staying in Moscow for the winter, but also the difficulties and dangers to which he would be subjected by postponing the retreat. Napoleon visualised all this, but remained inactive during the Moscow conflagration, at first hoping to shatter the resolve of Emperor Alexander, and then, out of concerns, very much justified, that from the first backwards step by the French, the common belief in their invincibility would be destroyed, and that all their enemies, held in obedience by fear, would cast off the shackles imposed by their conqueror.

All that being said, however, defeated by the forces of circumstance, Napoleon began to prepare for departure, but instead of the movement he had previously proposed towards Volokolamsk, he decided to head south towards Kaluga, engage Kutuzov in combat, and then, depending on the results of the battle, settle down for the winter in Kaluga, or retreat beyond the Dnieper via Yelnya, through country that had not yet been devastated. The wounded from the Moscow hospitals, and so-called trophies (i.e. Turkish Colours, a gilded cross from the bell tower of Ivan the Great and ancient weapons looted from Moscow), were directed back down the Smolensk road. The corps under Davout, Ney and the Viceroy were ordered to assemble in Moscow, while the troops of the *Vieille Garde* were ordered to be ready to march. Mortier was ordered to strengthen the armament of the Kremlin, fortify several posts suitable for the defence of Moscow and garrison the city with a detachment entrusted to him, consisting of a division of the *Jeune Garde*, under the command of General Delaborde, four battalions formed from cavalrymen who had no horses, a cavalry brigade of 500 men, two sapper and one artillery companies. Meanwhile, Murat had sent one of his aides de camp, General Rossetti [Joseph Marie Thomas Rossetti], to Napoleon with a report about the miserable state of his cavalry and the dangers of his position on the Chernishnya river, he was permitted

---

2 '… *Ceplan fut vraissemblablement conçu dans les derniers jours de Septembre…*' (This plan was probably conceived in the last days of September).
3 As Napoleon stated, speaking of Daru's recommendation: '*Ce conseil est un conseil de lion…*' (This advice is the counsel of a lion). Thiers, XIV, 497.

to retreat to Voronovo, if necessary, and take up a position there with his infantry, placing cavalry behind them in order to give them a rest and end the losses they were suffering from the exhausting mission of facing our vanguard.⁴

French historians claim that Napoleon resumed negotiations with Prince Kutuzov simultaneously with these preparations for the retreat from Moscow, probably with the aim of diminishing our commander's vigilance. According to their statements, on 1 (13) October, General Lauriston arrived at Miloradovich's outposts, under the pretext of enquiring about our Tsar's response to a letter sent by Napoleon. Kutuzov, as the French themselves admit, did not give this *parlementaire* a definite answer, confining himself to expressing hope that negotiations might begin as soon as a response from Emperor Alexander were received.⁵ A second meeting between Prince Kutuzov and Lauriston is not mentioned either in our official records or in the notes by personalities who were in Kutuzov's headquarters, but French historians state that, after this meeting, Murat, hoping for a truce, remained in his disadvantageous position on the river Chernishnya.⁶ But Kutuzov, having arrived in Tarutino himself, before the battle with Murat, at the entrance to the hut where he had received the French *parlementaire* said: 'I told Lauriston here that we would never agree to peace.'⁷

Murat's unfavourable position with the vanguard of the French army, 60 *versts* from Moscow, seemed to be an invitation to Kutuzov to strike. This vanguard consisted of no more than 20,000 men, including some 8,000 cavalry, with 187 guns.⁸ The enemy force, exhausted by hunger and the hardships of outpost service, could not offer stubborn resistance; while the terrain on which they were located did not present any obstacles convenient for strengthening the defence and contributed to the covert approach march by our troops: the river Chernishnya, conveniently passable via fords, did not constitute a significant barrier, and therefore, during Murat's occupation of Vinkovo [Chernishnya], his troops were located on both banks of

---

4   Chambray, II, 204-207. Orders for the King of Naples, dated 13 and 14 October, new style, and to the Chief of Staff of the *Grande Armée*, dated 18 October, new style.
5   '*Il en résulta une suspension d'armes par une espèce de convention tacite...*' (This resulted in a suspension of hostilities by a sort of tacit agreement). Chambray, II, 209.
6   Chambray, II, 209. Thiers, XIV. Gourgaud, *Examen critique de l'ouvrage de M-r le comte de Ségur, Livre VIII, Chap. XI*.
7   From notes by A.A. Shcherbinin [Liprandi comments: 'In Tarutino there were no longer any traces of buildings by 1 [13] October, the remaining huts having been dismantled for firewood in the camp and therefore it must be assumed that a mistake has crept in. The allocation of huts for firewood lay under my direct responsibility; consequently, what I have stated is well known to me, and there may be other witnesses to it].
8   The number of men in Murat's vanguard, according to returns submitted to Napoleon on 8 (20) September and according to an approximate estimation, were as follows: 6,923 in Poniatowski's *5e Corps*; 2,862 in Claparède's Division; 4,997 in Dufour's Division (including the light cavalry division from *1er Corps*); 2,721 in Nansouty's *1er Corps de cavalerie*; 4,263 in Sébastiani's *2e Corps de cavalerie*, with the light cavalry from *3e Corps*; 3,000 in Saint-Germain's *3e Corps de cavalerie*; 1,775 in Latour-Maubourg's *4e Corps de cavalerie*, for a total of 26,541 men. Chambray, taking into account the losses suffered by the vanguard of the French army, from 8 (20) September to 6 (18) October, believes that on the day of the Tarutino action, the strength of Murat's force did not exceed 20,000 men. Chambray, II, 215 & 230.

this river, as follows: Claparède's Division was forwards of the Chernishnya, in Vinkovo; on his flanks were a division each from the corps under Saint-Germain and Nansouty; Poniatowski's *5e Corps* was in Teterinka and to the right of this village; on the other bank of the river were: Saint-Germain's *3e Corps de cavalerie* and Dufour's Division to the right and left of the highway, respectively; Nansouty's *1er Corps de cavalerie* was further to the left, while Latour-Maubourg's *4e Corps de cavalerie* was four *versts* behind the right wing, between the highway and the Nara.[9] The extensive forest, on the left flank of the enemy position, left the French vulnerable to a surprise envelopment. Unable to occupy it, the enemy had to protect themselves from the left flank by sending patrols at least, but this was not done, both due to the extreme exhaustion of the cavalry, and due to Murat's negligence. The Cossacks, scouting in all directions, riding through the forest, approached the enemy camp and noted the French omissions, reporting on this to the headquarters. On the basis of this intelligence, Quartermaster General Toll, accompanied by one of the officers of the quartermasters department, Lieutenant Traskin, reconnoitred the forest several times in full detail. He drew up a plan of attack on the enemy position, on the basis of this survey himself.[10] But it was not easy to get consent for this from the old Field Marshal, who would not dare to take any action that might bring Napoleon out of Moscow and result in a general battle. On the other hand, it was obvious that Napoleon could not stay in Moscow for long even without this and that he would soon have to fight him, therefore one should not miss any opportunity to weaken him: such were Toll's arguments, and many of our generals shared his opinion. Among them was Konovnitsyn; Baggovut in particular insisted on not postponing the attack. Bennigsen himself, despite his dislike for Toll, approved of his proposal, and among other arguments in favour of the plan of action drawn up by him, he cited that it was necessary to attack the enemy before Victor's *9e Corps* arrived to assist them. Bennigsen submitted a note to Prince Kutuzov on the same subject in which he argued for the need to attack Murat's vanguard, and wishing to dispel the Field Marshal's concerns for the success of this enterprise, he mentioned that Napoleon remained in Moscow with the entire *Garde* and that Murat had little artillery and no more 8,000 cavalry.[11]

---

9   Chambray, II, 217-218.
10 The general opinion is to credit Toll for the importance of his contribution to the action at Tarutino. Emperor Alexander I, in rewarding this meritorious act, subsequently honoured him with a Rescript, which stated: 'as a reward for surveying the enemy positions, drawing up a disposition for an attack and indicating the routes for a 100,000 strong army right to the enemy outposts...' Toll was awarded the Order of St Anne, 1st class.
11 General Bennigsen's note to Prince Kutuzov, dated 3 [15] October 1812: '*Monsieur le Marchal! Il parait d'après tous les renseignemens et les rapports que nous avons reçus, que les renforts que l'ennemi attend, sous les ordres du maréchal Victor, se trouvent effectivement en marche et peu eloignés de nous; il me parait donc que les intérêts de notre Souverain et de l'Etat demandent que nous attaquions, sans perte de temps, avec toutes les forces concentrées sous les ordres de Votre Altesse, l'ennemi, qui se trouve vis-à-vis de nous sous les ordres du Roi de Naples, avant que ces renforts mentionnés puissent atteindre l'armée française. Cette mésure est, selon moi, d'autant plus nécessaire à prendre sans delai, que tous les avis que nous avons reçus, portent que Napoléon lui même, avec tout le corps de ses gardes, se trouve encore à Moscou, et que le*

Kutuzov, eventually agreeing to the proposed attack, instructed Bennigsen to command the force assigned to envelope the enemy position; the main body, under the personal command of the Field Marshal, was to conduct the frontal attack. The disposition compiled by Toll contained the following orders:

> The army is to depart camp on 4 [16] October,[12] at six o'clock in the afternoon. II Corps, III Corps and IV Corps (assigning one battery and two light artillery companies to each), and ten Cossack regiments with a company of Don horse artillery, under Adjutant General Count Orlov-Denisov [Vasily Vasilevich Orlov-Denisov], to whom the Lifeguard Dragoons, Lifeguard Ulans, Lifeguard Hussars, and Nezhin Dragoons are assigned as reinforcements, with a half-company of horse artillery, under the command of Major General Meller-Zakomelsky, are to move in four columns from the camp to the village of Spaskoe, where they are to cross the Nara river via three bridges, and are then to halt in column, at intervals of 150 paces from one another, having the cavalry column on the right side of III Corps.
>
> VI Corps, VII Corps, VIII Corps and V Corps, with the artillery organic to them, are to cross at the village of Tarutino via two bridges and deploy: VI Corps, VII Corps and VIII Corps in the first wave; V Corps behind them in reserve: each in regimental columns of division [two company frontage]; both cuirassier divisions behind the second corps. VI Corps, having crossed the right bridge at Tarutino, are to move along the road leading to the forest on our right flank, in which they are to halt in concealment in regimental columns of division at full interval. Of course, each corps is to form up in two waves.
>
> II Cavalry Corps, III Cavalry Corps and IV Cavalry Corps,[13] co-located with the vanguard are to close up to the vedette screen before dawn and will be under the command of Major General Korf.
>
> The four columns of the right flank are to move forward, leaving the enemy held forest to their left, behind our vedette screen, and after passing some distance, IV Corps is to make a change of direction to the left and move right up to the vedette screen, where it is to halt without a sound in column of divisions.

Roi de Naples a peu d'artillerie avec lui et que toute sa cavalerie se monte, tout au plus, à 8,000 hommes.
Votre Altesse, qui certainement mieux que moi saura juger l'importance de la proposition que je prends la liberté de lui faire, daignera, dans le cas qu'Elle approuvera mon projet, me donner Ses ordres, pour que je puisse avoir l'honneur de Lui presenter pour Son approbation la disposition de cette attaque, qui sera d'autant plus facile à exécuter que nous n'avons que des plaines devant nous entremelées de quelques petites forêts. Je crois nécessaire d'ajouter ici que l'ennemi, depuis quelques jours, a forcé la chaine de nos avant-postes et qu'il a placé la sienne sur une hauteur de la quelle chacune de ses vedettes peut voir ce qui se passe dans notre camp.' Archive of the Military Topographic Depot, No. 46,692, folio 4.
12 Subsequently, as will be explained, the attack was delayed until the following day.
13 II Cavalry Corps and III Cavalry Corps were amalgamated into a single corps (II Cavalry Corps), under Korf's command; IV Cavalry Corps was commanded by Vasilchikov in Sievers' place.

II Corps and III Corps are to march on further, striving to bypass the main part of the forest then changing direction to the left at the village of Khorosino.

The cavalry column, under the command of Adjutant General Count Orlov-Denisov, is to go around the forest even further; the 20th Jäger Regiment is attached to this column to march at its head. All jäger regiments located with the corps are to march at the head of the columns, in skirmish order with supports in front of the columns until they reach the forest, even then without drums and without words of command, so that the enemy cannot discover our approach to their left flank.

The jägers, having entered the forest, even if it happens that the enemy, having discovered them, fire warning shots to signal this, they are not to return fire, but are to strive to completely take possession of the entire forest, which is not more than half a *verst* deep, at the double, and having reached the further edge of the forest, they are to halt and wait for the arrival of the columns, which, having closed up to the jägers, are to emerge under their covering fire from the forest and direct the heads of the regimental columns to the left; the jägers must protect this movement.

VI Corps, VII Corps, VIII Corps and V Corps are also to close up to our forward screen before dawn, having II Cavalry Corps, III Cavalry Corps and IV Cavalry Corps to their front; once we hear that the action has begun on our right flank, the entire cavalry, with the exception of the cuirassiers, are immediately to go on the attack. The infantry columns are to follow them at a rapid pace. VI Corps, situated on the right flank, is to move up to the forest, having jägers in the lead, who are to occupy the forest immediately and establish communications with the corps under Lieutenant General Count Osterman [IV Corps]. As the offensive progresses, all formations of the force are to establish communications with each other as they close up.

The positioning of the artillery during the action is left to the corps commanders.

All movements should be conducted quickly and without a sound; use cold steel, and do not engage in extended firefights.

III Corps constitutes the reserve for the columns on the right flank, while V Corps is the reserve for the columns on the left flank.

All columns on the right flank, consisting of II Corps, III Corps and IV Corps and the cavalry column under Count Orlov-Denisov, are commanded by General of Cavalry Bennigsen; the columns on the left flank, VII Corps, VIII Corps and V Corps, as well as II Cavalry Corps, III Cavalry Corps and IV Cavalry Corps and the two cuirassier divisions, comprise the command of General of Infantry Miloradovich; the Commander in Chief of the army will also accompany them. The central column, composed of VI Corps, will be placed under the command of General of Infantry Dokhturov; as the advance closes with the enemy, this column will join IV Corps, and then both IV Corps and VI Corps, will come under his command. The entire cavalry will be commanded by Adjutant General Uvarov.

All regimental drummers and musicians are to be left in the camp and are to sound reveille at the appropriate time. Fires are to be lit, no more and no fewer than usual; leave the huts which are not at all to be burned; in any case, this will remain the responsibility of the corps and divisional commanders; leave one non-commissioned officer with three privates from each company, and one officer from each regiment in the camp for this.

Battery and light [artillery] companies, remaining from II Corps, III Corps and IV Corps, are to cross the river over the same bridges where their corps are to cross, but remain in reserve at the crossing points. The horse artillery of the entire army, excluding those companies mentioned above, are to cross after V Corps, VI Corps, VII Corps and VIII Corps and form a reserve behind the cuirassiers, except for two companies sent with the cavalry corps. The rest of the artillery is to remain in camp as a reserve, as is all the transport.

The Lifeguard Dragoons, Lifeguard Ulans, Lifeguard Hussars, and Nezhin Dragoons with the half-company of horse artillery are to set off at seven o'clock in the afternoon to the village of Spaskoe to link up with the column under Count Orlov-Denisov.

All the jäger regiments on the flanks, except for 4th Jägers, are to join their divisions at five o'clock in the afternoon, leaving their huts intact.

Do not light fires at halts during the march and pipes are also not to be smoked.'[14]

The detachment under General Dorokhov, which was stationed at Kamenskoe, was ordered to link up with the detachment under Figner, to move to Voronovo, destroy the two regiments stationed there and block the line of retreat of the enemy vanguard.[15]

Thus, it was intended to strike Murat at dawn on 5 (17) October. The reality was somewhat different. The officer sent from headquarters by Konovnitsyn with the disposition for General Yermolov could not find him anywhere in the camp, because Yermolov had gone to visit Duty General Kikin [Pëtr Andreevich Kikin] that day, in a village lying three *versts* from the left flank of the camp.[16] Meanwhile, Kutuzov set off to the camp from Letashevka on a *drozhki* [lightweight open wagon],[17] where he hoped to see the troops at full readiness for action, but to his extreme surprise he found men, for the most part, sleeping, the horses unsaddled; not a single gun was limbered; none of the generals were in their command posts. The Field Marshal, enraged by the failure to carry out the orders issued by him, showered insults on

---

14 Archive of the Military Topographic Depot, No. 46,692, folio 4.
15 Orders for Dorokhov dated 4 [16] October (log of outgoing documents, No. 154).
16 Shcherbinin's notes mention that Lieutenant Pavlov of the Yekaterinoslav Cuirassiers was sent to Yermolov with the disposition, but, according to other eyewitnesses, these orders were given to Lieutenant Gersevanov of the Glukhov Cuirassiers by the Field Marshal himself, who was with him as an orderly, who went looking for General Yermolov for a long time, and, eventually, found him in the village of Spaskoe, with General Shepelev. Prince A.B. Golitsyn's notes.
17 [The village, just south-west of Tarutino, was completely destroyed during World War II].

THE BATTLE OF TARUTINO (ON THE RIVER CHERNISHNYA) 331

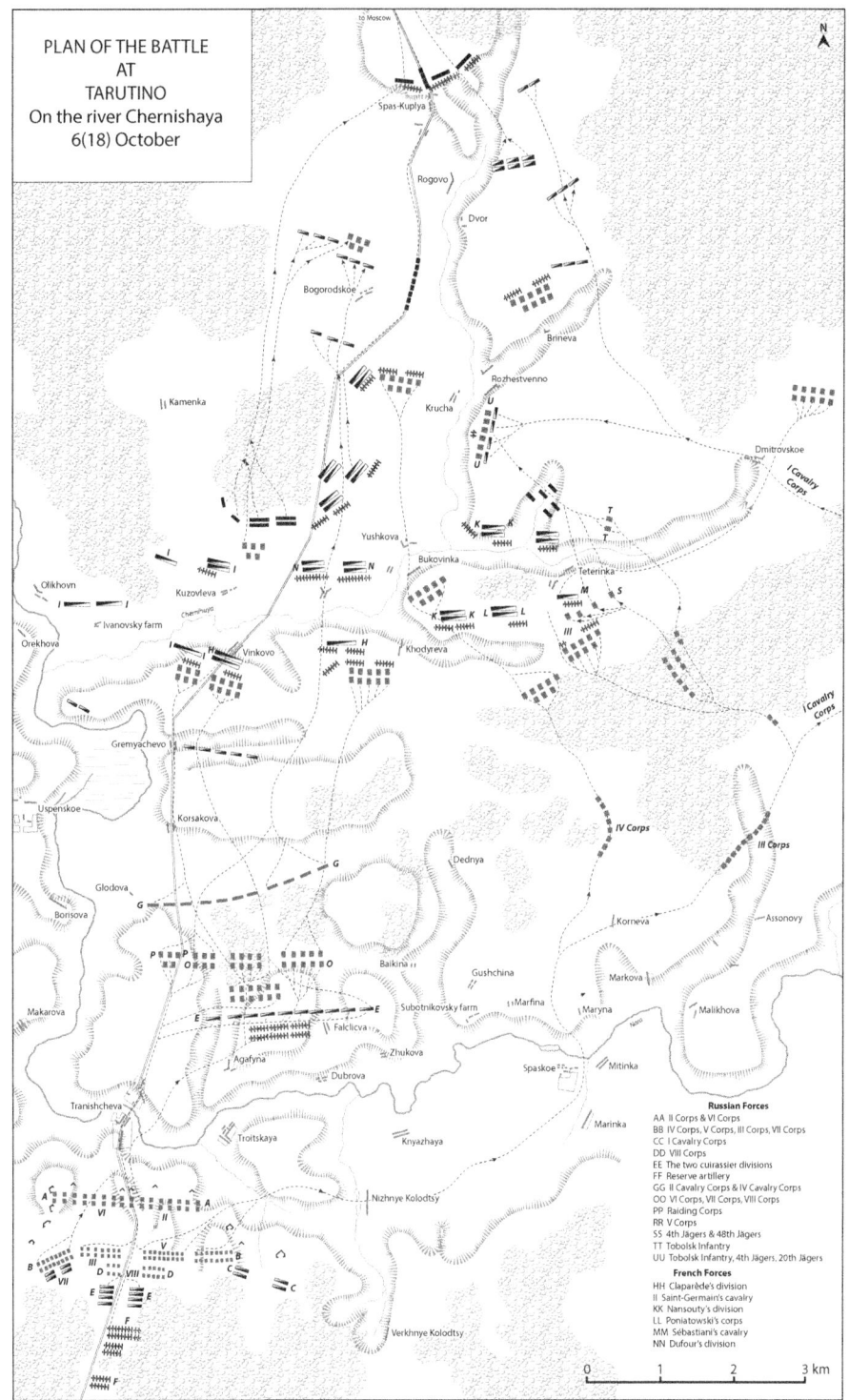

Plan of the Battle at Tarutino, 18 October 1812.

the first officer of the quartermaster's department that caught his eye, Lieutenant Colonel Eichen [Fëdor Yakovlevich Eichen].[18] The formation commanders offered to leave camp somewhat behind schedule, but Kutuzov, who had not willingly agreed to the proposed offensive, postponed it for a full 24 hours, of which Dorokhov was also informed.[19]

Bennigsen, for his part, issued a disposition to the troops entrusted to him, the essence of which was as follows: First Column (starting from the right flank), consisting of ten Cossack regiments and 20th Jägers, with one horse artillery battery, under Count Orlov-Denisov's command, was tasked to reach the edge of the forest that flanked the enemy position and halt at the village of Stromilovo; Second Column, consisting of II Corps, under General Baggovut's command, moving along the road leading from Spaskoe to Teterinka, was to halt at the edge of the forest, to the left of First Column; while Third Column, comprising IV Corps and 2nd Cuirassier Division, under Count Osterman's command, was to move further to the left, staying level with Second Column. The reserve was to consist of Count Stroganov's III Corps and General Meller-Zakomelsky's I Cavalry Corps, having orders to proceed behind II Corps. Colonel Toll was to take over the direction of the first two columns assigned to strike the enemy from the flank and rear. The troops were ordered to move without a sound and to reach the points assigned to them while it was still dark. At dawn, II Corps were to launch an attack on the 14 gun battery, which was forwards of the left flank of the enemy position, at Teterinka. At that very moment, First Column was also tasked to race towards Voronovo, behind enemy lines; IV Corps, which would serve as the link between V Corps and the main body, was to halt at the edge of the forest and await further orders; while III Corps were to proceed behind II Corps and serve as their reserve.[20]

These orders were very thorough, but, as frequently happens, they could not be executed precisely. The approach march at night by a significant number of troops met with unexpected difficulties, and the desire to coordinate the movements of several columns constantly forced them to halt and delayed the march to such an extent that II Corps needed about 12 hours to move less than 15 *versts* and arrived at the edge of the forest near the village of Khorosino not before seven o'clock in the morning. As IV Corps were still far behind at this time, II Corps postponed their attack. The situation had changed: instead of debouching the troops from the forest in the dark of night, it was necessary to commit them in daylight, and, having deployed into combat formation from a deep column of 16 battalions, cross about 1,000 paces under fire from an enemy battery. In order to facilitate the deployment of the corps, Prinz Eugen von Württemberg proposed to commit the force from the forest in three columns, so that the centre column, consisting of four battalions from Pillar's [Yegor Maximovich Pillar] Jäger brigade, with two artillery companies, having entered the open ground before the others, would be located in the first wave, while the flanking columns, from 4th Division and 17th Division, each consisting of six battalions with one artillery company, would support the centre column and

---

18 Shcherbinin's notes.
19 Prince A.B. Golitsyn's notes.
20 Prinz Eugen von Württemberg's diary (archive of the M.T.D. No. 47,344).

envelope the enemy on their left flank. Baggovut himself, who had a heated argument with Toll (dissatisfied at the imprecise execution of the issued disposition) immediately before this, led Pillar's brigade forwards, moving at the head of 4th Jäger Regiment, of which he was the Colonel in Chief. He said to the prince: 'I ask Your Highness to deploy the force, while I shall stay with my jägers; I have lived with them, I shall die with them. I shall go at the battery first.' Prinz Eugen von Württemberg, parting from him, moved to the right with the Tobolsk Infantry and with a light artillery company, while 17th Division headed to the left of the jägers.

It was already seven o'clock. Meanwhile, as the infantry of II Corps was preparing to attack the enemy, Count Orlov-Denisov, having passed through the village of Dmitrovskoe before dawn, concealed his Cossacks in the forest, waiting for our other columns to enter the open ground. Once it was fully daylight, concerned about being discovered, he ordered the troops to attack. With loud shouts, the Cossacks charged into Sébastiani's bivouacs, taking a cuirassier division by surprise and, having driven three regiments (*1er régiment de carabiniers*, *2e régiment de carabiniers* and *1er régiment de cuirassiers*) back over the Ryazan ravine, captured 38 guns. The attack was so unexpected that pots of hot coffee were found on the campfires; next to them – as evidence of the lack of food supplies – stood cauldrons of horse meat. Horror and indignation seized our warriors when they saw large icons being used by the enemy as tables and benches. Unfortunately, instead of relentlessly pursuing the disordered troops, the Cossacks began to loot the French baggage, which allowed the cuirassiers to recover. Deploying into line, they went on the attack, and were engaged with fire by the Cossack battery in Orlov-Denisov's detachment. At that very moment, Prinz Eugen von Württemberg emerged from the forest with the Tobolsk Infantry and three guns. Utter chaos was noticeable in the enemy camp; to the right of the prince, Cossacks were prowling behind the enemy lines; cannon fire rang out to the left. It was obvious that Baggovut was already committed to combat, and therefore Prinz Eugen, together with Toll at his side, without waiting for the arrival of the rest of his force, led the regiment that was with him against the enemy.

General Baggovut emerged from the forest with 4th Jägers and 48th Jägers, formed in column. As soon as this force appeared on the open ground, they were engaged by the fire of an enemy battery stationed near the village of Teterinka and suffered significant casualties. Baggovut himself was mortally wounded by one of the first shots. A warrior at heart, the courageous Baggovut was adored and respected in the army. His was a combination of courage and composure, extraordinary kindness and fortitude. All those who knew General Baggovut spoke positively of his sincere qualities, while his last letters to his wife,[21] in which he expressed the hope of devoting the rest of his life to his family after the war, serve as evidence that even among the valiant hardships of combat, he dreamed of love and companionship.

The death of Baggovut had a negative effect on the operations by II Corps, assigned to deliver the decisive blow to the enemy. The jägers, who had suffered heavy casualties from the enemy bombardment while in deep formation, scattered and continued to advance in a dense screen, not supported by an adequate reserve.

---

21 In September 1812, he wrote to her ten times.

The French *carabiniers*, taking advantage of this, charged at the 48th Jägers and cut down many of the men. Bennigsen, arriving at this point, was so baffled by this particular failure that, instead of going around the enemy position, he cared only about holding on to the ground he had seized. To that end, in order to assist the jägers he pulled together not only the entire 17th Division under Olsufiev, but also the infantry from 4th Division behind the Tobolsk Infantry with Prinz Eugen von Württemberg: all these troops, crowded in a small space, some still in the forest, some standing inactive, were under fire from enemy artillery for an hour. From our side, Frisch's Battery Artillery Company was placed on high ground and also opened a bombardment. Meanwhile, Osterman's IV Corps had not yet arrived at their appointed place, and therefore Bennigsen, worried about losing touch with the main body advancing against the enemy from the front, ordered Count Stroganov's III Corps (instead of moving to the right, to reinforce II Corps and enveloping the French from the flank), to head to their left and push the battery under Colonel Taube [Karl Karlovich Taube] onto the high ground: thus, on the decisive point of the battlefield there were only Cossacks with a Don artillery battery and two battalions of the Tobolsk Infantry with three guns. The direction given to III Corps was all the more mistaken because at that time our main body was already closing on the enemy position and General Vasilchikov's cavalry was preparing to attack.

As in the meantime, there was still no word of Osterman, General Konovnitsyn, who had joined Bennigsen on the right wing, volunteered to find IV Corps and set off back through the forest with the officers who were with him. Having travelled some distance, he noticed infantry making their way along the edge of the forest, up the road from the village of Gushchina towards Teterinka. Konovnitsyn, believing that this column belonged to IV Corps, sent Danilevsky (later historian of the war of 1812) to meet them, ordering him to ask who commanded these troops and to speed up their movement. Danilevsky rode up to the column, but was greeted with gunfire and seriously wounded. It turned out that the infantry moving through the forest were two Polish battalions retreating without resistance in front of the troops of IV Corps towards the Chernishnya, which they managed due to the slowness and disjointed nature of our offensive. Meanwhile, Konovnitsyn, having travelled around the enemy column via a roundabout route, eventually found Osterman and gave him Bennigsen's order – to hurry to the exits from the forest. Danilevsky, who had fallen with his horse shot under him, was saved by Lieutenant Shcherbinin [Alexander Andreevich Shcherbinin] and some Cossacks, who took him to Tarutino.

As soon as IV Corps approached the edge of the forest, Bennigsen, having ridden out to meet them, positioned them to the left of III Corps: thus, 46 battalions were concentrated against Teterinka. But by this time, the enemy troops were already retreating from all points.

It was mentioned above that Prinz Eugen von Württemberg, having left the forest, decided to attack the enemy with two battalions of the Tobolsk Infantry and with three guns, not waiting for the arrival of more troops from his division, but hoping for their assistance and that of III Corps under Count Osterman, which, according to disposition, was to be following II Corps. Crossing the Desenka river via a ford, the Prince moved to the left against the French cuirassiers retreating behind the Ryazan ravine, while the Cossacks circled behind the enemy; 4th Jägers, who had managed to pass to the right of Teterinka, where Polish troops were still holding, linked up with the left flank of the Tobolsk Infantry. Thus, Prinz Eugen, outflanking the Poles, ordered the three guns with him to open fire. From the opening shot, the enemy evacuated Teterinka and, changing front with the left flank refused, began to retreat behind the Chernishnya, while the cuirassiers, also retreating beyond this river, formed up forwards of the Moscow road.[22] Following this, 20th Jägers, which belonged to the right column, joined the Prince's force; but these six weak battalions, supported by the Cossacks, were unable to operate decisively, and the enemy owed their salvation to this circumstance. Murat's force stretched out in a long column past our weak detachment, which was unable to cut off their retreat, but, eventually, Colonel Toll managed to bring up Göring's [Pëtr Khristianovich Göring] horse artillery battery across the river near the village of Krucha and open fire on the cavalry screening the movements of the column. Count Orlov-Denisov raced to the right of the village of Brineva with several Cossack regiments and Meller-Zakomelsky's regular cavalry and started engaging the cavalry under Latour-Maubourg and Valence at Bogorodskoe; the French cavalry, and especially *6e régiment de cuirassiers*, fought very bravely, but were forced to retreat. Meanwhile, Prinz Eugen's infantry had also crossed the Chernishnya. 20th Jägers, under the command of Colonel Gorikhvostov [Alexander Zakharyevich Gorikhvostov], marched towards an enemy battery singing and captured it,[23] but being attacked by French carabiniers, lost the guns they had captured and were driven back with significant casualties. During these actions, the enemy troops that had remained in positions facing Vinkovo, went around the ravine near Bogorodskoe through the forest and reached the village of Spas-Kuplya, where Murat rallied his troops and reformed them once more.

On the left wing, where Kutuzov was stationed himself, the troops, on closing up to the Chernishnya, were ordered to halt. Miloradovich and Yermolov begged the Field Marshal for permission to attack the enemy, but without success. Kutuzov emphatically refused these requests. It was said that the reason for this was the arrival of an *Uryadnik* from Zhirov's Cossacks under Colonel Prince Kudashev, who was at Podolsk with one of the partisan detachments, with an intercepted order from Berthier to General d'Argence [Pierre Jacques Jean Hector du Bousquet d'Argence], about sending all carts to Mozhaisk. Having received this intelligence, Kutuzov became convinced of Napoleon's intention to retreat from Moscow, but in which direction he intended to go was unknown to the Field Marshal. It could

---

22 '*Toutes les troupes qui occupaient les bords de la Tchernichna avaient effectué précipitamment leurs retraite, moins par suite de l'attaque de front qu'elles avaient essuyée, qu'à cause de celle que les Russes dirigeaient sur leurs derrières...*' Chambray, II, 221. (All the troops holding the banks of the Chernishnya had retreated hastily, not so much as a result of the frontal attack which they had endured, rather because of those Russians that were directed into their rear).
23 In Prince Kutuzov's Army Orders dated 10 [22] October, No. 46 it states: 'the courage and speed with which the 20th Jäger Regiment, on the 6th of this month [18 October], attacked the enemy and, having driven them back, pursued them throughout the entire battle, inflicting severe losses on them at every step, obliges me to declare my total gratitude to all the gentlemen officers and lower ranks of this regiment, and as an encouragement to these latter, I award five paper roubles per man.'

easily turn out that Napoleon planned to envelope us from their right flank, and in this case, by pursuing Murat, we would have facilitated the execution of any plan drawn up by the enemy, or we would have been in danger of encountering Napoleon's main force.[24] This is how the stubborn inaction of our commander was explained, but one can hardly concur with this point of view. It is much more likely that the failure of the flanking movement undertaken by Bennigsen convinced Kutuzov of the need to avoid a critical action and forced him to refuse to deliver the decisive blow to the enemy.

It was only after the enemy had completely abandoned the banks of the Chernishnya that Bennigsen led II Corps, III Corps and IV Corps to the Desenka and upper Chernishnya. At the same time, Miloradovich's vanguard and Vasilchikov's corps crossed the river. Enemy infantry still occupied the forest along the highway, and therefore, to clear it, six battalions of jägers were sent from the vanguard, supported by two grenadier regiments from VIII Corps.

The Cossack regiments under Count Orlov-Denisov pursued the enemy as far as Spas-Kuplya; II Corps and IV Corps and the cavalry under Korf and Vasilchikov stopped at Bogorodskoe, under the command of Miloradovich; all the rest of our troops were withdrawn to the Tarutino camp. The detachment under Dorokhov, tasked with cutting off Murat's line of retreat, were unable to reach the Moscow road, and only *Uryadnik* Filatov of Vlasov's Cossack Regiment, sent by him with a fighting patrol, took part in the pursuit of the enemy, killing the cavalry general Dery [Pierre César Dery].[25] Murat's force, retreating to Voronovo, took up a rather advantageous position there.

Although it is difficult to report anything reliably about the losses from both sides in the action at Tarutino, however, most of the information available in this regard shows losses to the French: between 500 to 1,000 killed and wounded, and 1,500 men captured; taken by Russian troops: one cavalry standard, 38 guns, 40 ammunition caissons and many wagons. Among the dead were: the commander of the King of Naples' bodyguard, General Dery and General Fiszer [Stanisław Fiszer].[26] For our part, in the returns signed by Colonel Kikin, the following losses appear: one general, one subaltern, 72 lower ranks killed; 17 field officers and subalterns, 411 lower ranks wounded; 700 lower ranks missing, overall, our losses extended to 1,200 men. Our generals, and in particular Konovnitsyn and Toll, were very dissatisfied with the outcome of the action, in which, in their opinion, it should have been possible to destroy the entire enemy vanguard.[27] In contrast, the influence of

---

24 The Field Marshal himself thought so. From the notes by Prince A.B. Golitsyn.
25 War Diary signed by Prince Kutuzov (archive of the M.T.D. No. 46,692, folio 4). The Commander in Chief, on Dorokhov's recommendation, promoted Filatov to cornet and awarded him the Order of St Anna, 3rd class.
26 These figures were taken from Prinz Eugen von Württemberg's *Erinnerungen aus dem Feldzuge des Jahres 1812 in Russland*, because in French documents and official information, the losses from Murat's force are shown very imprecisely. On the day after the battle, a letter from General Borelli was sent to our outposts, in which he asked, on behalf of the King of Naples, for permission to bury the body of General Dery and take his heart. In response, he was told that Dery's body could not be found.
27 From Shcherbinin's notes.

the battle of Tarutino on the Russian forces was very favourable, because we had managed to drive back the enemy with a small force[28] and capture many guns.[29]

Bennigsen visited Kutuzov immediately after the fighting had ceased, but received his congratulations on the victory very coolly, and did not even dismount from his horse under the pretext of the contusion he had received. He believed that Kutuzov not only kept the left wing of the army but also Osterman's corps inactive, with the intent of depriving him of the glory of a decisive success. Such speculation was completely unfounded, but Bennigsen, nevertheless, from that day on became an implacable enemy of Kutuzov and armed himself against him through his subsequent actions. Bennigsen's report to the Field Marshal on the battle at Tarutino opens with the words:

> I hasten to inform Your Grace of yesterday's battle, which I had the honour of opening, executing and ending, and the consequences of which are already known to you.

Further on it stated:

> I had hoped that circumstances would allow Your Grace to be, as I was, a witness of the order and courage with which the troops entrusted to me made numerous attacks, in which they covered themselves with glory and honour.[30]

It was quite natural for Kutuzov to be dissatisfied with such an exclusive appropriation of the feats accomplished, and a consequence of this was the removal of Bennigsen from all duties associated with the appointment of Chief of Staff of the Army.

The battle at Tarutino did not satisfy Kutuzov's expectations,[31] but he, not wanting to weaken the moral influence of a success won by our army, presented it triumphantly

---

28 From our side, just eight battalions from the Tobolsk Infantry, 4th Jägers, 20th Jägers and 48th Jägers, ten Cossack regiments under Count Orlov-Denisov, a light cavalry division under General Meller-Zakomelsky and IV Cavalry Corps under General Vasilchikov actually participated in the battle: a total of 5,000 infantry and 7,000 regular and irregular cavalry.

29 The following sources were used for the description of the action at Tarutino: Prince Kutuzov's report on this action to the Tsar and Bennigsen's to Kutuzov. Prinz Eugen von Württemberg's *Erinnerungen aus dem Feldzuge des Jahres 1812 in Russland*, 110-116. Prinz Eugen von Württemberg's war diary (archive of the M.T.D. No. 47,344). Shcherbinin's notes. Buturlin, II, 139-148.

30 [Liprandi comments: 'Here it remains only to regret that General Bogdanovich did not publish Bennigsen's most humble letter in its entirety, which, languishing in the folders of the General Staff, could have thrown light on this matter; since it must not be forgotten that Bennigsen himself, as Commander-in-Chief, had commanded at Pultusk and Preußisch Eylau, and, I will add, had been facing a strong, fresh enemy, and not such as this latter was on the Chernishnya; Bennigsen's authority, therefore, is unquestionable'].

31 [Liprandi comments: 'Does this mean, therefore, in the sense that it emerged that Kutuzov expected even more confusion from the flanking movement, in which some units got lost at night, in a forest, which somewhat slowed down the general emergence of its constituent units

as a decisive victory. On 7 (19) October, a thanksgiving service was held in all units of the force, during which the Field Marshal was present with the Lifeguard Corps along with many generals.[32] In his report to the Tsar on the battle at Tarutino, Prince Kutuzov stated:

> With the discovery by our partisans of an opportunity to attack the corps under the King of Naples, numbering 50,000 men, our army set out from their positions at Tarutino in several columns, on 5 [17] October, at seven o'clock in the evening. The right wing, under the command of General Bennigsen, consisting of 20th Jägers and ten Cossack regiments, led by Count Orlov-Denisov, with support from three regiments of Lifeguard light cavalry, one dragoon regiment and II Corps, III Corps and IV Corps, crossing the river Nara at midnight, reached the points assigned to them and at dawn, passing through the forest, raced at the enemy.

Having described the course and outcome of the action in a few lines, the Field Marshal ended his report with the following handwritten postscript:

> The most flattering of all during this victory was the silence and order preserved by all the columns. Some witnesses liken the actions of this day to a training manoeuvre carried out with enthusiasm.[33]

The report to the Tsar about the victory at Tarutino, together with the cavalry standard [*1er régiment de cuirassiers*] captured from the enemy, was sent with Colonel Michaud, who, by the will of Emperor Alexander I himself, was to be the herald of the first victory won by our army (see chapter XXV). After explaining the details of the battle, about which it had been impossible to extract detail from the very brief report by the Field Marshal, Michaud asked permission to convey the wishes of the army to the Tsar. He stated:

> The victory we have won, the excellent condition of your troops, their spirit and general devotion to you, reinforcements daily approaching the army, the plight of Napoleon; the measures taken by Your Majesty to cut off his retreat: all this gives undoubted hope that Napoleon will be expelled from Russia in disgrace. The troops, confident of success, know that they owe everything to the efforts of Your Imperial Majesty and ask a single favour; that you personally take command of the army. Your Majesty's presence would make them invincible.

---

at their assigned locations; yet, in spite of all this, Kutuzov could not only have corrected all this, but could also have delivered a decisive blow to the enemy, but refused to do so?'].
32 War Diary signed by Prince Kutuzov (archive of the M.T.D. No. 46,692, folio 4).
33 Prince Kutuzov's report to Emperor Alexander I, dated 7 [19] October (archive of the M.T.D. No. 46,692, folio 4).

The gracious Monarch, deeply moved by this expression of devotion from 100,000 soldiers ready to die in defence of the Tsar and the Fatherland, answered:

> The entire nation aspire to this; I frankly admit that I do also, no less than others, and if I were to be carried away by this emotion now, I would sit in a carriage with you and go to the army. Taking into account the disadvantageous situation into which we have drawn the enemy, the excellent spirit of the army, the inexhaustible resources of the Empire and the directions I have given to the Army of the Danube, I am undoubtedly sure that we shall win and that, after all that has been done, all that remains for us, as you say, is to reap the laurels. I know that if I am with the army, then all the glory of success will reflect upon Me, and that I will take a place in history. But when I think how little experience I have in military matters compared to Napoleon, and that despite My good will, I could make a mistake from which the precious blood of My children would be shed, then, in spite of My aspirations, I am ready and willing to sacrifice personal glory for the good of the army. Let those who are more worthy than I reap the laurels. Return to the Field Marshal, congratulate him on his victory and tell him to drive the enemy out of Russia.[34]

A few days before the battle of Tarutino, Emperor Alexander I, being dissatisfied with the inactivity of our main force, had sent a handwritten rescript to Prince Kutuzov as follows:

> Prince Mikhail Ilarionovich. Moscow has been in enemy hands since 2 [14] September. Your latest reports are dated the 20th, and during the whole time not only has nothing been done to operate against the enemy and liberate this capital city, but according to your latest reports, you have retreated still further. Serpukhov has already been occupied by an enemy detachment while Tula with its famous factories absolutely vital to the army, is in danger.
>
> According to reports from General Wintzingerode, I see that an enemy 10,000 man corps is moving along the St Petersburg road. Another several thousand are also going to Dmitrov. A third has moved forward along the Vladimir road. A fourth rather significant is stationed between Ruza and Mozhaisk. Napoleon himself was in Moscow on the 25th.
>
> According to all this intelligence, since the enemy has divided his forces with strong detachments, since Napoleon himself is still in Moscow with his *Garde*, is it possible that the enemy forces in front of you are significant and prevent you from operating on the offensive.
>
> On the contrary, it is easy to believe that they are pursuing you with detachments, or at least with a corps much weaker than the army entrusted to you. It seems that, taking advantage of these circumstances, you could

---

34 From Michaud's handwritten notes.

profitably attack an enemy weaker than you and destroy them, or at least cause them to retreat, keeping a meaningful part of the governorate in our hands, which is now occupied by the enemy, and thereby avert the danger to Tula and our other internal cities.

You will remain answerable if the enemy is able to send a significant corps to St Petersburg, to threaten this capital in which few troops remain, since you have every means to avert this new misfortune with the army entrusted to you, acting with determination and activity.

Remember that you still owe an answer to the offended Fatherland for the loss of Moscow.

You have experienced My willingness to reward you. This readiness will not weaken in Me, but I and Russia have the right to expect all the diligence, resolve and success from you that your mind, your military talents and the courage of the troops led by you portend to us.

I remain forever grateful to you.

St Petersburg, 2 [14] October 1812. Alexander.

Upon receiving a report on the victory at Tarutino, the Sovereign granted Kutuzov a Golden Sword, with diamonds and a laurel wreath, and honoured him with the following handwritten rescript:

The victory won by you over Murat has made me indescribably happy. I flatter myself with the hope that this is the beginning that must bring results of even greater importance. The glory of Russia is inseparable from your own and from the salvation of Europe.

General Bennigsen was awarded diamonds to the Order of St Andrew for his actions and received a lump sum of 100,000 roubles. Encouraged by the Monarch's goodwill, Bennigsen sent a letter to the Tsar in which he accused Kutuzov not only of deliberately not supporting him with the troops of the left wing in the Tarutino action, but also of the insidious inaction of the army in general, despite all the proposals that – according to Bennigsen – were made by him to the Field Marshal. Not satisfied with these accusations, Bennigsen went into the details of Kutuzov's private life, exposing him as a sybarite, wallowing in bliss and pleasure. But Emperor Alexander did not pay any attention to this denunciation, and even forwarded Bennigsen's letter to the Field Marshal, which resulted in his removal from the army.[35]

On the occasion of the arrival of General Tormasov at headquarters on 8 (20) October, he was entrusted with command of III Corps, V Corps, VI Corps, VII Corps and VIII Corps, the light cavalry (I Cavalry Corps) under Meller-Zakomelsky and both cuirassier divisions that were under the command of Prince Golitsyn. As before, Miloradovich commanded the vanguard, composed of II Corps, entrusted to Prince Dolgorukov [Sergei Nikolaevich Dolgorukov] after the death of Baggovut,[36]

---

35 Bernhardi, *Denkwürdigkeiten des Grafen v. Toll*, II, 230.
36 He had recently arrived in the army from Naples, where he had been a diplomat.

IV Corps, II Cavalry Corps under Korf and IV Cavalry Corps under Vasilchikov, instead of Sievers, who had been sent to Malorussia by Prince Kutuzov.

French historians, in trying to justify the negligent disposition of Murat's force before the battle of Tarutino, argue that since the arrival of Lauriston at our headquarters, a truce had been concluded, and a pledge was made by both sides to notify each other in the event of a resumption of hostilities. Napoleon himself published the pretext for accusing us of treachery, declaring in one of his bulletins that: 'The Russians shamefully violated the truce between the vanguards (*une trève d'avant-garde*).'[37] The very expression: *a truce between the vanguards* shows that the whole thing was limited to a condition that the sentries who were in the forward outposts not shoot at one another. There was no truce between the armies, and this is most convincingly demonstrated by our partisan operations, which were not suspended even for a single day. The French themselves did not attach great credibility to the accusation contained in the bulletin: Fain [Agathon Jean François Fain], who was under Napoleon in 1812, mentions the truce before the Tarutino action with doubt,[38] while Gourgaud [Gaspard Gourgaud] and Thiers, although they speak of it in the affirmative, do not support their opinion with any evidence.[39] Ségur wrote that Napoleon had ordered Murat to resume hostilities; that, by mutual agreement, it was enough to give three hours warning to the opposite side, and that the truce existed only on the army's front and did not extend to the flanks.[40] With all of the evidence above, there is no need to justify the Russians for the accusations made of them.

---

37 From 26th Bulletin, dated 23 October, new style: '... *L'ennemi a non-suelement éprouvé une perte superieure à la notre, mais il a la honte d'avoir violé une trève d'avant-garde, ce qu'on ne vit presque jamais...*' (The enemy has not only suffered greater losses than ours, but is ashamed of having violated a vanguard truce, which is almost unheard of).

38 Fain, *Manuscrit de 1812*, 135-136: '*Il paraît que depuis la mission du général Lauriston, des communications s'etaient maintenues entre nos avant-postes et ceux de Koutousoff; qu'on était d'accord de ne pas s'attaquer sans se prévenir, et que les Russes ne se sont pas fait scrupule de mettre à profit notre extrême sécurité...*' (It appears that since General Lauriston's mission, communications had been maintained between our outposts and those of Kutuzov; that we agreed not to attack each other without warning, and that the Russians had no qualms about taking advantage of our extreme security).

39 Gourgaud, *Examen critique de l'ouvrage de Mr. le comte de Ségur, Livre VIII*, Chapter XI. Thiers, XIV, *Édit. de Brux.* 506.

40 Ségur, *Histoir de Napoléon et de la grande armée pendant l'année 1812*, 4me édit, II, 86-87.

Appendix I

Prince Bagration's correspondence with Count Arakcheev

'Dear Sir, Count Alexey Andreevich,
I am not to blame for any of this: they stretched me at first like a gut string, until … the enemy broke in towards you without a shot; we began to retreat, why I don't know; one cannot reassure anyone either in the army or in Russia that we will not be sold out. I cannot defend the whole of Russia alone. First Army must set off immediately and advance towards Vilna without fail; what is there to fear? I'm completely surrounded and I can't say where I'm going to break out; God will provide, but I shall not be caught napping; may my health hold out; I've been feeling really rough for a few days now. I ask you as a friend to attack without fail, otherwise it will be bad from the enemy, and perhaps one shouldn't be larking about at home. And the Russians must not flee. We have become worse than the Prussians at this. I shall find myself a place to break out, of course, but at a cost; but you should be ashamed, having a fortified camp at your back, open flanks, and weak corps facing you. We need to attack. My tail–end is in a fight every day now, but I cannot get to Minsk or Vileyka, due to the forests, swamps and wretched roads. I have no peace and have no life of my own; as God is my witness, I am glad to do it all; but both conscience and justice must be satisfied. You will fall back, and I shall break out. If they cannot tolerate my character in order to do this, it would be better to deliver me from the yoke around my neck, and send another to command; but why torture the troops without purpose and without relief. I recommend that you come at once. Don't listen to anyone. The bullet is a fool – the bayonet is a champion! This I dare to say. The wit of Mr Phull…
… Take pity on the Tsar and Russia. Why must we dance to the tune of the enemy, when we can defeat them; it is very easy to do – order the move forwards; make a reconnaissance in force with the cavalry and advance with the entire army. That is honour and glory. Otherwise, I assure you, one cannot hold out even in a fortified camp. They will not attack head on, but will envelope. Advance, for God's sake! The troops are in good spirits. I have already given several orders to fight, yet we are fleeing. This is the open expression of my love for my Tsar and Fatherland to you. If you don't like it, spare me, as I don't wish to witness the miserable consequences. It is all

very well to retreat 500 *versts*; but it is clear that there is a demon with the Sovereign and Russia, that is offering death to us. And so – farewell! I have told you everything, as a Russian to a Russian; but if my opinion is otherwise understood, I beg your pardon.'

'Dear Sir, Count Alexey Andreevich,
Your Excellency's brother, Pëtr Andreevich, has delivered a Directed Order to me, so that he could be with the army entrusted to me, and he also brought me your letter, about which I was very pleased. As for your brother, I assure you that, in all fairness, I shall devote myself to being helpful to him in any event. There is nothing newsworthy. The enemy cavalry are very cautious and wary of the Cossacks; rumours are circulating in 2nd Division, that Tormasov has been sent to engage them, since he has beaten them and is marching back towards them. I think that Oudinot is also displeased that Count Wittgenstein has nipped him; Davout is equally ashamed that he has not trapped me. Now our leader has been raised to his feet; God bless and good luck. I believe the enemy is assembling in strength somewhere out of reach, because their cavalry is withdrawing from all points. We shall discover this no sooner than the day after tomorrow. The whole army is publicly asking me to be overall commander; but I have not given any reply; as it is in the gift of my Tsar, even though, between you and me, I am personally extremely distressed by the Minister; but he has came to his senses and wrote asking for forgiveness for that. I forgave him and dealt with him not as a senior, but as a subordinate. I did this and act precisely out of my affection for the Tsar. I recommend to you that the Army of Moldavia hasten to come to us, for God's sake. Move Tormasov closer, and place that army there in place of Tormasov's, as the cavalry is especially needed. May God preserve us until the autumn, that we may break the habit of running away, then I may congratulate you upon Napoleon finding a second Egypt in Russia and his own downfall. That is how I see things. I confess to you frankly that however pleasing it was for me to link up with First Army, it is equally distressing; as the provisions for me are very poor. When it was just me on the march, I had everything. With my true respect, etc.
   July 26, [7 August] on the march in the village of Katan. Signed: Prince Pëtr Bagration.'
   (Noted in Count Arakcheev's handwriting: received on 3 [15] August).

'Dear Sir, Count Alexey Andreevich,
I shall tell you truly and conscientiously that I am making no pretence, but I am treated so deceitfully and so unpleasantly that it is impossible to list it all. It is the will of my Tsar. I cannot do this together with the Minister. For God's sake, send me somewhere else, even just to command a regiment, in Moldavia, or in the Caucasus, but I cannot stay here; the entire headquarters is filled with Germans, such that it is impossible for a Russian to live, if only there were some. It's up to you, or put me on leave at least so I can rest for a month. By God, they have driven me crazy with

their constant changes; I cannot find it in myself. This so-called army is only about 40,000 strong, but they still stretch it out like a thread then drag it back or to the side. Divide my army into two corps, give them to Raevsky and Gorchakov, and dismiss me. I truly thought that I was serving the Tsar and Fatherland, but in reality it turns out that I am serving Barclay. I confess it, I don't want to.

With my true respect etc.

29 July [10 August]. Signed: Prince Bagration.'

(Noted in Count Arakcheev's handwriting: received in Åbo 15 [27] August).

'Dear Sir, Count Alexey Andreevich,

I believe that the Minister has already reported about leaving Smolensk to the enemy. It hurts, sadly, and the whole army is in despair that this most important of places has been abandoned unnecessarily. I, for my part, pleaded with him personally, in a most persuasive manner; finally, I wrote to him, but he agreed to nothing. I swear to you on my honour that Napoleon was in such a dead-end as never before, that he could even have lost half the army and not have taken Smolensk. Our troops fought, and are fighting like never before. I held with 15,000 for over 35 hours and beat them; but he did not want to stay even 14 hours. It's a shame and a stain on our army; while it seems to me, he should not live on this Earth himself. If he reports that the casualties were heavy, it is not true; maybe about 4,000, no more, or not even that. Even then, if it had been ten, this is war! But having said that, the enemy losses were profound.

Napoleon, no matter how hard he tried and no matter how viciously he strove, and even issued or promised large sums as rewards to the commanders just to break in, but they were driven back everywhere. Our artillery, my cavalry, truly operated in such a manner that the enemy was stumped. What would it have been worth to stay for two days? They would have left at least; as they had no drinking water for men or horses. He gave me his word that he would not retreat, but suddenly sent a disposition that he was leaving in the night. Thus it is impossible to fight, and we might soon be bringing the enemy to Moscow; in this case, the Tsar should not delay. Wherever the new troops are, assemble them in Moscow, from Kaluga, Tula, Orël, Nizhny, Tver, wherever they are, and hold Moscow in readiness. I am sure that Napoleon will not get to Moscow soon; as he is exhausted, as is his cavalry, and his provisions are poor; but one should not look at this, while one must certainly hurry, prepare the people, at least 100,000, so that if he approaches the capital, the entire nation will fall on him – either beating him, or laying themselves down at the walls of the Fatherland. That is my assessment; there is no other way. Rumour has it that everyone is thinking of peace. Of reconciliation. God forbid! After all the sacrifices and after such an extensive retreat – to make peace: that would put the whole of Russia against us, and make each of us wear our uniform in shame. That we have come this far, we must fight while Russia still can and while the people are on their feet; as the war is no longer conventional, but of national survival, and one must uphold one's honour and all the glory of the Manifesto and the orders issued. We must have unity of command, and not division. Your Minister, may be good for the Ministry; but as a general he is not, he is bad, even worthless, yet the fate of our entire Fatherland was given to him… I'm going out of my mind with frustration; forgive me for writing so boldly. It can be seen that he does not love the Tsar and wishes the death of us all, who recommends making peace and command of the army by the Minister. And so I write you the truth: prepare the *opolchenie*. Because the Minister is leading our guests to the capital in a most skilful manner. There is major distrust throughout the whole army of Mr *Flügel–Adjutant* Wolzogen. He is, they say, more Napoleon's than ours, and he advises the Minister on everything. I am not only courteous towards him, but I obey like a corporal, although I am senior to him. It pains me; but out of love for my Benefactor and Tsar, I obey. Imagine that by retreating we are losing men from fatigue and more than 15,000 from hospitals; while if we were advancing, there would be none. Tell me, for God's sake, that our Russia – our mother – would say that we are so fearful and that is why we are giving such a good and faithful Fatherland to scum and instil hatred and shame in every subject. Of what are we afraid and of whom are we afraid? It is not my fault that the Minister is indecisive, a coward, stupid, pedantic and has every bad quality. The entire army is weeping utterly, and wishes him dead. Poor Pahlen is in a fever, dying of sorrow; Knorring was killed by a cuirassier yesterday; by God, calamity, and everyone is driven mad from disappointment and sorrow.

Hurry up and send us more men as replacements. It would be better to reassign the police to our regiments. Let us assimilate them. And much better, while if you keep them as a unit, it will be bad. Let us have horses. The cavalry are in need.

I have poured out my heart to you. Tomorrow I shall be with the army in Dorogobuzh and will halt there; while First Army is dragging behind me. He did not dare to stand at Smolensk with 90,000. Oh, it's sad, it hurts! We have never been so offended and distressed as now. All our faith is in God. I would rather go to war as a soldier than to be a Commander in Chief alongside Barclay. I have described the whole truth to Your Excellency here, to the former minister, and now Duty General, to a constant good friend. Read this and throw it in the fireplace.

7 [19] August, on the march, in the town of Mikhailovskoe. Signed: Prince Bagration.'

Appendix II

Biography of Kutuzov

Kutuzov, having graduated as an Ensign of Engineers at 15 years of age (1760), was promoted from captain, to the rank of prime major by Rumyantsev, for outstanding service rendered in the post of Chief Quartermaster, in the battles of Larga and Kagul [both in 1770]. In 1774, at the time when the Küçük Kaynarca peace had already been signed, but before the news of this had reached Constantinople, the Turks, having landed on the Crimean coast, fortified themselves ten *versts* from Alushta, in front of the village of Shumy. Kutuzov, fighting under the command of General Count Musin–Pushkin, broke into the fortified village with a Colour in his hands, and at that very moment was hit by a bullet, which, entering the left temple, exited through his right eye. The most skilled doctors doomed him to die, but, to everyone's surprise, he survived, having lost only his eye. Having set off to foreign lands, on the orders of the Empress, for his eventual convalescence from his wound, Kutuzov came to the attention of renowned military men of that era, Frederick the Great and Field Marshal Laudon, and talked with them several times.

Returning to the fatherland, Kutuzov became known to Suvorov and was employed by him, for several years, during the conquest of the Crimea; while in 1788, during the siege of Ochakov, he suffered another gunshot wound, where the bullet entered through his cheek, exiting to the rear; and on this occasion, just as before, Kutuzov, contrary to all expectations, survived. Providence itself, preserving the life of our warrior, in a truly miraculous way, seemed to predestine him for a great cause. The Empress advised Kutuzov to take care of himself, but, having barely recovered from his wound, he hurried back to the army, received command of an independent detachment operating on the Dniester, and defeated a significant Turkish force there.

In 1790, Kutuzov, during the assault on Izmail, led the left column, which was intended to break into the fortress after capturing the Kiliya Gates. Our troops were repulsed from this point twice. Kutuzov informed Suvorov of this. 'Tell him,' replied the hero of Rymnik, 'that I have already sent a report to the Empress about the conquest of Izmail, and that I am appointing Kutuzov commandant of Izmail.' Kutuzov, at the head of the Kherson Grenadiers, made a last ditch effort, and took possession of the two nearest bastions. Reporting on the capture of Izmail, Suvorov stated: 'Kutuzov marched on my left wing, but was my right hand.' Kutuzov asked Suvorov: what did the words he said during the assault mean, whereupon he received in reply: 'nothing! Kutuzov knows Suvorov, and Suvorov knows Kutuzov. If Izmail had not been taken, we would both have died under its walls.'

Kutuzov was indeed made commandant of Izmail, and took command of the forces stationed on the lower Danube. After that, having joined the army led by Prince Repnin, he dispersed a strong Turkish detachment at Babadag, brilliantly participated in the victory at Machin and received the Order of St George 2nd class as a reward.

At the beginning of 1793, Kutuzov was summoned to St Petersburg. Empress Catherine, who had an extraordinary ability to judge people, in discussions with 'Her Kutuzov' about various subjects, discovered diplomatic talents in him and great knowledge of the foreign policy of European states. The consequence of this was the appointment of Kutuzov as Ambassador Extraordinary to Constantinople. There he charmed the entire Divan with his intelligence and courtesy, gained the friendship of the mother of the Sultan and the Grand Vizier, and outwitted the French diplomats. The following year, returning to the northern capital by the will of the Empress, Kutuzov was first appointed Commander Land Forces and Fleet in Finland, and then, after the death of Graf von Anhalt, Director General of the Landed Gentry (now First) Cadet Corps. Despite the change in duties and occupations, Kutuzov, being equally keen and helpful in every place, took care, like a child-loving father, of his pupils, taught Tactics and Military History to the cadets himself, spending entire days with the corps, and evenings at the Hermitage gatherings, to which the Empress invited people of outstanding intelligence and merit.

During the reign of Emperor Paul, Kutuzov very successfully fulfilled the diplomatic mission given to him at the Court of Berlin and was appointed to replace Hermann as Commander Russian Forces in Holland. But as soon as he arrived in Hamburg, he learned about the evacuation of the allies from Dutch territory, and therefore returned to Russia. At the beginning of 1801, he took command of the army assembled in Volhynia; but upon the accession to the throne of Emperor Alexander I, he was appointed Military Governor of St Petersburg and Inspector of Forces stationed in Finland. Kutuzov did not hold this position for long: exhausted not so much by age as by labour and wounds, he requested a leave of absence from service and spent three years in the circle of his family in the quiet of rural life.

Then came 1805. Emperor Alexander confronted Napoleon for the first time. Kutuzov was entrusted with the command of an army which was intended to link up with the Austrians. But the forces whom the Russians had been assigned to assist were destroyed before our army arrived in the theatre of war. Kutuzov, with 50,000 men remained facing Napoleon's 150,000 strong army, being forced to avoid a decisive engagement, retreated over a distance of 400 *versts* in decent order; several times the Russian troops halted and delivered a strong rebuff; while at Krems they caused significant damage to one of the French divisions. The consequence of the prudent actions of our commander was the union of his army with the force under Buxhoeveden; but our allies were not able to take advantage of their situation. Our troops, located on Austrian territory, suffered a shortage of rations and starvation threatened. Kutuzov proposed to retreat to meet reinforcements and resupply; the Austrian generals preferred to operate on the offensive. Emperor Alexander, taking into account, on the one hand, that the Austrians ought to know the properties of the theatre of war and of Napoleon's *modus operandi* better than us, and on the other hand, that we were simply assisting them in this war, granted them overall command and control. Thus, Kutuzov, bearing the title of Commander–in–Chief, was reduced to being a witness to the defeat suffered by the allies at Austerlitz. None of the Russians ever thought of blaming Kutuzov for this failure. His merits in the military and diplomatic fields, his courage in his youth, courage in the prime of his life, experience in old age, his miraculous escapes from death: all this had made him a household name. All of Russia respected him and had confidence in him.

In 1806, Kutuzov was appointed military governor of Kiev; from 1807 to 1809, he was in the Army of Moldavia, as an assistant to Field Marshal Prince Prozorovsky, who was exhausted from old age, while in 1809 he was appointed military governor of Lithuania and, setting off from the banks of the Danube for Vilna, spent a year and a half there.

In the spring of 1811, Kutuzov took command of the army operating against the Turks, at a time when our Army of Moldavia had been reduced by half, and when the Sultan, prompted to continue the war through the intrigues of Napoleon, did not want to hear about any concessions in favour of Russia. All this notwithstanding, however, Kutuzov ended the long running war with a decisive blow and concluded a glorious peace, in the words of Emperor Alexander, granted by God to Russia.

Extracted from the work 'Emperor Alexander and His contemporaries in 1812, 1813, 1814 and 1815.' Biography of General Field Marshal Prince Kutuzov of Smolensk.

Appendix III

Standing Orders for the Tver *Opolchenie*

'To the Mounted Cossack Regiment, 5th *Sotnia* under Major and Chevalier Figlev.

Seeing from the regimental reports that among the number of men proceeding from the *Uezd* [districts] to the prescribed *opolchenie*, there remains a very small number short, and officials who have not yet arrived must be sent out without delay. Therefore, the regiments, upon being properly constituted, should immediately busy themselves in the following manner:

1. The horse regiment is to train the men to dress promptly and neatly, care for the horses, keep them in good condition, be able to fit the saddle and horse furniture, ride as individuals, knowing the turns, riding in various directions, parrying enemy thrusts, working with the lance, thereafter by platoons, and the whole front, deploying the *Sotnia* by platoons, and reforming the *Sotnia* by platoons, dispersed attacks and, finally, to swiftly and rapidly assemble at the rendezvous point and form up following a dispersed attack.
2. In the evenings, take the roll call, in which you must always inspire the men that they constitute the walls of strength of the interior, that they are to strike terror into the enemy and defeat his rage, in defence of the Faith, the Tsar, the Fatherland and their families, and that their *opolchenie* is temporary only until our foe has been expelled from the Russian frontier. In any event, they must form a single–minded brotherhood and show eagerness and courage of spirit, to unite with the cross over their hearts and weapons in hand; whereupon no human force shall overcome them.
3. Maintain good order at all levels of service, subordination between officers, and discipline between lower ranks, which is the most important factor for each of them and is revered as the soul of the service.
4. Treat the veterans of the lower ranks and warriors more with mildness than with strictness and punishment, as of these the former has already been earned due to their respectable length of service and good conduct, while others have earned it according to wounds received; the latter, as newly recruited men, in order to make them willing to serve, to make diligent and observant in their knowledge, then to accustom them to good order by the easiest means, reminding them often: about being God fearing and about loyalty to the Tsar and obedience

to their commanders; about friendly agreement and unanimity with their brothers in arms; about lenient treatment of the townsfolk, while keeping them from any kind of riot, quarrel, fighting, from drunkenness, theft and every kind of rage and atrocity, from depraved and wasteful gaming with strangers and among themselves and from debauchery, causing harm and intolerance in the community.

5. Inspect the soldiers' uniforms and footwear every day, and make whichever of them turns out to be faulty or torn, mend and wash their linen, and accustom them to keeping themselves in good order and cleanliness, for which they themselves are often to be inspected.
6. Check the availability of uniform and footwear issued to the soldiers, so that whichever of them is deficient but has not lost or squandered it, they should be trusted, for whose integrity the battalion and *Sotnia* commanders are obliged to answer.
7. The townsfolk should not suffer any insult, harassment, bitterness, self–will or arrogance without justice, and take nothing from anyone without payment or under duress, inevitably they will answer for any act contrary to this.
8. The soldiers are to form *artels* [collective Messes] and hold all to account with collective responsibility to keep them from deserting among themselves, and instruct them from the military regulations, those appropriate articles which determine the punishment for desertion.
9. The regiment is to have a true and accurate nominal roll of field officers and subalterns, lower senior ranks and soldiers, with notes in it of arrivals and departures, from the beginning of their formation, and for those mounted, an inventory of horses; every warrior's weapons and uniform and equipment.

After the roll call, which should always be so scheduled that no work would be needed thereafter, and the mounted men, after grooming the horses and, according to what has been done, as mentioned above, indoctrination about their service, after reading them a prayer, such as the one attached, dismiss them to their quarters, ordering most rigorously from them not to go anywhere and not to wander along the streets, but for everyone to be in their place, and those on duty with the battalions and *Sotnia* are to watch closely so that there is total silence. So that each soldier knows the identity of the commanding general, the designation of his regiment, battalion and *Sotnia*, the rank and surname of his regimental, battalion and *Sotnia* commander.

As these initial rules for the training of the warrior, in the current military situation, it is very necessary that these are swiftly brought to the knowledge of the men, thereafter I ask the gentlemen of the regiment, and in general all the commanders, to use every possible and vigilant effort to bring them into the proper order, upon which each commander is dependent upon his own honour and the attention of the chief authorities will be on him, to whom, for my own duty, I shall not neglect to inform about such events.

Yamogi village, 7 [19] September, 1812. Commanding General of the Tver Military Forces. Signed in original: Lieutenant General Tyrtov.'

Appendix IV

Composition of the Don Cossack Host

From Returns submitted to the Tsar on 3 [15] March 1812.

The Don regiments comprised:

In Lieutenant General Count Wittgenstein's Corps:
    Colonel Rodionov 2nd's
    Major Selivanov 2nd's
    In Lieutenant General Baggovut's Corps:
    Major General Ilovaisky 4th's
    Lieutenant Colonel Platov 4th's

In Lieutenant General Essen 1st's Corps:
    The Ataman's
    Major General Denisov 4th's
    Major General Denisov 7th's
    Major General Karpov 5th's
    Colonel Gordeev's
    Lieutenant Colonel Ilovaisky 8th's
    Suvorov's Don Horse Artillery Company

In the army under General of Infantry Prince Bagration:
    Major General Ilovaisky 5th's
    Colonel Dyachkin's
    Colonel Sysoev 3rd's
    Colonel Ilovaisky 10th's
    Colonel Ilovaisky 11th's
    Colonel Ilovaisky 12th's
    Lieutenant Colonel Slyusarev 2nd's
    Lieutenant Colonel Andriyanov 2nd's
    Lieutenant Colonel Barabanshchikov's
    Major [*Voyskovoy Starshina*] Vlasov 2nd's
    Major Platov 5th's
    Tatsyn's Don Horse Artillery Company
    Giving a total of 21 regiments and two artillery companies on the western borders of the Empire

In Moldavia (Army of the Danube):
    Major General Grekov 8th's
    Colonel Grekov 4th's
    Colonel Lukovkin's
    Colonel Melnikov 5th's
    Lieutenant Colonel Kuteinikov 4th's
    Lieutenant Colonel Astakhov 4th's
    Major Kireev's
    Major Isaev 4th's
    Major Panteleev's
    Major Melentiev 1st's
    Giving a total of ten regiments in the Army of the Danube

Under Lieutenant General the Duc de Richelieu:
    Lieutenant Colonel Yanov 2nd's, in Odessa
    Lieutenant Colonel Melentiev 2nd's
    Major Chikilev's, in Tavria [Crimea]
    Giving a total of three regiments in Novorossiya

Under Lieutenant General Rtishchev's command on the Caucasus Line:
    Major Ageev 3rd's
    Major Krasnov 2nd's
    Major Safonov's
    Lieutenant Colonel Ilyn's
    Major Petrov's
    Major Ryabinin's
    Major Rybashkin's
    Major Sychov 3rd's
    Major Samoilov's
    Major Molchanov's
    Lieutenant Colonel Arakantsov's

In Georgia:
    Colonel Balabin 1st's
    Lieutenant Colonel Ezhov 1st's
    Lieutenant Colonel Ageev 2nd's
    Major Pozdeev 8th's
    Major Popov 16th's
    Lieutenant Colonel Izvalov's
    Lieutenant Colonel Bogachev's
    Major Danilov's

In Derbent:
    Major Sysoev 2nd's
    Giving a total of 21 regiments under General Rtishchev's command

In Finland:
> Colonel Isaev 2nd's
> Lieutenant Colonel Loshchilin's
> Major Kiselev 2nd's

Giving a total of three regiments.

In Moscow:
> Major Grekov 21st's
> Two regiments newly sent from the Don, under lieutenant colonels Vlasov 3rd and Kharitonov, en route for Grodno

In Kazan:
> Two *Sotnia* under the command of *Essaul* [Captain] Tatsyn

In Novocherkassk:
> Two regiments

Moreover, shown under the various ranks:
> Major General: 1
> Field Officers: 17
> Subalterns: 90
> *Uryadniki* & Cossacks: 2,267

Appendix V

Troop strengths of the *Grande Armée*

Chambray, *Histoire de lexpédition de Russie*, II, 15–18.
From Returns dated 23 August, new style:

Corps	Grand Total	Artillery & Cavalry	Remarks
Vieille Garde	6,812	–	
Jeune Garde	12,925	–	including Claparède's division.
Cavalerie de la Garde	–	4,208	
Artillerie de la Garde	2,500	1,000	approximately.
1er Corps	40,622	–	
3e Corps	16,053	–	
4e Corps	32,823	–	including the Bavarian cavalry.
5e Corps	11,857	–	
8e Corps	12,686	–	
1er Corps de cavalerie	–	5,700	
2e Corps de cavalerie	–	3,859	
3e Corps de cavalerie	–	4,930	excluding Doumerc's division.
4e Corps de cavalerie	–	4,000	approximately & excluding Dąbrowski's force.
TOTAL:	136,278	23,697	

Therefore – 159,975 men overall. While if we exclude Delaborde's Division, of around 4,500 men left in Smolensk, from this total, it emerges that there were 155,475 men in the *Grande Armée* at the time.

Appendix VI

Dispositions for First and Second Western Armies, at the village of Borodino, issued on 24 August [5 September] 1812

'The armies, having subsumed all the reinforcements that arrived from Kaluga and Moscow, are to anticipate an enemy attack at the village of Borodino, where they are to give battle.

The armies are now in position as follows, starting from the right flank:

- II Corps, IV Corps, VI Corps, while VII Corps and 27th Division located on the left flank, make up the *corps de bataille* and are to be positioned in two echelons.
- Behind them the cavalry corps are to be located, joining the *ordre de bataille*, in regimental columns, as follows: behind II Corps – I Cavalry Corps; behind IV Corps – II Cavalry Corps; behind VI Corps – III Cavalry Corps; behind VII Corps – IV Cavalry Corps i.e. the cavalry regiments of Second Army.
- The reserve is stationed in the centre of the fighting position, behind the Cavalry Corps, in battalion columns at full interval, in two echelons, as follows:
- In the first echelon; III Corps, with Lifeguard V Corps and the Combined Grenadier Battalions of 4th Division, 17th Division, 1st Division and 3rd Division behind them.
- 2nd Grenadier Division and the Combined Grenadier Battalions of Second Army are to be stationed behind IV Cavalry Corps and constitute the reserves of Second Army. The jäger regiments of First Army, currently with the rearguard, as well as those attached to the *corps de bataille*, are to pass through it and go to the right flank of the army behind II Corps, where some are to occupy the forest located on the right flank, and some are to make up the reserve of the right flank of the army. All cuirassier regiments of both armies during the action must stand behind Lifeguard V Corps, also in regimental columns.
- The artillery in the reserve constitutes the reserve for the entire fighting line.
- Commanders of the *Corps de Bataille*.

The right flank, of II Corps and IV Corps, is under the command of General of Infantry Miloradovich.

The centre, of VI Corps, is under the command of General of Cavalry [sic] Dokhturov.

The left flank, of VII Corps and 27th Division, is under the command of Lieutenant General Prince Gorchakov 2nd.

The Commanders in Chief of the armies lead the troops of their respective armies as before.

Lieutenant General Prince Golitsyn 1st is to command 1st Cuirassier and 2nd Cuirassier divisions, who are to link up behind V Corps in column.

In this battle formation I intend to draw the forces of the enemy upon us and operate in reaction to their movements. Not being able to be omnipresent during the action, I rely on the renowned experience of the gentlemen Commanders–in–Chief of the armies, and therefore I leave them to make operational decisions in order to defeat the enemy. Placing all faith in the assistance of the Almighty and upon the courage and fearlessness of the Russian soldiers, upon a fortunate repulse of enemy forces, I shall issue my own orders to pursue them, to which end I shall expect incessant reports on operations, being located behind VI Corps.

In any case, I consider it not superfluous to present to the gentlemen Commanders in Chief that the reserves should be preserved for as long as possible, because a general who still retains a reserve will not be defeated. In the event of a counter-offensive during the action, it should be carried out in attack column, in which case they are not to engage in a firefight at all, but to act swiftly with cold steel.

In the intervals between infantry columns, there are to be some cavalry units, also in columns, which should support the infantry.

In the event of an unsuccessful action, General Vistitsky is to hold several routes open, which will be communicated to the gentlemen Commanders in Chief and along which the armies must retreat. This last point is for the eyes of the gentlemen Commanders in Chief only.

Signed in original: General Prince Kutuzov.

Headquarters, Tatarinovo Manor, 24 August [5 September] 1812.

Appendix VII

Reports on the Battle of Borodino

1

'General Barclay de Tolly reports to His Grace, Commander in Chief of all armies, Sir, Field Marshal General and Chevalier Prince Golenishchev–Kutuzov:

> On the 24 [5 September], in the afternoon, the troops of the army entrusted to me which were in the rear guard, under strong pressure from the enemy, retreated into position and rejoined their corps. Their crossing of the river Moskva was facilitated by the Lifeguard Jäger Regiment, who held the village of Borodino and a battery on the right bank of this river.[1]
>
> Irregular troops from the army entrusted to me remained on the left bank of this river to observe and shield the right flank, and on this day, as well as on the 25th [6 September], prevented the enemy from extending their positions in this direction.
>
> On the 24 [5 September], the enemy made repeated efforts to capture the village of Borodino, but each time was foiled in this objective by the valiant Lifeguard Jägers and Yelisavetgrad Hussars. This latter regiment, under the command of its courageous Colonel in Chief, Major General Vsevolodsky [Alexey Matveevich Vsevolodsky], despite the strong enemy attack and the operations of their artillery, held its position and thereby carried out the orders given to them from me precisely, to hold out until nightfall, no matter what the costs, until they were reinforced by three Cossack regiments, expected back from the left flank of Second Army.
>
> On that same evening of the 24 [5 September], III Corps, which formed part of the reserve of First Army, received orders from Your Grace to proceed to the left flank of Second Army to shield it from the increasing enemy strength along the old Smolensk road.
>
> On the 25 [6 September], apart from minor skirmishes in which several prisoners were taken, nothing important happened. On the morning of the 26th [7 September], before dawn, a report was received from the commander of the Lifeguard Jäger Regiment, Colonel Bistrom, that movement had been detected in an enemy position facing the village of Borodino and shortly

---

1   *Sic*. Clearly the Kolocha is meant.

thereafter, the enemy assaulted this village with superior numbers and forced the Lifeguard Jäger Regiment to abandon the village and beat a hasty retreat across the bridge, which they did not have chance to burn. The enemy pursued this regiment and quickly began to increase in strength.

I ordered Colonel Vuich, commander of the Jäger Brigade from 24th Division, to attack this enemy right flanking. This brave officer charged with bayonets fixed, and in an instant the enemy who had crossed over to our bank, were driven back. The Lifeguard Jäger Regiment joined this brigade and drove the enemy back across the river; the bridge was burned down, in spite of fierce enemy fire.

Meanwhile, a strong cannonade and musket fire continued on the left flank under Second Army, and the centre of both armies, that is, the mound was already under attacked, on which a battery had been emplaced, consisting of 18 heavy guns under escort by 26th Division; Prince Bagration demanded reinforcements and the remainder of First Army's reserve, i.e. the Lifeguard Infantry Division, was tasked with that. Following this, the entire II Corps and three cuirassier regiments of 1st Cuirassier Division were sent there. By noon, Second Army, the whole of VIII Corps and the Combined Grenadier Division, having lost most of their generals and having also lost their Commander-in-Chief, were driven back, all the fortifications of the left flank had been taken by the enemy, who threatened the left flank and rear of VII Corps and VI Corps with his full strength.

In this situation, I decided to place IV Corps, which had been moved from the right flank closer to the centre, following the detachment of the reserve forces, step by step to the left flank of VII Corps, adjoining their left flank to the Lifeguard Preobrazhensky and Lifeguard Semenovsky regiments stationed there, and behind this line were II Cavalry Corps and III Cavalry Corps.

These troops stood in this position, under crossfire from enemy artillery; from the right side by the formation operating against the centre of the army and the aforementioned mound, and this enemy artillery also enfiladed our line, and from the left side by the formation that had seized the entire position of Second Army; but in order to form a barrier to the enemy advances and to hold the rest of the posts we still occupied, this disadvantage could not be avoided, as otherwise we would have to abandon the aforementioned mound, which was the key to our entire position, and these brave troops, under the command of General of Infantry Miloradovich and Lieutenant General Count Osterman, withstood this terrible fire with astonishing courage.

Shortly after the capture of all the fortifications on the left flank by the enemy, they launched an attack on the central battery shielded by 26th Division, under covering fire from a massive cannonade and crossfire from their numerous artillery. They managed to close with and drive off the above-mentioned division, but the Chief of Staff of First Army, Major General Yermolov, with his customary determination, taking just Third Battalion, Ufa Infantry, stopped those fleeing and this host, reformed into column, struck with fixed bayonets. The enemy defended themselves vigorously, their batteries wreaked terrible devastation, but nothing could withstand us. Following the aforementioned battalion, I sent another battalion to the right of this battery to hit the enemy in the flank, and I sent the Orenburg Dragoon Regiment in support, even further to the right to shield their right flank and to cut into the enemy columns following in support of their assault force. Third Battalion, Ufa Infantry and 18th Jäger Regiment rushed against them directly towards the battery, 19th Jägers and 40th Jägers to their left, and in a quarter of an hour the audacity of the enemy had been punished: the battery was under our control, all the high ground and the fields around it were covered with enemy corpses. *Général de brigade* Bonnamy was one of the enemy who were granted mercy, and the enemy was pursued way beyond the battery. Major General Yermolov held it with a small force until the arrival of 24th Division, which I had ordered to relieve 26th Division, which had been disordered by the enemy attack and had previously been defending the battery, and entrusted this post to Major General Likhachëv.

During this incident, enemy cavalry, cuirassiers and lancers, launched an attack on the infantry of IV Corps, but the valiant infantry engaged them with unexpected resolve, allowing them get within 60 paces, and then opening such rapid fire that the enemy was completely driven off and, greatly disordered, they sought salvation in flight.

At the same time, the Pernov Infantry and 34th Jägers especially distinguished themselves, for which each company was awarded three marks of distinction.

The Sumy Hussars and Mariupol Hussar, and behind them the Irkutsk Dragoons and Siberia Dragoons pursued and drove the enemy right back on their reserves, but coming under fierce cannon and musket fire here, they were forced to retreat. The enemy cavalry, having received reinforcements from their reserves, pursued our men and, breaking through the intervals between our infantry squares, got completely into the rear of 7th Division and 11th Division; but this matchless infantry, not disordered in the least, received the enemy with fierce and rapid fire, and the enemy was scattered. Meanwhile, our cavalry reorganised again and the enemy was completely driven from this point once more and retreated behind their infantry, to the extent that we completely lost sight of them. After this, only the artillery was active on both sides, and on the left flank of IV Corps and the Lifeguard Division, skirmishing continued between the tirailleurs. It could be seen that the enemy was preparing to make another decisive assault; they moved their cavalry forward again and formed a number of columns. I foresaw that the men of our II Cavalry Corps and III Cavalry Corps, having suffered greatly in the previous attacks, would not be able to withstand so strong a new blow and I therefore sent for 1st Cuirassier Division, which, however, unfortunately, had been sent to the left flank by persons unknown to me, and my aide de camp could not find them at the place where I had supposed them to be. He reached the Chevalier Garde and Lifeguard

Horse Regiments, which trotted towards me: but the enemy had managed to achieve their objective in the meantime: the enemy cavalry hacked into the infantry of 24th Division, which had been placed to shield the battery on the mound, while from the other side, strong enemy columns stormed this mound and captured it. After this, all the enemy cavalry turned on the infantry of IV Corps and 7th Division, but were engaged on this spot by the Lifeguard Horse and Chevalier Garde regiments and halted in their operation; meanwhile, the Pskov Dragoons and the rest of the regiments of II Cavalry Corps and III Cavalry Corps joined these two regiments, whereupon a fierce cavalry battle ensued, which ended by five o'clock with the enemy cavalry completely driven back and retreating totally out of our sight, while our troops had held their ground, with the exception of the mound, which remained in enemy hands. Enemy infantry still remained within sight of ours, but towards evening, when it began to get dark, they disappeared. The cannonade continued until night itself had fallen, but from our side for the most part and to no small loss to the enemy; while the enemy artillery, having been completely defeated, also fell completely silent towards evening. During all these incidents, four regiments of jägers and a number of artillery pieces remained on our extreme right flank, under the command of Colonel Potemkin, whom I ordered to join 7th Division in the evening. Your Grace's I Cavalry Corps having been assigned to the left bank of the Moskva river and operated there together with the irregular troops under General of Cavalry Platov's command.[2]

I had the honour to present the report by Lieutenant General Uvarov on the operations by these troops in original to Your Grace.

Following the end of the battle, noticing that the enemy had begun to withdraw their troops from the places they had seized, I ordered the following positions to be held: the right flank of VI Corps resting on the high ground near the village of Gorki, on which a battery of ten heavy guns had been emplaced, and on which, moreover, it was intended to construct a closed redoubt that night. The left flank of this corps took the direction to the point where the right flank of IV Corps was stationed.

General Dokhtorov, who had succeeded Prince Bagration in command, was instructed to assemble the infantry of Second Army, deploy them on the left flank of IV Corps and hold the interval between this corps and the force under Lieutenant General Baggovut, who was on the extreme left flank with II Corps and III Corps, and by evening he had reoccupied all those places that had been held by him in the morning.

The cavalry corps were ordered to stand behind this line. Behind them, the Lifeguard Infantry Division was appointed in reserve facing the centre, while the cuirassier divisions were behind them. I instructed General Miloradovich to re–occupy the mound before dawn, with several battalions and artillery lying facing the centre.

---

2 *Sic*. Clearly the Kolocha is meant.

At midnight, I received Your Grace's command to retreat.

At the same time, I have the honour to present our casualty returns for this bloody day, and lists of all distinguished officers presented to me by the corps commanders.

Kaluga, 26 September [8 October] 1812.'

2

'Sir, Major General Yermolov reports to Commander in Chief First Army, General Barclay de Tolly:

On 26 August [7 September], being engaged in the execution of orders from Your Excellency and, in fact, with various instructions in accordance with my appointment, around noon I was sent to the left flank by His Grace, to inspect the artillery positions and reinforce them as dictated by the situation. Passing the centre of the army, I saw the fortified high ground on which a battery of 18 guns had been stationed which constituted the right wing of Second Army, in the hands of the enemy, who were already settling on it in large numbers. Enemy batteries already dominated the approaches to this high ground, and columns hurried from both sides to exploit the successes they had achieved. Our skirmishers were fleeing in many groups, not only in disorder, but even without resistance, 18th Jägers, 19th Jägers and 40th Jägers, completely overwhelmed and retreating in disorder, had allowed the enemy to consolidate themselves. This high ground commanded the entire area on which both armies were deployed; the 18 guns inherited by the enemy were too important a factor not to try to make good the losses suffered. I resolved to take it on. Audacity was required and, to my good fortunate, I achieved this. Taking only Third Battalion, Ufa Infantry Regiment, I stopped those fleeing and this crowd struck in the form of a column with fixed bayonets. The enemy defended themselves savagely, their batteries caused terrible devastation, but nothing could withstand us. Third Battalion, Ufa Infantry and 18th Jägers rushed straight into the battery, 19th Jägers and 40th Jägers to the left of it, and in a quarter of an hour the insolence of the enemy had been punished: the battery was under our control, the entire high ground and the fields surrounding it were covered with corpses, and *général de brigade* Bonnamy was one of the enemy who was granted mercy. The enemy was pursued far beyond the battery. But the intermingling of the regiments, in greater confusion than before, and the overwhelming enemy forces nearby that were going to reinforce their own, even more so forced me to withdraw the pursuers. It was only with difficulty that I forced the men to form themselves into columns, as good order alone could hold the battery threatened from all sides, until Your Excellency managed to send regiments from VI Corps.

I found that the 18 guns and, indeed, the whole battery had just two rounds of canister. Most of the artillery had been replaced twice. The officers and crew with the guns had been struck down and, eventually, using men from the battalion of the Ufa Infantry, we held off the strong enemy attempts for an hour and a half. The commander of 24th Division, Major General Likhachëv, had been called and, having handed over the battery to him, making ready to go to the left flank, I was wounded in the neck.

The recapture of this battery is owed to the decisiveness and valour of the officers and the extraordinary courage of the soldiers. I complete my duty by presenting the names of these brave men. In recommending them for awards, I ask for due consideration of their excellent merits.

I have the honour to present a list of those who have distinguished themselves and of drawing Your Grace's favourable attention, as their commander, I especially draw attention to the commander Third Battalion, Ufa Infantry, Major Demidov, commander 18th Jägers, Lieutenant Colonel Chistyakov, and the aide de camp of the late Major General Count Kutaisov, Lieutenant Pozdeev, all of them as most excellent and worthy officers, while Pozdeev, as an exemplary officer, remained in command of the battery until the end of the battle.

No. 152, 20 September [2 October] 1812.'

3

'Sir, Commander I Cavalry Corps, Lieutenant General Uvarov reports to General of Infantry, Commander in Chief First Army and Chevalier, Barclay de Tolly:

On the day of the battle, on the recent, unforgettable 26 August [7 September], 1812, I was sent in person by the overall Commander in Chief of all armies, His Grace the Prince, to cross the river with I Cavalry Corps and attack the enemy left flank,[3] in order at least to delay somewhat the forces who were so eager to attack our Second Army, which was on the left flank of the position. Having received this command, I crossed the river, leading an attack on the enemy with the Yelisavetgrad Hussars and Lifeguard Cossacks, supported by: the Lifeguard Dragoons, Lifeguard Ulans, Lifeguard Hussars and Nezhin Dragoons, notwithstanding the unfavourable terrain, as it was necessary to cross a deep ravine and a river and, having ascended, immediately engage the enemy; enemy infantry occupied a village on the left side, and the forest on the right, nevertheless, the attack was carried out in full view of the whole army with surprising success; the enemy were driven back on contact, a battery barely had time to escape, from which two guns were captured by the Yelisavetgrad Hussars; if it hadn't been for such unfavourable terrain, then they would certainly have been dragged away; the enemy were pursued taking heavy losses and therefore were forced to withdraw some of the troops from those locations where they were attacking

---

3   The Kolocha.

our positions so forcefully; thereafter, the enemy, having received such reinforcements at this point, tried by all means possible to eject me from the locations I held at the time, using cavalry and infantry for this, and placing batteries on the high ground; but no matter the increased intensity, they did not succeed in this; the moment that I saw enemy infantry striving to cross the river and attack our remaining infantry on the right flank of the position, I decided to attack them with hussars, although I must admit that, due to the unfavourable terrain for cavalry, this attack was a partial success, but, having said that, the enemy intent was frustrated, and these enemy infantry remained inactive the whole time; following this, having received orders, both from His Grace, and from Your Excellency, that if I were unable to resist the enemy, then to retreat and recross the river, but otherwise, if I saw the opportunity I was to remain in place, giving the appearance to the enemy that I was still undertaking to attack them through my movements, I held out, despite the overwhelming enemy numbers, until I was obliged to execute the decision to return to our positions.

It remains my duty to do justice to the regiments and the horse artillery company under Lieutenant Colonel Göring, which operated throughout with great success and also knocked out the enemy guns. I present for your Commander's attention; and I have the honour to convey herewith the casualties and those who have distinguished themselves.

3 [15] September, 1812.'

4

'Sir, Adjutant General Baron Korf reports to Commander in Chief First Army, General of Infantry and Chevalier Barclay de Tolly:

During the battle of 26 August [7 September], II Cavalry Corps and III Cavalry Corps, under my command, were located behind IV Corps and VI Corps; at around noon, once the enemy had turned all their forces on the left flank of our army, then, in accordance with Your Excellency's orders, I detached the Sumy Hussars, Mariupol Hussars, Courland Dragoons and Orenburg Dragoons, under the command of Major General Dorokhov, to support the left wing. Major General Dorokhov, approaching the entrenchments and their infantry with these regiments, found that enemy cavalry had begun to surround our infantry and batteries in superior numbers; immediately forming line, he swiftly struck with the Orenburg Dragoon Regiment in the centre, and with the Mariupol Hussars and Courland Dragoons into the flank of the enemy cavalry, who were driven back by the speed of this attack and pushed right back to their batteries. Here, the enemy reserves, supporting their fugitives, halted our cavalry, whereupon Major General Dorokhov immediately brought up the Sumy Hussar Regiment, which was in reserve, and, sounding the recall for the other regiments, deployed III Cavalry Corps in two waves and attacked and drove off the advancing enemy cavalry once more. In this action, the Sumy Hussars saved eight of our guns, which had been completely abandoned by our men. Meanwhile, the Siberia Dragoons and Irkutsk Dragoons had been placed to protect the large battery in front of our centre; from eight o'clock in the morning until noon they remained under a most severe cannon bombardment, and when at that time a strong column of enemy cavalry and infantry tried to take possession of this battery, these regiments, striking swiftly at the enemy, drove them off and thereby contributed to holding the place. At three o'clock in the afternoon, the enemy, directing all their efforts at the centre of our army, began to pressure our infantry, and then, upon the orders from Your Excellency, I hurried there with II Cavalry Corps to support this location. As I arrived at this place, I saw that the enemy, having a strong column of infantry in the centre, cuirassiers and carabiniers on the left, and horse grenadiers on the right, under covering fire from a battery, was advancing strongly on our infantry located there, and by their efforts had forced our skirmishers to retreat in disorder. I immediately ordered the Izyum Hussars and Poland Ulans, under the command of Major General Panchulidzev 2nd, to trot forwards, and, forming line, to strike at the enemy carabiniers and cuirassiers; but these regiments had not yet had time to form up when they themselves were attacked by the enemy and were thus thrown into disarray. In this action, I consider it my duty to mention my aide de camp and chief quartermaster, Captain Schubert, who helped me to rally and reform the cavalry regiments which had been thrown into disorder; the following distinguished themselves in particular: my aide de camp Captain Yakovlev and from the Izyum Hussars, Captain Loshkarev, who, having rallied a squadron of this regiment, immediately struck the enemy once more. Eventually, having managed to reform these two regiments, they halted the rapid enemy cuirassiers' and carabiniers' advance, and thus gave time for the infantry, which was also in disorder, to reform and move forwards; meanwhile, I ordered the Pskov Dragoon Regiment to move forwards more to the right, while the Moscow Dragoon Regiment was to stand behind in reserve. Colonel Zass, commander of the Pskov Dragoons, seeing that the enemy infantry and horse grenadiers were rapidly moving forward and thus threatened the right flank of the Izyum Hussars and Poland Ulans, which had not yet been reformed, went at this enemy cavalry at a trot, attacked and despite their superiority in numbers, drove them off and put them to flight. After this attack, Colonel Zass assembled the regiment sounding the recall directly under fire from the enemy, which was carried out very successfully and in the greatest order. It would be desirable for every cavalry regiment to carry out its mission so well. Meanwhile, the enemy cavalry, which had been in reserve, was approaching, whereupon Colonel Zass again went on the attack with his regiment, also driving this cavalry off and cutting into the left flank of the enemy infantry, which had turned all its fire on this regiment; at that very moment, His Highness' aide de camp, Colonel Prince Kudashev, brought up four guns of the Lifeguard Horse Artillery, who immediately fired several very accurate rounds of canister, such that this column was forced to retreat. After this latest and fiercest attack, which ended at about five o'clock, Major General Dorokhov had already joined me with his cavalry and was a perfect aid to me in holding the place. And after that, the enemy did not dare to attack any more, simply firing fiercely with canister at our cavalry, which, however, stood unshakably until nightfall. Your Excellency was yourself obliged to be an eyewitness to the disorder into which our infantry had already been brought, and had the cavalry not halted the enemy efforts at this point, the infantry would inevitably have been driven back, which would have been to the detriment of the entire army. May Your Excellency give full justice to the cavalry and not leave the distinguished officers unrewarded, of whom I have the honour to enclose a list. I consider it in particular my duty to recommend Major General Dorokhov to Your Excellency, who, having been detached with four regiments, commanded with great distinction throughout the battle, and Colonel Zass, who with his regiment decisively repulsed the enemy. I also dare to ask Your Excellency to issue five Military Order medals to each squadron and ten to each horse artillery company, to be distributed to the most outstanding and bravest, in order to encourage the lower ranks.

9 [21] September, 1812. Village of Krasnaya Pakhra.'

5

'Sir, Major General Borozdin reports to Commander in Chief First Army, General of Infantry and Chevalier Barclay de Tolly:

In the battle of 26 August [7 September] near the village of Gorki, due to the illness of the divisional commander, Your Excellency knows that I had the honour to command 1st Cuirassier Division, composed of: the Chevalier Garde, Lifeguard Horse, His Imperial Majesty's *Leib* Cuirassiers, Her Imperial Majesty's *Leib* Cuirassiers and Astrakhan Cuirassiers, as well as the Lifeguard Horse Artillery Company, which had been detached at the start of the battle, by order of the noble commander of the cuirassier regiments, Lieutenant General Prince Golitsyn: three regiments were directed to the left flank, while the Chevalier Garde and Lifeguard Horse, under the command of Major General Shevich, were in the centre; the Chevalier Garde and Lifeguard Horse, under the command of Major General Shevich, believed this day, having received orders from Your Excellency, that by attacking the enemy who had already taken possession of our battery, with whom, having driven them off, contributed to the salvation of the battery, having wiped out most of those who had encroached on this objective. This halted their efforts on our centre, and some of our infantry, who were already behind the enemy cavalry, were saved; in this attack they had the misfortune to lose: the excellent Colonel Löwenwolde, who was killed instantly, and Colonel Levashov took command; Colonel Arseniev [Mikhail Andreevich Arseniev] of the Lifeguard Horse, whom Major General Shevich recommends as outstanding for his presence of mind and courage in leading the Lifeguard Horse Regiment entrusted to him, and who, having received a contusion of the left shoulder from a round shot at the end of the attack, was forced to leave the front line, while Colonel Leontiev [Ivan Sergeevich Leontiev] took his place in command. His Majesty's *Leib* Cuirassiers, Her Majesty's *Leib* Cuirassiers and Astrakhan Cuirassiers, directed by me to the left flank, under the command of: Colonel in Chief, Colonel Baron Budberg [Karl Vasilevich Budberg or Carl Ludwig Freiherr Budberg–Bönninghausen], Colonel in Chief, Colonel Baron Rosen [Alexander Vladimirovich Rosen], and regimental commander, Colonel Karataev [Vasily Ivanovich Karataev] respectively, were placed as protection for our batteries, under heavy fire, where, despite the fearsome fire from enemy batteries, they defended our own with outstanding valour. Their fearlessness was so strong that even heavy losses of men and horses killed and wounded were unable to disorder their ranks, which closed every time in order. The enemy tirailleurs, having decided to approach them and our batteries, being supported by infantry columns, two squadrons were sent from the Astrakhan Cuirassiers on my orders, under the command of Lieutenant General Prince Golitsyn, and attacked and drove them off with heavy losses to the extent that Lieutenant Colonel Nemtsov, who was commanding them, crashed into those infantry columns in support, where he received a severe wound of a bullet in the left arm, from which the bone was fractured; these squadrons, returning under heavy enemy fire, were reformed behind the batteries; thereafter, in a follow up attack executed with the same valour, Major Kostin was killed, and Major Belavin was wounded in the chest by a bullet; the regimental commander Colonel Karataev, leading the regiment courageously, firstly suffered a severe contusion to the shoulder, but, despite this, returned to the front line, where he soon suffered another to the leg, but even then he remained at his post. This example inspired the fervour of his subordinates, and the regiment, defending its batteries, made courageous attacks, in which Captain Lvov, commanding a squadron, performed perfectly, as did Captain Rebinder, Staff Captain Zadonsky [Voin Dmitrievich Zadonsky], who took the place of squadron commanders, as did lieutenants: regimental adjutant Goyarin, Patkul, Trithoff, Ivashkin, who showed outstanding bravery and valour, in particular Patkul and Goyarin, fulfilling their duty according to their rank, were together with everyone in the attack; of those, the following were wounded: Lvov, Zadonsky and Goyarin suffered contusions; Rebinder, Patkul and Trithoff gunshot wounds, while Patkul was also gashed; the former remained at his post, while Trithoff and Patkul, due to the severity of their wounds, were sent to His Imperial Majesty's *Leib* Cuirassier Regiment, under the command of Baron Budberg, were attacked several times, at which time the gentleman Colonel was wounded by a round shot to the thigh, and the regimental commander Lieutenant Colonel Slepchenkov [Pëtr Ivanovich Slepchenkov] took a bullet to the leg, and once the regiment, on the orders of Lieutenant General Prince Golitsyn, was transferred to support 2nd Cuirassier Division, under the command of Colonel Kostin, where, protecting the batteries, Major General Duka had been sent to attack an enemy battery, charging upon it, the Colonel in Chief's squadron, under the command of Captain Vlasenko, drove the enemy away; here, although Captain Vlasenko and Lieutenant Skorobogaty were killed, two guns were taken by lieutenants Dershau [Karl Fëdorovich Dershau], Kaleny 2nd, and Sambursky and delivered to the headquarters. During these actions, Captain Melikov constantly distinguished himself, but unfortunately this brave officer's arm was torn off by round shot; Staff Captain Selyaninov was wounded in both legs by round shot, for which it must be assumed that a procedure has already been done; Lieutenant Vsevolozhsky 2nd [Matvey Matveevich Vsevolozhsky] was hit in the leg with a bullet, Vsevolozhsky 3rd [Dmitry Alexeevich Vsevolozhsky], whose leg was broken by round shot, Rodolchin, who performed his duty with honour in the role of regimental adjutant, received a severe contusion from round shot; Kalen 2nd and Cornet Count Minich 1st also suffered contusions to the left arm. Regarding those killed in the battle, Captain Vlasenko and Lieutenant Skorobogaty, who left their wives with no inheritance, I dare to ask Your Excellency to provide them with a means of subsistence. Her Imperial Majesty's *Leib* Cuirassier Regiment, under Baron Rosen's command, in protecting the batteries and enduring heavy enemy fire, did not lose their presence of mind in the slightest; Colonel Baron Rosen, being outstandingly brave, served as an example to his subordinates when the enemy attempted to attack our infantry ahead of us, and when he, Rosen, on the orders of Lieutenant General Prince Golitsyn, was sent by me to attack with two squadrons, which was done with great endeavour, from which the enemy cavalry suffered greatly, especially when Baron Rosen attacked them from behind; in a word, the enemy column was driven off and suffered heavy casualties. In recommending Baron Rosen, I must also testify to the outstanding courage of: squadron commander Major Wisterholz, who suffered a contusion; staff–captains Schlippenbach [Anton Andreevich Schlippenbach] and Gedeonov, wounded in the leg by round shot; lieutenants: regimental adjutant Kirilov, Rudkovsky 2nd and Koshenbar 2nd, the latter two suffering contusions. Regarding the other two squadrons from this regiment, Baron Rosen has informed me that Major Sologub, remaining on the left flank with them, attacked the batteries twice, striking down the enemy each time; also recommended for his outstanding courage and valour is squadron commander, Captain Hagen. The latter, during the bravely executed attack, was badly wounded in the arm by canister shot; Lieutenant Milevsky, who suffered a contusion to the head, also distinguished himself in these attacks. Then, having linked up with me, Major General Shevich with the regiments under his command, the Chevalier Garde Regiment, under the command of Colonel

Levashov, swiftly charged the enemy cuirassiers, instantly driving them off and, in pursuit, struck them down mercilessly; at the same time the Lifeguard Horse Regiment, under the command of Colonel Leontiev, supported this attack from the left side, and despite the batteries targeting them fiercely, struck the enemy, reformed under canister fire and was constantly at the ready. Major General Shevich, in leading these two regiments, through his commands and fearlessness, contributed to their complete rout; he was an inspiration; the valour of this general is already well known. He, Shevich, recommends the following gentlemen regimental commanders, who showed outstanding courage and valour: Chevalier Garde: regimental commander Levashov, Kablukov 1st, [Platon Ivanovich Kablukov], wounded in the right arm, Kablukov 2nd [Vladimir Ivanovich Kablukov]; Lifeguard Horse: who took over the command of the regiment after Colonel Arseniev (who has already been recommended above), Leontiev, Andreevsky [Stepan Stepanovich Andreevsky], Soldam and Prince Golitsyn 1st; captains: Chevalier Garde: Borozdin, Uvarov and Davydov, all wounded: the first in the left leg by canister shot, the second with a sabre cut to the head, while Davydov suffered a sword wound below the knee; Stahl and regimental adjutant Khrapovitsky; Lifeguard Horse: Sorochinsky [Ilya Stepanovich Sorochinsky], Salov, Ramm and Orlov 1st, who suffered gashes to the side and head; Lifeguard Horse Staff–Captain Count Tyshkevich, who suffered a sabre cut to the right knee and a contusion below the knee from canister shot; lieutenants: Chevalier Garde: Baron Garbs–Hoven and from the Lifeguard Horse; Mirkovich 1st, [Fëdor Yakovlevich Mirkovich], Charlemont, wounded: the first by sabre to the face and arm, the second, round shot to the left thigh and a contusion to the same leg, while Charlemont suffered a stab wound to the chest and a gash to the shoulder; cornets: Chevalier Garde: Sheremetev [Sergei Vasilevich Sheremetev], Yazykov 1st, [Dmitry Semënovich Yazykov], von Smitten [Gustav Gustavovich von Smitten], Pashkov [Andrey Ivanovich Pashkov] and Lifeguard Horse; Prince Golitsyn 3rd, also wounded: Sheremetev with a sabre cut to the face and a contusion to the left arm, Yazykov with a bullet to the left leg, von Smitten with a bullet to the right knee, Pashkov with a contusion to the lower back from round shot, while the latter had a serious contusion to the chest. Having described operations by 1st Cuirassier Division and the distinguished officers involved, it remains now to report on the Lifeguard Horse Artillery. Under Colonel Kozen's command, they occupied the interval left by our troops facing enemy cavalry and artillery three times our strength, which caused terrible destruction, to the Astrakhan Cuirassiers in particular. Colonel Kozen, in spite of heavy casualties, being skilled in his craft and brave, enduring as long as possible, harmed the enemy; eventually, in order to intensify the blows on the enemy battery, he, Kozen, with the permission of His Grace, the Commander in Chief of the Armies, reinforced that location with the battery company under Lieutenant Colonel Dietrichs 4th. The fire was intensified and the enemy battery was forced into silence and withdrew. Kozen attests to the outstanding bravery of these gentlemen officers: Captain Rall 2nd, Staff Captain Stolypin; lieutenants: Bartolomei, Divov, Baron Korf, Kupriyanov, and especially Bistrom [Philip Antonovich Bistrom], Helmersen and Gizhitsky, who, on the complete disordering of the battery by enemy canister fire, held on with four guns for a long time; Lieutenant Härbel 5th [Vasily Vasilevich Gerbel] and Sub Lieutenant Garder, who were with them, and who, having been sent for guns, gathered eleven of them from various companies, and placing them in convenient sites, caused great harm to the enemy. While *Portepée–Junker* [Sub Ensign] Pereira, taking the place of the killed officers, commanded the guns and distinguished himself in this action, for which he is presented for promotion to ensign in the army artillery. Also, Major General Shevich, colonels: Baron Rosen and Karataev, recommended the following for commissioning as officers for their outstanding bravery and courage, firstly – from the Chevalier Garde Regiment *Standart–Junkers*: Turgenev, Sheremetev; *Junkers*: Shepelev, Danilov and Turgenev; Lifeguard Horse *Standart–Junkers*: Count Manteuffel, Kulikovsky, Kalugin, Rodzyanko, Timiryadzev 3rd, Renne and Tomson; secondly, entrusted to them from Her Majesty's *Leib* Cuirassier Regiment *Wachtmeister* [Sergeant–Major] Ribas, and finally, *Junker* Rimovich from the same regiment; moreover, Baron Rosen wrote regarding Ribas that, being badly wounded, he remained on the front line to the point of collapse. In addition, I have the honour to recommend Conductor of non–commissioned rank Burnashov from His Imperial Majesty's Suite for the Quartermaster's Department, who, being with me throughout the battle, carried out my orders with precision and courage, and being wounded in the arm by a bullet, after dressing he returned to the field of battle once more. I dare to ask Your Excellency most humbly, for his diligence in the service of His Imperial Majesty, to be awarded officer's rank.

In accordance with my duty and obligations with regard to all that happened on 27 August [8 September] last, I have reported to the commander of the cuirassier regiments Lieutenant General and Chevalier Prince Golitsyn, on the day of battle. On the same date, having received Your Excellency's orders, delivered to me by the Chief of Staff of First Army, I have the honour to submit all this to the discretion and consideration of Your Excellency, with the application of a list of names, both named in the report here, and of other officers who have shown their distinction, I dare to recommend with regard to their courage and bravery; justice also demands that we testify that all of them, equally the lower ranks, were so courageous in this vicious battle that they appeared to have decided to sacrifice their lives, and I, to complete my duty, dare most humbly to ask for a reward for them.

With regard to the killed, wounded and missing from that day, I have the honour to present a brief dedicated return.

No. 8. Village of Kutuzovo. 7 [19] September, 1812.'

6

'Major General Count Sievers reports to His Grace, General Field Marshal, Commander in Chief of all armies and Chevalier, Prince Golenishchev–Kutuzov:

> Your Grace, I have the honour to report that on the 24th [5 September], I arrived on the left flank of the position of Second Army with the rearguard entrusted to me from Second Army, appearing before his excellency the Commander in Chief; on the orders of his excellency, Lieutenant General Prince Gorchakov, a battery of eight horse artillery guns from 9th Company assigned to me was deployed on the high ground to the left side of the large redoubt, and another of four guns on the high ground to the right side of the large redoubt; cavalry was stationed behind each battery for protection; meanwhile, regiments of jägers occupied the village and forest in front of each of these batteries. Following this, Cossacks announced the approach of the enemy along the Yelnya road; they soon appeared in large columns of cavalry, infantry and artillery, and clearly showed their intention to attack the left flank of the army. Colonel Emmanuel twice attacked the enemy flankers and supporting columns with the Kiev Dragoon Regiment entrusted to him, and drove them back.
>
> Enemy *tirailleurs* and our marksmen, as well as the batteries, began to operate on both sides; two squadrons of the Akhtyrka Hussar Regiment, located as the protection for the left battery, under the command of Captain Alexandrovich, struck one infantry column approaching the battery, driving it off; Captain Bibikov stopped the enemy flankers intending to go around the flank, with our flankers; whereupon, the enemy, crossing the Kolocha river in strong columns, from their left flank along the Smolensk road, proceeded through the village and forest lying in front of our batteries; in order to support our jägers already retreating from the forest and the village, I ordered the Novorossiya Dragoon Regiment, under the command of the regimental commander, Major Terenin, to cross the gap between the forest and the village and attack the enemy infantry columns that were in support of their *tirailleurs*; this regiment, animated by ardour for service and a desire to distinguish itself, fulfilled this command with outstanding valour: the first squadron, under Count Sievers' command, attacked one infantry column; the second squadron, under Lieutenant Stanyukovich's command attacked another; the third squadron, under the command of Major Borgraf, in support of both squadrons attacked the enemy cavalry; the fourth squadron, under Major Milfeld's command took on the enemy *tirailleurs* from behind; each squadron achieved complete success. Being a witness to this heroic feat, I took five bullets in my left side and leg, but only a severe contusion from one, and my horse was wounded; the Novorossiya Dragoon Regiment drove off the enemy at their first attempt, after the attack, Major Terenin reformed the regiment quickly and boldly attacked the advancing enemy cavalry for a second time, drove them back, pursuing and destroying them; but having encountered infantry advancing from all

sides from the forest and not being supported by our infantry, which had retreated from the forest and the village to the redoubt, I managed to cover the retreat of our infantry and the removal of the guns from the nearest high ground through this attack. The casualties to this regiment during these attacks were very significant in field officers, subalterns and lower ranks. Under the command of his excellency, Lieutenant General Prince Golitsyn, the entire cavalry of Second Army was deployed in battle formation behind the battery and redoubt on the left flank; due to the intensified enemy advance, despite the operations of the artillery, the redoubt was abandoned by our heavy artillery; along with them, some of the escorting infantry retreated, while the light artillery on the right side of the redoubt remained in action. Artillery Major General Löwenstern, having observed the retreat of the heavy guns, returned them to the redoubt without delay, as well as the retreating infantry battalions. The enemy offensive was halted for some considerable time, but having received reinforcements, they took possession of the redoubt; although its defence was not entrusted to me, and although the infantry was not under my command, I strove, through persuasion and encouraging by my own example, to force the reluctant battalions to take the redoubt back, I was twice in the ditch at the parapet myself, being exposed to the greatest danger, but my efforts were in vain. We counter–attackers were reinforced by several grenadier regiments from 2nd Division, which Lieutenant General Prince Gorchakov led against the enemy himself; in this situation, having examined the enemy's bold operation – within sight of our cavalry, taking our infantry attacking the redoubt, in the flank and rear with two strong columns between the redoubt and the village, advancing rapidly, – I rushed to the right flank of the cavalry line under my command consisting of the two cuirassier regiments that arrived deployed ahead of the line; their courageous commander, Colonel Tolbuzin 1st came to me; I pointed out to him the columns of enemy infantry advancing to close range; that was enough for him, the Malorussia Cuirassier Regiment was in the first wave; he struck one column with this regiment; the Glukhov Cuirassiers struck the other column; both columns were instantly driven back and pursued as far as the enemy battery, which these brave regiments captured and the cannon they took were presented by them to their commander.

The Kharkov Dragoons and Chernigov Dragoons were ordered to support the cuirassiers by me; that is, to protect their right flank, which was threatened by two infantry columns; on the other side of the village, two squadrons of Kharkov Dragoons, under the command of Major Zhbakovsky, and two squadrons of Chernigov Dragoons, under the command of Major Musin–Pushkin [Sergey Kladevich Musin–Pushkin], appeared, struck these columns and, driving them back, took possession of two cannon, with which the enemy had begun to deploy in battery in support of their infantry, but did not have chance to fire a single shot. The attacking cuirassier and dragoon squadrons, having pursued the enemy, reformed in good order; the enemy did not dare to take the slightest action against these regiments; darkness was already approaching; yet the operations by the infantry near the redoubt continued for some time; the grenadier regiments that had taken possession of the redoubt left it at night and were withdrawn, as were the rest of the infantry, to the main position, while the cavalry, formed up in two waves, remained in place, they put out a screen and before dawn, leaving that part in place, also withdrew to their former positions. Due to the absence of Lieutenant General Prince Gorchakov, who was commanding the attacked left flank of Second Army, and was wounded on 26 August [7 September], I, in pursuance of the subsequent order from the former Commander in Chief of Second Army, the late Prince Bagration, have the honour to present to Your Grace this report of mine on the operations by the regiments of IV Cavalry Corps entrusted to me, during the fighting on the 24th [5 September], and a list of distinguished field officers, subalterns and lower ranks, I most humbly ask for a worthy reward for the diligence and outstanding courage shown by them, each according to their merits.

No. 276, 26 September [8 October], 1812.'

7

'Major General Count Sievers reports to His Grace, General Field Marshal, Commander in Chief of all armies and Chevalier, Prince Golenishchev–Kutuzov:

I have the honour to inform Your Grace that after the army took up positions on the 25th of this month [6 September] in the morning, the enemy attacked the left flank of the army on the morning of the 26th [7 September], following orders from His Excellency the Commander in Chief of Second Army to detach several cavalry to support the infantry located in two *flèches* forwards of the position, the Novorossiya Dragoons and Akhtyrka Hussars were ordered by me to move forward; the Novorossiya Dragoon Regiment, under the leadership of the regimental commander, Major Terenin, executed a bold attack on the enemy, and Major Terenin, setting an example of courage, encouraged the lower ranks and, being greeted with canister and musket fire, hacked into and drove off the enemy infantry columns; Captain Count Sievers, with the squadron commanded by him, with outstanding courage, was the first to hack into the enemy columns, ascending to an enemy battery of 12 guns, which, however, the regiment was not able to drag away, because advancing enemy cavalry, with support from more infantry coming out of the forest, prevented that enterprise; on this battery, the bold Captain Count Sievers was seriously wounded by a bullet in the leg and a sabre cut to the head; his horse was killed under him; the regiment retreated in good order under the protection of its flankers, covering the retreat of the infantry and being forced to abandon the trophies acquired for the glory of its fearless valour to the enemy; the entire regiment, on retreating, halted behind our forward batteries, and then halted in the front line on the left flank of the position as the protection for the battery and the regiment was under fierce bombardment by the enemy until the very end of that day; during the day they lost a very significant number of killed and wounded.

Colonel Vasilchikov directed two squadrons of Akhtyrka Hussars to drive off the cavalry which had surrounded the forward *flèche* on the left flank, already held by the enemy, while he supported them with two squadrons himself; Major Prince Castriot charged valiantly at the enemy cavalry, drove them off, and then, having put the infantry to flight, re–took the *flèche*. Our infantry had not supported this attack, and Colonel Vasilchikov was forced to retreat behind the rear *flèche*, where he held off enemy cavalry attempting to get around the flank into the aforementioned place several times; Major Duvanov charged with outstanding courage at the enemy infantry column with four squadrons, driving them back, but was engaged by another column with fierce musket fire and was seriously wounded. Colonel Vasilchikov, observing the enemy cavalry advancing in strength, struck them in the flank with four squadrons, and, having driven them off, pursued them as far as the enemy batteries before withdrawing behind our batteries with the regiment. Once the two forward *flèches* had been abandoned by our troops, I observed the intention of the enemy to envelope our left flank in several columns of infantry and cavalry proceeding, under the cover of *tirailleurs*, by which they might get into the rear of our entire position and cut off the corps under Lieutenant General Baggovut. At that moment, I took two heavy guns and three light ones from the nearest battery, and placed this battery far ahead of the position of Second Army, on a knoll near the forest itself; the effect of their canister fire on these columns was so striking that the columns were driven back and the enemy no longer dared to repeat the attack, but upon quickly discovering the battery, they tried to knock out the one I had set up near the forest, but did not manage to do it, but instead, this battery, with the help of others on our left flank, caused great harm both to the enemy battery and to their troops. Once the batteries had fired their last charges, efforts to replenish the shells from anywhere were in vain; one caisson, through the diligence and quick wits of the regimental clerk of the Lithuania Ulan Regiment, who stayed with the regiment throughout the entire action, was brought up in the nick of time, and when the enemy made a new attempt on the battery, the guns were worked so well once more that the enemy was forced to retreat in haste and perfect disorder. Despite the shortage of ammunition, these five guns were held by me under the protection of jägers and infantry, under the command of Major General Shakhovsky, and the Lithuania Ulans until the evening. In accordance with my thoughts, Lieutenant General Baggovut, who was with Lieutenant General Tuchkov's corps to my left along the old Smolensk road, seconded six guns of 4th Battery Company under the command of Lieutenant Weide to me. I ordered him to hold the high ground on the right side, and this battery operated successfully and silenced the enemy battery which had greatly harmed our cavalry; the enemy infantry column and cavalry were confined to a ravine by the canister fire that greeted them; this battery, having also fired off its ammunition, so as not to be exposed in the open to the recently renewed operations by enemy batteries, retreated from the high ground only when the centre of Second Army pulled back. Once the enemy attempted to attack the battery of five guns located by the forest for a third time, due to a lack of ammunition with the guns, there was nothing with which to engage the enemy; so I ordered that the five guns be brought in, which was done under the cover of an attack by the Lithuania Ulans on the enemy infantry column; but another column, proceeding through dead ground along the edge of the forest, forced the ulan regiment to retreat, which, having passed the scrub, attached itself again to the batteries on the left flank of the cuirassier division; meanwhile, both infantry regiments under Major General Prince Shakhovsky's command, supported by a regiment from General Baggovut's corps, held off the enemy attempts until nightfall.

In accordance with the subsequent orders from the former Commander in Chief Second Army, the late Prince Bagration, having the honour to submit this report of mine to Your Grace on the operations by the regiments and artillery that were under my command in the battle on the 26th [7th September], I am enclosing a list of those who distinguished themselves to the discretion of Your Grace, for the awarding of deserving rewards, which I most humbly ask for everyone, to encourage those who distinguished themselves, and to all my other subordinates.'

8

'Commander V Corps, Lieutenant General Lavrov reports to General of Infantry and Chevalier Dokhturov:

In accordance with the orders issued to me by Your Excellency, dated 1 [13] September, No. 920, in order for me to report on the situation and actions of the formation entrusted to me on the day of the battle at the village of Borodino, I have the honour to present to Your Excellency: that on the day of battle on 26 August [7 September], at five o'clock in the morning, the entire Lifeguard Infantry Division, on instructions from Colonel von Toll of the Quartermaster's Department, sent by Commander in Chief First Army, General of Infantry, Minister of War and Chevalier Barclay de Tolly, took up positions behind the right flank of Second Army in order to support them; half an hour later I received orders from General of Cavalry Bennigsen to direct the Lifeguard Izmailovsky and Lifeguard Lithuania regiments from the Lifeguard Division entrusted to me, and the combined grenadier brigade, under the command of Colonel Khrapovitsky of the Lifeguard Izmailovsky Regiment; the other regiments: Lifeguard Preobrazhensky, Lifeguard Semenovsky and Lifeguard Finland, under Major General Baron Rosen's command remained, being ordered to move up closer to Second Army's front line, which was immediately executed. From that point on, the columns under the command of Major General Baron Rosen were under continuous fierce fire and changed their locations as necessary, and for 14 hours were under cannon, canister, and finally also musket fire. At four o'clock in the afternoon, the enemy cavalry which had broken through reached the columns under Major General Baron Rosen, who led them forward with drums beating and greeted the enemy cavalry with fixed bayonets, from which a few were run through, and the rest were put to flight.

After this incident, I received orders from Your Excellency to take these columns to the left, and having taken up the position assigned to me, I was notified in person by Adjutant General Vasilchikov that the marksmen sent by the enemy, who were holding the edge of the forest, were harming his cavalry, and that the enemy was enveloping our left flank; in order to hold them back, a battalion from the Lifeguard Finland Regiment was sent to support the cavalry, under the command of Colonel Gervais [Alexander Karlovich Gervais]; and as the enemy marksmen in the forest had been reinforced, and had already begun to harm the columns under Major General Baron Rosen, I detached two more battalions from this regiment, under the command of Colonel Kryzhanovsky [Maxim Konstantinovich Kryzhanovsky], to drive the enemy away. Colonel Gervais, holding the enemy with the battalion entrusted to him, with marksmen spread out in a screen, half an hour later let it be known that the enemy had entered the forest in two columns and, under the cover of skirmishers, was advancing threateningly. Whereupon Colonel Kryzhanovsky reinforced his battalion with skirmishers under the command of Sub–Lieutenant Marin, who was killed by canister shot; Sub–Lieutenant Schöning, who inherited this mission, struck the enemy screen with fixed bayonets, while Colonel Kryzhanovsky, approaching with the 3rd and 2nd battalions, also ordered the enemy columns to be struck with bayonets fixed. Colonel Steven with 2nd Battalion, and Gervais with 3rd Battalion, shouting 'Hurrah!' charged with the bayonet with outstanding courage, pushed the enemy back and drove them to the edge of the forest, where they positioned marksmen, on whom a battery opened fire from the enemy side, under the protection of cavalry, which fired fiercely with canister, whereupon Captain Ogarev [Alexander Gavrilovich Ogarev] was wounded with canister shot in the knee, whose place was taken by Staff Captain Baikov [Sergey Vasilevich Baikov].

Aware of the strengthening of the enemy on his right flank, Colonel Kryzhanovsky ordered the commander of 1st Battalion, Captain Ushakov [Pëtr Sergeevich Ushakov], to send in the skirmishers; they were sent in under the command of Staff Captain Rahl 4th, who drove back the enemy screen; thus in one hour the entire forest was cleared; At that moment, orders were received from Your Excellency, via Adjutant General Vasilchikov, to clear the forest and hold it at all costs.

The enemy were reinforced several times in order to repulse our skirmishers, but without any success; the musket and canister fire was fierce from the enemy side; but in order to hold the enemy and not allow them to break into the forest again, Staff Captain Afrosimov 4th was sent with a company to assist the screen, and then Staff Captain Akhlestyshev also with a company. The skirmishers maintained their screen at the edge of the forest at all times; at nine o'clock in the evening the gunfire began to subside and ended by ten o'clock, and all three battalions remained on the battlefield seized from the enemy, protecting the entire Lifeguard Infantry Division with their screen.

The Lifeguard Izmailovsky and Lifeguard Lithuania regiments and the combined grenadier brigade fought in the presence of Your Excellency, which is why I acknowledge the submitted reports as best and true from colonels Kutuzov [Alexander Petrovich Kutuzov] and Udom regarding the exploits of the regiments entrusted to them, to submit to the discretion of Your Excellency, remaining confident that everyone will receive a reward according to their merits.

The Lifeguard Jäger Regiment, as it had been seconded by order of Commander in Chief First Army on 23 August [4 September] and fought on the right flank at the village of Borodino, this report was submitted to the Commander in Chief about them.

Doing full justice to the valour and unshakable resolve of all ranks, it is my duty to present to Your Excellency in particular with regard to Major General Baron Rosen, and regarding the regimental commanders, colonels: Khrapovitsky, Udom, Kryzhanovsky, Driesen and Postnikov; of battalion commanders, as well as field officers and subalterns, to whom, by the authority of Your Excellency's command, I most honourably present the list; as a mark of their outstanding courage, I humbly ask Your Excellency for five crosses per company of the Military Order for the lower ranks.

No. 1116, 3 [15] September, 1812.'

9

'Commander VI Corps, General of Infantry Dokhturov reports to His Grace, Commander in Chief of the armies, General of Infantry and Chevalier, Prince Golenishchev–Kutuzov:

Your Grace is not unaware of the operations by the troops in the centre from the beginning, formerly under my command; I left them after a short time, having been appointed, by the will of Your Grace, to command the army, instead of the wounded General Prince Bagration; which is why I make it my duty to report that, having arrived with them, I found the high ground and redoubts, previously occupied by our troops, had been taken by the enemy, as well as the ravine that separated us from them.

Having set myself the most important objective of holding in the present positions, I issued the orders necessary in this event, instructing the formation commanders to repulse the enemy attempts by whatever means and not to give up any current locations; everyone accomplished this with outstanding discretion, and although the enemy, who had decided without fail to drive back our left flank, made an attack with all their might under fearsome artillery fire, these attempts were completely disrupted by the measures taken and the matchless courage of our troops.

The Lifeguard Lithuania, Lifeguard Izmailovsky and Lifeguard Finland regiments, during the entire battle showed bravery worthy of Russians and were the first who, with their outstanding courage, holding back the enemy attempts, struck them everywhere with fixed bayonets; the other regiments; Lifeguard Preobrazhensky and Lifeguard Semenovsky, also contributed to the repulse of the enemy.

In general, all the troops that day fought with their usual reckless courage, such that from my assumption of command until nightfall stopped the battle, almost all points were retained, except for some locations, which were conceded due to the need to withdraw the troops from the fearsome canister fire, which had caused great harm; but this retreat was of a very short distance, conducted with due order and with the infliction of casualties on the enemy in this event. The gentlemen generals, commanding the units entrusted to them, about whom I am presenting this list, with my remarks on the exploits of each, their prudent orders and their own example of outstanding fearlessness, that repelled the attacking enemy everywhere. I have the honour to recommend to Your Grace these worthy generals, who have rendered me the greatest service in the diligent and outstanding performance of their duties; I have recommended that they deliver to me with haste the lists of those who have distinguished themselves in this battle; once received, I shall not hesitate to present them to Your Grace; enclosing a list of officers who were with me with remarks on their exploits, I humbly ask for them to be awarded for the distinction that they have demonstrated.

No. 935, September 1812.'

10

'A copy of the report by Lieutenant General Raevsky to General of Infantry and Chevalier Dokhturov:

> I was on the left flank with the corps entrusted to me in positions near the village of Borodino, initially in two waves, the right flank leaning against the mound on which I had placed the Battery Company of 26th Brigade. Seeing from the lie of the land that the enemy would launch an attack on our flank and that this battery of mine would be the key to the whole position, I fortified this mound with a redoubt and reinforced it with as many guns as the location allowed. My prediction came true. On the 26th [7 September], at dawn, the enemy began to move around my flank, and I was ordered to change front, leaning the right flank on this same redoubt:

four infantry regiments from 26th Division, under the command of Major General Paskevich, were assigned to protect it; two regiments of infantry from 12th Division occupied the scrub to my front; the left flank of both lines adjoined a village fortified with batteries, where the Commander in Chief Second Army, Prince Bagration, was located, who immediately let me know that if he needed troops, he would take them from my second line. This prompted me to demand reinforcements, which I received, comprising three regiments of jägers, under the command of Colonel Vuich; I positioned all these troops behind the redoubt in such a way that, when attacked by the enemy, they could take their columns from both flanks, while the regiments located in the scrub would take their places in the front line. The enemy, having arranged their entire army in front of our eyes, so to speak, in a single column, went straight at us frontally; approaching us, strong columns separated from their left flank and went straight at the redoubt, and despite fierce canister fire from my guns, their forward troops climbed over the parapet without firing a shot; at the same time, from my right flank, Major General Paskevich's regiments attacked the left flank of the enemy who were behind the redoubt with bayonets fixed. Major General Vasilchikov did the same to their right flank, while Major General Yermolov, taking a battalion of jägers from the regiments led by Colonel Vuich, struck with fixed bayonets straight at the redoubt, where, having wiped out all those in it, he took the general leading the column prisoner. Major generals Vasilchikov and Paskevich pushed the enemy columns back in the blink of an eye and drove them into the scrub so hard that hardly any of them escaped.

Regarding the further operations by my corps, it remains for me to describe in a nutshell that after the destruction of the enemy, returning again to our positions, we held out there until facing the repeated attacks by the enemy, until we were reduced by the killed and wounded to complete insignificance and my redoubt had just been occupied by Major General Likhachëv. Your Excellency himself knows that Major General Vasilchikov, having rallied the scattered remnants of 12th Division and 27th Division, and with the Lifeguard Lithuania Regiment, held the vital high ground located at the left extremity of our entire line. I cannot describe the deeds of every general, field officer and subaltern, and their outstanding courage is proved by the fact that almost all of them were wiped out at their posts. I ask Your Excellency most humbly to award the field officers and subalterns, of whom I have the honour to present. Awards for the three generals: Vasilchikov, Yermolov and Paskevich, as corps commanders are not given the authority to submit for promotions, I ask Your Excellency to fulfil this. You know yourself that there were no cases where they did not show outstanding courage, diligence and military talent. I have the honour to enclose a list of field officers and subalterns who have shown themselves to be outstanding.

No. 280, 11 [23] September 1812, Lukovno village.'

11

'Regarding the operations by the troops of II Corps, under the command of Lieutenant General Baggovut:

> On 26 August [7 September], once the enemy had launched an attack on our left flank, I, by order of Your Excellency, went to reinforce them with the infantry regiments of II Corps.
> Having reached the centre of the army, on the orders of Your Excellency to reinforce them, I left four infantry regiments from 4th Division, under Major General Prinz Eugen von Württemberg, while I proceeded on to the left flank with the remaining four regiments of 17th Division.
> A little to the left of the centre was the detachment under Major General Count Sievers, whose horse artillery occupied the high ground, which, due to the lightness of its calibre, could not cause sufficient harm to the enemy, which is why I ordered them to be replaced by 17th Battery Company, commanded by Colonel Dietrichs 2nd, giving him the protection of the Ryazan Infantry Regiment, and in order to prevent the enemy from occupying the scrub located nearby to the left side of this battery, I ordered the Brest Infantry Regiment to scatter skirmishers through it and to hold the enemy without fail.
> As soon as everything had been set up, a few shots from the aforementioned battery forced the enemy to open a strong bombardment on it, bringing their batteries closer to our batteries, under the protection of three strong columns of infantry, but the successful operations of our artillery in an instant cooled their ardour and at the same time this column retreated behind the forest and the artillery also withdrew.
> Lieutenant General Tuchkov 1st informed me that the enemy was pressing him and their immediate objective, as noted, was to take the high ground from him, located on the left flank; to that end, the Belozersk Infantry and Wilmanstrand Infantry were sent to reinforce them with six guns from 17th Battery Company, which were taken from the above mentioned battery, in place of which six guns from 33rd Light Company were sent; This detachment was commanded by Lieutenant General Olsufiev.
> This detachment, having arrived at the place assigned to them, came under the immediate command of Lieutenant General Tuchkov, who ordered the aforementioned six guns to occupy the high ground. The enemy, noticing this movement, opened heavy fire on our battery, sending marksmen forward under the protection of a strong column, trying not to let the high ground be taken, as it was important to them; the hail of canister and round shot produced by the enemy batteries could not stop the swiftness of Lieutenant Shchepotyev, commander of those artillery pieces, who, with astonishing composure, took the place assigned to him and operated with incredible good fortune, such that there was no shot that did not cause more harm to the enemy, and in the shortest possible time, the enemy columns, which had so quickly marched on our battery, were forced to

retire; the enemy battery, despite the fact that two caissons were blown sky high by Lieutenant Shchepotyev, however, did not stop their fierce operations, both against our battery and on our columns; the enemy, seeing the failure of their infantry column, sent another stronger than the previous one, which wanted to take our battery without fail and already their skirmishers were at the foot of the hill; whereupon Lieutenant General Olsufiev sent Lieutenant Colonel Kern [Yermolay Fëdorovich Kern] with a battalion of the Belozersk Infantry Regiment, which, being supported by the Pavlov Grenadiers, rushed with determination at the column and the enemy skirmishers with bayonets fixed, forcing them to turn back and seek salvation in flight; here the canister from our battery completed their total destruction, and thus ended their audacious attempt; the enemy dual attack did not achieve the results they desired, which is why they were forced to retire behind the forest, and their battery fell completely silent. During these events, Lieutenant General Tuchkov 1st had been wounded by a bullet, after which, due to my seniority, I took command of the left wing of the army. During this time, Major General Prinz Eugen von Württemberg reached me with two regiments, Kremenchug Infantry and Minsk Infantry, which I placed between our left flank and the detachment under Major General Count Sievers, thus establishing a link with this general; the artillery, which arrived with him, comprised: six guns from 4th Battery Company, together with 17th Battery Company, while another six guns were directed to Count Sievers' detachment.

During this time, the enemy moved from our left flank in the direction of the detachment under Count Sievers; upon noticing this, I sent a strong fighting patrol from Major General Karpov's Cossack Regiment to flush out the enemy on our left flank; the Cossacks, approaching a village where they took up positions, found them hidden in the forest with several columns and artillery; the enemy perceiving this as an attack, immediately advanced their guns, sending out skirmishers, and opened fire on the Cossacks.

Meanwhile, the enemy had launched an attack on the brigade under Major General Count Ivelich. This general closed on the enemy column with four companies of the Brest Infantry Regiment, firing a volley of musketry before charging with fixed bayonets; but the superiority of the enemy guns in the column prevented him from executing his intention, even more so because, having suffered a severe wound from a bullet in the shoulder, he had to fall back a little, content only with the fact that he had not allowed our batteries to be shot up, meanwhile notifying me of this incident, and asking for reinforcements, for which I commanded Major General Vadkovsky [Yakov Yegorovich Vadkovsky] with the Wilmanstrand Infantry Regiment, sending him 500 men from the Moscow *Opolchenie* in support, and also ordering him to link up with the Ryazan Infantry and drive the enemy back without fail, and having barely appeared with this detachment, despite strong small arms fire, charged with bayonets fixed and drove back the enemy, suffering a severe contusion, while Colonel Sukharev, commander of the Wilmanstrand Infantry Regiment, was wounded by a bullet.

At the very moment that this was happening, two strong enemy columns with four guns were making their way through the forest between our left flank and the brigade under Count Ivelich, in order to completely cut the latter off from linking up with me and to get into their rear. A battalion of the Tauride Grenadier Regiment, which was in their way, engaged the enemy with fierce musket fire and thus stopped them, then, deploying two companies as skirmishers, withdrew onto the road that connected us with the centre of the army with the remaining two companies. Having been notified of this, I tasked Major General Prince Shakhovsky [Ivan Leontevich Shakhovsky], ordering him to repulse the enemy with the Minsk Infantry Regiment without fail, he executed this mission very successfully, as the enemy immediately retreated. The Colonel in Chief of the Minsk Infantry Regiment, Colonel Krasavin [Alexey Fëdorovich Krasavin], was wounded in this action.

The enemy, seeing the failure of their operation from this action, finally decided to launch a decisive blow on our left flank, arranging a strong column of infantry, placing cavalry on its flanks, charged at our battery, commanded by Staff Captain Leskov, and with exemplary speed their cavalry found themselves already halfway up the hill, and with one more push, our guns would serve as trophies for the enemy; but the valiant Colonel Pyshnitsky, with exemplary fearlessness, charged at the enemy with the Kremenchug Infantry Regiment with fixed bayonets, setting an example of personal courage for his subordinates, and in one minute the enemy was driven from the battery, and their impudence was so punished by Russian bayonets that this hill was littered with enemy corpses, and the rest fled.

After that, I ordered the troops to assemble on the road leading to the city of Mozhaisk, so that, if necessary, I could rejoin the army; for this eventuality, the battery was to be removed from the high ground; the enemy, taking advantage of this opportunity, rushed all his forces up to pursue me, which is why I was forced to reform the troops a second time on both sides of the road, while four guns from Lieutenant Colonel Bashmakov's [Flegont Mironovich Bashmakov] company were ordered to fire upon the enemy, while our skirmishers moved onto their flank from the direction of the forest, which caused them to flee back the way they came; we pursued them a little, halting because the darkness of the night did not allow us to exploit this opportunity any further, sending only a Cossack patrol to monitor their retreat, who then returned and informed me that the enemy had retreated beyond Moskva river,[4] leaving mastery of the battlefield completely to the Colours of His Imperial Majesty.'

---

4   Possibly the Kolocha?

12

'General of Cavalry, Military Ataman of the Don Host, Platov, reports to His Grace, Supreme Commander General Field Marshal, Commander in Chief of all active armies and Chevalier Prince Mikhail Ilarionovich Golenishchev–Kutuzov:

> On the former 26 August last [7 September], near the village of Borodino, the general battle with the enemy, I was, by order of Your Grace, with the Cossack regiments on the right flank of our army, and of the action against the enemy left flank, Your Grace by personal presence is aware; I, on the other hand, have made it my duty to testify in all truth to Your Grace of the tireless activity and outstanding courage shown during the entire duration of the battle by the commander of the Cossack regiments, Major General Ilovaisky 5th [Nikolai Vasilevich Ilovaisky], and the regimental commanders and their regimental field officers and subalterns who distinguished themselves in this battle, attaching herewith a list of names, I humbly ask for your consideration and respect as a commander, for their reward according to their merits.
>
> No. 1206, 25 September [7 October], 1812.'

Appendix VIII

Michaud's letter to former *Flügel–Adjutant* Mikhailovsky-Danilevsky

A copy is held in the Archives of the Military Topographic Depot, No. 47,352, folio 2.

'Mon cher Colonel! Après l'entretien que nous eumes hier sur les évènemens de la guerre de l'année 12, je crois vous faire plaisir, très cher Colonel, en vous faisant connaitre une petite conversation que j'eus l'honneur d'avoir avec Sa Majesté notre très gracieux Empereur le 8. 7re 1812. Elle devrait faire époque dans l'histoire par la connaissance qu'elle donne de la force d'ame de notre Souverain qui a été bien mal jugé par ceux qui l'ont cru au moment de conclure la paix après la perte de Moscou.

Vous savez, mon cher chevalier, que je fus envoyé à St.–Pétersbourg par le maréchal Koutouzoff pour porter la nouvelle à Sa Majesté de l'abandon de Moscou dont les flammes éclairerent ma route jusqu'au delà de Mourom: jamais voyageur n'a eu le coeur plus sensiblement touché qu'a été le mien dans cette occasion: Russe de coeur et d'ame quoique étranger, porteur d'une des plus tristes nouvelles au meilleur des Souverains, traversant un pays au milieu d'un demi–million et plus d'habitans de toutes classes qui émigraient n'emportant avec eux que l'amour de la patrie, l'espoir de la venger et un dévouement sans bornes pour leur adoré Souverain, frappé tour à tour par la douleur de ma mission, de tout ce que je voyais, et par la joie de tout ce que j'entendais autour de moi de l'entousiasme national, j'arrivais le 8 au matin à la capitale tout plein de chagrin par les tristes nouvelles qu j'allais donner. Admis à l'instant par Sa Majesté dans Son cabinet, l'Empereur jugea d'abord par mon air que je n'avais rien de consolant à Lui apprendre... m'apportez–vous de tristes nouvelles Colonel, me dit–il?... bien tristes, lui repondis–je, l'abandon de Moscou... mais aurait–on livré mon ancienne capitale sans se battre? Sire, les environs de Moscou n'offrant aucune position à pouvoir hasarder une bataille avec des forces inferieures, le maréchal a cru bien faire en conservant à Votre Majesté une armée, dont la perte sans sauver Moscou aurait pu être de la plus grande consequence, et qui, par les renforts que Votre Majesté vient de lui procurer et que je viens de rencontrer de toutes parts, se verra bientôt à même de reprendre l'offensive et faire repentir l'ennemi d'avoir pénétré dans le coeur de Ses états... l'ennemi est–il entré en ville?... Oui Sire et elle est en cendre à l'heure qu'il est, je l'ai laissée toute en flammes. A ces *mots les yeux du Souverain me firent si bien connaitre l'état de Son ame que j'en fus ému à ne pouvoir tenir... Je vois, colonel, par tout ce qui nous arrive, que la Providence exige des grands sacrifices de nous; je suis pret à me soumettre à toutes ses volontés, mais dites moi, Michaud, comment avez vous laissé l'esprit de l'armée en voyant abandonner ainsi Mon ancienne capitale sans coup ferir; est-ce que cela n'a pas influé sur le moral du soldat? N'avez-vous pas aperçu du découragement... Sire, me permettez Vous, lui repondis-je, de Vous parler franchement en loyal militaire... Colonel, je l'exige toujours, mais dans ce moment surtout je vous prie de me parler comme vous l'avez fait autrefois; ne me cachez rien; je veux savoir absolument ce qu'il en est... Sire, j'ai laissé toute l'armée depuis les chefs jusqu'au dernier soldat sans exception dans une crainte épouvantable, effrayante... Comment-ca? reprit le Souverain d'un air indigné; d'ou peuvent naitre les craintes? Mes Russes se laisseroient-ils abattre par quelques malheurs... Jamais, Sire, ils craignent seulement que Votre Majesté par bonté de coeur ne se laisse persuader de faire la paix; ils brullent de combattre et de Lui prouver par le sacrifice de leur vie et par leur courage, combien ils Lui sont devoués... ah! vous me tranquilisez, colonel; (en frappant de la main sur mon épaule) eh bien, retournez à l'armée, dites à nos braves, dites à tous mes bon sujets, partout ou vous passerez, que quand je n'aurais plus aucun soldat, je me mettrai moi même à la tête de ma chère noblesse, de mes bons paysans et j'userai ainsi jusqu'à la dernière ressource de Mon empire, il m'en offre encore plus que mes ennemis ne pensent, mais si jamais il fut écrit dans les décrèts de la divine Providence que ma dinastie dut cesser de regner sur le trone de mes ancetres, alors après avoir épuisé tous les moyens qui sont en mon pouvoir, je me laisserai croitre la barbe jusqu'ici (en portant la main sur la poitrine) et j'irai manger des pommes de terre avec le dernier de mes paysans plutôt que de signer la honte de ma patrie et de ma chère nation dont je sais apprecier les sacrifices qu'elle Me fait... puis allant jusqu'au fond de Son Cabinet et revenant à grands pas, le visage tout plein de feu, serrant de Sa main mon bras... Colonel Michaud, n'oubliez pas ce que je vous dis ici; peut-être un jour nous nous le rappellerons avec plaisir... Napoléon ou Moi, ou lui, ou Moi, nous ne pouvons plus regner ensemble; j'ai appris à le connaitre; il ne me trompera plus... Sire, lui repondis-je, le coeur entousiasmé de tout ce que je venois d'entendre, Votre Majesté signe dans ce moment la gloire de la nation et le salut de l'Europe.'*

Appendix IX

The Tsar's general plan of operations

The general plan of operations, in the form in which it was sent by the Tsar to Prince Kutuzov, consisted of the following Supreme Commands addressed to Chichagov, Tormasov, Count Wittgenstein and Count Steinheil:

1. 'To Admiral Chichagov. The distance of the enemy main body beyond the Dnieper, our resources prepared and already united there being sufficient to fix and defeat them, gives us the opportunity to deliver a powerful blow behind enemy lines and operate on his line of operations: from the north across the Dvina, into the Vilna Governorate and Minsk Governorate, by two armies, Count Steinheil's and Count Wittgenstein's; from the south, into the Grodno Governorate and Minsk Governorate, also with two armies, one, formerly Tormasov's, and the other, under your command. The liberation and salvation of Russia must result from this general offensive against the enemy outlined here. If, over such a wide area, every part in general, and each one in particular, do not move towards the objectives assigned to them, in accordance with the best outcome of the whole, then even the most beneficial operation could prove prejudicial. Any uncoordinated movements by our forces, in their present positions, would produce nothing more than the loss of men, without significant gains, if they are merely independent, and not general and consistent with the whole and with all the other independent formations, and even that must be done in such a way that the operations performed everywhere are also at specific times and towards specific locations. And so, with common efforts and with the cooperation of one another, the actual successes will be achieved beyond doubt, and the consequences will be more beneficial and more important. Of course, we should take advantage of the remoteness of the enemy main body to restore our severed communications, and turn our superior numbers, on the one hand, from Polotsk beyond the Dvina to the left flank of the enemy corps under Oudinot and MacDonald, located along the Dvina, and, isolating them from the enemy main body, smash them and drive them onto the advancing force led by Count Steinheil. This force, completing the destruction and relieving the corps under Count Wittgenstein, will give them the means to quickly turn to the northern part of the Minsk Governorate, to link up with you. Meanwhile, from the other direction, the army, formerly under Tormasov, taking care to fight off the two corps under Prince Schwarzenberg and Reynier, will hold them on the road from Pruzhany to Slonim, until you have chance to arrive in Pinsk with the army led by you. From here, screened by the movements of the

army formerly under Tormasov, you must quickly advance via Nesvizh to Minsk, and thereby cut Schwarzenberg and Reynier off from the enemy main army, then rejoin the army formerly under Tormasov, between Smolensk and Nesvizh, so that the troops under Schwarzenberg and Reynier would be all the more completely and surely cut off from the Minsk Governorate, and subsequently, from the other direction, via Minsk, also link up with Count Wittgenstein, at the same time attaching the corps from Mozyr at Minsk, so that, with the unbreakable unification of all our forces in Lithuania, it will be possible to drive them back and force them to turn: the Saxons into the Duchy of Warsaw, and the *Kaiserlichen* into Galicia, the Prussians and Württembergers behind the Neman, while the French are eradicated to the last man. When executing this important plan, one should always take into account the movements of the enemy with our common objective, and over time, where whatever formation of our forces might be at the time, or currently is, and therefore, for your information and consideration, copies are attached here of these instructions to the commanders of our forces, who must mutually notify one another, not only about the movements of the enemy, but also about the locations of their positions, who is doing what and where they intend to be over the next few days, so that everyone can always see the course of operations being carried out by common efforts, they will verify them with the general plan, and, accordingly, bring everything to the desired outcome.

I acknowledge it as good to prescribe for your unconditional and precise execution:

a) From Ostrog, turn the army led by you towards Pinsk, where it is vital that you arrive by 25 September [7 October], as one of the main objectives of the entire operation is: screened by Tormasov's movements drive Reynier's and Schwarzenberg's corps several stages from Pinsk, Nesvizh and Minsk, so that, by forestalling them in these locations, you will cut them off from the Minsk Governorate, the Berezina and the enemy main army completely.

b) Not later than 1 [13] October, and the earlier, the better, the army led by you must be in Nesvizh. Here, having established communications with the army formerly under Tormasov, you are to strengthen it by 5 [17] October, if necessary, with a detachment from your force, and thus put them in a better state to strike and pursue Schwarzenberg and Reynier, driving them into the Duchy of Warsaw or into Galicia.

c) By 9 [21] October, at the latest, and if earlier, so much the better, your main force should be in Minsk, where by the same day the detachment from Mozyr should arrive. From Minsk, as soon as possible, on one side, hold the river line of the Berezina and Borisov, where you must establish a fortified camp, furthermore, also holding the forest defiles along the road from Borisov to Bobr, and fortifying all places suitable for this along the entire route, so that on the return route of the enemy main army, pursued by our forces, strong resistance may be offered at every step, while on the other side, by 15 [27] October, link up with Count Wittgenstein in the direction of Dokshitsy, with which your direct communications, both with St Petersburg and with Kiev, will be completely confirmed and secured.

d) Thus occupying the centre with the three armies combined, and having a fourth in reserve at Vilna, under Count Steinheil's command, meanwhile, incidents in the main armies will reveal everything that cannot be foreseen, and then, according to the wishes of the enemy, our three armies must also link up to repulse the enemy, either in the centre or on either flank, either to the left, across the Ula, or to the centre, through Bobr or Borisov and the Berezina, or to the right towards Bobruisk.

In a word: wherever they might make an attempt, always forestalling them with energy and speed, at least in equal forces, and maintaining the dispositions of our troops in such a way that nothing could reach the main enemy army from outside our borders, and so that couriers, or spies, could not exfiltrate anywhere from it, and not the slightest element of that enemy main army, which has gone so far inside our borders, so exhausted by the losses already suffered, defeats and harsh marches, how else should they suffer, except utter defeat and complete annihilation, not being able to retreat from our borders. Finally, if the enemy having been ejected from Moscow attempts to turn towards Kiev or St Petersburg, then even here from your central position it is possible to turn in one direction or another, holding on either the Dnieper or the Volkhov, and forestalling the enemy there, who, on the other hand, will be continuously and relentlessly struck from behind by Our combined main armies, under the command of Prince Kutuzov. Until that time, being here in unbreakable communications and continuous correspondence with all other elements of Our forces, in this position you should anticipate what might happen in the main armies, and in due course you will not be left without further instructions on those events.'

2. 'To the army formerly under Tormasov. I am forwarding herewith, copies of instructions, issued by Me to the generals: Chichagov, Count Steinheil and Count Wittgenstein, on the occasion of the general advance of Our troops into the Lithuania Governorate, for your information and comment; having converted them into orders, at the same time, I acknowledge it as good to prescribe for your unconditional and precise execution:

   a) By 25 September [7 October], Chichagov will be in Pinsk. On 1 [13] October, he will enter Nesvizh; therefore, you are to be in Pruzhany between 25 to 30 September [7 to 12 October], and thereby divert the enemy as far as possible, from Pinsk and Nesvizh, and then from 1 [13] October you are to start offensive operations against the enemy, having assembled and absorbed all your detachments beforehand, pressuring, or breaking them, or, if they take a strong position, then, outflanking them to the right, on 5 [17] October, linking up with reinforcements from Nesvizh, and then defeating the enemy with combined forces.
   c) The objectives for your army are: to mask Admiral Chichagov's advance such that he has time to get out of Pinsk without being discovered by the enemy, and enter Nesvizh, thereby cutting off Schwarzenberg's and Reynier's corps

from the Minsk Governorate and from the main French army. Thereafter it is up to you to split those corps apart and drive them away, leaving only warning outposts along the Shchara river, from its confluence with the Neman, through Slonim to Pinsk, such that Count Wittgenstein is given the opportunity to link up with Chichagov's army between Minsk and Dokshitsy without interference. Thereafter you are to place your army at Nesvizh, from where you may equally observe towards the Shchara in one direction, and to Bobruisk and the Berezina, near Borisov in the other, being in unbreakable communications and frequent correspondence with the forces in Vilna and Minsk.

c) In this situation, it may be necessary to wait for events to unfold in the main armies, and in due course you will not be left without instruction on these incidents.'

3. 'To Count Wittgenstein. Having attached herewith copies of the instructions issued by Me to generals: Tormasov, Chichagov and Count Steinheil, on the occasion of the general advance of Our forces into the Lithuania Governorate, for your information and comment, converting these instructions and ordering you, moreover, I acknowledge it as good to prescribe for your unconditional and precise execution:

   a) By 25 September [7 October], 11,000 men of the St Petersburg *opolchenie* will arrive in Sebezh to reinforce the corps led with such renown by you personally.
   b) Between 20 and 24 September [2 and 6 October], 9,000 infantry, cavalry and artillery will assemble in Velikie–Luki from St Petersburg, and 8,000 men from the Governorate of Novgorod's *opolchenie*, which you will see in more detail from the schedule attached herewith, and I entrust this corps to your command.
   c) Without losing any time, issue preliminary orders to supply all these troops with mobile magazines and reserve artillery parks. There should be a provisions magazine in Velikie–Luki, assembled and delivered from the Pskov Governorate, since our main army had been intended to halt at Vitebsk.
   d) From 25 September [7 October], with all these newly arrived troops, and having assembled all your detachments, not otherwise needed due to the offensive operations by Count Steinheil, arrange their movements such that the Velikie–Luki Corps proceeds through Nevel along the Polotsk road, while the St Petersburg *opolchenie* advances from Sebezh to your concentration area. Once these latter are close to your camp, detach 5th Division from your corps with several of the best replacement battalions and most of the cavalry, with sufficient artillery, and you will personally depart with the headquarters yourself in order to join the Velikie–Luki Corps with these troops on the way to Polotsk, wherever you regard it as appropriate, at your best discretion, since the offensive mission of this formation is very important; entrust the right hand corps, under your overall command, to Lieutenant General Prince Iashvili.

e) By 1 [13] October, the corps from Velikie–Luki, reinforced by the elite troops that you are to attach to it, are to move at least 35,000 men onto the left bank of the Dvina. Anticipating difficulties in assaulting Polotsk frontally and avoiding wasting men in attacking fortifications, by means of this crossing you will not only take Polotsk from the rear, but also isolate Oudinot's Corps completely from the main enemy army, while Prince Iashvili will proceed simultaneously along the right bank of the Dvina towards Polotsk. Your crossing of the Dvina may take place between the mouth of the Obola river, which flows into the Dvina, protecting the crossing from the direction of Vitebsk and the main enemy army with this river on the right bank of the Dvina, while on the left bank by the river Ula and by Polotsk, screening your intentions from the enemy with demonstrations indicating that you want to take Polotsk from the right bank of the Dvina by assault.

f) Having liberated Polotsk from behind, having annihilated the enemy there and re–attached the corps under Prince Iashvili, you are to move, as quickly as possible, to destroy Oudinot, isolated from the main enemy army, trapping them against the troops under Count Steinheil, who by this time, having beaten back MacDonald, will already have closed up to Vidtsy and Sventsiany. Here Count Steinheil, having relieved you, is to continue to destroy the remnants of the enemy, and if he does not have chance to mop up everyone, then he is to drive them beyond the Viliya and the Neman, and, having occupied Vilna, is to monitor the Neman from the Prussians blockading Riga and at the same time is to serve as a reserve for the three combined armies across the Berezina and in the Minsk Governorate.

g) Having thus isolated Oudinot and secured yourself from the opposite direction through the operations by Count Steinheil, quickly direct yourself towards Dokshitsy, where you should arrive by 15 [27] October, and from there, having established communications with Minsk and linking up with Chichagov, across the Berezina, occupy Lepel and the entire course of the Ula, from the Berezina to its confluence with the Dvina.

h) The choke–points here should be fortified in the strongest manner, to which you are to direct all your efforts, as it is impossible to predict to where the enemy, when retreating from behind the Dnieper, will decide to move. Remaining in uninterrupted communications and frequent correspondence with all our other forces, later, once everything is linked up and established, it will be possible to gather intelligence for oneself about the state of the enemy in Vitebsk, and make an effort there, to deny to the enemy every location which he might rely on during his retreat. From this position, it will be necessary to wait for events with the main armies, and in due course you will not be left without further instructions on those events.'

4. 'To Count Steinheil. I am forwarding herewith, copies of the instructions issued by Me to generals: Tormasov, Chichagov and Count Wittgenstein, on the occasion of the general advance of Our forces into the Lithuania Governorate, for your information and comment, converting them into your instructions. Moreover, I acknowledge it as good to prescribe for your unconditional and precise execution:

a) Once the troops from Finland have arrived in Riga, Essen will instruct Löwis to set out with the Riga garrison, 20,000 men, along the left bank of the Dvina, and, proceeding along the road through Eckau and from there to Friedrichstadt, clear the area of the enemy and settle down there, awaiting further dispositions from you. In the meantime, he is not to tolerate the presence of any enemy detachment at a distance of less than two marches from Friedrichstadt, and must try to destroy everything that comes towards this city, so that the attention of MacDonald is drawn and he is distracted from Count Wittgenstein before the arrival of the Finland Corps in Riga. If superior enemy forces assemble against Löwis, which, however, is not foreseen, then upon the arrival of the Finland Corps in Riga, you will be able to provide him with strong support.

b) Once all your troops have landed in Reval, hasten to Riga via Pernau, where, in accordance with intelligence from beyond the Dvina, make arrangements so that if, in the event of the enemy combining against Löwis, it would be difficult for them to independently generate an offensive into the Vilna Governorate, then once you leave Riga, up to Eckau, keeping in mind the destruction of the enemy artillery, and linking up with Löwis' Corps, if the combination of superior enemy numbers so demands, or move via Bausk to Birzhi, Löwis is to be ordered, staying level with you, to go from Friedrichstadt to Nerft. From this position, being inextricably linked with each other, having supplied yourselves with necessities, a mobile replacement park and a provisions magazine, from 20 September [2 October], launch the most powerful offensive operations, keeping in mind working in such a way as to best divert MacDonald's attention and strength away from Count Wittgenstein.

c) If few enemy troops remain on the right bank, which is likely, because even from the first movements by General Löwis towards Friedrichstadt, they might be diverted from Mitau, to join with those who were in Kreutzburg and Jakobstadt, it is self-evident that, with such a movement, they must be prevented from uniting, and must be be defeated in detail. However, if Victor's Corps assembling at Tilsit does not force you to take other measures, then the Finland Corps is always to keep to the left, towards the Vilna Governorate, in the direction of Vyzdy and Sventsiany, where you should arrive by 4 [16] October in order to engage Oudinot, who will have been defeated and pursued by Count Wittgenstein, you are to relieve the latter, to annihilate the enemy, and, having driven the remnants of their forces beyond the Neman, halt in Vilna, and from there monitor the Neman for the Prussians blockading Riga. From this position, Our troops will serve as a reserve for the three combined armies near the Berezina.

d) Having been in continuous communications and frequent correspondence with all other formations of Our forces there, await developments from our main armies, and in due course you will not be left without further instructions on those developments.'

Appendix X

Prince Kutuzov's letter to the Head of Kaluga City

'My dear Ivan Vikulich! Your commendable diligence, coupled with prudence, which is necessary under the present circumstances, has granted me the pleasant duty of expressing my gratitude to you. At the same time, I ask you to reassure the inhabitants of the city of Kaluga and be assured that the condition of our army, as always, is in a trustworthy position. Our forces are not only preserved, but also increased, and the hope of the certain defeat of our enemy has never left us. Your citizen Mr Muromtsov was an apparent witness to the disadvantages of the enemy, which they meet with the destruction of their forces at every step. Lack of food and complete destruction are inevitable for them, and then my years and love for the Fatherland give me the right to demand your trust, by which I assure you that the city of Kaluga is and will be perfectly secure. Your warm prayers to the Almighty and the courage of our troops will result in the pleasure which I hope, and which, to the general joy, will follow the campaign, which is due to end in a short time.'

And again:

> 'My dear Ivan Vikulich! With heartfelt gratitude, coupled with pleasure, I see your enthusiasm for our dear Fatherland and, adding my warm prayers to yours, I ask the Almighty to send down help to our armed forces to defeat and deliver the final blow to the insidious enemy, who dared to enter the Russian lands. At present, we see God's mercy towards us in abundance: our demons are surrounded on all sides; free departure from the camp is completely prohibited by raiding parties sent by us everywhere; men and horses are exhausted by hunger, and every day from all locations they are losing some 500 men killed and captured, which your private citizens, Mr Eliseev and Mr Lebedev, can confirm. After that, you will see that our prayers have been heard, and that the right hand of the Almighty sends His blessing to us, which, with our continuous exclamations to the King of Kings, having intensified, to give us new proof of how much our Fatherland is preserved by Him, and how little the enemy will find a chance to be proud of their short–lived superiority over the troops of the God–given All–August Monarch! I ask you to express my enthusiasm to your community and gratitude to your spouses for delivering lint – a feature of such laudable diligence, worthy of them alone in every respect.

Appendix XI

Supreme Orders to the Chancellor of State Count Rumyantsev, dated 12 [24] October (archive of the M.T.D. No. 46,692, Annex 5)

On this occasion, Rumyantsev's memo to Graf Metternich read:

'Une des chances de la guerre vient de mettre à la disposition de Sa M.I. – le trois étendards du célèbre regiment d'Orelly chevauxlégers; il les avait reçu de l'Imperatrice Marie–Therese; il doit les regretter; il les a toujours illustrés par sa valeur. Le frère de notre Empereur, le grand Duc Constantin, dans plus d'une circonstance a été temoin de leur eclat, lorsque l'armée russe en Italie les a vûs flotter avec honneur à coté de ses propres bannières dans cette arène de gloire que parcouraient alors ensemble, pour le même intérêt, les soldats des deux Empereurs contre la France qui est parvenue à les désunir aujourd'hui.

Sa Majesté par la voye de cette lettre, que par Son ordre j'écris à V.E. sollicite S.M. l'Empereur d'Autriche de vouloir bien lui rendre un service amical, celui de reprendre ces étendards et les faire restituer aux braves, aux quels ils ont appartenus, que révère Son armée et qu'Elle même honore d'une estime particulière.

L'Empereur Alexandre demande à l'Empereur François le secret sur la demarche qu'il vient de faire et trouvera plaisir à le lui garder de Son coté. Le courrier qui porte les drapeaux ignore de quel bien eil est chargé; nul esprit de jactance, nul desir de réciprocité, null envie d'être citée, n'a conduit Sa Majesté à prendre le parti au quel Elle S'est determinée. C'est tout uniment, Mr. le Comte, la main de l'amitié qui écarte d'auprès e'elle des preuves cetaines, que cette intimité dont les Souverains d'Autriche faisaient tant de cas, dont leur armée se charmait autant que nos propres troupes, a fait place de nos jours à une guerre sans motifs.

Sa Majesté le confesse, Elle éprouverait trop de peine à mettre sous les yeux de Ses sujets, ce qui devrait servir à perpétuer le souvenir d'une époque que l'Empereur voudrait voir éffacée des annales de l'Histoire.

15 (27) d'octobre, 1812.'

In response to this memo, Graf Metternich wrote to the Chancellor:

'Monsieur le Comte!
Je me suis empressé de mettre sous les yeux de l'Empereur a lettre que V.E. m'a fait l'honneur de m'adresser par Mr. Peterson.

Sa M.I. m'ordonne de Vous prier, Mr. le Comte, d'être, près de l'Empereur votre auguste Maître, l'interprête de Sa sensibilité toute particulière à la marque d'attention que Sa M.I. Lui donne par le renvoi des étendards du régiment d'Oreilly que les chances de la guerre avaient mis au pouvoir de l'armée russe.

S'il est indubitable que la position actuelle des choses n'a pu s'établir, qu'après que l'Empereur mon Maître avait épuisé toutes les chances pour l'empêcher, il ne l'est pas moins que les voeux les plus chers de Sa M.I. appellent des tems où les rapports entre l'Autriche et la Russie ne seront plus entravés par des circonstances independantes d'Elle.

L'Empereur croit ne pouvoir mieux témoigner à Sa M.I. de toutes les Russies combien Il attache de prix à toute preuve de Ses sentimens personnels pour Lui. Il ne saurait mieux rendre justice aux motifs qui ont dicté la détermination de l'Empereur Alexandre, qu'en acceptant des trophées conquis par la valeur et rendus par l'amitié.

Vienne, le 1–er Decembre 1812.'

Appendix XII

The composition of the Force from the Army of the Danube that set off from Wallachia for Volhynia on 19 [31] July

(war diary of the leading detachment of the Army of the Danube, renamed Third Army, under Admiral Chichagov's command. Compiled by Chief Quartermaster 4th Corps, Lieutenant Colonel Malinovsky):

1st Corps – General of Infantry Count Langéron:
Vyborg Infantry, two battalions; Vyatka Infantry, three battalions; Staroskol Infantry, two battalions; 29th Jägers, two battalions; 45th Jägers, three battalions.
St Petersburg Dragoons, four squadrons; Livland Dragoons, four squadrons.
Grekov 4th's Cossacks; Panteleev 2nd's Cossacks; 1st Ural Cossacks.
22nd Battery Artillery Company; 41st Light Artillery Company; 42nd Light Artillery Company; 14th Horse Artillery Company; 7th Pontoon Company; pioneers – half–company.

2nd Corps – Lieutenant General Essen 3rd:
Arkhangelogorod Infantry, two battalions; Schlüsselburg Infantry, three battalions; Staroingermanland Infantry, two battalions; Ukraine Infantry, two battalions; 37th Jägers, three battalions.
Smolensk Dragoons, four squadrons; Seversk Dragoons, four squadrons.
Grekov 8th's Cossacks; 2nd Ural Cossacks.
8th Battery Artillery Company; 14th Light Artillery Company; 15th Light Artillery Company; 15th Horse Artillery Company; 8th Pontoon Company; pioneers – half–company.

3rd Corps – Lieutenant General Voinov:
Kursk Infantry, two battalions;[1] Crimea Infantry, two battalions; Bialystok Infantry, three battalions; 8th Jägers, two battalions; 39th Jägers, two battalions.
Belorussia Hussars, eight squadrons; Kinburn Dragoons, four squadrons.

---

1 From the orders of Admiral Chichagov, it is evident that the Kursk Infantry marched to Volhynia independently, under the command of their Colonel in Chief, Major General Agalin, and were left in Khotyn.

Melnikov 5th's Cossacks; 3rd Ural Cossacks; 4th Ural Cossacks.
10th Battery Artillery Company; 38th Battery Artillery Company; 18th Light Artillery Company; 50th Light Artillery Company.

4th Corps – Major General Bulatov:
Okhotsk Infantry, two battalions; Kamchatka Infantry, two battalions; Mingrelia Infantry, two battalions.
Chuguev Ulans, eight squadrons; Dorpat Dragoons, four squadrons; Pereyaslavl Dragoons, four squadrons; Tiraspol Dragoons, four squadrons.
Melnikov 3rd's Cossacks; Kuteynikov's Cossacks.
18th Battery Artillery Company; 39th Battery Artillery Company; 31st Light Artillery Company; 17th Horse Artillery Company; pioneers – half–company.

Reserve – under Army Chief of Staff, Lieutenant General Sabaneev:
Olonets Infantry, three battalions; Yaroslavl Infantry, three battalions; 7th Jägers, three battalions. Olviopol Hussars, eight squadrons.
Lukovkin's Cossacks.
16th Horse Artillery Company.

Appendix XIII

Order of Battle of the Third Army

1st Corps – Major General Count Lambert:
Kozlov Infantry, two battalions; Yakutsk Infantry, two battalions; Ryazhsk Infantry, two battalions; Kolyvan Infantry, two battalions; Apsheron Infantry, two battalions; 10th Jägers, two battalions; 13th Jägers, two battalions; 38th Jägers, two battalions.
Alexandria Hussars, eight squadrons; Belorussia Hussars, eight squadrons; Tatar Ulans, eight squadrons.
Grekov 4th's Cossacks; Chikilev's Cossacks; Bashkirsky's Cossacks; Barabanshchikov 2nd's Cossacks.
9th Battery Artillery Company, 12 guns; 11th Horse Artillery Company, 12 guns; 12th Horse Artillery Company, 11 guns.

2nd Corps – Lieutenant General Markov:[1]
Nasheburg Infantry, two battalions; Vitebsk Infantry, two battalions; Courland Infantry, two battalions; Vladimir Infantry, two battalions; Tambov Infantry, two battalions; Dnieper Infantry, two battalions; Kostroma Infantry, two battalions; 14th Jägers, two battalions; 28th Jägers, two battalions; 32nd Jägers, two battalions.
Starodub Dragoons, four squadrons; Tver Dragoon, two squadrons; Vladimir Dragoon, four squadrons; Taganrog Dragoons, four squadrons; Pavlograd Hussars, eight squadrons.
Dyachkin's Cossacks; 2nd Kalmuk Regiment.
15th Battery Artillery Company, 12 guns; 18th Battery Artillery Company, 12 guns: 13th Horse Artillery Company, 12 guns.

3rd Corps – General of Infantry Count Langéron:
Vyatka Infantry, three battalions; Staroskol Infantry, two battalions; Vyborg Infantry, two battalions; 29th Jägers, two battalions; 45th Jägers, three battalions.
Lubny Hussars, eight squadrons; St Petersburg Dragoons, four squadrons; Livland Dragoons, four squadrons; Serpukhov Dragoons, four squadrons; Arzamas Dragoons, four squadrons.
Grekov 8th's Cossacks; 4th Ural Cossacks.

---

1 Later Prince Shcherbatov, and finally Lieutenant General Saken.

22nd Battery Artillery Company, 12 guns; 34th Battery Artillery Company, 12 guns.

4th Corps – Lieutenant General Essen 3rd:
Arkhangelogorod Infantry, two battalions; Ukraine Infantry, two battalions; 37th Jägers, three battalions; combined grenadiers, six battalions.
Vlasov's Don Cossacks; 1st Kalmuk Regiment; Yevpatoria Tatars.
8th Battery Artillery Company, 12 guns; 15th Horse Artillery Company, 12 guns.

Lieutenant General Voinov's Corps:
Kursk Infantry, two battalions; Crimea Infantry, two battalions; Bialystok Infantry, three battalions; Yaroslavl Infantry, three battalions; Saratov Infantry, two battalions; 8th Jägers, two battalions; 39th Jägers, two battalions.
Dorpat Dragoons, four squadrons; Kinburn Dragoons, four squadrons.
3rd Ural Cossacks; Kireev's Cossacks; Panteleev's Cossacks.
10th Battery Artillery Company, 12 guns; 16th Horse Artillery Company, 6 guns; 38th Battery Artillery Company, 4 guns.

Major General Bulatov's Corps:
Okhotsk Infantry, two battalions; Kamchatka Infantry, two battalions; Mingrelia Infantry, two battalions; 27th Jägers, three battalions; 43rd Jägers, three battalions.
Chuguev Ulans, eight squadrons; Pereyaslavl Dragoons, four squadrons; Tiraspol Dragoons, four squadrons.
Melnikov 3rd's Cossacks; Kuteynikov's Cossacks.
16th Battery Artillery Company, 12 guns; 19th Battery Artillery Company, 12 guns; 17th Horse Artillery Company, 12 guns.

Major General Engelhardt's Detachment:
Schlüsselburg Infantry, three battalions; Staroingermanland Infantry, two battalions.
Tver Dragoons, two squadrons; Zhitomir Dragoons, two squadrons.
Melnikov 5th's Cossacks.
38th Battery Artillery Company, 8 guns.

Reserve – Lieutenant General Sabaneev:
Olonets Infantry, three battalions; 7th Jägers, three battalions; 12th Jägers, two battalions.
Olviopol Hussars, eight squadrons.
Lukovkin's Cossacks.
16th Horse Artillery Company, 6 guns.

Appendix XIV

Liprandi's assessment of Bogdanovich's four sources for the Fall of the Central Battery

'As a close eyewitness to the described episode, I made it my duty to look into the sources indicated by the honourable author.

Hoffmann, originally in Prussian service, was a Captain on our General Staff in 1812 and, during the battle of Borodino, was with the force operating around Utitsa, almost four *versts* from the central battery. At the end of the war, being a Colonel, he transferred back to Prussian service, and as a Lieutenant General, just 34 years after the aforementioned battle, described it and published it in 1846, dedicating his work to Prinz Eugen von Württemberg.[1] Hoffmann openly states that he owes information on the capture of the central battery and on the cavalry attacks to Schreckenstein, who was in Thielmann's brigade.[2] It would seem that, after this statement, a reference to him ought not to be placed together with a reference to Schreckenstein, whose account, as we shall see, is itself inconclusive. But since General Bogdanovich found this combination appropriate, one should also look into Hoffmann's account, which, perhaps, adds something that he witnessed himself.

On page 61 of the source to which General Bogdanovich refers, Hoffmann states that Caulaincourt entered the fortification not through the gorge, which would have been 'impossible because of the steep slope,' rather that the cuirassiers entered over parts of the parapet which had already been trampled down.[3] Hoffmann, having said that the infantry stationed behind the ravine (General Bogdanovich writes simply to the rear or in the ravine), soon drove out Caulaincourt's cuirassiers with their fire, adding that the Saxon *Garde du Corps* followed in their wake, also over the

---

1   *Die Schlacht von Borodino mit einer Uebersicht des Feldzug von 1812, v. General v. Hoffmann.* Koblenz, 1846. Prinz Eugen von Württemberg also published his book that same year.
2   It should be noted here that Schreckenstein's book only appeared in 1855, i.e. nine years after Hoffmann's book; consequently, whatever Hoffmann extracted from Schreckenstein could only refer to a manuscript that had not yet been published, or perhaps an incomplete draft, or perhaps even from interviews, which is very plausible, as we shall see from Schreckenstein's published account.
3   The rampart, especially along the flanks, was not yet complete when the battle began, and then the action of the enemy artillery, and especially in the struggle with General Bonnamy's brigade that had broken into the fortification, followed by the pursuit of those who were escaping, ruined the parapet in general, especially the flanking sections, where not every embrasure had been revetted with gabions; all this shows the reality of the ease of entering it.

trampled parts of the parapet, where the slope was not so steep, entered the fortification, which was still producing heavy fire, and that eventually the Viceroy's infantry alone seized the fortification and captured Likhachëv. Consequently, Thielmann's cavalry appeared inside the fortification but could not have captured it. Yet, as we shall see, the appearance of Thielmann's cavalry inside the fortification really was under completely different circumstances.[4] Let us take a look at the second source.

Bernhardi is the publisher and editor of Memoirs of Graf von Toll, which appeared in 1851.[5] Much of the contents of the Graf's memoirs are not first–hand, and of course there are also additions by the publisher, a non–military man and a German who tries to belittle the Russians everywhere, which has been noted by General Bogdanovich himself; but that is not the point: let us turn our attention to his account, which is used as a source by our historian. Bernhardi, in describing this episode, just like Hoffmann, declares he has borrowed from Schreckenstein and also from some French Staff Officer, adding: 'I am reliant upon these accounts.' It thus seems strange to reference Bernhardi at all! He should have left it at Hoffmann: he, at least, participated in the battle of Borodino and, being far from the central fortification, may have heard of these events from his comrades; but Bernhardi had barely come into the world; Graf Carl Friedrich [Toll] should not need to resort to Schreckenstein's testimony of what was happening to us. He was one of the main participants on this great day.

But be that as it may, Bernhardi states (Vol. II, page 101–103 and so on) that Caulaincourt entered the fortification over the parts of the ditch and parapet which had been demolished by the artillery and trampled down by previous attacks and therefore it was much easier than through the gorge in which he was killed. Once the French cuirassiers had been forced to abandon the fortification, then the Saxon *Garde du Corps*, despite the fact that the fortification was still producing heavy fire, broke into it over the ditch and parapet. It goes without saying that after Caulaincourt this would have been even easier to do. Bernhardi adds that the wounded General Likhachëv was taken prisoner here, while the Viceroy, with three infantry divisions, hurried to the fortification and entered it from the direction of the embankment. Overall, the account of this episode is extremely inconsistent, and Mr. Bernhardi apparently piles all the glory onto his countrymen. He states something that Graf Toll would not have said, not least because it is contrary to all the evidence, suggesting that 'some of the Russians defending the fortification fled (!), while some fought at the guns, but had to yield to the on–rushing Saxon cavalry.' The former never happened, while the latter is true only insofar as the gunners, armed only with rammers and gun spikes, as is well known, also had no desire to surrender, preferring death to captivity.

---

4   The author adds that, during the fierce attacks by French cavalry on our infantry (after the fortification had been captured), he saw Barclay staying with the Pernov Infantry (10th Division) for a long time, being attacked from all sides: 'he seemed to be seeking death.' The arriving regiments of 23rd Division (IV Corps) repulsed all attacks, but, according to the author, Barclay was too weak to do anything against the captured fortification.

5   *Denkwürdigkeiten aus Leben der Kaiserl-Russisch. General von den Infanterie Carl Friedrich Grafen von Toll*. Theodor von Bernhardi, Leipzig, 1856.

Buturlin's account is accurate, and completely opposed to the accounts by the other three referred together with him.

This is how D.P. Buturlin describes this episode (History Of Emperor Napoleon's Invasion, translated from the French by Major General A. Khatov, St Petersburg, 1823. Vol. 1, page 281): 'General Caulaincourt had managed to break through beyond the lunette with the cuirassier regiments from Wathier's division, and even broke into it from the rear with the *5e régiment de cuirassiers*, and found his death there, while his cuirassiers were forced to abandon this fortification. *2e* and *3e corps de cavalerie* pursued the enemy cavalry... While (page 283) these successful charges were being executed on one side of the lunette, on the other, the infantry columns under the Viceroy of Italy; the *21e régiment d'infanterie de ligne* from Gérard's division and *17e ligne* from Broussier's division, attacked it frontally and on the flank. The battalions from Major General Likhachëv's 24th Division defending this fortification, already weakened by losses suffered previously, could resist no longer. The Viceroy, having enveloped the lunette on the left with *9e* and *35e régiments*, took possession of it; while the Russians who were in the fortification would not surrender, so they were beaten to the ground. General Likhachëv, suffering from illness and covered with wounds, nevertheless, charged into the enemy ranks,' and so on. This is clear and accurate.

Schreckenstein wrote his book about the action of the cavalry in this battle 43 years after the fact.[6] The episode of the struggle at the central battery is on pages 81 to 94 inclusive.[7] In carefully examining this book, one comes to the conclusion that in order to compile this, for the episode of the capture of the central battery at least, General Schrekenstein did not have complete notes, but was writing from memory after 43 years; while if he had any notes, then they were only in the form of the most brief comments, and I base this on the following: firstly, according to statements by Hoffmann and Bernhardi, they owe all the information related to the struggle at the central battery to General Schrekenstein, as a participant during its capture. Hoffmann published his book nine years before the publication of Schreckenstein's book. Consequently, Hoffmann had to have been content with verbal accounts and wrote them down, or looked through any brief comments that Schreckenstein might have had. The same is true of Bernhardi, who, although he published his book in 1856, i.e. shortly after the appearance of Schreckenstein's book, yet, it goes without saying that in such a short period of time he could not have amended what was already included in the manuscript (which amounted to three thick printed volumes), which at that time, very likely, was already at the printing house. Yet from this a lot of things cited by Hoffmann and Bernhardi, as if they had come from Schreckenstein, do not agree with what is expressed in his book; and secondly, the author of this latter book states himself that when the Zastrow regiment halted

---

6   *Die Kavalerie in der Schlacht an der Moskwa (von den Russen: Schlacht bei Borodino gennant) am 7 September 1812. Nebst einigen ausfürlichen Nachrichten über den Leistungen des 4 Kavalerie Corps unter der Anführung des General Latour-Maubourg*. Von General-Leutnant Freyherrn Böth von Schreckenstein. Münster, 1855.
7   General Bogdanovich has referenced pages 84 to 124. The episode actually does begin on the former, but 124 has a list of the officers killed in the battle of Borodino in general!

and was unable to do anything to the infantry stationed in the ravine (Tsybulsky's detachment), General Schreckenstein continues, 'I followed those who had entered the (central) fortification. It was so full of cavalry that I could not make progress, and having noted simply that a violent melee was taking place in it,[8] I returned to the Zastrow regiment. It seems that I wanted to find General Thielmann, but to tell the truth I have only a vague memory of all this. In such situations one usually follows instinctive urges; one does not quite know what one is doing, and after hearing accounts, one muddles them with what one saw first-hand, and so on.' In general, the account is largely inconclusive; thus, one constantly encounters, for example: 'it seems; maybe; I did not notice; I could only note that the Viceroy's infantry was moving into the fortification; I do not remember; I suppose; as far as I recall.' He expresses doubt that French cuirassiers were in the battery before Thielmann; then he provides Chambray's evidence, who clearly states that Wathier's division, after retreating from the redoubt, took up its former position on the Viceroy's right flank; as the latter and Thielmann advanced towards the fortification, which was firing fiercely; 'as far as I could tell, many more men were falling around the fortification; as the Saxon *Garde du Corps* approached, a hail of bullets rained down on them;' while later it is mentioned that 'it was likely that the infantry were not permanently inside the fortification, because the artillery occupied every space and, it seems that they expected to move into the fortification from the ravine behind it,[9] but the swift attack by the cavalry from all sides did not allow much of this plan to be fulfilled;' but he remembers very well that many of his comrades who were in the fortification before him told how they 'saw the garrison leaving through the gorge and some of them were cut down.' What nonsense! Who was showering them with bullets? With whom did Caulaincourt and then Thielmann fight? If the French, and then Saxon, cuirassiers and others were not fighting with these same artillerymen; then how, as the enemy were fighting in the fortification, were some of the garrison able to leave it through the gorge! Everyone who was in the fortification, I repeat, preferred death to captivity and, of course, no longer thought of escaping from it. He states himself that he heard how 'one Russian officer, who had the cross of St Anna around his neck, defended himself on a gun carriage and was cut down.' General Schreckenstein continues somehow to say a lot, but very little conclusively: 'It seems I am able to claim that General Thielmann probably took part in the attack personally. What happened behind the entrenchment[10] and in the lower part of the ravine (near Tsybulsky) was not visible through the smoke; I believe the attack failed. It seems that then came the Polish cuirassiers. That attempt must have failed. What happened in this event, I do not know; I only know that Colonel Małachowski was very pleased with the deeds of my cuirassiers.'

I shall desist from recounting similar evidence from General Schreckenstein (and its 'embryo from Hoffmann and Bernhardi'), whom General Bogdanovich preferred even to marquis Chambray, whom he declared in the preface to be a more impartial

---

8   It is clear that the cavalry were unable to defeat the defenders of the fortification.
9   It is likely that General Bogdanovich extracted the infantry stationed in the ravine behind the fortification from Schreckenstein, as noted above.
10 This is how he refers to our central battery almost everywhere.

historian than any other, and made more references to him than to others on that basis, he is not mentioned here. Why? Only he and Allah know. But be that as it may, let us turn to the main objective of the capture of the fortification. General Schreckenstein says that the *Garde du Corps* broke into it over the collapsing ditch dug in loose sand and the crumbling parapet. The next day, General Schreckenstein examined the fortification, of which he had 'a vague memory' regarding its form (layout). Yet he adds that 'since this entrenchment had been hastily built and consisted of spoil and clay, it was amazing how it had been damaged and in the end could only provide a little cover for the defenders. The soil had slipped into the ditch, such that it became very shallow.[11] The lines consisted only of a parapet and a narrow ditch, which was almost completely filled in. The guns stood inside the works and I think that the parapet was made only to protect the infantry.' What kind of nonsense again: either there were no infantry, or it was made for the infantry? And here once more: General Schreckenstein recounted on the the guns in the fortification; his total does not agree with other historians, which is not a problem; but he says that our guns were ten–pounders, which we have never had, and in 1812 at least, did not exist.

Buturlin wrote something completely different from that which Hoffmann, Bernhardi and Schreckenstein have stated, and has been cited by General Bogdanovich. What was the purpose of the reference to Buturlin, together with the three Germans mentioned, when only that which the latter three wrote was included in the account by the Gentleman Historian and not a word from Buturlin? A combination of such references might co–exist, but then it would have been necessary to critically examine the contradictory evidence and lead the reader to a conclusion, even if only approximate to the truth; not as has been done here, off the cuff, as they say! Buturlin has been cited solely to state that our infantry defended the fortification desperately, which has been unanimously confirmed by all sources, without exception, foreign and ours.

---

11 And he gives the initial depth as three feet.

Appendix XV

The conclusion of Liprandi's detailed assessment of available evidence on the Fall of the Great Redoubt

'Upon careful consideration of all the descriptions given, having discarded the stock phrases of the French and the boastful exaggerations of some German authors, in essence everyone has come to similar conclusions on this episode: 'it was not cavalry, but infantry that took possession of it.' Whether it was due to the mutual agreement between Murat and the Viceroy, or by orders issued by Napoleon himself to attack the central battery, it makes no difference. Murat sent strong masses of cavalry onto the high ground at Semenovskaya, and at the same time the Viceroy was directed at the central battery with three infantry divisions, his flanks protected by cavalry. Meanwhile, Caulaincourt's *2e corps*, after the successful attack on our lines in the sector between Semenovskaya and the central battery, had passed the latter, which was now to their left rear; and here again it makes no difference whether it was by order of Murat or Napoleon himself or, much more likely, on his own initiative, upon Caulaincourt's own instincts, who saw that the Viceroy was in full advance to the front of the central battery, at the same time, wanted to take advantage of his position to assist them by attacking the same location from the opposite direction, and to that end he turned sharply to the left about (*brusquement se rabat à gauche*), and at the head of the *5e régiment de cuirassiers* reached the gorge. Some of the cuirassiers broke through into the battery, where they met a rebuff; the vast majority crowded into the gorge and were subjected to heavy fire from the infantry stationed beyond the ravine, and were in a hurry to get away from the fortification in which Caulaincourt had just been killed. At this point, the Viceroy's infantry, having closed up to the battery, were fighting with its defenders, while the cavalry advancing alongside them swarmed around the fortification from the flanks, and although several horsemen broke into the battery, it was simply on impulse and did not gain them control of it in any way until such time as the infantry had surrounded the battery from all sides (and some of them even broke in through the gorge): only then was full control of the fortification achieved. This is the conclusion that all those who have written about it come to without exception, despite chicanery by some German historians who want to introduce Thielmann into this drama with his Saxon *Garde du Corps*, as if he had played something like Caulaincourt's role. But even this effort is also unsuccessful, because they have stated themselves that Thielmann would have been in a most critical situation if the Viceroy's infantry had not come up at that moment. Thielmann's appearance at the battery was very natural: he was in Latour–Maubourg's *4e corps* with his brigade, which was protecting the Viceroy's infantry, and therefore, while they were fighting on the ramparts and some of them were beginning to envelope the fortification, the horsemen were able to move into it, as it no longer constituted a viable defensive barrier along the entire length of its perimeter, and again I repeat to those same German narrators who so triumphantly have Thielmann leaping across the ditch and parapet, I say that these obstacles no longer existed, that they had been battered down, and that Thielmann could not have survived had the infantry not already taken possession, and so on. This is what all the tales by German authors boil down to. It goes without saying that the French commentators do not say a word about Thielmann as he did not play an independent role, being in the corps under Latour–Maubourg, all of whom were involved in the Viceroy's mission.

At the conclusion of this episode, it is impossible not to note once again that our honourable historian, relying on the evidence of Schreckenstein alone (who had the goodwill, however, to confess that everything just written by him was vaguely recalled memories), yet chose him in preference to every other source for the presentation of this episode! And from this arbitrary, selection, without critical assessment of those significant failings that so amaze anyone who wishes to get an accurate understanding of this, the most singular feat for all sides in the whole war. Indeed, one wonders how, for example, the honourable historian, on the basis of the above mentioned Schreckenstein alone, has Caulaincourt, after his successful attack on our lines, turn to the right in order to get to the battery, while every commentator who recounts this episode in any detail, clearly states that Caulaincourt turned to the left about, and it could never have been otherwise; since, by turning to the right, he would have arrived in Utitsa. Of the 63 sources cited above, 83 percent say that Caulaincourt entered the battery through the gorge, from the rear, while our honourable historian, on the basis of the 'vaguely recalled memory' of Schreckenstein and his compilers, Hoffmann and Bernhardi, assure us that Caulaincourt crossed over the ditch and parapet, and at the same time reveal that they have also stated that the ditch and parapet had been battered almost level and that it was more difficult to enter via the gorge because of its slope! Fourteen of the authors cited say that Caulaincourt was killed by round shot, and some even add that it was one of the last to be fired from the battery, and even more: his death from round shot was also confirmed in the bulletin, while only two mention a bullet, and two wrote that he was killed by a *Biscaïen*! That is, by a fortress weapon that could never have been used at Borodino;[1] it was incomparably larger. The remainder limit themselves to using the word killed, which, in my opinion, would be a more fluent statement than referring to a 'bullet,' contrary to the evidence of the majority. Thielmann is mentioned by 12 sources, exclusively Germans, including Hoffmann and Bernhardi, who borrowed it from Schreckenstein, which is also how it entered our History, while the 51 other commentators, many of whom were involved in the episode, among whom there are also some Germans, not a word is said about Thielmann.'

---

1   Here is how they are defined in the artillery dictionary: '*Biscaïen. Mousquet de biscaye de fort calibre, ou fusils de rampart. On donné aussi ce nom au plus petit des boulets du canon.*' Consequently, the latter two authors, calling it a *Biscaïen*, could be referring to a small calibre round shot.

Appendix XVI

Liprandi's rebuttal of Bogdanovich's claim that there was no reliable evidence for French produced counterfeit Russian Banknotes being brought into circulation

General Bogdanovich could have deduced the contrary from Danilevsky (Vol. 3, page 259), that once the French had been ejected from Moscow and other places, 'when the inhabitants presented French produced hundred–rouble banknotes, which they had acquired on various occasions during the enemy occupation, to the military authorities, they were so skilfully forged that even the Assignation Bank took them for genuine at first glance; they differed from Russian banknotes only in the signature that was engraved on them.

If General Bogdanovich could not accept this account, because Danilevsky did not confirm it with a source, then Danilevsky himself could already serve as the source, as an eyewitness to what he describes, and that all of us (that is, those who participated in this war) saw these counterfeit banknotes, as did the Cossacks, who found them on prisoners and in their wagons, and in Minsk, Vilna and in almost every Jewish settlement, and they were even encountered in Warsaw. They were also plentiful in St Petersburg, where many remember them very well. They could be distinguished from genuine notes only by the fact that they were printed on thicker paper, and the signatures engraved on them.[1] The old moneychangers could have given General Bogdanovich some interesting information. But in any case, a reference to Danilevsky is necessary, and, perhaps, his account might be refuted; for this, however, it would be necessary to inquire in the archives of the Assignation Bank; as the historian has referred to it, as it were. Danilevsky, in describing the escape of the commanders of the French army from Vilna beyond the Neman (Vol. 4, page 259), mentions Berthier's letter to Napoleon, where, in passing, he expresses his sorrow at the loss 'of his last carriage, in which there were top secret documents.' Danilevsky

---

1 The main thing, as far as I remember, to distinguish fakes from the genuine, was that on the real ones the stroke crossing back over the capital letter X stops on either side of the encountered stroke, while the counterfeiter drew it through the middle.

adds: 'In it we found obvious evidence of Napoleon's fraud: a plate for printing fake hundred–rouble banknotes.'

And is that not enough for General Bogdanovich to refer to Danilevsky? Then here is another example (Vol. 3, page 259): 'A large stock of this bad–faith was later found by us in Königstein. And so the ruler of the entire continent of Western Europe, master of the forces and wealth of twenty nations, brought by him to conquer Russia, was trading in fake banknotes!'

I repeat, is this still not enough, at least, to refer to Danilevsky? It should not be forgotten that Alexander Ivanovich Danilevsky, in 1812, served under Prince Kutuzov, while in 1813 (and subsequently in 1814 and 1815) under Prince P.M. Volkonsky, already as an equerry; therefore, he had the surest opportunity to know what he was talking about regarding counterfeit banknotes, both in 1812 and in 1813 about the stocks found in Königstein. Is it possible that General Bogdanovich did not find any trace of that which all of Russia knew in the source material provided to him and that he did not want to introduce it into his history, because, as one must assume, Danilevsky did not back up his account with a source?[2] Yet Danilevsky also commented that Lesseps suggested that Tutolmin accept cash in banknotes for the expenses of the Orphanage; Tutolmin did not accept the money and wrote in a report (Report by Tutolmin to Empress Maria Feodorovna, dated 11 [23] November):[3] 'This was done maliciously in order to lend me their fake banknotes, of which they brought a very large number with them, and they even, at the behest of Napoleon, issued them as pay to their troops.'

The cited report from Tutolmin, who remained in Moscow all the time it was occupied by the enemy, by its significance, cannot be suspected of fiction: he had every opportunity to learn everything that related to this subject and would not have dared to write fantasies in a report to the Empress. Danilevsky refers to that report, consequently, General Bogdanovich should have kept it in mind and, if he did not have time to delve further, should therefore also mention it in his history. But if the honourable author had taken on the task himself, or had time, as I noted above, to rummage through the archives, for example, of the Ministries of: Finance, War, Boards of Trustees,[4] Internal Affairs or in those later transferred to the Ministry of Police Affairs, in the archives of the Moscow and St Petersburg Military Governors General, and perhaps in the archives of the Ministry of Foreign Affairs and the General Post Office, then, of course, General Bogdanovich would have found an explanation of the situation and would have discovered that since the spring of 1812 we had known that Napoleon's Minister of Foreign Affairs, the duc de Bassano (Mare), had instructed the Warsaw banker Fraenkel to allow counterfeit banknotes for 20,000,000 roubles to be produced, prior to the entry of the French across our borders. On this point, there were 1,500,000 such banknotes in Brody alone. The Governor of Volhynia reported on this malicious practice independently of the

---

2   It is also known that many, taking advantage of certain developments, made themselves a huge fortune.
3   This was published in the Readings By The Imperial Society Of Russian History And Antiquities, 1860, book 2, issue 5, pages 161-184.
4   Danilevsky mentions these three departments. Were their Archives examined?

others. Count Guriev and Count Arakcheev, reported on Supreme Command; officials were sent to oversee this matter from beyond our borders from Riga to Radzivilov; but the Jews, so skilled in such cases and indispensable to everyone in this trade, had already managed to distribute some of them, both among the landowners and among the farmers before the entry of the French. Upon the French invasion, they used these banknotes in the places they occupied, and from October 1812 such banknotes began to turn up at the Bank.[5] The honourable author of this History, as he calls it, would have found in the archives that upon crossing our borders at the end of 1812, Count Arakcheev announced several Supreme Commands on this subject, as a result of which, following the occupation Warsaw, Kutuzov was also ordered to find the banker Fraenkel; he would have found the correspondence of Vyazmitinov, Marquis Paulucci and so on. I am not obliged to instruct the historian in the duties which he has taken upon himself; I note this situation here only so that readers can see that what General Bogdanovich wrote about counterfeit banknotes is based only on his own conclusions; as, in fact, it was vital, as I said above, to dig deeper, or not to mention it at all; in that event it would be only omission after omission, of which there are many in his work. I absolutely do not understand this omission and its expression on counterfeit banknotes!

All this overwhelmingly compelling evidence notwithstanding, back in 1846, the Old Believers exhibited two rooms at the Preobrazhensky Bezpopovshchinsky Cemetery in Moscow, in which there was a machine for making counterfeit banknotes while gendarmes were resident in the other.[6]

I cannot but add to this that rather than there being no reliable sources about counterfeit banknotes imported earlier and then brought into Russia by Napoleon, as I noted above, we have such sources in numerous departments, but the honourable author did not follow Danilevsky's guidance, and the only author he selected, from among foreigners, was the author of the *Histoire de la destruction de Moscou*, a German A.F. de B...ch, who worked in Russian service and wrote a book in his native language, a translation of which [by Jean–Baptiste–Joseph Breton] our honourable historian accepted as the sole authority, despite the fact that the whole book, as I noted below, is hostile to us Russians.

We could not leave such gaffes in this book by General Bogdanovich without comment out of respect for the truth.

---

5 Before the end of 1814, the Bank received about 12,000 genuine and more than 500,000 counterfeit notes, collected in Poland and Germany, from the Post Office from various persons who had served in the army and sent money from there. In that same year, upon the return of the troops, out of 1,500,000 in the *artel* [military messing funds], 300,000 turned out to be counterfeit, and so on. If I, as a private individual, could collect such information from the archives, then how much more could General Bogdanovich have found in the secret departments of the Ministries, to whom all of them had been opened?

6 This cemetery enjoyed special patronage by the French, because the schismatics there, upon the entry of the enemy, had sent deputies to the Commandant of the Kremlin, and so on. Napoleon had been in this cemetery. Murat and some of the Marshals repeatedly visited it. A guard detachment was assigned to the Old Believers who lived there, and all their chapels were preserved. I do not find it necessary to mention any further details here, indeed there is no reason to.

Index

Aa river [Lielupe]: 298-299.
Åbo [Turku]: iii, 20, 26, 28, 296, 344.
Airship - see Leppich.
Akinfov, Fëdor Vladimirovich: 201-203.
Åland Islands: 20, 26, 295-296.
Alekseev, Ilya Ivanovich: 296, 303.
Alexinki: 110, 126.
Arakcheev, Alexei Andreevich: 10-11, 17, 29, 187, 209-210, 216, 229, 407; correspondence with Bagration: iii, 342-345.
Artel: 36, 350.
Arzamas: 260.
Astrakhan: 59, 68.
Augereau, Charles-Pierre-François: 87.
Austerlitz, battle of: 127, 348.

Baggovut, Karl Fëdorovich: 86, 114, 145-147, 157-158, 327, 332-333, 340, 351, 360, 373-374, 379.
Bagration, Pëtr Ivanovich: 10-12, 16, 84, 107, 111-112, 117, 122, 131, 133-134, 136, 140, 142-143, 161, 167-168, 223-224, 240-241, 243, 249, 251-252, 351, 358, 360, 372, 374, 376, 378; correspondence with Arakcheev: iii, 342-345.
Bagration *fléches*: 106-108, 113, 123, 125-126, 129-131, 133-138, 140, 147, 160, 372-373.
Bakhmetev 1st, Alexey Nikolaevich: 114, 153, 162, 167, 175.
Bakhmetev 2nd, Nikolai Nikolaevich: 114, 153, 162, 167-168, 175.
Bakkarevich, Mikhail Nikitich: 29.
Balabin, Pëtr Ivanovich: 297.
Balabin, Stepan Fëdorovich: 239.
Balashov, Alexander Dmitrievich: 10, 29, 46, 216.
Barabanshchikov, lieutenant colonel: 351, 396.
Barclay de Tolly, Mikhail Bogdanovich: 8, 10-11, 16, 19, 83-85, 88, 90-94, 96, 107, 112, 114, 132-135, 140, 144-146, 148, 151-152, 154-156, 159, 161, 168, 172, 179-183, 199-200, 210, 234, 246, 249-250, 253, 309, 344-345, 357, 361-363, 365, 374.
Bashmakov, Dmitry Yevlampevich: 155.
Bashmakov, Flegont Mironovich: 381.
Bashutsky, Pavel Yakovlevich: 44, 260.
Bauer, Friedrich Wilhelm: 12.
Bauska: 297-300.
Beauharnais, Viceroy of Italy, Eugène Rose de: 84-85, 87-88, 97, 99, 102, 112, 120, 124-126, 129, 131-133, 142, 147- 153, 155, 157, 173, 179, 183, 198, 204-205, 219-220, 263, 324-325, 399-401, 403-404.
Bedryaga, colonel: 291, 295, 301.
Begichev, Ivan Matveevich: 43, 293, 302-303.
Belgard, Alexander Alexandrovich: 299.
Belliard, Augustin-Daniel: 99, 159, 162.
Belorussia: 73, 79, 276, 311.
Bely: 86, 98, 179, 279, 324.
Bennigsen, Leonty Leontevich: 12, 93, 97, 101, 105, 113, 130, 179-184, 209, 237, 244, 246-247, 249, 253, 273, 275, 327-329, 332, 334, 336-338, 340, 374.
Berestechko: 308, 311.
Berezina river: 17, 46-47, 242-243, 317, 321-322, 386-390.
Bernadotte, Jean-Baptiste, Crown Prince of Sweden: 20-28, 210, 231.
Bernhardi, Theodor von: 90, 95, 101, 112, 140, 166, 185-186, 238, 399-402, 404.
Berthier, Louis-Alexandre, prince de Neuchâtel: 99-100, 123, 125, 130, 135, 159, 200, 219, 335, 405.
Bessières, Jean-Baptiste, duc d'Istrie: 159, 219, 239, 246, 248, 254.
Beurmann, Frédéric-Auguste de: 131, 135.
Bezpopovsky (Old Believers) cemetery: 199, 407.
Bezubovo: 132, 150-151.
Biała: 318-320.

Białystok: 70-71, 73, 77, 321.
Bibikov, Alexander Alexandrovich: 43, 293, 302.
Bibikov, Dmitry Gavrilovich: 146, 370
Bistrom, Karl Ivanovich: 131, 357.
Bistrom, Philip Antonovich: 369.
Blesson, Johann Ludwig Urban: 90.
Bobruisk: 71, 321, 387-388.
Bogorodsk: 42, 254, 263, 283, 285.
Bogorodskoe: 335-336.
Boguslavsky, Alexander Andreevich: 131.
Boguslavsky, Police Chief: 279.
Bonnamy de Bellefontaine, Charles-Auguste: 142-144, 168, 359, 361.
Borisov: 71, 251, 386-388.
Borodino village, French attack on: v, 131-132.
Borovsk: 196, 209, 238, 247, 265, 267, 270.
Borovsky crossing: 237-238.
Borozdin 1st, Mikhail Mikhailovich: 118, 137, 168.
Borozdin 2nd, Nikolay Mikhailovich: 117, 140, 168, 365.
Brest-Litovsk: 314-321
Britain: 22, 24, 27, 214, 229, 260.
Bronnitsy: 239, 246, 265.
Broussier, Jean-Baptiste: 142, 152, 154, 240, 400.
Bruguière *dit* Bruyère, Jean-Pierre-Joseph: 135, 162.
Bryansk: 63, 209, 247, 261, 280.
Bucharest, Treaty of: 14, 23.
Bug river: 243, 258, 312-318, 321-322.
Buturlin, Dmitry Petrovich: 112, 183, 400, 402.
Buxhoeveden, Ivan Filippovich: 137, 347.
Buxhoeveden, Pëtr Fëdorovich: 309.
Byalka river: 319.

Cathcart, William Schaw: 45, 214.
Catherine the Great: 12-13, 15, 91, 279, 347.
Caucasus: 11, 59, 61, 127, 343, 352.
Caulaincourt, Armand de: 127, 272.
Caulaincourt, Auguste-Jean-Gabriel de: 152-153, 162, 398-401, 403-404.
Chaplits, Yefim Ignatevich: 80, 307-308, 317, 320-321.
Charles XIII, King of Sweden: 20, 22, 26-28.
Charukov: 308.
Chastel, Louis-Pierre-Aimé: 150, 152, 155-156, 162.

Chernavchitsy: 315-316.
Chernishnya river: iii, 254, 272, 325-327, 334-336.
Chernyshev, Alexander Ivanovich: 242-245, 313, 315, 317-319.
Chichagov, Pavel Vasilievich: v, 14, 16, 22, 49, 80, 97, 183, 191, 235, 238, 242-245, 252, 276, 295, 309-317, 320-323, 385, 387-389, 394.
Chigirin: 66, 322.
Chirikovo: 246, 248.
Claparède, Michel-Marie: 135-136, 151, 205, 254, 326, 354.
Clausewitz, Carl Philipp Gottlieb: 150, 234.
Colbert-Chabanais, Pierre-David de: 74, 254.
Compans, Jean-Dominique: 101, 110-112, 123-124, 126, 130-131, 133-134, 162.
Confédération du Rhin [Confederation of the Rhine]: 22.
Confederation of Poland-Lithuania: 71.
Constantinople [Istanbul]: 13, 346-347.
Courland: 55, 70, 297.
Crossard, Jean-Baptiste-Louis de: 181.

Dąbrowski, Jan Henryk: 276, 354.
Daendels, Herman Willem: 305.
Dahlenkirchen: 296, 298.
Dalmatia: 22.
Danube river: 13-14, 23, 310, 347-348.
Danzig [Gdańsk]: 82, 255, 297.
Davout, Louis-Nicolas, prince d'Eckmühl: 82, 84, 88, 97-100, 102, 110, 112, 120, 123-124, 126, 129-131, 133-135, 138, 141, 173, 205, 254, 256, 324-325, 343.
Davydov, Denis Vasilevich: 240-241, 265-267, 280, 282.
Davydov, Yevdokim Vasilevich: 155, 368.
Dednya: 254, 263
Defrance, Jena-Marie-Antoine: 144, 153-156, 162.
Dekhterev, Nikolai Vasilevich: 318.
Delaborde, Henri-François: 85, 163, 325, 354.
Delzons, Alexis-Joseph: 131-132, 254, 263.
Demidov, Flegont Pavlovich: 143, 362.
Demidov, Nikolai Nikitich: 32.
Denmark: 23, 27, 82.
Denisov 7th, Vasily Timofeevich: 265, 351.
Depreradovich, Nikolay Ivanovich: 108.
Dery, Pierre-César: 336.
Desenka river: 334, 336.
Desna: 239, 242, 245-246.

Dessaix, Joseph-Marie: 112, 123-124, 126, 130-131, 162.
Diebitsch und Narten 2nd, Hans Karl Friedrich Anton von: 303.
Disna [Dzisna]: 71, 301, 304.
Dmitrov: 42, 205, 254, 263, 265, 285, 339.
Dmitrovskoe: 333.
Dnieper District: 61.
Dnieper river: 8, 83-85, 92, 189, 194, 220, 251, 255, 289, 325, 385, 387, 389.
Dokhturov, Dmitry Sergeevich: 108, 115, 136, 159, 161, 168, 173, 182-183, 189, 329, 356, 374, 376-377.
Dokshitsy [Dokšycy]: 242, 295, 386, 388-389.
Dolgorukov, Sergei Nikolaevich: 340.
Dorogobuzh: 7, 19, 41, 84-87, 99, 189, 267, 276, 345.
Dorokhov, Ivan Semënovich: 135, 152, 168, 242, 247, 265, 267, 270-271, 330, 332, 336, 363, 365.
Doronino: 110-112, 123, 126.
Doumerc, Jean-Pierre: 304, 354.
Dragomilov gate (Moscow): 196, 199-200, 203-205, 218.
Driesen, Fëdor Vasilevich: 137, 376.
Drissa river: 291, 294.
Drohiczyn: 317-321.
Dubno: 310, 322.
Dufour, François-Marie: 173, 205, 254, 327.
Duka, Ilya Mikhailovich: 110, 119, 133-135, 168, 367.
Dukhovshchina: 84-86, 179, 280.
Dumas, Mathieu: 76, 227, 257.
Dünaburg [Daugavpils]: 55, 291, 296-297, 300.
Dünamünde [Daugavgriva]: 297-298.
Duppelin, Jean: 111, 133.
Durosnel, Antoine-Jean-Auguste: 205, 227.
Dvina [Daugava/Düna] river: 7, 24, 28, 55, 87, 166, 194, 220, 234, 242, 276, 291, 294-297, 300-301, 303-304, 324, 385, 389-390.
Dyachkin, colonel: 351, 396.

Eckau [Iecava]: 298, 301, 390.
Elbe river: 82, 87, 256.
Emmanuel, Georgy (Yegor) Arsenevich: 111, 370.
Engelhardt, Grigory Grigorevich: 315, 397.
Engelhardt, Pavel Ivanovich: 40, 280-281.
Ertel, Fëdor Fëdorovich: 97, 243-244, 313, 322.
Euler, Alexander Khristoforovich: 117.

Essen 1st, Ivan Nikolaevich: 55, 296-298, 300, 351, 390.
Essen 3rd, Pëtr Kirillovich: 310, 312, 315-316, 319-320, 394, 397.
Ezel island [Saaremaa]: 26, 56, 68.

Fatherland: 9-10, 15-16, 18-19, 21, 30, 32-35, 37, 40-41, 45-46, 49, 52-54, 57-59, 61-62, 64-65, 67, 92, 153, 161, 170-171, 175, 184, 188-189, 191, 193-195, 197, 202, 206-212, 222, 225-226, 240, 252, 259, 262-263, 276, 278, 280, 284, 286, 288, 290, 292-293, 311, 339-340, 342, 344-346, 349, 391.
Ferrier, Gratien: 71, 248.
Figner, Alexander Samoilovich: 265-266, 268-270, 330.
Fili: 179, 182, 186, 195-196, 198.
Finland: 21, 23, 26, 28, 44, 56, 242, 244, 295, 347, 353.
Finnish Army (Vyborg Jäger Regiment): 56-57.
Fire brigade: 196.
Fire-extinguishing equipment: 196, 221, 230.
Foch, Alexander Borisovich: 299.
Foch, Boris Borisovich: 168, 175.
Fomkino: 102, 110.
Förster, Yegor Khristianovich: 168, 249.
Foucher de Careil, Louis-François: 124, 130.
Fredrikshamn [Hamina]: 20.
Friant, Louis: 110-112, 124-126, 130, 136, 138, 140, 162, 173.
Friederichs, Jean-Parfait: 254.
Friedland, battle of: 127, 184.
Friedrichstadt [Jaunjelgava]: 297-298, 390.
Frolovsky Yam: 238, 246.

Garoza: 298-300.
Gaverdovsky, colonel of the Russian General Staff: 98, 132.
Gendarmes: 74, 76, 227, 407.
Gérard, Étienne-Maurice: 112, 124- 126, 142, 152, 154, 156, 400.
Gerbel, Karl Gustavovich: 300.
Gerbel 5th, Vasily Vasilevich: 369.
Gerngross, Rodion Fëdorovich: 298-299.
Girard, Jean-Baptiste: 305.
Glodova: 254, 263.
Glubokoe: 8, 71.
Golenishchev-Kutuzov, Pavel Vasilyevich: 213.
Golitsyn, Alexander Borisovich: 199.

Golitsyn, Alexander Nikolaevich: 216.
Golitsyn, Boris Andreevich: 35, 200, 284, 368.
Golitsyn, Dmitry Vladimirovich: 108, 117, 168, 340, 356, 365-367, 369, 371.
Gorchakov, Alexei Ivanovich: 12, 91-92, 216
Gorchakov 2nd, Andrey Ivanovich: 102, 108, 110, 117, 135, 162, 167-168, 344, 356, 370-372.
Gorki: 104-108, 122, 130, 132, 142, 151, 153-154, 157-158, 161, 164, 238, 248, 360, 365.
Gorodechno, battle of: 307, 322-323.
Gorodok: 303-304.
Gramoshche: 291, 294.
Grande Armée formations: iii, *1er Corps*: 84, 102, 110, 120, 123-124, 126, 133, 137, 141, 173, 256, 354; *1er corps de cavalerie*: 120, 125, 149, 327, 354; *1re Division*: 142, 152; *2e Corps*: 304; *2e corps de cavalerie*: 120, 125, 142, 152, 354, 400, 403; *2e Division*: 173; *2e division de cuirassiers*: 152-153; *3e Corps*: 84, 100, 112, 120, 124-126, 133, 173, 254, 263, 354; *3e corps de cavalerie*: 85, 120, 126, 150, 152, 155, 157, 327, 354, 400; *3e Division*: 142, 152; *3e division de cavalerie légère*: 152; *4e Corps*: 85, 87, 102, 112, 120, 122, 126, 173, 198, 205, 219, 240, 254, 263, 354; *4e corps de cavalerie*: 85, 120, 125, 149, 152-153, 327, 354, 404; *4e division de cavalerie légère*: 139, 153; *4e division de cuirasssiers*: 153-155; *5e Corps*: 76, 82, 85, 87, 102, 110, 112, 120, 126, 141, 158, 198, 205, 239, 246, 248, 327, 354; *6e Corps*: 304; *6e division de dragons*: 150, 155; *7e Corps*: 308, 311; *7e division de cuirassiers*: 152; *8e Corps*: 97, 112, 120, 124-126, 133, 135, 173, 276, 354; *9e Corps*: 86-87, 304-305, 324, 327; *10e Corps*: 82; *11e Corps*: 87; *14e Division*: 142, 152; *15e Division*: 173; *16e Division*: 141; *Légion de la Vistule*: 135, 151; *Réserve de cavalerie*: 97, 101-102, 120, 148-149, 152, 173, 254.
Grande Armée, national contingents:
Austrian (*Kaiserlichen*): 8, 310, 317-320, 323, 386; at Gorodechno: 312; Mohr's detachment: 321; O'Reilly Dragoons: 308-309;
Baden: *2. Infanterie-Regiment*: 142;
Bavarian: 132, 254, 292-293, 304, 354;
French: *Garde impériale* units: 8, 85, 97, 99, 102, 112, 120, 125-126, 129-130, 148, 150, 158-159, 164-165, 219, 231-232, 272, 324, 327, 339; *1er chevau-légers lanciers polonais de la Garde*: 74, 80; *2e chevau-légers lanciers de la Garde*: 74, 254; *3e chevau-légers lanciers de la Garde*: 74, 76, 317, 321; *Artillerie de la Garde*: 124-125, 149, 219, 354; *Artillerie à cheval de la Garde*: 240; *Chasseurs à cheval de la Garde*: 254; *Dragons de la Garde*: 240, 254, 267; *Jeune Garde*: 85, 120, 125, 141, 149, 151, 173, 204-205, 325, 354; *Marins de la Garde*: 256; *Tartares lituaniens de la Garde*: 76, 80; *Vieille Garde*: 120, 125, 173, 205, 325, 354;
Cavalry units: *1er chasseurs à cheval*: 201; *1er cuirassiers*: 333, 338; *3e chevau-légers lanciers*: 294; *5e cuirassiers*: 153, 400, 403; *6e chasseurs à cheval*: 150; *6e cuirassiers*: 335; *7e chasseurs à cheval*: 294; *7e dragons*: 155-156; *8e chasseurs à cheval*: 150; *25e chasseurs à cheval*: 150; *carabiniers*: 144, 155-156, 333-335, 364;
Infantry units: *9e ligne*: 154, 400; *15e légère*: 140; *17e ligne*: 400; *21e ligne*: 400; *24e légère*: 134; *25e ligne*: 111, 131; *30e ligne*: 142; *35e ligne*: 400; *48e ligne*: 140; *57e ligne*: 111, 131, 134; *61e ligne*: 111-112; *84e ligne*: 150; *92e ligne*: 132; *106e ligne*: 131; *111e ligne*: 111;
Italy, Kingdom of: 120, 122-123; *3e chasseurs à cheval*: 102; *Garde royale*: 120, 126, 150; *vélites de la Garde*: 240;
Lithuanian: Cavalry: *17 Pułk Ułanow*: 73, 75, 82; *18 Pułk Ułanow*: 73, 82, 75; *19 Pułk Ułanow*: 73, 75, 82; *20 Pułk Ułanow*: 73, 75, 82; *21 Pułk Strzelcow Konnych*: 76, 82; Infantry: *17 Pułk Piechoty*: 73; *18 Pułk Piechoty*: 73, 82; *19 Pułk Piechoty*: 73, 82; *20 Pułk Piechoty*: 73, 82; *21 Pułk Piechoty*: 73, 82; *22 Pułk Piechoty*: 73, 76, 82.
Prussian: 296, 298-300, 386, 389-390; *1. Preußisches Ulanen*: 205.
Saxon: with *7e Corps*: 308, 310-312, 317-320, 322-323, 386, 410; with *9e Corps*: 324; Thielmann's brigade: 139-140; *Garde du Corps*: 153, 155, 398-399, 401, 403; *von Zastrow Kürassiere*: 154-155.
Spanish: *Régiment de Joseph Napoléon*: 112.

Warsaw, Duchy of : 5 *Pułk Strzelcow Konnych*: 82; 6 *Pułk Ułanow*: 135; 9 *Pułk Ułanow*: 82; 10 *Pułk Huzarów*: 205; 12 *Pułk Ułanow*: 158; 13 *Pułk Huzarów*: 158; 14 *Pułk Kirasjerów*: 139, 153-154, 401; Westphalian: 78, 97, 129, 135, 140, 147, 153, 157-158, 173, 267, 271, 276, 324; *1. Kürassiere*: 139; *2. Kürassiere*: 139; Württemberg contingent of the *Grande Armée*: 131, 135, 386.
Grandjean, Charles-Louis-Dieudonné: 296-297, 300.
Grand Vizier: 13, 347.
Grekov 4th, colonel: 394, 396.
Grekov 8th, major general: 394, 396.
Gridnevo: 100-102, 112, 121, 174.
Grodno: 70-71, 73, 75-78, 317, 321, 353, 385.
Grouchy, Emmanuel de: 85, 87, 112, 120, 126, 129, 150, 152, 156-157, 162, 205.
Guerilla - see Partisans.
Gzhatsk [Gagarin]: 83, 90, 93-95, 98, 100, 102, 121, 166, 168, 190, 214, 240- 242, 276-277, 280.

Hamburg: 23, 82, 197, 347.
Harting, Martin Nikolaevich: 101, 247.
Helsingfors [Helsinki]: 57, 296.
Hessen-Philippsthal, Ernst von: 147-148, 175
Hilliers, Louis-Baraguey d': 256, 276-277.
Hogendorp, Diderik (Dirk) van: 70, 74, 80.
Horn, Heinrich Wilhelm von: 298.
Hünerbein, Friedrich Heinrich Karl Georg von: 297-298.
Hungary: 22, 309.

Ilovaisky 5th, Nikolai Vasilevich: 351, 382.
Ilovaisky 12th, Vasily Dmitrievich: 266, 351.
Ivelich, Pëtr Ivanovich: 147, 380-381.

Jomini, Antoine-Henri de: 71.
Junot, Jean-Androche: 85, 97, 99, 102, 112, 120, 123, 126, 129, 133, 135-136, 141, 173, 256, 277.

Kaiserov, Paisy Sergeevich: 97, 169, 182, 186, 200.
Kaluga: 37-38, 42, 86, 98, 172, 185, 191, 220, 241, 247, 250, 260, 264, 276, 280, 325, 344, 355, 361, 391.

Kamenka stream: 105, 108, 138, 140-141, 151, 153.
Kamenets: 291, 301.
Kamenets-Podolsky: 322.
Kamenskoe: 271, 330.
Karataev, Vasily Ivanovich: 366, 369.
Karpenko, Moses Ivanovich: 132.
Karpov 5th, Akim Akimovich: 108, 112, 120, 158, 351, 380.
Kashira: 42, 238-239, 246, 261, 267
Khorosino: 329, 332.
Khotyn: 310, 322.
Khrapovitsky, marshal of nobility: 279-280.
Khrapovitsky, Matvey Yevgrafovich: 138-139, 374, 376.
Kiev [Kyiv]: 48, 86, 317, 322, 348, 386-387.
Kikin, Pëtr Andreevich: 330, 336.
Kiselev 2nd, major: 44, 353.
Kleinmichel, Andrei Andreevich: 260.
Kleist, Friedrich Emil Ferdinand Heinrich von: 298-299.
Klin: 42, 191, 215, 261, 265.
Knyazkovo: 108, 145, 155.
Kobrin: 314-315.
Kochubey, Viktor Pavlovich: 10, 216.
Kolocha river: 102, 104-108, 110, 112, 122-123, 125-126, 129, 131-132, 142, 145, 147-148, 150, 151, 164, 173, 370.
Kologrivov, Andrey Semënovich: 34, 261.
Kolotsky Monastery: 100, 102, 110, 112, 121, 163, 169, 174, 240, 277.
Königsberg [Kaliningrad]: 171, 256.
Konopka, Jan: 74, 76, 80, 317, 321
Konovnitsyn, Pëtr Petrovich: 18, 88, 98, 101-102, 132-133, 136-138, 141, 158, 168, 175, 182-183, 238, 244, 249, 264, 273, 327, 330, 334, 336.
Konstantin Pavlovich, Grand Duke: 82, 84, 202, 260-261.
Korf, Fëdor Karlovich: 115-116, 152, 156, 168, 175, 246, 249, 253, 328, 336, 341, 363, 369
Korf, Nikolay Ivanovich: 155.
Kosiński, Antoni Amilkar: 307, 311.
Kostenetsky, Vasily Grigorevich: 154, 168.
Kostroma: 47, 58, 261.
Kovno [Kaunas]: 75, 86, 171, 255, 305.
Kozen, Pëtr Andreevich: 134, 136, 156, 368-369.
Kozula: 319-320.

Kozyany: 294-295.
Krasiński, Izydor Zenon Tomasz: 141.
Krasiński, Wincenty Jan: 74.
Krasnaya Pakhra: 239, 242, 247-249, 365.
Krasnov, Ivan Kosmich: 84, 86, 102.
Kremlin (Moscow): 203, 205, 218-221, 227-228, 230-231, 257, 275, 293, 325.
Kretov, Nikolay Vasilevich: 139, 167-168.
Kreutz, Cyprian Antonovich: 86, 88, 98, 116, 144.
Krymskoe, action at: 174-175, 179.
Krzna river: 319-320.
Kudashev, Nikolay Danilovich: 143, 156, 171, 265, 270, 335, 364.
Kudashev, Yusney: 58.
Kulakovo: 237-238.
Kurgan battery (Raevsky redoubt or central battery): iv, 104, 106, 108, 126, 129-130, 132-133, 142-146, 148-153, 155, 157, 159, 161-162, 358, 398, 400, 403.
Kurin, Gerasim Matveyevich: 283-285.
Kutaisov, Alexander Ivanovich: 143-145, 162, 362.

La Houssaye, Armand-Lebrun de: 150-151, 155, 248.
Lambert, Karl Osipovich de: 76, 82, 307-308, 311, 314-316, 396.
Langéron, Louis Alexandre Andrault de: 310-312, 315-316, 320, 394, 396.
Lanskoy, Sergey Nikolaevich: 312-314.
Lanskoy, Vasily Sergeevich: 185, 249.
Lariboisière, Jean-Ambroise-Baston de: 171, 256.
Latour-Maubourg, Marie-Victor-Nicolas de Faÿ de: 85, 112, 120-121, 126, 129, 133, 138-140, 149, 152-155, 205, 327, 335, 404.
Lauriston, Jacques-Jean-Alexandre-Bernard-Law de: 229, 272-276, 326, 341.
Lavrov, Nikolay Ivanovich: 116, 168, 374.
Lebedev, Nikolai Petrovich: 41, 101, 120.
Ledru des Essarts, François-Roch: 133-134.
Lefebvre, François-Joseph, duc de Dantzig: 219, 232.
Lelorgne d'Iderville: 204, 227-229.
Lepel: 389.
Lepel, August Hellmuth von: 140.
Leppich, Franz Xaver (Schmidt): 192-193, 221-222.
Lesna river: 314, 316-317.

Lesseps, Martin de: 205, 232-233, 285-286, 406.
Letashevka: 262, 330.
Levashov, Vasily Vasilevich: 155, 365, 368.
Liders, Nikolai Ivanovich: 321.
Lieven, Khristofor Andreevich: 211.
Likhachëv, Pëtr Gavrilovich: 116, 144-145, 153, 161-162, 175, 359, 362, 378, 399-400.
Lithuania: 243, 251, 320, 348, 386-389; French occupation of: 9, 70-71, 73-78, 80, 82, 276, 317, 323, 325.
Lobanov-Rostovsky, Dmitry Ivanovich: 35, 52, 95, 260.
Lobanov-Rostovsky, Yakov Ivanovich: 65.
Lopukhin, Pëtr Andreevich: 32.
Lopukhin, Pëtr Vasilevich: 10, 216.
Lorge, Jean-Thomas-Guillaume: 138-140, 152.
Loshchilin, lieutenant colonel: 295-296, 353.
Löwenhielm, Carl Axel: 22, 26-27, 231.
Löwenstern, Karl Fëdorovich: 117, 168, 249, 371.
Löwenstern, Vladimir Ivanovich: 144.
Löwenwolde, Karl Karlovich: 155, 365.
Löwis of Menar, Friedrich von: 55, 297-300, 390.
Lubino: 83.
Lublin: 317-318.
Luboml: 311-313.
Lüders, Nikolai Ivanovich: 310.
Lukovkin, Gavryl Amvrosievich: 317-318, 352, 395, 397.
Lukovnya: 239, 242.
Łuków: 318.
Lutsk: 73, 307, 311.
Luzhki: 86-87.

MacDonald, Étienne (Jacques-Joseph-Alexandre): 25, 27, 82, 86-87, 219, 242, 276, 291, 296-297, 300, 324, 385, 389-390.
Madatov, Valerian Grigorevich: 311.
Magazines: 7, 9, 34-36, 48-49, 51-52, 55, 63, 66-67, 76-77, 85, 96, 169, 172, 224, 231, 233, 256, 299, 305, 313-314, 317-318, 321, 388, 390.
Małachowski, Stanisław: 139, 153-154, 401.
Manifestos on the *Opolchenie*: 29-31, 33, 39-40, 54-55, 57- 62, 64, 66-67, 257, 260, 345.
Marauders: 74, 78-79, 179, 220, 231, 234, 278, 280, 303, 305.
Marchand, Jean-Gabriel: 133.

Maret, Hugues-Bernard, duc de Bassano: 255, 406.
Markov, Yevgeny Ivanovich: 315, 396.
Martin, Thomas Byam: 297.
Mayevsky, Sergei Ivanovich: 17.
Mecklenburg-Schwerin, Carl August Christian zu: 108, 110-111, 118, 133-134, 137, 162, 168.
Melissino, Alexey Petrovich: 318.
Melnikov 3rd: 395, 397.
Melnikov 5th, colonel: 312, 352, 395, 397.
Meller-Zakomelsky, Pëtr Ivanovich: 42, 44, 239, 249, 261, 293-294, 328, 332, 335, 340.
Mesothen [Mežotne]: 299.
Metropolitan Platon (Pëtr Georgievich Levshin): 193-195, 290.
Michaud de Beauretour, Alexandre: iii, 207-210, 217, 237, 338, 383-384.
Międzyrzec: 317-318.
Mikhailovsky-Danilevsky, Alexander Ivanovich: iii, 166, 208, 334, 383, 405-407.
Military Order medal: 278-279, 365, 376.
Miloradovich, Mikhail Andreevich: 94, 97-98, 100, 107, 114, 146, 148, 161, 168, 174, 182, 186, 191, 199-207, 236-237, 239, 242, 245-246, 248-249, 253-254, 260, 262, 273, 280, 326, 329, 335-336, 340, 356, 358, 360.
Minsk: 25, 38, 65, 70-71, 73, 75-77, 82, 86, 171, 243, 251, 255-256, 305, 313, 321, 342, 380-381, 385-386, 388-389, 405
Mitau [Jelgava]: 25, 297-301, 390.
Mocha river: 246-248, 253, 270.
Modlin: 82, 317.
Mogilev: 70, 73, 79-80, 86, 238, 244-245, 251, 313.
Mohr: Johann Friedrich von: 313-314, 321.
Moldavia: 11, 97, 343, 352.
Monakhtin, Fëdor Fëdorovich: 145.
Moniuszko, Ignacy: 76,82.
Montbrun, Louis-Pierre de: 110, 112, 120-121, 126, 129, 133, 142, 144, 152, 162, 205.
Morand, Charles-Antoine-Louis-Alexis: 110-111, 124-126, 133, 142, 144, 152, 154, 162.
Morkov, Irakli Ivanovich: 32, 100, 120, 170-171, 191.
Mortier, Adolphe-Édouard-Casimir-Joseph: 173, 205, 228, 325.
Moskva river: 104, 107-108, 123, 164, 173, 179-180, 198-199, 218-219, 225, 237-239, 357, 360, 381.
Mosty: 321.
Mourier, Pierre: 131.
Mozhaisk: v, 42, 97, 105, 124, 140, 161, 167-169, 171-174, 179, 183, 191, 239-240, 242, 247, 254, 256, 265-268, 270-271, 276-277, 324, 335, 339, 381.
Mozyr: 65, 97, 238, 243-244, 313, 322, 386.
Musin-Pushkin, Pëtr Klavdievich: 322.
Musin-Pushkin, Sergey Klavdievich: 371.
Mstislavl: 85, 305.
Mukhavets: 314, 316.
Murat, Joachim, King of Naples: 84-85, 87-88, 98, 100-102, 111-112, 120, 125, 133, 135, 138, 141, 146, 159, 172-175, 190, 200-207, 239, 245-248, 253-254, 269, 272-273, 275, 324-327, 330, 335-336, 338, 340-341, 403.
Murom: 260.

Nansouty, Étienne-Marie-Antoine-Champion de: 110, 112, 120, 126, 129, 133, 135, 138-139, 149, 162, 205, 327.
Nara river: 174-175, 253, 262, 327-328, 338.
Narbonne-Lara, Louis-Marie-Jacques-Amalric de: 23-24, 100, 229.
Neipperg, Adam Albert von: 21.
Neman river: 87, 97, 242, 245, 258, 321, 386, 388-390, 405.
Nemchinino: 246, 248.
Nepeitsyn, Sergey Vasilevich: 294-295, 302.
Nesvizh [Niasviž]: 76, 243, 386-388.
Nevel: 291, 294, 303, 388.
Neverovsky, Dmitry Petrovich: 84, 108, 111, 118, 133-135, 141, 162, 168.
Ney, Michel, duc d'Elchingen: 84, 99-100, 102, 123, 125, 129, 133-136, 138, 140-141, 159, 163, 205, 324-325.
Nikitin, Alexey Petrovich: 143, 152.
Norway: 22-23, 27-28.

Olai [Olaine]: 296, 298-300.
Oldenburg, Peter Friedrich Georg (Georgy Petrovich) von: 31, 34, 46, 168.
Olsufiev, Zakhar Dmitrievich: 114, 147, 168, 334, 379-380.
Opolchenie: iii, 12, 15, 29-30, 51-54, 68-69, 121, 161, 168, 170, 175, 181, 187, 212, 214, 260-263, 279, 289, 345; Arkhangelsk: 57; Astrakhan: 59, 68; Caucasus: 61; Chernigov: 65, 68, 261; Don Host: 60, 68; Estland: 56, 68; Finland: 56, 68; Kaluga:

39-40, 261; Kazan: 49; Kharkov: 64; Kherson: 62, 68; Kiev: 66, 68; Kostroma: 48; Kursk: 63; Lifland: 55, 68; Moscow: 31-33, 95, 100, 106-107, 113, 120, 141, 167, 171, 175, 186, 194, 199, 248, 261, 380; Nizhny Novgorod: 48-49, 261; Novgorod: 46-48, 213, 261, 294, 302-303, 388; Olonets: 57, 68; Orël: 63; Orenburg: 68; Pavlova: 284; Penza: 50-51; Perm: 58; Podolsk: 66-68; Poltava: 64, 68; Pskov: 54; Refugee: 214; Roslavl: 280; Ryazan: 36, 42, 51, 261, 263; Saint Petersburg: 42-46, 213, 293-294, 301-303, 388; Saratov: 59; Siberia: 67-68; Simbirsk: 50; Smolensk: 40-42, 100, 107, 113, 120, 261; Tambov: 63; Taurida (Crimea): 61; Tula: 37-39; Tver: iii, 33-34, 213, 261, 266, 282, 349; Vladimir: 35, 284; Vologda: 57-58, 68; Vyatka: 49; Yaroslavl: 31, 35, 42, 51, 261; Yekaterinoslav: 62.
Order of Saint-Alexander Nevsky: 168.
Order of Saint-Andrew: 340.
Order of Saint-Anne: 168.
Order of Saint-George: 168, 347
Orlov-Denisov, Vasily Vasilevich: 328-330, 332-333, 335-336, 338.
Ornano, Philippe-Antoine d': 132, 150.
O'Rourke 1st, Joseph Cornelius: 310-311, 314-315.
Osma river, action on: 88.
Osterman-Tolstoy, Alexander Ivanovich: 114.
Ottoman Porte (Sultan): 13-14, 22-23, 348.
Oudinot, Nicolas-Charles-Marie: 27, 276, 343, 385, 389-390.

Pahlen, Pëtr Alexeevich: 12.
Pahlen, Pëtr Petrovich: 116, 345.
Pajol, Pierre-Claude: 121, 141, 162.
Pakhra river: 238, 242, 246, 248.
Panchulidzev 2nd, Semën Davydovich: 156, 168, 364.
Panki: 200, 236-237.
Panteleev, major: 352, 394, 397.
Paris: 23-24, 39, 82, 97, 226, 233, 256-257.
Parlementaire: 132, 201-202, 205, 273, 326.
Partisans: iii, v, 42, 240-241, 254-256, 265-271, 275, 280, 282-285, 289-290, 293-295, 304, 308, 318, 325, 335, 338, 341.
Partouneaux, Louis de: 305.
Paskevich, Ivan Fëdorovich: 82, 108, 117, 142, 144, 168, 246, 378.

Paul I Petrovich: 15, 347.
Pavlova: 283-285.
Pelet-Clozeau, Jean-Jacques-Germain: 137.
Perkhushkovo: 198, 242.
Pernety, Joseph-Marie de: 124, 130
Pernov [Pärnu]: 55.
Petrovsky Palace (Moscow): 205, 219-220, 227.
Pillar, Yegor Maximovich: 332-333.
Pillau [Baltiysk]: 297, 305.
Pino, Domenico: 163, 173.
Pinsk: 313, 321-322, 385-388.
Piszczac: 319.
Platov, Matvey Ivanovich: 60, 84-86, 107, 117, 122, 147, 151, 173-174, 360, 382.
Platov 4th: 351.
Platov 5th: 351.
Plauzonne, Louis-Auguste-Marchand de: 132.
Podolia: 321, 323.
Podolsk: 42, 191, 238-239, 242, 246-247, 254, 317, 335.
Poklonnaya Gora: 179, 181-182, 195, 200, 203-204, 223-224.
Poland: 71, 75, 82, 229, 321.
Polga river: 174-175.
Polotsk: 46, 242, 291, 294-295, 300-301, 303-304, 385, 388-389.
Poniatowski, Józef Antoni: 76, 82, 85, 87-88, 97, 99, 102, 110-113, 120, 122-124, 126, 129, 135, 141, 147, 158, 173, 198, 204-205, 239, 246, 248, 254, 327.
Porechye: 41, 92, 179, 251, 278, 280.
Porkhov: 293, 302.
Potëmkin, Yakov Alexeevich: 174, 200, 262, 360.
Pridruisk [Piedruja]: 300-302.
Priluki: 314-315.
Prussia: 48, 82, 86, 211, 342.
Prut river: 13, 23.
Pruzhany: 314, 317, 321, 385, 387.
Psarevo: 108, 146.
Pskov: 214-215, 219, 291-293, 302, 388.
Pyshnitsky, Dmitry Ilych: 146, 381.

Raevsky, Nikolay Nikolaevich: 117, 133, 136, 142-144, 146, 168, 182, 184, 189, 237-239, 242, 246, 248, 344, 377.
Raevsky redoubt - see Kurgan battery.
Ragusa [Dubrovnik]: 22.
Rakhmanov, Pavel Alexandrovich: 36.

Rakhmanov, Vasily Sergeevich: 295.
Rapp, Jean: 133, 162.
Ratno: 313-314.
Razout, Louis-Nicolas de: 133.
Refugees: 199, 206, 214, 237.
Repninsky, Sergei Yakovlevich: 322.
Reval [Tallinn]: 28, 56-57, 242, 244, 296, 300-301, 390.
Reynier, Jean-Louis-Ébénézer: 235, 307-308, 311-313, 316, 319-320, 385-387.
Rezvoy, Dmitry Petrovich: 17.
Ribas y Boyons, Don Jose de: 17
Ribas, *Wachtmeister* from Her Majesty's Cuirassiers: 369.
Riga: 25-26, 28, 55-56, 87, 215, 220, 242, 244, 295-301, 389-390, 407; garrison of: 25, 295, 297, 299, 303, 390.
Rodionov 2nd, Mark Ivanovich: 179, 294-295, 351
Rogachev: 238, 244, 313.
Roguet, François: 141, 151.
Rosen, Alexander Vladimirovich: 366-367, 369
Rosen, Fëdor Fëdorovich: 298
Rosen, Grigory Vladimirovich: 84, 168, 173, 374-376
Rossi, Ignaty Petrovich de: 146.
Rostopchin, Fëdor Vasilevich: 31, 63, 136, 168-171, 181-182, 185-189, 191-193, 195-199, 202, 207, 209, 221-228, 230, 253, 286.
Rożniecki, Aleksander Antoni Jan: 138-139, 153.
Rudnya offensive: 10.
Ruhenthal [Rundāle]: 297, 299.
Rumyantsev-Zadunaisky, Pëtr Alexandrovich: iii, 12, 23, 27, 210, 346, 392.
Russian armies:
 Army of the Danube/Moldavia: iii, iv, 7, 14, 25, 66, 80, 97, 242-243, 260, 276, 309-313, 323, 339, 343, 348, 352, 394;
 First Army: iii, 11, 24, 55, 84-86, 88, 97, 101, 107, 122, 134, 143-144, 161, 249-250, 253, 294, 342-343, 345, 355, 357-358, 361-363, 365, 369, 374, 376;
 Second Army: iii, 24-25,66, 84-86, 88, 97, 107-108, 122, 136, 140, 143, 146, 150, 152, 158-161, 209, 243, 249, 313, 355, 357-358, 360-362, 370-375, 378;
 Third Army: iii, iv, 66, 97, 243, 310, 313-315, 317, 394, 396.

Russian cavalry corps:
 I Cavalry Corps: 85-86, 101, 107-108, 115, 122, 147-148, 150, 173, 239, 254, 262, 332, 340, 355, 360, 362;
 II Cavalry Corps: 86, 88, 107, 115, 148, 152, 156, 175, 246, 254, 262, 328-329, 341, 355, 358-360, 363-364;
 III Cavalry Corps: 86, 108, 116, 135, 152, 156, 175, 246, 254, 328-329, 355, 358-360, 363;
 IV Cavalry Corps: 108, 113, 118, 131, 134, 237-238, 262, 328-329, 341, 355, 372.
Russian infantry corps:
 I Corps: 7, 243-244, 260-261, 291-295, 302-303, 385;
 II Corps: 85-86, 97, 107-108, 114, 133, 145, 158, 172-173, 247, 249, 262, 328-330, 332-334, 336, 338, 340, 355-356, 358, 360, 373-374, 379;
 III Corps: 86, 108, 113, 119-120, 122, 133, 141, 158, 247, 249, 262, 328-330, 332, 334, 336, 338, 340, 355, 357, 360, 373;
 IV Corps: 86, 97, 107-108, 114-115, 142, 146, 148-149, 152, 154, 158, 246, 248-249, 253-254, 262, 328-330, 332, 334, 336, 338, 355-356, 358-360, 363;
 V Corps (Lifeguard): 86, 108, 116-117, 136, 158, 247, 249, 262, 328-330, 332, 338, 340-341, 355-356, 374;
 VI Corps: 86, 108, 115-116, 125, 142, 144-145, 148, 153-154, 158, 247, 249, 262, 328-330, 340, 355-356, 358, 360-361, 363, 376;
 VII Corps: 108, 117-118, 133, 144, 152, 237-238, 246, 249, 253, 262, 328-330, 340, 355-356, 358, 377-378;
 VIII Corps: 108, 118, 239, 249, 253-254, 262, 328-330, 336, 340, 358;
 Finland Corps: 57, 242, 244, 260, 295-301, 303, 390.
 2nd Reserve Corps: 66.
Russian cavalry divisions: 1st Cuirassier Division: 108, 117, 134, 248-249, 262, 328-329, 340, 356, 358-360, 365, 368; 2nd Cuirassier Division:110, 113, 119, 133-134, 139, 248-249, 262, 328-329, 332, 340, 356, 360, 367, 374;
Russian infantry divisions: 1st Grenadier Division: 113, 119, 141, 147; 2nd Combined Grenadier Division: 108, 112-113, 119,

INDEX 417

355, 358; 2nd Grenadier Division: 108, 110-111, 113, 118, 133, 138-139, 160, 355; 3rd Division: 88, 113, 119, 133, 135, 137, 175, 355; 4th Division: 114, 145-146, 172, 332, 334, 355, 379; 5th Division: 260, 302-303, 388; 6th Division: 27, 260, 295; 7th Division: 113, 115, 155, 359-360; 8th Division: 322; 10th Division: 322; 11th Division: 114, 132, 175, 359; 12th Division: 118, 134, 142, 144, 378; 13th Division: 310; 14th Division: 260, 302-303; 17th Division: 114, 145, 332-334, 355, 379; 21st Division: 27, 260, 295-296; 22nd Division: 322; 23rd Division: 112, 114, 153, 162, 175; 24th Division: 113, 116, 132, 144, 146, 154, 175, 358-360, 362, 400; 25th Division: 27, 260; 26th Division: 108, 117, 140, 142, 144, 246, 358-359, 378; 27th Division: 108, 111, 113, 118, 131, 133-134, 138, 141, 355-356, 378;

Russian artillery units: Pioneers: 117, 119, 121, 263, 301, 303, 311-312, 394-395; Pontoniers: 117, 119, 263, 303; Reserve: 86, 108, 117, 119, 160, 261-262, 388;

Battery companies: 1st Battery: 119; 2nd Battery: 118; 3rd Battery: 119; 4th Battery: 114; 7th Battery: 115; 8th Battery: 319, 394, 397; 9th Battery: 396; 10th Battery: 395, 397; 11th Battery: 114; 15th Battery: 396; 16th Battery: 397; 17th Battery: 114; 18th Battery: 395-396; 19th Battery: 397; 21st Battery: 296; 22nd Battery: 394, 397; 24th Battery: 116; 26th Battery: 117; 34th Battery: 397; 38th Battery: 312, 395, 397; 39th Battery: 395; Lifeguard Battery: 134.

Horse companies: 1st Lifeguard Horse: 134, 365; 2nd Lifeguard Horse: 155-156; 2nd Horse: 150; 4th Horse: 115; 5th Horse: 115; 9th Horse: 116; 10th Horse: 118; 11th Horse: 396; 12th Horse: 396; 13th Horse: 396; 14th Horse: 394; 15th Horse: 312, 319, 394, 397; 16th Horse: 395, 397; 17th Horse: 395, 397; 23rd Horse: 301; Suvorov's Don Horse: 351; Tatsyn's Don Horse: 351; Tula *Opolchenie* Horse: 37.

Light companies: 1st Light: 119, 139; 2nd Lifeguard Light: 140; 2nd Light: 119; 3rd Light: 118; 5th Light: 119; 6th Light: 119; 11th Light: 296, 299-300; 14th Light: 394; 15th Light: 394; 18th Light: 395; 31st Light: 395; 35th Light: 293; 41st Light: 394; 42nd Light: 394; 44th Light: 114; 47th Light: 117; 49th Light: 293, 303; 50th Light: 395.

Russian cavalry units:
Cossacks: Bashkirs: 58, 246, 248; Bug: 62, 265, 267; Don: iii, 44, 60, 68, 117, 262, 265, 267, 328, 334, 351-353, 382, 397; Kalmuks: 396-397; Lifeguard: 115, 150-151, 202, 206, 265, 362; Orenburg: 58, 68; Simferopol Tatars: 267; Teptyar: 58, 267, 282; Tver: 349; Ural: 312, 394-395, 396-397; Yevpatoria Tatars: 397;

Cuirassiers: Astrakhan: 117, 134, 140, 160, 365-366, 368; Chevalier Garde: 117, 152, 154-156, 233, 359-360, 365, 367-369; Glukhov: 111, 119, 371; Her Majesty's *Leib*: 117, 134, 140, 365-367, 369; His Majesty's *Leib*: 117, 134, 140, 365-366; Lifeguard Horse: 49, 117, 134, 152, 154, 156, 360, 365-366, 368-369; Malorussia: 111, 119, 371; Military Order: 119, 139; Novgorod: 119; Yekaterinoslav: 119, 139;

Dragoons: Arzamas: 308, 396; Chernigov: 110-111, 118, 371; Courland: 116, 135, 363; Dorpat: 311, 395, 397; Finland: 295-296, 299; Ingermanland: 115, 294; Irkutsk: 86, 98, 116, 144, 156, 359, 364; Kargopol: 115; Kazan: 280; Kharkov: 108, 110-111, 118, 265, 371; Kiev: 110-111, 118, 370; Kinburn: 394, 397; Lifeguard: 115, 150, 242, 267, 328, 330, 362; Livland: 394, 396; Mitau: 293, 303; Moscow: 115, 156, 364; Nezhin: 115, 150, 328, 330, 362; Novorossiya: 110-111, 118, 131, 135, 370, 372; Orenburg: 116, 135, 144, 156, 359, 363; Pereyaslavl: 395, 397; Pskov: 115, 156, 360, 364; Riga: 294; St Petersburg: 394, 396; Serpukhov: 396; Seversk: 394; Siberia: 86, 116, 144, 156, 359, 364; Smolensk: 319, 394; Starodub: 396; Taganrog: 396; Tiraspol: 395, 397; Tver: 396, 397; Vladimir: 396; Yamburg: 294, 303; Zhitomir: 319-320, 397;

Hussars: Akhtyrka: 110-111, 113, 118, 131, 135, 140, 240, 265, 370, 372-373; Alexandria: 308-309, 396; Belorussia: 311, 394, 396; Consolidated: 291, 301; Grodno: 293; Irkutsk: 32; Izyum: 102, 115, 156, 179, 206, 364; Lifeguard: 115,

150, 201, 248, 328, 330, 362; Lubny: 318, 396; Mariupol: 116, 135, 156, 265, 270, 359, 363; Moscow: 32; Olviopol: 318, 395, 397; Pavlograd: 396; Sumy: 116, 135, 156, 269, 359, 363-364; Yelisavetgrad: 115, 150, 242, 267, 280, 357, 362;
Lancers: Chuguev Ulans: 395, 397; Lifeguard Ulans: 115, 150, 328, 330, 362; Lithuania Ulans: 118, 135, 265, 373-374; Mamonov Ulans: 32; Poland Ulans: 115, 156, 265, 269, 293, 302, 364; Tatar Ulans: 308, 396;

Russian infantry/grenadier regiments:
Alexopol Infantry: 118; Apsheron Infantry: 396; Arakcheev's Grenadiers: 119, 141, 147; Arkhangelogorod Infantry: 394, 397; Astrakhan Grenadiers: 118, 137; Azov Infantry: 295, 299; Belozersk Infantry: 114, 147, 379-380; Bialystok Infantry: 394, 397; Brest Infantry: 114, 147, 158, 379-380; Bryansk Infantry: 295-296; Butyrsk Infantry: 116, 175; Chernigov Infantry: 119; Courland Infantry: 396; Crimea Infantry: 394, 397; Dnieper Infantry: 396; Fanagoria Grenadiers: 118; Kamchatka Infantry: 395, 397; Kaporsk Infantry: 119; Kexholm Infantry: 114, 153; Kiev Grenadiers: 118, 137; Kremenchug Infantry: 114, 145-146, 158, 380-381; Kolyvan Infantry: 396; Kostroma Infantry: 59, 396; Kozlov Infantry: 396; Kursk Infantry: 394, 397; Ladoga Infantry: 117; Leib Grenadiers: 119, 141, 147; Libau Infantry: 115, 174; Lifeguard Izmailovsky: 116, 134, 137-140, 158, 374, 376-377; Lifeguard Finland: 116, 134, 137, 140, 158, 374-375, 377; Lifeguard Lithuania: 116, 134, 137-140, 374, 376-378; Lifeguard Marines (Equipage): 166, 132, 263; Lifeguard Preobrazhensky: 116, 152, 358, 374, 377; Lifeguard Semenovsky: 116, 152, 358, 374, 377; Lithuania Infantry: 296; Malorussia Grenadiers: 118; Marines: 44, 213, 293, 303; Mingrelia Infantry: 395, 397; Minsk Infantry: 114, 145-146, 157-158, 380-381; Moscow Garrison: 197, 203; Moscow Grenadiers: 118, 137; Moscow Infantry: 115; Murom Infantry: 119; Narva Infantry: 118; Nasheburg Infantry: 396; Neva Infantry: 296, 299; Nizhegorod Infantry: 117; Nizov Infantry: 295, 299; Novoingermanland Infantry: 118; Odessa Infantry: 110, 118; Okhotsk Infantry: 395, 397; Olonets Infantry: 395, 397; Orël Infantry: 117; Pavlov Grenadiers: 119, 141, 147, 380; Pernov Infantry: 114, 153, 359; Petrov Infantry: 296, 299; Podolsk Infantry: 296; Polotsk Infantry: 114, 303; Poltava Infantry: 117; Pskov Infantry: 115; Reval Infantry: 119, 137; Ryazan Infantry: 114, 147, 158, 379-380; Ryazhsk Infantry: 396; Rylsk Infantry: 114; Saint Petersburg Grenadiers: 119, 141, 147; Saratov Infantry: 310, 397; Schlüsselburg Infantry: 318, 394, 397; Selenginsk Infantry: 114; Shirvan Infantry: 116; Siberia Grenadiers: 118, 137; Simbirsk Infantry: 110, 118; Smolensk Infantry: 118; Sofia Infantry: 115, 174; Staroingermanland Infantry: 394, 397; Staroskol Infantry: 394,396; Tambov Infantry: 396; Tarnopol Infantry: 110, 118; Tauride Grenadiers: 119, 141, 381; Tobolsk Infantry: 114, 146, 172, 333-335; Tomsk Infantry: 116, 144, 175; Ufa Infantry: 116, 143, 358-359, 361-362; Ukraine Infantry: 394, 397; Vilna Infantry: 110, 118; Vitebsk Infantry: 396; Vladimir Infantry: 396; Volhynia Infantry: 114, 146; Voronezh Infantry: 44, 293, 302; Vyatka Infantry: 394,396; Vyborg Infantry: 394, 396; Wilmanstrand Infantry: 114, 147, 379-380; Yakutsk Infantry: 396; Yaroslavl Infantry: 395, 397; Yekaterinoslav Grenadiers: 119, 141, 147; Yekaterinburg Infantry: 114; Yelets Infantry: 114;

Russian jäger regiments:
1st Jägers: 114, 132; 2nd Jägers: 59, 296; 3rd Jägers: 295, 299; 4th Jägers: 108, 114, 174, 330, 333-334; 5th Jägers: 108, 110-111, 117; 6th Jägers: 118; 7th Jägers: 395, 397; 8th Jägers: 312, 394, 397; 10th Jägers: 396; 11th Jägers: 108, 113, 115, 174; 12th Jägers: 310, 397; 13th Jägers: 396; 14th Jägers: 396; 18th Jägers: 114, 142-143, 168, 359,

361-362; 19th Jägers: 116, 132, 142-143, 155, 359, 361; 20th Jägers: 108, 113, 119, 329, 332, 335, 338; 21st Jägers: 108, 113, 119; 22nd Jägers: 310; 27th Jägers: 397; 28th Jägers: 396; 29th Jägers: 394, 396; 30th Jägers: 86, 114, 174, 297; 32nd Jägers: 396; 33rd Jägers: 114, 153; 34th Jägers: 108, 114, 174, 359; 36th Jägers: 115, 174; 37th Jägers: 319, 394, 397; 38th Jägers: 396; 39th Jägers: 394, 397; 40th Jägers: 116, 132, 142-143, 155, 359, 361; 41st Jägers: 108, 113, 118; 42nd Jägers: 117; 43rd Jägers: 397; 44th Jägers: 296; 45th Jägers: 394, 396; 48th Jägers: 86, 114, 174, 333-334; 49th Jägers: 108, 110, 118, 141; 50th Jägers: 108, 110, 118, 141; Lifeguard Jägers: 107, 116, 131-132, 357-358, 376;
Ruza: 173, 179, 183, 265, 277, 339.
Ryazan ravine (Tarutino): 333-334.
Ryazan, road to: 185-186, 196, 205-207, 229, 236-241, 246, 265, 267.

Sabaneev, Ivan Vasilevich: 310-311, 315, 395, 397.
Saint-Cyr, Laurent de Gouvion: 8, 86-87, 219, 229, 242, 276, 292, 297, 300, 304-305, 324.
Saint-Germain, Antoine-Louis-Decrest de: 138, 162, 327.
Saint-Priest, Armand-Charles-Emmanuel Guignard de: 66-67.
Saint-Priest, Guillaume-Emmanuel Guignard de: 11, 136, 162.
Saken, Fabian Wilhelmovich Osten-: 97, 317, 319, 322.
Salamanca, battle of: 123.
Saltanovka, battle of: 10.
Saltykov, Alexander Nikolaevich: 216.
Saltykov, Nikolai Ivanovich: 10.
Saltykov, Pëtr Ivanovich: 32.
Samus, hussar (Fëdor Potapov): 280.
Sapieha, Aleksandr Antoni: 72-73.
Satino: 246, 248.
Schlock [Sloka]: 296, 298, 301.
Schubert, Fëdor Fëdorovich: 156, 364.
Schwarzenberg, Karl Philipp zu: 21, 86, 235, 242, 276, 307-308, 310-314, 316-319, 321-323, 385-387.
Sébastiani, Horace-François-Bastien: 201-202, 205-206, 239, 333.
Sebezh: 244, 291, 293, 302, 388.

Semenovka stream: 104-105, 138-140, 142, 144, 147, 152-153.
Semenovskaya: 105-108, 113, 122, 129, 131, 133-142, 146, 149, 151-152, 157-159, 403.
Semlevo: 86, 88, 267.
Senate: Finland Senate: 26; Governing Senate of Russia: 29, 31-32, 92.
Septinsular Islands [Ionian Islands]: 22.
Serbia, Russian forces in: 310.
Serpukhov: 42, 185, 246-247, 265, 270, 339.
Seslavin, Alexander Nikitich: 265.
Setun: 175, 179.
Setun river: 180, 238.
Shakhovskoy, Ivan Leontevich: 113, 131, 141, 147, 157, 168.
Shakhovskoy, Pëtr Ivanovich: 54, 214.
Shcherbatov, Alexey Grigorevich: 315-317.
Shcherbinin, Alexander Andreevich: 334.
Sheepskin coats: 32, 38, 41, 52, 55, 264.
Shevardino: v, 102, 105, 107-108, 110-113, 121-122, 125-126, 129, 133, 151, 161-162, 169.
Shevich, Ivan Yegorovich: 86, 154, 168, 365-369.
Shishkov, Alexander Semënovich: 29.
Shubin, Semën Ivanovich: 280-281.
Siberia: 67-68, 127, 208.
Siedlce: 317-318.
Siegenthal, Heinrich Bersina von: 313-314.
Sievers, Fëdor Fëdorovich: 55
Sievers, Karl Karlovich: 111, 118, 131, 134, 140, 168, 341, 370, 372, 379-380.
Sievers, Yegor Karlovich: 301.
Slonim: 65, 80, 317, 321, 385, 388.
Smolensk, battle of: 7, 10, 92, 189, 224, 251-252; Smolensk, French occupation of: 84-87, 171, 220, 256, 276-277, 305; Smolensk icons: 126, 192; Smolensk partisans: 278-280; Smolensk, Russian magazines in: 38, 96.
Sołtyk, Roman: 71, 78.
Sorbier, Jean-Barthélemot de: 124, 130-131, 133, 149.
Sparrow Hills - see Vorobievo.
Spaskoe (on the Nara): 328, 330, 332.
Spas-Kuplya: 253-254, 335-336.
Stein, Heinrich Friedrich Karl vom und zum: 210.
Steinheil, Fabian Gotthard von: 44, 56, 235, 242, 244, 295-302, 385, 387-389.

Stockholm: 21, 24.
Stolypin, Afanasy Alexeevich: 140, 369.
Stonets stream: 104-105, 107, 152.
Stroganov, Pavel Alexandrovich: 119, 147, 168, 332, 334.
Stulov, Yegor Semënovich: 284-285.
Styr river: 7, 238, 307-310, 323
Subsidies: 24.
Sukhtelen, Pëtr Kornilovich: 21, 24.
Suvorov-Rimniksky, Alexander Vasilevich: 12-13, 17, 91, 136, 206, 230, 279, 346.
Suvorov, *Starshina* of Don artillery: 351.
Sventsiany [Švenčionys]: 251, 295, 389-390.
Sweden: 20-24, 26-28.
Swedish Pomerania: 20.
Sychyovka: 279, 289.
Synod (Holy Synod of Russia): 29-30.
Sysoev 2nd, major: 352.
Sysoev 3rd, colonel: 351.

Tambov: 50, 261.
Tarutino: iii, v, 247, 253, 262-264, 266, 273, 319, 326, 328, 334, 336-341.
Tatarinovo: 108, 130, 160, 356.
Tawast, Johan Henrik: 23.
Taxes: 30, 42, 65-66, 72, 75
Terenin, Alexei Kuzmich: 111, 131, 370, 372.
Terespol: 315, 317-319.
Teste, François-Antoine: 131.
Teterinka: 327, 332-335.
Thielmann, Johann Adolf von: 139-140, 153, 401, 403-404.
Thiers, Adolphe: 17-18, 112, 162, 341.
Tilsit [Sovetsk]: 87, 305, 390; Treaty of: 229, 289.
Tirailleurs: 74, 359, 366, 370, 373
Tolbuzin 1st, Mikhail Ivanovich: 111, 371.
Toll, Karl Wilhelm von: 83, 88, 97, 105, 107, 113, 136-137, 145, 148, 160, 181-183, 185, 237-238, 244, 247, 327-328, 332-333, 335-336, 374, 399.
Tolstoy, Pëtr Alexandrovich: 47-48, 261.
Tormasov, Alexander Petrovich: v, 7, 11-12, 16, 86, 97, 183, 191, 235, 238, 243-245, 249, 252, 276, 307-308, 310-313, 315, 322-323, 340, 343, 385-389.
Trekhgorka (Moscow): 195, 197.
Tsarevo-Zaimishche: v, 83, 88, 90, 92-95, 98, 168, 241, 252, 307.
Tsybulsky, Ivan Denisovich: 401.

Tuchkov 1st, Nikolay Alexeevich: 113, 119, 122, 129, 133-134, 141, 147, 162, 167, 373, 379-380.
Tuchkov 3rd, Pavel Alexeevich: 241.
Tuchkov 4th, Alexander Alexeevich: 137, 162.
Tula: 185, 209, 220, 241, 247, 260-261, 339-340, 344; Tula road: 239-240, 247, 268.
Turisk: 311.
Turiya river: 308, 311.
Tutolmin, Ivan Akinfievich: 227, 228, 406.
Tver: 34, 42, 46, 86, 169, 194, 213, 215, 261, 282, 344.
Tyrtov, Yakov Ivanovich: 33-34, 213, 350.

Udom, Ivan Fëdorovich: 139, 316, 376.
Ula river: 243, 295, 387, 389.
Ushakov, Ivan Mikhailovich: 137, 260.
Ushakov, Pëtr Sergeevich: 375.
Usvyatie: 83-84.
Utitsa: 105-108, 111, 113, 123, 126, 135, 141, 147, 158, 398, 404.
Uvarov, Fëdor Petrovich: 115, 148, 150-152, 175, 182-183, 239, 249, 329, 360, 362, 368.
Uzha river: 83-84.

Vadbolsky, Ivan Mikhailovich: 265, 270.
Valence, Jean-Baptiste-Cyrus de Timbrune de Thiembronne de: 138, 335.
Valueva: 102, 110, 112.
Valutina Gora (Lubino), battle of: 7, 97, 123, 179, 224.
Vandamme, Dominique-Joseph-René: 78.
Vasilchikov, Dmitry Vasilevich: 131, 373.
Vasilchikov, Illarion Vasilevich: 86, 118, 142, 144, 168, 237-239, 241, 246, 248-249, 334, 336, 341, 375, 378.
Velikie-Luki: 215, 244, 293, 302-303, 388-389.
Velyaminov, Ivan Aleksandrovich: 299.
Vereshchagin, Mikhail Nikolaevich: 197.
Vereya: 42, 238, 247, 270-271, 282.
Victor, duc de Bellune (Claude-Victor Perrin): 86-87, 164, 219, 256, 276, 304-305, 324, 327, 390.
Vileyka: 71, 342.
Vilna [Vilnius]: 25, 38, 242, 251, 253, 342, 348, 385, 387-390; French occupation of: 8, 70-71, 73, 75-77, 80, 86, 171, 255-256, 276, 305, 405.
Vinkovo: 326-327, 335.

Vistitsky, Semën Stepanovich: 41, 97, 101, 168, 356.
Vistula river [Wisła]: 27, 87, 318.
Vitebsk: 55, 70, 79-80, 86, 127, 163, 179, 388-389.
Vlasov 2nd, major: 308, 351, 397.
Vlasov 3rd, lieutenant colonel: 336, 353.
Voinka stream: 104, 122, 131, 150-151.
Voinov, Alexander Lvovich: 310, 314-316, 394, 397.
Volga river: 24
Volhynia: iv, 7, 70, 73, 166, 234-235, 242, 260, 276, 308-310, 313, 317, 321-323, 347, 406.
Volkonsky, Pëtr Mikhailovich: 207, 272-273, 275, 406.
Volokolamsk: 179, 265-266, 324-325.
Vorobievo: 179, 181-183, 200, 238.
Vorontsov, Mikhail Semënovich: 108, 110, 113, 119, 131, 133-134, 160, 162, 167-168.
Voronovo: 183, 253-254, 269, 326, 330, 332, 336.
Vorontsovo: 193, 221.
Vuich, Nikolay Vasilevich: 132, 142, 358, 378.
Vyazema: 171, 175, 200.
Vyazma: v, 86-88, 94, 224, 256, 265, 267, 276-277, 279.
Vyazmitinov, Sergey Kuzmich: 10, 216, 407.

Wallachia: iv, 309, 313.
Warsaw: 71, 74, 82, 256, 317-318, 320, 405-407; Duchy of: 48, 71, 82, 310, 313, 317, 323, 386.
Wathier (Wattier), Pierre: 152-153, 156, 400-401.
Węgrów: 317-318, 320.
Wellington, Arthur Wellesley, 1st Duke of: 17.
Wilson, Robert Thomas: 9.
Wintzingerode, Ferdinand Fëdorovich von: v, 41, 84, 86, 179, 186, 206, 213, 215, 229, 261, 265-266, 271, 339.

Wittgenstein, Pëtr Khristianovich: iii, 7, 11, 27-28, 55, 86, 179, 213, 219, 229, 234-235, 242-245, 260-261, 276, 291-295, 300-305, 313, 343, 351, 385-390.
Włodawa: 312, 318, 322.
Wolzogen, Justus Philipp Adolf Wilhelm Ludwig von: 159, 345.
Württemberg, Alexander Friedrich Karl von: 136.
Württemberg, Friedrich Eugen Karl Paul Ludwig von: 95, 114, 145, 149, 166, 168, 181-182, 199, 332-334, 379-380, 398.

Yaroslavl: 32-33, 207, 214, 260-261, 265.
Yauza river: 199-200, 203, 205.
Yefremov, Ivan Yefremovich: 202, 238-239, 265, 267.
Yelisavetgrad [Kropyvnytskyi]: 322.
Yelnya: 38, 85, 102, 105, 110-112, 276, 280, 325, 370.
Yemelyanov, major, partisan leader: 279.
Yermolov, Alexey Petrovich: 17, 143-146, 150, 160, 162, 168, 181-184, 207, 237, 249, 330, 335, 358-359, 361, 378.
Yorck, Johann David Ludwig von: 211, 296-299.
Yukhnov: 38, 267, 279-280.

Zadonsky, Voin Dmitrievich: 366.
Zalesie: 318-320.
Zamość: 50, 65, 311.
Zass (Saß), Alexander Pavlovich: 310.
Zass (Saß), Andrey Andreevich: 156, 364-365.
Zechmeister von Rheinau, Theophil Joseph: 308.
Zhirov, Ivan Ivanovich: 265, 335.
Zhitomir: 97, 317, 322.
Zhukovo: 172-173.
Zubtsov: 93, 214, 282, 324.
Zvenigorod: 42, 179, 196, 198, 209, 268, 282.

From Reason to Revolution – Warfare 1721-1815

http://www.helion.co.uk/series/from-reason-to-revolution-1721-1815.php

The 'From Reason to Revolution' series covers the period of military history 1721–1815, an era in which fortress-based strategy and linear battles gave way to the nation-in-arms and the beginnings of total war.

This era saw the evolution and growth of light troops of all arms, and of increasingly flexible command systems to cope with the growing armies fielded by nations able to mobilise far greater proportions of their manpower than ever before. Many of these developments were fired by the great political upheavals of the era, with revolutions in America and France bringing about social change which in turn fed back into the military sphere as whole nations readied themselves for war. Only in the closing years of the period, as the reactionary powers began to regain the upper hand, did a military synthesis of the best of the old and the new become possible.

The series examines the military and naval history of the period in a greater degree of detail than has hitherto been attempted, and has a very wide brief, with the intention of covering all aspects from the battles, campaigns, logistics, and tactics, to the personalities, armies, uniforms, and equipment.

Submissions

The publishers would be pleased to receive submissions for this series. Please email reasontorevolution@helion.co.uk, or write to Helion & Company Limited, Unit 8 Amherst Business Centre, Budbrooke Road, Warwick, CV34 5WE

You may also be interested in:

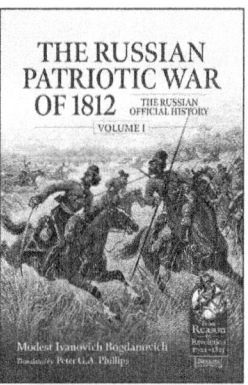

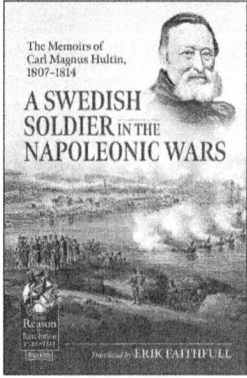